Youth and Authority

Youth and Authority

Formative Experiences in England
1560–1640

PAUL GRIFFITHS

CLARENDON PRESS · OXFORD
1996

Oxford University Press, Walton Street, Oxford OX2 6DP
Oxford New York
Athens Auckland Bangkok Bombay
Calcutta Cape Town Dar es Salaam Delhi
Florence Hong Kong Istanbul Karachi
Kuala Lumpur Madras Madrid Melbourne
Mexico City Nairobi Paris Singapore
Taipei Tokyo Toronto
and associated companies in
Berlin Ibadan

Oxford is a trade mark of Oxford University Press

Published in the United States
by Oxford University Press Inc., New York

British Library Cataloguing in Publication Data
Data available

Library of Congress Cataloging in Publication Data
Griffiths, Paul, Dr.
Youth and authority : formative experiences in England, 1560–1640
/ Paul Griffiths.
p. cm.
Includes bibliographical references.
1. Youth—England—History—16th century. 2. Youth—England—
History—17th century. 3. Authority—History—16th century.
4. Authority—History—17th century. I. Title.
HQ799.G72E55 1996
305.23'5'094209032—dc20 95-40416
ISBN 0-19-820475-2

1 3 5 7 9 10 8 6 4 2

Typeset by Graphicraft Typesetters Ltd., Hong Kong
Printed in Great Britain on acid-free paper by
Bookcraft (Bath) Ltd., Midsomer Norton

For Mavis Griffiths,
1932–1992
and Tessa Jones,
1907–1988

ACKNOWLEDGEMENTS

My first debt is to the staff of the various record offices and libraries I have visited since 1987 to gather material for this book. Only so much can be collected by one person, however, and (like many others before me) I have been greatly helped by the kindness of other scholars who have given both references and encouragement. They include Bernard Capp, Paul Cartledge, David Cressy, Bob Scribner, Jim Sharpe, and Andy Wood. My first flush of enthusiasm for early modern social history was sparked in the second year of my undergraduate degree at York; Jim Sharpe continues to be a good colleague and friend. Other debts are mentioned in my footnotes.

Money is another rather vital form of support, and I have been lucky enough to be generously supported by a number of institutions. The British Academy funded the three years of doctoral research from which this book has finally emerged. I must also thank the master and fellows of Jesus College, Cambridge, who further subsidized my doctoral years. In 1991 I was elected into a research fellowship at Clare College, Cambridge. Further research for this book was completed at Clare, and much of it was written in privileged comfort in that friendly place—my warm thanks to the master and fellows of Clare. More recently, my colleagues in the Economic and Social History Department, University of Leicester, have kindly eased my entry into the department to allow me to complete my book.

The final shape of this book owes much to exchanges which took place when various versions of the following chapters were read to seminars in Bangor, Cambridge, Liverpool, London, Oxford, Toronto, Warwick, Wolverhampton, and York. Ian Archer, Patrick Collinson, David Cressy, Adam Fox, Ian Gentles, Ian Green, Brian Outhwaite, Ulinka Rublack, Roger Schofield, and Paul Slack have all read certain chapters in draft, and I am grateful for their very constructive comments. I had one large stroke of good fortune when Keith Wrightson was appointed to supervise my Ph.D.; I owe him much more than a few words on paper. Ruth has been my other main prop in the last few years. The greatest debt of all is to the two much-loved and much-missed Liverpool women to whom this book is dedicated. No single sentence can convey the warmth and encouragement they still bring.

P.G.

Liverpool, Cambridge, Leicester
1987–94

CONTENTS

LIST OF FIGURES AND TABLE

ABBREVIATIONS

APC   Acts of the Privy Council
BCB   Courtbooks of the Court of London Bridewell
BIHR   Borthwick Institute of Historical Research, York
CH   Clothworkers' Hall, London
CLA   Canterbury Cathedral Library and Archives
CLRO   Corporation Record Office, London
CSPD   Calendar of State Papers Domestic
CSPV   Calendar of State Papers Venetian
CUL   Cambridge University Library
EDR   Ely Diocesan Records
ERO   Essex Record Office
FHL   Friends' House Library, London
GCL   Goldsmiths' Company Library, London
GL   Guildhall Library, London
Jour.   Journals of London Common Council
NAM   Minute Books of the Norwich Assembly
NCQS   Norwich City Quarter Sessions
NMC   Courtbooks of the Norwich Court of Mayoralty
NRO   Norfolk and Norwich Record Office
ORO   Oxfordshire Record Office
PCBP   Proceedings of the Court of the Official of Banbury
             Peculiar
PRO   Public Record Office, London
Rep.   Repertories of the London Court of Aldermen
SP   State Papers Domestic
SRO   Somerset Record Office
STAC   Star Chamber
TT   Thomason Tracts
YCA   York City Archives

INTRODUCTION

Early Modern Youth and History

It is well known that early modern England was a relatively youthful society;[1] that full independent adulthood (marriage and setting up in a craft, workshop, or business) came rather late in life;[2] and that the substantial numbers of people aged between childhood and full adulthood were regarded as being completely under the authority of male adults who possessed formal authority in both domestic and public institutions.[3] All this renders the young a particularly interesting section of early modern society. Yet surprisingly it is only recently that a monograph has been devoted squarely to a full investigation of the problems which this situation might raise.[4]

Despite extensive literatures on the social history of childhood, education, and service in this period, the history of youth has until recently remained a relatively neglected issue, and it has largely been written as the history of adult conceptions, or the position of the young within familiar institutions like the family or service.[5] In so doing, some historians have often reproduced the mandates of contemporary governors. Historical youth, therefore, emerges as a passive social construct of the dominant adult society.[6] Thus one recent historian has wrongly argued that what he calls childhood was 'discovered' in England by an adult movement (Puritanism) which for the first time fully recognized the significance of the

---

[1] E. A. Wrigley and R. S. Schofield, *The Population History of England and Wales 1541–1871: A Reconstruction* (1981), esp. 215–19, 443–50. The age-structure of the population, however, was never constant, and the proportion of young people was higher in some periods.

[2] See below, esp. p. 5.

[3] See Keith Thomas, 'Age and authority in early modern England', *Proceedings of the British Academy*, 62 (1976), and Ch. 2 below.

[4] Ilana Krausman Ben-Amos, *Adolescence and Youth in Early Modern England* (New Haven, 1994).

[5] Cf. Margaret Pelling, 'Apprenticeship, health and social cohesion in early modern London', *History Workshop Journal*, 37 (1994), 33, 'The history of childhood is flourishing, but—for the early modern period especially—it is largely the history of the child within the confines of the family. Moreover, the child tends to be largely passive.'

[6] Cf. C. John Sommerville, *The Discovery of Childhood in Puritan England* (Athens, Ga., 1992), 3.

rising generation of young people, and organized them for change accordingly. Pre-adult stages of life had to be 'discovered' in former centuries.[7] The institutional and ideological setting constructed by adult males was of great consequence for the lives of early modern youth. Nevertheless, we must not relegate their story to that narrated by the requirements of dominant ideologies and institutions alone. That was merely one side of youthful experiences, the prescriptive and normative, though it was a pattern of behaviour that always remained one possibility. We should retain interpretative flexibility and a measure of imagination in our approach to sources and ideas, and seek to free historical youth from the oppressive grip of prescriptive ideologies and institutions when it is appropriate to do so. There was, after all, a wide variety of adult opinions about youth. Similarly the history of youth was neither scripted nor inevitable. This book seeks to recover the creative potential of youth in early modern society by exploring some of the problems raised by attempting to socialize young people of the lower and middle ranks in the period *c.*1560–*c.*1640.

It is certainly not the case that youth had been wholly neglected by historians before the publication of Ilana Krausman Ben-Amos's *Adolescence and Youth in Early Modern England* in 1994. We now possess a large and growing continental literature, and a recent general survey.[8] In England too, youth was trumpeted as a historical and contemporary problem in the 1960s, discussed in countless inches of column space in newspapers and magazines, and explored by historians who tended to enter the debate at a rather late hour, prompted by the theories of social scientists[9] and a concern with the historical family and social structure. They pored over the sources in search of an explanation of the all too visible problems raised by post-war youth, though the major portion of their time was given to the generations of young people after 1700. They 'discovered' youth in a wide variety of social and institutional situations in nineteenth- and twentieth-century society—in factories, play, clubs, schools, and more 'shameful' bouts of juvenile delinquency—which gave that

[7] Ibid. 10, 22, and ch. 2 *passim.*

[8] Michael Mitterauer, *A History of Youth*, trans. Graeme Dunphy (Oxford, 1992). There is a useful summary of the recent historiography of youth in John Springhall, 'The history of youth reaches middle age', *Social History Society Bulletin*, 19 (1994).

[9] The work of Erik Erikson, in particular, retains significance, influencing the work of historians on both sides of the Atlantic. The 1960s and 1970s witnessed a stream of books and articles about youth and childhood which often took Erikson's ideas as a conceptual point of entry. There is a useful commentary on the development of this literature in Linda Pollock, *Forgotten Children: Parent–Child Relations from 1500 to 1900* (Cambridge, 1983), ch. 1.

age historical precision and meaning.[10] Youth had finally arrived on the historical stage, but it was more often summoned by historians of the past two centuries with no interest in 'merrie England' except to place great distances between the 'modern' and 'early modern' period, which was remote and different. The emergence of a distinctive group of youth was attributed to the 'modernizing' processes associated with industrial and educational advances after 1750. If historians wandered back to early modern society it was to proclaim the existence of a 'new world' of costume and play for eighteenth-century children; that juvenile delinquency was a nineteenth-century 'discovery';[11] that youth tightly bound by the institutional chains of service and the family was stripped of historical agency; or even more dramatically, that youth did not exist as a separate stage of life in early modern society because young people dressed in adult costume and were missing from contemporary pictures, the generational casualties of early exposure to the monotonous rhythm of the adult timetable of work and a particular alignment of social structure and relations.[12]

In his *Centuries of Childhood* (first published in France in 1960 and translated into English in 1962), Phillipe Aries associated harsh parental discipline, a formal, distanced parent–child relation, and the absence of a separate idea of childhood and youth before some rather ill-defined point in the seventeenth century (or after) with broader trends of social and structural change. He suggested that the gradual emergence of the nuclear family and organized education in the seventeenth and eighteenth centuries cultivated warm sentiment where previously there had been little or none, and the recognition of distinctive pre-adult stages of life. A number of historians, most notoriously Lawrence Stone and Edward Shorter, have traced a similar pattern of rising familial sentiment. Again, an almost magical break in mentalities and structures is located somewhere in the seventeenth or eighteenth centuries. People were different then, we are told, they fell in love with each other, cared for their nearest and dearest, and lived together as a settled nuclear group inside the same four walls.[13] In this particular evolutionary tale, a 'dark

[10] See J. R. Gillis, *Youth and History: Tradition and Change in European Age-Relations, 1770 to the Present* (1981).
[11] See below, Ch. 3.
[12] See J. H. Plumb, 'The new world of children in eighteenth-century England', *Past and Present*, 67 (1975); Phillipe Aries, *Centuries of Childhood: A Social History of Family Life*, trans. R. Baldick (New York, 1962); Gillis, *Youth and History*.
[13] Lawrence Stone, *The Family, Sex and Marriage in England 1500–1800* (1977); Edward Shorter, *The Making of the Modern Family* (1976). Pollock, *Forgotten Children* (esp. chs. 1–2),

age' of parental neglect, scant recreation, and 'lost' childhood and/or youth precedes the brilliant illumination of the eighteenth century, though the seventeenth century is often introduced as a transitional phase. The history of mentalities is divided into convenient periods in which the pace of change gradually gathers momentum, so that family life and growing up could never quite be the same again.

These rather negative assessments of the fortunes of youth before structures altered form and parents had a change of heart encouraged some historians to consult contemporary sources. They in fact discovered significant continuities in familial emotions and forms, thereby revealing the suspicious interpretative and methodological assumptions which informed the work of Aries, Stone, Shorter, and other 'pessimists' of past family life.[14] Alan Macfarlane helped to restore emotion and sympathy to the early modern household in his study of the Essex clergyman Ralph Josselin (1971). The proper place of affection, joy, and grief was firmly readmitted in Linda Pollock's study of childhood in contemporary literary sources (1983), and it has now become a commonplace in textbooks investigating the nature of early modern society.[15] Another central plank in the Aries/Stone thesis, the missing nuclear family which gradually emerged to assume shape at some point in the seventeenth century, had already been exposed as an error before Stone put pen to paper to write *The Family, Sex and Marriage in England 1500–1800* (1977). In 1972 Peter Laslett and Richard Wall published a series of articles in *Household and Family in Past Time* which traced the history of the nuclear family as far back as sources permit.[16] Such research now allows us to establish the contours, structures, and mentalities by which to study young people in early modern society.

discusses the broad preference among English, French, and American historians to present an evolutionary model of progressive and changing attitudes towards childhood. Again, the critical period is often towards the close of the seventeenth century, though there is some disagreement about the timing and causes of this 'novel' set of structures and emotions.

[14] Cf. Shulamith Shahar, *Childhood in the Middle Ages*, trans. Chaya Galai (1990), 3, 'it is . . . highly doubtful whether any "emotional revolution" has occurred in the attitude of parents to their children'; and Alan Macfarlane's highly perceptive remarks in his review of Stone's *Family, Sex and Marriage* in *History and Theory*, 18 (1979).

[15] Alan Macfarlane, *The Family Life of Ralph Josselin, a Seventeenth-Century Clergyman: An Essay in Historical Anthropology* (Cambridge, 1970); Pollock, *Forgotten Children*, esp. chs. 4–5; J. A. Sharpe, *Early Modern England: A Social History 1550–1750* (1987), ch. 2; Ralph Houlbrooke, *The English Family 1450–1700* (1984); Keith Wrightson, *English Society 1580–1680* (1982), ch. 4.

[16] Peter Laslett and Richard Wall (eds.), *Household and Family in Past Time* (Cambridge, 1972). Cf. Alan Macfarlane, *The Origins of English Individualism: The Family, Property and Social Transition* (Oxford, 1979), esp. chs. 6–7.

The significance of youth at this time is also an issue of numbers. There was a large number of young people and a rather late age at first marriage in Tudor and Stuart society. Wrigley and Schofield have discovered that the age-structure of the population becomes increasingly youthful as we go back in time from 1671 to the middle of the sixteenth century, when 36–40 per cent of the population were under 15, and a mere 6.5–7 per cent were above 60 years of age. They chart a peak in the youthful population in 1556 (in age-groups they designate as *childhood* and *young adulthood*), which is followed by a further peak in 1576, and a sustained rise until 1621. One result of the near doubling of the population at this time was a rise in the numbers of young people. They became more visible. 'As you walke in the streetes', Bishop Goodman invited his readers in 1616, study the complexions of passers-by, 'or looke into the register booke of your churches, and you shall finde more living under the age of thirtie than above.'[17] The greater visibility of youth at a time of prolonged socio-economic difficulty raised sharper anxieties about young people and orderly socialization.

Not only was the proportion of young people in the population notably high, the age at which they made the shift into full adulthood came rather late. There is also evidence that the authorities interfered with marriage entry as well as passing regulations about setting up in trade. There was a statutory stamp, for example, upon the minimum age of departing apprenticeship (24 for males and 21 for women, or marriage), and on the length of formal apprenticeship (seven years at least). Mindful of economic competition and the glut of young people, the authorities often attempted to safeguard the fortunes of settled adult craftsmen and retailers by monitoring entry into service and prolonging journeywork, thereby extending the subordination of youth.[18] The average age at first marriage was also high. In a sample of twelve parishes in the period 1600–49, the mean age for males was 28, and for women 26, though figures are complicated by local social and economic structures.[19]

As we have seen, other historians have tracked the course of parent–child relations from child-rearing, through education, service, the

---

[17] Wrigley and Schofield, *Population History of England*, 215–19, 443–50. See esp. figure 7.4, 216, and table 10.6, 447, though the latter figure is based on the *dependency* ratio and includes older folk also; Godfrey Goodman, *The Fall of Man, Or the Corruption of Nature Proved by the Light of Our Natural Reason* (1616), 83–4.

[18] See Steve Rappaport, *Worlds within Worlds: Structures of Life in Sixteenth-Century London* (Cambridge, 1989), 322–9.

[19] Wrigley and Schofield, *Population History of England*, 257–65, 423–4; Houlbrooke, *English Family*, 63 ff.; Sharpe, *Early Modern England*, 40.

nature of inheritance customs, to the rather troubled issue of courtship and match-making. They have discovered warm sentiment
(upset it must be said by the occasional thug or rebel) in which
young people experienced degrees of independence according to
gender, social class, or the acquisition of skills. We also possess
work which explores some aspects of the position of young people
in non-parental households as servants or apprentices, which often
tends to represent youthful experiences in distant polarities with
little middle ground. On one side, there is the story of abuse, fear,
and intimidation, and on the other, a rosier picture of domestic
calm and 'inevitable socialization'.[20] The potential problems presented by service are raised as historical orthodoxies in the first
view, and more or less neglected in the second. It is only recently
that some historians have offered a more flexible interpretative
model, which catches these two extremes and explores ambiguities
in age-relations, including the ways in which governors intervened
to settle unsteady households.[21] A functional interpretation of life-
cyclical progress, which merely repeats the requirements of adults
in places of authority is of limited value. The optimistic story of
'inevitable socialization' in which young people move through the
life-course and fully accept the values of the normative socializing
process is often recycled, though rarely questioned.[22] There were
many different ways of growing up in early modern society, and
they were affected by social class, gender, the state of labour markets, customary access to the land,[23] and, above all, the responses
of the young. In fact, the familiar account of socio-economic difficulty in the period *c.*1560–*c.*1640 and increasing urbanization and
migration could have raised particular problems of youth or further concentrated the attention of the authorities upon that age.
Youth was more visible in this time of religious change, rapid population growth, deeper poverty, greater vagrancy, agrarian change,
and urban growth. Reformation, demographic pressures, and other
changes elevated concern with familial- and age-relations. Pressure

[20] The principal contributions are discussed in Ch. 6.
[21] See, for example, Pelling, 'Apprenticeship, health and social cohesion'; Paul Seaver,
'A social contract? Master against servant in the Court of Requests', *History Today*, 39 (Sept.
1989).
[22] One interpretation which is clearly affected by the inability to distinguish between
prescriptive attitudes and institutions and youthful experiences is Rappaport's survey of the
structures of life in sixteenth-century London, *Worlds within Worlds*.
[23] Cf. The interesting remarks of John Walter, 'A "rising of the people?" The Oxfordshire
rising of 1596', *Past and Present*, 107 (1985), 123–5.

upon dwindling resources reduced opportunities, and pushed many young people to move to find work in service.[24]

Other young people spent the greater part of their teenage years in some type of formal education, though beyond basic literary skills our knowledge of Tudor and Stuart education is largely confined to the offspring of the upper and middle ranks at the grammar schools, universities, and Inns of Court.[25] We should not expect to find many of the youth of the lower classes who are one subject of this book resident in these quarters. Scholars rarely appear in the following pages, which are filled instead with servants, apprentices, and maids. Service and apprenticeship are treated here as the representative experience of most young people of the lower classes. Peter Laslett has argued that service was the 'characteristic' experience of early modern youth, and we possess some impressive statistical and literary proofs.[26] Others have questioned the universality of service, and even suggested that in some cases it was the preserve of certain groups (e.g. orphans or migrants).[27] Yet even if some allowance is made for the differing experiences of town and country, or the impact of different economic and social structures, it still seems that the majority of *plebeian youth* entered some form of service, and that servants composed the largest single body in the workforce.[28] So, my discussion is largely confined to the fortunes of apprentices and servants at the expense of schoolchildren and the parent–child relation, though service need not imply a complete break from the parental home. Communications were frequently maintained. Young people could also make a series of departures

[24] See A. L. Beier, *Masterless Men: The Vagrancy Problem in England 1560–1640* (1985), esp. chs. 2–3.

[25] A useful survey of the social history of education in this period is provided by Rosemary O'Day, *Education and Society: The Social Foundations of Education in Early Modern Britain* (1982).

[26] Peter Laslett, *Family Life and Illicit Love in Earlier Generations: Essays in Historical Sociology* (Cambridge, 1977), 44. Graham Mayhew has conveniently summarized much of the recent research in his 'Life-cycle, service and the family unit in early modern Rye', *Continuity and Change*, 6 (1991).

[27] See especially Mayhew, 'Life-cycle, service and the family unit'; Richard Wall, 'Leaving home and the process of household-formation in preindustrial England', *Continuity and Change*, 2 (1988). Yet Mayhew's chief source, Rye's muster rolls, are not without flaws, as they do not include people under 16 years of age and those who departed the town to serve elsewhere (he is, however, aware of these problems, 207). Moreover, can we be sure of the typicality of Rye's households? In that town sons were generally well provided for, and often followed their father's occupation, so that there was a clear option to service in another household ready at hand. Rye does not seem to be the most promising location from which to construct theories about the extent of service in this period.

[28] See Ann Kussmaul, *Servants in Husbandry in Early Modern England* (Cambridge, 1981), 3; Beier, *Masterless Men*, 23.

from home, and they often returned at the close of a term of service.[29]

As well as histories of education and service, youth has also been touched on in the study of other phenomena, some of which have been depicted as age-related. They will be more fully explored in the following chapters, and include the impact of the Reformation, which (it has been argued) had special appeal for some sections of the young, though involving others in struggles with ecclesiastical authorities;[30] recreation (and the nature of youth culture);[31] the drift to urban and industrial areas, which was in large part a movement of youth;[32] illegitimacy and infanticide, which have both been explored as problems of poor household discipline;[33] and the high number of servants among suicides, who were often victims of physical abuse.[34]

So, the rescue of youth (or what some historians have called 'childhood') from historical obscurity is in fact rather advanced in some respects. Youth has been extricated from a number of interpretative muddles, which in the pursuit of linear progresses have relegated histories of familial- and age-relations to anachronistic cycles of development. Nevertheless, some problems linger. One regular ambiguity in the existing historiography is the reluctance (or failure) to follow contemporary opinion about the different ages and, above all, to distinguish adequately between youth and childhood. One historian who claims to have 'discovered' childhood

[29] Cf. Richard Wall, 'The age at leaving home', *Journal of Family History*, 3 (1978).

[30] Susan Brigden, 'Youth and the English Reformation', *Past and Present*, 95 (1982); Patrick Collinson, *The Religion of Protestants: The Church in English Society 1559–1625* (Oxford, 1982), 224–30; id., *The Birthpangs of Protestant England: Religious and Cultural Change in the Sixteenth and Seventeenth Centuries* (Basingstoke, 1988), chs. 3–5; Martin Ingram, *Church Courts, Sex and Marriage in England 1570–1640* (Cambridge, 1987), 123, 354–5.

[31] R. W. Malcolmson, *Popular Recreations in English Society 1700–1850* (Cambridge, 1973); S. R. Smith, 'The London apprentices as seventeenth-century adolescents' and Bernard Capp, 'English youth groups and *The Pinder of Wakefield*', both of which can be found in Paul Slack (ed.), *Rebellion, Popular Protest and the Social Order in Early Modern England* (Cambridge, 1984).

[32] A. L. Beier, 'Vagrants and the social order in Elizabethan England', *Past and Present*, 64 (1974); Paul Slack, 'Vagrants and vagrancy in England 1598–1664', in Peter Clark and David Souden (eds.), *Migration and Society in Early Modern England* (1987), 54.

[33] Keith Wrightson and David Levine, 'The social context of illegitimacy in early modern England', in Peter Laslett, K. M. Oosterveen, and R. M. Smith (eds.), *Bastardy and its Comparative History* (1980), 163–9; Keith Wrightson, 'Infanticide in earlier seventeenth-century England', *Local Population Studies*, 15 (1975).

[34] Michael Macdonald and Terence R. Murphy, *Sleepless Souls: Suicide in Early Modern England* (Oxford, 1990), 252–3; S. J. Stevenson, 'Social and economic contributions to the pattern of "suicide" in south-east England, 1530–1590', *Continuity and Change*, 2 (1987), 229.

in Puritan England even comments that early modern people rarely followed such distinctions, and that they 'used the term "childhood" to describe the entire period of social and economic dependence'.[35] (There are in fact a few scattered remarks in contemporary sources to support this view.[36]) To complicate matters still further, an ill-defined border between childhood and youth is crossed with worrying ease by historians in their use of age-titles. Many of them simply forget to consider age-differentials and related changes in contemporary responses to children and youth. The risk of such numerical and conceptual imprecision is that we confuse two separate ages and misread contemporary perceptions. Historians like Pollock, Thomas, Jordanova, and Sommerville, who use the far more specific term 'childhood' as a catch-all to gather people falling into pre-teenage and teenage years, distort contemporary age-description.[37] The issue is more pressing still because the existence of youth itself is in doubt when Plumb, Aries, and Gillis introduce the attitudes of adults and opportunities for recreation as definitional measures of that age. In fact, most contemporary authors fully recognized distinctions in the interval between infancy and adulthood. Youth and childhood were usually treated apart. It was on this basis that they drafted their work, proposing strategies and conceptualizations of these two ages. There were special texts for young people, which were intended to turn the offspring of corrupt humanity into pious and civil members of society. This genre conveyed prescriptive theories and distinctive sets of ideas and strategies turning on the particular properties of childhood, youth, and adulthood.[38] In George Gascoigne's *Glass of Government* (1575), Gnomaticus discussed the 'great difference betweene children and young men'. Henry Cuffe typically defined an age as 'a period and tearme' of life in which 'natural complexion and temperature . . . is evidently changed'. The difference of ages clearly mattered. It was important to the meaning

---

[35] Sommerville, *Discovery of Childhood*, 15, 78.

[36] For example, the child in Thomas Ingelhard's *A Pretie and Mery Enterlude Called the Disobedient Child* (1569), who was of marriageable age; Henry Cuffe, *The Difference of the Ages of a Man's Life* (1607), 117–22.

[37] Pollock, *Forgotten Children*; Keith Thomas, 'Children in early modern England', in Gillian Avery and Julia Briggs (eds.), *Children and Their Books: A Celebration of the Work of Iona and Peter Opie* (Oxford, 1989); Ludmilla Jordanova, 'New worlds for children in the eighteenth century: problems of historical interpretation', *History of the Human Sciences*, 3 (1990); Sommerville, *Discovery of Childhood*.

[38] See S. R. Smith, 'Religion and the conception of youth in seventeenth-century England', *History of Childhood Quarterly*, 2 (1975).

and ordering of daily experiences, and helped contemporaries to understand their world and social order.[39]

A further problem is that the range of contemporary materials consulted by previous historians is often socially biased and fragmentary. This limitation which naturally affects interpretations can only provide a restricted view. The sources for the history of pre-adult stages of life have been overwhelmingly literary and secondary hitherto—autobiographies, letters, diaries, pictures, and medical and moralizing books. Historians have been rather reluctant to journey beyond the literate and socially privileged quarters.[40] We are now reasonably familiar with some aspects of the history of young people of the middle and upper classes. Records of formal apprenticeship offer the best-documented experience of youth at this time, and they have been well researched in a number of articles. In some respects, these are histories of the 'middling sort' of young people,[41] and this book too makes extensive use of these types of sources. A formal seven-year apprenticeship offered young men whose families could afford to pay the premium a route to full citizenship and a responsible place in the economic and political life of their community. Calls for closer regulation of formally apprenticed young people, therefore, can be interpreted as preoccupations with the position and cultural preferences of 'middling' youth (or aspiring 'middling' young people);[42] the calibre of the rising generation of magistrates; and the values of civic order which were partly defined in the training of tomorrow's civic notables.

Apprentices feature prominently in the following chapters, but whenever it is possible I have attempted either to bring in the

[39] George Gascoigne, *The Glass of Government*, 1575 (Tudor Facsimile Texts, New York, 1970), fo. G3ʳ; Cuffe, *Difference of the Ages*, 115.
[40] Pollock, *Forgotten Children*, 22; Jordanova, 'New worlds for children', 74. Ben-Amos's recent full-length study, which is based on a case-study of apprenticeship in Bristol and nearly seventy contemporary autobiographies, contains many of these limitations.
[41] Cf. Christopher Brooks, 'Apprenticeship, social mobility and the middling sort, 1500–1800', in Jonathan Barry and Christopher Brooks (eds.), *The Middling Sort of People: Culture, Society and Politics in England, 1550–1800* (Basingstoke, 1994); and R. A. Houston, *Social Change in the Age of Enlightenment: Edinburgh 1660–1760* (Oxford, 1994), 92, 'Apprentices can be seen as representatives less of the lower orders than as a young section of the middling ranks who might ultimately become masters and incorporation, or even town officials in their own right'. It should also be said that the social profile of apprenticeship was becoming more 'exclusive' in the course of the seventeenth century as more young people of the upper classes entered formal seven-year terms and costs gradually increased. See Brooks, 'Apprenticeship', esp. 61–2 , 64–5, and 70.
[42] I feel that Brooks is arguably overstating his case when he calls apprenticeship 'a distinctive institution of the middling sort' ('Apprenticeship', 78), but there is no doubt, however, that most apprentices in the period *c.*1560–*c.*1640 were of 'middling' status.

experiences of male and female servants and parish apprentices or to signpost their different expectations and fortunes. Yet the experiences of more humble youngsters at this time are less clear, and they often remain distant characters in this and other studies. The worlds of letters and commerce are, of course, interesting, but we might wonder if they are representative. Other priorities and sources, including the full range of judicial records, for example, would not only offer a point of entry to the experiences of lower class youth, but would also help us to fashion a more sensitive explanatory framework for the social history of young people in former centuries. It is hoped that in places this book touches the experiences of 'all sorts' of early modern youth.

Above all, previous historians have tended to treat youth rather obliquely or tangentially, as a single or subsidiary aspect of the particular issue under review; a plot within a plot. They have not squarely focused upon the age of youth, which is rarely explored as a problem in itself.[43] The experiences of youth are frequently neglected in the hurry to discuss the demographic and institutional systems which regulated age-relations. Young voices, therefore, are distant and silent. Ludmilla Jordanova believes that 'an unfocused sentimentality about giving children a voice' wrongly distracts attention from the whole culture and society. Indeed, it is 'regrettable' that historians should seek to portray a world of children, for 'there is no such separate and private world, as there is no autonomous, authentic voice of children in which a separate history of childhood could be rooted'.[44] Jordanova is surely right to request a composite and rounded interpretation of childhood, which fully incorporates exchanges with the adult population. Yet historians have tended to underplay the significance of formative experiences of youth in early modern society, and the extent to which contemporaries described a distinctive problem of youth with particular causes, situations, and solutions. It is necessary to recover these identities in the course of tracing the critical familial, communal, and societal aspects of the social history of youth.

It is now well known that there was a separate age of youth in early modern society (and before), so the principal concern of current work should be with the nature of experiences of youth—the level of independence, formative experiences, peer association, and so on. A rather literal reading of contemporary prescriptive

---

[43] Cf. Pollock, *Forgotten Children*, 58 ff. One notable exception, as already stated, is Ben-Amos's *Adolescence and Youth in Early Modern England*.

[44] Jordanova, 'New worlds for children', 78–81.

texts, especially by historians of later centuries seeking to identify the distinctive characteristics of youth in an age of factories and compulsory schooling, has encouraged an impoverished view of 'housebound' early modern youth. In distant centuries, young people had little free space or time. Their cultural experiences were severely limited by the formal authority of householders whose province, the orbit of their rule, also established the rough contours of their world. It is not a great step from this ordered existence to deny the reality of youth, or to paint young lives in grey and dreary colours. The majority of early modern contributions are free of this rather stale and narrow image. But even here there has been considerable reluctance to abandon this infatuation with authority structures. The story of dominated and passive youth is still retold. The oppressive grip of household authority continues to hover over early modern youth, structuring their allegiances and territories. Even the most recent work still argues that 'the lack of a marked spatial and temporal segregation of the young and old' 'undermined' formative experiences of youth.[45] This is partly a question of the choice and use of sources. Literary sources such as autobiographies and diaries, for example, are not the best place to seek formative experiences of youth outside the household. In such sources it is rare to see young people of the lower classes expressing opinions, falling in love, drinking, walking, playing, and so on. Yet studies of courtship have long suggested that they exercised a high degree of freedom and spontaneity.[46]

This book seeks to clarify some of the linguistic and conceptual muddles which have scarred discussions of youth hitherto; to depict the distances between youth and other age-groups which would have been familiar to early modern people; and to demonstrate the significance of formative experiences of youth at this time. Yet to write a comprehensive history of youth is beyond the scope of a single study, and I can only hope to draw the contours of the problem of age and authority, describe some formative experiences of youth, and invite further work. So, I have chosen to describe what I understand, perhaps arbitrarily, to be the most pressing problems requiring elucidation at this present time as a prolegomenon to a more complete knowledge of the social history of early modern youth. On the one hand, youth can be interpreted as a social construct of the dominant adult society (a problem of socialization and

---

[45] Ben-Amos, *Adolescence and Youth in Early Modern England*, 205–6.

[46] For example, Keith Wrightson and David Levine, *Poverty and Piety in an English Village: Terling 1525–1700* (1979); Ingram, *Church Courts*, esp. 225–6. See also below, Ch. 5.

discipline), while on the other, we need to study the nature of youthful experiences, how the young interpreted the implications of their appointed inferiority. All societies have to manage the transition from youth to adulthood (socialization) and the problems raised by this progress. The problem of youth was an issue of authority and socialization. In Tudor and Stuart society (but not only then) the household and service were the most widely discussed forms of disciplining youth. Contemporary moralists, therefore, generally defined problems of youth in terms of the collapse of domestic discipline or restraint, and its 'natural' repercussions—licentiousness and independence. As we shall see, they commonly depicted youth in binary polarities as 'contested territory'[47]—a struggle between right and wrong, liberty and control, or conformity and dissent. This freedom, which was portrayed as a problem by the authorities, was often nothing more than harmless conviviality and play. By approaching the history of youth through close study of judicial sources, and complicating the discussion of socialization by exploring in depth the responses of young people, it is hoped that a positive image will emerge which emphasizes creative formative experiences of youth at this time.

Judicial records must be treated with care. Just as our interpretation of the problem of youth as an issue of authority or conformity implies conflict and the need to resolve disputes, so court records can tell us much about aspects of youth which adults in places of authority found distasteful, threatening, and in need of reform. There is a risk here of depicting age-relations in terms of universal strife, and that would be a mistake. Young people responded in all sorts of ways to the pressures of service, for instance, or religious instruction. There was consensus, consent, and conformity, though they only make sparse appearances in judicial records. They can, however, be teased out by exploring their obverse or supplementary sources. This book hopes to offer an interpretative model which catches the happy as well as darker side of life—negotiation, mediation, opposition, or conformity. The young could also move between these positions, so that there can be no simple and polished interpretation. Even the most conforming godly youth sometimes slipped away to join the fun on the green or in the alehouse. A more accurate portrait of the representative experiences of early modern youth would be a complex collage with numerous subsets and splashes of colour. This book instead seeks to discuss the principal

---

[47] See below, Ch. 1.

contours of the problems raised by the position of youth within
authority structures. No single interpretation of youth will emerge,
but we will see that there was a politics of age-relations. Age was a
further principle of order in early modern society. Yet even on this
point there was disagreement. The terms of this politics were being
.continually renegotiated and redefined. To complicate matters still
further, adult men and women freely interpreted these principles
of authority, and were often content to allow their young charges
a degree of tolerance which raised fears in the circles of magistrates
and moralists. There was no rough age/youth polarity in early
modern society. A grand plan of socialization may have existed, but
householders, and on occasion ecclesiastical and secular authorities, disagreed about its precise form and objectives.

In pursuit of early modern youth and contemporary conceptualizations of the problem of age and authority, I have consulted a number
of different types of sources in a tactical eclectic fashion seeking to
bring in as many experiences as possible in the course of my narrative. Contemporary printed books (and the forms of policy and
prosecution) provided a point of entry to the conceptual world of
ministers and magistrates. Yet as we shall see, conversion rhetoric
and political order also required another more positive image of
youth. These same texts often presented a contrary picture of virtuous young people residing in godly if imagined households, which
retailed as moral exemplar. This image of sober youth was also
recycled in the statements of secular courts and institutions as a
pattern for imitation. The records of church and secular courts,
which were chiefly consulted in manuscript (though supplemented
by a sampling of printed materials to contribute further geographical breadth), permit us to test the fictional image of youth presented in texts against the 'hurly burly' of daily life. The archives
have characteristic flaws, they reproduce a hierarchical dialogue
between youth and age. But minute books and depositions can also
help us to depict the essential characteristics of formative experiences
of youth which stirred unease in pulpits, studies, and courtrooms.

Clearly, perhaps inevitably, much of England is touched on lightly,
and some topographical distinctions have not been pursued here.
Broad expanses of rural society and the invitation to distinguish
between wood-pasture and arable regions have been passed over
for the present. Nevertheless, an attempt has been made to gain a
reasonable spread of sources and locations, though an urban bias
lingers and affects my interpretation of the problem of youth. This
urban nuance can be partly justified by both the evident quality

and relevance of rich urban materials. The towns also had relatively large youthful populations, and a series of problems which were clearly age-related, including petty crime, vagrancy, and the potential difficulties of household life. Interestingly, in 1552 in London, before in-migration gained pace and became a quick march, 56.25 per cent of the male population were under 30 years of age.[48] The authorities were well aware of these problems, which are most evident in urban materials. They were not the exclusive property of urban society. They do not allow us to produce neat contrasts between town and country. Differences were more an issue of contextualization; of degree rather than kind, though there were arguably more opportunities for youthful sociability in the towns, and young people were more visible in the more congested spaces of the townscape. With this in mind, I turned to the records of London, York, and Norwich. Norwich was investigated in some depth, especially in Chapter 7, which deals with the experiences of 'masterless' young people. This East Anglian city was chosen because its principal judicial sources extend in fine consecutive sequence for the period 1560–1645, which permits us to pass observations and quantify and tabulate with a degree of confidence.

The problem of age and authority in this period carries us to many experiences and places. This book is an introduction to this many-sided topic, and it inevitably adopts a 'broad-brush' approach and the method which is sometimes disparaged as 'source mining'. Yet this type of enquiry is simply necessary to open up the problem of youth more generally. A broad canvas permits us to raise themes of critical national significance, like the nature of collective experiences; sex in the long interval between the first stirrings of puberty and late marriage; and age as a further dimension of the problem of order in Tudor and Stuart society. The obvious alternative method of an intensive local community study investigating people in small spaces would be of limited value at present. It would reduce the scope of what can be addressed to the particular problems of one region or community, and it would be unlikely to contribute further to what we already know about aspects of the the experiences of youth which can be well approached by this method (e g inheritance, illegitimacy, and literacy). A study which is partly exploratory must cast its net far wider, and hunt in dispersed sources and locations to propose starting-points for further exploration. Nevertheless,

[48] The figure is given by Rappaport, *Worlds within Worlds*, 388–93, esp. table A1.2, 392. Cf. Ian Archer's remarks about the problems raised by young people in London in this period, *The Pursuit of Stability: Social Relations in Elizabethan London* (Cambridge, 1991), 242–3.

I have tried to compensate for my particular 'broad brush' by using some good sets of courtbooks intensively, and by being reasonably thorough in providing comparative references in the hope of journeying beyond the merely impressionistic to establish that the issues under review here are neither unique nor eccentric.

On the basis of the above strategy of central questions and sources of evidence, this book will proceed by discussing conceptualizations of youth and the responses of the young to the preoccupation with socialization. Different characterizations of youth, which express not only a prescriptive (Chapters 1–2), but a highly critical attitude also (Chapters 3–7) will be explored in turn. The progress from prescription to criticism is also that from ideal to reality. As chapters unwind, different stages of youthful independence and creativity will come into view—the freedom to play and socialize, resistance, irreverence, and some choice about the terms of entry into service. The often equivocal attitudes of different sections of adult society will be treated throughout. The first chapter explores contemporary definitions of youth and the construction of distinctive sets of attitudes towards different stages of the life-course. Chapter 2 seeks to establish age as a further dimension of principles of authority at this time, and to place prescriptive attitudes to young people within discussions of their ideal position in the social order. Ministers and magistrates saw their images of virtuous youth as being to some extent out of sorts with the preferences of the young. The remaining chapters, therefore, will compare the fictional and ideal construct of youth in literary materials with the nature of experiences of youth. We will investigate the principal characteristics of the world of conviviality and play (Chapters 3–4), religious commitment (Chapter 4), sexual behaviour and courtship (Chapter 5), master–servant relations (Chapters 4–6), and the identification and social milieu of 'masterless' young people (Chapter 7). In fine, this book seeks to demonstrate that there was no single, straight, or smooth path to full adulthood in Tudor and Stuart society. The experience of growing up was rarely predictable at a time when young people were highly visible, creative, and resourceful.

Attitudes towards Youth

At some point in every investigation of youth in early modern Europe the author still has to confront the suggestion that pre-adult stages of life as we understand them did not exist in the centuries under review. It is said that contemporaries juggled with childhood, adolescence, youth, and adulthood, confusing their definitions and identities, with the result that the borders between different ages were often vague and ill-defined, or even more dramatically, certain ages had either not yet emerged or remained to be discovered. Significant differences have been posited between distant centuries and societies. Aries argues that a long childhood was followed by a quick leap into adulthood, though it is difficult to discover a place in time when he considers the age of youth (adolescence in his terms) to have finally 'arrived'. Gillis and others describe the gradual emergence of adolescence only in the recent past. Thus the histories of childhood, adolescence, and youth have been written according to the rhythms of 'modernizing processes'; as a long evolutionary tale.[1] At particular points in the development of the historiography of pre-adult stages of life we have been invited to 'discover' one or more of these age-groups in former centuries. We find scholars hunting in the sources left behind by early modern people or their modern 'descendants' to find when childhood or youth was 'discovered'; a point in time when the experiences of young people and adults can be adequately distinguished from each other, and contemporaries produced clear cultural and social

---

[1] Phillipe Aries, *Centuries of Childhood: A Social History of Family Life*, trans. R. Baldick (New York, 1960), esp. part 1, and part 3, ch. 2. Aries complicates matters still further by not making a firm definition of youth; when does it begin and end? He quotes contemporaries who hold that youth begins at 25 (but rarely offers the same precision himself), and then discusses a 'long childhood' which 'soaks up' teenage years (ibid. 21, 26, 128); John Gillis, *Youth and History: Tradition and Change in European Age-Relations 1770 to the Present* (1981), 1–2. See also Linda Pollock, *Forgotten Children: Parent–Child Relations from 1500 to 1900* (Cambridge, 1983), esp. chs. 1–2; Michael Mitterauer, *A History of Youth*, trans. Graeme Dunphy (Oxford, 1992), 15; V. C. Fox, 'Is adolescence a phenomenon of modern times?', *Journal of Psycho-History*, 5 (1977), esp. 271–5.

distances between children and youth.[2] Yet all of these things existed
long before Luther posted up his ninety-five theses.[3]

This chapter will explore contemporary conceptions of youth in
Tudor and Stuart England, and describe some of the preoccupations which prompted magistrates and moralists to define a particular problem of youth. In so doing, they drew upon a set of intellectual
and social assumptions which clearly distinguished that age from
other stages of the life-cycle. These ideas attributed specific characteristics to each age, with the result that there were attitudes towards youth which permit us to distinguish it from childhood as
well as adulthood in the sentiments of adult observers. The age of
youth raised problems for which particular solutions were proposed.
None of these difficulties were peculiar to youth; it was often a
question of scale, and the pressing opinion that youth presented
the best opportunity to produce good Christians and citizens. The
problem of youth, therefore, was in large part a problem of authority and socialization. It was interpreted in terms of lust, liberty,
licence, and critically, time. Youth was depicted as 'contested territory'; a struggle for conformity in which piety and civility stood
at polar points to impurity and independence. One vital aspect of
the 'official' discourse about age-relations from which a politics of
age directly derived was the political necessity of regulating youth.[4]
Attitudes towards youth help us not only to understand how magistrates and moralists defined that age, but also their interpretations of social order, immorality, and criminality.

Images of youth at this time were usually conceived in religious
language and symbols.[5] The principal sources for this chapter, therefore, will include the treatises, legislation, autobiographies, and
diaries which articulated the religious principles and social morality
of protestant England. Nevertheless, the meaning and representation
of youth to some extent depends upon the nature of the source
before us. Cheap print, for example, may offer another impression.
This chapter seeks to present a rounded portrait of youth which is
drawn from a range of sources, and investigates the particular

[2] Most recently, C. John Sommerville, *The Discovery of Childhood in Puritan England* (Athens,
Ga., 1992).
[3] Cf. Shulamith Shahar, *Childhood in the Middle Ages*, trans. Chaya Galai (1990); Barbara A.
Hanawalt, *Growing up in Medieval London: The Experience of Childhood in History* (New York,
1993).
[4] The politics of age is discussed in Ch. 2.
[5] See S. R. Smith, 'Religion and the conception of youth in seventeenth-century England',
History of Childhood Quarterly, 2 (1975), 495; John Morgan, *Godly Learning: Puritan Attitudes
towards Reason, Learning and Education* (Cambridge, 1986), 144.

preoccupations of different genres (if any) and the common ground between them. Above all, magistrates and moralists presented youth as 'contested territory'. Their conceptualizations were tactically ambiguous, and turned on the interplay between sets of polarities, including good and bad, hope and despair, and right and wrong. Later sections of this chapter will explore both the optimistic and pessimistic portraits of youth, which were intended to coexist in meaningful tension. Youth was a tempestuous age which required careful taming, but it was also a hopeful age of promise and quickening physical and mental faculties. It was this essential ambiguity which allowed moralists to produce differences between youth and other age-groups when they discussed the problem of authority. The idea of 'contested territory' will also be further explored and related to the concern that order depended upon the smooth succession of the generations—the process of socializing young people. But it is with contemporary definitions that we will begin. The opening section seeks to establish the strategies for defining the age of youth throughout this book, and explores a range of numerical and social definitions of age-groups, including the concept of the 'ages of man', and a number of age-titles which were directly derived from the life-cycle.

1. *Defining the Age of Youth*

Rehearsals of the different 'ages of man' regularly featured in texts which assisted in establishing theories of conventional age-relations in early modern society. The understanding of life as a progress from one age with its own particular properties and functions to another is, of course, of ancient origins. The politics and rhythm of generational development were of great interest to Aristotle and Horace, as well as Augustine, Bede, and Chaucer. Visual and literary depictions of different ages took standard forms linking otherwise remote centuries and societies. The political treatises, sermons, medical handbooks, encyclopedias, astrological books, poetry, wall paintings, tapestries, decorations, and stained glass of medieval England were all potential introductions to the different 'ages of man'.[6] Authors often disagreed about the number of ages between

---

[6] J. A. Burrow, *The Ages of Man: A Study in Medieval Writing and Thought* (Oxford, 1986), 43, 45, 92, and chs. 1–2 *passim*; Samuel C. Chew, *The Pilgrimage of Life* (New York, 1973), 146; Aries, *Centuries of Childhood*, esp. 18–19; Merry E. Wiesner, *Women and Gender in Early Modern Europe* (Cambridge, 1993), 41; Hanawalt, *Growing up in Medieval London*, 109.

the cradle and the grave, and their title and duration also. Classical authors described, three, four, six, and seven ages.[7] The medical writers of medieval Europe commonly presented four, though their philosopher colleagues tended to divide life into seven ages, and other literary and visual materials also portrayed this numerical imprecision.[8]

Tudor and Stuart commentators generally followed the schemes and sources of medieval authors.[9] They also could not agree about numbers. Thomas Fortescue, Walter Raleigh, Jaques in *As You Like It*, William Vaughan, and John Smith, for example, all described seven ages. Smith portrayed individuals fleeing from infancy to childhood, 'from thence to youth . . . strength', full age, declination, and finally, old age.[10] Samson Price, John Carpenter, and the author of *The Office of Christian Parents* (1616) divided life into six distinct phases—infancy, childhood, youth, manhood, gravity, and old age.[11] Matthew Griffith and Richard Steele noted five ages.[12] While William Gouge commented that 'many distinguish the whole course of a man's life into foure parts 1. childhood 2. youth 3. manage [and] 4. old-age'. There was a contemporary ballad called 'The Foure Ages of Man', a scheme which was also followed by Francis Lenton, William Guild, and Thomas Brooks, though Thomas Vincent confined himself to merely three.[13] By contrast, a woodcut accompanying the ballad 'The Age and Life of Man . . . From Seaven Till Seaventy', depicted eleven ages of man.

This numerical imprecision was one aspect of early modern discourse about age-differentials. Nevertheless, no matter how many ages they discussed as they fetched people from the cradle to the grave, contemporaries nearly always distinguished a stage of life between childhood and adulthood which they usually called youth.[14]

[7] Chew, *Pilgrimage of Life*, 146.   [8] Burrow, *Ages of Man*, 37, 46–7.
[9] Chew, *Pilgrimage of Life*, ch. 6; Burrow, *Ages of Man*, 50.
[10] Thomas Fortescue, *The Forest, Or Collection of Historyes* (1576), 37–8; Walter Raleigh, *The History of the World in Five Books* (1614), 26; *As You Like It*, 2. 7; William Vaughan, *Directions for Health* (1626), 120–1; John Smith, *The Pourtract of Old Age* (1676), 11.
[11] Samson Price, *The Two Twins of Birth and Death* (1624), 9; John Carpenter, *The Plaine-Man's Spiritual Plough* (1607), 87; anon., *The Office of Christian Parents* (Cambridge, 1616), 43–4.
[12] Matthew Griffith, *Bethel, Or a Forme for Families* (1634), 472; Richard Steele, *A Discourse Concerning Old Age* (1688), 4–6.
[13] William Gouge, *Of Domesticall Duties* (1622), 525; Francis Lenton, *The Young Gallant's Whirligigg, Or Youth's Reakes* (1629), 352; Thomas Vincent, *Words of Advice to Young Men* (1688), 32.
[14] Cf. Vaughan, *Directions for Health*, 120–1, who does not use the title 'youth' to describe the age-group 14–30 years of age, even though he is clearly familiar with the conception of youth and introduces it at a later point in his discussion (see ibid. 123).

The nature of this conception of youth, however, was somewhat blurred by the fact that authors disagreed not only about the number of ages of man but also about their numerical definition. Thomas Fortescue commented that youth extended from 22 to 42 years of age. The author of *The Office of Christian Parents* presented a more typical definition—from 14 to 28—while Richard Mulcaster brought forward the beginning of youth—from 'seven till one and twenty'.[15] There was an occasional gendered dimension to these numerary quarrels, which could imply a sense of different rates of physical development for young men and women. The author of *The Office of Christian Parents* claimed that childhood ended at 12 for 'maids' and two years later for 'boys', while Richard Steele believed that 'females are reckon'd to attain' to youth 'four years sooner than the males'.[16] Nevertheless, we still encounter a broad range of definitions of pre-adult stages of life when people, sometimes glancing back over their lives in an autobiography, tell the story of their youth.[17]

A further area of confusion was the correct place (or otherwise) of the age of adolescence in early modern age-schemes. The proper ordering of adolescence and youth has raised difficulties for both early modern people and recent historians. Both adolescence and youth were adapted by classical and early modern commentators to describe the period of 'growing up'. Thomas Fortescue, for example, situated people aged between 14 and 22 years of age in 'adolescency' before they started a 'long youth', which stretched until the late age of 42. This particular structuring of adolescence and extended youth was familiar to Thomas Elyot, who produced a dictionary in 1538, and to an early eighteenth-century lexicographer also.[18] Other authors reversed the process and placed youth before

[15] Fortescue, *The Forest*, 37; anon., *Office of Christian Parents*, 43; Richard Mulcaster, *Positions wherein Those Primitive Circumstances be Examined Which are Necessarie for the Training up of Children* (1581), 118.

[16] Steele, *Discourse Concerning Old Age*, 5; anon., *Office of Christian Parents*, 136.

[17] For some examples from other genres see Richard Gough, *The History of Myddle*, ed. David Hey (Harmondsworth, 1981), 116; anon., *A Warning to Young Men, Or a Man of Blood* (1680), 5; Joseph Alleine, *Christian Letters Full of Spiritual Instruction* (1671), 17; Sir Thomas Smith, *De Republica Anglorum: A Discourse on the Commonwealth of England*, ed. L. Alston (Cambridge, 1906), 11–12.

[18] Fortescue, *The Forest*, 38; Sir Thomas Elyot, *Dictionary*, 1538 (Scolar Press Facsimile, Menston, 1970), s.v. 'adolescentia'; N. Bailey, *An Universal Etymological English Dictionary* (1721), s.v. 'adolescency'; id., *Dictionarium Britannicum* (1736), s.v. 'adolescency'. Cf. Sir Thomas Elyot, *The Castel of Health* (1541), fo. 13ʳ; Henry Cuffe, *The Difference of the Ages of a Man's Life* (1607), 117–22; Price, *Two Twins*, 9; and the remarks of Thomas Wythorne quoted by Lawrence Stone, *The Family, Sex and Marriage in England 1500–1800* (1977), 512. A number of medieval and classical portrayals are discussed by Burrow, *Ages of Man*, 14, 23, 85, 91–2 (Aristotle called youth the period of growth, 6).

adolescence.[19] These descriptions were by no means uncommon, but they were not widely used.

The precise number of ages to be included in these accounts of the 'ages of man' clearly placed limits upon vocabulary. Nevertheless, despite some linguistic plasticity, a majority of early modern observers used the age-title 'youth' when they wished to draw attention towards people who were in their teens and twenties. This description of pre-adult years coexisted with a contrary but less widely used version which called the 'age of growth' adolescence.[20] Early modern people possessed age-titles which suggest that they distinguished between different phases of youth and development—'boy', 'girl', 'lad', 'wench', 'great boy', 'young man', and 'youth', for example, often indicated a particular place in the progress from youth to adulthood, and imply that some contemporaries recognized differences in the early and later stages of youth.[21] But formal descriptions of the 'ages of man', however, especially those consisting of four or five stages, tended to exclude adolescence,[22] the main point of dispute being about the timing of youth. Authors often depicted generational tension or the pressing necessity of moral reform as a dialogue between age and youth.[23] More significantly perhaps, if we turn from literary sources to certain judicial records,[24] it is very rare to find a mention of adolescence. In fact, I have seen no trace of the term in the courtbooks that I have so far consulted. By contrast, youth is used with impressive regularity. Insufficient attention has been paid to contemporary description and modes of expression hitherto, and previous historians have tended to use youth and adolescence interchangeably in discussions of age-relations in early modern society in a manner which may well have been unfamiliar to most early modern people, and to classical society also.[25]

[19] Rachel Speight in her poem of 1621, 'Mortalities Memorandum', places youth before adolescence (Chew, *Pilgrimage of Life*, 163).

[20] Cf. Aries, *Centuries of Childhood*, 'Until the eighteenth century, adolescence was confused with childhood'; 'an ambiguity remained between childhood and adolescence on the one hand and the category known as youth on the other. [In early modern society] People had no idea of what we call adolescence, and the idea was a long time taking shape', 25, 29.

[21] Cf. the discussion of the 'vocabulary of age' below and Table 1.1.

[22] See, for example, the accounts provided by the author of 'The Foure Ages of Man', and William Gouge, Francis Lenton, and Richard Steele (cited above nn. 12–13), and Richard Mulcaster, *Positions*, 118.

[23] Keith Thomas, 'Age and authority in early modern England', *Proceedings of the British Academy*, 62 (1976), 210.

[24] Naturally I have in mind the judicial sources upon which this book is based, and they include a number of borough courts, hospital records, and, in particular, the records of the church courts which are full of references to 'the youth'.

[25] Cf. N. Kleijwegt, *Ancient Youth: The Ambiguity of Youth and the Absence of Adolescence in Greco-Roman Society* (Amsterdam, 1991); R. Garland, *The Greek Way of Life* (1990).

The two even appear side-by-side in the title of a recent important study.[26]

Nevertheless, there was a measure of contemporary imprecision, and Aries has produced several examples of this 'irregular' vocabulary as firm linguistic evidence that early modern people made no distinction between childhood and other pre-adult stages of life.[27] The use of terms like 'child' or 'boy' was a purely random and arbitrary exercise depending upon individual fancy, so that there was no evident standard or deliberate selection. In fact, age-titles were often confused, and Aries suggests that 'child' or 'boy' could imply any stage in the long 0–30 years age-range.[28] John Gillis has commented that the 'language of age in pre-industrial Europe is hopelessly vague'. He claims that *garçon* or *knabe* 'referred to boys as young as 6 and as old as 30 or 40'.[29] This reading of the causal connection between significant age-titles suggests that for young people at least there is little evidence of an age-specific vocabulary. Moreover, linguistic and numerical inconsistency implies that early modern people had no sense of a stage of life in the long interval between childhood and adulthood, or that if they did, they did not define it in strictly numerical fashion. Gillis draws further support from a narrow reading of child labour in this period in which children were rudely pushed into the monotonous rhythm of adult work and society by the age of 10. These 'tiny adults' and 'forgotten youth' joined the apparently undifferentiated and grey world of adult work, having lost any remote sense of distinctive and sympathetic experiences, character, and sentiment in their 'lost youth'.[30]

[26] Ilana Krausman Ben-Amos, *Adolescence and Youth in Early Modern England* (New Haven, 1994). However, Ben-Amos comments that 'The term *adolescentia* was well known to early modern writers and commentators, but on the whole it was less frequently used' (ibid. 9), yet she still uses the title freely throughout her book. Other historians also regularly use adolescence to describe the period of youth, and they include Hanawalt, *Growing up in Medieval London*, *passim*; Mitterauer, *History of Youth*, *passim*; Alan Macfarlane, *The Family Life of Ralph Josselin, a Seventeenth-Century Clergyman: An Essay in Historical Anthropology* (Cambridge, 1970), 92; Thomas, 'Age and authority', 227; Fox, 'Is adolescence a phenomenon of modern times?', *passim*. Still others confuse childhood with youth.

[27] Aries's argument is, of course, rather more complex than this. It is also based upon substantial investigations of other methods and sources, including visual representation of children and other age-groups, though he has also attracted criticism in these areas of enquiry. See Anthony Burton, 'Looking forward from Aries? Pictorial and material evidence for the history of childhood and family life', *Continuity and Change*, 4 (1989).

[28] Aries, *Centuries of Childhood*, 25–9.

[29] Gillis, *Youth and History*, 1–2. Cf. Hanawalt, *Growing up in Medieval London*, 217—some people 'carried the title of "boy" or "girl" far into their biologically mature years'.

[30] Gillis, *Youth and History*, 1–2. Cf. Mitterauer, *History of Youth*, 16: 'A temporary haziness in the use of the different terms for children and teenagers in French language is ... not satisfactory evidence that traditional European society prior to the seventeenth and eighteenth centuries had no clear concept of adolescence'; and Hugh Cunningham's recent

Nevertheless, in early modern England at least, there is another
type of source from which we can recover a 'vocabulary of age'.
Significant age-titles like 'child', 'servant', 'boy', 'girl', 'lad', 'maid',
or 'wench' which derive directly from the life-course often appear
in judicial records. Sadly, it is rare to discover a precise age attached to these titles. But in the records of the Norwich Court of
Mayoralty (1565–1646), Christ's Hospital, London (1556–80), and
a few supplementary sources there are 249 cases in which the clerk
recorded the age of the offender before the court. The sample is
not large (or exhaustive), but it will at least convey an impression
of the sentiments and conceptualizations of governors as they resorted to a 'vocabulary of age'. The results are set out in Table 1.1.

Some clear trends emerge from this survey of the application of
age-titles in a number of English courts. Perhaps the most significant for us is that in London and Norwich governors allocated
certain titles almost exclusively to people in their teens, with the
result that there is little sign here of the rough and irregular use of
age-titles, which caused both Aries and Gillis to doubt the reality of
youth in early modern society. In fact, all of the mentions of 'boy',
for example, are gathered in the age-range 6–18 years old. Yet
significantly, sixty-three of the seventy usages (90 per cent) are
clustered in the age-belt 10–18.[31] Every 'girl' and 'maid' is aged
between 10 and 24 years of age. While all of the 'lads' are in the
11–19 cohort. Five of the six 'wenches' are aged between 11 and
13 years old. The one 'youth' was 13. These courtbooks also provide
linguistic support for there being a distinctive conception of childhood in this period. 'Child' was used to describe 120 people, 102
of whom were in the age-range 0/1–10 years old (85 per cent),
although the examples of 13 (two times), 14 (three times), 15, 20,
and 21 years old (one each) remind us that there was a degree of
plasticity in age-definition. Sixteen other people who were in the
age-group 0/1–3 years old were called 'infants'. If we confine discussion to titles other than 'infant' or 'child', eighty-three of the
remaining 113 examples of age-description are clustered in the 12–
16 age-range (73.5 per cent). The conceptual world of clerks and
magistrates in these courts included a 'vocabulary of age', which

emphasis upon child unemployment, 'The employment and unemployment of children in
England *c*.1680–1851', *Past and Present*, 126 (1990). See also Shahar, *Childhood in the Middle
Ages*, 245, who very plausibly suggests that there is much evidence of 'contemporary aware-
ness that a child could not undertake the same tasks as an adult peasant'.

[31] Cf. pp. 101–3 and 136, below.

Table 1.1 *The 'Vocabulary of Age' in Early Modern England*[a]

Age	Lad	Maid	Boy	Girl	Wench	Child	Youth	Infant	Total
0–1						23		10	33
1–2						15		2	17
2						8		1	9
3						12		3	15
4						9			9
5						7			7
6			1			11			12
7					1	3			4
8			4			7			11
9			2			4			6
10		1	5	1		3			10
11	3	1	6		1	5			16
12	4	1	14	1		5			25
13	1	2	13	2	4	2	1		25
14	3	2	9	2		3			19
15			2	1		1			4
16	5	1	9						15
17		2							2
18			3						3
19	3								3
20						1			1
21						1			1
24		1			1				2
Totals	19	9	70	7	7	120	1	16	249

[a] The sample includes 204 examples from the records of the Norwich Mayor's Court and the Court of Christ's Hospital in London, thirty-nine from the Norwich Census of the Poor, a further five from vol. 5 of the courtbooks of London Bridewell, and one example from the minute books of Norwich City Quarter Sessions.

placed people in particular age-groups and helped to construct borders between them.

Nor was public familiarity with the different 'ages of man' merely confined to large cities. Roger Lowe of Lancashire attended a play called *The Ages of Man*, 'concerning the life of man from his infancie to old age'.[32] The presence of youth in early modern society can be confirmed both by adult observation and sentiment (including literary prescription, conversion rhetoric, the pressures of socialization,

[32] *The Diary of Roger Lowe of Ashton-in-Makerfield, Lancashire, 1663–1674*, ed. W. L. Sachse (1938), 106.

and prosecution), and the collective sympathies and experiences of young people themselves. These twin proofs of observation and participation permit us to grant youth a distinctive place in early modern society and an active historical role. Youth was one target of Protestant reformers, for example, and there was a particular genre of conduct literature which was intended to further salvation and civility among the youth. The more humble balladeer and carrier of chapbooks crossed the country circulating moral codes for young people in a convenient, small, and cheap package as well as representations of the 'ages of man'.[33] Outside the printed page, we often encounter a group in judicial records—the object of complaint and prosecution—who are formally given the collective title the 'youth' by the scribe. Witness the howls of outrage at the dubious influence of the alehouse, for example, or the casual resort to catechizing.[34]

Age was a badge of political and social differentiation at all levels of Tudor and Stuart society. The distribution of poverty and authority, for example, or decisions about prosecution and punishment were affected by considerations of age and the life-course.[35] A vital aspect of popular expressions of age-relations (and youth) was the distance between the married and unmarried members of a community. A number of ceremonies and social events ritually depicted movement along the life-cycle.[36] In addition, the sense of youth as a distinct experience in early modern society was encouraged by a regular succession of festive and cultural moments— sporting combat between married and unmarried people, youth feasts (usually for male youth), the great youth holidays of May Day and Shrove Tuesday, and children's games which served as an everyday, informal guide to the 'ages of man'. The distinctions of age were also drawn by formal structuring and interference. Different

---

[33] See Tessa Watt, *Cheap Print and Popular Piety, 1550–1640* (Cambridge, 1991), esp. 99, 138, 162, 190, 248; Margaret Spufford, *Small Books and Pleasant Histories: Popular Fiction and its Readership in Seventeenth-Century England* (Cambridge, 1981), esp. 202–3.

[34] For instance CUL EDR, B/2/10, fos. 59, 62; B/2/25, fo. 6; D/2/10, fos. 14, 22ᵛ, 24, 28, 29ᵛ, 34, 46ᵛ. A great deal of additional evidence is presented in subsequent chapters.

[35] The life-cyclical aspects of poverty and social policy are discussed by Tim Wales, 'Poverty, poor relief, and the life-cycle: some evidence from seventeenth-century Norfolk', in Richard M. Smith (ed.), *Land, Kinship and Life-Cycle* (Cambridge, 1984). The political and ideological significance of age and authority is explored in the next chapter. John Beattie has argued that age was one 'discretionary' aspect of the enforcement of the law in early modern England, which influenced choices about prosecution and sentencing, *Crime and the Courts in England 1660–1800* (Oxford, 1986), esp. 440, 611.

[36] See Ben-Amos, *Adolescence and Youth in Early Modern England*, esp. ch. 9, and below, Ch. 3.

age-groups were sometimes allocated different functions and places in civic ritual. While church seating plans often provided further visual validation of age-categories and hierarchies by placing the congregation according to age.[37]

The structures of life and work gave permanent institutional expression to youth; service and apprenticeship being generally seen as a 'natural' sequence of steps to full adulthood. Guild ideologies and practices, including ceremonies and patterns of residence and tutelage for young people, reaffirmed economic and social distances between youth and adulthood.[38] It has been argued that there was a distinctive apprentice culture in urban society, which contributed yet another cultural stamp to age-categories.[39] As we have seen the significance of youth as a timeless step in the life-cycle was also understood by pious authors of conduct books. Though they rarely could agree about a specific numerical definition of youth, when contemporaries used the title they normally had in mind people who were in their teens and twenties. They also possessed a vocabulary which placed people in the same age-group, though a measure of inconsistency always lingered. But there was far more consensus and precision about defining the age of youth in terms of life-cyclical progress. Youth was often conceptualized as a time of dependency and socialization; as preparation for adulthood.[40] 'One and twentie years pass', Bishop Goodman remarked, 'when we live under the custodie and tuition of others.' John Strype simply stated that young people should be 'under tutors and governors'. While the author of *The Office of Christian Parents* discussed how maids and boys 'enter into that age' when 'body and mind are preparing to that state of life where they themselves may be governors of others'.[41]

Youth was widely held to be a preparative period in which individuals acquired the wherewithal to participate fully in the adult world of work, commerce, marriage, and parental responsibility. Yet the texts and records upon which our recovery of the process of socialization depends envisage very different experiences for

---

[37] See below, pp. 104–9.

[38] See Steve Rappaport, *Worlds within Worlds: Structures of Life in Sixteenth-Century London* (Cambridge, 1988), esp. ch. 7; Felicity Heal, *Hospitality in Early Modern England* (Oxford, 1990), 332.

[39] See below, pp. 161–9.

[40] Cf. Mitterauer, *History of Youth*, esp. 33, 84; Shahar, *Childhood in the Middle Ages*, 28.

[41] Godfrey Goodman, *The Fall of Man, Or the Corruption of Nature* (1616), 83; John Strype, *Lessons Moral and Christian for Youth and Old Age* (1699), 9; anon., *Office of Christian Parents*, 136.

young men and women. Marriage was a point of departure from youth for both men and women, though given the virtual absence of the idea of a female occupational career at this time it was 'the most common female exit'.[42] Matthew Griffith, however, informed his audience that 'an unmarried man is but halfe a man'.[43] Yet conduct books placed a far greater emphasis upon marriage and the acquisition of domestic skills for young women. The period of youth is a critical point in the social construction of gender when young men and women are introduced to particular functions and roles to crush any 'natural similarities'. It was hoped that young men would depart youth with the appropriate wisdom, prowess, and resources to become householders, employers, husbands, fathers, or magistrates; young women would emerge from youth as competent mothers, wives, and domestic workers. The training of youth is one 'political context in which masculine and feminine is "socially determined"'.[44] The author of *The Office of Christian Parents* typically suggested that from 12 years of age 'till the age of marriage', women should be taught 'the points of huswifery'. By contrast, young men were to be trained from 14 'till marriage' in a trade or calling.[45] This was the world of formal work and authority; a finely defined structure in which later careers and responsibilities were clearly charted. It was expected that women would not make this sort of occupational progress.[46] They were refused entry 'to any publik function in the church or commonwealth' because their future course was in theory limited to the 'conscionable performance of household duties',[47] even if this was everywhere contradicted by women engaging in casual work, informal training, and formal apprenticeships.[48] Nevertheless, moralists simply continued to advise maids and daughters 'to be keepers at home', to follow 'wife-like sobriety', modesty, mildness, courtesy, and obedience; and

[42] Hanawalt, *Growing up in Medieval London*, 12–13.

[43] Griffith, *Bethel*, 19. Cf. Mitterauer, *History of Youth*, 37.

[44] I am quoting from Wiesner, *Women and Gender in Early Modern Europe*, 6, 240. Cf. ibid. 3.

[45] Anon., *Office of Christian Parents*, 136–7, 142.

[46] Cf. Ben-Amos, *Adolescence and Youth in Early Modern England*, 133.

[47] Gouge, *Domesticall Duties*, 18–19. Cf. Mitterauer, *History of Youth*, 37, and the remarks of Barnabas to Dalila in *Nice Wanton*, in Leonard Tennenhouse (ed.), *Two Tudor Interludes: Nice Wanton and Impatient Poverty* (The Renaissance Imagination, 10, New York, 1984), 49–50.

[48] See Linda Pollock, '"Teach her to live under obedience": the making of women in the upper ranks of early modern England', *Continuity and Change*, 4 (1989); Ilana Krausman Ben-Amos, 'Women apprentices in the trades and crafts of early modern Bristol', *Continuity and Change*, 6 (1991); ead., *Adolescence and Youth in Early Modern England*, ch. 6.

to spend time studying to become a valuable 'fellow helper' to their husbands.[49]

For young women, therefore, the progress from youth to adulthood was in large part measured by their performance in the domestic theatre and the reception of certain 'wife-like' qualities and virtues, including obedience and chastity.[50] Interestingly, although abstinence was recommended as a moral standard for the 'younger sort' more generally, chastity was more usually depicted as a desirable female asset in conduct books and in circulated cheap advice like ballads.[51] Because marriage was the most common point of departure from youth for women, female sexuality was more closely monitored. A concern which was sharpened in certain cases by the transfer of parcels of property and money.[52] Dod and Cleaver cautioned that young women should be constantly reminded 'that the best portion, the greatest inheritance and the most precious jewell that they can bring with them on the marriage day is shamefastnes; the want thereof is most hurtfull in all women'. By contrast, young men required 'many things: as wisdom, eloquence, knowledge of things, remembrance, skill in some trade or craft', justice, courage, 'and other things and qualities . . . too long to rehearse'. These qualities shaped constructions of masculinity and assisted in establishing the character of male socialization. They could not be the property of mere maids. Instead, a woman was asked to treasure honesty, without which she is 'like a man'. Chastity was 'all things', and if a woman should happen to be unchaste, Dod and Cleaver further instructed their readership, then 'call her whore and noughtie packe', and 'with that one word you have taken all'.[53] Virginity was sometimes defined by age-titles which implied female youth; a sharp reminder of the close association between the

[49] Griffith, *Bethel*, 140–1, 114, 139; John Dod and Robert Cleaver, *A Godlie Forme of Household Government* (1612), 59, 217; Richard Baxter, *A Christian Directory, Or a Sum of Practical Theologie and Cases of Conscience* (1673), 552. For some typical expositions of the duties of wives see Francis Billingham, *Christian Oeconomy or Household Government* (1609), 9–11; Griffith, *Bethel*, 322–3, 412 ff.

[50] Cf. Sylvia Hull, *Chaste, Silent and Obedient: English Books for Women 1475–1640* (San Marino, Calif., 1982).

[51] For a few examples of this sort of advice in contemporary ballads see 'The Maiden's Tragedy' in William Chappell (ed.), *The Roxburghe Ballads* (Ballad Society, 14 vols.; London, 1869–95), iii, part 2, 356–9; 'A Warning to Youth' and 'A Warning for Maides' in ibid. iii, part 1, 36–46; W. C. Day (ed.), *The Pepys Ballads* (Cambridge, 1987), 314–15, 336, 500–1; Peter J. Seng (ed.), *Tudor Songs and Ballads from MS Cotton Vespasian A-25* (Cambridge, Mass., 1978), 82–3. Cf. Shahar, *Childhood in the Middle Ages*, 166.

[52] Cf. Hanawalt, *Growing up in Medieval London*, 12–13.

[53] Dod and Cleaver, *Godlie Forme*, 351–2.

construction of femininity and chastity in youth. The clerk at the
Court of London Bridewell used the title 'maid' to infer virginity.
On occasion the process of 'naming' virgins was reversed. Thomas
Brooks, for example, wrote his book for 'young men and virgins'.[54]

Magistrates and moralists also constructed an image of pious and
civil male youth, though rarely if at all do they introduce chastity
as a measure (or 'prize') to evaluate the successful shift from youth
to adulthood for young men. For them the pace of movement
through the life-cycle was measured by the slow though sure transition from pupil to teacher—young underlings became qualified
craftsmen and fathers. Full participation in a trade and marriage
defined the border at which young men left behind the idealized
dependency of youth and accepted the responsibilities of adulthood and a fresh habit of independence. This new maturity
was solemnized and given ritual expression in feasting, drinking,
and ceremonies like the taking of the oath of citizenship, and some
of the customary celebrations of marriage or setting up a fresh
household.[55]

These gendered descriptions of youthful development raise important questions about audience. Who were authors actually address-
ing when they called the youth to general obedience? A substantial
number of texts were addressed either to young men or women.[56]
But a much larger number of authors announced that their prescriptive materials were intended for a group they variously called
the 'youth', 'young men and maydens', 'young and tender plants',
'the younger sort', 'the young', and 'younger'. Others directed their
attention to young people of both sexes in the course of their
advice.[57] These authors were preoccupied with the age of youth in
the first instance, and they often expressed anxiety about what
Matthew Griffith called 'the single life'. All 'singlepersons', he advised, should 'be hewed and squared' by the axe of God's word.
Both ministers and balladeers regularly cautioned single folk to
follow a course of abstinence, 'the pillar of fortitude . . . the bodies

---

[54] Thomas Brooks, *Apples of Gold for All Young Men and Women and a Crown of Glory for Old Men and Women* (1662), Epistle Dedicatory, fo. 4.

[55] See, for example, Alan Macfarlane, *Marriage and Love in England: Modes of Reproduction 1300–1840* (Oxford, 1986), 313–15.

[56] For a discussion of texts which were intended to be read by women see Pollock, ' "Teach her to live under obedience"'; Hull, *Chaste, Silent and Obedient.*

[57] For example, Strype, *Lessons Moral and Christian*, 3, 5, 7, 11, 30, 34; John Shower, *Seasonable Advice to Youth* (1692), 8, 30; Dod and Cleaver, *Godlie Forme*, 363; Brooks, *Apples of Gold*, 31, 32, 39, 44, 52, 57, 96, 103; Gouge, *Domesticall Duties*, 560; Griffith, *Bethel*, 141, 142, 159, 160, 208.

bridle', and 'a shield against lusts'.[58] If they could not resist the terrible temptations of the flesh, young people were invited to seek safe refuge in marriage.[59]

Moralists targeted the 'single life'. Yet many like Thomas Brooks, who in his *Apples of Gold* (1662) addressed himself 'to all young persons throughout the nations, especially those (of both sexes) who begin to turn their faces towards Zion', and who also referred to 'young men and women', constantly relegated the far more comprehensive 'youth' to 'young men' alone. Other authors lapsed from 'young men and maydes' to 'young men', or from the 'younger sort' and 'youth' to 'young man', often in the same paragraph or sentence.[60] Thus the sins of youth became the sins of young men.[61] Some authors reversed the process and casually slipped from 'young men' to 'youth'.[62] Such terms were frequently used interchangeably, and as they steered their young audience through the hazards of pride, flattery, folly, excess, temptation, time, scoffing, or 'carnal reasoning', authors tended to converse with male youth.[63] Richard Turner was a rare example of an author who introduced the age of youth in the feminine.[64] This habit of introducing the problem of youth in gendered language was one reflection of the more urgent preoccupation with socializing young men into private and public places of formal authority, and the reflexes of a society pervaded by patriarchal sentiment and modes of expression. Young men, after all, were future heads of household and employers of young underlings. The moralists' drive to tame youth and raise good citizens had a particular gendered aspect. Nevertheless, it cannot be relegated to a gender-specific tune. Some of the attitudes which are discussed in this chapter are more easily explained by the preoccupation with sexuality. Youthful liberty raised great problems for moralists, and was depicted in a frantic vocabulary of moral depravity and imminent ruin. Yet when we turn from moral commentaries

[58] Griffith, *Bethel*, 164, and 163 ff.; Seng, *Tudor Songs and Ballads*, 87; Day, *Pepys Ballads*, 232.

[59] For example, Dod and Cleaver, *Godlie Forme*, 136; Griffith, *Bethel*, 164 and 237 ff.

[60] See Brooks, *Apples of Gold*, Epistle Dedicatory, fo. 4; Shower, *Seasonable Advice*, 8, 9, 26; Strype, *Lessons Moral and Christian*, 133, 141. Thus Brooks in *Apples of Gold* has male-orientated section headings to guide the reader, including 'The Young Man's Duty and Excellency', 'Good Counsel to Young Men', 'The Old Man's Doubts Resolved', 'Encouragements to Young Men', and 'The Young Man's Objections Answered'.

[61] See Brooks, *Apples of Gold*, 98–101.

[62] Examples of this regular interchange between 'young men' and 'youth' throughout one text can be followed in William Guild, *A Young Man's Inquisition or Trial* (1608).

[63] A very good example is Brooks, *Apples of Gold*, 84–5, 91, 97, 141, 178, 189, 199.

[64] Richard Turner, *Youth Know Thyself* (1624), fos. B1^v–B2^r.

to the records of prosecution we discover that it was independent young women who were charged with some offences with greater frequency.[65] Single women did not fit comfortably into patterns of authority in which marriage and the household were the starting-points for good order.[66] One moral commentary made the connection between female independence and inevitable immorality. There were particular gendered discourses about sexuality, the distribution of authority, and occupational careers, for example, but hovering over all of these 'narrower' debates was the universal concern that youth required close regulation, that young people should be socialized in appropriate fashion, and that good order turned on the succession of generations.

The life-cyclical definition of youth and the apparent teens–twenties consensus are two ways in which this book will locate young people in early modern society. The borders between childhood, youth, and adulthood were sometimes imprecise and blurred.[67] They were widely observed but sometimes neglected, or in fact were unattainable for some people in tough socio-economic conditions. Marriage, setting up an independent household, and full participation in a trade marked various points at which young men and women crossed into adulthood. The timing of the passage into youth was more uncertain. For plebeian youth, entering service or work were significant transitional experiences, and we shall shortly see that they often had interesting correspondences with contemporary opinion about the timing of puberty and the 'age of discretion'. Many early modern people regarded service and its subordinate status as a stage of life. To complicate matters still further, courtbooks like those of the Norwich Court of Mayoralty, which in some cases record the age of offenders, are unfortunately rare, though these records can be supplemented by other judicial materials (e.g. those of London Bridewell) which also provide ages with greater regularity. But it has been argued that even these entries may be suspect because people have slippery memories, and numeracy, like literacy, was an art which had to be acquired. Contemporaries tended to 'round up' figures, with the result that there was an 'unconscious preference' for multiples when recording ages.[68] However, the

---

[65] See below, Ch. 7.

[66] Cf. Patricia Crawford, 'Public duty, conscience and women in early modern England', in John Morrill, Paul Slack, and Daniel Woolf (eds.), *Public Duty and Private Conscience in Seventeenth-Century England: Essays Presented to G. E. Aylmer* (Oxford, 1993), 59; and below, Ch. 7.

[67] Cf. Hanawalt, *Growing up in Medieval London*, 217.

[68] Keith Thomas, 'Numeracy in early modern England', *Transactions of the Royal Historical Society*, 5th ser., 37 (1987), 126.

judicial records I have consulted reveal no strict numerical pattern, and ages are drawn from the entire range of possibilities for youth at least. They have, therefore, been treated as a legitimate indication of age.

Nevertheless, in the absence of precise ages, it is often necessary to turn to the 'vocabulary of age' and its choice of titles which derive directly from the life-cycle. There is, however, an inevitable element of risk involved because these titles may be only approximate indications of age. Apprenticeship, for instance, was in theory an institution which trained single people to be employers and parents. But we sometimes discover married or older apprentices in the sources. Some young people claimed that they had served for more than sixteen, eighteen, and even twenty-one years.[69] Christopher Pennington of London is a fairly remarkable example of somebody who had a long youth. In 1631 he petitioned for the freedom of the city at the ripe age of 66, having been apprenticed to a 'forraine weaver' for fourteen years, 'and hath kept servant there above fortie yeares'.[70] Nevertheless, the overwhelming majority of apprentices in the sources fall within the teens–twenties age-bracket. The life-cyclical character of apprenticeship would place most of them in this age-group, though we must allow for some irregularities.

The case is not so clear with the age-title 'servant', which was frequently used to describe agricultural, domestic, and craft workers, including perhaps the elderly Christopher Pennington. Service could in fact imply work, though it was clearly age-related.[71] The term was sometimes used to describe older bachelors, spinsters, widows, or widowers returning to residential work. There is mention of a familiar figure, the 'ancient servant' and trusty retainer in the London sources.[72] Yet there is a great deal of evidence which suggests that most of those who were called servants in this period were young people in their teens and twenties.[73] Ann Kussmaul has carefully characterized service in husbandry as an important stage in the progress from youth to adulthood in the countryside. In London, only 9.2 per cent of the male servants who were buried in the large

---

[69] See CLRO Reps. 34, fo. 459; 37, fo. 138ᵛ; 47, fos. 343ᵛ–4.
[70] CLRO Rep. 45, fo. 445.   [71] See below, Ch. 7.   [72] CLRO Rep. 45, fo. 112ᵛ.
[73] Cf. Marjorie Keniston McIntosh, *A Community Transformed: The Manor and Liberty of Havering, 1500–1620* (Cambridge, 1991), 54. Hanawalt writing about medieval London has commented that 'the age-range [of servants] was from seven to seventy, with the majority being in their teens or early twenties' (*Growing up in Medieval London*, 173). See also P. J. P. Goldberg, *Women, Work and Life-Cycle in a Medieval Economy: Women in York and Yorkshire c.1300–1520* (Oxford, 1992), 168–72, esp. table 4.3.

parish of St Botolph's, Aldgate, in the period 1584–1601 were older than 25 years of age at death. While in Norwich, the clerk of the Court of Mayoralty recorded the age of servants in only a handful of cases, though all of these offenders were under 27 years of age. Significantly, servants were often grouped together with apprentices and children by courts imposing household curfews upon the young, for instance, or by clerical officials attempting to persuade the youth to attend catechizing.[74]

This 'vocabulary of age' helped to anchor a firm conception of youth in early modern minds. Yet as we shall shortly see, there are interesting contradictions and a deliberately ambiguous attitude towards youth in the rhetoric of conversion and political socialization. That age was usually conceived in terms of seemingly distant polarities, and it is by no means uncommon to find these shifting meanings in the same page or paragraph, as authors press the urgency of seeking conformity in youth. On the one hand, youth was depicted as a time of great hope and promise, but on the other it was a 'dark and licentious age', which threatened to bury good prospects under layers of pessimism and despair. We will explore each aspect of this two-sided image in turn, though it must be remembered that it was the correspondence and communication between these two poles which provided the pivotal point for discussions of authority. Darkness and light, and despair and hope required each other and meant less when they were treated apart. But we will begin with the 'dark' and 'dangerous age'.

2. The 'Dark' and 'Dangerous Age'

The 'dark' and 'dangerous age' is a regular refrain in contemporary moral commentaries in which authors try to catch in language and imagery the worst sides of the age of youth. The author of *The Office of Christian Parents* commented that youth was 'the worst and most dangerous time of all'. Richard Greenham and Richard Burton both portrayed youth as 'the dangerous season', and Thomas Brooks called it 'the slippery age'. Matthew Griffith held youth in similar contempt, it was a 'dark age'. A hostile image he shared with Walter

---

[74] Ann Kussmaul, *Servants in Husbandry in Early Modern England* (Cambridge, 1981), 3–11; Jeremy Boulton, *Neighbourhood and Society: A London Suburb in the Seventeenth Century* (Cambridge, 1987), 133–4; NRO NMC 7, fo. 334; 8, fo. 89; 10, fo. 177. Cf. McIntosh, *A Community Transformed*, 53–4. Household curfews and catechizing are discussed in Ch. 2.

Pringle, who described the age of youth as 'years of darkness, deadness, and sinfulness'.[75] These rather inflammatory and crude denunciations were clearly intended to advertise the disreputable characteristics of youth which stirred anxiety in the studies, pulpits, and courtrooms of early modern England. In fact, contemporaries attributed particular qualities to each age. Pierre Charron, for example, identified 'many discommodities and miseries common, ordinary, and perpetual' in the life of man, but also other 'particular and distinct' characteristics 'according to the diversity of the parts, ages, and seasons', which he defined as 'infancy, youth, virility, and old age'.[76]

Moralists assigned the 'dark age' particular characteristics, sins, and vices; 'its peculiar corruptions, levity, wantonness, and headiness'.[77] They were by no means the exclusive property of the young. It was more often an issue of degree rather than kind. The author of *The Office of Christian Parents* typically stated that every age had its own season, 'as unto children a certain weaknes', to youth 'lustie and stoutnesse, gravitie to constant age, and to old age a certain ripeness'.[78] Thomas Vincent noted '20 sins of youth'. While Thomas Brooks discussed only five—pride, sensual pleasures and delights, mocking and scoffing at religious men and things, rashness, and lustfulness and wantonness. These were the '5 sins of youth; yet they are not all the sins of youth, for youth is capable of and subject to all sins whatsoever', but they were the 'special sins of youth'.[79] Similar catalogues of sins featured in the plays, ballads, and advice books retelling the tale of the 'prodigal son',[80] and in the literature

[75] Anon., *Office of Christian Parents*, 159; Richard Burton, *The Apprentice's Companion* (1681), 88; Richard Greenham, *The Works of the Reverend and Faithful Servant of Jesus Christ Mr Richard Greenham*, ed. H[enry] H[olland] (1601), 262; Brooks, *Apples of Gold*, 98; Griffith, *Bethel*, 161. Pringle's description is included in W. K. Tweedie (ed.), *Select Biographies* (Wodrow Society, 2 vols.; Edinburgh, 1845–7), ii. 424.

[76] Shower, *Seasonable Advice*, 6; Pierre Charron, *Of Wisdome, Three Bookes*, trans. S. Lennard (1630), 122. See also Goodman, *Fall of Man*, 125.

[77] Samuel Crossman, *The Young Man's Calling, Or the Whole Duty of Youth* (1678), 122. See also Shower, *Seasonable Advice*, 5; Vincent, *Words of Advice*, 77.

[78] Anon., *Office of Christian Parents*, 43.

[79] Vincent, *Words of Advice*, 92; Brooks, *Apples of Gold*, 84–101. Cf. Griffith, *Bethel*, 161–2; Shower, *Seasonable Advice*, 6.

[80] For example, *The Interlude of Youth* in I. Lancashire (ed.), *Two Tudor Interludes* (Manchester, 1980); Turner, *Youth Know Thyself*, fos. B1ᵛ–B2ʳ; 'Four Ages of Man'; Lenton, *Young Gallant's Whirligigg*, esp. 5–8, 10, 12, 14–17; *Nice Wanton* in Tennenhouse, *Tudor Interludes*; George Gascoigne, *The Glass of Government*, 1575 (Tudor Facsimile Texts, New York, 1970), fo. N1ʳ, and *passim*; Chappell, *Roxburghe Ballads*, ii, part 1, 393–8; iii, part 1, 63–8; iv, part 1, 49–50. Cf. Watt, *Cheap Print and Popular Piety*, 120; and the comments of Natascha Wurzbach, *The Rise of the English Street Ballad 1550–1650*, trans. Gayna Walls (Cambridge, 1990), esp. 124–5, 141.

reporting the 'last dying words' of the felon at the gallows as he told the story of his youth to explain his sorry descent to the hanging tree; a penitential narrative of irreverence, 'lewd play', theft, and illicit sex, in which perpetual sinning and law-breaking became a metaphor for misspent youth.[81] The peak of depravity was touched in youth, and this became a powerful representation of the 'wicked' side of that age. Shakespeare's old shepherd echoed the despair of many pious authors in wishing that 'there were no age' between 10 and 23, 'or that youth would sleep out the rest', for youth was nothing but 'getting wenches with child, wronging the ancientry, stealing', and fighting.[82]

These anxieties were articulated in a variety of print media, and they were intimately affected by the particular problems raised by service and an image of profane youth engaging in violence, recreation, opposition, and irreverence, which could spill over into generational tension. 'The most part' of young people, William Guild commented, 'walketh and loveth to walketh in that broad byway of liberty, where there is no restraint or curbing of the affections and lusts of the flesh'. The youth of England were like wild colts and heifers leaping and kicking in wide fields. Anthony Stafford introduced the same simile. A young man 'is like a wilde horse', charging over broad expanses unfettered, 'who, if he wants a curbe will runn himself to death'. Gerrard Winstanley and Shakespeare also used the metaphor of the young colt. Arviragus in *Cymbeline* fondly recalled his 'leaping time'.[83] This image of unshackled youth pervaded conversion rhetoric, and it can also help us to conceptualize the preoccupations behind secular legislation like The Statute of Artificers (1563), which was introduced to curb 'the unadvised rashness and licentious manner of youth'.[84] Contemporaries often

[81] George Chapman *et al.*, *Eastward Ho*, 1605 (Tudor Facsimile Texts, New York, 1970), esp. fo. G3ʳ. Cf. Charles MacKay (ed.), *A Collection of Songs and Ballads Relative to the London Prentices and Trades* (Percy Society, 1, 1841), 51–3; Day, *Pepys Ballads*, 115–16, 128–9; Chappell, *Roxburghe Ballads*, iii, part 1, 1–5, 23–41, 155–9; vii, part 1, 61–6, 70–5, 100–2. Cf. Wurzbach, *Rise of the English Street Ballad*, esp. 112–13, 126, 129; J. A. Sharpe, ' "Last dying speeches": religion, ideology and public executions in seventeenth-century England', *Past and Present*, 107 (1985).

[82] *The Winter's Tale*, 3. 3.

[83] Guild, *Young Man's Inquisition*, 20–1; Anthony Stafford, *Meditations and Resolutions, Moral, Divine, Political, Written for the Instruction and Bettering of Youth* (1612), 109–10; Winstanley is quoted by Thomas, 'Age and Authority', 16; *Cymbeline*, 4. 2; *Richard II*, 2. 1; *2 Henry IV*, 4. 2; *The Merchant of Venice*, 5. 1. See also Chapman *et al.*, *Eastward Ho*, fo. H3ʳ; anon., *Office of Christian Parents*, 135; Strype, *Lessons Moral and Christian*, 7–8; Greenham, *Works*, 262; Brooks, *Apples of Gold*, 99.

[84] This aspect of service is more fully explored in Ch. 7.

passed comment upon the violent and reckless nature of young people.[85]

New decades and generations slipped by but different authors and governors continued to interpret the problem of youth as a question of authority and discipline. Young people 'cannot bear any restraint', John Strype complained towards the close of the seventeenth century.[86] It was the great distance between youthful autonomy and the policy of containing spontaneity within the structures of the life-cycle by prolonging dependence, which explains much of the hyperbole which characterized conceptualizations of 'dangerous' youth in early modern society. Youthful independence and its baggage of moral lapses was in many respects criminalized. In fact, as we shall shortly see, the control of youth was essential to social order more generally. Thomas Brooks simply stated that youth required 'very violent reins'. While William Guild observed that youth 'is carried with a more headlong force unto vice, lust, and vaine pleasures of the flesh', and therefore 'hath need of straiter discipline, more carefull watching . . . harder brydling, and more diligent instruction by the word of God'.[87]

A further guide to the preoccupations affecting this concept of youth is provided by the language and imagery used to depict this 'rash age'. These descriptions tended to employ sensual and vivid imagery—heat, excess, noise, lust, riot. Young people were 'hotspurs'. 'Their pots are boiling', William Higford declared. Robert Abbot portrayed youth as 'a seething pot which casts out scum'. While another author discussed the 'naturall heat and vigour which is most predominant in youth'. An age, Bishop Goodman commented, which 'desireth nothing more than the noyse of the drumme, or the sound of the trumpet'.[88] Youth was sometimes presented as the hot and humid summer which chills in the cool autumn of wise adulthood and maturity.[89] Contemporary theory about humours and heat in the different 'ages of man', which associated separate stages of the life-cycle with hot, warm, cool, mild, and cold

---

[85] For example, Conyers Read (ed.), *William Lambarde and Local Government* (Ithaca, NY, 1962), 158–61.

[86] Strype, *Lessons Moral and Christian*, 7–8.

[87] Brooks, *Apples of Gold*, 100; Guild, *Young Man's Inquisition*, 20–1.

[88] Brooks, *Apples of Gold*, 93; Higford is quoted by Thomas, 'Age and authority', 218; Robert Abbot, *A Christian Family Builded by God* (1653), 24; the fourth quotation (by Braithwait) is quoted by Smith, 'Religion and the conception of youth', 499; Goodman, *Fall of Man*, 126. See also *The Diary of Alexander Jaffray*, ed. J. Barclay (1833), 5.

[89] Cf. Chew, *Pilgrimage of Life*, 155.

temperatures, usually portrayed youth as the 'hot' phase of life.[90] Some of Shakespeare's characters share these sentiments, though youthful 'heat' can also mean something more positive; a vital energy which can be tapped for productive purposes.[91] The 'hot' temper of youth was sometimes mere boasting and posturing by heroic officers, or by young sparks and gallants. It could even have been a key stratagem of conversion rhetoric. But in the portrait of the 'dark' side of youth it was deeply disturbing and threatening. The typical complaint about the teeming sensuality of youth suggests that moralists were chiefly preoccupied by a fear (or ignorance) of youthful energy and sexuality. Their complaints may have been prejudiced gestures to comprehend the physical developments associated with puberty.

A number of works published in early eighteenth-century England reported that puberty or the 'ripe age' began at 13 to 15 years of age for girls—'when female spirits were brisk and inflam'd'— and 16 for boys, when they were full of 'vital strength'.[92] Such remarks provide a clue to contemporary thought, but there does not seem to have been any clear and considered medical opinion about sexual development in the earlier period *c.*1560–*c.*1640,[93] and much of what we find is a chorus of condemnation which was largely fashioned by ignorance and a moral crusade to reform the perceived negative qualities of youth. Authors spend page after page dwelling upon youthful lust, licentiousness, and the flesh. John Shower vividly portrayed 'the young sinner . . . burning in lust' and 'drowning in sensuality'. Henry Cuffe was only producing a conventional wisdom in claiming that it was Venus (and the pursuit of pure pleasure) who guided 'our blossoming, lustfull age'.[94] Moralists

---

[90] See, for example, Cuffe, *Difference of the Ages.*

[91] See *Richard II*, 2. 1; *1 Henry IV*, 5. 2; *The Merchant of Venice*, 5. 1.

[92] See anon., *Aristotle's Compleat Masterpiece in Three Parts Displaying the Secrets of Nature in the Generation of Man* (23rd edn., 1749), 28–9; anon., *Aristotle's Book of Problems* (13th edn., 1775), 66. Both of which have been edited by R. Trumbach in the Garland Series: Marriage, Sex and the Family in England 1660–1800, 11 (1986). Natalie Davis suggests that sixteenth-century French opinion situated the age of puberty at 14 for males, 'Some tasks and themes in the pursuit of popular religion', in C. Trinkaus and H. O. Oberman (eds.), *The Pursuit of Holiness in Late Medieval and Renaissance Religion* (Leiden, 1974), 319–20. Merry Wiesner suggests that 'somewhere around fourteen was probably about average, with poorer girls starting later than wealthier ones' (*Women and Gender in Early Modern Europe*, 44). Cf. Peter Laslett, 'Age at sexual maturity in Europe since the Middle Ages', in his *Family Life and Illicit Love in Earlier Generations: Essays in Historical Sociology* (Cambridge, 1977).

[93] A point suggested to me by Adrian Wilson, who tells me that he is not aware of any fully developed medical interpretation of puberty and related physical development before 1650.

[94] Shower is quoted by Smith, 'Religion and the conception of youth', 499; Cuffe, *Difference of the Ages*, 121.

may not have had medical textbooks close to hand on their shelves, but they would have had easy access to treatises which offered them a decidedly pessimistic account of human nature and potential.

All of the 'ages of man' could wallow in worldly slumber and sensuality, though most authors agreed that there was one age in which the 'lusts of the flesh' raged most fiercely. It was 'chiefly in youth', William Guild remarked, 'that man's nature . . . affecteth libertie of the flesh'. Young people were intoxicated by pleasure and licentiousness, and subject, Henry Hesketh observed, to 'irregular sensual passions'. They possessed 'a great deal of nature' but little grace; much vigour and heat but little civility.[95] Youth was considered a 'time of discovery' in a number of respects. Both intellectual and physical powers were quickly developing and approaching their full potential, and one aspect of this was a version of physical development in which 'natural man' first asserted himself in youth. 'And on the other side of all ages', William Guild observed, it was 'youth *having newly begun and unacquainted* with these terrifying lets [i.e. "lets and hindrances of the affections and alluring lusts of the flesh"]', who were 'easiest by nature to be drawn away and perswaded to the inticing and sweet pleasures of the flesh'. 'Tis true', Shower commented, that nature's corruption 'doth usually and with great violence discover itself in unsanctified youth by there lusts of the flesh.'[96] Moralists quickly made the connection between the first bursts of 'these terrifying lets', strength, vigour, heat, sensuality, lust, and the urge for liberty.

The unpredictable temper of 'the flesh' contributed to an orthodoxy regarding the malleability and essential instability of youth. It was a 'most unsettled age'. Dod and Cleaver described the young as 'tender and tractable, their minds flexible and ready to anything'. William Guild characterized them as 'greene and flexible'. For 'the most part', Shower remarked, young people 'are changeable and unsteady, heedless and unweary'.[97] This concern with the

[95] Guild, *Young Man's Inquisition*, 267; Henry Hesketh, *The Importance of Religion to Young Persons* (1683), 5. See also Richard Sibbes, *Works*, ed. A. B. Grossart (Edinburgh, 1973), 283; Francis Billingham, *The Young Man's Scripture* (1609), fos. 20ᵛ–1ʳ; Strype, *Lessons Moral and Christian*, 7–8. Cf. Roger Ascham, *The Scholemaster* in *English Works*, ed. W. A. Wright (1970), 226–7; Brooks, *Apples of Gold*, 88.

[96] Guild, *Young Man's Inquisition*, 106–7; Shower, *Seasonable Advice*, 6.

[97] Smith, 'Religion and the conception of youth', 497; Shower, *Seasonable Advice*, 9; Guild, *Young Man's Inquisition*, 87; Dod and Cleaver, *Godlie Forme*, 265. Cf. the remarks of Sommerville, *Discovery of Childhood*, 34; Turner, *Youth Know Thyself*, fo. B2ʳ; Oliver Heywood, *Autobiography, Diaries, Anecdote and Event Books*, ed. J. Horsfal Turner (4 vols.; Brighouse, 1882), i. 160; and the remarks of Charity in *The Interlude of Youth*, in Lancashire (ed.), *Two Tudor Interludes*, 551–2.

mercurial and shifting moods of young people is an interesting footnote to the rising levels of actual physical movement they were making at this time. Francis Lenton made this connection when he commented upon 'the vagrant will and thirsting appetite of youth'.[98] This flexibility was a vital aspect of the two-sided vision of youth because it meant that the fate of young people was in the balance; they could swing either way, towards conformity or opposition. The obstacles were formidable, though there was a glimmer of hope. The matter was still more urgent because magistrates and moralists followed the tactical argument that the time of youth provided the best opportunity to save souls and plant political conformity.

3. The 'Spring' of Life

Thomas Vincent cautioned people to seek salvation 'in the morning of your life, in the spring of your years, in the flower of your youth'. Samuel Burrowes preached that youth was 'the fittest and most choicest time', for Christ 'doth come awooing . . . now you are strong and quick and full fed'.[99] Young bodies and minds were fresh, strong, and active, and young converts offered 'a great kindnesse' to God because they inhabited 'a world of self-denial', and left behind a profane world laced with pleasure, corruption, and temptation before they 'tasted of the honey'.[100] Special sermons for the young naturally paid close attention to this point. Thomas Powell reminded 'the younger sort'—'being such for the most part that were present when this sermon was preached'—that God coveted 'the first fruits of our green and flourishing age'. Burrowes warned his audience of 'apprentices and maids' that God 'will have you come in in green yeares'.[101]

Such pastoral commentaries represent the local application of a far wider belief that the smooth progress of sound religion and civil society was greatly assisted by the active participation of young people. Cranmer reminded Edward VI 'that there is nothing more necessary' than ensuring 'that the youth and tender age of your

[98] Lenton, *Young Gallant's Whirligigg*, 17.

[99] Vincent, *Words of Advice*, 21; Samuel Burrowes, *Good Instruction for All Young Men and Maids* (1642), 5.

[100] Quotations are from Burrowes, *Good Instruction*, 8; Greenham, *Works*, 424. Cf. Guild, *Young Man's Inquisition*, 51; Vincent, *Words of Advice*, 22–4.

[101] T. Powell, *The Beauty, Vigour and Strength of Youth Bespoke for God* (1676), 54; Burrowes, *Good Instruction*, 4. Cf. Brooks, *Apples of Gold*, 47.

loving subjects' are 'brought up and traded in the truth of God's holy word'. These appeals doubtless fell on sensitive ears at a time of bitter confessional struggle. In 1600 the Privy Council wrote to the mayor and aldermen of York about the apparent disturbing rise of recusancy in the city. They encouraged the civic fathers 'to have care of the good education of all youthes and children' in their charge, that they 'be instructed and seasoned at the first with the trew knowledge of God and religion whereby they are likelie to become good members of the Church and Commonweale'. John White of Dorchester firmly believed that 'all the hope is in training up the youth *in time*', and his words were translated into action in the imposing form of an hospital in which young people were introduced to the godly life of tutored work, order, and piety.[102]

The political subordination of youth was necessary because 'natural man' who first asserted himself in that age proposing sensual corruption and temptation, also advocated levelling notions like parity and disobedience.[103] It was hoped that people would be weaned away from such insolent habits in youth, otherwise each might prove a potential Tyler or Kett in later life, unfit for any 'place' or office in the commonwealth. 'Hence it comes to passe', Roger Mainwaring commented, that people who were 'never subdued with a religious awe' in early life, 'nor acquainted with any reverence or godly fear towards their superiour', grow up to 'become so desperate and audacious, so lewd and licentious, as to be so far from honouring the person of the ruler, that they doe, with great boldnesse, traduce his actions'. It was of some meaning for the preservation of social order that people should be 'broken and bridled' in the time of their youth 'by good nurture'.[104]

These troubled sentiments were driven by a sharp sense of the enduring nature of custom and habit. Magistrates and ministers had to interfere with the natural course of life to encourage a fresh commitment to piety and civility. 'The custom of sinne', one author declared, 'is in a manner made natural by long continuance', and

[102] Thomas Cranmer, *Miscellaneous Writings and Letters*, ed. J. E. Cox (Cambridge, 1846), 267; YCA B/32, fos. 79ᵛ–80; David Underdown, *Fire from Heaven: Life in an English Town in the Seventeenth Century* (1992), 109–13. Cf. John Vowell [Hooker] *Orders Enacted for Orphans and for Their Portions within the Citie of Exeter* (1575), Epistle Dedicatory; anon., *Office of Christian Parents*, 11.

[103] Issac Bargrave, *A Sermon Preached before King Charles . . . [on] March 27, 1627* (1627), 1–2, 4.

[104] Roger Mainwaring, *Religion and Allegiance; In Two Sermons Preached before the King's Majestie . . . [on] 4 July 1627* (1627), Second Sermon, 7. See also Robert Shelford, *Lectures or Readings upon the 6 Verse of the 22 Chapter of Proverbs Concerning the Vertuous Education of Youth* (1606), 15–16.

'custom, if once it be rooted, cannot easily be plucked up and expelled'. Custom was treated as 'a second nature'. Arthur Dent strongly believed that custom 'maketh another nature and taketh away all sense and feeling of sinne'.[105] Souls had to be won early because as each year passed by individuals became more familiar with the world of fallen humanity. Experience taught that it was 'a hard thing to irradicate old habits'.[106] By contrast, those who turned to God in youth were treasured converts because their life stretched before them, and they had a long time in which to glorify him. A careful education was typically seen as an opportunity to construct a 'second nature in man'.[107] More urgent still, it was generally held that a 'second nature' proved more decisive in shaping the course of life.[108]

The problems of salvation and political conformity, therefore, were presented as issues of time, which gave them a particular 'age-aspect' and added a strategic sense of pressure. The clock was ticking at birth; the race against time had begun. Time was an instrument of moral reformation and a regular theme of Sunday sermons.[109] If 'young men and women' hoped to escape an eternity of suffering, Thomas Brooks cautioned, they must put 'precious time' to good purpose. These valuable minutes and hours were not to be squandered in drinking, or carding and dicing. Nor were young people to swear, lie, or whore away the day, because 'time was a talent that God will reckon with you for'.[110] These sentiments also coloured works about poverty and reformation like John Gore's *The Poor*

---

[105] John Northbrooke, *A Treatise wherein Dicing, Dauncing, Vaine Playes and Enterludes . . . are Reproved,* 1577? (facsimile, Garland Series: The English Stage: Attack and Defence, 1577–1730, New York, 1974), fos. 3ᵛ–4ʳ; Arthur Dent, *The Plaine-Man's Path-way to Heaven,* 1601 (facsimile, The English Experience, 652, Amsterdam, NJ, 1974), 330. See also Francis Fuller, *Words to Give the Young Man Knowledge and Discretion* (1653), 103; Billingham, *Young Man's Scripture,* 28; Vincent, *Words of Advice,* 24–5; W.P., *The Prentise's Practise in Godlinesse and His True Freedome* (1613), fo. 22ᵛ; William Martyn, *Youth's Instruction* (1612), 31.

[106] Vincent, *Words of Advice,* 24–5.

[107] Ibid. 22–4; Guild, *Young Man's Inquisition,* 47–8, 87–8; W.P., *Prentise's Practise,* fos. 3ᵛ–4. Cf. Thomas Floyd, *The Picture of a Perfit Commonwealth* (1600), 98–9; Richard Baxter, *The Poor Man's Family Book* (1674), 302; Gouge, *Domesticall Duties,* 537, 544; John Milton, *Of Education* in *Prose Works,* ed. K. M. Burton (1958), 320–1.

[108] See Dod and Cleaver, *Godlie Forme,* 108–9; Floyd, *Picture of a Perfit Commonwealth,* 98; Guild, *Young Man's Inquisition,* 101; Richard Baxter, *Compassionate Counsel to All Young Men* (1681), 9.

[109] For example, in sermons preached by Henry Newcome, *The Diary of the Reverend Henry Newcome from September 30 1661 to September 29 1663,* ed. T. Heywood (Chetham Society, 18, Manchester, 1849), 112, 124, 146, 192.

[110] Brooks, *Apples of Gold,* 24. See also John Downame, *A Guide to Godlynesse* (1629), 256; Dod and Cleaver, *Godlie Forme,* 78; Baxter, *Christian Directory,* 567.

Man's Hope (1646), and can help us to conceptualize criticisms of alehouses, idleness, and plebeian recreation.[111]

The right use of time and the image of pious and civil youth were standard subjects of the scripted 'last dying speeches' at the gallows. Contemporary accounts of habitual criminality tended to follow conversion rhetoric and present a *domino theory* of character in which youthful lapses moulded a 'second nature'—the more serious capital crimes quickly followed on the heel of youthful misdemeanours. The story of the fall into crime closely paralleled the slide into sin. In *Eastward IIo*, Touchstone lectures Quicksilver, his apprentice who is shortly to hang at Tyburn, 'you see the issue of your sloth. Of sloth cometh pleasure, of pleasure cometh riot, of riot comes whoring, of whoring comes spending, of spending comes want, of want comes theft, of theft comes hanging.'[112] These moral narratives, which were spoken from the gallows and circulated in pamphlets, plays, and ballads, were composed for the example of young people (and especially young men), so that that they could declare with George Saunders in a moment of tragic self-knowledge: 'I have sinned', 'I am a sinner', and so kneel down in humble fashion, repent, and begin a 'second life'. They would learn to obey magistrates and parents, and to ask God to bless the monarch, clergy, nobility, and the State.[113]

An early conversion in youth was a source of joy in later life, but to remain in sin could only be a source of remorse. A near proverbial wisdom held that what was sown in youth was reaped in age.[114] A misspent youth resulted in sobs, sighs, and tears in old age. We can almost hear the regrets and laments of diarists and spiritual

---

[111] John Gore, *The Poor Man's Hope* (1646), esp. 41. Cf. W.P., *Prentise's Practise*, fo. 28ᵛ; Brooks, *Apples of Gold*, 28; Philip Stubbes, *An Anatomie of Abuses*, 1583, ed. A. Freeman (Garland Series: The English Stage: Attack and Defence 1577–1730, New York, 1973), 87; Fuller, *Words to Give the Young Man Knowledge*, 56.

[112] Chapman *et al.*, *Eastward Ho*, fo. G3ᵛ. Cf. Chappell, *Roxburghe Ballads*, iii, part 1, 1–5, 25–8, 36–41; J. A. Sharpe, *Crime in Early Modern England 1550–1750* (1984), 162–4; id., ' "Last dying speeches"'; Lincoln B. Faller, *Turned to Account: The Forms and Functions of Criminal Biography in Late Seventeenth- and Early Eighteenth-Century England* (Cambridge, 1987), esp. chs. 2, 3, and 5; Philip Rawlings, *Drunks, Whores and Idle Apprentices: Criminal Biographies of the Eighteenth Century* (1992), esp. chs. 19–22.

[113] Day, *Pepys Ballads*, 129; Chappell, *Roxburghe Ballads*, vii, part 1, 72–5; iii, part 1, 155–9; Lenton, *Young Gallant's Whirligigg*, 21. See also Chappell, *Roxburghe Ballads*, iii, part 1, 23–41; vii, part 1, 61–6, 70–3, 100–2; Day, *Pepys Ballads*, 115–16; MacKay, *Songs and Ballads Relative to the London Prentices*, 35–50, 51–3.

[114] For example, Shower, *Seasonable Advice*, 7; Guild, *Young Man's Inquisition*, 58; Brooks, *Apples of Gold*, 14; Baxter, *Compassionate Counsel*, 40; Fuller, *Words to Give the Young Man Knowledge*, 56.

autobiographers as they glanced back and remembered nutting on the sabbath, or dancing around a maypole. Ralph Josselin's 'youthful vanities' plagued him 'to this day'. While George Trosse's youthful lapses were 'an hospital of diseases' in his 'elder yeares'.[115] To complete their case, many authors suggested that salvation in later life, though still a faint possibility, was much more difficult to obtain. Sin and crime had become a custom, and both physical and intellectual powers were a faint shadow of their former youthful excellence. In addition, a late repentance was viewed with suspicion, especially the final gasps of dying men and women.[116]

Time was measured in years, the comparison between youth and later life, and in hours and minutes, the warning to put time to good purpose rather than sinking in worldly ease and seeing the grave as a distant prospect.[117] Attention was firmly shifted into the present because past time could not be redeemed, and future time could not be trusted.[118] Even 'the best of us', Thomas Powell warned his audience of young men, 'cannot promise ourselves a day'. 'The present time only is ours, the morrow we are not sure of', and so he advised his young hearers to 'improve your time while you are young'. 'Start today while it is called today', John Shower advised the mourners of the 'younger sort' who had gathered to bury their friend, every day is a delay. 'Bee new men now', the author of *The Prentise's Practise* ordered his readers, 'this day, this night, this hour in which thou art admonished'. Preaching by example, Thomas Powell wasted no time upon words; 'upon this monosyllable now', he declared, 'depends eternity'.[119] Young people were frequently invited to 'strike while the iron was hot'.[120]

[115] *The Diary of Ralph Josselin 1616–1683*, ed. Alan Macfarlane (British Academy Records of Social and Economic History, New Series, 3, 1976), 144, 151, 185, 243–4; Isaac Gilling, *The Life of George Trosse* (1715), 131; *The Autobiography of Henry Newcome*, ed. R. Parkinson (2 vols.; Chetham Society, 16–17, Manchester, 1852), 68, 74. See also *The Notebook of the Reverend Thomas Jolly a.d. 1671–1693*, ed. H. Fishwick (Chetham Society, 33 Manchester, 1895), 81; Jaffray, *Diary*, 3; Sommerville, *Discovery of Childhood*, 74–5.

[116] For the possibility and difficulty of late salvation see Brooks, *Apples of Gold*, 351, 359–60; Shower, *Seasonable Advice*, 34–5; Powell, *Beauty, Vigour and Strength of Youth*, 53–4; Strype, *Lessons Moral and Christian*, 117–18. Typical suspicions of late repentance are voiced by Newcome, *Diary*, 13; Stubbes, *Anatomie of Abuses*, fo. R3ʳ; Powell, *Beauty, Vigour and Strength of Youth*, 55; Brooks, *Apples of Gold*, 54.

[117] Greenham, *Works*, 422; Powell, *Beauty, Vigour and Strength of Youth*, 68; Griffith, *Bethel*, 143.

[118] Brooks, *Apples of Gold*, 31–2; W.P., *Prentise's Practise*, fo. 66; Downame, *Guide to Godlynesse*, 461; Sibbes, *Works*, 43.

[119] Powell, *Beauty, Vigour and Strength of Youth*, 61, 56; W.P., *Prentise's Practise*, fo. 28ᵛ; Shower, *Seasonable Advice*, Epistle Dedicatory, fos. A2ʳ, 35, 37.

[120] For example, by Fuller, *Words to Give the Young Man Knowledge*, 88; Abbot, *Christian Family*, 23; Powell, *Beauty, Vigour and Strength*, 63; Griffith, *Bethel*, 159.

To counter youthful complacency moralists were never slow to introduce the threat of an early death. John Shower cast a reproachful eye over his young audience and told them that though they all seemed to be in apparent good health, 'may not the same be said of those who died last week?'[121] Preachers dissected the body establishing its multiple frailties and remarking in an ominous tone how one small fault could lead to an unwelcome early grave. In his *Compassionate Counsel to All Young Men* (1681), Richard Baxter reminded his readers that 'thousands go out of the world in youth', and proceeded to discuss the rapidity of seizures and the myriad complications of veins, nerves, humours, and arteries.[122] These chilling reminders were often introduced in funeral sermons as the speaker reviewed the lost life of a close friend and anticipated the future of those young comrades he or she left behind. John Shower mentioned the risks of smallpox on such occasions.[123] Like the last words at the gallows, these dramas of mortality with their doubtless hushed and reverential audience provided a unique moment in which to preach by precept and example, and hope as Ralph Josselin put it, 'to do young men good by it'. Josselin preached at the funeral of Sarah London in 1672 and 'endeavoured to stir up young persons to be good', and he took full advantage of the opportunity presented by another funeral sermon 'to presse young men to be religious early'.[124] 'Bending' and 'curbing' were the inevitable morals of conversion rhetoric and this rather bleak portrait of youth. Nevertheless, there was still some hope. Attitudes towards youth, after all, were highly ambiguous.

4. 'The Beauty, Vigour and Strength of Youth'

On the one hand moralists poured scorn on youth and called it the 'dark age', but on the other they clearly recognized that the same stage of life presented a final chance for most people to learn the ways of piety and conformity before the customs of a wicked world intoxicated their hearts and minds. The 'deadly' and 'dangerous' season was only one-half of attitudes towards youth. One convention of contemporary investigation and discourse was that of binary

---

[121] Shower, *Seasonable Advice*, 38–9. Cf. Brooks, *Apples of Gold*, 51.
[122] Baxter, *Compassionate Counsel*, 6.
[123] Shower, *Seasonable Advice*, 40, 57. Cf. Baxter, *Christian Directory*, 546.
[124] Josselin, *Diary*, 593, 562, 579. Cf. Newcome, *Diary*, 99.

opposition—a subtle interplay of right and wrong[125]—and it is by no means unusual to discover authors manipulating counter-images, and placing a far more generous portrait of youth alongside a stream of passionate invective. In his *The Importance of Religion to Young Persons* (1683), for example, Henry Hesketh presented the commonplace of 'leaping colts' and 'boiling flesh', but a strong counter-rhythm beats against this gloomy tune because he was also able to portray youth as a 'fair and beautiful creature with which a cherubim might fall in love', and as a near ally of Jesus Christ, who 'the blessed spirit of God inspires, and for whom all the glories of Heaven are prepared'.[126]

This more favourable, even indulgent, image of youth is also present in other works and genres. A number of Shakespeare's characters heap lavish praise upon youth. It was a grave, fresh, stainless, and honourable age. In *All's Well that Ends Well*, the French king praises Helena for possessing all that life rates, 'youth, beauty, wisdom, courage, all | that happiness in prime can happy call'. Walter Raleigh called youth 'the strong, flourishing, and beautiful age of man's life'.[127] 'Youth is a time of joy', one balladeer boldly proclaims, 'let pleasures lead thee through | the blossomes of thye youth.' Riotous gallants and flaunting bachelors parade through other ballads: 'I am a lively, joviall lad', one character announces, 'And for thy sake I will swagger.' These songs were often spiced with salacious matter to satisfy consumer taste, but they also retained an equivocal satirical note throughout, and can be interpreted as a critique of the leisure preferences of male youth of the middle and upper classes in particular.[128] Other texts presented an image of valiant and heroic youth as moral exemplar. Ballads and chapbooks related the memorable histories of courageous apprentices who joined the crusade against the Turk or the war against the French for 'famous England', the greater glory of the monarch, and their city of London, earning battle honours and quick promotion

---

[125] See Stuart Clark, 'Inversion, misrule and the meaning of witchcraft', *Past and Present*, 87 (1980).

[126] Hesketh, *Importance of Religion*, 22.

[127] *All's Well that Ends Well*, 2. 1; *Othello*, 2. 3; *Titus Andronicus*, 4. 2; *Anthony and Cleopatra*, 3. 13; *Twelfth Night*, 1. 5; Raleigh is quoted by Burrow, *Ages of Man*, 52. Cf. Shahar, *Childhood in the Middle Ages*, 27.

[128] Seng, *Tudor Songs and Ballads*, 111; Wurzbach, *Rise of the English Street Ballad*, 174; Day, *Pepys Ballads*, 281; and 'The Bachelor's Delight . . . The Happiness of a Single Life' and 'The Bachelor's Triumph', both of which can be found in Chappell, *Roxburghe Ballads*, iii, part 2, 423–6, 427–9. A similar view of male youth pervades contemporary commentaries on prostitution. See my 'The Structure of Prostitution in Elizabethan London', *Continuity and Change*, 8 (1993), esp. 41, 55, n. 134.

through the ranks to captain. It has been argued that this literature cultivated a sense of 'apprentice culture' and identity.[129] Another secular moral narrative is that of the diligent, virtuous, and pious apprentice, who loyally attends his master and completes an exemplary passage to full adulthood as a prelude to a spectacular elevation to Lord Mayor, or another lofty civic position.[130] These stories of courageous and virtuous young men were intended to encourage (and blend) patriotism, masculinity, civility, civic identity, and order, by drawing attention to the positive aspects of youthful strength and vigour. Yet this young soldier and aspiring civic leader sits uneasily alongside the wenching profligate, who also made many appearances in both contemporary literature and daily life.[131]

The apparent contradictions in juggling pessimistic and optimistic portraits of youth can be comfortably accommodated within the standard binary discourse. This fund of pliable images belonged to a studied, manipulative vocabulary, which conveyed a spectrum of possible meaning to satisfy particular sentiments and strategies. This ambiguity permitted youth to be seen as a 'hopeful age' while retaining an alternative vocabulary which reminded young people of the eternal struggle against 'fleshly' temptations and the dreadful fate of those who remained complacent and content. The strategic comparison between virtuous and disobedient youth was a principal feature of conversion rhetoric and political instruction, being a common theme of both cheap print and the contemplations of ministers and magistrates.[132] Ilana Krausman Ben-Amos has recently suggested that 'we must turn' to popular literature 'if we are to glimpse a set of images encapsulating the beauty, strength, vigour, and wit of youth, rather than its follies and sins'. These 'sentiments', she continues, 'stood in sharp contrast to the images of youth conveyed in didactic and religious literature'. The 'two-sided'

---

[129] Spufford, *Small Books and Pleasant Histories*, ch. 9; S. R. Smith, 'The London apprentices as seventeenth-century adolescents', in Paul Slack (ed.), *Rebellion, Popular Protest and the Social Order in Early Modern England* (Cambridge, 1984); Laura Caroline Stevenson, *Praise and Paradox: Merchants and Craftsmen in Elizabethan Popular Literature* (Cambridge, 1984), 112–13, 187; Sommerville, *Discovery of Childhood*, 81. For some examples of the genre see 'The Honour of a London Prentice' in Mackay, *Songs and Ballads Relative to the London Prentices*, 22–8; 'The Loyall London Prentice' in Chappell, *Roxburghe Ballads*, iv, part 1, 840–9; 'The Honourable Prentice, Or This Taylor is a Man' (1615), esp. 1–2; Chapman *et al.*, *Eastward Ho*; Thomas Heywood, *The Foure Apprentices of London* (1600?), and the works of Deloney and Rowley discussed by Smith, 'London apprentices', 224.

[130] Stevenson, *Praise and Paradox*, 144, 147–8, 188, 190–1, 193–4; Smith, 'London apprentices', 224. Cf. 'The Foure Ages of Man'.

[131] See Charles W. Camp, *The Artisan in Elizabethan Literature* (New York, 1923), 115.

[132] This use of contrary images implies that Sommerville's recent 'discovery' of childhood in sympathetic portrayals of children is perhaps misleading.

representation of youth, therefore, is in part a question 'of the
respective biases of the genres'.[133] It may well be true that a rosier
picture of youth is more likely to emerge from popular literature,
though there are many texts which oppose competing images of
youth in the form of their principal characters.[134] Yet this partition
of optimistic and pessimistic images is misleading because it obscures the tactical note of ambiguity which featured prominently in
political and religious rhetoric. Thomas Powell published a sermon
he preached to 'young men' as *The Beauty, Vigour and Strength of
Youth* (1676).

Attitudes towards youth in many respects generated purpose and
intensity by weaving together sets of polarities in the same moral
commentary. The image of youth in didactic texts reproduced the
deep gulf between fallen and restored humanity; a polarity which
was felt more acutely in that promising yet 'dark' age. Dod and
Cleaver remarked that at 'fifteene or sixteene' people were 'most fit
for reprehension, because then by all reason it should soonest enter;
and which time againe is most dangerous because then our affections are most strongest in us'. Richard Greenham also noted an
'aptnesse' in youth which was double-edged, for it could encourage
vice as well as 'such things as are good'. Moved by the repentance
of his wayward apprentice, Touchstone in *Eastward Ho* commented
that 'The ragged colt may prove a good horse'.[135] Authors still cling
to 'hope', and freely lace their work with qualifying words like
'may', 'might', 'could', or 'possible'. The 'dark side' of youth was
partly balanced by a dash of hope and some bright colours. There
is anguish, but also caution and promise. They may not have possessed scientific theories of physical and intellectual development
in youth, but moralists believed that in that age there was a promise
which was both a departure from childhood and a talent which was
easily squandered in later life.

The rhetoric of conversion and political conformity was squarely
rooted in contemporary pedagogy. The majority of commentators
agreed that the ability to acquire knowledge and skill was far greater
in youth. Children could make some progress. Indeed, there were
a few exemplary cases of pious and bright children, and the stories

[133] Ben-Amos, *Adolescence and Youth in Early Modern England*, 23, 28. Ben-Amos also writes
that 'In devotional literature, as in the medieval preaching tradition, youths were chastised
and addressed moralistically; in some types of popular literature, as in medieval chivalric
romance, young heroes were idolized, satirized, or scolded leniently' (ibid. 28).

[134] For example, see below, p. 55.

[135] Dod and Cleaver, *Godlie Forme*, 289; Greenham, *Works*, 289; Chapman *et al.*, *Eastward
Ho*, fo. H3ʳ.

of these mirrors of piety were printed and circulated for imitation by both adults and young people.[136] Nevertheless, it was more generally felt that children rarely possessed the intellectual capacity to choose, reason, and remember. 'Before we come to tenne yeares of age', Bishop Goodman remarked, 'we have no judgment at all, therefore we cannot pass our judgment.' Gouge thought that teaching young children was like teaching a parrot 'or such like unreasonable creatures: they may learne what is taught them but they cannot conceive it'. Yet he still advised that people should be instructed 'before they can well conceive' and 'discerne betwixt good and evil' otherwise they would enter their critical teens as 'perverse and headstrong, much like a strong bigge arme of a tree than a twig'.[137]

Childhood was portrayed according to theories about intellectual progress as an introduction to doctrines and precepts; as a first blast and preparation for the approaching 'age of discretion'.[138] 'Let them have wordes taught them when they are able to heare and speake words', John Dod advised, and 'afterwards when they come to more discretion they will conceive and remember the sense'. William Gouge believed that the 'apprehension' was 'much helped' by early guidance.[139] Thus it was certainly worthwhile catechizing children, for example, even if most of them could not yet decipher meanings. 'Some sparkes of the holy and heavenly fire', John Bruen commented, 'may on occasion break out from the hearts and lips of young children', but 'by reason of their weakness of understanding and want of judgment, they neither know whence they are, nor what they mean'. Richard Greenham and Alexander Jaffray both made the same point. Henry Cuffe observed that children possessed 'slippery and short memories', and 'no evident use of their reason'.[140]

While children were prevented from reasoning by their limited though potentially acute faculties, the story of adulthood was the slow decline of the physical and intellectual skills which had blessed the age of youth. Most adults were too rooted in the wicked routine

[136] Sommerville, *Discovery of Childhood*, ch. 2. See also below, p. 183.
[137] Goodman, *Fall of Man*, 185; Gouge, *Domesticall Duties*, 545, 547. Cf. Shahar, *Childhood in the Middle Ages*, 177.
[138] Anon., *Office of Christian Parents*, 59–60, 66, 100–2.
[139] John Dod, *A Plaine and Familiar Exposition of the Ten Commandments* (1606), 144–5; Gouge, *Domesticall Duties*, 545.
[140] William Hinde, *A Faithfull Remonstrance of the Holy Life and Happy Death of John Bruen of Bruen Stapleford in the County of Chester* (1641), 8–9; Greenham, *Works*, 88; Jaffray, *Diary*, 2; Cuffe, *Difference of the Ages*, 125, 127. Cf. Ian Green, ' "For children in yeeres and children in understanding": the emergence of the English catechism under Elizabeth and the early Stuarts', *Journal of Ecclesiastical History*, 37 (1986), 110.

of a profane world; complacent, content, and ignorant.[141] The miserable and declining state of age was a regular theme in discussions of the ages of man and conversion rhetoric.[142] In old age, Thomas Powell commented, 'all the abilities of the mind shall be decayed'. The author of *The Pourtract of Old Age* (1676) pointed out that 'the directing part, which usually is called the understanding', and 'the executing parts' were corrupted or missing in old age. That stage of life was a sad 'receptacle of all manner of maladies'. Imagination, understanding, and memory were fast declining, and physical ills were numerous. John Smith spent a few pages describing the sorry state of the mind, teeth, limbs, and so on. '*Sans* teeth, *sans* eyes, *sans* taste, *sans* everything', was Jaques's abrupt summary in *As You Like It*.[143] The sympathetic and optimistic attributes of youth had faded and become a faint memory.

This unkind critique of age was a rhetorical ploy to establish the value of an early conversion. In fact, moralists often distinguished between different stages of the ageing process, presenting the middle ground of early adulthood between youth and old age, which they called man age (or manhood), full age, middle age, or virility, as a time of wisdom, strength, maturity, and responsibility. The 'Foure Ages of Man' depicted the progress from youth to early adulthood as a movement into office. Richard Steele called the 'ripe age' before old age the best and settled course.[144] Again, depending upon the number of ages to be discussed, commentators could insert an age which was generally called 'declination' or 'gravity' before 'decrepit old age'.[145] An ordered scheme of life-cyclical progress was contrasted with the worldly trek from an 'ill-advised and ill-nurtured' youth to the profane customs of adulthood and the shortcomings of old age. The alternative pious life charted a smoother course from a promising childhood to a godly and civil youth, a mature adulthood spent in office, and wise old age. When they were proposing an argument for conversion in youth, moralists strategically depicted childhood and adulthood as partners in deficiency.[146] The main concern here was with taming the 'dangerous

---

[141] See Gouge, *Domesticall Duties*, 67, 448; Vincent, *Words of Advice*, 33; Cuffe, *Difference of the Ages*, 131.

[142] For example, Smith, *Pourtract of Old Age*, 23, 54, 151, 202, 260; Powell, *Beauty, Vigour and Strength of Youth*, 53–4.

[143] Powell, *Beauty, Vigour and Strength of Youth*, 57–9; Smith, *Pourtract of Old Age*, 38–9, 43–9, 51; *As You Like It*, 2. 7.

[144] Steele, *Discourse Concerning Old Age*, 4–6.

[145] For some examples see the accounts of the 'ages of man' proposed by Samson Price, Henry Cuffe, and the author of *The Office of Christian Parents*.

[146] See the remarks of John Donne in M. Seymour-Smith (ed.), *The English Sermon, An Anthology*, i:*1550–1650* (Cheadle, 1976), 349.

season' of youth. The steady advance of old age presented a sharp contrast, and it could be mocked as a time of 'infant weaknesse'. Shakespeare's Jaques called old age 'second childishness and mere oblivion'.[147]

By contrast, conversion rhetoric offered a more generous view of capable youth with the ability to reason and make a choice. Thus William Guild advocated the 'study, exercise and desire' of God's holy word 'to youth (*the first age capable of the same*)'. John Downame commented that the age of youth 'above all others is most fit to receive and retain instruction in the ways of the Lord'. It was 'most strong and able to receive' good teaching. Thomas Brooks applauded youth's strong memory, lively parts, and vigorous nature. In the opinion of Francis Fuller, youth was 'most fit for work, the body being most active and vigorous, the fancy and invention most quick, the memory most strong . . . the will most pliable, and the heart (as not hardened by custom in sin) most soft'.[148]

In youth there was still a faint glimmer of hope because young people were still malleable.[149] The manipulative nature of contemporary pedagogy drew upon this alleged malleability, portraying youth as a young twig or plant; something which in the course of growth could be nurtured and crafted. 'Best to bend while tis a twig' was a proverbial wisdom. Richard Shelford advised 'that while the plant is young and tender a man may winde and bende it which way he will', and 'ever so it is in the education of youth' because 'now they will bend, now they be pliable, now they will worke'.[150] People were to be planted in good virtue 'while they are tender and flexible in youth'.[151] Moralists also introduced a wax metaphor to

[147] Thomas Bancroft is quoted by Chew, *Pilgrimage of Life*, 149; *As You Like It*, 2. 7.

[148] Guild, *Young Man's Inquisition*, 22; Downame, *Guide to Godlynesse*, 337, 335; Brooks, *Apples of Gold*, 47; Fuller, *Words to Give the Young Man Knowledge*, 51–2. Cf. Cuffe, *Difference of the Ages*, 116, and the remarks of John Donne in Seymour-Smith, *English Sermon*, 340.

[149] Cf. Gerald Strauss's interpretation of sixteenth-century German thinking about youth and Edmund Morgan's discussion of New England Puritanism. Strauss suggests that malleability and discretion were seen as characteristics of childhood in sixteenth-century Germany: 'At seven the age of reason, the senses were in working order, memory alert, understanding intact, habits still unset.' At 14, the 'age of pubescence, opportunity had passed unless sound ideas, good habits and correct responses had already been firmly implanted (*Luther's House of Learning: The Indoctrination of the Young in the German Reformation* (1978), 106, 101–2). Edmund Morgan quotes the ideas of John Cotton of New England, who comments that children 'are flexible and easy bowed [and that] it is far more easy to train them up to good things now than in their youth and riper years' (*The Puritan Family: Essays on Religion and Domestic Relations in Seventeenth-Century New England* (Boston, 1944), 52 and 52 ff.).

[150] F.R., *A Collection of English Proverbs* (Cambridge, 1670), 61; Shelford, *Lectures or Readings*, 126. Cf. Josiah Nicholls, *An Order of Household Instruction* (1596), To the Reader; Dod and Cleaver, *Godlie Forme*, 265; Griffith, *Bethel*, 159.

[151] Guild, *Young Man's Inquisition*, 87.

conceptualize the reform of youth; a substance, which 'as long as it is soft and clammie', William Vaughan reported, 'receiveth any impression or seale, but being hardened it receiveth none'. 'So likewise', he cautioned masters and parents, 'imprint discipline' in young hearts and 'bow' them 'to what instruction thou wilt'. Yet a note of ambivalence lingered, for young people could also 'bend to vice like wax'. By contrast, the author of *A Discoverie of Youth and Age* (1612) commented that in later life 'there is no such waxe, but only inviolable constancie' because old folk 'never change colour.'[152] These views affected advice about vital life-cyclical moments. William Lambarde warned overseers to put people in service 'while they be young and tractable, and before they be corrupted with vice and idleness'. While Thomas Fortescue advised 25-year-old men to marry young maids rather than older women because 'in tender youth they are flexible and bending to whatsoever man would have them, obedient and subject still to his will and pleasure'.[153]

Youth was not only malleable, it was also portrayed as an age of discretion when people first obtained the wherewithal to judge options and choose accordingly.[154] It was in youth, John Downame commented, that we first 'come to knowledge and discretion'. John Lydgate produced the same observation; the capacity to choose entered when youth reached discretion. By contrast, John Dunton noted that it took children 'a long time' to comprehend 'the different nature of good and evil'.[155] Moralists often agreed when they came to attach particular years to the first stirrings of discretion. Dod and Cleaver and Shelford dated its first entry to 15 or 16.

[152] William Vaughan, *The Golden-Grove* (1600), third part, fo. V8^r; anon., *Office of Christian Parents*, 159; anon., *A Two-Fold Treatise, the One Decyphering the Worth of Speculation, the Other Containing a Discoverie of Youth and Age* (Oxford, 1612), 21–2. See also *Nice Wanton* in Tennenhouse, *Tudor Interludes*, 544; Stubbes, *Anatomie of Abuses*, fo. 7^v.

[153] William Lambarde, *The Duties of Constables, Borholders* . . . (1602), 129; Fortescue, *The Forest*, 46. Cf. Crossman, *Young Man's Calling*, 3.

[154] Cf. Shahar, *Childhood in the Middle Ages*, 24, who writes that in the Middle Ages 'Most authors specify the age of 7' as the time when 'the child can express himself properly, distinguish between good and evil, and choose between them. He has reached "the years of choice and discretion".' But Shahar then proceeds to add significant qualifications to this definition of the 'age of discretion' . First of all it is stated that other authors attributed the same characteristics to older and younger ages (ibid. 24). Shahar also makes the important point that the years after age 7, witness an intensification of 'the predilection to sin', and also the development of 'the power of judgment, the ability to distinguish between good and evil, and the intellect' (ibid. 27). Further points about criminal responsibility, penance, giving evidence in civil courts and oath-taking raise the age at which governors and moralists considered people to be fully capable of 'discretion' to age 12 or 14 (ibid. 25–7).

[155] Downame, *Guide to Godlynesse*, 337; Lydgate is quoted by Chew, *Pilgrimage of Life*, 177; John Dunton, *The Life and Errors of John Dunton Late Citizen of London* (1705), 19. Cf. Morgan, *Puritan Family*, 47.

Thomas Floyd proposed 14 years of age. In fact, the 14–16 age-range was a common interpretation.[156] Further guidance can be gleaned from the age at first communion. Early modern people frequently made the connection between preparation for the first reception of the host (which was itself a vital moment in the 'life-calendar' of the church) and discretion. Again, age 16, the age at which people could have been presented if they failed to communicate at least once a year, marked the point at which it was felt that most of them acquired full powers of discretion.[157] Perceptions of intellectual progress assisted in directing the primary evangelical thrust towards children and youth. They can also help us to conceptualize the shifting concerns of the pastoral ministry such as the growing preoccupation with catechizing young people towards the close of the sixteenth century.[158]

These competing conceptions of different ages were partly derived from a fund of pliable images and a manipulative vocabulary which could be easily adjusted to fit specific rhetorical purposes. Youth could be weak or strong, or intelligent or simple depending on the particular point being introduced. Above all, it was the interface between these extremes which was described in some detail. Young people as well as magistrates and moralists could exploit this versatile and adaptable impression of youth in their testimonies, petitions, and appeals before the authorities. A petition on behalf of a young follower of Essex who took to the streets of London in support of his master's botched conspiracy pleaded with the queen

[156] Dod and Cleaver, *Godlie Forme*, 288–9; Shelford, *Lectures or Readings*, 40; Floyd, *Picture of a Perfit Commonwealth*, 100. Terence R. Murphy has suggested that 14 was also the age at which people assumed 'full criminal responsibility'; that to be capable of public wrong one had to be 'of years of discretion' and fully able to comprehend right and wrong (' "Woful childe of parents rage": suicide of children and adolescents in early modern England', *The Sixteenth Century Journal*, 17 (1986), 262–3). Shahar writes that in the Middle Ages 'According to secular legislation, boys and girls under 14 or 12 respectively did not yet bear criminal responsibility', and that 'According to the authors of confessors' manuals, young people from the age of 14 were made to do penance for sins of a sexual nature' (*Childhood in the Middle Ages*, 25). Cf. Hanawalt, *Growing up in Medieval London*, 202, 'Criminal law, canon law and taxation set twelve to fourteen as the age of entrance into legal liabilities'; Margaret Pelling, 'Apprenticeship, health and social cohesion in early modern London', *History Workshop Journal*, 37 (1994), 84.

[157] See S. J. Wright, 'Confirmation, catechism and communion: the role of the young in the post-Reformation Church' in Wright (ed.), *Parish, Church and People: Local Studies in Lay Religion 1350–1750* (1988), esp. 213–14, 217. The relation between age at first communion, discretion, and confirmation is more problematic, though Wright offers evidence that after the Reformation 'the emphasis' on the age at confirmation 'gradually shifted from childhood to adolescence' (ibid. 213). These issues will be more fully discussed by Ian Green in his forthcoming study of catechizing.

[158] See below, Ch. 2.

'to esteame him a younge plante', and to attribute his fault 'rather to the sparkes of youthe than willfull disobedience'. William Seymour wrote to King James from his prison cell asking him 'to cast your mercifull eyes upon the most humble and penitent wretch that youth and ignorance have throwne into transgression'. In 'time and riper years' he would grasp 'the true sense and feelings of his errors', but now he sat in misery in his cell with a sentence of death hovering over him, falling to his knees to confess 'the grevious offences of my youth' in the hope that the monarch would 'take home a lost sheepe'. George Merifield was languishing in prison in 1635 when he wrote to Laud explaining that he had 'unadvisedly' issued a writ against Sir Henry Martyn and other judges of the Royal Commission. He was now 'hartily sorry' and begged 'for mercy, he being a young man'. What he had done was indeed unforgivable, but it had 'proceeded out of ignorance' rather than 'willfull-nesse or contempt against authority'.[159] These young petitioners also moulded pliable images of youth to present themselves as weak, stupid, ignorant, and naturally naïve. Yet they could only successfully squeeze sympathy from the authorities if it was held that youth was also a promising age of 'beauty, vigour, and strength'. That element of hope which prompted governors to pardon the capital crimes of some young people always lingered. It would quickly expire as the ways of a wicked world wrestled the young away from the right path to salvation. But for ten years or more there was an opportunity to be seized. As we have seen, moralists and magistrates coined particular rhetorics and strategies to tame young people. Above all, youth was represented as 'contested territory'.

5. *'Contested Territory'*

The pressures of time and the golden opportunity provided by the first sparks of discretion and malleability in youth permitted that age to be depicted as a time of 'contested territory' in which people chose either to start out along the long and winding road to heaven or to bask in worldly slumber and secure an awful fall into hell.[160] Richard Burton described youth as 'the season' of man's 'greatest trial, wherein nature will soon discover itself whether filthiness or holiness; the righteous commands of God or the wretched lusts of

---

[159] PRO SP 12/279/284; 14/86/1; 16/282/39. Cf. 16/278/43; Florike Egmond, *Underworlds: Organised Crime in the Netherlands, 1650–1800* (Oxford, 1993), 26.
[160] Cf. Hanawalt, *Growing up in Medieval London*, 109.

the flesh shall be dearer to him'. The author of *The Prentise's Practise* (1613), invited 'every young man' to choose between 'the way of life' or 'religious profession', in which the lusts of the flesh 'may be restrayned' and affections bridled, and 'the way of death', which granted 'full libertie and full head . . . to youthful affections' and lusts. 'Two waies are proposed', Henry Crosse cautioned, the difficult passage to virtue or the much easier path to vice.[161] Some authors gave these 'waies' specific personalities. The moral of a play, for example, could turn on the contrasting fortunes of profane and pious characters, and the final twist when virtue is asserted and morality restored. Thus in *Eastward Ho* opposing moralities are identified and the pattern of the play established when Touchstone announces, 'I have two prentises: the one of a boundless prodigalitie, the other of a most hopeful industrie'.[162] On the title-page of Braithwait's *The English Gentleman* (1630) youth is pictured standing between virtue holding up a palm branch and pleasure represented by a naked woman holding a comb and mirror—the tools of mere vanity.[163] 'Contested territory' also offers a conceptual setting for the discussion of some familiar aspects of spiritual autobiography. Authors of these retrospective life-studies often presented their youth as a time of perpetual backsliding between contrary peaks of comfort and despair.[164]

Youth, therefore, was frequently called the *choosing time.* 'Men have seldom above one chusing time', John Chishul advised in 1658, and Scripture associated that moment of decision with the age of youth. Thomas Vincent, Benjamin Keach, and Samuel Crossman all called youth 'the choosing time'.[165] Young people were asked to make choices in their youth—a suitable calling, for example, or a spouse—and each fresh choice was a further step along the life-cycle.[166] The pressures of choice, which were driven

[161] Burton, *Apprentice's Companion*, 88–9; W.P., *Prentise's Practise*, fos. 3ᵛ–4ʳ; Henry Crosse, *Vertue's Commonwealth*, 1603, ed. A. B. Grossart (Edinburgh, 1878), 44. See also Vincent, *Words of Advice*, 13; Guild, *Young Man's Inquisition*, 19, 47–8.

[162] Chapman *et al.*, *Eastward Ho*, fo. A3ʳ. See also Gascoigne, *Glass of Government; The Interlude of Youth* in Lancashire, *Two Tudor Interludes*; and *Nice Wanton* in Tennenhouse, *Tudor Interludes*. Cf. the dialogue form used in such ballads as 'The Foure Ages of Man'.

[163] Olien, *Pilgrimage of Life*, 180 (and Augustine and Theodore de Bry's portrait of youth, 178, 180).

[164] Cf. Spufford, *Small Books and Pleasant Histories*, 74–5.

[165] Chishull is quoted by Sommerville, *Discovery of Childhood*, 83 (Cf. the remarks of John Maynard on the same page); Vincent, *Words of Advice*, 18; Benjamin Keach, *War with the Devil, Or the Young Man's Conflict with the Powers of Darkness* (1684), 22; Crossman, *Young Man's Calling*, 4.

[166] Choice is one conceptual point of entry for Ilana Krausman Ben-Amos's recent important work on the 'maturation process' in early modern England. See esp. 'Service and the

by the concern with custom and time, also framed the dialogue between moralists and the young. Salvation and political conformity were age-related. Thomas Brooks called youth the 'acceptable time', and 'the time of salvation'. 'There is the place', Roger Ascham directed, 'in yougthe is the time.'[167]

Youth was presented as a time of 'contested territory' in a variety of print media, including moral commentaries and plays, but one of the most vivid insights into this struggle for souls is provided by conversion narratives which often begin in youth when the author first experienced the stirrings of grace. 'If you look abroad in the world', Brooks observed, 'you shall hardly find one saint among a thousand but dates his conversion from the time of his youth.' It was 'ten to one, nay an hundred to one if ever they are converted, if they are not converted when they are young'. Long experience of pastoral care had convinced Baxter that most people first encountered the sensations of conversion 'at 14, 15, or 16 years of age'.[168] The memories of senior saints provide evidence of the youth of recent converts.[169] F. W. B. Bullock has collected the conversion narratives of thirty-six Protestants. Putting to one side the conversions from the old Catholic faith, we have the ages of twenty-nine people at the point at which they claimed a firm conviction of saving grace. Seven were aged between 12 and 19 years old (24.1 per cent), sixteen between 20 and 29 (55.1 per cent), while only five were above 30 years of age (17.2 per cent).[170] These narratives tell the story of what Richard Sibbes called 'going out of yourself', escaping the 'state of nature' to join combat with the flesh and become a 'new man' or a 'second Adam'. They describe the interior struggle between righteousness and 'natural man' to mould a 'second nature'.[171] John Cotton was converted when hearing Dr Sibbes 'preaching a sermon about regeneration . . . opening the state of a meer civil man'. James Fraser became a 'new man' after

coming of age of young men in seventeenth-century England', *Continuity and Change*, 3 (1988); ead., *Adolescence and Youth in Early Modern England*.

[167] Brooks, *Apples of Gold*, 53; Ascham, *The Scholemaster*, 210.

[168] Brooks, *Apples of Gold*, 53 (the second quotation is from Sommerville, *Discovery of Childhood*, 83); Richard Baxter, *Reliquiae Baxterianae, Or Mr Richard Baxter's Narrative of the Most Memorable Passages of His Life and Times* (1696), 89.

[169] For example, *A Short History of the Life and Times of John Crook, Written by Himself* (1706), 17; FHL MS Box 10/10, 1–3, fo. 4; William Kiffin, *Some Remarkable Passages in the Life of William Kiffin*, ed. W. Orme (1823), 60; Tweedie, *Select Biographies*, ii. 91; James Janeway, *Death Unstung: A Sermon Preached at the Funeral of Thomas Mowsley* (1669), 116.

[170] The remaining convert, Sir Alan Broderick, was in fact 52 years old, F. W. B. Bullock, *Evangelical Conversion in Great Britain 1516–1695* (St Leonard's-on-Sea, 1966).

[171] Sibbes, *Works*, 22, 254, 257, 259, 288.

reading 'a book called *The Practice of Piety* concerning the misery of natural man'. While Adam Martindale first felt saving grace after hearing one Mr Smith preach at St Helen's Church (Lancashire) 'about the desperateness and damnablenesse of a natural estate without conversion'.[172] All of these converts struggled with 'natural man', who vigorously asserted himself in their youth.

The pressures of choice and time remained constant throughout the sixteenth and seventeenth centuries, and doubtless beyond. In fact, the image of youth as 'contested territory' in the conduct books was not significantly rephrased or redrawn in the half-centuries before and after the English Revolution, and it remains to relate this commonplace to everyday life.[173] Some of its more energetic proponents were producing near formulaic writing about youth after 1660. Thomas Brooks's *Apples of Gold* was published in 1662, Samuel Crossman's *The Young Man's Monitor* in 1664, Thomas Powell's *The Young Man's Conflict with and Victory over the Devil* in 1675, and his *The Beauty, Vigour and Strength of Youth* in 1676, Richard Burton's *The Apprentice's Companion* in 1681, Henry Hesketh's *The*

---

[172] Samuel Clarke, *A Collection of the Lives of Ten Eminent Divines* (1662), 57–8; Tweedie, *Select Biographies*, ii. 2, 99 (cf. 417–18); *The Life of Adam Martindale Written by Himself*, ed. R. Parkinson (Chetham Society, 4, Manchester 1845), 36; Bullock, *Evangelical Conversion*, 48.

[173] One can also add that this was a mode of conceptualization which straddled confessional divisions between Protestants and Catholics, and 'factional struggles' between Anglicans and Puritans. Attitudes towards youth and the resulting stratagems appear to demonstrate similar content and purpose within the allegedly 'warring battalions' of the Protestant Church. Much the same sentiments about youth were expressed by all shades of Protestants. Richard Greenham (1535?–94?) was a Puritan. Godfrey Goodman (1583–1656) is perhaps best described as a rather 'idiosyncratic Anglican' and a near 'crypto-catholic', who managed to offend both Laud and his King. Both Thomas Brooks (1608–80) and Samuel Crossman (1624?–84) were ejected in 1662. Brooks possesses the 'classical' Emmanuel College training. He was chaplain to Thomas Rainborough and preached pro-Parliament sermons. Crossman subsequently conformed and he was eventually elevated to the lofty heights of King's chaplain and prebendary of Bristol (1667). Henry Cuffe (1563–1601) was secretary to Essex and was executed for his part in his patron's attempted coup. William Gouge (1578–1653), the strongly Puritan minister of St Anne's, Blackfriars, refused to read The Book of Sports in 1618 and in 1633. He was a presbyterian member of the Westminster Assembly of Divines. Abraham Jackson (1589–1646?) was promoted by Laud, being admitted prebendary of Peterborough in 1640. This may seem to be a veritable 'soup' of authors, and I offer my interpretation of 'contested territory' as a basis for further enquiry. Yet I am persuaded that an emphasis upon socialization and salvation in youth pervades all shades of Protestantism other than some of the more radical revolutionary sects. Cf. Sommerville *Discovery of Childhood*, 107, who arguably misreads contemporary mentalities in claiming that the group he calls Puritans 'showed scarcely any interest' in 'occupational preparation, for their concentration was on moral and spiritual development'. Contemporaries may not have recognized the distinction that Sommerville proposes, and the 'moral and spiritual' aspects of socialization and service are accordingly discussed below, esp. Chs. 5–8. There are indeed a large number of Puritans who discuss preparation for adulthood and the ideal image of pious, moral, and civil youth. Much evidence has been presented throughout the course of the present chapter.

Importance of Religion to Young Persons in 1683, and John Shower's *Seasonable Advice to Youth* in 1692. There were also new editions of these and earlier works. Caleb Trenchfield's *A Cap of Grey Hairs for a Green Head* was in its fifth edition by 1710. Some authors freely borrowed from each other, and this exchange of material and ideas is one indication of the extent to which sentiments and strategies were pooled. We could argue that one continuous tradition stretches across the long seventeenth century bringing together Richard Greenham, who was writing in the mid/later sixteenth century, and Dod and Cleaver, who were plagiarizing him in 1612, and perhaps still more significantly, between William Gouge, whose *Of Domesticall Duties* was first published in 1622, and Richard Burton, who was plainly borrowing language and imagery from that famous domestic guide in 1681.[174]

Burton's liberal use of Gouge suggests that the dialogue between moralists and youth did not substantially alter in this period. This was, after all, a rhetoric of conversion, and saving souls was a time-less concern. One recent study argues that rival groups of Protestants viewed youth in different ways. Puritanism is interpreted as a lively opposition movement, which targeted young people and in so doing 'discovered childhood' in a wave of revolutionary fervour.[175] Yet we could also credit early Protestants like Cranmer or Latimer with this 'discovery' because they also believed that the stormy way ahead was best negotiated by appealing to young people at the dawn of reform. One convention of recent sociological research is that youth delights in novelty and enthusiasm of all shades, and that movements of this sort strategically target young people.[176] Different Protestants provided competing interpretations of par-ticular aspects of childhood and youth. Original sin and childhood innocence being one point of dispute. Yet shining through this alleged fog of sectarian confusion was the bright image of youth as 'contested territory', which was drawn by Protestants of all sorts as one aspect of their conversion rhetoric. Sommerville misrepresents generations of godly authors by claiming that Anglicans 'tended

---

[174] Compare Dod and Cleaver, *Godlie Forme*, 300, with Richard Greenham quoted by E. H. Emerson (ed.), *English Puritanism from John Hooper to John Milton* (Durham, NC, 1968), 149–50, and also Gouge, *Domesticall Duties*, 503, 603–4, with Burton, *Apprentice's Companion*, fos. 3ᵛ–4, 27–8, 167.

[175] Sommerville, *Discovery of Childhood*. See below, Ch. 4 n. 3.

[176] See below, p. 178. Cf. Sommerville, *Discovery of Childhood*, 24, 'By contrast, Henry VIII's Reformation was not so much a popular movement as an act of state. Capturing the minds of the young was not seen as crucial until Puritan opinion outran religious policies and turned the Reformation into a movement.'

towards a greater concentration on youthful vice and submission to authority', and that Puritans did not refer to 'breaking the will' of the child before 1700.[177] They may have used other language and imagery—the 'leaping colt', for example, the pliant twig or branch, or manipulating wax—but the meaning is much the same. It also existed in purposeful tension with a more sympathetic view of youth which was driven by the concern that 'hopeful' young people should not join the tribe of 'slaves and drudges of Satan'.[178]

This two-sided image and the preoccupation with saving souls in youth are also conveyed in other genres and media. Chapbooks, ballads, and plays were written for the guidance of youth, and they occasionally gave the two sides of 'contested territory' a personality. There was some pooling of languages and images across different genres. Nevertheless, the seventeenth century witnessed a fall in the proportion of religious ballads in the registers of the Stationers company, which suggests that the pressure to save and socialize young people was increasingly being represented in different forms in popular literature; in the more secular setting of 'last dying words', for example.[179] These genres also related the adventures of young gallants and sparks (though a moral subtext often ran through the story), and they sometimes offered a more tolerant view of such habitual youthful 'occupations' as courtship, recreation, and illicit sex.[180] So, there were shifting images of youth, which could be redrawn to fit particular purposes and meanings; civic identity, for example, socialization, patriotism, or salvation. One task of this book is to complicate interpretations of youth. The portrait of youth before us often depended upon the particular point an author was trying to introduce. In fact, images could be manipulated even on the same page. It is misleading, therefore, to produce a final or 'closed' image of youth. To complicate matters still further, the perceptions of the population contributed a further note of ambiguity. Attitudes towards youth were a point of tension between people, clergy, and magistrates. The authorities had frequent occasion to compare their static vision of pious elders and reverential juniors with the 'undue' measure of toleration which was extended to young people. The apparent spontaneity and freedom of the

[177] Sommerville, *Discovery of Childhood*, 26, 94.

[178] These quotations are from Baxter, *Compassionate Counsel*, 25; Hesketh, *Importance of Religion*, 18; Burton, *Apprentice's Companion*, 162.

[179] See Wurzbach, *Rise of the English Street Ballad*, 221, 238; Watt, *Cheap Print and Popular Piety*, 47.

[180] See below, esp. Chs. 3–5.

young was one uncomfortable token of that 'dark' and 'dangerous age', which thirsted after licentiousness and spurned restraint.

This chapter has suggested that there was a widely held (if disputed) conception of youth in early modern society, which could take on a variety of forms and meanings in the rhetoric of ministers and magistrates; a 'vocabulary of age'; some cultural and ritual events, which added additional social meaning to age-differentials; and the socializing aspects of life-cyclical progress, which supplied a structural account of youth. The age of youth tended to be associated with people who were in their teens and twenties and with the state of dependence; a specific stage of the life-cycle. It was the near coincidence of the ages at which people first left the parental home and the first stirrings of discretion, malleability, and puberty, which moulded understanding of the start of youth in early modern minds.[181] Sir Thomas Smith remarked that his contemporaries called '*puberes* . . . the age of discretion'.[182] In youth, the intellectual and physical glides almost imperceptibly into the social and economic spheres of life. These vital connections anchored distinctions of pre-adult stages of life in early modern society. It is arguably easier to map the end of youth with reference to the life-cycle. Marriage (the setting-up of a new household and a new hierarchy) and full participation in a trade marked the border between youth and adulthood, though marital status alone was far more important as a female milestone in the theories of magistrates and moralists.[183]

The articulation of a distinctive set of attitudes towards youth helped to fix that age as a perennial problem in early modern minds with particular solutions. Above all, the problem of youth was an issue of sexuality, disobedience, lust, and excess. Contemporaries proposed several remedies, including the subordination of youth in service. Youthful spontaneity and 'heat' had to be tamed and channelled towards useful purposes to safeguard conventional age-relations and the vital process of socialization. Subsequent chapters will investigate how this preoccupation with youthful lust and excess ushered in a chorus of demands to closely regulate the world of youthful conviviality and play (Chapters 3–4), sexual behaviour, courtship, and household relations (Chapters 5–6), and 'masterless' young people (Chapter 7). Increasing levels of vagrancy, illegitimacy, or young people discovered 'out of service' or idle were

---

[181] Cf. Mitterauer, *History of Youth*, 37, 69, 72–4; and Aries, *Centuries of Childhood*, 26, writing of the seventeenth century, 'nobody would have thought of seeing the end of childhood in puberty'.

[182] Smith, *De Republica Anglorum*, 128. [183] Cf. Mitterauer, *History of Youth*, 37–8.

all diagnosed as terrible instances of worldly slumber and corrupt humanity. The characterization of youth as 'contested territory' was not only drawn in the pages of conduct books, dramatists, and cheap print, it was also present in the courtroom in constructions of criminality and order. In fact, the successful negotiation of the 'perilous' period of youth was essential to social order more generally since age-relations were an important dimension of contemporary theories of hierarchy and order. The desire to craft young citizens and Christians from very unpromising raw materials was one political impulse of a society in which age was a further principle of order. To the first characterization of the assorted risks and potentials of youth ('contested territory') we must now turn to a second; the ideal place of youth in the social order. The manner in which the ordering principle of age was conceived and derived ideological legitimacy is the subject of the next chapter, which explores the meaning of the politics of age in early modern society.

2

The Politics of Age

Contemporary literary descriptions of early modern society were the product of a stream of exchanges between prejudice and experience. Yet these formal attempts to comprehend and structure English social order did not always gel with everyday realities. Authors did not keep pace with complicated processes of socio-economic alteration and differentiation. The benefit of hindsight permits us to see not only these complexities, but also that the experience of socio-economic difficulty was rendered more intricate by distinctions of age, gender, class, and geographical area. Nevertheless, this broad spectrum of experiences was not so evident to the small group of men who wrote formal descriptions of the social structure. The writings of William Harrison, Sir Thomas Smith, and Edward Chamberlyne, for example, catch little of either the dynamism and diversity of early modern society, or the potential sources of antagonism to which socio-economic transition gave rise. They provided in the main a depiction of a basically enduring and stable social order.

This chapter will investigate contemporary perceptions of the social order and the strategic allocation of distinctive functions and responsibilities to particular social groups, including age-groups. Early modern England had a politics of age which communicated static and durable representations of orderly age-relations. It was expected that wise age would tame the rash temper of youth. This politics of age was one aspect of conventional patterns of social relations, and it was closely related to other theories of authority, including familial and gender ideologies, from which it drew support and further legitimacy. Nevertheless, the meaning and form of this politics was also framed by a particular discourse about youth—the subject of the opening chapter. It was also communicated in certain selected vocabularies, teaching, and carefully choreographed rituals or ceremonies which trumpeted the merits of conventional patterns of authority. This chapter seeks to explore these portrayals of the politics of age. It enters a number of territories and institutions, including the household, the civic community, the church, and the guild, though it is chiefly concerned with representation—with choreography, theatre, and discourses of authority. The picture that emerges, therefore, is formal, formulaic, and mostly stagnant. Nevertheless, it was in many respects a still life, and there was in fact an underlying tension. The politics of age was sometimes disputed, redefined, and renegotiated (the principal subject of Chapters 3–7).

The first section of this chapter will briefly review the forms and significance of the conventions of formal social description. Early modern people did not only seek to describe the world in which they lived, but also to navigate potential problems by proposing languages of order which conveyed conventional patterns of social relations. It will be suggested that these portraits of hierarchy reveal a dimension of the problem of order which has received little attention hitherto; the politics of age. Later sections will explore representations of this politics; its institutional and ritual expression (e.g. church seating plans), and a few points of contact between figures of authority and young people, including catechizing. Governors clearly valued stable age-relations. They passed gloomy forecasts about unshackled youth in periods of uncertainty like the English Revolution, produced close correspondences between age and authority, and allocated responsibility accordingly. Youth implied incompetence and inadequacy; age implied seniority, proficiency, and knowledge. 'Boy' or 'youth' with their accusations of inferiority were terms of insult in adult discourse. This chapter will also examine this vocabulary of insult as one part of a much broader discussion of the varied relationships between age, competence, and office-holding. The politics of age mattered, and we will first turn to rhetorics of authority to sketch its linguistic and institutional expressions.

1. The Politics of 'Place'

A number of recent historians have charted the changing vocabularies of social description in the long transition from a society of 'estates' and 'degrees' to one of 'sorts' and 'classes'. These accounts of linguistic permutations have largely been confined to the limits imposed by the principal objectives of social description, which gave expression to social polarities without necessarily proposing solutions for problems of order and authority.[1] The language of 'sorts of people', for example, which Keith Wrightson argues offered a far more sensitive picture of daily life than 'study-rooted' terms like 'degree' or 'estate', provided a means to consolidate identities in opposing social groups, and to depict potential enemies outside those closed quarters. Its changing conventions paid lip-service to social alteration, but they also created a vacuum which was filled by other languages which expressed theories of authority and order in everyday situations.

The language of 'sorts of people', however, was a significant point of departure from the conventions of earlier social description, even though it could coexist with other conceptions of the social order. By contrast, one language of authority which also existed alongside changing perceptions of social structure did not represent such radical discontinuity. Yet the language of *'place'* did none the less represent a reworking of customary conceptions. Familiar structures and vocabularies can of course gain fresh vigour in fast-changing conditions. They can be reanimated and redefined to fit altering circumstances and expectations. While the institutions and relations by which authority is mediated can themselves be affected in difficult periods. This was indeed the case with the particular conception of authority and order embodied in what I will call the language and structure of 'place'.

We have become familiar with the image of late sixteenth-century England as a troubled society struggling to comprehend the experience of deep demographic and socio-economic strain, which elicited sharp anxieties about order.[2] Magistrates, pushed into action to safeguard the fabric of their social world, drew upon a vocabulary of authority which offered reassuringly conventional ideas about a person's 'place' in a society which was both stable and consensual. As is well known, the family was the basic unit of political

[1] The more important contributions include Keith Wrightson, ' "Sorts of people" in Tudor and Stuart England', in Jonathan Barry and Christopher Brooks (eds.), *The Middling Sort of People: Culture, Society and Politics in England, 1550–1800* (Basingstoke, 1994); id., 'Estates, degrees and sorts: changing perceptions of society in Tudor and Stuart England' and Penelope Corfield, 'Class by name and number in eighteenth-century Britain', both of which can be found in Corfield (ed.), *Language, History and Class* (Oxford, 1991); David Cressy, 'Describing the social order of Elizabethan England', *Literature and History*, 3 (1976); and Susan Amussen, *An Ordered Society: Gender and Class in Early Modern England* (Oxford, 1988), esp. ch. 2.

[2] David Palliser has recently offered a rather more optimistic interpretation of the fortunes of late Tudor society in his *The Age of Elizabeth: England under the Late Tudors 1547–1603* (2nd edn., 1992).

authority and economy in early modern society.[3] Magistrates and ministers perpetuated a patriarchal fiction in which the family was presented as a 'little commonwealth', 'the picture of a commonwealth', or a 'little' and 'lesser church'.[4] It was typically represented as a scaled-down model of both Church and State, the 'seminary' and 'nursery' of the commonwealth, the 'first and natural beginning' of all 'civil societies', and a vital theatre of social discipline.[5] The fortunes of sound religion and political order rested upon domestic poise and equilibrium. According to this near formulaic rhetoric, society consisted of 'severall houses, and if the severall houses which are so many members be not well ruled', William Jones commented, 'how can the whole body be well ordered?' A slow Reformation and civil instability were both attributed to the abuses common in 'a rabble of disordered families'. Daniel Cawdrey simply cautioned his readers that 'the long desired and by some much desired reformation sticks here'.[6]

It was hoped that reform would be conducted on a number of strategic fronts (including the family, church, school, and the courts), creating a sweeping wave of evangelistic fervour which would break over traditional commitments yet boost existing theories of order.[7] It was often remarked that the critical territory was the household.[8]

---

[3] Anthony Fletcher and John Stevenson, 'Introduction', in Fletcher and Stevenson (eds.), *Order and Disorder in Early Modern England* (Cambridge, 1985), 31–2; Martin Ingram, *Church Courts, Sex and Marriage in England 1570–1640* (Cambridge, 1987), 125; Patrick Collinson, *The Birthpangs of Protestant England: Religious and Cultural Change in the Sixteenth and Seventeenth Centuries* (Basingstoke, 1988), 60–1.

[4] For example, *The Works of the Faithfull Servant of Jesus Christ, Dr Thomas Taylor* (1653), 190; John Dod and Robert Cleaver, *A Godlie Forme of Household Government* (1612), 13; William Gouge, *Of Domesticall Duties* (1622), 17–18; John Downame, *A Guide to Godlynesse, Or a Treatise of Christian Life* (1629), 329–30; Daniel Cawdrey, *Family Reformation Promoted* (1656), 24–5; *The Work of William Perkins*, ed. I. Breward (Courtenay Library of Reformation Classics, 3, Appleford, 1970), 418; Francis Billingham, *Christian Oeconomy or Household Government* (1609), fo. 43ᵛ.

[5] Sir Thomas Smith is quoted by Collinson, *Birthpangs*, 60. Cf. Richard Baxter, *A Christian Directory, Or a Sum of Practical Theologie and Cases of Conscience* (1673), 513, 515, 519; Cawdrey, *Family Reformation Promoted*, 45; Matthew Griffith, *Bethel, Or a Forme for Families* (1634), 2.

[6] William Jones, *Briefe Exhortation to All Men to Set Their Houses in Good Order* (1631), 5, 11; Cawdrey, *Family Reformation Promoted*, 46. For discussions of the important role of the household in winning order and reformation see Lewis Bayly, *The Practice of Piety* (30th edn., 1632), 340–1; Robert Abbot, *A Christian Family Builded by God* (1653), Epistle Dedicatory, fo. 4ʳ; Josiah Nicholls, *An Order of Household Instruction* (1596), To the Reader; Baxter, *Christian Directory*, 513–14.

[7] Cf. Lyndal Roper, *The Holy Household: Women and Morals in Reformation Augsburg* (Oxford, 1989).

[8] Downame, *Guide to Godlynesse*, 330; Richard Baxter, *The Poor Man's Family Book* (1674), 295; Cawdrey, *Family Reformation Promoted*, 46.

The domestic scene was therefore depicted in familiar images as a 'communion or fellowship of life betweene the husband, the wife, the parents, and the children, and betweene the master and the servant'.[9] Nevertheless, familial relations were always conceptualized in terms of firm instruction and restraint.[10] The male householder enjoyed his magisterial function as a gift from God for which he would one fateful day be held to account. He was God's 'deputy' and a 'God to his wife, children, and servants'. No conduct book was complete without a long list of the responsibilities of the householder, including domestic instruction, which was a vital aspect of the grand design of socializing young people into the world created by their elders.[11]

A common thread running through conventional theories of authority which attempted to structure early modern society was the political significance of familial rhetoric, metaphor, and example.[12] This imagery could be stretched to wrap the whole of society in an accessible and familiar familial fabric, or it could be reduced to focus upon particular families. Magistrates became fathers and fathers became magistrates.[13] The parent–child relationship was proposed as a pattern for imitation, thereby casting all social relations in a paternal hue, while retaining the valued qualities of perpetual subordination and education. The language of 'place' provided one way of articulating this familial ideology, which was also given institutional precision and permanence in the 'place' structure. Yet this familial meaning was only one aspect of a far broader concern with 'place' in early modern society. Each individual had an appointed, divinely ordained 'place' in a subject relationship as governor or governed, in which authority was allocated according to progress along the life-course (e.g. husband/wife, parent/child, and master/servant). The 'place' structure offered a tidy demonstration

---

[9] William Vaughan, *The Golden-Grove* (1600), fo. M7^r. See also Baxter, *Christian Directory*, 498; Perkins, *Work*, 416; Griffith, *Bethel*, 7, 223.

[10] See Perkins, *Work*, 417, 436–7; Thomas Floyd, *The Picture of a Perfit Commonwealth* (1600), 94; Downame, *Guide to Godlynesse*, 147; Baxter, *Christian Directory*, 498; Griffith, *Bethel*, 394–5, 405–6.

[11] For a few typical discussions of the role and significance of the householder see Downame, *Guide to Godlynesse*, 328–9; Cawdrey, *Family Reformation Promoted*, 21–3, 51–9; Perkins, *Work*, 436–8.

[12] Cf. John Morgan, *Godly Learning: Puritan Attitudes towards Reason, Learning and Education* (Cambridge, 1986), 154.

[13] Floyd, *Picture of a Perfit Commonwealth*, 36; Sir Thomas Smith, *De Republica Anglorum: A Discourse on the Commonwealth of England*, ed. L. Alston (Cambridge, 1906), 24; Peter Barker, *A Learned and Familiar Exposition upon the Ten Commandments* (1633), 266; Dudley Digges, *The Unlawfulnesse of Subjects Taking up Arms against Their Sovereigne* (Oxford, 1643), 61.

of patterns of authority. This at least was the theory; the ordered if imaginative household of elite choreography. 'God hath so disposed everyones severall place', William Gouge commented, 'as there is not anyone, but in some respect is under another.' The politics of 'place' were widely circulated in the Homily *Concerning Good Order and Obedience,* in many other sermons and treatises, and late on Sunday afternoon if the minister catechized as required by ecclesiastical articles.[14] Theologus in Arthur Dent's *The Plaine-Man's Path-way to Heaven* (1604) declared that 'it is a most excellent and glorious thing',

when every man keepeth his standing, raunge and his rancke. When all men with care and conscience performe the duties of their places. When the husband doth the dutie of an husband, and the wife of a wife. When the father doeth the dutie of a father, and the childe of a childe. When the maister doeth the dutie of a master, and the servant of a servant. When everyman setteth God before his eyes in doing those things which specially belong unto him. For herein consisteth the honor of God, the glory of the Prince, the crowne of the Church, the fortune of the Commonwealth, the safetie of cities, the strength of Kingdomes, and the very preservation of all things.[15]

Each 'place' had its political value and obligations, and 'everymans place is the best'. The rhythm of civil society turned on 'the consistency of its particulars in their own place'. If this sequence was disrupted, if superiors failed to educate their juniors, or subordinates elected to evade or even resist appointed authority, there would be utter confusion. Individuals were therefore warned not to step out of 'place'.[16] Richard Allestree offered a glimpse of Heaven to those who 'constantly attend to all those things which are the duties' of their 'place'. But others who flouted the conventions of this significant politics could only expect to be 'shut out of Heaven'.[17]

The 'place' model was a tightly constructed web of checks and correspondences. It displayed the 'goodly order of God', so that magistrates and ministers made the connection between 'place' and piety, and produced a sequence of correspondences between

---

[14] Gouge, *Domesticall Duties,* 5; *The Two Books of Homilies Appointed to be Read in Churches,* ed. J. Griffiths (Oxford, 1849) [hereafter, *Homilies*], 105–17.

[15] Arthur Dent, *The Plaine-Man's Path-way to Heaven,* 1604 (facsimile, The English Experience, 652, Amsterdam, NJ, 1975), 197–8.

[16] Baxter, *Christian Directory,* 567; Anthony Farindon, *The Sermons of the Reverend Anthony Farindon* (4 vols.; 1849), i. 332–3, 335.

[17] Richard Allestree, *The Whole Duty of Man* (1658), 325. Cf. Farindon, *Sermons,* i. 351; William Ames, *Conscience with the Powers and Cases thereof* (1639), 159; Gouge, *Domesticall Duties,* 13, 17.

salvation, obedience, and hard work. God was served 'in magistrates, in parents, in tutors and in all those whom . . . [he] has placed
over us'.[18] The language of 'place' also possessed the sort of institutional fixity required by a rhetoric of order. Close contemporary
approximations included 'office',[19] 'steed',[20] or 'room'.[21] These words
were often coupled, and their close affinity reveals the significance
attached to institutional definition.[22] Early modern people also
twinned 'place' and 'function'.[23] This was a formal language which
was used in discussions of authority in contemporary texts. It was
also common currency in administrative circles as evidenced in
court materials which show the term 'place' being used to introduce a variety of positions of authority in both central and local
government, including wardmote foreman, beadle, constable, scav-
enger, raker, churchwarden, muster master, collector, sheriff, mayor,
alderman, lieutenant of the Tower of London, and the Spanish
ambassador.[24] The language of 'place' implied precedence, authority, and superiority,[25] though it was also used by witnesses when they
gave their testimonies before the courts.

John Downame considered that 'superiours in authority are such

---

[18] Anthony Stafford, *Meditations and Resolutions Moral, Divine, Political, Written for the Instruction and Bettering of Youth* (1612), 77, 252; Nicholas Bownde, *The Doctrine of the Sabbath Plainly
Layde Forth* (1595), 281; Farindon, *Sermons*, i. 338; *Homilies*, 105. Cf. the remarks of William
Lambarde in Conyers Read (ed.), *William Lambarde and Local Government* (Ithaca, NY, 1962),
117.

[19] For some examples of 'place' being coupled with 'office' see CLRO Reps. 26(1), fos.
107, 135ᵛ, 234ᵛ; 26(2), fos. 283, 364, 453; 27, fos. 100ᵛ, 151ᵛ, 254, 285ᵛ, 294ᵛ; 31(1), fos. 20ᵛ,
54, 107ᵛ, 164ᵛ; 32, fos. 200, 347ᵛ; 34, fos. 125, 209, 454ᵛ, 504ᵛ; 37, fos. 191, 257ᵛ, 277; 44,
fos. 82, 145, 259; 48, fos. 113, 432ᵛ; 50, fos. 81ᵛ, 293, 309; 53, fos. 50ᵛ, 173ᵛ, 312; CLRO
Jours. 26, fo. 127; 27, fos. 72, 97ᵛ; 29, fos. 127ᵛ, 282, 284; 32, fo. 127ᵛ; GL MS 11,588/2,
fo. 771; YCA, B/33, fo. 89; B/34, fos. 23ᵛ, 288ᵛ, 289; PRO STAC 8 54/15; 71/17; 159/23;
249/18.

[20] See CLRO Reps. 31(1), fo. 154; 32, fos. 56ᵛ, 166, 348; 33, fo. 320ᵛ; 45, fo. 346ᵛ; 46, fo.
65ᵛ; 48, fos. 398, 399.

[21] See CLRO Reps. 25, fos. 220ᵛ, 241ᵛ; 26(1), fos. 139, 161ᵛ; 26(2), fos. 476ᵛ, 489ᵛ; 27, fos.
28, 258ᵛ; 31(1), fo. 21ᵛ; 31(2), fo. 425ᵛ; 33, fo. 93; 34, fos. 31ᵛ, 162; 36, fos. 208ᵛ, 220; 39,
fo. 286; 42, fo. 70; 45, fo. 47ᵛ; 46, fos. 57, 268ᵛ; 53, fo. 147; 54, fos. 278–78ᵛ; 55, fo. 246
(irregular pagination); GL MS 11,588/2, fo. 747.

[22] See the use of all three terms in one sentence in CLRO Reps. 27, fos. 8ᵛ, 30ᵛ; 36, fo.
169ᵛ. Contemporaries also twinned 'room and steed', or 'room and office', and there are
countless individual usages of all of these terms in contemporary sources.

[23] For example, Farindon, *Sermons*, i. 338.

[24] For example, CLRO Jours. 26, fos. 49–9ᵛ; 28, fos. 293–3ᵛ; 29, fos. 5ᵛ, 121ᵛ; 32, fo. 127ᵛ;
33, fos. 36, 130; 35, fos. 240, 267ᵛ, 455; 37, fos. 30, 126ᵛ, 340; 38, fo. 284; Reps. 27, fos. 11ᵛ,
57, 74, 107ᵛ, 166, 232, 292, 335; 28, fos. 21, 35ᵛ, 51, 76, 189, 221, 240, 300; GL MSS 5770/
1, fos. 31, 48, 69, 390, 421, 438ᵛ; 5770/2, fos. 126, 171, 434, 515, 530; 5602/1, fo. 21; CUL
EDR B/2/21, fo. 133; B/2/36, fo. 145; BIHR CV/CB2, fo. 97ᵛ; BIHR YV/CB2, fo. 48.

[25] See CLRO Jours. 28, fo. 307ᵛ; 30, fos. 382–3; 35, fos. 226ᵛ–7; Reps. 43, fo. 70ᵛ; 45, fos.
560–0ᵛ.

as have not only a place of excellence but also of power and juris-diction as our governours'.[26] In the house that the moralists built, institutional authority or 'place' effectively depersonalized its occu-pier, because the simple fact of authority was of far greater conse-quence than the character of whoever happened to possess it. Magistrates ruled by 'vertue of their place', so that authors often pressed the necessity of paying respect to a higher 'place'.[27] The language of 'place' possessed institutional strictness within the struc-tures of central and local government, courts, livery companies, and family life. Yet it also had a similar but far broader resonance in the less institutionally defined rhythm of daily life, serving as a blueprint for the distribution of authority in a sharply differenti-ated but functionally interdependent society.

Unlike descriptive terms such as 'sort' or 'degree', which tended to express social distance, 'place' espoused a sympathetic sense of unity and mutuality. The Homily *Concerning Good Order and Obedi-ence* attempted to persuade hearers that 'everyone hath need of [each] other', so that each part could 'dwell together in unity'.[28] The 'place' structure was deliberately two-sided. This calculated malleability permitted both identification and differentiation within the same set of social relations because the distribution of authority was coated with a familial gloss. Writing in 1652, John Bradford invited his readers to rest contentedly in the 'benefit of peace and most seemly quietness and order', which would surely issue forth if 'highe and lowe . . . accompt themselves as parents and children'.[29] Carefully chosen paternal sentiment encouraged a sense of com-mon aspirations. A further way of bridging the substantial distance between governors and governed was to offer the comfort of spiritual equality. Everybody had a chance of salvation, and in matters divine 'there is no high and low'. Yet mere humanity could not be ex-pected to remain obedient and pious. Anthony Farindon therefore reminded his listeners that God 'hath assigned every man in his place and calling'. The 'place' structure institutionalized inequalities. 'In the kingdom of the world', Farindon continued, 'every man is not fit for every place. Some must teach and some govern, some must learn and some obey.' Such 'disproportion' was a prerequisite

[26] Downame, *Guide to Godlynesse*, 146–7.

[27] See Gouge, *Domesticall Duties*, 595, 458, 592; John Calvin, *Institutes of the Christian Reli-gion*, ed. J. T. McNeill (2 vols.; Library of Christian Classics, 20–1, 1961), ii. 402; Dod, *Plaine and Familiar Exposition*, 184–6; Richard Burton, *The Apprentice's Companion* (1681), 10.

[28] *Homilies*, 105. Cf. Farindon, *Sermons*, i. 319.

[29] John Bradford, *Godlie Meditations upon the Lordes Prayer, the Beliefe and Ten Commandments* (1652), fo. G8ʳ.

for order because that 'equality which commendeth and upholdeth a commonwealth ariseth from the difference of its parts moving in their severall measures and proportions, as music doth from its discords'.[30]

The politics of 'place' provided a vocabulary for expressing the concern with class, authority, and pedagogy. Those in places of authority were asked to urge the virtues of salvation and obedience in youth as a matter of routine. Sermons and texts were littered with exhaustive guides to facilitate the turning of theory into practice, identifying precise roles for parents and children,[31] and masters and servants.[32] They retailed images of ordered households which would help secure the smooth succession of generations and the progress of society, and also repeated the strategic value of remaining within the physical and political boundaries defined by 'place'.[33] Social mobility was no friend with its individual aspirations and progresses. To distract attention away from social climbing and fix it upon present time and place, moralists manipulated sets of polarities—pride/humility, ambition/patience, idleness/diligence, and damnation/salvation. Subordinates were not to be tempted away from appointed inferiority.[34] Idleness was also out of step with the politics of 'place', corrupting young people and setting in motion the chain of events which inevitably led to the fatal hanging tree. In fact, young people were asked to display neither creativity nor spontaneity. They were expected to observe the limits of household discipline, and steer clear of the alehouse and dancing green, and other sites of 'lewd' recreation. The 'place' rhetoric added further ideological substance to the stream of bitter invective against unregulated recreation,[35] and helped to fuel the backlash against

[30] Farindon, *Sermons*, i. 334–5. Cf. Morgan, *Godly Learning*, 147.

[31] For some conventional discussions of parent–child relations see Dod and Cleaver, *Godlie Forme*, 274–9; John Dod, *Plaine and Familiar Exposition*, 188–93; Griffith, *Bethel*, 369–72; Allestree, *Whole Duty of Man*, 286–305; Gouge, *Domesticall Duties*, 427–588. See also Linda Pollock, *Forgotten Children: Parent–Child Relations from 1500 to 1900* (Cambridge, 1983), chs. 5–6. Ralph Houlbrooke, *The English Family 1450–1700* (1984), chs. 6–7.

[32] Typical expositions of the 'ideal' nature of master/servant relations are given by Perkins, *Work*, 432–3; Ames, *Conscience*, 160–1; Allestree, *Whole Duty of Man*, 323–8; Dod and Cleaver, *Godlie Forme*, 366–77; and Gouge, *Domesticall Duties*, 589–693.

[33] See Perkins, *Work*, 418–19; Baxter, *Christian Directory*, 14; Griffith, *Bethel*, 17. Cf. Christopher Hill, *Society and Puritanism in Pre-revolutionary England* (1964), 444–5.

[34] Cf. Vaughan, *Golden-Grove*, fo. F8r; Perkins, *Work*, 470; Dod and Cleaver, *Godlie Forme*, 72–3; Floyd, *Picture of a Perfit Commonwealth*, 282.

[35] See Dent, *Plaine-Man's Path-way*, 187; Thomas Hall, *Funebria Florae: The Downfall of May Games* (1661); Keith Wrightson, *English Society 1580–1680* (1982), 206–21; David Underdown, *Revel, Riot and Rebellion: Popular Politics and Culture in England 1603–1660* (Oxford, 1985), 48–84.

the Book of Sports (1633) because the 'King's book' drew young people away from the guiding eye of a responsible elder.[36]

Physical mobility also presented difficulties, especially in this period of ever increasing movement. It is no accident that the politics of 'place', with its static and immutable character, possessed a geographical as well as an institutional meaning and setting. Stability was one prerequisite of its successful operation. Movement elevated anxieties. Every young person was in theory the property and subject of an adult householder. To stray outside the compass of his government rendered a servant or apprentice out of 'place', 'masterless', and effectively beyond appropriate discipline. This close fit between political and geographical 'place' provided contextualizations for the identification of criminal young people. A close correspondence was proposed between instruction, diligence, stability, and order, and in addition between piety and civil order.

In fine, the 'place' structure was a carefully crafted mosaic of closely connected social relations, one intention of which was to dam up youthful heat and licentiousness, and prevent it from spilling over and turning scripted age-relations upside down. Government in households and society more generally tended to be bolstered by additional sources of power. The distribution of authority in early modern society traced distinctions of age, gender, and social class.[37] A further form of potential regulation was the economic hold masters and parents could extend over their young charges. All of these political arrangements were also situations in which age governed youth. Outside the walls of the household, the web of duties which tied magistrates and teachers to their subjects and pupils could also be anchored by an ordering age-dimension. Whether by immediate interpersonal relations or a more distant metaphorical allusion, it was intended that the politics of age should operate as one principle of order in early modern society.

2. *The Politics of Age*

Writing in troubled times, the anxious author of *The Case of the Army Soberly Discussed* (1647) commented that 'The new doctrine of the

---

[36] Hill, *Society and Puritanism*, 193; Anthony Fletcher, *Reform in the Provinces: The Government of Stuart England* (1986), 230, 239; Underdown, *Revel, Riot and Rebellion*, 29; William Hunt, *The Puritan Moment: The Coming of Revolution in an English County* (1983), 253.

[37] Cf. Howard Becker, *Outsiders: Studies in the Sociology of Deviance* (New York, 1963), esp. 12–13, 128.

people's sovereignty' threatened to upset conventional social relations because it handed authority to servants and children as well as their parents and masters.[38] The near symmetry between radicalism and confusion was much repeated in conservative rhetoric at this time, which drew upon familiar theories of orderly age-relations. Sensitivity to inversions in customary age-relations was widespread. The family, the basis of social order and the arena in which young people were supposed to be preparing for participation in adult society, was menaced by a motley crew of religious radicals, who were charged with intoxicating wives, children, and servants with their 'nonsense' about equality and independence. They also contaminated the smooth flow of generations with their 'irregular' ideas about sexual ethics, polygamy, and divorce. Both royalists and parliamentarians derived much value in accusing the other side of conscripting young people who should have remained in safe and close dependency.[39] Religious toleration was portrayed as a 'chaos', another Amsterdam and Munster. While a succession of prophets produced forecasts about the collapse of 'political, ecclesiastical, and oeconomicall' relations.[40]

This chorus of anxiety was only the nerve-end of a society in which age was one principle of authority. Investigations of social structure and the ordering of early modern society hitherto have explored the nature of relations between different social groups. Nevertheless, the significance of the politics of age is little explored, and it still remains peripheral to most studies.[41] We do not possess a book-length survey which adequately explores the forms in which age affected the articulation and enforcement of authority in early modern society. The politics of age must take its place in historical enquiry alongside the more familiar concerns of class and gender. There is a risk, however, of producing a confusion of languages of

[38] TT E 396 (10), 6.
[39] For some typical expressions of contemporary concern see Thomas Edwards, *The First and Second Parts of Gangreana* (1646), esp. 24–5, 70, 83, 85; Ephraim Pagitt, *Heresiography, Or a Description of the Hereticks and Sectaries of These Latter Times* (4th edn., 1647), 11–12. This sensitivity about inversion in social relations and fears about conscripting young people are more fully explored by Christopher Hill, *The World Turned upside down: Radical Ideas during the English Revolution* (Harmondsworth, 1975), esp. 188–90, and chs. 9–10, and 15; Keith Thomas, 'Women and the civil war sects', *Past and Present*, 13 (1958); J. C. Davis, *Fear, Myth and History: The Ranters and the Historians* (Cambridge, 1986), esp. ch. 5; Ian Gentles, 'The struggle for London in the second civil war', *Historical Journal*, 26 (1983); Christopher Durston, *The Family and the English Revolution* (Oxford, 1989), esp. chs. 6–7; Underdown, *Revel, Riot and Rebellion*, esp. 88–9.
[40] For example, Edwards, *Gangreana*, 57–8, 83, 100.
[41] But see Keith Thomas, 'Age and authority in early modern England', *Proceedings of the British Academy*, 62 (1976).

authority—a veritable political Babel. One contemporary solution was to refer to the conventions of 'place', which revealed some conceptual flexibility gathering at least three principles of authority within a single ordering language.

Age, therefore, was a further principle of order in early modern society, and one means of communicating the significance of age-relations was provided by the rhetoric of a person's 'place', which could be age-specific. Robert Abbot, for example, typically divided the family into 'foure sorts. 1. Old men 2. Old women 3. Yong men [and] 4. Yong women'.[42] Age was intended to govern the more turbulent temper of youth. This age-hierarchy was extended beyond the immediate familial setting in a series of metaphors, which depicted conventional patterns of authority in terms of the dialogue between age and youth. Richard Greenham commented that 'By father and mother, I do not understand only my natural parents', but also magistrates and ministers 'whom God hath set over me for my good'.[43] Ministers and magistrates often used the metaphor of age and authority in works discussing relations between governors and governed,[44] household texts, and in conventional expositions of the fifth commandment.[45] There were two principal ways in which age functioned as a principle of authority; in a direct relationship in which an elder guided a junior, and in a metaphorical fashion in which expressions of authority were given a paternal edge by disguising superiors as fathers—'political fathers'—and subordinates as children.[46] Contemporary descriptions of the social order excluded the young because they possessed no authority, and were therefore unworthy of inclusion in these ladders of rank and status. They were thought by some to be outside the reach of the law because of their low status. In 1616, for example, a Dorsetshire gentleman interrupted 'a company of disordered persons' who were 'cutting, spoyllinge and throwing down' his fences and ditches, who told him that they were 'cast downe by woemen and boyes', and that he 'should have noe remedy against them'.[47]

---

[42] Abbot, *Christian Family*, 11.

[43] *The Workes of the Reverend and Faithful Servant of Jesus Christ Mr Richard Greenham*, ed. H[enry] H[olland] (1601), 216. Cf. Dod and Cleaver, *Godlie Forme*, 131–2, 366; Gouge, *Domesticall Duties*, 487.

[44] For example, Dudley Digges, *Unlawfulnesse of Subjects*, 61; Henry Parker, *Vox Populi, Or a Discourse wherein Clear Satisfaction is Given, As Well Concerning the Right of Subjects as the Right of Princes* (1644), 32; Smith, *De Republica Anglorum*, 24; John Swan, *Redde Debitum: Or a Discourse in Defence of Three Chief Fatherhoods* (1640), 9.

[45] See below, pp. 88–9.   [46] Barker, *Learned and Familiar Exposition*, 266.

[47] PRO STAC 8, 298/12.

In his *Picture of a Perfit Commonwealth* (1600), Thomas Floyd remarked that the

authority not onely of masters over their servants, but also of parents over their children, was very necessary throughout all dominions by which means . . . the commonwealth long to have stood. Doubtles if parents over their children and masters over their servants had such authority, that in respect thereof the commonwealth flourished, then the supreme governor should in equitie have farre greater preeminence, being of both parents, children, masters, and servants a commaunder . . . unto whom all should bee most obedient whereby the estate of the commonwealth might perfectly stand, and that it might be stayed in respect of this obedience, as it was of a certain man coming to Sparta, who beheld what honour, obedience and reverence, the younger sort did to the elders and the elders to their superiours, and said it is expedient to be an old man and of authority . . . (by which means) the commonwealth should of necessity long continue.[48]

This exemplary Spartan society provided a pattern for imitation. Age governed youth, and age in its turn obeyed the civil magistrate. Indeed, Keith Thomas has characterized early modern society as being affected by gerontocratic theories and modes of expression. Young people were expected to honour and reverence their elders and betters.[49] Richard Baxter typically commented that 'in all duties' both nature and Scripture 'tell us that the younger owe much duty to the elder'. He proceeded to present an ideal image of youth submitting to their elder's judgement, 'supposing that ordinarily they are wiser than the yonger, and therefore living towards their elders in a humble and learning disposition'. Age was to be given 'preheminence . . . in the procuring of the common good, and providing for the maintenance and credit thereof'.[50] This was, after all, a society in which 'older and wiser' was a nugget of proverbial wisdom.[51]

Moralists justified the rigid subordination of young people by portraying youth as the 'dark and dangerous season', and introducing the significance of the life-course for order. There were many like Baxter who believed that stability 'lyeth in a good succession of

---

[48] Floyd, *Picture of a Perfit Commonwealth*, 193–5.

[49] Thomas, 'Age and authority', *passim*.

[50] Richard Baxter, *Compassionate Counsel to All Young Men* (1681), 181. Cf. Thomas Vincent, *Words of Advice to Young Men* (1668), 29–30; John Strype, *Lessons Moral and Christian for Youth and Old Age* (1699), 96–7; William Guild, *A Young Man's Inquisition or Trial* (1608), 83; George Gascoigne, *The Glass of Government*, 1575 (Tudor Facsimile Texts, New York, 1970), fos. D2^{r-v}, D3^v, H2^r.

[51] F.R., *A Collection of English Proverbs* (Cambridge, 1670), 126.

the generations'. Young misfits became poor parents and the sorry cycle of adult negligence repeated itself.[52] Young people were therefore fed a staple ideological diet of honour and reverence, and prominent among the tools of persuasion was, of course, the fifth commandment. Further confirmation could be found at other places in Scripture, perhaps most notably Ephesians 6: 1, 'children obey your parents in the Lord for this is right'. These scriptural injunctions provided much support for contemporary authors, who discussed age-relations at some length.[53] The family (and service) was allocated a key role in the process of raising pious and civil individuals. It provided a means to check 'presumption in yougthe' and the multiple vices which contaminated young people 'by reason of age'.[54] Parents had a 'double-regard' to bring up their young charges 'civilly' and 'religiously', and they were to proceed by instruction and restraint.[55] Young people were expected to surrender spontaneity and creativity. Full independence (and membership of adult society) was reserved for those who had departed the economic and social security of a parent's or master's household.

The preoccupation with the licentious humour of youth in 'improving' texts also found expression in secular courts and institutions. The records of urban guilds and corporations, for example, reveal a preoccupation with the 'natural inclinations of youth'.[56] They articulated a vision of civil and sober youth which they were prepared to defend in the courts by prosecuting young people who fell short of these qualities. The process of socialization was also defined and managed by these authorities. One significant aspect of the movement from youth to adulthood was a transition in attitudes towards play, time, and work. The period of service was experienced as a collision between the free impulses of young people and adult preoccupations with tutored time, work, and order.[57] Both the courts and guilds took a leading part in the regulation of

---

[52] Baxter, *Compassionate Counsel*, 11–19 (esp. 13); Francis Cheynell, *A Plea for the Good of Posterity* (1646), 16; Robert Shelford, *Lectures or Readings upon the 6 Verse of the 22 Chapter of Proverbs Concerning the Vertuous Education of Youth* (1606), 19–20, 137.

[53] See Pollock, *Forgotten Children*, esp. chs. 4–6; Houlbrooke, *English Family*, esp. chs. 5–7; Wrightson, *English Society*, ch. 4.

[54] Roger Ascham, *The Scholemaster* in his *English Works*, ed. W. A. Wright (1970), 209–10; W.P., *The Prentise's Practise in Godlinesse and His True Freedome* (1613), 38.

[55] Griffith, *Bethel*, 345–60 (the quotation is at 345); Gouge, *Domesticall Duties*, 158. Cf. Dod and Cleaver, *Godlie Forme*, 342, 347; Henry Hesketh, *The Importance of Religion to Young Persons* (1683), 28; Guild, *Young Man's Inquisition*, 75.

[56] J. Dunlop and R. D. Denman, *English Apprenticeship and Child Labour: A History* (1912), 188.

[57] See below, esp. Ch. 7.

the period of youth and service, punishing youthful indiscretions which were considered a waste of time, a poor application to work, and a violation of civic codes.

The institution of service (and the household), therefore, was a vital agency of social discipline—'a title . . . of politike or civil discipline'.[58] The Newcastle Merchant Adventurers instructed that every apprentice should 'be well and godly brought up in the feare and love of God' to know 'his duty towards his master and mystres' and the responsibility of juniors to 'reverence' all their superiors. A memorandum on the Statute of Artificers (1563), the principal statutory stamp for compulsory service, claimed that its 'effectual execution' would 'banish ydlenes' and 'reforme the unadvised rashness and licentiousness of youth'. It was hoped that young people would serve 'for seven yeares at the least', so that 'younge men [who] lead a ryotouse life' would be reformed, 'for then the aged should be guides unto youth'.[59] The proposed repeal of the Statute in the early nineteenth century was greeted with gloomy forecasts in some quarters. One strong defence against repeal was that it would be 'ruinous to the morals of youth' because traditional patterns of authority would be swept away. Who would now regulate the morals of youth?[60]

Young people, therefore, were pressured into entering service. Structured work (and time) offered one solution to the many problems raised by disorderly youth.[61] Apprenticeship indentures communicated a strong sense of impeccable youthful behaviour. They defined a strict moral standard by which young people could be evaluated and prosecuted if found wanting. In 1565, for instance, William Bothill of Liverpool was apprenticed to the tailor Oliver Garnet. The terms of his indentures (a moral compact between the civic authorities, the master, and the apprentice)[62] envisaged a life of obedience and abstinence for Bothill in the years ahead. He promised to serve his master 'well, truelie, faythfullie

---

[58] Edmund Bolton, *The Cities Advocate*, 1629 (facsimile, The English Experience 175, Amsterdam, NJ, 1975), 13–14, 28. Cf. Ilana Krausman Ben-Amos, 'Service and the coming of age of young men in seventeenth-century England', *Continuity and Change*, 3 (1988). Michael Mitterauer has recently contextualized these problems in a far broader western and central European setting ('Servants and youth', *Continuity and Change*, 5 (1990)).

[59] J. R. Boyle and F. W. Dendy (eds.), *Extracts from the Records of the Merchant Adventurers of Newcastle-upon-Tyne* (2 vols.; Surtees Society, 93, 101, Durham, 1895, 1899) [hereafter *Newcastle Merchant Adventurers Records*), i. 21; R. Tawney and E. Power (eds.), *Tudor Economic Documents* (3 vols.; 1924), iii. 363, 345, 356.

[60] The concern with the repeal of the Statute of Artificers is more fully explored below, Ch. 7.

[61] See below, Ch. 7.   [62] See below, Ch. 6.

and diligentlie as a true apprentice', and to reject the illicit lure of 'cardes, dice, bowlis', and other 'unlawful games, hores, harlots, alehowses . . . tavernes', and 'unlawful and suspicious places' and fornication. Nor would Bothill absent himself 'from his mayster's howse, labour [and] busyness . . . by nyght nor day'. Thus William Bothill, in a typical indenture of apprenticeship, pledged himself to twelve long years of stringent abstinence.[63]

The strict note of the indenture was repeated in company ordinances and defended in the courts. In 1603 the Newcastle Merchant Adventurers instructed 'that from henceforth no brother or sister' of the company 'shall permit or suffer his apprentice' to 'daunce, dice, carde, mum, or use anie undecent apparell but plaine', or to 'weare their haire longe, nor locks at their eares like ruffians'. 'Disobedyent apprentices' were to be dispatched to a 'speciall gaol or prison'.[64] In 1617 the Eastland company at York passed an 'acte against evill rule of apprentices' who frequented 'whorehouses' and 'dishonest and unlawfull company', or played 'cards, dyce, or any other unlawfull games or gameinge for money'. Swift action was also proposed against young people who remained outside their master's household at night.[65] Similar codes of appropriate youthful conduct were introduced at other places and times. Significantly, they were sometimes reissued in times of 'great disorder' like the 1550s and 1650s in Newcastle.[66]

In the larger towns a descending chain of command connected the Guildhall, company hall, and other such 'middlemen' like the wardmote inquest and parish vestry to the politically vital household. Proclamations were often read or issued to householders and their young charges. It was hoped that this organization would help navigate household disorders and curb the worst excesses of youthful conviviality and play. It was to the court, the market-place, or the company hall, that the householder travelled (sometimes signing a register of attendance)[67] to listen to orders regulating his servants' clothing, for example, or playhouses and football. In large

[63] J. A. Twemlow (ed.), *Liverpool Town Books: Proceedings of Assemblies, Common Councils, Portmoot Courts 1550–1603* (2 vols.; Liverpool, 1918, 1935), i. 526–7. See also ii. 937–9, 952–4, 968–72. Interestingly, female apprentices in Liverpool were also pledged to the same moral commitments, though at least in Liverpool the clauses regarding illicit sex were not included in female indentures of apprenticeship.

[64] *Newcastle Merchant Adventurers Records*, i. 22–3.

[65] Maud Sellers (ed.), *The Acts and Ordinances of the Eastland Company* (Camden Society Publications, 3rd ser., 11, 1906), 27.

[66] *Newcastle Merchant Adventurers Records*, i. 20, 22. See also ibid. 23–5, 27–8, 153, 159.

[67] For example, CH minute books 1558–81, fo. 253ᵛ; 1581–1605, fos. 49, 51ᵛ.

centres like London this grapevine offered the quickest route to the perceived source of disorder. An efficient guild structure was a valuable asset, and in such circumstances the first shudder of disorder encouraged the prompt dispatch of a regulatory order. In some cases civic officials were sent to the company halls to instruct householders to keep their apprentices safe indoors. Periodic curfews applied the housebound ideology, confining young people within the political compass of their master's authority and directly controlling their time. In London, curfews extending for one or two nights, and sometimes for as long as a week, were often introduced in tense periods like the May Day or Shrovetide holidays, or as a response to attacks upon foreigners, servingmen, or the young men of the Inns by groups of servants and apprentices.[68] Night-time curfews were imposed as a matter of routine in many areas, and they were sometimes prefaced by remarks portraying the aggravated dangers of darkness.[69] In 'the dead of night' the young could slip into the shadows to join 'lewd company' at some 'evil' house, or to hide from their master. The simple fact of being on a street at night could attract a chorus of concern. A conception of 'unreasonable', 'unseasonable', 'unlawful', and 'extraordinary' time regulated the hours of darkness when morals adopted a particular and more sinister nocturnal meaning.[70] Young people who were found outside in these suspect hours 'wythout just cause' or 'lawful businesse' were assumed to be *en route* to some disorderly gathering, or to have committed some other mischief.

Time was strictly regulated in youth. That age was, of course, measured in years (a period of transitional training for the adult world of work) and in hours, days, and weeks (the pressure to put time to good use and comprehend appropriate notions of work

[68] See below, pp. 149, 156.

[69] For some examples of night-time curfews upon apprentices, servants and children see CLRO Jours. 21, fo. 356; 22, fo. 421; 24, fos. 28ᵛ, 141ᵛ; R. Sharpe Francis (ed.), *Ormskirk Sessions Order Books*, in *A Lancashire Miscellany* (Lancashire and Cheshire Record Society, 120, Blackpool, 1965), 33–4; R. Savage (ed.), *Minutes and Accounts of the Corporation of Stratford-upon-Avon and Other Records 1553–1620* (Dugdale Society Publications, 1, Oxford, 1921), 146–7; J. P. Earwaker (ed.), *The Court Leet Records of the Manor of Manchester from 1552 to 1686* (6 vols.; Manchester, 1884) [hereafter *Manchester Court Leet Records*], i. 159, 192; J. C. Atkinson (ed.), *North Riding Quarter Sessions* (9 vols.; North Riding Record Society, 1–9, 1884–92), ii. 193; Twemlow, *Liverpool Town Books*, i. 246; ii. 163, 457, 576, 808; R. S. Ferguson (ed.), *Some Municipal Records of the City of Carlisle* (Cumberland and Westmorland Antiquarian and Archaeological Society, 4, Kendal, 1887), 295.

[70] See PRO STAC 8, 190/13; 220/13; 288/14; 303/7; YCA B/35, fo. 173; City & Ainsty Quarter Sessions minute book, 1638–62, fos. 33, 85; NRO NMC 7, fo. 269; 8, fo. 186; 14, fo. 166; CLRO Jours. 21, fos. 127–7ᵛ; 26, fo. 71; 27, fo. 19; 29, fo. 109ᵛ; GL MS 4069/1, fos. 147ᵛ, 214, 216.

and morality). The differences between night and day added a further ordering dimension. Magistrates understood limited or disinterested participation in service to be evidence of immorality and even resistance. Youthful indifference to pressures to enter service was interpreted not only as an absence of subordination to appointed authority, but also as another form of socialization. We can perhaps see the rough contours of the problem of youth; the closely related secular and religious moral and political codes which connected tutored work, time, and virtuous youth, were felt to be threatened by an exuberant youth culture, which was beyond the 'safe' compass of structures of authority. This youth milieu was described at considerable length in menacing terms. It was criminal, profane, and promiscuous. This was just one-half of attitudes towards youth,[71] and its opposite, conformity, makes few appearances in judicial sources. The campaign to tame the 'lusty' age of youth and turn young people into pious and civil citizens met with mixed fortunes. Nevertheless, some of them responded more enthusiastically to the demands of service and the authorities' understanding of time, order, and 'place'.

We possess extensive literatures on theories of domestic relations which usually confine discussion to the literate and socially privileged quarters of Tudor and Stuart society.[72] This means that the issue of the extent to which such advice engaged the enthusiasm of householders is likely to remain unresolved for the greater portion of the population, who rarely left trace of their thoughts and actions. Did the 'godly' or ordered household remain a paper image or an exception; 'a copy and model' for the rest of the parish?[73] It has been suggested that there was some interest in buying householder tables in ballad form which offered advice about household discipline.[74] 'Little churches' did exist, and we find some heads of household treating the task of reformation with vigour. His nuptials completed, Nehemiah Wallington duly purchased a copy of Gouge's *Domesticall Duties* (1622), 'so everyone of us may learn and know our duties and honour God, everyone in his place where God has set them'. We glimpse Henry Newcome taking copious notes from Gouge and other conduct books.[75] A sufficient

[71] Cf. above, Ch. 1.

[72] For example, Pollock, *Forgotten Children*; Houlbrooke, *English Family*.

[73] Here I am quoting George Herbert, *Priest to the Temple* in *The Works of George Herbert in Prose and Verse* (2 vols.; 1859), i. 180.

[74] Tessa Watt, *Cheap Print and Popular Piety 1550–1640* (Cambridge, 1991), 234.

[75] Paul S. Seaver, *Wallington's World: A Puritan Artisan in Stuart England* (Stanford, Calif., 1985), 79; *The Diary of the Reverend Henry Newcome from September 30 1661 to September 29 1663*,

sample of contemporary materials survives to retrieve the principle and occasionally the practice. Yet whether such moral persuasion with its theories about pious life had a substantial circulation outside the ranks of sympathetic readers like Wallington, Newcome, Ralph Josselin, and other godly folk—from whence our empirical proofs tend to derive—is a matter which remains highly ambiguous and decidedly unproven. Some light could be shed by the frequent complaints about profane householders, though they may have served a specific rhetorical purpose. The slow and uneven pace of reform was often blamed on householders who set a poor example by failing to teach 'family duties'.[76]

It is difficult to tease out the precise moral meaning affecting their thoughts and actions, but some contemporaries were clearly concerned about the conduct of domestic relations, including those between age-groups.[77] Joan English of Great Mongham in Kent was presented for using 'her tonge inordinatlie toward hir elders and betters'. While Daniel Clarke of Thetford (Norfolk) was summoned before the Ely Church Courts for carrying himself 'very unseemly and uncivilly towards divers ancient men and parishioners'.[78] Michael Macdonald has described 'a popular conception of insanity', which caused 'ordinary villagers to identify defiance towards elders and superiors within the family as a sign of madness'.[79] One author claimed that it was both 'unnatural and cruel' for a child to deny a parent love. It was for considerations of this nature that Edward Aspland found himself charged at the Ely Archdeaconry Court with 'abusing and unnaturally using his father by bad words'. Another

ed. T. Heywood (Chetham Society, 18, Manchester, 1849), 6, 8, 55, 56, 82. See also Claire Cross, 'A man of conscience in seventeenth-century urban politics: Alderman Hoyle of York', in John Morrill, Paul Slack, and Daniel Woolf (eds.), *Public Duty and Private Conscience in Seventeenth-Century England: Essays Presented to G. E. Aylmer* (Oxford, 1993), 207; Ilana Krausman Ben-Amos, *Adolescence and Youth in Early Modern England* (New Haven, 1994), 63.

[76] See Gouge, *Domesticall Duties*, 602, 613, 651, 668; Abraham Jackson, *The Pious Prentice, Or the Prentise's Piety*, 1640 (facsimile, The English Experience, 746, Amsterdam, NJ, 1975), 34; W.P., *Prentise's Practise*, fo. 44ᵛ; Thomas Sparke, *A Treatise to Prove that Ministers Publickely and Householders Privately are Bound to Catechize Their Parishioners and Families* (Oxford, 1588), 47–8.

[77] For the contemporary concern with gender-relations inside the 'private world' of the family see Martin Ingram, 'Ridings, rough music and the "reform" of popular culture in early modern England', *Past and Present*, 105 (1984); E. P. Thompson, 'Rough music' in his *Customs in Common* (1991). Cf. Roper, *Holy Household*, esp. ch. 5.

[78] CLA X.1.7, fo. 174; CUL EDR B/2/29, fo. 146ᵛ. In Florence at this time some young people were sent to prison for disobeying their parents. See John K. Brackett, *Criminal Justice and Crime in Late Renaissance Florence, 1537–1609* (Cambridge, 1992), 54, 109.

[79] Michael Macdonald, *Mystical Bedlam: Madness, Anxiety and Healing in Seventeenth-Century England* (Cambridge, 1981), 127–8.

youngster had been presented at the same court in 1620 'for most unnaturally usinge himselfe in beatinge of his owne mother and father-in-lawe'. While Ludovic Wate was presented in 1598 for 'unnaturally and against all christianity . . . abusing his mother by wordes' and giving her 'strokes'.[80] In January 1634 George Lasells petitioned the Privy Council to complain about his 'unnatural son', who had enjoyed 'plentiful allowance' and had been 'tenderly and carefully educated' at school, the university, and Inns of Court at a cost of £1,000. Yet Lasells had had a poor return, and his son was 'rebellious, disobedient, and unnatural', taking possession of 'a great parte' of his father's estate, spoiling it 'to the value of' £300, 'and frightening away tenaunts'. He 'humbly prayed' that 'he may not be enforced contrary to the lawe of nature to be subject to his owne sonne'.[81]

Such words as 'monstrous', 'unnatural', 'unchristian', and 'inhumane' were part of an emotive vocabulary which could be used to define appropriate standards of familial conduct, including relations between husbands and wives,[82] and masters and servants. Thomas Parnel was accused of inflicting 'strange and inhumane cruelty' upon his apprentice. While a London embroiderer found himself before the mayor and aldermen for his 'unnatural usage' of his apprentice by 'unreasonable correction'.[83] People who disrupted the smooth course of domestic life could expect to be carried before a court. Ecclesiastical visitation articles inquired after 'sowers of discord between man and wife' and parents and children. Thus Dorothy Wate was presented in 1584 'for making debate between man and wife'.[84]

3. Catechizing Youth

The politics of age and 'place' were widely circulated and understood in Tudor and Stuart society. They could have been preached at sermons,[85] presented in cheap print, defended in the courts, and

[80] Anon., *The Office of Christian Parents* (Cambridge, 1616), 224; CUL EDR B/2/39, fos. 50ᵛ, 65; B/2/15, fo. 173ᵛ. See also Griffith, *Bethel*, 378.

[81] PRO SP 16/269/79.

[82] For example, CLRO Reps. 25, fo. 192; 29, fo. 5ᵛ; PRO SP 16/325/81.

[83] CLRO Reps. 29, fo. 52; 33, fo. 331.

[84] W. H. Frere (ed.), *Visitation Articles and Injunctions of the Period of the Reformation 1536–1575* (3 vols.; Alcuin Club Collections, 14–16, 1910), iii. 7; CUL EDR B/2/13, fo. 101ᵛ. See also EDR B/2/20, fo. 9; D/2/9, fo. 129. Cf. below, Ch. 6.

[85] Many of the texts intended for youth were first preached as special lessons and sermons for young people. Thomas Powell's *The Beauty, Vigour and Strength of Youth* (1676), for instance, had been 'lately preached to young men'. Henry Hesketh's *Importance of Religion to*

given full expression in the face-to-face meeting between youth and the ministry at catechizing. In fact, with regard to the size of the potential audience and direct experience, the catechism served as an important introduction to the principles of 'place' and age. It offered the 'best meanes to work knowledge of God and his service in the hearts of inferiours'.[86] It is well known that pedagogy was seen by contemporaries as a vital aspect of reform, and a means to steer young people away from centuries of darkness and ignorance, and the invitations of 'natural man'. The catechism was a principal component of a system of mass education which was assembled by ministers and magistrates in the period 1536–53, only to be disrupted by the interfering clerics of restored Catholicism, though it resumed apace under Elizabeth.[87] The period 1580–1640 has recently been portrayed as a critical phase, which witnessed a substantial rise both in pastoral endeavour and in the publication and reprinting of catechisms and pastoral advice books.[88]

The catechism very quickly became established in the pastoral round as one part of a broader evangelical thrust in company with fasting, preaching, and praying,[89] and familiar institutions such as

Young Persons (1683) and John Shower's *Seasonable Advice to Youth* (1692) were preached at the funerals of young folk. Samuel Burrowes's *Good Instruction for All Young Men and Maids* (1642) was preached at St Stephen's Church, Coleman St., London, 'at the earnest request of divers young men and apprentices'. Finally, William Gouge's *Domesticall Duties* (1622) was in its first form a course of sermons which he preached in his Blackfriars parish in London.

[86] Cawdrey, *Family Reformation Promoted*, 37. Cf. Vincent, *Words of Advice*, 57; anon., *A Catechisme or Brief Instruction in the Principles of Christian Religion* (1617), Epistle Dedicatory, fo. A2ᵛ.

[87] G. Schochet, 'Patriarchalism, politics and mass attitudes in Stuart England', *Historical Journal*, 12 (1969), 423; P. Tudor, 'Religious instruction for children and adolescents in the early English Reformation', *Journal of Ecclesiastical History*, 35 (1984), 391 and *passim*.

[88] This significant increase in the production of catechisms is discussed by Ian Green, '"For children in yeeres and children in understanding": the emergence of the English catechism under Elizabeth and the early Stuarts', *Journal of Ecclesiastical History*, 37 (1986). Robert Cawdrey referred to the catechism in a near millennial or at least revivalist fashion: 'the catechisme is in these last times come again as it were by right of recovery', *A Short and Fruitfull Treatise of the Profite and Necessitie of Catechising* (1580), fo. D2ᵛ. I must thank Ian Green not only for allowing me to see chapters of his forthcoming study of the pastoral ministry in advance of publication, but also for reading this chapter and offering very helpful comments. Dr Green's book will be the standard discussion of catechizing for a long time, and I cannot hope to match the fuller knowledge and subtleties of his work in this short account.

[89] Green, '"For children in yeeres"', 146; Patrick Collinson, 'Shepherds, sheepdogs, and hirelings: the pastoral ministry in post-Reformation England', in W. J. Sheils and D. Wood (eds.), *The Ministry: Clerical and Lay* (Studies in Church History, 26, Oxford, 1989), 190. Indeed, Collinson has suggested that we can only dismiss the effectiveness of the pastoral ministry when we have 'carefully considered the almost universal practice of the catechism and found it wanting', 202.

schools,[90] bridewells, and hospitals,[91] and, above all, the family.[92] It was expected that public catechizing would take place every holy day and each Sunday before evening prayer.[93] Some enthusiastic ministers followed up their sabbath day endeavour by visiting households during the week.[94] Thomas Sparke provided a typical description of a catechism; 'a forme of instruction, brieflie, soundly and plainly conteining the first principles of the Christian religion'.[95] These 'pithy and lively exhortations'—the 'ABC of our religion'— were intended as a first introduction to reformation of life and the means of salvation. They were a 'first draught' and a necessary first course before the 'stronger meat' of the sermon, without which preachers vainly 'built castles in the ayre'.[96] It was the task of the catechizer to proceed by question and answer, and to 'oppose' 'adversaries' and propose sound doctrine. It was hoped that he would engage catechumens in examination, 'expansion', and 'repetition', 'as by the reflex of an echo', 'twentie times over and over againe'. The skilful minister patiently crafted 'precept upon precept', so that his advice could be committed to memory as 'a proverbe in everyones mouth'.[97]

[90] See H. E. Salter (ed.), *Oxford Council Acts 1583–1625* and M. G. Hobson and Salter (eds.), *Oxford Council Acts 1626–1665* (Oxford Historical Society, 87, 95, Oxford, 1928, 1933) [hereafter *Oxford Council Acts* vols. i and ii], ii. 227; Z. Crofton, *Catechizing God's Ordinance* (1656), 60–74; K. S. Martin (introd.), *Records of Maidstone Being Selections from Documents in the Possession of the Corporation* (Maidstone, 1926) [hereafter, *Records of Maidstone*], 125; Edward Cardwell (ed.), *Synodolla: A Collection of Articles of Religion, Canons and Proceedings of Convocation in the Province of Canterbury* (2 vols.; Oxford, 1966), i. 291; Frere, *Visitation Articles*, iii. 99–100, 342.

[91] Some bridewells had 'house' ministers. See NRO NMC 14, fo. 421ᵛ; BCB 6, fo. 363; 7, fos. 26, 315; 8, fo. 12ᵛ; C. H. Mayo (ed.), *The Municipal Records of the Borough of Dorchester, Dorset* (Exeter, 1908) [hereafter *Dorchester Municipal Records*], 515; F. Rose-Troup, *John White: The Patriarch of Dorchester* (1930), 12.

[92] See Griffith, *Bethel*, 360; Crofton, *Catechizing God's Ordinance*, 60–74; Jones, *Briefe Exhortation*, 16 ff.; anon., *Office of Christian Parents*, 102. Sparke commented that the householder must catechize less the 'seed . . . sowen by the minister come to nothing', *Treatise*, 30 and 28–9.

[93] Although this is the practice *as it emerged* in the later sixteenth century, there were some ambiguities. The Prayer Book of 1549, for example, asked ministers to catechize every six weeks (See Wright, 'Confirmation, catechism and communion', 204), while the Royal Injunctions of 1559 as well as some early visitation articles suggested that they should catechize every second Sunday. See Frere, *Visitation Articles*, iii. 223–4, 296, 299, 305, 371, 376.

[94] For example, Baxter, *Reliquiae Baxterianae*, 83; Joseph Alleine, *Christian Letters Full of Spiritual Instruction* (1671), esp. 40–1.

[95] Sparke, *Treatise*, 3.

[96] Crofton, *Catechizing God's Ordinance*, 13 and 10–13, 36, 37, 56–7; Richard Bernard, *Two Twinnes or Two Parts of One Portion of Scripture* (1613), 19, 8. Cf. Sparke, *Treatise*, 11–13.

[97] Herbert, *Priest to the Temple*, 207; Sparke, *Treatise*, 4; Greenham, *Works*, 289; Bernard, *Two Twinnes*, 10–11 (cf. 8, 23–4); Crofton, *Catechizing God's Ordinance*, 12, 75, 84–5. The

A further benefit was that by teasing out 'echoes' and repetitions, the catechizer could mould responses and check spontaneity and creativity. The construction of orthodox identities, a new set of 'proverbs' or a 'second custom', was one objective. The monotonous, didactic pulse of catechizing was well tuned to the restraint of youth in this still largely pre-print world of word and mouth.[98] One author remarked that it was the minister's duty to put 'words into their mouths'. At the Westminster Assembly of Divines, Mr Seaman advised that 'the greatest care should be taken for the answer', which must 'be formed not to the model of knowledge that the child hath, *but to that he ought to have*'[99] [emphasis mine].

Authors often announced that their catechisms had been written for the benefit of every 'sort', 'degree', and age; for 'babes in yeeres and babes in knowledge'. Thus Luther declared, 'I stay forever a child'.[100] Nevertheless, the primary pastoral thrust was directed towards children and youth 'in yeeres'. Crofton, for example, requested that ministers catechize 'all that are ignorant', but especially 'youth and children to be the subject of it'. Luther delivered his view in blunt fashion—'especially the young'. While Richard Baxter thought that all ignorant people had a pressing 'need to learn', but that 'nature hath put children under a necessity of it'.[101] When we turn to reports of failures to catechize in ecclesiastical court materials, calls to greater efficiency were regularly accompanied by some further statement about the intended audience. In exactly 100 complaints in the parishes of Ely Diocese in the period 1574–1638, for example, sixty-three mention youth alone. Only one report coupled youth with children, six mention children or children and

quotations from Samuel Crook and Arthur Dent can be found in Stanley Fish, *The Living Temple: George Herbert and Catechizing* (1978), 19, 18 (see also 11–25).

[98] Cf. Gerald Strauss, *Luther's House of Learning: The Indoctrination of the Young in the German Reformation* (1978), 154, 172; Tudor, 'Religious instruction', 399.

[99] Crofton, *Catechizing God's Ordinance*, 17, and 58–9; A. F. Mitchell and J. Struthers (eds.), *Minutes of the Sessions of the Westminster Assembly of Divines* (1874) [hereafter *Westminster Assembly of Divines*], 93.

[100] The first quotation is from Bishop Freke's Articles for Rochester Diocese (1572) which can be found in Frere, *Visitation Articles*, iii. 342. The second is from Bernard, *Two Twinnes*, 10. Luther is quoted by Strauss, *Luther's House of Learning*, 159. Bernard also wrote that 'everyone is to be taught according to his capacitie whatever yeares hee bee of' (*Two Twinnes*, 10). Ian Green has plausibly argued that a careful reading of the prefatory remarks of English catechisms suggests that the majority of them were written for ignorant people of all ages, ' "Children in yeeres" ', esp. 402, 408–9. Cf. Fish, *Living Temple*, 14; Herbert, *Priest to the Temple*, 208.

[101] Crofton, *Catechizing God's Ordinance*, 112. Luther is quoted by Strauss, *Luther's House of Learning*, 160; Richard Baxter, *The Catechizing of Families: A Teacher of Householders How to Teach Their Households* (1683), 3.

servants. Thirty entries give no specific designation. In a single visitation of the Archdeaconries of Norfolk, Norwich, and Suffolk in 1597, Bishop Redman received 115 complaints of pastoral neglect, ninety-seven of which referred to youth alone (84.3 per cent).[102] We must remember that some churchwardens may have strictly followed the letter of the question asked of them when they filed their returns. In this case, are 'the youth' being instructed? They could have been *predisposed* to refer to youth in their returns.[103] A more rounded impression is that children, servants, and youth were the majority of actual catechumens, and that problems of bad behaviour and non-attendance were more likely to spring from these quarters. Visitation articles frequently addressed 'youth' and 'children' alone. Sadly, the returns rarely supply ages. The original articles, however, often draw attention to the age-group 6 or 7–20 years old.[104] Some bishops inquired after householders who did not send their 'children, young men, and maidens, and servants above six years and under twenty', and parish authorities were requested to keep a regular record of attendance and performance.[105] The majority of calls to attend catechizing were issued for youth and children, who on occasion were asked to rehearse questions and answers before their elders as moral exemplar. Bishop Parkhurst instructed churchwardens in Norwich Diocese to encourage 'the elder married folkes to be present, both for the good example of youth, and also to learn themselves by hearing'.[106] It has also been

[102] The sources are the CUL EDR B/2 and D/2 series, and J. F. Williams (ed.), *Diocese of Norwich: Bishop Redman's Visitation 1597* (Norfolk Record Society, 18, Norwich, 1946) [hereafter *Bishop Redman's Visitation*].

[103] A point carefully outlined for me by Ian Green. It is even more important because Green suggests that the wording of visitation articles changes in response to the 1604 Canons, in which canon 59 dealing with catechizing translated *iuventutem et plebem rudiorem* as 'youth and ignorant persons'. Green suggests that before 1604 the more common description of catechumens in the articles was 'children, apprentices and servants'. 'Youth' was used, but less frequently. See esp. ch. 1 of Green's forthcoming book.

[104] For example, Frere, *Visitation Articles*, iii. 220, 258–9, 299, 305–6, 371.

[105] See ibid. 223–4, 107, 213, 238–9, 275, 296, 299, 305–6, 342, 371, 380; Oliver Heywood, *The Life of John Angier of Denton* (Chetham Society, 97, Manchester, 1937), 77; *The Life of the Reverend Mr George Trosse*, 1714, ed. A. W. Brink (facsimile, Montreal, 1974), 115; *The Injunctions and Other Ecclesiastical Proceedings of Richard Barnes* (Surtees Society, 22 Durham, 1850) [hereafter *Barnes Injunctions*], 15–16. A significant distinction is often made in visitation articles. Bishops sometimes enquired after 'young folkes that cannot say the catechism, or elderly folkes that cannot say the Lord's Prayer, the Belief, and the Ten Commandments in the English tongue', though elderly often means those above 20 or 24 years of age. See Frere, *Visitation Articles*, iii. 259, 276, 297, 372.

[106] Alleine, *Christian Letters*, 112; John Strype, *Annals of the Reformation and Establishment of Religion* (4 vols.; 1725–31), ii. 91; Frere, *Visitation Articles*, iii. 100. Cf. Strauss, *Luther's House of Learning*, 167–9; John Whitgift, *Works*, ed. Revd J. Ayre (3 vols.; Cambridge, 1851–3), iii. 610.

argued that older folk resented forced attendance at catechism classes, which they understood to be principally intended for their young charges.[107]

Nor need we rely only upon stories of pastoral experiences in ecclesiastical court materials. The drive to catechize young people was encouraged by contemporary pedagogy and the pressing urgency to sow the seeds of faith in that malleable age at a time of religious strife. In 1586, for example, the vicar of Prescot (Lancashire) wrote in a despondent tone that 'the onlie reformation that we can hope for in this corrupt countrie is that children be truly and diligently catechised' because 'superstition is grounded in the aged'. Crofton remarked that 'the want of catechizing' raised fears about the youth 'turning pagan or papist'.[108] Indeed, the significance of the smooth succession of generations for order was linked to ideas of intellectual and physical development in youth. Malleability promised a degree of flexibility and fertile earth to work the manipulative aspects of catechizing. In a circular to the Bishops of Canterbury province 'for the better observance of catechizing and confirming of youth' (1591), Whitgift cautioned that 'the youth, being as it were the fry and seminary of the Church and commonwealth', should be taught to 'learn their duty' to God, their Prince, and neighbours, 'especially in these tender yeares, when things might best be planted in them, and would become most hardly to be afterward removed'. In his guide to catechizers, Crofton advised that 'whilest youth have souls rationall and capable of education, let them not want instruction in those things that may make them serviceable to God'.[109]

Catechizing and education more generally were to begin in infancy, 'as early as possible'.[110] It was hoped that these first stumbling steps towards civility and piety would gain pace and become a quick march in the years of 'discretion'. The ceremonies of the Church also marked this progress through early life. Discretion, catechizing, confirmation, and communion were related in a sequence of

[107] See Christopher Haigh, 'The Church of England, the Catholics and the People', in Haigh (ed.), *The Reign of Elizabeth I* (1984), 217. Cf. Strauss, *Luther's House of Learning*, 174–5.

[108] F. A. Bailey (ed.), *A Selection from the Prescot Court Leet and Other Records 1447–1600* (Lancashire and Cheshire Record Society, 89, Blackpool, 1937), 300–1; Crofton, *Catechizing God's Ordinance*, Epistle Dedicatory. Cf. Cawdrey, *Short and Fruitfull Treatise*, Epistle Dedicatory; Tudor, 'Religious instruction', 393.

[109] Whitgift, *Works*, iii. 610; Crofton, *Catechizing God's Ordinance*, 131, and 83. Cf. the remarks of Dod and Cleaver, *Godlie Forme*, 283.

[110] See Tudor, 'Religious instruction', esp. 394–400; Wright, 'Confirmation, catechism and communion', 204–5.

steps in which full understanding of the catechism was a necessary preparation for both confirmation and first communion.[111] The *Book of Common Prayer* warned that it was only with discretion and patient catechizing that individuals could 'with their own mouths and with their consent ... ratify and confirm' the promise made on their behalf at baptism. Nobody was to be admitted to communion 'until such time as he can say the catechism and can be confirmed'. Guest's articles for Rochester Diocese (1565) requested that people 'be not admitted to the Holy Communion before the age of xiii or xiiii years of good discretion and well instructed in the catechisme'.[112] A degree of care is appropriate. There are reports of great neglect in confirming young people.[113] In addition, although the great majority of confirmed were in the age-range 10–14 years, younger children and older adults also received the bishop's touch.[114]

We have already seen how the age of youth was seen to offer the best chance to cultivate fresh standards of discipline and piety.[115] Catechizing provided a further means of socializing young people and putting the case for conversion in early life.[116] The successful catechizer raised 'dutifull and obedient children', 'faithfull and diligent subjects', fashioned 'civil respect' for 'degrees and distinctions of men', and persuaded young people to pick up the virtues of 'humility, obedience, and good manners, [and] to reverence and give place to their elders and betters'.[117] By contrast, it was said

[111] Cf. Kenneth Fincham, *Prelate as Pastor: The Episcopate of James I* (Oxford, 1990), 123.

[112] Fish, *Living Temple*, 110–11, and 111–14; Frere, *Visitation Articles*, iii. 161. These important interrelations are explored in greater detail in Wright, 'Confirmation, catechism and communion'. Cf. Green, ' "For children in yeeres" ', 410–11; Tudor, 'Religious instruction', 395–6, 403; Whitgift, *Works*, 610; Bernard, *Two Twinnes*, 16; Sparke, *Treatise*, 13–18; Cawdrey, *Short and Fruitfull Treatise*, fo. C5ʳ. Visitation articles often asked parish officials to 'repel and put back' from communion those who could not say their catechism. See Frere, *Visitation Articles*, iii. 62, 156, 220, 373. Some articles also banned people who could not repeat their catechisms from marrying or from becoming godparents, Frere, *Visitation Articles*, iii. 48–9, 220, 259–60, 276–8, 378; *Barnes Injunctions*, 14–15; BIHR Wis/1. For some examples of prosecutions see CUL EDR B/2/13, fo. 70; B/2/35, fo. 257; D/2/51, fo. 11. Cf. EDR B/9/5; B/9/9; B/9/15; *Barnes Injunctions*, 122, 125, 126, 130.

[113] Kenneth Fincham, however, writes that 'There is no doubt ... of the immense popularity that confirmation enjoyed amongst all age-groups' (*Prelate as Pastor*, 128).

[114] See Whitgift, *Works*, iii. 610–11; Wright, 'Confirmation, catechism and communion', 210 and *passim*. Bishop Bentham's injunctions for his visitation of Coventry and Lichfield in 1565, instructed parish officials to present 'all children ... being full seven years of age and not yet confirmed', Frere, *Visitation Articles*, iii. 163. However, the editor notes that this is the youngest age mentioned for entry to the ceremony.

[115] See above, Ch. 1.

[116] For some typical statements about this significance of catechizing see Crofton, *Catechizing God's Ordinance*, 80–3 and Sparke, *Treatise*, 6–25.

[117] Anon., *A Catechisme or Briefe Instruction*, Epistle Dedicatory, fo. B2ʳ; Frere, *Visitation Articles*, iii. 214, and 166, 211, 281; Allestree, *Whole Duty of Man*, 71–2.

that 'the want of catechising' bred confusion, disorder, idleness, drunkenness, whoredom, swearing, filthy communication, and 'all other wickednesse'.[118] Bitter experience had taught Crofton 'that such are most apt to rebellion and disobedience towards men who are not catechised in the doctrine of God'. It was hoped that catechizing would provide 'a check to youthful lust'. The upright youth who parades through moral treatises and apprenticeship indentures was also portrayed in catechisms in which the short and simple phrases of the fifth and seventh commandments (in particular) were liberally interpreted to urge high standards of obedience and moral character. The first table of the decalogue discussed 'faith' and 'matters ecclesiastical'. The second, 'obedience', and 'civil matters', or 'mediate service'—that which 'at second hand redounded to God by serving of men'. Joseph Alleine taught his flock 'relative duties' for 'a long time'. This pious youth was expected to be obedient, meek, quiet, peaceable, just, chaste, temperate, righteous, and 'moderate in their degree'.[119]

Expositions of the fifth and seventh commandments provided opportunities for political and social comment. The fifth expressed the more urgent 'relative duties' of the second table because 'all disorders in the other doe flow from hence; that superiours are diligent . . . or else inferiours are proud and stubborn', envious, and ambitious.[120] Discussions of the fifth precept often began with a simple statement of intent: 'The first general doctrine' is 'that all duties are to be performed to our superiours' in the 'family, school, church, and commonwealth'.[121] The young were expected to obey all those above them in age, 'place', 'office', and 'excellency'.[122]

[118] Jones, *Briefe Exhortation*, 18; Crofton, *Catechizing God's Ordinance*, 68; Cawdrey, *Short and Fruitfull Treatise*, fo. C1ᵛ.

[119] Issac Bargrave, *A Sermon Preached before King Charles . . . [on] March 27 1627* (1627), 18–19; John Eliot, *Christian Commonwealth*, 1659 (facsimile, Research Library of Colonial Americana, New York, 1972), 3; Alleine, *Christian Letters*, 110; Cawdrey, *Family Reformation Promoted*, 17. Cf. John Calvin, *The Catechisme or Manner to Teache Children the Christian Religion* (1598), fo. C5ʳ; *The Book of Common Prayer* (1620), fo. R8ᵛ; M. Nicholes, *A Catechisme Composed According to the Order of the Catechisme in the Common Prayer Book* (1642), 30; Richard Bernard, *A Double Catechisme* (Cambridge, 1607), 27–8.

[120] Dod, *Plaine and Familiar Exposition*, 181. Cf. Thomas Granger, *The Tree of Good and Evil: Or a Profitable and Familiar Exposition of the Commandments* (1616), 15.

[121] Dod, *Plaine and Familiar Exposition*, 182; John Cotton, *Milk for Babes* (1646), 4. Cf. *The Book of Common Prayer*, fo. R8ᵛ; anon., *A Short Catechisme for Householders with Praiers to the Same Adioyning* (1614), fos. A5ʳ⁻ᵛ; anon., *A Catechism or Brief Instruction*, 34; Nicholes, *Catechisme*, 31–2; Richard Alleine, *A Briefe Explanation of the Common Catechisme* (1630), 20.

[122] John Ball, *A Short Treatise Contayning All the Principall Grounds of Christian Religion by Way of Questions and Answers* (1633), 91; Bernard, *Double Catechisme*, 28; John Stallham, *A Catechisme for Children in Yeeres and Children in Understanding* (1644), 15; Nicholes, *Catechisme*, 31; Edward Elton, *A Forme of Catechizing* (1620), 15.

The scope of authority was extended in familiar fashion by calling all superiors by the 'sweet and pleasant names' of father and mother. Authors distinguished between 'parents by nature . . . dignity and office', and age.[123] The periodic Sunday recital of the fifth precept reaffirmed the politics of age. Outside the household, 'in civill life', young people were advised by catechisms to honour and revere elders 'for yeares', especially those of age sufficient to be their parents.[124]

Explanations of the fifth commandment presented an opportune moment to lecture about the politics of 'place'. The catechumen was instructed to honour both 'spiritual' and 'bodily' 'place' and age. The 'summe' of the fifth precept, Dod commented, 'is to shew what duties we owe one another in respect of their and our place'. Nicholes remarked that its meaning required 'that we carry ourselves as becomes us in our places, and give unto others that honour and respect that is due unto them in regard of their places and degrees'.[125] These representations of authority confirmed the hierarchical dialogue between youth and age. The fifth precept 'reproved' disobedient servants and children, and provided scriptural ammunition for fiery broadsides against young 'murmurers' and other 'masterful and arrogant' young people, who ran away from their masters, paraded in fine and rich clothing, or married without parental consent.[126]

The stern tone of the seventh commandment helped to construct

---

[123] Ball, *Short Treatise*, 191; Gervase Babbington, *A Very Fruitfull Exposition of the Ten Commandments* (1596), 98. Cf. Alexander Nowell, *A Catechism or First Instruction and Learning of Christian Religion*, trans. T. Norton (1570), 14; *The Humble Advice of the Assembly of Divines . . . Concerning i a Confession of Faith ii A Larger Catechism iii A Shorter Catechism* (1648), 35; George Gifford, *A Catechisme Containing the Summe of Christian Religion* (1583), fos. G2^{r-v}; *The New Catechisme According to the Form of the Kirk of Scotland Very Profitable and Useful for Instructing of Children and Youth* (1644), 14; Edmund Allen, *A Catechisme, That is to Say a Christian Instruction of the Principall Points of Christian Religion* (1551), fos. D1–D2; Robert Openshaw, *Short Questions and Answers, Conteyning the Summe of Christian Religion* (1614), fo. B3^r; Calvin, *Catechisme*, fo. D3^v; John Ball, *Short Questions and Answers Explaining the Common Catechism in the Book of Common Prayer* (1655), fo. B4^r; Schochet, 'Patriarchalism', 431.

[124] George Estye, *A Most Sweete and Comfortable Exposition uppon the Ten Commandments* (1602), fos. 101^{r-v}; Ball, *Short Treatise*, 194. Cf. Babbington, *Very Fruitfull Exposition*, 102; Gifford, *Catechisme*, fo. G6^r; Ball, *Short Questions and Answers* fo. B4^r

[125] Estye, *Most Sweete and Comfortable Exposition*, fo. N8^v; John Mayer, *The English Catechism Explained, Or a Commentarie Set Forth in the Booke of Common Prayer* (1623), 310–11; Ball, *Short Treatise*, 191–2; Dod, *Plaine and Familiar Exposition*, 181–2; Nicholes, *Catechisme*, 31; Babbington, *Very Fruitfull Exposition*, 99; *Humble Advice of the Assembly of Divines . . . Concerning . . . A Shorter Catechism*, 11.

[126] Dod, *Plaine and Familiar Exposition*, 183; Bernard, *Double Catechisme*, 41–2; John Stockwood, *A Sermon Preached at Paules Crosse on St Bartholomew's Day, 24 August 1578* (1578), 26.

a sexual and moral code for both the married and unmarried members of the population.[127] 'Singlepersons' were warned to 'beat downe the body and bring it into subjection'. The pious and virtuous individual followed a strict regime of 'temperance, chastity, and sobernes', and fought long and hard to keep his 'body holy and pure'.[128] Moralists produced this precept to caution against 'all impurity and fleshly pollution' in 'speech, gesture', 'act, or desire'.[129] Many young people would have become familiar with the sorry tale of man's fall and the awesome struggle for regeneration against 'lustful and fleshly nature'—'the occasion of this commandment'— late on Sunday afternoon at catechism class.[130] They would also have heard their pastor trumpeting the value of chastity as one safeguard in that eternal and fateful combat with man's 'first nature'.

The seventh commandment was a vivid point of entry to the rigorous morality of reformed religion and its preoccupation with sin. Young people were instructed to check 'inward . . . unchaste lusts'—such as fornication, masturbation, sodomy, bestiality, and incest—and 'outward wantonness'—'things pertaining to the body', which provoked lust like 'a rolling eye', 'costly' and 'strange apparel', idleness, drunkenness, 'excessive diet . . . sleepiness', stage-plays, love-books, 'unchaste and wanton songs', 'lascivious pictures', 'filthy words', 'houses of open whoredome', and 'mixt dancing of men and women' with 'unchast touches', 'wanton touches', and 'ridiculous motions'.[131] The proposed remedies included solitary prayer, thorough self-examination, and profitable structured work (which was institutionalized in service and bridewells).

It must be said that these expositions can tell us a great deal about the image of youth drawn by authors, but much less about the words and lessons spoken by the minister as he catechized. I have tended to mingle quotations from a variety of catechisms ranging from the standard form in the Prayer Book to more difficult, lengthy, and advanced manuals. This strategy can, however, give

---

[127] Cf. Strauss, *Luther's House of Learning*, 104.

[128] Mayer, *English Catechism*, 359–60, 357. Cf. Ball, *Short Treatise*, 202; id., *Short Questions and Answers*, fo. B4ᵛ; Openshaw, *Short Questions and Answers*, fo. B3ᵛ.

[129] Samuel Crooke, *Brief Direction to True Happinesse* (1643), 19; Ball, *Short Treatise*, 203; id., *Short Questions and Answers*, fo. B4ᵛ.

[130] Bernard, *Double Catechisme*, 29.

[131] I have juggled quotations from different catechisms and treatises. They are Ball, *Short Questions and Answers*, fo. B4ᵛ; Bernard, *Double Catechisme*, 2; Dod, *Plain and Familiar Exposition*, 280; Barker, *Learned and Familiar Exposition*, 357, 366; anon., *Short Catechisme for Householders*, fo. A6ʳ; Openshaw, *Short Questions and Answers*, fo. B3ᵛ.

us a sense of the line of exposition pursued by the pastor as he expanded upon the short phrases in the Prayer Book catechism— the catechism which most children and even youth were likely to encounter.[132] The minister's words may be lost, but we can trace the theory behind catechizing. Another missing part of the scene is the responses of young people. The question of authentic pastoral experiences is an elusive topic. Much of our evidence is retrieved from the chorus of complaint in pastoral advice books and church court records. Here we see little of the routine, unspectacular performance which probably characterized much ministerial labour. The orthodox is buried beneath tales of irreverence and omission. Thomas Sparke commented that 'scarce the twentieth minister and hundreth householder doth performe his duty'. Neglect and contempt were common, and 'deeply rooted in the hearts of the most'. Catechizing is 'everywhere neglected', Daniel Cawdrey lamented in 1656, and only a 'few' young people received guidance. In 1635 the King complained that 'the necessary duty of catechising' had been 'much neglected' in Norwich for 'divers yeares'.[133] We should be cautious before producing such concern as evidence of neglect. Such howls of outrage could have been calls for greater pastoral energy.[134] They may have been fuelled by political (and religious) uncertainty, or by more 'precise' godly tempers. To complicate matters still further, each parish had its particular circumstances, politics, and personalities. Visitation returns and the records of the church courts, however, seldom reveal widespread indifference and dereliction of duty. Nevertheless, the casual and trouble-free report *omne bene* or a blank return is highly ambiguous, and could disguise both pastoral passivity and contempt, *or* the completion of the catechizer's task.

Yet scattered amongst these ambivalent omissions and formulaic 'all's well', there are reports in which pastors were rebuked for not catechizing. Some of them elected to drink and/or play cards,[135]

---

[132] These points about basic, intermediary, and advanced catechisms and their intended audience will be fully explored by Ian Green in his forthcoming book.

[133] Sparke, *Treatise*, 1–2; Cawdrey, *Family Reformation Promoted*, 137; NRO NMC 20, fos. 97ᵛ– 8. Cf. Bernard, *Two Twinnes*, Epistle Dedicatory.

Cf. Green, *For children in yeeres*.

[135] CUL EDR B/2/11, fo. 84; D/2/10, fo. 14; W. Hale (ed.), *A Series of Precedents and Proceedings in Criminal Causes Extending from the Year 1457 to 1640: Extracts from the Act Books of the Ecclesiastical Courts in the Diocese of London*, 1847 (facsimile, Edinburgh, 1973), 186; Williams, *Bishop Redman's Visitation*, 82, 90; F. G. Emmison, *Elizabethan Life: Morals and the Church Courts* (Essex Record Office Publications, 63, Chelmsford, 1973), 225, 228; Baxter, *Reliquiae Baxterianae*, 20.

still others grumbled about a heavy pastoral load.[136] We discover ministers who had not catechized 'sence . . . being incumbent', 'of late', or 'never at all'.[137] Others had not taught their flock for several months or years.[138] While some ministers catechized seldom, 'divers tymes', 'when he seemeth good', 'sometymes', 'now and then',[139] only during the season of Lent,[140] or at Easter.[141] Church-wardens and pastors were also presented for not bothering to call the youth.[142] While still others attracted the hostile attention of the courts for not keeping a record of attendance and performance.[143] Some confessed, regretted their fault, and announced that they would 'purpose speedily to apply . . . thereunto'. Others complained that the blame lay elsewhere because they had been 'alwaies readye to do' their 'dutie' but the parishioners 'will not send their youthe'.[144] One minister 'endeavoured . . . to the utmost, but could never yet obtain the tenth part'. In other places the young came 'by fitts and starts', some tempted perhaps by such experienced tacticians as Joseph Alleine who dangled the bait of money and apples before 'all children that came to be catechised'.[145]

These narratives from the archives can help us to shine some pale light upon a grey area, but in the absence of well-kept registers of attendance (and recorded ages) we have little option but to turn

[136] Some served two benefices. For example, CUL EDR D/2/10, fos. 153ᵛ, 155; S. A. Peyton (ed.), *The Churchwarden's Presentments in the Oxfordshire Peculiars of Dorchester, Thame and Banbury* (Oxfordshire Record Society, 10, Oxford, 1928), 217; Williams, *Bishop Redman's Visitation*, 43, 82, 115, 125.

[137] CUL EDR B/2/10, fo. 62; B/2/25, fo. 6; B/2/35, fo. 260ᵛ; B/2/52, fo. 61ᵛ; Williams, *Bishop Redman's Visitation*, 133, 150–1.

[138] NRO Diocesan Records Wis 7/1 (unpaginated); Williams, *Bishop Redman's Visitation*, 121–3, 138, 155–6.

[139] CUL EDR B/2/11, fo. 119ᵛ; B/2/24, fo. 9; B/2/29, fo. 121ᵛ; B/2/35, fo. 131ᵛ; D/2/10, fos. 5, 26, 28; D/2/35, fos. 22, 135; Williams, *Bishop Redman's Visitation*, 39, 50, 52, 66, 76, 93, 101, 143.

[140] CUL EDR B/2/24, fo. 51; D/2/35, fo. 132ᵛ; D/2/51, fos. 10, 40, 43, 52, 65, 68; B/2/52, fos. 58, 137; Peyton, *Churchwarden's Presentments*, 244, 249, 264.

[141] Williams, *Bishop Redman's Visitation*, 43, 64; Peyton, *Churchwarden's Presentments*, 249.

[142] BIHR CV/CB1, fo. 16ᵛ; ERO D/ACA 30, fos. 171, 185ᵛ; 32, fo. 175ᵛ; 48, fo. 154; Williams, *Bishop Redman's Visitation*, 64, 119.

[143] CUL EDR B/2/10, fo. 62; D/2/10, fos. 14, 22ᵛ, 24ᵛ, 28, 29ᵛ, 34, 46ᵛ.

[144] The first remorseful minister is quoted by H. Johnstone (ed.), *Churchwarden's Presentments (Seventeenth Century), Part 2, Archdeaconry of Lewes* (Sussex Record Society, 50, Lewes, 1949), 35. The details of the second case can be followed in CUL EDR B/2/11, fo. 119ᵛ. See also EDR B/2/10, fo. 59; B/2/11, fo. 125ᵛ; B/2/13, fo. 138; B/2/15, fo. 94ᵛ; B/2/25, fo. 6; B/2/31, fo. 97; B/2/32, fos. 62ᵛ, 72ᵛ; B/2/33, fo. 68; B/2/36, fos. 200ᵛ–1; B/2/38, fo. 58; D/2/10, fos. 14, 26ᵛ, 46ᵛ, 64ᵛ, 153ᵛ, 167, 177ᵛ; D/2/10a, fos. 7ᵛ, 37ᵛ; D/2/35, fos. 125, 132ᵛ; D/2/51, fo. 11ᵛ; BIHR CV/CB2, fos. 73, 76; Williams, *Bishop Redman's Visitation*, 139, 145, 149, 152.

[145] John Pruett, *The Parish Clergy under the Later Stuarts: The Leicestershire Experience* (1978), 116–17; Alleine, *Christian Letters*, 87.

to records of visitation and literary sources. Yet even here, among the stream of invective retailing stories about false starts and utter negligence, we can discover reports that catechizing is continuing.[146] It is difficult to evaluate these sources and produce confident interpretations about success and failure. Nevertheless, some recent historians have judged the rising tide of catechizing at the close of the sixteenth century 'a qualified success'.[147] The calibre of pastors was improving in this period. It was more likely that they would be resident graduates, though local experiences should be catered for.[148] Yet the regular litany of complaint throughout subsequent decades must not be dismissed lightly and devalued as pastoral polemics. They at least raise doubts about the wholesale triumph of this rather ambitious attempt to turn 'rude' youth into pious and civil folk.

Pastoral experiences are often obscured by the nature of the sources, but it is even more difficult to penetrate the minds of long dead catechumens.[149] Authors criticized the humdrum monotony and simplicity of learning by rote, which encouraged parrot-like repetition and empty formality rather than curiosity and persuasion.[150] One contributor to the debate about the new catechism at the Westminster Assembly of Divines commented that the great majority 'answered as a parrot . . . not understanding the thing'. William Harrison observed that although 'many' were taught the duties of the two tables, they 'carelessly omit them as if they never heard them', and 'content themselves with bare and idle hearing'. George Herbert also called these 'ignorant and silly souls' parrots. His long experience in the pastoral ministry had persuaded him that only a few ever 'pierced into the sense of it'.[151] He therefore invited ministers to be inventive. They could introduce a spark of colour and topicality if they freely borrowed from daily metaphors and comparisons. The order of the catechism could be easily

[146] For example EDR B/9/12; B/9/5; B/9/8; B/9/10; B/9/52. We also see ministers and householders catechizing as instructed in such sources as diaries and autobiographies. For example, *The Diary of Ralph Josselin 1616–1683*, ed. Alan Macfarlane (British Academy Records of Social and Economic History, New Series, 3, 1976), 9, 282, 517, 547. Henry Newcome's diary often reveals him teaching and catechizing at home.

[147] Wright, 'Confirmation, catechism and communion', 205; Ian Green, 'Reformed pastors and *bon cures*: the changing role of the parish clergy in early modern Europe', in Sheils and Wood, *Ministry*, 262.

[148] See Green, 'Reformed pastors'; Wrightson, *English Society*, 206 ff.

[149] Cf. Strauss, *Luther's House of Learning*, chs. 10–11.

[150] See ibid. esp. 154–5, 173–5; Fish, *Living Temple*, 11–25.

[151] Mitchell and Struthers, *Westminster Assembly of Divines*, 92; William Harrison, *The Difference of Hearers: Or an Exposition of Certayne Sermons* (1614), 160; Herbert, *Priest to the Temple*, 208–9.

adjusted to accommodate fluctuations in individual capabilities. In fact, Ian Green has suggested that such compromises with presentation and form were commonplace. They were a practical and tactical response to actual pastoral experiences.[152]

Yet we still encounter examples of the 'people's contempt of catechizing and [the] catechizer'.[153] One commentator reported that 'dayly experience proveth' how the majority felt only utter contempt for 'earnest' and interfering pastors, who took active steps to call the parish to catechizing. They preferred instead, 'carelesse pastors', 'pot companions', and the like, who 'make shipwrack of their salvation'. 'Many' could 'scarcely say the Lordes Prayer, the Articles of the Faith, and the Ten Commandments'. The godly few inhabited scattered settlements in a worldly desert in which active piety was a distinguishing mark. Those who duly attended catechizing were 'laughed at by the rest of their fellowes who out of prophaneness keep away from it themselves'.[154] Church court materials reveal many examples of youthful irreverence and jocularity. A number of young people simply refused to be catechized. Giles Revell, 'a proud unmarried youthe' of West Wratting in Ely Diocese for example, 'beinge asked by the vicar whether he could rehearse the articles of his beleef, after some misbehaviour answered stubbornly before all the company [of youth] . . . that he could doe it, but wold not'. The minister of Ickelton in the same Diocese asked John Cakebread, a servant, 'many questions [but] he returned noe answere at all' and 'turned his head and laughed at him'.[155]

Other young people gave their ministers 'contumacious speeches' and 'contemptuous answers', 'irreverent words and outragous slanders'.[156] In January 1604 the vicar of Barklowe in Ely Diocese watched Joanne Guy, a servant, pass 'sondrie tymes' through his churchyard in suspicious carefree fashion. When he attempted to discover her purpose, Guy responded 'unreverentlie and saucily' in words 'unfit for anie man's servant . . . scorning to turn her face towards him'. Such open discourtesy merited a swift reprimand. The minister

---

[152] Herbert, *Priest to the Temple*, 208–9; Green, 'Reformed pastors', esp. 282.

[153] Bernard, *Two Twinnes*, 3.

[154] Cawdrey, *Short and Fruitfull Treatise*, fos. B1^r–B2^r; Crofton, *Catechizing God's Ordinance*, 116.

[155] CUL EDR B/2/28, fo. 179^v; B/2/36, fo. 115^v. See also ERO D/ACA 32, fo. 179; 43, fo. 137; 54, fo. 6^v; CUL EDR B/2/10, fo. 23^v; B/2/15, fo. 123; B/2/16, fo. 128; B/2/25, fo. 2^v; B/2/35, fos. 257^v, 258; B/2/38, fo. 57^v; B/2/52, fo. 16^v; D/2/9, fo. 179^v; D/2/51, fo. 58^v; BIHR CV/CB2, fos. 28^v, 59^v; Hale, *Series of Precedents*, 242; Peyton, *Churchwarden's Presentments*, 117, 162; Emmison, *Elizabethan Life: Morals*, 143.

[156] See Peyton, *Churchwarden's Presentments*, 162; CUL EDR B/2/52, fo. 13; D/2/10, fo. 10; BIHR YV/CB2, fo. 36^v.

asked the maid 'what was the 5 commandment?', to which Guy replied, 'she would tell me when she saw cause'. To counter this display of youthful independence Guy was ordered to attend catechism class on the following Sunday, where not surprisingly the issue to be discussed was the meaning of the fifth commandment— 'that the word honor did extend to magistrates and ministers . . . as well as her natural father and mother'. But Guy was far from being the sorry penitent. She followed another script, and refused the requisite deference and humility, standing and staring at the pastor with 'a bold face in ye chancell . . . after a laughing manner'. John Simonson of Bagby in York Diocese also spoke 'disgraceful words' to his minister, 'sayinge he was a proud stitchill, and that he would not come at him to be catechised'. He also informed the minister that 'he cared not a fart for him'.[157]

Other ministers were interrupted by 'wrangling in the church porch', 'skoffes and mocks', 'chiding and brawling', 'quarreling', and 'uncivil speeches', and by people walking 'aboute the church or neere the church'.[158] Agnes Cross of Elme in Ely Diocese forced the pastor to 'leave off' catechizing the youth by 'most maliciouslye raylinge, cursing, and slaunderinge' him with 'lewd talkinge and laughinge', and openly taunted the churchwardens 'in scoffinge manner bursting out into laughter' and 'deridinge all authoritie'. John Peacock of Abbes Rooting in Essex 'disclaimed at the minister's catechising, saying that he did nothing but prattle'.[159]

Peacock and the rest can help us to recover the atmosphere of irreverence and jocularity which often clouded the minister's endeavours. They at least permit us to construct a more flexible explanatory framework, which incorporates a wide range of responses from the orthodox to the flatly hostile. Pious youth make few appearances in these sources, and when they do they are usually complaining about an inadequate minister. The 'servants and children' of Steeple Morden in Ely Diocese, for example, 'much misliked' their pastor, who catechized 'in such bad manner and sort' shattering the solemnity of the event with his 'frivolous and impertinent questions'. While the youth of St Nicholas parish in Colchester made their feelings apparent by voting with their feet

[157] CUL EDR B/2/40, fo. 29ᵛ; BIHR CV/CB2, fo. 123ᵛ. See also CUL EDR B/2/17, fo. 171ᵛ; B/2/15, fo. 15ᵛ; Hale, *Series of Precedents*, 246.
[158] See NRO Diocesan Records Wis 7/1 (unpaginated); CUL EDR B/2/32 fo. 62ᵛ; B/2/14, fo. 140ᵛ; B/2/35, fo. 162; B/2/52, fo. 17ᵛ; ERO D/ACA 52, fo. 186ᵛ; H. Johnstone (ed.), *Churchwarden's Presentments (Seventeenth Century), Part 1, Archdeaconry of Chichester* (Sussex Record Society, 42, Lewes, 1948), 28.
[159] CUL EDR B/2/27, fo. 5ᵛ; Emmison, *Elizabethan Life: Morals*, 143.

and travelling to another nearby parish for 'instruction' because
their minister displayed 'simplicity' rather than active commitment.[160]

The sombre note of the fifth commandment with its prohibitive
ethos could elicit the desired response. Early one morning in 1629,
15-year-old William Kiffin ran away from his master's house without
good reason. 'Wandring up and down the streets' of the capital,
Kiffin followed some people into St Antholin's Church where in a
truly ironic twist, one Mr Foxley was 'preaching upon the fifth
commandment and shewing the duty of servants to masters'. His
troubled mind turning over every pregnant phrase, the gloomy
Kiffin thought the preacher looking down at him from the pulpit
'had known me', and was directing his stern advice to the poor
runaway at the back of his church. Persuaded, the penitent and
remorseful apprentice chose to 'immediately return' to his master.[161] On this occasion the politics of age and 'place' emerged
triumphant, and the appointed age-hierarchy was restored as the
apprentice retraced his steps back to his master's house. Whether
preaching or catechizing, ministers could press the necessity of
conformity upon the young, and present age-relations as an
appropriate metaphor to catch the form and manner of authority
more generally. This politics of age and 'place' was not only
communicated in word and print because it was also given public
expression in the close affinity between age and office, in
orchestrated processions and other visual displays of authority, in
punishments, and in the vocabulary of insult and injury.

4. *Age and Authority*

Institutional authority was generally held to be the preserve and
perhaps even the automatic right of older men. The hierarchical
dialogue between age and youth was granted solid institutional
character and meaning in the formal allocation of authority. In
James Harrington's Republic youth (all those aged between 18 and
30) was deemed 'not capable of civil administration'. While John
Strype commented that 'we expect to find wisdom and counsel in
the aged and therefore princes usually make use of the aged for
their counsellors' and 'the younger sort for action'. Again, youthful

---

[160] CUL EDR B/2/11, fo. 63ᵛ; Emmison, *Elizabethan Life: Morals*, 143.

[161] *Some Remarkable Passages in the Life of William Kiffin*, ed. W. Orme (1823), 3. Cf. S. R.
G. Gardiner (ed.), *Reports of Cases in the Courts of Star Chamber and High Commission* (Camden
Society Publications, New Series, 39, Westminster, 1886), 200–1.

'heat' had to be channelled for the use of the State.[162] As we have already seen, life-cyclical progress for males was measured by the elevation from subjection to responsibility and office. Mere 'boys' had not yet made this progress and were unfit for office. In 1595 Richard Edey, a Marshalsea porter, was standing in a shop door when he was told by a Knightsbridge husbandman that 'there was a great stirre in London'—the apprentices 'had pulled downe the pillorye in Cheapsyde'. The porter reflected that 'it was a good comonwealthe wheare boyes must be governors'.[163] It was, after all, an age-old wisdom that the middle range between youth and old age was the autumn and prime of life; a time of great sense and maturity, which was best suited to formal responsibility and office-holding.[164] Young people were rash and impatient, unsuited to office, and not 'fit to write cases of conscience'.[165]

Keith Thomas has produced evidence which demonstrates that people tended to rise to high office as privy councillors, bishops, aldermen, and sheriffs, for example, after 40 years of age.[166] These were the lofty heights of officialdom. Much the same concerns affected the rather unspectacular sort of administrative routine in the corporation, guild, and parish, in which considerations of age clearly moulded the distribution of authority, and provoked disputes, suspicions, and criticisms.[167] Considerations of this nature prompted contemporaries to produce a sequence of correspondences between age, 'place', worthiness, precedence, honour, seniority, and authority. In 1634 it was the 'auntientest alderman' in London who took

[162] James Harrington, *Seven Models of a Commonwealth Ancient and Modern* (1659), 12 (Harrington reserved civil administration for 'all elders being thirty years and upwards'); Strype, *Lessons Moral and Christian*, 88–9. Cf. Bishop Babbington quoted by Thomas, 'Age and authority', 208.

[163] PRO SP 12/252/94ii.

[164] J. A. Burrow, *The Ages of Man: A Study in Medieval Writing and Thought* (Oxford, 1986), 8–10.

[165] Paul Slack, 'The public conscience of Henry Sherfield' (conveying Sherfield's ideas), 166; Keith Thomas, 'Cases of conscience in seventeenth-century England' (conveying the ideas of Charles I), 35. Both of these essays are in Morrill, Slack, and Woolf (eds.), *Public Duty and Private Conscience*.

[166] Thomas, 'Age and authority', *passim*.

[167] See NRO NMC 7, fo. 192ᵛ; YCA B/34, fo. 102ᵛ; BIHR YV/CB2, fo. 481; CV/CB2, fo. 73; CUL EDR D/2/32, fo. 73; Newcome, *Diary*, 162; Felicity Heal, *Hospitality in Early Modern England* (Oxford, 1990), 332; Paul Slack, *Poverty and Policy in Tudor and Stuart England* (1988), 10; Nicholas Alldridge, 'Loyalty and identity in Chester parishes 1540–1640', in Wright, *Parish, Church and People*, 107–8; H. G. Tibbut (ed.), *The Minutes of the First Independent Church (Now Bunyan's Meeting) at Bedford 1656–1766* (Bedfordshire Historical Society, 55, Bedford, 1976), 105; W. J. Sheils (ed.), *Archbishop Grindal's Visitation, 1575: Comperta et Detecta Book* (Borthwick Texts and Calendars: Records of the Northern Province, 4, York, 1977), 85; William Prynne, *Minors no Senators* (1646), 6 and *passim*.

the 'place' of the sick mayor. Seventeen years earlier it was reported that there was 'much question and controversie' in the city because 'young men of less experience and sufficiencye' had been chosen as wardmote officers instead of 'discreet, honest, and hable' house-holders to 'the dishonor' of city government and the 'disgrace of that service'. It was later claimed that jurymen were inappropriately young, possessing far too little experience and understanding. A concern with the quality of constables, in particular that they were of no estate and too young, lay behind the demand that they should not be sworn until the 'full age' of 21. Another source of anxiety was the capital's alehouses, and it was thought that those under 25 years of age were 'unfit' to keep these dens of 'sedition and vice'.[168] By contrast, old age was a tactical plea used by individuals seeking to obtain dispensation from office or from engaging in trade.[169]

The more humdrum or risky tasks were often handed to the junior or younger members of a guild or civic corporation. In York it was the youngest aldermen who supervised the watches when plague threatened the city. One Mr Latham, the clerk of the or-phans, 'being the youngest clark' in the London Lord Mayor's court, was asked to inform the mayor and aldermen of the timing of 'speciall courts to be holden for the reading of Acts of Common Council'.[170] The periodic round of promotions proceeded according to age and seniority in a manner familiar to all societies which reward long and loyal service. Thus in 1640 Rowland Backhouse of London, 'his age being neere fourscore' years, 'whoe accordinge to his precedencie ought next to succeed', was required to offer his services in the 'great place and office of maioralty'. Nicholas Barnsley of London was nominated upper warden of the Grocers in 1607, 'in respect of' his 'auncyntie and place', but begged to be excluded from the succession because he was 'not able to go forth' without a staff, and desired to end his 'wearysome and paynefull dayes' in his 'native [Staffordshire] soyle'. While in 1619 Norwich was rocked by a squabble about the 'election of ye chiefest magistrate' in which 'new' figures attempted to leap up the ladder of preference over 'ye auncientest aldermen' to enter high office. The King was told

[168] CLRO Rep. 48, fo. 112ᵛ; Jours. 30, fo. 257; 37, fo. 116; Reps. 28, fo. 64; 49, fo. 33; Remembrancia, V, fo. 85.

[169] For example, CLRO Reps. 30, fo. 14ᵛ; 32, fo. 170ᵛ; 33, fo. 182; 34, fos. 293–5; 35, fos. 132ᵛ–3; 43, fo. 291ᵛ; 44, fos. 368ᵛ–9; 45, fo. 537; 48, fos. 118–18ᵛ; 49, fos. 206ᵛ, 343ᵛ; 52, fo. 104; 53, fos. 59ᵛ, 69ᵛ; 55, fos. 34, 56ᵛ; GL MSS 3016/1, fos. 21, 51, 54, 73, 158, 168, 181, 347; 11,588/2, fo. 500; PRO SP 16/31/24.

[170] YCA B/34, fo. 149; B/35, fo. 133; CLRO Rep. 31(2), fo. 439. See also Reps. 32, fo. 280ᵛ; 44, fo. 152ᵛ; GCL minute books O2, fos. 380–1; O3, fo. 444.

of this confusion in the 'natural order of things'—'the imploying of divers of ye younger sort [who were] eyther weake in meanes or unexperienced in government' was a 'disgrace to ye more auncient and able citizens'. The mayor requested a restoration of precedence —that the 'auncientest alderman in ranke . . . in his turne . . . may be allwayes preferred to ye office of mayoralty'. His appeals were sympathetically received by central government, and the correct sequence of precedence was re-established.[171]

The cycle of promotion ('the rising of office')[172] and the aspirations, jealousies, and resentments to which it gave rise, naturally turned on matters of 'ancienty and degree', and experience.[173] The near symmetry between age, reputation, and authority could issue forth in a flash of resentment, or a suit for rightful precedence and ranking. Such deep sensitivity to age and authority could shatter the peace of institutions. A quick rise to power by some young upstart, or a lengthy period of immobility on the ladder of ranking watching others leap-frog into higher places, could severely wound pride and reputation. In 1618, for example, a dispute sliced the London Cutlers into two camps of 'younger' and 'ancient' brothers. The 'auncient' masters and others 'of the auncients' petitioned the Court of Aldermen about their master 'combyning himself with the younger sort' of the company, 'who for their voices exceede the nomber of the auncient'. This unholy alliance had 'committed diverse wrongs'. The 'ancients' being especially troubled by the election of a young man as rentor ahead of one of their number whose just elevation was a matter of 'right'. The company had been affected by a similar dispute in 1614.[174]

In 1611 the Court of Aldermen in London received a petition from divers plasterers complaining about their master and wardens for choosing Richard Fisher, one of the 'younger sort', as warden before the petitioners 'who are all his auncientes' in the livery. The matter was sent to a committee to be closely examined. Counter-charges followed on the heel of accusations of bribery and other unsavoury electioneering, and the twists and turns of the dispute can be followed in the city sources for at least seven months. Fisher was accused of 'corrupt dealinge' and 'bargaining for offices'

---

[171] CLRO Rep. 54, fos. 109–9ᵛ; GL MS 11,588/2, fos. 469–70; PRO SP 14/108/80. The Norwich dispute is more fully explored in J. T. Evans, *Seventeenth-Century Norwich: Politics, Religion and Government* (Oxford, 1979), 66–73. See also CLRO Reps. 53, fo. 25; 49, fo. 201; 34, fo. 179ᵛ; GL MSS 11,588/1, fos. 418ᵛ, 420; 11,588/2, fos. 198, 413, 512–13, 522, 530, 777–8, 806, 836; 11,588/3, fos. 45–6, 165, 166.

[172] CLRO Reps. 52, fo. 291ᵛ; 55, fos. 148ᵛ, 177. [173] GL MS 11,588/2, fos. 777–8.

[174] CLRO Reps. 33, fo. 245ᵛ; 31(2), fo. 344.

under cover of making a payment towards the tax for the Irish Plantation. The court decided that Fisher was indeed 'inferior' to many in the livery, and that he had been elected contrary to 'auncyent orders'. A new election was arranged and Fisher was restored to his former ranking, and an 'ancient' duly elevated. Yet wounds and injuries must have simmered and festered, because in October 1611 the master and wardens were committed to Newgate for flatly refusing to co-operate, and offering instead a stream of 'contemptuous and disgracefull speeches against the authoritie of the court'.[175]

Early modern institutions further extended familiarity with the use of age-titles as a guide to status by representing the allocation of authority in age-metaphors. Vocabularies of age offered a means of depicting the sequence of precedence. Thus some parish vestries, including St Bartholomew-by-the Exchange, St Dunstan-in-the-West, and St Margaret Lothbury (in London) appointed 'younger' and 'older' collectors and churchwardens.[176] The London guilds elected 'younger' and 'older' or 'upper wardens', and they included the Pewterers, Plasterers, Basket-Makers, Goldsmiths, Scriveners, Coopers, and Cutlers. If two candidates received the same number of votes, the Pewterers ordered 'that the elder man shall have the office'.[177] Inferior officers were also allocated the titles 'young clerk', 'younger yeoman', or simply, as in the household of London's Lord Mayor, 'young man'.[178] Such titles are usually more helpful as an indication of status and function rather than precise ages, just as commentaries on the fifth commandment appropriate the vocabulary of age to represent the distribution of authority. Yet in both cases meaning could only be retained if formal authority was indeed usually allocated to older people.

These struggles between the 'younger and meaner sort'[179] and 'ancients', show how the delicate interplay between age, precedence,

[175] CLRO Rep. 30, fos. 97ᵛ, 116ᵛ, 179ᵛ–80, 194ᵛ, 201. See also Rep. 43, fos. 202–4ᵛ.
[176] E. Freshfield (ed.), *The Vestry Minute Book of the Parish of St Margaret Lothbury in the City of London 1571–1677* (1887), 1, 3, 6, 38, 57–8, 61; id. (ed.), *The Vestry Minute Book of the Parish of St Bartholomew-by-the-Exchange in the City of London 1567–1676* (1890), 37, 60–2, 83, 87–8, 130; GL MS 3016/1, fos. 56, 112, 114, 180, 191, 224, 360, 414.
[177] GL MSS 7090/2, fos. 37, 47, 56, 64, 74ᵛ, 112ᵛ, 120, 127ᵛ, 134ᵛ, 141ᵛ; 7090/3, fos. 29ᵛ, 39, 52ᵛ, 64, 73ᵛ, 81ᵛ, 99; 7090/4, fos. 18, 36ᵛ, 50, 90; 11,588/2, fos. 18ᵛ, 40ᵛ, 41, 151; GCL minute books O2, fo. 109; O3, fos. 704, 717; P1, fos. 59ᵛ, 75ᵛ; P2, fos. 198, 256ᵛ, 261ᵛ, 282; CLRO Reps. 30, fos. 183ᵛ–4; 31(1), fo. 16; 31(2), fos. 377, 430ᵛ; 34, fo. 179ᵛ; 37, fo. 130; Steve Rappaport, *Worlds within Worlds: Structures of Life in Sixteenth-Century London* (Cambridge, 1989), 252, 253.
[178] CLRO Reps. 30, fos. 183ᵛ–4; 36, fos. 125ᵛ, 159, 235ᵛ, 256; 37, fos. 256, 259ᵛ, 270ᵛ; 40, fos. 84, 209ᵛ; 43, fos. 297, 299ᵛ; 47, fos. 45, 391ᵛ–2; 48, fos. 61ᵛ, 243–3ᵛ, 416ᵛ; 49, fos. 137ᵛ, 344; 51, fos. 93ᵛ–4, 295ᵛ; 52, fo. 260ᵛ.
[179] CLRO Rep. 29, fo. 232ᵛ.

'place', and authority affected the meaning of public reputation and character in male society at least.[180] 'If I be a brother you make a younger brother of me', one grocer told his company court on deciding that he could find no justice there. The fragile pride of another grocer was wounded when he was called a 'younger brother'. Here the deep sense of injury was communicated in age-titles.[181] Yet these disputes were not merely generational squabbles. They sometimes were simply that. But we must not assume that this rhetorical and tactical use of age-titles can always be directly related to actual ages. 'Young' and 'old', and 'man' and 'boy', were key terms in a vocabulary of insult, which played on sensitivity to public appearance and self-esteem. They helped to cast aspersions and trim reputations in a society in which age was one principle of order. The simple fact that they occurred at all renders these disputes significant, but equally interesting is the way in which rival parties conceptualized authority and formulated their responses in terms of age.

'Young' and 'youth', therefore, were often hurled as insults. Bishop Sandys called his Presbyterian foe 'foolish young men'. The heresiographer Thomas Edwards possessed a formidable repertoire of insults to expose the 'fanatical' errors and inadequacies of his sectarian enemies, and they included 'young' and 'youth'. Their 'foolish' opinions were the stuff of immature rashness and fantasy, and could have no place in responsible adult society. Ballad sellers also stirred suspicions and much speculation about their chosen course of life, for they roamed outside the conventions of formal authority. These misfits were again labelled 'boyes' and 'idle youths'.[182] Youth was also coined to draw attention to unsatisfactory performance in administrative spheres. London Common Council sometimes questioned the talents and commitment of watchmen. In 1633 it was claimed that the safe keeping of the city was in the hands of 'boyes yt are readier to take part' with nocturnal pilferers or vagrants. These complaints could flow in the opposite direction. The tables were firmly turned by a Dorchester watchman, who sneered that his godly town was in the charge of 'a company of boys'.[183]

---

[180] For some other examples see CLRO Reps. 29, fo. 232ᵛ; 31(1), fo. 161; 31(2), fo. 430ᵛ; 01 for 66–7 191· 95 fo 217· 11 fo 910ᵛ· 12 fos 21ᵛ–5· 18 fos 217ᵛ–8· 51 fos 228ᵛ–0· 55, fos. 215–16. Cf. *Titus Andronicus*, 1. 1, 8.

[181] GL MS 11,588/1, fo. 376ᵛ; PRO STAC 8 26/1.

[182] Kenneth Parker, *The English Sabbath: A Study of Doctrine and Discipline from the Reformation to the Civil War* (Cambridge, 1988), 57; Edwards, *Gangreana*, 32, 35; Natascha Wurzbach, *The Rise of the English Street Ballad 1550–1650*, trans. Gayna Walls (Cambridge, 1990), 251, 260, 261.

[183] CLRO Jour. 36, fo. 59; David Underdown, *Fire from Heaven: Life in an English Town in the Seventeenth Century* (1992), 150. Cf. Helen Stocks (ed.), *Records of the Borough of Leicester Being a Series of Extracts from the Archives of the Corporation of Leicester 1603–1688* (Cambridge, 1923), 59.

In adult discourse terms like 'boy' or 'lad' belonged to a vocabulary of insult, and their potential to trim reputations turned on their more usual application to people in pre-adult years, and their association with immorality and inadequacy.[184] William Cheshire of Rix (in Essex) called Thomas Stowe 'rascally knave and boy' in the public stage of his parish church and found himself before the Archdeaconry Court for 'swearing, banning [i.e. cursing] and railing'. Thomas Mesaunte, an Essex churchwarden, is shown in the sources rudely wrestling the church bell from one William Gassock, and in so doing 'offered to trip up his heels'. He trumpeted his hard-won triumph and precedence in the churchyard by heaping a chorus of abuse upon Gassock: 'Sirrah boy, I will use you like a boy.' Wounded and worse still, in full public gaze, Gassock responded in kind taunting the churchwarden: 'Boy, boy on your face for I am as good a man as you.'[185] Hugh Porrye of London challenged William Goodwin to fight 'in single combat'. Goodwin refused, and Porrye 'in most unseemely mann[er]' poured scorn upon his enemy, calling him 'coward and boy', and 'with a loud voyce affirmed that he kept better men . . . to wype his bootes and shewes'. Other 'base and opprobrious termes' which were used to trim reputations included 'rogue, rascall, scurvye prentize boy', and 'upstart boy'.[186]

'Boy' was hurled between rivals to imply inequality and incompetence, taunting and pruning masculine sensitivities, pride, and esteem. The distance between 'boy' and 'man' was as great as the imposing border between youth and adulthood. Even in these heated moments, as tempers boiled and insults were traded, early modern people exposed the difference of ages by shifting the attributes of one age to another. The prayers and devotions of parishioners were rudely interrupted in a Nottingham church. John Spencer 'before many gentlemen and townsmen' called Robert Malin (the sheriff), 'jack-boye' and 'proud boye', and informed the watching congregation that 'he was as good a man as hee setting his place or office aside'. The attention of neighbours was doubtless gripped by this volley of abuse. Malin was then called a 'shitten boye' and 'a lad' in the full glare of publicity, and informed that 'it was never [a] good world since such boyes as he bore office in the towne'. The sheriff could not permit public review of his reputation to pass

---

[184] This particular form of abuse in adult discourse has also been discussed by James C. Scott, who remarks on 'the use of boy' by people who possess authority 'when speaking with inferiors' (*Domination and the Arts of Resistance: Hidden Transcripts* (New Haven, 1990), 32).

[185] Emmison, *Elizabethan Life: Morals*, 114, 137.

[186] PRO STAC 8 158/10; 156/1; 26/1; SP 16/197/23–4.

unpunished, and so he responded by having his vociferous critic bound to keep good order.[187]

The character of Spencer's chosen insult, uttered in the full knowledge that it would maximize injury, and the sheriff's concern that his reputation should not be exposed to the vicious snap judgement of local gossip, reveals the significance of age and authority in the public sphere. This particular vocabulary of insult could touch a raw nerve, especially in public places. Highly structured visual representations of social order were an important aspect of the articulation of authority at this time. Studies of civic ceremony and identity have made us familiar with ritual interpretations of the distance between governors and governed.[188] When Oxford's élite assembled to greet the King in 1636 they were arranged in strict order 'according to their places'.[189] These choreographed rituals served as a visual reminder of 'place' and social categories, including age-relations.

It was not sufficient that young people were depicted as the subordinate party in dominant adult discourse, they also had to be *seen* to be obedient and passive creatures. This visual dimension was one territory in which the contest between youth and age was enacted. Age-relations were constantly being renegotiated and redefined. Governors attempted to impose conformity upon the young by proposing rules regulating what clothes they put on, for instance, how they should wear their hair, or where they should sit in church.[190] Visual display was choreographed to represent conventional theories of age-relations.[191] Processions and feasts sometimes gave a further cultural badge to age-differentials by assigning different age-groups separate places and functions. The 'younger sort', for example, were often relegated to 'the lower end of the table'.[192]

[187] W. H. Stevenson *et al.* (eds.), *Records of the Borough of Nottingham* (9 vols.; Nottingham 1882–1956) [hereafter *Nottingham Borough Records*], v. 275–6.

[188] See Mervyn James, 'Ritual drama and the social body in the late medieval English town' in his *Society, Politics and Culture: Studies in Early Modern England* (Cambridge, 1986); Charles Phythian-Adams, 'Ceremony and the citizen: the communal year at Coventry 1450–1550', in Peter Clark and Paul Slack (eds.), *Crisis and Order in English Towns 1500–1700: Essays in Urban History* (1972); Miri Rubin, *Corpus Christi: The Eucharist in Late Medieval Culture* (Cambridge, 1991), esp. 243–71.

[189] *Oxford Council Acts*, i. 166–7, 212, 213; ii. 67, 163, 284, 310.

[190] The significance of clothing and hair is further explored in Ch. 4.

[191] James C. Scott discusses how governors manage 'visual and audible displays of rank, precedence and honour' by interfering with the 'terms of address, demeanour, speech levels', and clothing (*Domination and the Arts of Resistance*, 105).

[192] GL MSS 5770/1, fo. 315; 5770/2, fo. 111; Heal, *Hospitality*, 332; Phythian-Adams, 'Ceremony and the citizen', 63–4; Susan Brigden, *London and the Reformation* (Oxford, 1989), 584. Cf. Edward Muir, *Civic Ritual in Renaissance Venice* (Princeton, 1981), esp. 303.

A further opportunity to advertise appointed age-hierarchies was provided by the 'public' and 'open' punishments of disobedient young people with their well-scripted visual and verbal statements of offence and repentance, which are further explored below.[193]

Among the best-documented forms of visual representation of age and authority are the seating plans of churches, and partly for this reason they have received considerable attention from historians, who have tended to explore these neat compartmentalizations of the Sunday congregation through the prism of local social structure—class, wealth, and office.[194] They are said to provide a map of the distribution of status and authority. In fact, the sources offer ample confirmation of the preferential treatment which was extended to those of 'quality' and 'ability', who were often allocated superior positions at the front of the church where they could glance back through the middling ranks to the humble poor who gathered on the back benches.[195] If we turn to church court materials, we sometimes see the self-styled 'better' and 'chiefest' inhabitants filing petitions against their audacious inferiors, who blurred social categories by slipping into the front and best pews. They also complained about the sheer press of numbers, and obscured sound and vision.[196]

A dispute gripped the parish of Wistow in York Diocese in the period 1640–2. Tempers had been stirred by a recent uprooting of church seating—'the seates or stalles' having 'bene of late much altered'. Petitions were rushed to York. In a letter to the Archbishop, the vicar-general explained that 'the people of inferiour ranke sit in the chiefest seates . . . without respect or givinge place to their superiours', and he predicted a bleak future of 'much contention and controversies' if the petitioners were not appeased. His warning fell on sympathetic ears because further disputes were avoided, and Wistow's élite were restored to their visually vital front pews. But a further quarrel animated parish life in the years after

---

[193] See below, Ch. 6.

[194] Margaret Aston writes that seating plans 'opened opportunities for both social advertisement and social control', 'Segregation in church', in W. J. Sheils and D. Wood (eds.), *Women in the Church* (Studies in Church History, 27, Oxford, 1990), 281. See also Underdown, *Revel, Riot and Rebellion*, 29–33; Amussen, *An Ordered Society*, 137–44; Alldridge, 'Loyalty and identity', 94–8; Jeremy Boulton, *Neighbourhood and Society: A London Suburb in the Seventeenth Century* (Cambridge, 1987), 146–7; R. A. Houston, *Social Change in the Age of Enlightenment: Edinburgh 1660–1760* (Oxford, 1994), 64–9.

[195] See ERO D/ACA 32, fo. 80; 45, fo. 172; 47, fos. 125, 147; 48, fo. 172; 51, fo. 207; Aston, 'Segregation in church', 289.

[196] ERO D/ACA 43, fos. 106ᵛ, 114ᵛ, 120ᵛ, 126ᵛ, 165; 44, fos. 14, 16ᵛ; 45, fos. 174ᵛ, 261, 266ᵛ; Emmison, *Elizabethan Life: Morals*, 130–8.

the Restoration. On this occasion the pulpit had been moved, and in a petition seeking 'good order and amity' in the church, eight inhabitants who had been 'dispossessed of their antiente seates', requested that they be 'duelie and carefully provided for, and placed in the said church accordinge to their degrees and qualities'. The social geography of the parish was accordingly recast.[197]

The social élite's preoccupation with public performance and the uppermost seats implies that investigations of 'qualities' and 'degrees' pay insufficient attention to the middle and rear of the church. The poor often assembled here in the 'lower part' of the church, and it is from the back benches that most reports of jocular and irreverent behaviour derive.[198] The size of the church was in fact one significant variable. The smaller churches effectively placed physical limits on the number of social distinctions which could be introduced in a social map of this type. Indeed, the growing fashion for family pews was cutting into the broad spaces which had previously accommodated separate social groups.[199] In this case, the boundaries of the possible were set by money and physical space. Yet in larger churches social segregation could take on more ambitious forms, which more accurately represented the significance of age and gender in the social order. Officials could carve up the congregation into tidy social pockets. The extra space and galleries allowed them to distinguish between the sexes and ages by placing them in 'the middle alley' or 'other lower places'.[200] Keith Thomas writes that 'the generations were segregated with young persons consigned to the back of the aisles'. The politics of age could also determine the sequence of precedence in the front rows among the social élite. In some churches the average age of occupiers of each bench increases the closer we approach to the minister.[201]

The churchwarden's accounts for the parish of St Botolph's in Cambridge reveal payments for '3 formes [i.e. benches] for youth to sit on, 2 longe [and] 1 short'. Some parishes constructed galleries for 'youth to sit in', a fashion which worried Ephraim Udall, who

---

[197] BIHR D/C CP 1640–2; Wis/1. In one church the parishioners were restrained from ~~ambitious displays of deference. Officials reported that 'there is no abuse used in our~~ church by the rising up of the people in prayer time at the comeinge in of men of abilitie ... Justice Dalton and his wife and some of his family and wee desire it may be amended', CUL EDR B/2/52, fo. 52. Cf. B/2/35, fos. 212–14.

[198] See below, Ch. 4.   [199] Aston, 'Segregation in church', 286 ff.

[200] See ERO D/ACA 48, fo. 107ᵛ.

[201] Thomas, 'Age and authority', 7; Alldridge, 'Loyalty and identity', 95–6. Alldridge comments that 'Older inhabitants could rely on a certain tribute being paid to their authority', 96.

considered it a much safer option for them 'to stand at their masters and dames pew doores'. (In one York parish adult males sat with their family and servants 'to the entent' that they 'myght see the conversation of the sayd prentises'.[202]) In London, the parish of St Botolph, Aldersgate, constructed a 'young mans gallery' and a 'maidens gallery'. St Brides, Fleet St., had a gallery 'fitted for mens daughters' in which boys 'intruded'. While in 1647 the vestry of St Margaret, New Fish St., instructed that 'the gallery should be made fitt for the youth'.[203] Various concerns affected the construction of generational spaces, not least the visual representation of social differentiation. Some officials believed that young people could not fully participate in the service. Thus in one Durham parish the churchwardens declared 'that no young man, journaman nor prentice . . . shall presume in the quire to sit or above the cross alleye . . . excepte he can read and helpe to say the service'.[204] Of equal concern was youth's predilection for irreverence and rough play. Despite Udall's anxiety, many parishes clearly saw an advantage in pushing the young to one section of the church. Some appointed special officers. Thomas Hickucke of St Botolph's, Aldersgate, was paid twenty shillings 'for rulinge the apprentices sittinge over the belfrey for the yeare', and widow Bromley received 6*s.* 8*d.* 'for overseeing the maydes'. In 1634 the governors of London Bridewell ordered that a seat 'be made in the walle neare weare the place where the boyes sitt' for an artisan to sit in who 'shall aveighe and rebuke them there', and inform the governors about apprentices who 'will not be reformed'. Artisans and governors were strategically placed in the chapel on other occasions to reduce the volume of noise, and to cut short the antics of young mockers and scoffers.[205]

Uppermost in the minds of parish officials when they drew these social maps was the public expression of age-differentials. There is much evidence in church court records which suggests that at least some sections of the adult population valued these representations

---

[202] J. C. Cox (ed.), *Churchwarden's Accounts from the Fourteenth Century to the Close of the Seventeenth Century* (1913), 191; Udall is quoted by Aston, 'Segregation in church', 289; David Palliser, 'The parish in perspective', in Wright, *Parish, Church and People*, 23. See also GL MS 1175/1, fo. 126 (a seating plan for the congregation which shows the space reserved for servants).

[203] GL MSS 1454/74; 6554/1, fo. 202; 1175/1, fo. 84ᵛ. See also GL MS 3570/2, fo. 27.

[204] Cox, *Churchwarden's Accounts*, 191.

[205] GL MS 1454/97; BCB 7, fo. 377ᵛ. See also BCB 7, fo. 237; 8, fo. 162ᵛ; E. G . O'Donoghue, *Bridewell Hospital, Palace, Prison and School from the Death of Elizabeth to Modern Times* (1929), 66–8. See also Alldridge, 'Loyalty and identity', 94. Some other examples of these special officers are given below, p. 195.

of status, and that they were prepared to go to the trouble and
expense of issuing petitions or suits to safeguard social distinctions.
Formal descriptions of the social order rehearsed the fine status
distinctions of the adult male society, and tended to exclude children and servants as a matter of course.[206] Churchwardens revealed
the same social bias when they pushed young people to inferior
benches, thereby providing the occasion for disputes between generations. In 1653 the parish authorities of Newbould-upon-Avon
filed a petition at Warwick Quarter Sessions complaining about

divers of the most substantial inhabitants . . . having no seats in the church,
and other seats in the church [being] so narrow . . . the parties cannot
kneel down at prayer, and that some of the best part of the church is filled
with servants and boys whilst the aged people and others of better rank,
are seated near the door in so cold a part of the church standing upon
a hill that they are not able to endure the cold in the winter time.

The churchwardens were ordered to place the petitioners in some
'convenient seats having respect unto their ages and degrees'. A
similar complaint affected a Chichester congregation who made
their feelings plain about Stephen Grigges and his wife, who were
promptly presented for 'letting out seates' in church and taking
money to place 'girles in seates . . . thereby displacing ancient men
and women'. 'Great disorder' interrupted worship in the church of
Much Hadham in Hertfordshire when a group of 'boyes and younge
men' caused a great deal of trouble by 'placing themselves very
disorderly amongst the aunscient sort of parishioners there'[207] The
distance between youth and age had to be protected. These arbitrary movements around the church in which young people casually
crossed the border between youth and adulthood were resented
by some adults, who were keen to uphold public representations of
age-categories in the order of seating. Such points of conflict illuminate the form of potential generational tension, and also return
us to the significance of popular ideas about the life-cycle.[208] The
master was not to be confused with his servant, or married folk with
single persons. George Watson was presented at York Archdeaconry
Court in 1634, for 'he being but a servant will sit where he will in

[206] See Keith Wrightson,'The social order of early modern England: three approaches', in
Lloyd Bonfield, Richard Smith, and Wrightson (eds.), *The World We Have Gained: Histories of
Population and Social Structure: Essays Presented to Peter Laslett* (Oxford, 1986), 182; Cressy,
'Describing the social order', 30, 31–4.
[207] S. C. Ratcliff and H. C. Johnson (eds.), *Warwick County Records* (9 vols.; Warwick, 1935–
64), iii. 162; Johnstone, *Churchwarden's Presentments . . . Chichester*, 74; Aston, 'Segregation in
church', 288.
[208] See above, esp. Ch. 1.

the church'. 'A greate disorder' upset worship in the parish of Elme in Ely Diocese in 1604, servants and children caused great offence by 'shouldring up and thrusting into seats ... whereby divers inhabitants and parishioners there (marryed folkes) are displaced and destitute and have no seates to sitt in'. While a 'fitt person' was appointed in the London parish of St Dunstan-in-the-West to stop 'servingmen, apprentices, and other servantes and boyes' slipping into the pews reserved for 'the auncientest and better sort of the parishioners'.[209]

Unmarried women often sat apart from the wives of the parish.[210] The sources refer to the 'married womens seates', 'womens stooles' and pews, 'mens daughters' seats, and to the 'maids stoole' or pew.[211] In some churches women sat apart from men on one side of the church, sometimes arranged in a pattern which carefully traced the male social hierarchy.[212] Again, there are cases in which members of the congregation and the authorities took steps to preserve borders between age-groups. The officers of Harlton in Ely Diocese reported that Mary Hartley refused to sit in 'a very convenient seat ... but sitteth among the maides very undecently being a maryed wife'. Similarly, Elizabeth Carder of Abington Magna was presented in 1591 for leaving her 'accustomed seate' among the wives to 'sytte in the maides stoole ... there being not sufficient roome', prompting Margery Amye, 'singlewoman', to 'contend and strike' for her seat.[213] Theories of gender were juggled with ideas about age and social class in the drawing of seating plans. The church-wardens of Impington in Cambridgeshire reported that in their church 'men and women doe not sitt promiscuously together'.[214]

---

[209] BIHR CV/CB2, fo. 73ᵛ; CUL EDR B/2/20, fo. 76ᵛ; GL MS 3016/1, fos. 124–5. Cf. CUL EDR B/2/18, fo. 192ᵛ; PRO SP 16/288/72; Peyton, *Churchwarden's Presentments*, 186; Alldridge, 'Loyalty and identity', 96; Aston, 'Segregation in church', 288.

[210] See Aston, 'Segregation in church'. Aston also explores some of the reasons for the segregation of the sexes, esp. 240, 259, 263.

[211] For example, CUL EDR B/2/17, fo. 88ᵛ; B/2/31, fo. 37; B/2/35, fos. 207–10; B/2/52, fo. 26; ERO D/ACA 46, fo. 101ᵛ; 48, fo. 107ᵛ; PRO SP 16/117/56; GL MSS 1175/1, fos. 25, 47; 1431/2, fo. 77; 3570/1, fos. 12, 21; 4165/1, fo. 29; 4415/1, fo. 88; 6554/1, fo. 173.

[212] Seating plans do survive. There are a number in the vestry book of the London parish of St Margaret, New Fish St. which show men and women sitting in different sides of the church. See GL MS 1175/1, fos. 8ᵛ, 25, 30, 33, 47, 96, 107. In 1584 the Oxford corporation 'agreed' that any widowed freewoman who 'marries agayne ... shall have her place both in the church and in other places according to the decree of her husbande which she doth marrie, and not other wise', *Oxford Council Acts*, i. 11. See also ORO PCBP 1626–36, fo. 119ᵛ.

[213] CUL EDR B/2/18, fo. 18ᵛ; B/2/11, fo. 175ᵛ. Cf. GL MS 6554/1, fo. 202; Cox, *Churchwarden's Accounts*, 191; Hale, *Series of Precedents*, 241–2.

[214] CUL EDR B/9/52. Cf. J. Barmby (ed.), *Churchwarden's Accounts of Pittington and Other Parishes in the Diocese of Durham from A.D. 1580–1700* (Surtees Society, 84, Durham, 1888), 23; Cox, *Churchwarden's Accounts*, 191.

When they devised seating plans, parish authorities had to wrestle with the sequence of precedence, and with the complicated interplay between an ideological triumvirate—age, gender, and class. Historians of early modern social structure and order should follow their example. All three ordering principles could dissect the Sunday congregation, constantly meeting at points of resolution and conflict. In 1662, for example, the churchwardens of Dry Drayton on the western fringes of Cambridge, reported that 'our men and women and younger people sett distinctly'.[215] Church seating plans kept age-categories in full public gaze. The archives permit us to trace the contours of this social map, though we only glimpse its felt significance when the public representation of age-relations had become a topic of debate. Distinctions of age clearly possessed meaning; church furniture conveys a social archaeology also. It is another example of elite choreography. The herding of the congregation into arranged spaces extended familiarity with the life-cycle and the social distance between young and old. It confirmed identities, reputations, sympathies, and distances. Young people who trespassed onto forbidden adult space upset householders and ratepayers, who responded with cautions in church and petitions in court. These whispers, warnings, and threats in church, and subsequent court action, reveal not only the petitioner's thinly disguised pride in maintaining social distinctions, but also their recognition of a group of people they called 'the youth'. Age could only be a principle of authority in a society in which such differences and oppositions were formulated, valued, defended, and occasionally contested.

This chapter has explored the politics of age and 'place' in early modern society, and attempted to convey some of the cultural, ideological, and social significances of the division between youth and adulthood. It has trawled through a number of sources and locations to discover the meaning of age—in languages of precedence and authority; the widely held concern (in popular conceptions of family life and other rhetorics) that conventional social relations must be respected; catechizing; the allocation of formal authority and its metaphorical representation; the vocabulary of insult and injury; and visual representations of social order. The complex importance of age is apparent in these sources, though it has been relatively neglected hitherto. Age was a further principle of order in early modern society, and we should review our

[215] EDR B/9/15.

approach to the social order accordingly. The successful negotiation of the 'troubled' time of youth was vital to social order more
generally, for magistrates and ministers associated youthful independence with disorder. They drew upon a vocabulary of 'place'
which strongly inferred institutional authority and function, and
proposed a close correspondence between age, authority, the sequence of precedence, reputation, and subordination. The language
of 'place' sliced through the diversity of everyday experiences to
depict conventional social relations in clear terms of hierarchy and
pedagogy, but also mutuality and inclusion, catching differentiation
and identification in the same phrase. In so doing, it assisted in
defining the ideal place of youth in the social order.

Yet the recovery of political rhetoric or choreographed visual
display is of limited use because it can only tell us about one side
of the story of youth; the normative and prescriptive. It only expressed élite characterizations of youth and scripted patterns of
social relations. This is a still-life or model, which assumes a great
measure of conformity and passivity. Yet this was only one way of
growing up, and it offers a rather singular and narrow rendering of
youthful experiences which has a tendency to relegate the aspirations, frustrations, and responses of young people to an interesting
footnote or subplot in the history of adult constructions and institutions. The authentic voice of youth is frequently silent and
remote. But youth was not a passive experience in Tudor and Stuart
society; young people possessed creativity, invention, and agency.
Again, the social history of youth is neither scripted nor inevitable.
To draw a rounded impression and see the young as historical
actors, we must construct a more flexible and sympathetic explanatory model for the social history of age- and familial-relations, and
travel beyond the well-trodden terrain of privileged and élite circles,
which are well approached by literary and secondary sources. These
sources, locations, and constructions are an important aspect of
my history of age and authority, but they need to be supplemented
to expand historical coverage and contemporary significance. We
have already caught a glimpse of the potential spectrum of youthful
responses in the face-to-face meeting with the ministry at catechizing, and in the arbitrary meanderings of some young people through
the Sunday congregation. The next chapter will continue the pursuit of creative youth. We will depart the orchestrated society of the
'place' structure for the rather more mercurial and diverse theatre
of daily life, in search of youth's responses and a fresh characterization of that age—'ill-advised and ill-nurtured youth'.

3

'Ill-Advised and Ill-Nurtured Youth'

In the history of intergenerational relations one lament remains constant, even eternal: 'the world is full of ill-advised and ill-nurtured youth'.[1] Every society confidently proclaims that its youth are 'the very worst youth'. Centuries pass by, the forms and structures of societies change irrevocably, new characters appear on the historical stage, but this generational refrain continues its regular rhythm. 'Youth were never more sawcie', Thomas Barnes commented in 1624, 'yea never more savagely saucie . . . the ancient are scorned, the honourable are contemned, the magistrate is not dreaded.' A generation earlier, a typically irate Philip Stubbes declared, 'was there ever seen less obedience in youth of all sorts, both mankind and womenkind towards their superiours, parents, masters, and governors'. John Locke thought that 'the early corruption of youth' had become a general complaint.[2] Such complaints might be commonplace; one still point in an otherwise changing world. Nevertheless, they retain much significance helping us to locate a perennial preoccupation which sharpened in a period of swift change and uncertainty[3] like the English Revolution, or one of prolonged socio-economic difficulty such as the close of the sixteenth century.[4] Nor

---

[1] Thomas Beard, *The Theatre of God's Judgment* (1631), 216.

[2] Thomas Barnes, *The Wise-Man's Forecast against the Evill Time* (1624), 59 (cf. 53); Stubbes is quoted by David Underdown, *Revel, Riot and Rebellion: Popular Politics and Culture in England 1603–1660* (Oxford, 1985), 48; John Locke is quoted by C. John Sommerville, *The Discovery of Childhood in Puritan England* (Athens, Ga., 1992), 101. This generational complaint is made by many other contemporaries. See, for example, Richard Allestree, *The Whole Duty of Man* (1658), 287; Matthew Griffith, *Bethel, Or a Forme for Families* (1634), 208; Roger Ascham, *The Scholemaster*, in *English Works*, ed. W. A. Wright (Cambridge, 1970), 209; Thomas Becon, *A New Catechism Set Forth Dialogue Wise* (Cambridge, 1864), 350; John Strype, *Lessons Moral and Christian for Youth and Old Age* (1699), 12; and the complaints of the attorney general in PRO STAC 8 20/10. For latter-day expressions and fears about youth see Stephen Humphries, *Hooligans or Rebels? An Oral History of Working Class Childhood and Youth 1889–1939* (Oxford, 1981), 98; Geoffrey Pearson, *Hooligan: A History of Respectable Fears* (Basingstoke, 1983).

[3] Cf. Pearson, *Hooligan*, esp. chs. 7–8.

[4] For contemporary anxieties about age-relations during the English Revolution see above, Ch. 2, and the much-quoted remarks of Edward Hyde, Earl of Clarendon, *The Life of Edward Hyde, Earl of Clarendon* (3 vols., Oxford, 1827), i. 358–9.

should the universality of this particular grievance reduce its importance. In fact, its very persistence as centuries slip by renders the problem of age, youth, and authority more worthy of serious investigation. Nevertheless, historians have tended to neglect it hitherto, or to relegate its meaning to the routine antics and postures of an age-group who were predisposed to create problems for the dominant adult society. Again, societies experience change and bequeath fresh contexts and ideologies to succeeding generations. The problem of youth was always being recontextualized and redefined in new situations and periods of history.

In the opening chapter we discussed contemporary definitions of youth—its risks and potential—and we have also seen how magistrates and ministers regarded the ideal place of youth in the social order. Yet a great deal of contemporary comment was not only prescriptive, but also highly critical. Moralists saw their prescriptive ideals—their vision of civil and pious youth residing in godly households—as being to a considerable extent threatened by a youth culture or milieu (a world of conviviality and play), which merited only their hostile invective and negative commentaries. These cultural moments and spaces provided a good opportunity for young people to express a certain measure of autonomy and creativity. They can help us to define early modern youth. A number of historians who have not questioned the existence of youth in this period have recently followed the suggestions of many contemporary authors and presented youth as the 'one social group which exercised the moralist above any other'.[5] This chapter will begin to explore this characterization of 'ill-advised and ill-nurtured youth', and its principal purpose is to open our discussion of formative experiences shared by young people at this time. These youth spaces and places were one important aspect of growing up. They contributed a further cultural and social progress to the moral and economic adulthood envisaged by theories of socialization. Youthful identities and experiences clearly did not spring from dominant ideologies alone, and the issue of youth culture can help us to see how some young people clarified the implications of their instituted inferiority. The ideal place of youth in the social order was often a matter of dispute. Later sections of this chapter, therefore, seek to trace these formative experiences of youth by exploring the forms and meaning of some games and sports played by young

[5] I am quoting Patrick Collinson, *The Religion of Protestants: The Church in English Society 1559–1625* (Oxford, 1982), 224. Cf. Martin Ingram, *Church Courts, Sex and Marriage in England 1570–1640* (Cambridge, 1987), esp. 123, 354–5.

people; some ritual celebrations of movement along the life-cycle; the great 'youth holidays' of May Day and Shrove Tuesday; and some of the evidence for the presence (or otherwise) of youth groups and other forms of collective activity by and on behalf of early modern youth. But we will begin with a number of potential conceptual and methodological problems which complicate our pursuit of historical youth.

1. *Youth Culture?*

Young people were ubiquitous in early modern society[6] and we will soon see them on the move, spilling onto fields and streets, playing, damaging property, going to church, drinking, having sex, trading punches and slanders, and hurling abuse at adults and each other. Nevertheless, despite extensive literatures on the history of popular culture in Tudor and Stuart society, the question of youth culture has only recently received full scholarly attention. A number of historians have attempted to define the contours of a distinctive apprentice culture in urban society. Still others have pored over the sources in the hope (as yet unrealized) of discovering an English equivalent of the age-related charivaris and formal youth groups, which appear to play a prominent part in the organization of a number of continental societies.[7] These quests are important, but youth groups may prove to be an elusive quarry. The form and meaning of cultural experiences can assist us in tracing the sympathies and identities of young people. But critical questions linger and require further exploration. Was there a distinctively youthful cultural milieu in early modern society with a set of attitudes and values which rescored or even proposed alternatives to conventional preoccupations with order, including socialization?

The tale of housebound youth is still retold; the 'great enclosure' of early modern youth remains a theme of some recent historiography. The door of the household marked a cultural and social frontier, which presented boundaries for young people who remained inside. They could look through windows and watch the world go by, or step gingerly outside on a task, but they did so at the call of the householder who framed the horizons of their world.

---

[6] See Keith Thomas, 'Children in early modern England', in Gillian Avery and Julia Briggs (eds.), *Children and Their Books: A Celebration of the Work of Iona and Peter Opie* (Oxford, 1989), esp. 82.

[7] See below, pp. 169–74.

Barbara Hanawalt has argued that there were few clear indications of youth culture in medieval London. 'With only one or two apprentices in a household,', she writes, 'it was hard for the young men to form a strong youth culture in defiance of their masters'. This decisive 'enclosure of youth' shattered any faint association between young underlings who were dispersed in scattered households. 'They were locked into a close, quasi-familial relationship with their masters rather than forming separate youth groups.'[8] Hanawalt concludes that 'No full-fledged youth subculture in which peers were the chief influence on an adolescent's life existed in the Middle Ages.'[9]

In his recent *History of Youth* (first published in German in 1986 and translated into English in 1993), Michael Mitterauer argued that there was no competition between the family and peer group in what he calls 'traditional society'. 'In service [he continues,] there was no such thing as a private sphere independent of working relationships.' In this rather narrow view, the 'leisure activities of young people' are said to be 'completely under the control of the householder'. They faced only the dim prospect of 'comprehensive subordination' which cast a dark shadow over their lives both inside and outside the household.[10] Mitterauer, making arguably unhelpful comparisons with generations of young people who sit glued to the television screen or with an ear tuned to the radio, paints a bleak and rather impoverished portrait of early modern youth, who came of age in a world in which 'shared formative experiences were minimal'. An even more distant prospect, he continues, 'was the possibility of developing shared attitudes and values, particularly ones which might distinguish them from an older generation'. Unlike latter-day innovations in communications which permit new fashions and modes of expression quickly to enter private homes, the 'primitive' communication systems of early modern society 'trapped' youth in households and local communities. They possessed few outlets for expression.[11] The high rate of migration, however, was one way in which young people crossed these alleged obstacles.[12] Others were the shared cultural and social moments in

[8] Barbara A. Hanawalt, *Growing up in Medieval London: The Experience of Childhood in History* (New York, 1993), 137.
[9] Ibid. 11.
[10] Michael Mitterauer, *A History of Youth*, trans. Graeme Dunphy (Oxford, 1993), 115, 131.
[11] Ibid. 236.
[12] Cf. Ilana Krausman Ben-Amos, *Adolescence and Youth in Early Modern England* (New Haven, 1994), 175–6, who argues that the 'frequent mobility of youths hindered the formation of strong ties based on the communities and neighbourhoods where they lived . . .'

the 'particular worlds' in which they lived and served. These experiences were not enjoyed by all young people in equal measure, and we shall shortly explore some of this variety. But they permit us to produce confident interpretations of distinctive experiences of youth in Tudor and Stuart society.

Ilana Krausman Ben-Amos argues that 'there were concrete elements in the social life which undermined the formation of a cohesive youth subculture, even in the largest towns' of early modern England. 'Among these', she suggests, 'were the lack of a marked spatial and temporal segregation of the young and old, intricate and growing divisions in the social standing and lifestyles of the young themselves, division along gender and occupational lines, and finally, the great mobility of the young.'[13] In this case, one problem is raised by the limited nature of sources consulted which also restricts interpretation.[14] Another, is how we choose to define youth culture (there is little discussion of this point in Ben-Amos's book). Is it best approached through the study of peer association? This is a useful point of entry, though we must not 'reduce' our interpretation to the formal, organized youth groups described by Davis.[15] We need to discover whether youth had 'both independent income from wages and freedom to decide how to dispose of its leisure time'.[16] (It should be remembered that money is not a vital prerequisite for all forms of leisure.) We encounter many situations in contemporary sources in which young people came together to drink, play, walk, and talk. These formative experiences of youth, for that is what they were, should make us pause before finally consigning youth culture to the dustbin.

It is also unrealistic to require youth culture to cross borders of rank, occupation, and gender, and even the territory of a single town. A more 'modest' definition may be appropriate. Ben-Amos and others turn to occupational and gendered fissures to propose that there was no youth culture at this time. But this is a rather closed and unsubtle interpretation, however, and it is uncomfortably

---

[13] Ibid. 205–6.
[14] Ben-Amos's book is based upon her Stanford Ph.D thesis which studied apprentices in Bristol and nearly seventy contemporary autobiographies. Autobiography has many good qualities as a source, but it may not be the best place to seek cultural experiences of this sort. A fuller study may well be necessary which consults the sources of more than one town, including church court records.
[15] This seems to be one problem in the work of Barbara Hanawalt, who uses the term 'youth group' when seeking formative experiences of youth, *Growing up in Medieval London*, 137.
[16] I am again quoting Hanawalt, who also argues that youth in medieval London 'had neither' the income nor the freedom (ibid. 12).

close to the image of shackled housebound youth. It is a definition which requires far too much—a calm surface with no ripples or rough edges—and it has very little that is positive to say about the experience of youth. It is true that young people formed occupational or gendered allegiances, but in countless well-documented episodes they did so in the company of people of the same age. They also moved between different identities, from single-sex to occupational cultures, for example, or from territorial affiliations to courtship. But we should not forget that they were formative experiences of youth, and that youth was one point of reference for people who were in their teens and twenties. The common identity of youth is complicated by these multiple identities, but this does not mean that youth was not an emotional and social bond in early modern society. For these reasons it is very unhelpful to dismiss the idea of youth culture without offering to put something in its place. We can split youthful experiences into 'narrow clusters', which could function apart or in some sort of correspondence. But these ties of courtship, work, gender, residence, and play were experiences of youth, and they were recognized as such by early modern commentators, who not only associated these cultural spaces with values which complicated orderly socialization, but also produced collective identifications like the 'apprentices' or 'youth'. The common identity of youth was also furthered by conviviality and play, the role of the young on festive days, and life-cyclical rituals. Youth culture has rough edges. It is 'scarred' by the regular appearance of adults and the aforementioned 'clusterings'. But if its principal features include formative experiences of youth, the freedom to organize free time, and common cultural and social moments, then we shall see in the course of this book that it is not an entirely unhelpful term. The accent on formative experiences is at least positive.

Like its older (historiographically speaking) cousin popular culture, youth culture will prove to be a term which is riddled with all kinds of conceptual and methodological problems. Just as interpretations of popular culture should be refined to accommodate élite participation, so youth culture is affected by contact with other age-groups. Young people, after all, were one subgroup within another amorphous category—popular culture. They were one aspect of plebeian culture.[17] We require a supple definition of youth culture

[17] Cf. Bob Scribner, 'Is a history of popular culture possible?', *History of European Ideas*, 10 (1989). The most recent discussion of cultural pluralism in early modern England is in Tim Harris, 'Problematising popular culture', in Harris (ed.), *Popular Culture in England, c.1500–1850* (Basingstoke, 1995), esp. 10–14. However, Harris does not include youth in his analysis.

to take to contemporary sources, which is able to integrate exchanges with the adult population. In fact, there is a risk in interpreting play in stark terms as a contest or opposition between age-groups. Different games and rituals had particular meanings. The same procession, dance, song, or game could have multiple interpretations and discrete meanings for different groups. Free time exposed ill-will and distance between sections of youth,[18] but it could also bring together young people and adults in shared cultural and social moments, which were expressions of communal and plebeian identity more generally.[19] Finally, the social distance between young and old people was communicated in conviviality and play, which offered colourful public confirmation of the differences of the ages of man. In some areas sporting events were arranged between wives and spinsters or maids, and between husbands and bachelors.[20]

It has been argued that the young were granted a measure of irresponsibility and toleration which was withdrawn from full adult members of the community.[21] This concession exposed their adult friends and relations to the charge of upsetting 'place' relations and the politics of age—social pariahs who were guilty if only by association. Adults had a number of pivotal roles as participators, providers, and spectators. In his bitter condemnation of *Dancing and Minstrelsie* (1581), Thomas Lovell makes plain his opinion that the fault lay with the whole of the community—the young dancers for their profane antics, and the older 'providers' who gave their consent, and food and drink. 'The youth', he declared, 'doo service' to dancing 'with their bodyes', and 'the elder sort offer sacrifice unto it' by providing wheat, malt, barley, money, and other victuals, thereby 'shewing themselves shamelesse bawds to maintain their children and servants in this spiritual whoredome being by duetie bound to bring them up as chaste virgins and undefiled members of the Church'.[22]

The vital energy and exuberance of youth granted young people a lively presence on festive occasions. Yet these physical attributes, which were viewed with deep suspicion by moralists, did not purchase

---

[18] See below, pp. 165–8.   [19] This point is developed in the following pages.
[20] See F. G. Emmison, 'Tithes, perambulations and sabbath-breach in Elizabethan Essex', in F. G. Emmison and R. Stephens (eds.), *Tribute to an Antiquary: Essays Presented to Marc Fitch by Some of his Friends* (1976), 204; T. F. Thistleton-Dyer, *British Popular Customs Present and Past* (1876), 90–1.
[21] See, for example, Ingram, *Church Courts*, 354.
[22] Thomas Lovell, *A Dialogue between Custom and Veritie Concerning Dancing and Minstrelsie* (1581), Epistle Dedicatory, fo. A5^r.

them a monopoly over the festive life of the community.[23] Nicholas Blundell has left behind an account of May Day festivities at Little Crosby in Lancashire in 1715. 'The little boyes and girles of this town diverted themselves with rearing a maypole in the West Lane', and they had a 'morrys dansing and a great many came to it both old and young'—

> The lasses and louts
> with smirkings and shouts
> . . . cried merrily
> Hey for Crosby
> Hey Sefton!
> Hey Thornton!
> Hey for Netherton!

Then towards the close of day, 'being weary, they stopped' and 'poured down' the ale and 'greedily chewed' the cakes and stewed prunes prepared by the watching adults.[24]

Older members of the community had easy access to a rich repository of local knowledge, customs, and stories. They also possessed the greater share of money and managed economic resources, including baking, brewing, and victualling. The young picked up practical skills from parents, relatives, and neighbours, as well as the history of the community, its topography, legends, proverbs, and other worldly wisdom. It was adults who drew upon local customs and traditions to plan parish ales and festivities like the one at Liverpool—'and what entertainments those country gatherings offered both to children and their adults', Nicholas Blundell exclaimed.[25] John Aubrey described the place of the 'church house' in the ale, 'to which belonged spits, crooks [and] utensils for dressing provisions. Here the housekeepers met and were merry and gave their charity', while the 'young people' danced before them on the green. The Whitsun Church ale or wake provided one opportunity for the young to sport and dance. Aubrey recalled the days of the ale when 'the young people . . . had dancing, bowling, shooting at butts etc., the ancients sitting gravely by looking on'. Yet as Aubrey's typically nostalgic tone indicates, the ale was being replaced by a parish rate in many places in the seventeenth

---

[23] Cf. Malcolmson, *Popular Recreations*, 55–6.

[24] *The Great Diurnall of Nicholas Blundell of Little Crosby*, ed. J. J. Bagley (3 vols.; Lancashire and Cheshire Record Society, 110, 112, 114, Preston, 1968–72), ii. 140; William Blundell, *Crosby Records, A Cavalier's Notebook*, ed. T. Ellison Gibson (Liverpool, 1952), 235, 237.

[25] M. Blundell (ed.), *Blundell's Diary and Letter Book 1702–1728* (Liverpool, 1952), 52.

century.[26] A report of a Whitsun revel at Rangeworthy in Gloucestershire presented an idyllic scene—'a few young people' are dancing to the tune of some local musicians, while 'some of the old inhabitants linger to watch on their way home from the sermon'.[27] Young people played a physical and boisterous part on such occasions; the older folk watching from the fringe of the green, smoking, drinking, eating, talking, and perhaps passing comment on the events in view, reminiscing of former times when they would have taken the role of the dancers. Nevertheless, they sometimes joined in the fun on the green. Eight morris dancers at a Hertfordshire 'maying', for example, could allegedly claim an average age of one hundred years each![28]

There are many examples in contemporary sources of adults being charged with 'incouraging' and 'enticing' young people to dance and other 'unlawful pastimes'. They included a Cambridgeshire father who 'incouraged' his three sons 'to daunce the morrice about the towne he himselfe following'; William Rochester of Norwich, who kept 'a daunsing skole . . . lodging and teaching' servants, journeymen, and children, 'withowte lycence of there parents and masters'; and an Essex rector who was suspended for playing the part of 'a Lorde of misrule or Christmas Lorde amongste certein youngelings'. Others were reprimanded for providing 'bowls, balls, or cudgells'. While reports of householders entertaining young people at a late hour to drink, dice, dance, and play are commonplace in contemporary sources.[29] The alehouse keeper was a prominent character,

[26] Aubrey is quoted by Underdown, *Revel, Riot and Rebellion*, 45, who also gives an account of the decline of the ale in chs. 3–4. See also Ronald Hutton, *The Rise and Fall of Merry England: The Ritual Year 1400–1700* (Oxford, 1994), esp. chs. 4–5; F. W. Weaver and G. N. Clark (eds.), *Churchwarden's Accounts of Marston, Spelsbury, Pyrton* (Oxfordshire Record Society, 6, Oxford, 1925), 18, 19, 23, 24, 25, 30; John Brand, *Observations on the Popular Antiquities of Great Britain*, revised by Harry Ellis (3 vols.; Bohns Antiquarian Library, 8–10, 1849), i. 276–84; Joseph Strutt, *The Sports and Pastimes of the People of England*, ed. J. C. Cox (Cambridge, 1923), 289–91.

[27] The account of the Rangeworthy revel can be found in Underdown, *Revel, Riot and Rebellion*, 45, 62. Cf. Morris Marples, *A History of Football* (1954), 19; and Stubbes's hostile account of May Games in his *Anatomie of Abuses*, fos. P3ᵛ–P4ʳ.

[28] Brand, *Popular Antiquities*, i. 252.

[29] CUL EDR B/2/35, fo. 28; NRO NMC 8, fo. 355; William Hale (ed.), *A Series of Precedents and Proceedings in Criminal Causes Extending from the Year 1475 to 1640: Extracts from the Act Books of the Ecclesiastical Courts in the Diocese of London*, 1847 (facsimile, Edinburgh, 1973), 213. See also BCB 1, fo. 116; NRO NMC 12, fos. 172–3, 203; CUL EDR B/2/15, fo. 54; CLRO Jour. 21, fos. 206ᵛ–7; J. C. Atkinson (ed.), *North Riding Quarter Sessions* (9 vols.; North Riding Record Society, 1–9, 1884–92), ii. 34; F. G. Emmison (ed.), *Elizabethan Life: Disorder* (Essex Record Office Publications, 56, Chelmsford, 1970), 223, 330; Underdown, *Revel, Riot and Rebellion*, 269; C. H. Cooper and J. W. Cooper (eds.), *Annals of Cambridge* (5 vols.; 1842–1908), iv. 305.

crossing generations, offering food and drink, and a selection of 'unlawful games'.

Youth, a time of significant physical, emotional, and social altera-tion, had its particular aspirations and preoccupations—conviviality, play, courtship, intimate moments of first love and sex, and the pressures of socialization in service. It is, after all, as some modern sociologists tell us, a 'restless age' which is characterized by a long search for self-identity and a taste for novelty.[30] Youth was one as-pect of plebeian culture, but young people were not mere orna-ments. They were in fact creative proposers of cultural and social options. We can allocate them historical agency and separate spheres, but not at the expense of the cultural and social exchanges with the adult society. Adults appear in contemporary sources not only as figures of authority—as magistrates, officers, masters, and parents—policing, punishing, and prosecuting young people, but also as planners, providers, participators, and innovators—as teachers, friends, spectators, players, tapsters, bawds, fiddlers, cooks, and so on—arranging festivities, telling stories, passing on wisdom about marriage, work, customs, and beliefs. For those who articulated the strict standards of the politics of 'place' and age, these points of contact between young people and adults were a shocking negation of authority—the 'shamelesse' adult bawd was 'by duetie bound' to raise young people 'as chaste virgins and undefiled members of the Church'.

Patriarchy was interpreted in many different forms. There was in fact no single response to youth, and the preoccupations of magis-trates and moralists could be as far removed from the opinions of artisans, craftsmen, and labourers in villages and towns, as from the young people whom they placed at an opposite point of the com-pass and attempted to reform. Most adults would have agreed with moralists that young people should obey their parents and masters, and pick up valuable experience and training under their close tutelage. Nevertheless, they often parted company over issues like appropriate recreation, Sunday observance, acceptable sexual behaviour, and courtship. Clearly the 'inevitable' strife between magistracy and youth was not a simple youth/age polarity. Young people participated in events in the alehouse and on the green or close with at least the tacit consent of a parent or guardian.[31] The chorus of complaints in prescriptive sources about 'overmuch

[30] For example, by Erik Erikson, 'Youth, fidelity and diversity', in Erikson (ed.), *Youth, Change and Challenge* (1963), 20.

[31] Cf. the case from Grand Tey in Essex discussed by Malcolmson, *Popular Recreations*, 112.

liberty', therefore, possess much more value than mere rhetoric. They also raise questions about the nature of youth culture and the household as a reliable agency of socialization. The youth were one subgroup in plebeian culture. As such, it can be inappropriate to expect them to make a complete break from that culture. They participated in protests, charivaris, wakes, fairs, ales, and other communal celebrations; they drew inspiration from occupational or single-sex cultures.[32] Historians of youth need to complicate the cultural identity and commitment of their subjects. We have seen that games and sports were not the exclusive property of young people. Nevertheless, moralists associated games and institutions like the alehouse or the bawdy house with the utter ruin of youth, not only because they neutralized wise instruction, but also because young people were principal participants and customers.

Youth culture, therefore, lacks definite shape. It prompts us to think about the young, but it also disguises inconsistency and variety by catching different forms and characters within its large circumference. The age of youth stretches over complicated and passionate formative years which witness many biological and emotional changes. It is an age in which people are constantly shifting. Attitudes towards play, sex, work, money, clothes, and the forms and sites of social life, for example, alter as individuals progress through mid-teens to their twenties.[33] Even the very young grow older and aspirations, habits, needs, and capabilities change to suit the ever expanding mental and physical landscape. Young and old recognized these permutations on the passage from puberty to late marriage. Early modern youth, after all, was a *long youth*—it took longer to complete the move to full adulthood.[34] In addition, men and women experience different emotional and biological changes at a different pace. We must chart the different fortunes of young men and women which elicited contrasting responses from governors. They may have often met in a common courtship culture, but how distinctive were male and female experiences? The neat impression of youth culture is spoilt still further by the enduring differential of class which admitted a bewildering variety of experiences, though my present subject is the youth of the lower and middle

[32] See below, esp. pp. 161–9 and Ch. 4.

[33] Cf. J. R. Gillis, *Youth and History: Tradition and Change in European Age-Relations, 1770 to the Present* (1981), esp. ch. 1. Gillis argues that in early modern society there was only one long youth and little or no recognition of different experiences and stages within that age. This suggestion deserves careful consideration, but I believe that it again suffers from the reluctance of some historians to fully contextualize youthful experiences in this period.

[34] See above, Ch. 1.

classes. But even here, at the lower reaches of Tudor and Stuart society, there were many different ways of growing up. Did urban youth differ greatly from their rural cousins? Perhaps not as much as first sight might imply because so many young people left the countryside for the town, and many of them returned home in later life with fresh skills, likes and dislikes, and stories to tell. In the town they would have discovered a much higher number or concentration of shops, alleys, bawdy houses, alehouses, playhouses, temptations, apprenticeships, and young companions to share these experiences. The young were more visible in the crowded townscape. A further complication was posed by religious belief. We will shortly meet a number of godly young people, who announced their intention to withdraw from their 'profane' peers. Their youth was a tortuous time in which doubt, guilt, and unease mingled with flashing moments of joy and realization. They read and worshipped, but many of them were sorely tempted by the counter-attractions of conviviality and play. Thus age, gender, class, geography, and beliefs indicate a spectrum of potential youthful experiences. Again, there were many different ways of growing up in early modern society.

2. Mocking and Scoffing Youth

Youth culture suddenly appears a rather more untidy interpretative term and in need of rescue. It can disguise as much as it reveals. None the less, despite these problems it is possible to depict the characteristics of the youth culture or milieu which created some unease in the pulpits, courtrooms, and studies of early modern England. Again, we should reduce our expectations, and construct a more subtle explanatory framework, which draws attention to a few subcategories in the long age of youth (e.g. class, gender, and work), and exposes the participation of adults in various guises in this world of conviviality and play. Above all, we should not 'close' interpretative options. My interpretation may appear rough and untidy. Yet it has the value of squarely focusing upon formative experiences in 'ordinary' places like the alehouse, street, field, and other recreational spaces. It was here that young people met with each other often on equal terms, and followed interpretations or values which troubled people in places of authority.

The essential attributes of a youth culture or milieu included a different sense of place and time, and an alleged preference for play and leisure. Youth was a period of transitional training for the adult world of work in which people were expected to digest appropriate notions of time and labour discipline. The majority of early modern people were introduced to the fresh rhythm of work in youth. One of the perennial tensions in the socialization process, therefore, was the dispute about time; a conflict between work and leisure. The whims of youth often contradicted 'adult' concerns with 'place', discipline, property, time, and work, and provoked collisions between the preoccupations of adults and young people. Magistrates and ministers made the connection between the pastimes of youth and immorality, insolence, rough play, and pranks. They were quite simply a waste of time.

Clearly formative experiences of youth were not a light and innocent diversion from the socializing process. They also presented a potential unwelcome alternative to the more rigid ideas of time, work, and discipline held by magistrates and ministers. Attitudes towards youthful pastimes were naturally coloured by a deep concern with age-relations, and the difficult task of turning the children of fallen humanity into civil and pious youth. Again, the age of youth is depicted in terms of a contest or negotiation. Irreverent pastimes like dancing and football, or the pull of the alehouse and playhouse, threatened to upset 'place' relations and interfere with generational succession.[35] Dancing attracted howls of outrage and forecasts of moral corruption.[36] This 'mother of all evill' was 'an introduction to whoredome' and 'a preparative to wantonness'; 'a friend to wickednesse' and 'a provocation to fleshly lust'; the 'storehouse and nurserie of basterdie', and a constant cause of brawling, 'miserable murthers', idleness, pride, and drunkenness.[37]

Worse still, it was thought that young people often had a casual

---

[35] See Stubbes, *An Anatomie of Abuses*, fos. L5ʳ–L8ᵛ; John Northbrooke, *A Treatise wherein Vaine Dicing, Dauncing, Vaine Playes and Enterludes . . . Are Reproved*, 1577? (facsimile, Garland Series: The English Stage: Attack and Defence 1577–1730, New York, 1974), 62; Francis Lenton, *The Young Gallant's Whirligigg, Or Youth's Reakes* (1629), 8; M. J. Goombridge (ed.), *Calendar of the Chester City Council Minutes* (Lancashire and Cheshire Record Society, 106, Blackpool, 1956), 79–80; Keith Wrightson, 'Alehouses, order and reformation in rural England 1590–1660', in Eileen Yeo and Stephen Yeo (eds.), *Popular Culture and Class Conflict 1590–1914* (Brighton, 1981); Peter Clark, *The English Alehouse: A Social History, 1200–1830* (1983), chs. 7–8. See also below, ch. 4.

[36] Cf. Collinson, *Religion of Protestants*, 224–6; Jeremy Goring, *Godly Exercises or the Devil's Dance: Puritanism and Popular Culture in Pre-Civil War England*, Friends of Dr William's Library, 37th lecture (1983).

[37] Northbrooke, *Treatise*, 123, 127, 135, 140; Stubbes, *An Anatomie of Abuses*, fo. M7ʳ. See also William Hinde, *A Faithful Remonstrance of the Holy Life and Happy Death of John Bruen of Bruen Stapleford in the County of Chester* (1641), 'The end [is] bastardy and beggary'; George Widley, *The Doctrine of the Sabbath* (1604), 106.

or even insolent attitude towards their elders, religion, property, and authority. A number of adult observers claimed that the young were 'naturally' disposed to be disobedient and irreverent. The struggle between age and youth had begun at the birth of man and would continue until his final moments. The problem of youth, therefore, was timeless. Young people had always found 'the ways of religion . . . unpleasant and abhorring from our nature'.[38] John Northbrooke's 'youth' tells 'age' that church 'is more fit for such olde fatherly men as you are, than for such young men as I am'. The grave was a distant prospect; youth represented the carefree present. 'How many young persons', John Shower asked towards the close of the seventeenth century, 'despise the Holy Scripture, make light of sabbaths, sermons, and all good counsel?' Even young John Bunyan found the regular round of prayer and worship 'grevious': Heaven and Hell were both 'out of sight and mind, and as for saving and damning [he declared], they were least in my thoughts'.[39]

Mocking and scoffing at religious men and things ranked fourth in Thomas Brooks's catalogue of the sins of youth.[40] Contemporary sources reveal young people damaging church furniture and the sacred building itself, stealing holy books, swearing, cursing, and blaspheming.[41] John Harris, a London apprentice, claimed that John Foxe's *Book of Martyrs* contained 'xx lyes'; that those who perished in the flames died for mere 'vaine glorie'; and that Mr Foxe was a 'folysh fellowe'. In August 1612 Percival Brook, a York alderman, was strolling by the green in North Street when he caught sight of Matthew Wilton, an apprentice, 'playeing at tenn bones . . . and blaspheming the name of God by outragious oathes swearinge Gode's life [and] Gode's wound', which terrible utterances did 'greave' the alderman who proceeded to 'reprehend' the apprentice for his 'grevious oathes' and for playing with 'a young boy at such unlawfull games'. But Wilton refused to be that pious youngster represented in the indenture of apprenticeship, and he became even 'more vehement in oathes', announcing that he would 'sweare in spite of the devil' and 'in the spite of the old shaggy dog', meaning the unfortunate Brook. This public insult deserved

[38] W.P., *The Prentise's Practise in Godlinesse and His True Freedome* (1613), fos. 57ᵛ-8.
[39] Northbrooke, *Treatise*, 1; John Shower, *Seasonable Advice to Youth* (1692), 31; John Bunyan, *Grace Abounding to the Chief of Sinners* (1928), 9.
[40] See above, p. 35.
[41] For example, BCB 5, fos. 61, 324, 347; ERO D/ACA 32, fos. 58ᵛ, 184ᵛ; BIHR YV/CB 2, fos. 49ᵛ, 51ᵛ; E. Freshfield (ed.), *The Vestry Minute Book of the Parish of St Margaret Lothbury in the City of London 1571–1677* (1887), 1–2, 16, 34.

a swift and public reprimand. The apprentice was quickly dispatched to the House of Correction with 'a paper on his head with these wordes written in great letters . . . "for blaspheminge God by outragious and spitefull oathes"'.[42]

Like Wilton, Edward Gill of Norwich, a hatter's servant, uttered 'monstrous oathes' to his local civic and guild officials. Gill was presented at the Mayor's Court in 1573 for being out of his master's service, 'frequentyng the alehowses, and abusing the wardens of [the] hatters in this court, callying them shepe and sayeing that Whight the warden is a murderer and carryeth a knyfe in his hose to kyll him that wilbe drunk before hym'.[43] In such disputes magistrates were seeking to uphold notions of civic order, including the idea of civil and pious youth extending appropriate obedience. What greater contrast could there have been than that between Samuel Clarkson of London, a model of civic virtue, 'a civill and quyett man beinge a howseholder and long freed', and Thomas Vicars, an apprentice, who assaulted and wounded Clarkson in 1610? Opposing values were clearly identified in this case, and it is the role of governors to separate them by bringing the young stray back within the civic fold. Such scornful words as these were often spoken in the heat of the moment; a reckless outburst which was occasionally inspired by alcohol.[44] Yet the ease with which blasphemous language with its seditious tinge slipped into daily discourse and was used to taunt and lampoon figures in places of authority raised concern. These irreverent speeches were an all too visible display of youthful indifference. Young people found many opportunities to meet and swap salacious and cheerful gossip about each other, but also to express dissatisfaction and more 'insolent' and 'subversive' opinions about a particular calling or master. We find Roger Lowe and John Chaddocke sitting by a 'great pitt' in Horseshoe Field and later at West Leigh Heath on the same Sunday, 'conversing together of our great greefes concerning our callinge'.[45] Such confidences created loyalties, solidarities, and enmities.

Cases of youthful insubordination are presented in all subsequent chapters, and they should not be treated lightly and dismissed as the momentary gestures of a troublesome generation from whom

[42] GL MS 12,806/2, fos. 172-2ᵛ; YCA B/33, fos. 310-10ᵛ. See also BCB 5, fos. 43ᵛ, 130ᵛ, 377ᵛ, 394ᵛ; NRO Diocesan Records Vis 7/1 (unpaginated); GL MS 5770/1, fo. 11; ERO D/ACA 30, fos. 102, 113ᵛ, 206ᵛ, 287; 32, fo. 227ᵛ.

[43] NRO NMC 11, fo. 143.   [44] For example, BCB 5, fos. 43ᵛ, 377ᵛ.

[45] Roger Lowe, *The Diary of Roger Lowe of Ashton-in-Makerfield, Lancashire 1663–1674*, ed. W. L. Sachse (1938), 59.

nothing else should be expected. On occasion these 'vile wordes' may appear rudely satirical, rash, and vulgar. But they retain significance because the words of the young are seldom reported in contemporary sources. In these heated exchanges between young people and figures of authority the hidden sentiments of the inferior party in a hierarchical dialogue finally come to the surface. We see the often impulsive and open expression of a darker truth of festering tension.[46] Linguistic behaviour usually follows conventions which represent the nature of the social relationships between the speakers. All speech should be contextualized. In this particular case, it was the product of social distance and it can tell us much about how some young people interpreted their appointed inferiority.[47]

The significance of public expressions of youthful opposition, however, should not be exaggerated. We cannot generalize about the experience of youth from the few recorded cases in which young people hurled abuse at magistrates,[48] although we glimpse one response to authority. In the records of London we see young servants and apprentices throwing punches and threats at constables, disturbing the watch, throwing stones at the dog-killer, impugning the honour of the courts, and issuing libels against aldermen.[49] In April 1621 the London beadles were ordered to instruct householders 'to take care and order' that their apprentices, servants, and children 'from henceforth civilly and orderly behave and demeane themselves towards all embassadours and strangers' and subjects 'without ill or unseemly gestures or language', and, above all, that they allow the coaches of peers, nobles, and gentlemen to pass through the streets without the usual volley of abuse. These measures may well have been prompted by the 'bold and insolent' actions of a tailor's apprentice, who was presented at the Court of Aldermen in the same month for calling the Spanish ambassador a 'divell'. Robert Marshall, a glazier's apprentice, was arrested at the same spot, 'houldinge a loafe in his hands towardes' one of the ambassador's servants, and announcing 'that he could finde it in his heart to throw it at his choppes'. While a bricklayer's apprentice,

---

[46] Cf. James C. Scott, *Domination and the Arts of Resistance: Hidden Transcripts* (New Haven, 1990), esp. p. 87.

[47] Cf. David Garrioch, 'Verbal insults in eighteenth-century Paris', in Peter Burke and Roy Porter (eds.), *The Social History of Language* (Cambridge, 1987), esp. 104–5, 118.

[48] The more 'private' world of the household is another matter altogether, and we shall return to this domestic sphere to observe the nature and quality of household life and master/servant relations in subsequent chapters.

[49] CLRO Reps. 25, fo. 177ᵛ; 27, fo. 114ᵛ; 29, fo. 34; 30, fos. 191ᵛ, 293ᵛ; 33, fos. 106ᵛ, 162ᵛ; 35, fo. 215ᵛ.

Richard Taylor, threw a brickbat at the same servant. These three offenders were 'publiquely' whipped from Aldgate, 'a longe by the place where the affront was', and so to Fleet Street and Temple Bar. Precautionary measures were also introduced on festive occasions, and also to safeguard the honour of the city during civic and royal ceremonial. In October 1621, for example, Common Council issued orders 'for my Lord Maior's day'. Again, householders were asked to 'strictly charge and admonish all and every their children, servants, and apprentices' to permit ambassadors, noble persons, ladies, gentlemen, and all others to pass unmolested:

and should neither throwe nor shoote anythinge at them, nor misbehave themselves towards them either in gesture, wordes or acon, nor should use in the Exchange nor in any streete or lane . . . any uncivill sports as trapp, squibbes, football or the like . . .

Many previous complaints had been made, and 'divers persons . . . daily founde delinquent' therein.[50] London's young people (like the young people of Norwich)[51] had always had a delicate relationship with foreigners, and the memory of 'Evil May Day' (1517) when they took advantage of the holiday to launch wholesale plunder of the capital's alien population was perpetuated in a tradition of holiday disorder and in the concerns of later generations of governors.[52] Some young people who fell into the clutches of the Law were rescued by their companions. One servant who was rescued by 'divers of his associates' ran into a nearby house saying 'he would either kill or be killed before he would be taken'. In the town of Ashford in Derbyshire, a group of 'young people' in 'verie ryottous and unlawfull manner' broke open the stocks to free their friend, Stephen White. One witness reported that 'there was much glorying in that outragious deliverance'. He further deposed that White 'did publiquely affirme and saie after he was so delivered lett us see whether' the constable 'dare now sett him in the stocks agayne'.[53]

[50] CLRO Jours 31, fos. 303, 303ᵛ-4, 317-18ᵛ; 32, fo. 221ᵛ; Rep. 35, fos. 141ᵛ-2. See also Jours 25, fo. 22; 26, fo. 387; 27, fo. 114ᵛ; 30, fo. 48ᵛ; 32, fos. 256ᵛ-7. John Chamberlain's account of the 1621 disturbance is in PRO SP 14/120/74. See also PRO 16/126/64; CLRO Reps. 30, fos. 20ᵛ, 317; 34, fo. 132.

[51] NRO NMC 14, fos. 290ᵛ, 291, 315; 11, fos. 209, 670, 671.

[52] See CLRO Rep. 12, fo. 90ᵛ, Ian W. Archer, The Pursuit of Stability: Social Relations in Elizabethan London (Cambridge, 1991), 94, 243; Susan Brigden, London and the Reformation (Oxford, 1989), 130-1; and the 'Evil May Day' ballad in Charles Mackay (ed.), A Collection of Songs and Ballads Relative to the London Prentices and Trades (Percy Society, 1, 1841), 11-22. Barbara Hanawalt describes a few earlier incidents (Growing up in Medieval London, 127).

[53] CLRO Rep. 30, fo. 18ᵛ; PRO STAC 8, 168/25. The Derbyshire incident is further explored below, pp. 149-50 (I must thank Andy Wood for this reference). Cf. CLRO Reps. 24, fos. 246-6ᵛ; 26(2), fos. 399, 408ᵛ; 28, fo. 211ᵛ.

Juvenile delinquency naturally has a long and chequered history. The crash of breaking glass was a familiar accompaniment to youthful games and sports. There are many examples of young people damaging property—churches and schools were favourite targets—stealing from orchards,[54] issuing punches, threats, and insults. We find 'rude youths' riding horses 'violently and desperately' along Maidstone's high streets; taking pot-shots at passing dogs; 'discharging gonnes' to the 'dangerous hurte' of London's peaceable residents; 'cutting and taking lanthornes from mens doores'; 'casting rockets into the aire'; damaging conduits; throwing turnips; rolling timber onto highways, ploughs and harrows; pulling up pales, stiles, and rails; abusing and threatening teachers as well as smashing windows; fighting among themselves and with others, including soldiers; snowballing passers-by; pulling down the gallows in Oxford; 'abusing' the pupils at an Exeter school; and throwing squibs, fireworks, and other 'wild fire' into passing coaches and onto the streets as ceremonial processions filed by (similar complaints were made as late as 1814).[55]

Nevertheless, some historians of later centuries refer to the 'birth' or the 'full emergence' of juvenile delinquency as late as the close of the eighteenth century or after. It was only then that ' "juvenile delinquency" became a major social problem and a focus of great anxiety amongst the propertied'.[56] Again, we are reminded of the

[54] NRO NMC 8, fos. 433, 521; 9, fo. 31; 11, fo. 35; 13, fo. 351; 16, fos. 160ᵛ, 445; CLRO Rep. 22, fo. 394ᵛ; Freshfield, *Vestry Minute Book of the Parish of St Margaret Lothbury*, 1–2; Richard Baxter, *Reliquiae Baxterianae* (1696), 2; John Dunton, *The Life and Errors of John Dunton Late Citizen of London* (1705), 12.

[55] K. S. Martin (intro.), *Records of Maidstone Being Selections from Documents in the Possession of the Corporation* [hereafter, *Records of Maidstone*] (Maidstone, 1926), 156; *The Diary of Ralph Josselin 1616–83*, ed. Alan Macfarlane (British Academy Records of Social and Economic History, New Series, 3, 1976), 591; BCB 5, fo. 239; CLRO Jour. 22, fos. 170, 177; NRO NMC 14, fo. 103; J. P. Earwaker (ed.), *The Court Leet Records of the Manor of Manchester from 1552 to 1686* [hereafter *Manchester Court Leet*] (6 vols.; Manchester, 1884–90), i. 159; J. M. Guilding (ed.), *Reading Records: Diary of the Corporation* (4 vols.; Reading, 1886), ii. 392–3; iii. 129–30, 352, 353; iv. 36–7; J. W. Willis Bund (ed.), *Worcestershire County Records: Division 1, Documents Relating to Quarter Sessions; Calendar of the Quarter Sessions Papers*. i: *1591–1643* (Worcester, 1900), 81, 366; A. E. Gibbs (ed.), *The Corporation Records of St Albans* (St Albans, 1890), 20; C. H. Mayo (ed.), *The Municipal Records of the Borough of Dorchester, Dorset* [hereafter *Dorchester Municipal Records*] (Exeter, 1908), 670; F. A. Bailey (ed.), *A Selection from the Prescot Court Leet and Other Records 1447–1600* (Lancashire and Cheshire Record Society, 89, Blackpool, 1937), 177; H. Stocks (ed.), *Records of the Borough of Leicester* (Cambridge, 1923), 285; PRO SP 16/232/36; 14/184/39; CLRO Jours. 29, fo. 63; 31, fos. 164ᵛ, 354; 32, fo. 86ᵛ; 36, fo. 217; PD 10/72; 10/74a; 10/86; 10/88; 10/99; 10/100; 10/167; 10/149; BCB 6, fo. 326.

[56] I am quoting from Peter King and Joan Noel, 'The origins of "the problem of juvenile delinquency": the growth of juvenile prosecutions in London in the late eighteenth and early nineteenth centuries', *Criminal Justice History*, 14 (1993), 17, 18, 35. The more important contributions include M. May, 'Innocence and experience: the evolution of the concept of

narrow image of early modern youth circulated by historians who seek to present the experiences of Georgian or Victorian youth as entirely distinctive. Peter King and Joan Noel argue that youth was not 'seen as a particularly distinctive or threatening subgroup' before the late eighteenth century.[57] In places this argument is rather imprecise and inconsistent.[58] Another problem is what is meant by juvenile delinquency. King and Noel base their discussion on property crime and distinctive forms of trial and punishment for young offenders, a fairly restricted rendering of antisocial or criminal behaviour by youth. There is certainly no evident reason to relegate the complexities of juvenile delinquency to property offences in early modern society. The term may have been first coined in a later period, but we must sketch this problem in broad terms as it was identified by contemporary governors, who felt that the youth were a 'threatening subgroup' in their world. Their concerns mainly turned on the problems created by service, and encompassed behaviour regarded as antisocial because it complicated the progress to adulthood, including irreverence, immorality, domestic disorders, or even the 'seditious' implications of conviviality and play.

Nor can we agree (with Martin J. Wiener) that the high (and rising) proportion of young people in the population of early nineteenth-century England presented 'a new problem'. This demographic situation had existed in former centuries. In fact, Wiener's chosen point of comparison is with the closing years of the seventeenth century, but the population becomes increasingly youthful as we go back in time to the middle years of the sixteenth century.[59] To complicate matters still further, the meaning and form of juvenile delinquency changes as centuries roll by and new patterns of work, socialization, or leisure, for example, slowly take the place of existing

juvenile delinquency in the mid-nineteenth century', *Victorian Studies*, 17 (1973); John Gillis, 'The evolution of juvenile delinquency in England 1890–1914', *Past and Present*, 67 (1975); S. Margery, 'The invention of juvenile delinquency in early nineteenth-century England', *Labour History*, 34 (1978); P. Rush, 'The government of a generation: the subject of juvenile delinquency', *Liverpool Law Review*, 14 (1992).

[57] King and Noel, 'The origins of "the problem of juvenile delinquency"', 17.

[58] It may be a question of semantics and finding the right terms to describe this problem. When King and Noel write that 'Early modern observers were well aware of the existence of young offenders and youth related social problems, and [that] particular attention was paid to the problems of youth during the years of rising anxiety about crime and vagrancy between 1560 and 1640' (ibid. 17), one feels that there is only a thin line between their depiction and the idea of early modern youth as 'a particularly distinctive and threatening subgroup'. However, this first approach is not fully incorporated into their interpretative model.

[59] Martin J. Wiener, *Reconstructing the Criminal: Culture, Law, and Policy in England, 1830–1914* (Cambridge, 1990), 17.

practices. The politics of age in Tudor and Stuart society drew attention to the vices and misdemeanours of youth; to certain abuses and crimes which were commonly associated with this stage in the life-course. In addition, age-related terms were coined to describe offences which were principally associated with young people.[60]

The busy market-places of London were a regular venue for youthful pranks. Some fishmonger's apprentices tested the patience of shoppers, passers-by, and their masters, and repeatedly crossed the fine line between rough play and crime. Commerce, conversation, and communication were all interrupted by apprentices fighting and brawling in the market-place; throwing 'cuttings of fishe'; offering 'lewde speeches and throwing water' to the great offence of good and honest people and the 'general slander and discredit' of the company; striking women 'openly in the markett with a staff and breaking heads'; and wishing 'a poxe of God' to fall on the heads of a passing 'gentlewoman' and her daughter, knocking off the hat of the mother and striking the daughter in the face 'and making her nose bleed'.[61] In October 1610 the Fishmongers' court took swift steps to punish 'dyvers apprentices for dyvers abuses and mysdemeanours by them commyted at dyvers and severall tymes in the markett place and elsewhere to the great dislike of neighbors and others that use to come to the same markett'. Nathaniel Prestbury was one offender. He 'openly in the markett place of Stocks threwe cuttings' of fishtails at other apprentices, 'and did throwe them about' hitting 'dyvers strangers almost an houre together so as no man could stand or passe by without a clarp in the face with a fishtayle . . . or such like stuff'. Prestbury had only scornful words for a freeman of the company who 'willed him to leave it off', telling him to 'kisse his tayle'. The clerk reported that 'dyvers [similar] complaynts' had been made hitherto. One of Prestbury's companions, Jonas Bond, 'a comon dycer and player' who sometimes spent 'whole nights together' in the alehouse 'drawing other mens apprentises' there to drink and play, was presented 'for beating of a woman with childe and fighting and brawling with a customer openly in the streete'. He had 'dyvers tymes' mocked the company's officer when he served notice to attend the court. William Withington's apprentice also upset market folk. He was presented 'for commonly abusing himself in the markett scoffying and deryding the markett folkes and for pourying of water into the

---

[60] See below, Ch. 7.   [61] GL MS 5770/1, fos. 396, 149–50, 589, 420–1, 476–7.

necke of a weake child . . . and for vile and stubborn usage' in the market and his master's household.[62] In 1631 the company beadles 'were warned to looke better hereafter that yonge men stood more decently in the markett with their white sleeves according to ancient custom'.[63]

Again, it would be foolish to pass observations about the quality of age-relations from such scattered cases. They show us that young people *could* in certain circumstances scorn authority, take bold stances, hurl defiance, and issue challenges. These encounters may seem unremarkable, they were, after all, quickly forgiven and forgotten. Yet there is something more serious here also. Such youthful disorders often elicited sharp responses from governors, who issued stern rebukes, applied a number of punishments (including choreographed public rituals), and curfews at sensitive points in the year (and at night).[64] The problems raised by the young were *perceived* to be more than high spirits because they stirred anxieties and encouraged a particular discourse about youth, which related general concern with stability and reformation to orderly socialization. In larger towns like London with more visible clusters of youth these fears were more frequently articulated, but the concern with orderly socialization touched all communities.

One troublesome aspect of the transition from childhood to youth and full membership of adult society was a transformation in attitudes towards work, time, and play. This reordering of priorities and fresh expectations together with the more pronounced concern with age- and familial-relations associated with the Reformation and the particular socio-economic configurations of the period 1560–1640 provide the pressing circumstances in which we should study these bursts of youthful energy and exuberance. They were more than a mere nuisance. It should be remembered that youth was *the* 'choosing time'.[65] The vices of youth possessed clear ideological significance in a society in which age was one principle of order.

---

[62] GL MS 5770/1, fos. 593–4. The carefully staged public punishment of these fishmongers is described below, p. 346. The 'wild' behaviour of all three apprentices was largely blamed on the inadequacies and weaknesses of their masters. Prestbury was apprenticed to 'either his brother or nere kynsman [who] will not correct him'. The court was told that Bond's master 'doth not dare correct him', and that William Withington's apprentice 'will not be governed' by his master and mistress.
[63] GL MS 5770/2, fo. 869.   [64] See above, p. 78, and below, pp. 341–7.
[65] See above, Ch. 1.

3. 'All Manner of Unprofitable or Idle Games'

A large minority of children attended some sort of school, others were pressured to work (generally by familial circumstances). Nevertheless, most of them would have been encouraged to play. Socialization for adult roles was not yet a dominant issue in these pre-teenage years, although preparation was made as each year passed by and people approached puberty, discretion, and service. Opportunities for leisure were in theory reduced in service as spare time was limited by the adult timetable and calendar. This was why some courts restricted play at particular games to people they called 'children'.[66] This could have been a task- rather than a time-orientated society.[67] But the misuse of time by young people raised concern about morality and work, and ultimately fatal issues like salvation and socialization. The more restrictive ethos of service and the apprenticeship indenture plunged young people into the working year, which was punctuated by a sequence of sabbaths, festivals, and communal and familial events in which they were principal actors. The transition from a child's sense of play to the regulated world of work (and time) in youth, however, has been interpreted as a squeeze on leisure time and a stumbling block to the formation of distinctive youthful experiences.

Tudor and Stuart children and youth had hundreds of games to choose from,[68] but did they find sufficient free time in which to play? The rhythms of life established by the school and household turned at their own pace, driven by a specific clock. Some schools like the free school at Maidstone created time for a weekly play day. Holidays could be quite generous. In 1658, for example, Bristol Grammar School 'limited' holidays to a fortnight at Christmas, ten days each at Easter and Whitsun, and another six days at the city's important fairs.[69] In 1718 the governors of London Bridewell allowed the house apprentices fifteen 'play days' every year.[70] The

---

[66] See below, pp. 136–7.

[67] See E. P. Thompson, 'Time, work-discipline and industrial capitalism', in his *Customs in Common* (1991).

[68] The dazzling diversity of children's games is recovered by Alice Bertha Gomme, *The Traditional Games of England, Scotland and Ireland* (2 vols.; 1894, 1898). See also Strutt, *Sports and Pastimes*, esp. book 4, ch. 4.

[69] *Records of Maidstone*, 150; John Latimer, *The Annals of Bristol in the Seventeenth Century* (Bristol, 1900), 284. See also Keith Thomas, *Rule and Misrule in the Schools of Early Modern England*, University of Reading Stenton Lecture, 9 (Reading, 1976).

[70] CLRO Misc. MS 58/35. These 'play-days' tended to be attached to festivals and holidays: three-and-a-half at Christmas, two-and-a-half at Easter and Whitsuntide, 1 day on election day, Restoration day and 30 January, and half-days on New Years day, Shrove Tuesday,

length of the working day depended upon the demands of work at certain points in the year or the form of work (e.g. employment in different types of agriculture, casual work, manufacturing work, or service in apprenticeship), and apprentices and servants may have been expected to work from 5/6 a.m. to 7/8 p.m. depending on the season of the year (at the close of the working day the curfew if it was applied was only one or two hours away),[71] though many of them would have had a shorter day, and possibly more free time for conviviality and play.

Despite these apparent restrictions, however, it is quite clear that young people found both time and space to meet outside the family, school, and workplace. Work in the tillage farms and dairies in the small Cambridgeshire village of Kirtling 'was usually done by noon',

and it was always the custom for the youth of the town who were men or maidservants and children, to assemble after horse baited, either upon the green or (after heysel) in a close accustomed to be so used, and there all to play till milking time, and supper at night. The men to football, and the maids with whom we children commonly mixed being not proof for the turbulence of the other party, to stoolball and such running games as they knew. And all this without mixing of men and women as in dancing with the fiddle but apart. No idle or lascivious frolics between them and at last all parting to their stations.

In this case, the limits of play were established by the rhythm of work, by baiting and milking ('their stations'), but there was still ample time for recreation.[72] The rolling fields of East Anglia provided a broad landscape in which to exercise lively imaginations and limbs. Young people also played on common land and waste. As in Kirtling, communal closes or fields were set aside as recreational space, though this public facility was increasingly fenced off

May Day, 2 August (King's accession), Bartholomewtide, 2 September, and 6 November (gunpowder treason).

[71] J. Dunlop and R. D. Denman, *English Apprenticeship and Child Labour: A History* (1912), 175; Charles Phythian-Adams, *Desolation of a City: Coventry and the Urban Crisis of the Late Middle Ages* (Cambridge, 1979), 74–6; David Palliser, 'Civic mentality and the environment in Tudor York', in Jonathan Barry (ed.), *The Tudor and Stuart Town: A Reader in English Urban History 1530–1688* (1990), 215. Bristol's carpenters required their journeymen and apprentices to be at work from between 5 and 6 a.m. to 7 p.m. (Ben-Amos, *Adolescence and Youth in Early Modern England*, 211). Cf. CLRO Rep. 42, fo. 299ᵛ.

[72] Roger North, *The Autobiography of the Hon. Roger North*, in his *The Lives of the Right Hon. Francis North, Baron Guildford . . . Together with the Autobiography of the Author*, ed. A. Jessop (3 vols.; 1890), iii. 9–10. See also FHL MS Box 10/10, 1–3. I must thank Margaret Spufford for allowing me to see a copy of this document—Josiah Langdale's autobiography—which is in her possession.

and newly defined as 'private' as the ethics of property and capital exerted stronger influence in the countryside.[73]

Contemporary sources supply much evidence of the regularity of play and its significance in the lives of young people. In the rest of this book we will see them meeting at the close of the day in the early hours of the evening, on Sundays and other holidays, and also follow them outside the household during the working day. Young lives were not solely structured by the physical boundaries of the household and the pressures of service. Many young people had freedom to organize leisure time, and thoughts quickly turned to play at the close of the working day.[74] The range of sports and opportunities for sociability were affected by geography. The countryside had larger expanses of green and water, and more hills, trees, hedges, ditches, and wildlife. Nevertheless, the town was only the thickness of its walls away from the rural world, and the townscape provided a distinctive environment for play. William Lilly recalled how 'every night' a hundred or more boys or youths of several London parishes gathered in the Strand at dusk, 'some playing, others as if in serious discourse', and stayed there playing and talking until darkness. Samuel Pepys's back yard was used as a venue for boys sports. While it was reported that markets and fairs drew gangs of 'knavish boies', and, in 1632, that on Sundays 'and all festival dayes the boyes and maydes and children' of two parishes close to St Paul's played 'till darke night'.[75] Urban materials reveal the dangers of play in the maze of alleys and streets which formed the townscape. In 1658, for example, the Wardmote Inquest of St Dunstan-in-the-West in London instructed residents to fill in wells and to close the hatches of cellars which were considered 'very dangerous for children to fall in' at night.[76]

This world of play has often been treated in rather condescending

---

[73] David Dymond, 'A lost social institution: the camping close', *Rural History*, 1 (1990), esp. 185. Dymond writes that the 'hey day' of the recreational close was from the fifteenth to the seventeenth centuries. 'Most' of them 'were out of use by the early eighteenth century' (ibid. 179). Robert Malcolmson attributes the steady decline of recreational space to enclosure, urbanization, and the increase in public thoroughfares (*Popular Recreations in English Society 1700–1850* (Cambridge, 1973), 108). The great disparities between traditional customary consciousness and use-rights, and the emerging ethics of property and capital have been recently explored by Jeanette Neeson, *Commoners: Common Right, Enclosure and Social Change in England 1700–1820* (Cambridge, 1993), esp. chs. 1–2, 6, 10.

[74] Cf. Thomas, 'Children in early modern England', 57–8.

[75] William Lilly, *William Lilly's History of His Life and Times* (1822), 45; *The Diary of Samuel Pepys*, ed. R. Latham and W. Matthews (11 vols.; 1970–83), iv. 433; *The Autobiography and Personal Diary of Simon Forman*, ed. J. O. Halliwell (1849), 8; PRO SP 16/214/94.

[76] GL MS 3018/1, fos. 12, 17ᵛ.

terms by adult observers, who see only innocence and nonsense in the sequence of chants, songs, expressions, and gestures which give form and meaning to games. Alice Gomme, however, has taught us to comprehend the rules, codes, and forms which govern the games played by long dead children.[77] The child's predilection and talent to imitate adult manners and pursuits is revealed in a rich range of parodies in which children re-created adult roles and responsibilities in their free time. Child's play rehearsed adult concerns with marriage, trade, and agricultural work.[78] Others trace movement along the life-course from a happy birth through a humdrum life of hard work, to a solemn funeral.[79] The bitter-sweet moments of courtship and first love were also enacted in play.[80] Still other games, like 'Round and Round the Village' which copied the Rogationtide ritual, assisted in introducing children to ideas of territory and contest, and perhaps aroused the first sensations of local and national identity.[81] Regional cultures (including patterns of speech), topographies, and disparate occupational structures contributed local colouring to many games. Some were played by either boys or girls alone.[82] Nevertheless, they retained a uniform purpose as an informal introduction to the differences of the ages of man, and the vocabulary, customs, and concerns of youth and adults.

We should be careful about producing generalizations from edited catalogues of children's games, which are arranged according to their editor's classifications and commentaries. Some games are well described and their histories are reasonably clear, though the origins of others are lost in time. It is even more difficult to enter the minds of contemporaries and discover what these games with their glosses on adulthood meant to young people. Were they played in a routine manner without thought being given to the lessons contained in their actions and words, or were they closely comprehended and accepted, mocked, or rejected?[83] Secondary and edited sources have uses as well as flaws, but we need to seek further

[77] Gomme, *Traditional Games*, esp. ii. 475 ff.

[78] Alice Gomme classifies games by 'the incidents which show the customs and rites from which . . . [they] descended', and by implication imitate, and by their 'dramatic forces'. See ibid. esp. 461–70. Marriage and trading games are discussed ibid. 305–6, and 438 ff. Gomme also considers the child's penchant for imitating adult roles 515 ff.

[79] The best example is 'When I Was a Young Girl', ibid. 372–4.

[80] See the list ibid. 461–2. 'Sally Water' is an excellent example of this type, 148–79.

[81] Ibid. 122–43, 477–8.

[82] Gomme sometimes remarks on the gendered nature of certain games or significantly assigns them to both sexes. See ibid. 460–1, 482, 483, and *passim*.

[83] Cf. Mary Elizabeth Perry, *Crime and Society in Early Modern Seville* (Hanover, NH, 1980), 206.

clarification in contemporary materials and see the games played by young people who lived in Tudor and Stuart England.[84] In addition, the discussion of recreation hitherto, has been hindered by the failure to distinguish adequately between the pastimes of youth and children. Other historians have tended to use a catch-all like 'children's games', which stretches over pre-adult years regardless of changes in forms and attitudes.[85] Yet as we depart childhood for the alleged physical vigour of youth, different aspirations and emotions affect the meaning of leisure and social life. Youth distances itself from childhood. One contemporary remarked that at 20 years of age, 'if anyone shall tell us of our childishness or call us by the most opprobrious name of boys, wee hold it a great disgrace'.[86]

Early modern people also recognized differences *within* the long age of youth, though this 'partition' of youth into younger and older segments is more difficult to document. Nevertheless, terms like 'boy', 'lad', 'wench', 'young man', 'great boy', and 'youth' imply that they distinguished between different stages of growing up. The same sentence could feature 'boys' and 'young men'.[87] These distinctions clearly held meaning for young people themselves who constructed hierarchies amongst fellow servants, and interpreted the purposes of leisure differently according to their place in the progress from puberty to marriage.[88] In youth, courtship and sexual pleasure became more important as each year passed by. There were also greater prospects of having money, which purchased access to the alehouse and bawdy house, and a very different world of drink, gossip, cards, and tables. Manners, play, and sport became more aggressive and physically demanding—children 'being not proof for the turbulence of the other party [i.e. youth]'. Children's games like 'Hide and Seek' and 'Kiss-in-the-Ring' were discarded for rough play at football, cudgels, wrestling, dancing, and so on. Physical strength, which was paraded in bouts of fighting, taunting, aggressive language, vandalism, and posturing was one aspect of a developing sense of manhood. It helped young men to distance themselves from children and young women, and to identify with older men.[89] Significantly, the Manchester Leet Jury banned those

---

[84] Cf. the discussion of the problems of sources for the study of calendrical festivals below.

[85] This is a rare blemish in the work of Alice Gomme. Joseph Strutt is another offender.

[86] Godfrey Goodman, *The Fall of Man, Or the Corruption of Nature* (1616), 185.

[87] Cf. Ch. 1.

[88] For some evidence of hierarchy amongst fellows in the same household see below, esp. pp. 297–8.

[89] Cf. Lyndal Roper, 'Blood and codpieces: masculinity in the early modern German town', in her *Oedipus and the Devil: Witchcraft, Sexuality and Religion in Early Modern Europe*

above 12 years of age from playing 'gede-gaddy or the cat's pallet'. Young people who ignored this ban faced two lonely hours in the 'dungeon', and their parents or masters were fined fourpence for each offence. Such light diversions were thought to be inappropriate for young people under the 'heavy hand' of socialization. This age-aspect to suitable recreation can be found in other places. In 1657, for example, the Kirkby Kendal Court Leet banned everyone above 12 years of age from playing 'in the street at a game commonly called Kattstick and Bullvett'.[90]

Nevertheless, habits change gradually, perhaps imperceptibly. When we turn to both urban and rural sources we see games which are identified by Gomme and others as belonging to children being played by apprentices and servants who were clearly in their teens and twenties. Games like nine holes, prison bars, football, cat and trap, quoits, or cudgels were first played by most people in their youth. They provided yet another source of identification with older people, and posted further distances from childhood. In 1560, for example, two servants were presented at London Bridewell 'for playing at ix holes in Finchfield', and punished 'for their lewd doyng'. A group of 'great boyes' fell victim to the Dorchester patriarch, John White, who discovered them playing at five and nine holes for a farthing a game on the sabbath. The thrill of play also tempted some of them away from church on the following Sunday. Oxford students also enjoyed playing nine holes, though the King was concerned that such diversions polluted 'bodies and mindes', and 'alienated the younger sort' from their studies. In 1604 'all manner of unprofitable or idle games', especially 'bull bayting, beare bayting, comon plaies, publick showes, enterludes', and 'nyne holes' were 'altogether restrained, inhibited, and forbidden'.[91] Roger Lowe of Lancashire told how the peace of Latchford Heath was rocked by 'a great company of persons with two drums' playing 'prison bars (prisoners base)'. He stayed 'awhile' to watch, 'but concluded it was

---

(1994); Hanawalt, *Growing up in Medieval London*, 114, 'Adolescents moved away from the games of childhood and began to experiment with wrestling, sword play and archery, which were adult male games. In addition, they began to frequent taverns and to learn such games as dice and checkers.'

[90] Earwaker, *Manchester Court Leet*, i. 205, 234; R. S. Ferguson (ed.), *The Boke of Recorde of Kirkbie Kendall* (Cumberland and Westmorland Antiquarian and Archaeological Society, extra series, 4, Kendal, 1892), 174. 'Kappstick' may be a lake county version of cat and dog.

[91] BCB 1, fo. 72; Mayo, *Dorchester Municipal Records*, 663; PRO SP 14/8/119. In the most common form of nine holes, nine holes were made in the ground and balls or marbles were thrown at them from a distance (Gomme, *Traditional Games*, i. 413–14). Joseph Strutt called nine holes 'a boyish game' (*Sports and Pastimes*, 222).

but vanitie'.[92] A Nottingham apprentice was arrested 'for quytteng [i.e. playing quoits] for monie'.[93]

These games were played by young people in fields, closes, greens, yards, alleys, and streets in both town and country. Prisoners bars had a long history in London. Tip-cat was also 'commonly played' on London's streets. Precepts were issued in 1567 'for the utter restraynt and taking away' of 'playinge buclere or crosse water in the open stretes and lanes'. It was also reported that boys 'trundling the hoop' were 'very troublesome' to passers-by.[94] In 1615 Common Council complained of the 'many hurts and other inconveniences' which 'daylie happen by [children, servants, and apprentices] playinge at . . . catt, trapp, or stoolball' in the streets. Two years later the same court passed orders 'for avoyding of tumults and breach of his majestie's peace and many hurts' caused by 'men and boys' playing at trap in the streets. Some unfortunate players had lost eyes in this rough play. The 'unlawful exercise' of trap and cat had been banned in 1591 when it was reported that apprentices carried cudgels and short staves 'under their cloakes in the evening' on their way to play in the fields causing 'great disorder'.[95] But games had caught the enthusiasm of young people and proved to be resilient. In 1618 it was ordered that 'from henceforth there shall not be any trapp, catt, or nyne holes playing' in Little Moorfields 'in regard of the hurt' to pedestrians. A further ban on 'play at cudgells' by apprentices was issued in 1632. While in 1636 a Finsbury farmer complained that he had 'susteined much losse and damage' by 'football play, trapp and catt, and other annoyances'.[96]

Even more unlucky were those passers-by who walked into a

[92] Lowe, *Diary*, 25. Prisoners bars or base was a team game. Each side had a prison or base (usually a stake driven into the ground), and the object was to capture the opposing team. Prisoners were set free if one of their teammates ran to the stake and touched them, though if the runner was himself touched by an opponent he also became a prisoner. The game was apparently very popular and is mentioned by both Shakespeare and Spenser (Gomme, *Traditional Games*, ii. 80–3; Strutt, *Sports and Pastimes*, 67–8).

[93] W. J. Stevenson *et al.* (eds.), *Records of the Borough of Nottingham* (9 vols.; Nottingham, 1882–1956), iv. 105. A quoit was an iron ring. An iron pin is driven into the ground and a second pin is placed at an optional distance from the first. The players then try to throw their quoits over their opponent's pin (Strutt, *Sports and Pastimes*, 63–4).

[94] Strutt, *Sports and Pastimes*, 68; CLRO Rep. 16, fo. 211. Tip-cat is described by Gomme, *Traditional Games*, ii. 294–5 (the quotation is from 295). See also Strutt, *Sports and Pastimes*, 303.

[95] CLRO Jours. 29, fo. 329ᵛ; 30, fo. 128ᵛ; 23, fo. 17; 35, fo. 485. Trap and cat, another team game, resembles cricket or rounders. The object of the game was to hit a ball as far as possible. The batsman was out if the fielding side either caught the ball or hit the trap or wicket when bowling (Gomme, *Traditional Games*, ii. 306–7). See also BCB 8, fo. 85; CLRO Jours. 31, fos. 317–18ᵛ; 32, fo. 221ᵛ.

[96] CLRO Rep. 33, fos. 302–2ᵛ; Jour. 35, fo. 485; Rep. 50, fo. 79.

football match, becoming trapped in a frantic confusion of noise and moving bodies. Football was roundly condemned as rough play, which created formidable obstacles for pedestrians—'overthrowing smalle children, aged and impotent poore personnes, and women great with childe'—and left a trail of injuries and damaged property after the final kick.[97] It was reported that 'divers dangerous disorders' rocked parts of London in January 1586 'by occasion of football play'. Householders were instructed to 'take order with all their servants and prentizes . . . that none of them hereafter presume to offend therein'.[98] Yet this drive failed to sweep young footballers off the streets. In 1593 Common Council reviewed the situation. Many precepts had been issued 'to inhibit the outragious playe at footeball', but every citizen could see that they had not 'wrought' the expected 'reformation', and pedestrians still had to steer a safe course through 'divers great ryotts' and 'unlawful assemblies'. In 1599 it was reported that football was played 'in everie part' of London, so that her majesty's subjects 'can hardlie passe through the streets'.[99] Later complaints (and instructions that householders restrain their young charges) were issued in 1600, 1602, 1605, 1611, 1621, 1623, 1628 (when it was reported that football still caused 'many hurts . . . extendinge even to the losse of the lives and limbs of people'), 1630, 1632, and 1633.[100]

The complaints and frustrations of London's magistrates were repeated in other places. Football (or its East Anglian relation 'camping') was played in closes or fields set aside for communal recreation, and often gave ritual expression to local identities and the differences between the ages.[101] Provincial magistrates also complained about damage and distress. The windows of All Hallows church in York were 'much broken' in March 1660 by a group of servants 'playing and strikeing at the football' in 'Owzegate and thereaboutes', who ignored an earlier 'admonition' from the justices. Two months later Quarter Sessions appointed 'an inquisition for football'. In 1618 the Manchester Court Leet appointed three 'officers for ye footeball'. The town had a recent history of 'great disorder' caused by 'that unlawfull exercise of playinge . . . footballe

[97] CLRO Jour. 20(1), fo. 27; Malcolmson, *Popular Recreations*, 34–40; Dymond, 'Lost social institution', 171–2, 181.
[98] CLRO Jour. 22, fo. 10.
[99] CLRO Jours. 23, fo. 225^v; 25, fo. 22. See also CLRO Jours. 22, fos. 156^v, 257; 23, fos. 4^v, 343^v.
[100] CLRO Jours 25, fos. 146, 166^v; 26, fos. 27, 143; 27, fo. 14^v; 28, fo. 160^v; 31, fo. 376; 32, fo. 221^v; 34, fo. 205; 35, fo. 259^v; 36, fos. 20, 181.
[101] Malcolmson, *Popular Recreations*, 112, 116; Dymond, 'Lost social institution', 179 ff.

in ye streetes', and local residents had been 'greatly wronged and
charged with makinge and amending of their glasse windowes broken yearely' by 'lewd and disordered' footballers.[102] The turbulent
and competitive character of football was well suited to the aggression which was evident in male youth. Like other boisterous games,
football presented young men with an opportunity to flaunt the
rowdy and competitive spirit which was one sign of their blossoming manhood. Nor were rough sports like football the exclusive
property of young people, though governors frequently targeted
apprentices and servants as principal players, or those about whom
they were most concerned.

In the next section we will turn from games to discuss some
rituals and festivals which further communicated the significance of
the difference of the ages of man, and exposed anxieties about
order and socialization which clearly affected the magistrates' response to youthful conviviality and play.

4. Some Rituals and the Festive Calendar

A series of rituals indicated movement along the life-cycle from
childhood through youth to adulthood, and they helped to give
firmer meaning to age-differentials.[103] These ceremonies traced
patterns of male and female progress which were outlined in the
first chapter.[104] For males of certain social rank childhood was
heralded by 'putting on breeches'.[105] The border between youth
and adulthood was crossed at marriage and full participation in a
trade. Ideas about occupational career shaped the forms of transition
for men and women, and in the plans of moralists at least marriage
was the principal point of exit for women. The end of an apprenticeship was one transitional moment for young men and it rarely
passed without a ritual farewell to youth—a feast or drinking. The
leap from 'bachelourship' to adulthood, from dependence to independence, imbued the person experiencing transition with a sense
of departing one age for another, for ahead stretched uncharted
territory—'a wide world to stand up on my legs'. John Dunton
recalled how his apprenticeship was 'just upon expiring' when he

---

[102] YCA City & Ainsty Quarter Sessions minute book, 1638–62, fos. 430, 432, 434–6;
Earwaker, *Manchester Court Leet*, ii. 239–40, 248, 432; iii. 4; iv. 209.

[103] There is a much fuller account in Ben-Amos, *Adolescence and Youth in Early Modern
England*, ch. 9. David Cressy is shortly to publish a major study of life-cyclical rituals in this
period.

[104] See above, esp. pp. 27–30.   [105] For example, Josselin, *Diary*, 407.

'invited a hundred apprentices to celebrate a funeral for it'. The older Dunton dismissed such ritual cheer as 'no more than a youthful piece of vanity; for all such entertainments are expensive'.[106] Other evidence suggests that such rituals were being trimmed in the seventeenth century because of a concern with the cost for the apprentice and the company in difficult times. In January 1613, for example, the Court of the London Pewterers announced that 'the custome' by which 'younge men of the companie at theire makinge free have in . . . to dyne the master, warden and assistants', should from 'henceforth . . . cease' because of the draining of company funds and the high cost to the apprentice who required money to set up in business. It was ordered that the feast should be replaced by a single fee of 6s. 8d. for 'the use of the Hall'. In 1614 the customary close of term breakfast was abandoned in Bristol, and the guilds were asked to content themselves with a 3s. 4d. fee thereafter.[107]

Such life-cyclical moments as these brought age and individual circumstances firmly to mind. Another ceremony which gave ritual form to the passage from youth into adulthood was of course marriage in which young people often had a symbolic role, the young men going in company with the groom to fetch his bride and escorting the couple to the church amidst bright colours and a volley of cheers and songs. John Aubrey reported that 'the young fellows that accompany the bride' would 'give a lusty bang with their truncheons'. They would sometimes be met by the bride's relatives and friends, 'strong and sturdy men', who acted out a ritual refusal barring the way of the groom and his party.[108] At the church the groom would leave behind the peer group of bachelors for householder status. On the Isle of Portland he bid a ritual farewell to his former youthful peers: 'Young men and bachelors I bid you all adieu | Old men and married men I'm coming to you.'[109] The bride's garter was a prize for young men who were prepared to struggle to obtain possession of it.[110] There are also examples of

[106] John Dunton, *The Life and Errors of John Dunton Late Citizen of London* (1705), 50. See also Hanawalt, *Growing up in Medieval London*, 207; Cynthia Maria Truant, *The Rites of Labor: Brotherhoods of Compagnonnage in Old and New Regime France* (Ithaca, NY, 1994), ch. 5.

[107] GL MS 7090/4, fo. 26; Latimer, *Annals of Bristol*, 46.

[108] John Aubrey, *Remaines of Gentilisme and Judaisme* (1686–1687), ed. James Britten (Folk-lore Society, 4, 1881), 171–2.

[109] Quoted by J. R. Gillis, *For Better for Worse: British Marriages 1600 to the Present* (Oxford, 1985), 70.

[110] For some marriage festivities see ibid. 58–63; Alan Macfarlane, *Marriage and Love in England: Modes of Reproduction 1300–1840* (Oxford, 1986), ch. 10; Ingram, *Church Courts*, 164; *The Courtship Narrative of Leonard Wheatcroft, Derbyshire Yeoman*, ed. G. Parfitt and R. Houlbrooke (Reading, 1986); Ferguson, *The Boke of Recorde of Kirkbie Kendall*, 89–93.

festivities in which the groom's young friends fetched the newly weds to their first home, dancing a morris or some other jig, to join in their first meal. In some places the authorities regarded what they considered to be excessive conviviality on such occasions with deep suspicion, and they attempted to limit the numbers attending the wedding drinking, feasting, and dancing.[111]

The working year was pleasantly interrupted by such ceremonies and a number of feasts and holidays in which young people had a prominent role. The reformed Church cast a sharp eye over the festive calendar reducing the seasonal complexity of medieval ceremonial to a monotonous rhythm of working days and sabbaths, which was punctuated by a sequence of holy days and other festivals which were far more secular in origin, including Shrove Tuesday and May Day.[112] These latter days largely remained 'youth festivals',[113] though the young lost their 'special role' on other festive days like Candlemas, All Souls, Frick Friday, and Whitsun processions.[114] Rogationtide processions in which members of the community marched to the furthest points of its boundaries in a symbolic representation of communal identity continued beyond the Reformation, and one purpose of this perambulation was to introduce young people to the shape and customs of their community.[115] Yet despite the Protestant revision of calendrical festivals and changing

[111] J. S. Purvis (ed.), *Tudor Parish Documents of the Diocese of York* (Cambridge, 1948), 167; Emmison, 'Tithes, perambulations and sabbath-breach', 201; Hale, *Series of Precedents*, 226–7; Earwaker, *Manchester Court Leet*, i. 103, 162, 220; ii. 193; iii. 86; Archer, *Pursuit of Stability*, 113; Gillis, *For Better for Worse*, 74.

[112] David Cressy, *Bonfires and Bells: National Memory and the Protestant Calendar in Elizabethan and Stuart England* (1989), ch. 2; Hutton, *Rise and Fall of Merry England*, esp. chs. 3–7; Malcolmson, *Popular Recreations*, ch. 2. See also Eamon Duffy, *The Stripping of the Altars: Traditional Religion in England 1400–1580* (New Haven, 1992), ch. 1; K. Thomas, *Religion and the Decline of Magic; Studies in Popular Beliefs in Sixteenth- and Seventeenth-century England* (1971), esp. ch. 3; François Laroque, *Shakespeare's Festive World: Elizabethan Seasonal Entertainment and the Professional Stage*, trans. Janet Lloyd (first published in France in 1988; Cambridge, 1993), esp. chs. 3–5.

[113] Patrick Collinson, *The Birthpangs of Protestant England: Religious and Cultural Change in the Sixteenth and Seventeenth Centuries* (Basingstoke, 1988), 55; Malcolmson, *Popular Recreations*, 54.

[114] Susan Wright, 'Confirmation, catechism and communion: the role of the young in the post-Reformation Church', in Wright (ed.), *Parish, Church and People: Local Studies in Lay Religion 1350–1700* (1988), 207.

[115] See ERO D/ACA 30, fos. 170ᵛ, 193ᵛ; 32, fo. 95ᵛ; 43, fos. 102ᵛ, 110ᵛ; 45, fo. 284; CLRO Jour. 21, fo. 352ᵛ; Hutton, *Rise and Fall of Merry England*, 142–3, 176, 247; Pepys, *Diary*, ii. 106; ix. 179; Marjorie Keniston McIntosh, *A Community Transformed: The Manor and Liberty of Havering, 1500–1620* (Cambridge, 1991), 202; Neeson, *Commoners*, 320. Ronald Hutton draws attention to the uneven chronology of Rogationtide survivals, which were more apparent after the reign of Elizabeth when they suffered 'plenty of difficulties' (*Rise and Fall of Merry England*, 142).

practices, a measure of licence was still extended to youth on festive days like Plough Monday, St Valentine's Day, New Year, Easter, and Christmas. John Aubrey, recalling his Wiltshire boyhood, declared that '*non obstante* the change of religion, the plough boys and also the schoolboys will keep up and retain their old ceremonies and privileges'. In 1654 Bristol's apprentices took to the streets to express their unhappiness about the abolition of Christmas (a reminder of the impact of the Interregnum on the festive calendar and the possibilities of cultural conflict). Boy bishops and Lords of Misrule were a distant memory in most places by the turn of the seventeenth century, though St Nicholas's day retained its time-honoured reputation for misrule.[116]

In some respects the rhythm of the year turned on the timing of calendrical festivals, some of which were said to have existed from 'time out of mind', or since the memory of man began. They were therefore traditional, though we are often rather uncertain about their particular histories, which are often lost in the distant past. One problem is raised by the nature of the sources used to study the experience and meaning of calendrical festivals hitherto. Much is left unsaid or accepted without question. Great faith has been placed in collections of 'traditional' customs and beliefs compiled by eighteenth- and nineteenth-century antiquarians, who in much the same periods (though in different contexts) have been shown attempting to retrieve a rapidly disappearing world, and in the process 'inventing' traditions by sketching new histories and attaching 'modern' significances to alleged customary practices.[117] The commentaries of ancient authors are sometimes juggled with references to practices which were current when antiquarians began committing oral culture and traditions to print.[118] We can at least recognize the risks of using later catalogues as evidence of early

[116] Gillis, *For Better for Worse*, 23 ff.; John Aubrey is quoted by Cressy, *Bonfires and Bells*, 15; Latimer, *Annals of Bristol*, 256; Aubrey, *Remaines*, 40–1. Plough Monday is also discussed by Brand, *Popular Antiquities*, i. 505 ff.; Strutt, *Sports and Pastimes*, 273–4; Duffy, *Stripping of the Altars*, 13. A number of St Valentine's day customs are described by Aubrey, *Remaines*, 74–5; Gillis, *For Better for Worse*, 24; while some Christmas and New Year rituals are described by Strutt, *Sports and Pastimes*, 272–3; Heal, *Hospitality*, 77; Bob Bushaway, *By Rite: Custom, Ceremony and Community in England 1700–1880* (1982), c. Other 'defences' of Christmas are noted by Hutton, *Rise and Fall of Merry England*, esp. 210–11, who also has much to say about the decline of boy bishops and lords of misrule, esp. 10–12, 53–4, 77–8, 90–1, 97–8, 114–15, 179–80, 242–3.

[117] Eric Hobsbawm and Terence Ranger (eds.), *The Invention of Tradition* (Cambridge, 1983); Charles Phythian-Adams, *Local History and Folklore: A New Framework* (1975). Cf. Cressy, *Bonfires and Bells*, 13; Hutton, *Rise and Fall of Merry England*, esp. introduction and ch. 2.

[118] Cf. Cressy, *Bonfires and Bells*, 13.

modern customs without further support from contemporary sources. These later commentaries often simply report the bare form of a festival and game. We rarely discover the actual sentiments of early modern people, and whether these events were greeted with active hostility, encouragement, or warm support. We can turn to court records to depict the hostility of some magistrates and ministers to calendrical festivals and sabbath day play. Yet the question of their continued vitality in seventeenth-century England is plagued by a wide spectrum of local experiences (e.g. survival, suppression, or abandonment). At least in some places the festive calendar may have been severely pruned. Asked in 1575 what sports and festivities were to be found in the capital, an apprentice answered that he 'knewe of none but two or three dromes and awnsientes and such like showes in Southwarke'.[119]

New dates took the place of former holidays, and contributed a distinctively national and Protestant flavour to the festive year. Gunpowder treason was an important aspect of political memory, and young people played a prominent part in celebrating this spectacular deliverance from catholic plotting, hurling crackers and fireworks, issuing threats, and making a nuisance of themselves at bonfires. For some 5 November 'became a day of mischief, an autumn analogue to the rowdiness of Shrovetide and May'. Bonfires also burned bright on 17 November—Queen Elizabeth's day. In London, apprentices took advantage of these memorial days to play tricks and pranks.[120] The Bridewell apprentices left the confines of the hospital to march around the city. As late as November 1718 witnesses reported the activities of 'the Bridewell boys' to governors. Issac Cox was told by a passer-by that 'they were comeing', and he later saw 'them knocking at the windows at Fleet Bridge'. Another witness saw them 'neere Fleet ditch . . . with staves and clubs and large sticks beating at the doors going to Bridewell'. A pedestrian going from Roebuck to Swan Lane at the upper end of Cheapside 'met the blewcoat boys' and he trailed them listening to their cries of 'High Church'. At a fire in Walbrook the Bridewell

---

[119] Quoted by Archer, *Pursuit of Stability*, 94.
[120] Cressy, *Bonfires and Bells*, 145, 173–5, 180 and chs. 8, 9, and 11 *passim*; Hutton, *Rise and Fall of Merry England*, 146–51; Bushaway, *By Rite*, 64–74; Tim Harris, *London Crowds in the Reign of Charles II: Propaganda and Politics from the Restoration until the Exclusion Crisis* (Cambridge, 1987), esp. 30–1; CLRO PD 10/72; 10/74a; 10/86; 10/88; 10/99; 10/100; 10/105, 10/167. Both Cressy (*Bonfires and Bells*, chs. 8–9) and Hutton (*Rise and Fall of Merry England*, esp. ch. 5), emphasize the differing fortunes of these celebrations of the accession dates and birthdays of different monarchs, and delivery from gunpowder treason, and their political utility.

crew 'cryed out that the Roebuck mob was coming', though this did not interfere with their cries of 'blew' which were returned with gifts of money from 'some people'. They were said to be at the head of 'neer 200 in Newgate' beating on doors and windows. This was the same gang who gathered at the upper end of Newgate crying 'High Church' and sacking 'the bonfeir at the end of Bow Lane'. The 'Bridewell boys' were also spotted going into alehouses to request money, 'and particularly went into the 3 Tunns at Snow Hill'. They 'had money given them at several places'. One apprentice told the governors that the Ludgate constable 'said nothing to them' and that their numbers never reached above thirty. Another, that 'they did not goe above 12 and thereabouts together'. In November 1715 the 'Bridewell boys' had been 'charged to keep to work and not stirr out of their master's houses on any holy day'; beadles were 'charged to keep ye gates shut'. They also upset the celebration of the coronation and the Prince's birthday when they 'blew up ye padlock of ye back gate with gunpowder and immediately ran out in a body together'. Complaints reached 'even his majesty's ears'.[121]

Despite the often ambivalent attitude of magistrates and moralists, a number of 'traditional' holidays continued to be celebrated in the early modern period and beyond, even if their particular form and meaning was affected by geographical location. They included the great 'youth holidays' of Shrove Tuesday and May Day. May Day was 'primarily a festival of unmarried young people', a colourful day of dance, mischief, and song in which young people were allegedly allowed free rein to follow their 'preoccupation with courtship and love making'.[122] May was a 'merry month' and the gateway to summer; a time of renewal which was well suited to the lusty and vigorous temper of youth. One ballad proclaimed that May 'is the moneth of pleasure'. 'A Pleasant Countrey Maying Song' told how 'love is in her chiefest prime' in this 'merry maying time', which ushered in the eagerly anticipated summertime.[123] The imagery on display was both colourful and symbolic, including depictions of community,[124] changing seasons, renewal, love, and lust.

[121] CLRO Misc. MSS 58/35.

[122] I am quoting Charles Phythian-Adams 'Ceremony and the citizen: the communal year at Coventry 1450–1550' in Peter Clark and Paul Slack (eds.), *Crisis and Order in English Towns 1500–1700: Essays in Urban History* (1972), 66. Cf. Malcolmson, *Popular Recreations*, 30; Gillis, *For Better for Worse*, 25; Laroque, *Shakespeare's Festive World*, 111–14; Cressy, *Bonfires and Bells*, 21–3; Hutton, *Rise and Fall of Merry England*, 27–30, 116.

[123] W. G. Day (ed.), *The Pepys Ballads* (Cambridge, 1987), 242–3, 337.

[124] There are examples of the young people of neighbouring communities fighting for possession of the maypole. See Gillis, *For Better for Worse*, 27; Brand, *Popular Antiquities*, i. 246, 236–7.

John Brand described the prominent function of traditional characters like Robin Hood, Maid Marion, and a Lord and Lady of May, who presided over the festivities.[125] The 'young maids' of Oxford carried 'garlands of flowers' around the town, which they later placed in a local church at twilight. Contemporaries also described milkmaids dancing and singing in the streets wearing bright blue, 'the universal symbol of constant love', alongside the vivid green of flowers and garlands.[126]

In many places in the early hours of May morning a stream of people walked to nearby fields and woods, some like Elizabeth Pepys to gather the precious first few drops of May dew—a coveted moisturizer[127]—others to fetch home branches or garlands. In a much-quoted commentary, the antiquarian Henry Bourne described how 'the juvenile parts of both sexes were wont to rise a little after midnight',

and walk to some neighbouring wood accompanied with music and blowing of horns where they break down branches from the trees and adorn them with nosegays and crowns of flowers; when this is done they return with their booty homewards about the rising of the sun, and make their doors and windows to triumph with their flowery spoils.

It is said that in Northumberland 'the young people of both sexes' rose from their beds 'early in the morning to gather the flowering thorn and the dew off the grass', and carried their spoils home 'with music and acclamations; and having dressed a pole on the town green with garlands, dance around it'.[128] The centre of attention on this day of dancing, singing, playing, and bright colours was the rural green or urban field with its maypole decorated, one antiquarian tells us, with green boughs, flowers, herbs, flags, strings, and handkerchiefs,[129] and the neighbourhood either dancing or watching from the edges of the green with the young taking the major part in the dancing. Churchwardens' accounts disclose payments 'in reward to the youth that brought in May', though official

[125] Brand, *Popular Antiquities*, i. 253–62; Roger B. Manning, *Hunters and Poachers: A Cultural and Social History of Unlawful Hunting in England 1485–1640* (Oxford, 1993), 22.

[126] Aubrey, *Remaines*, 18; Brand, *Popular Antiquities*, ii. 217; Pepys, *Diary*, viii. 193. I am quoting Phythian-Adams, 'Ceremony and the citizen', 66.

[127] Pepys, *Diary*, viii. 240; ix. 549, 551.

[128] Strutt, *Sports and Pastimes*, 275–6. Cf. Thistleton-Dyer, *British Popular Customs*, 257; Brand, *Popular Antiquities*, i. 213–15; A. R. Wright, *British Calendar Customs*, ed. T. E. Lones (3 vols.; 1936–40), ii. 201–4.

[129] Strutt, *Sports and Pastimes*, 276–7.

parish contributions appear to trickle away towards the close of the sixteenth century.[130]

One antiquarian tells us that in London Shrove Tuesday, a day of laughter, play, and misrule before the solemn season of Lent, was the apprentices' 'particular holiday'. In Cooke's *Greenes Tu Quoque* (1614) an apprentice dreams of becoming mayor of London and muses that 'Prentices may pray for that time; for whenever it happens I will make another Shrove Tuesday'.[131] Shrovetide was presented as 'a season for extraordinary sport and feasting', and Shrove Tuesday was a day for football, cock fighting, fighting with cudgels, and throwing at cocks. It was reported that the youth of Chester 'exercised themselves in manly sports of the age' like archery, running, leaping, and wrestling.[132] In 1653 Maidstone's governors objected against the 'many inconveniences' caused by people who gathered in 'rude and unlawful manner in the streetes and other open places' on Shrove Tuesday 'commonly playeinge at football and cudgells, tossinge of doggs, and setting forth and throwinge of libettes [sticks] at cocks and other poultry in a cruel unchristianlike manner'. They drew up a system of graduated fines—masters and parents being made liable for the offences of those under 21 years of age.[133] Orders were passed in Bristol in the 1650s banning Shrovetide sports—football, tossing of dogs, and throwing at cocks. When the bellman proclaimed the order for 1660 he was knocked about by a 'mob', who ripped his fine livery. The next day, in a provocative defence of customary activities, apprentices threw at hens and geese rather than cocks, and tossed cats and bitches in the air instead of dogs.[134] In other places, in similar fashion to the

---

[130] *Nottingham Borough Records*, iv. 175, 183; J. C. Cox (ed.), *Churchwardens' Accounts from the Fourteenth Century to the Close of the Seventeenth Century* (1913), 286; Brand, *Popular Antiquities*, i. 248–9. See also Cressy, *Bonfires and Bells*, 22.

[131] Brand, *Popular Antiquities*, i. 88. Cf. ibid. 67—'the boys of London had their particular times or seasons'; Cooke is quoted by Charles W. Camp, *The Artisan in Elizabethan Literature* (New York, 1923), 118. See also Brigden, *London and the Reformation*, 540; Malcolmson, *Popular Recreations*, 28–9; and Peter Burke's discussion of the cultural and social significance of the dispute between carnival and Lent in his *Popular Culture in Early Modern Europe* (1978), chs. 7–8.

[132] I am quoting Brand, *Popular Antiquities*, i. 64–5, 93. Joseph Strutt comments that 'the day before Lent was used to be a universal holiday given up to a variety of sports', *Sports and Pastimes*, 274. For some examples of the variety of Shrovetide sports and pursuits collected by later antiquarians see Hutton, *Rise and Fall of Merry England*, 18–19, 244; Laroque, *Shakespeare's Festive World*, esp. 61, 96–103; P. H. Ditchfield, *Old English Customs* (1901), 64; R. Chambers (ed.), *The Book of Days: A Miscellany of Popular Antiquities* (2 vols.; 1859), i. 238; Thistleton-Dyer, *British Popular Customs*, 62–91. See also Aubrey, *Remaines*, 40–1. Evidence from early modern materials is presented below.

[133] Martin, *Records of Maidstone*, 131.   [134] Latimer, *Annals of Bristol*, 260, 292.

'Bridewell boys' November rituals, the youth knocked on doors to request pancakes and other fare, throwing stones at the houses of reluctant folk until they capitulated and presented the customary food and drink. One collector of customs tells how after they finished throwing at cocks on Shrove Tuesday, the boys of St Mary's on the Scilly Isles would stone houses at dusk to obtain either pancakes or money, 'a privilege they claim[ed] from time immemorial' and enjoyed 'without control' to bring the day's sports to a happy end.[135]

We can mingle observations and examples from contemporary materials and later antiquarians to show early modern people (and their nineteenth-century descendants) dancing, eating, and participating in other holiday events. Again, the nature of the sources can obstruct our understanding of the popularity of these rituals and cast only faint light on their particular history. The purpose and form of rituals and ceremonies could be disputed between sections of the community, who viewed custom, crime, and pastimes in different ways, perhaps driven by a 'precise' religious temper or a strong commitment to property ethics. May games, the setting-up of a maypole,[136] or the ritual gathering of wood,[137] for example, could all result in controversy, violence, or prosecution, as contesting parties disputed the meaning of custom, common right, and the seasonal calendar. Contemporary records also show other youthful activities in holiday time catching the hostile attention of magistrates. In 1578 London's governors placed firm limits on Shrovetide festivities, ordering householders to stop their apprentices, servants, scholars, or any of their family joining 'unconveneyent multitudes', or making 'anye showtinge, hooping noyses, sounding of drumes or instruments, shootinge of gunnes or usinge of squibbes other then shalbe fytt for quyet and sober persones modestlye and dyscretlye usinge their tyme of honest recreation'. This sharp contrast between dishonest and honest Shrovetide celebration is good evidence of the disputed interpretation of how this holiday was to be observed.[138] In 1634 the bench of London Bridewell complained about the May Day antics of the hospital apprentices, who marched 'disorderly with bowes on their necks into the citty' with a drum striking before them. One ballad told how the 'youth of the city' marched

---

[135] Thistleton-Dyer, *British Popular Customs*, 76–8, 84–7; Strutt, *Sports and Pastimes*, 227; Wright, *British Calendar Customs*, i. 16–20.

[136] For example, PRO STAC 8, 21/12; 161/1; 262/11. See also Cressy, *Bonfires and Bells*, 22–3.

[137] See Bushaway, *By Rite*, 210–13.   [138] CLRO Jour. 20(2), fo. 388.

with great joy on May morning to the ceremonial tune of fifes and drums.[139]

Festive days provided an occasion for disorder,[140] and a cloud of anxiety hovered over May Day and Shrovetide in particular. The Venetian ambassador wrote that the London apprentices had 'two days of the year which are fatal for them, namely Shrove Tuesday and the 1st of May', when they 'display such unbridled will and are so licentious, that in a body three or four thousand strong they go committing outrages in every direction'.[141] Watches and curfews were set on sensitive days like Shrove Tuesday,[142] May Eve (and Day),[143] the Vigil of St John's Eve,[144] and Bartholomewtide.[145] There was a thin line between respectable behaviour and disorder. A 'May game or merriment' disturbed the peace of the town of Ashford in Derbyshire. William Hatfield, a local 'gentleman' who was 'yett litle hable to travel but with exceeding great payne', gave his version of events before Star Chamber. He claimed that he was attacked by a group passing through the town 'in most ryotous, routous and unlawful manner . . . armed with long staves, pitchforkes, swordes, daggers, and other offensive weapons' with a drummer marching at their head, who left him 'in great danger of his death' and 'great dispayre of his life'. His companion was stabbed 'into his bellye soe wyde and deepe with a daggar that the verie fatt . . . of his entrailles did passe and issue out'. A constable arrested one of the 'Mayers' but he was released from the stocks by his comrades. Several young men of the town appeared before Star Chamber charged with riot and assault. In a joint answer four of them explained that after evening prayer on Whit Sunday 'a certayne company of young people gathered togeather . . . goinge a Mayinge or aboute some May games . . . as they many tymes doe in that countrey and havinge amongest them a drumme'. Their 'understanding and their intent', they continued, was 'to be noe other end but to make merry'. The company was asked by Thomas Goodwin of Ashford 'to goe to

[139] BCB 7, fo. 377ᵛ; Day, *Pepys Ballads*, 242.
[140] Burke, *Popular Culture*, 204; Keith Lindley, 'Riot prevention and control in early Stuart London', *Transactions of the Royal Historical Society*, 5th ser., 33 (1983), 109; Brigden, *London and the Reformation*, 540.
[141] CSPV 1617–19, 246–7.
[142] The meaning and celebration of Shrove Tuesday, and the attitudes of governors, are further explored in my discussion of Shrovetide brothel sacks by apprentices.
[143] For example, CLRO Jours. 25, fo. 344ᵛ; 27, fos. 38ᵛ, 231ᵛ; 28, fo. 62ᵛ; 30, fo. 128ᵛ.
[144] For example, CLRO Jours. 25, fos. 273ᵛ, 356; 26, fo. 352ᵛ; 27, fo. 380; 28, fos. 95ᵛ, 226; 29, fo. 355; 30, fo. 192ᵛ.
[145] For example, CLRO Jours. 25, fos. 87, 189ᵛ; 30, fo. 228.

Churchdale [a nearby meadow] to make merry and to drynke of syllybowken theire as hath byn a longe tyme accustomed by younge people'. The 'companie' was above nine in number, and at some point they left the meadow and marched through the town in military style allegedly carrying a range of weapons. Another defendant told the Star Chamber that they 'did in a merriment and May Game goe upp and downe the towne with a drum as they used to doe in other yeares'.[146]

Some common threads run through these May Day and Shrovetide events. They offered an occasion for displays of collective activity by young people (or by groups primarily composed of young people, or identified as such by the authorities),[147] who took full advantage of the season to play, feast, drink, and in certain cases to request tributes from householders. A measure of ritual licence, we are told, was extended to young people. Structures of authority which held society together were suspended for a single day or longer. These exploits have been interpreted in terms of officially sanctioned misrule; a deliberate and tactical relaxation of conventional controls in the festive season when play and laughter replaced appointed hierarchy, and the social order was mocked and mimicked.[148] In England historians produce the example of the London apprentices, who were allegedly granted free rein by governors to sack bawdy houses and playhouses at Shrovetide, as evidence of a process of regulated 'ritual inversion'. Schoolchildren provide further evidence of Shrovetide misrule. In some schools authority and regulation were pushed to one side for a day or longer, and pupils were permitted licence to 'bar out' their teachers from the classroom. At Bromfield in Cumberland, for example, it was 'a custom time out of mind' in the beginning of Lent 'at a Fasting's Even to bar out the master for three days'. Classes were cancelled at Eton, and the scholars played rather than work in the classrooms.[149] But

---

[146] PRO STAC 8, 168/25. Further north in Newcastle in 1633, the Shrovetide season provided the occasion for 'an intolerable tumult' by 'an armed and unruly multitude of young men', most of whom it seems were apprentices. It was claimed that the 'tumult' was sparked by a number of causes, including the customary rights of the inhabitants to dry their clothes at a particular location which was also popular for 'walking after sermon', and 'a desire' for a more popular form of electing civic officials. The course and causes of the 'tumult' can be followed in PRO SP 16/233/60–1; 233/66; 233/78; 234/85.

[147] Cf. below, pp. 158–60.   [148] See esp. Burke, *Popular Culture*, ch. 7.

[149] Brand, *Popular Antiquities*, 72–3, 441–54; Chambers, *Book of Days*, i. 238; Aubrey, *Remaines*, 132; Thistleton-Dyer, *British Popular Customs*, 69, 72. Barring-out on this and other days in the year is explored in much greater detail by Keith Thomas in his *Rule and Misrule in the Schools of Early Modern England*, University of Reading Stenton Lecture, 9 (Reading, 1976). See also Laroque, *Shakespeare's Festive World*, 60–1.

it is the Shrovetide behaviour of London's apprentices which has most captured the imagination of historians, even though their interpretations are open to revision at a number of vital points which have important implications for interpretations of the collective behaviour of early modern youth.

5. *Sacking Brothels in London*

James Harrington reported that 'on Shrove Tuesday it was customary for the apprentices to rise and pull down brothels'. Ben Jonson's Lanthron Leatherhead, recalling his youthful feats, spoke of 'the rising o' the prentices; and pulling downe the bawdy houses' in Shrovetide. While another fictional apprentice regretted the loss of past times when he plucked down 'houses of iniquitie'.[150] The reported scale of the sacks with their armed brigades and selected targets implies a measure of organization and an information network. In 1631 a rumour rushed around old Paris Garden liberty in Southwark that Mr Holland's 'house of obscenity' as well as '20 other houses neere the same' were to be 'pulled downe' on Shrove Tuesday. 'Many thousands of scroles and papers' had been scattered in the city and suburbs 'for the aggrevating of apprentices and ydle persons to demolish' these particular dens of vice. Concern quickly spread and the residents of the liberty petitioned the Privy Council to request that the trained bands be kept 'in a readynes' to support the watch.[151] A number of literary sources told how bawds and prostitutes shivered as Shrovetide loomed near,[152] though it was not just the staff of the bawdy houses or their neighbours who feared that they were festive targets. In 1621 the Spanish ambassador retired to a house at Nonsuch 'to avoide the fear and furie of Shrove Tewsday'; he was 'not ignorant of the yll affection generally borne him' which could flare up on this 'furious' day.[153] It surprised Charles II that apprentices plundered brothels. 'Why', the perplexed monarch asked, 'Why do they go to them then?'[154]

---

[150] Harris, *London Crowds*, 22; Laroque, *Shakespeare's Festive World*, 97. Cf. the remarks of Matthew Hale also quoted by Harris in his 'The bawdy house riots of 1668', *Historical Journal*, 29 (1986), 549; John Taylor, *A Bawd, A Vertuous Bawd*, in his *Works* (2 vols.; 1630), i. 115. I must thank Bernard Capp for this reference. In fact, the bawdy house sacks were not confined to Shrovetide. See Lindley, 'Riot prevention and control', 109; Harris, 'Bawdy house riots'.

[151] PRO SP 16/205/33.

[152] For example, John Gwillim?, *The London Bawd with Her Character and Life*, 4th edn., 1711, ed. R. Trumbach (Garland Series: Marriage, Sex and the Family in England 1660–1800, 17, 1985), 8.

[153] PRO SP 14/199/90.   [154] Quoted by Pepys, *Diary*, ix. 130.

Much the same dilemma has taxed later generations of historians, who have usually resorted to some form of the anthropologically tested safety-valve theory to obtain their explanations, and like Peter Burke, Steven Smith, or Roger Manning characterize the sacks in vivid terms as 'festive misrule', 'carnivalesque misrule', or a 'ritualized' attack. In this season of misrule the apprentices were allowed to plunder dens of immorality, pull down brothels, and punish keepers, and in so doing they let off 'natural' steam, expelling lust, rage, and passion, thereby defining acceptable sexual conduct for the rest of the population to imitate.[155] Historians of England at least have arguably used terms like 'misrule' or 'inversion' rather uncritically hitherto, and have rarely addressed questions of contextualization and conceptualization. Misrule is a teasing word with its promise of subversion, parody, and comedy. It has been argued that it not only provides a way of understanding popular customs in former centuries, but also raises questions about the nature of youth culture. Yet the London Shrovetide sacks suggest that we must seek further clarification of the provenance and meaning of misrule.

The precise history of the sacks is unclear, one problem being the relative silence of medievalists on Shrovetide in the capital.[156] The absence of the records of City Quarter Sessions before the seventeenth century and the very irregular survival of Middlesex Sessions materials further obscures our sense of timing. So, poor documentation is one problem.[157] However, the journals and repertories of city government are complete, and charges of Shrovetide disorders enter the journals of Elizabethan London in the 1570s.[158] 'Football plaie' attracted as much hostile comment as

[155] The value of the safety-valve theory for the historian has been colourfully demonstrated by Peter Burke, *Popular Culture*, ch. 7. The quotations are taken from his 'Popular culture in seventeenth-century London', in Barry Reay (ed.), *Popular Culture in Seventeenth-century England* (1985), 35–6; S. R. Smith, 'The London apprentices as seventeenth-century adolescents', in Slack, *Rebellion, Popular Protest and the Social Order*, 231; Roger Manning, *Village Revolts: Social Protest and Popular Disturbances in England 1509–1640* (Oxford, 1988), 81. Cf. Cressy, *Bonfires and Bells*, 18.

[156] Hanawalt comments that 'The destruction of brothels associated with Shrove Tuesday in the early modern period does not appear in the medieval court records' (*Growing up in Medieval London*, 125).

[157] Cf. Archer, *Pursuit of Stability*, 3.

[158] But we should never assume that the records of government are themselves complete; an order may not have been entered for a particular year, for example. However, the long absence of such complaints in the Journals before 1570 is surely significant. Ronald Hutton writes about 'the development of Shrove Tuesday into a major time of misrule for London apprentices' at this time, though he is mainly relying on the research of other scholars (*Rise and Fall of Merry England*, 188).

any other disorder at this time. There are in fact no references to sacks in Elizabethan materials.[159] They enter the records of Middlesex Quarter Sessions in the early seventeenth century,[160] but the records of city government in that period usually restricted comment to generalized outbursts about Shrovetide disorders. If we seek some historical commentary in these sources we are left with vague remarks about the recent past. In 1622, for example, the Privy Council referred to 'disorders and tumults' committed in 'former years', and to 'insolencies and disorders' which had troubled the city 'for some years last past', and in 1629 wrote to the mayor and aldermen in a critical, satirical tone—'Although it is soe well knowne unto you as that it needes not to be repeated which have beene the insolencies and disorders comitted heretofore upon Shrove Tuesday'.[161] James Harrington called the brothel sacks 'customary', a word which carries a poignant sense of long continuance and distant origins. The precise chronology of Shrovetide brothel sacks is as yet unclear, though some historians suggest that their association with Shrove Tuesday belongs to the early years of the seventeenth century.[162]

The character and function of the sacks has received little detailed attention hitherto,[163] and most historians are often content simply to mingle a few contemporary phrases with appropriate anthropological references. We know little about official attitudes and the participants remain distant characters. It so happens that there is contemporary support for parts of the safety-valve explanation. Shrove Tuesday was, after all, the day of play before Lent. John Selden has left us an account of the meaning of Shrovetide—'What

[159] Archer, *Pursuit of Stability*, 3.

[160] For a chronology of the early Stuart sacks see Lindley, 'Riot prevention and control', 109.

[161] CLRO Remembrancia V, fos. 150–1; VIII, fos. 17ᵛ–18; IX, fo. 182. See also VIII, fos. 24–4ᵛ.

[162] For example, Rappaport, *Worlds within Worlds*, 10; Manning, *Village Revolts*, 213. Clearly many problems linger regarding the chronology of the sacks. We still possess no convincing explanation for the alleged 'sudden interest' in sacking brothels in the early years of the seventeenth century. On the other hand, I am not convinced by Archer's argument (following Yarborough) that 'it seems unlikely that the tradition was so recently developed because the most convincing explanation for the selection of the brothels as targets lies in the onset of the stricter moral regime associated with Lent, and the quest among apprentices for an outlet for their struggles with their sexuality' (*Pursuit of Stability*, 3). This argument depends on the sacks being seen within the sanction of official approval and tolerance of Shrovetide disorder, that the majority of participants were apprentices, and the rather dubious proposal that apprentices had few sexual options at this time. There is good reason to dispute all of these points, or at least to qualify them.

[163] However, Keith Lindley in his 'Riot prevention and control' has much to say about Shrove Tuesday as part of a broader discussion of policing and order in early Stuart London.

the Church debars us one day she gives us leave to take out another [that is, Shrove Tuesday]', he commented, 'first there is a carnival and then a Lent'. In 1627 a group of rioting sailors claimed that the apprentices were 'licensed to perform acts of violence' on Shrove Tuesday.[164] On occasion, the sackers were called the 'reformers of vice' and James Harrington claimed that the routs were part of the apprentice's 'ancient administration of justice at Shrovetide'.[165] 'A Ballad in Praise of London Prentices and What They Did at the Cockpitt Play-House in Drury Lane' (1617) praised the 'merry men' and 'brave prentices' for plundering the playhouse and 'far surpassing their previous 'chronicles of glory'. It presented the apprentices as vigilant moral commentators

> Now sing we laude with one accord
> To these most *digni laude*
> Who thus intend to bring to an end
> All that is vile and baudie
> All players and whores thrust at a' dores
> Seductive both and gawdie
> And praise we these bold prentizes.[166]

Indeed, apprentices appeared in other guises as overseers of justice and morality in London, taking a leading part in the food riots in the hungry 1590s, adopting a high profile in the anti-alien reaction which was partly motivated by perceived inequalities in the labour market, and protesting against unfair monopolies.[167]

The brothel sacks of early Stuart London arranged for the days before Lent with their cast of lusty young men seem to provide irresistible raw material for the meaning of the safety-valve theory. Yet we are never told exactly who is allowing the carnival to proceed and the day's sport to begin. Where does official permission come from; which bench of magistrates or governors is extending holiday misrule and permitting radical social inversions? At this point there is often significant silence, and historians tend to descend into unhelpful generalizations which mask more than they reveal. Thus Peter Burke simply refers to the 'upper classes'.[168] We search in vain in the records of central and city government for even a gesture of support for the actions of the Shrovetide sackers.

---

[164] Selden is quoted by John Brand, *Popular Antiquities*, ii. 64; CSPV 1626–8, 125.

[165] Sir Thomas Overbury is quoted in Brand, *Popular Antiquities*, ii. 90; James Harrington is quoted by Harris, *London Crowds*, 22.

[166] Charles MacKay (ed.), *A Collection of Songs and Ballads Relative to the London Prentices and Trades* (Percy Society, 1, 1841), 94–7.

[167] See Archer, *Pursuit of Stability*, 6; Manning, *Village Revolts*, 204, 206; Andrew Pettigree, *Foreign Protestant Communities in Sixteenth-century London* (Oxford, 1986), 292, and ch. 9.

[168] Burke, *Popular Culture*, 201.

There is no official favour or sympathy to be found in the words and orders of magistrates. Instead we discover a chorus of complaints and stringent measures to prevent disorder. In the holiday envisaged in the corridors of city government young people would not even be allowed to step outside their master's door unless they were sent on necessary business.

Writing to the mayor of London in 1631, the Privy Council poured anger upon the recent sacks adopting near formulaic rhetoric to present them as plain 'ryotts and tumults', 'insolencies', and 'disorders'. Common Council in turn issued orders to the trained bands in 1618 describing 'divers great and notorious outrages having of late yeares beene comitted in the tyme of Shrovetide'.[169] The troublemakers were variously called 'loose and dissolute', 'idle and loose', 'lewd and ill affected', 'idle and riotous', and portrayed as a 'disordered multitude'.[170] Patience was clearly limited if it had ever existed. Writing in 1617 John Chamberlain trusted that the company who 'pulled down seven or eight [bawdy] houses and defaced five times as many' would hang 'as yt is more than time they were'.[171] In the 'great sack' of that year extensive rioting broke out at four locations—Drury Lane, Wapping, Finsbury Fields, and St Katherine's. The crowd 'broke the prison' at Finsbury Fields and 'let out all the prisoners', and attacked officers ('beatinge the sheriffe from his horse') as well as the institutionalized immorality of bawdy houses and playhouses ('theyr cheefest spleene')—they 'entered the house and defaced yt cutting the players apparell all in pieces and all theyr furniture, and burnt theyr playbookes'.[172] The King was 'much moved' and 'appointed a publique sessions' as well as ordering that the trained bands 'be drawne out into the fields' in future years. This 'insolency' also prompted the Privy Council to urge the city authorities to fill the vacant office of provost marshal with people 'extraordinarie both of courage and discretion . . . assisted with a sufficient number of fellowes' to police the holiday season.[173] In fact, the next year was a quiet holiday and the 'prentises did litle harm'.[174]

---

[169] APC iii. 311; v. 208, 225; CLRO Jour. 30, fo. 283. There are many other similar references in the records of city and central government.

[170] For example, CLRO Remembrancia IV, fos. 91–3; V, fos. 150–1; VI, fo. 182; VIII, fos. 17ᵛ–18, 125ᵛ; Jour. 30, fo. 283. Again, these remarks can be discovered in many other places in the sources.

[171] PRO SP 14/90/105.

[172] Ibid.; PRO SP 14/90/135. These feats were recorded in the ballad 'In Praise of London Prentices', quoted above.

[173] CLRO Remembrancia IV, fos. 91–3.

[174] PRO SP 14/96/23. However, it was reported that 'they had a cast at New Bridewell beyond St John's Street, and pulled downe two or three houses at other places'.

Rather than breaking the dams of restraint and permitting misrule to have the upper hand, the Shrovetide season sharpened the
concern with order, youth, and family government—it was said that
'no proclamations, no authority [and] no force could disperse' the
1617 sackers.[175] London's governors attempted to keep young
people safe inside the household by issuing orders for curfews. In
March 1595, for example, Common Council issued one of a regular
series of Shrovetide precepts 'for preventing of sundry outrages
which through the negligence and want of care of the masters over
their families and servants might happen' in the city, liberties, and
suburbs. Aldermen were to instruct their ward beadles to give
'streight charge and commaundment in her majestie's name' to all
householders to 'keepe all their apprentices and servants in such
good order and due obedience' in Shrovetide. Nor were magistrates slow to introduce the threat of committal proceedings against
careless masters who permitted their young underlings to 'wander
abroade in the streetes or out of theire company' without any 'lawfull
and necessarie' occasion.[176] Curfews were introduced as part of a
general call to holiday order which also fixed watches at strategic
points like the gates and the traditional recreational areas, and
increasingly turned to the trained bands for additional assistance in
the early seventeenth century.[177] In 1618, for example, the city governors with the memory of the previous year stirring anxieties issued
a precept 'for mustering on Shrove Tuesday' to boost holiday defences. The 'discreet and hable' men of the trained bands armed
with pikes and muskets were to patrol potential trouble-spots from
5 a.m. to 9 p.m., adding their support to the household curfew and
the setting of a 'good and substantial double watch' in the same
hours 'to ryde and assist the sheriffs'. The trained bands were set
at 'fit' locations across the city. In 1623 400 were placed in
Moorfields, 200 in Smithfield, and a further 200 'on or neere Tower
Hill'. The eight captains were allocated fifty pounds of powder and
'a convenient quantitie of matche', and were paid thirty-five shillings each to prevent 'ryotts and tumults'.[178]

The Privy Council posted 'express and frequent direccons' to the
city about order in Shrovetide, and there is not even a whisper

[175] PRO SP 14/90/135, George Gerrard writing to Carleton.
[176] CLRO Jours. 23, fo. 370; 24, fo. 93ᵛ. See also Jours. 22, fos. 156ᵛ, 257, 366; 24, fos. 192,
274ᵛ; 25, fos. 28ᵛ, 147ᵛ, 238, 322.
[177] For examples of annual orders regarding Shrovetide watches and curfews see CLRO
Jours. 26, fo. 170ᵛ; 31, fos. 12, 152; 36, fo. 224ᵛ; 37, fos. 35, 268ᵛ.
[178] CLRO Reps. 37, fos. 105ᵛ–6. See also Reps. 38, fo. 61; 41, fos. 241ᵛ, 273ᵛ; 53, fos. 110ᵛ,
139ᵛ.

of official toleration in this stream of correspondence but only concern—the limits of misrule. The safety-valve was stopped up.[179] The sacks stained the image of the city, heaping 'blame and slander' on magistrates, and upsetting the 'royal peace' of the monarch who kept a close eye upon proceedings from his neighbouring royal seat.[180] Periodic reports about the poor performance of the trained bands raised further anxieties.[181] The routine form and punctuality of the Shrovetide decrees is one indication of the resolution of rioters in flocking each year to the scene of previous disorders. They often returned in numbers. In 1610 Robert Netherwood was charged with 'sondrie misdemeanours' at Bridewell. He had announced that 'he would bring 500 persons upon Shrove Tuesday to pull downe the Fortune playhouse'. Reports of the size of the crowd ranged from hundreds to thousands. The Venetian Ambassador described 'a body three or four thousand strong'. One witness claimed that 'nigh 10 or 12 thousand' sacked the playhouse in Drury Lane in 1617,[182] though figures can of course be manipulated to excite outrage, or to call for greater efficiency. On occasion, governors presented an image of a city under siege with 'great multitudes' combining to the 'great danger' of the city.[183] There were injuries on both sides and a few deaths.[184] This was no mere holiday prank. Shrovetide posed serious threats and the authorities attempted to construct defences and punish offenders. The crowd was not sheltered by a cloak of misrule.[185] The author of *The Book of Days* remarked that the sacks continued 'partly under favour of *a privilege which the common people assumed*' at Shrovetide 'of breaking down doors for sport'[186] [emphasis mine].

At least from the middle decades of the sixteenth century it appears that what approval existed for Shrovetide misrule derived from the people; that any earlier consensus about the nature of holiday conduct had long since shattered; and that governors and sections of the people disputed the meaning of customary rituals

[179] CLRO Remembrancia VI, fo. 182.
[180] CLRO Jour. 30, fo. 283; Remembrancia V, fos. 150–1.
[181] CLRO Rep. 37, fos. 108ᵛ–9. Cf. Rep. 46, fo. 126; Lindley, 'Riot prevention and control', 122–4.
[ ] BCB 5, fo. 410, CSP V 1617–19, 247; PRO SP 14/90/135, Lindley, 'Riot prevention and control', 110.
[183] For example, CLRO Jour. 30, fo. 283.
[184] For example, CLRO Reps. 27, fos. 169, 173ᵛ, 175ᵛ; 43, fos. 245ᵛ–6; Lindley, 'Riot prevention and control', 125, n. 80.
[185] Cf. Laroque, *Shakespeare's Festive World*, 101, 'The municipal authorities were also on the *qui vive* and were likely to intervene when things went too far'.
[186] Chambers, *Book of Days*, i. 239.

and holidays. In 1622 the Privy Council was seeking 'a reall reformacon of that lycentious and rude custome formerly used by base and lewd persons at Shrovetyde'. Thomas Dekker believed that the apprentices 'take the lawe into their owne hands and doe what they list'. Ben Jonson reported that 'they compell the time to serve their riot'. While the Venetian ambassador called Shrove Tuesday the day of their 'furious misrule and impetus'.[187] Pepys had in mind another holiday when he claimed that the crowd were only 'taking the liberty of these holidays to pull down bawdy houses'. Such shady places, after all, were illegal and, Pepys remarked, 'one of the great greviances of the nation'. So, to some extent they were a 'consensual target', conferring a degree of broadly interpreted if unorthodox legitimacy upon proceedings—the 'ancient administration of justice at Shrovetide'. A group of masters claimed that the sackers were only doing the magistrate's work.[188] But by 1560, if not before, the authorities had decided that clear rules needed to be imposed upon the popular taste for days of misrule.

The structure of participation in the sacks has also been relatively neglected hitherto because historians have tended to recycle the safety-valve theory almost as a matter of course, and interpret Shrovetide misrule as one aspect of the youthful struggle with sexuality in a society which offered young people few opportunities to escape the dull rhythm of the working year and the narrow limits introduced by close supervision. The sacks, therefore, were the timely antics of apprentices, peeling off excess lust before the season of abstinence. It is true that people made the connection between Shrovetide and youth, and that this holiday was in large part conceived of as a problem of youth and household discipline both in the representations in literary materials and magisterial endeavour. The curfew was intended to keep young people within the compass of their master's authority. But there is also much contemporary comment which suggests that apprentices were not the only group to take to the streets in Shrovetide to commit 'great and notorious outrages'. John Taylor remarked that 'the unruly rabble' who plundered the 'most famous bawdes' did 'falsely take upon the name of London prentices'. John Strype claimed that the leaders of the 'apprentices' were not apprentices but 'forlorn companions, masterless men, tradeless, and the like'. John Chamberlain accused 'the prentises, or rather the unruly people of the suburbs' of taking

---

[187] CLRO Remembrancia, V, fos. 150–1; Dekker and Jonson are quoted by Laroque, *Shakespeare's Festive World*, 99, 97; CSPV 1617–19, 247.

[188] Pepys, *Diary*, ix. 129–30; Harris, *London Crowds*, 24.

the main part in the sack of 1617, and there is other evidence that the crowd travelled from all points of the city and neighbouring areas. 'Like a flash of lightening', the Venetian Ambassador commented, 'they change from place to place.'[189]

The descriptions of the participants by the authorities must be treated with care for they were laced with invective. They are, however, interesting. The letters passing between the Privy Council and the Guildhall rarely stated that brothels were sacked by apprentices alone. In 1629, for example, the Council took steps to prevent 'ryotts or tumults' by apprentices 'joyneng with other loose and dissolute persons which abound in these parts'. 'Loose and dissolute' or 'lewd and ill affected' others are often described as significant participants. In 1617 the Council wrote to the mayor to review a recent Shrovetide 'insolencie' committed by 'a disordered multitude of which though manie were apprentizes yett the greatest number were roagues and vagabondes and vagrant persons'.[190] These identifications of the crowd could have represented attempts to disgrace the apprentices by associating them with a vagrant and disorderly fringe, and at one stroke tarnish the image of the Shrovetide crowd as a united company of youth and busy moral policemen. Yet they revealed a common anxiety in governing circles; that the apprentices would join with other troublesome groups for which there is much evidence on this and other occasions, including threats by unpaid sailors to join with the apprentices to plunder the capital's brothels.[191]

The judicial sources show that many Shrovetide rioters were indeed apprentices. In March 1606 fourteen males were committed to London Bridewell (and Richard Sheppard to Newgate) 'for their outrages and disorders comitted on Shrove Tuesday . . . in the Moorefields'. Eight 'aggrevators of the tumult' are named in the records. Sheppard was described as a masterless man; five others were described by their trades, and at least two of them were apprentices. Three people were arrested for their part in a 'riotus rout on Shrove Tuesday' in Finsbury Fields. Two are given no trade in the courtbooks and they were sent to Newgate. While a third, George Coles, a locksmith's apprentice, was dispatched to Bridewell.

---

[189] Taylor, *Works*, ii. 98; Strype is quoted by Manning, *Village Revolts*, 213; PRO SP 14/90/105; CSPV 1617–19, 247. See also Lindley, 'Riot prevention and control', 110, 116.
[190] CLRO Remembrancia IV, fos. 91–3; VI, fo. 182; V, fos. 150–1; VIII, fos. 17ᵛ–18, 125ᵛ; Reps. 27, fo. 173ᵛ; 37, fos. 105ᵛ–6; APC iii. 311; vi. 235.
[191] CSPV 1626–8, 125. Cf. Lindley, 'Riot prevention and control', 113, and *passim* for the broad spectrum of problems raised by disorderly apprentices and others in the period; Archer, *Pursuit of Stability*, ch. 1.

Another five apprentices were arrested in the Norton Folgate rout of 1608. Seven apprentices were bound over at Middlesex Quarter Sessions in 1615 for sacking Joan Leake's bawdy house in Shoreditch, though in 1610 one Katherine Brome was charged with 'ayding and assisting to the apprentices on Shrove Tuesday'.[192]

Sadly, the sources often give only the bare information of name and sometimes status and/or occupation, and rarely proceed to discuss matters of motivation and organization. The profile of the Shrovetide crowd and its contemporary description would repay further research. 'Apprentices', which is often used as a generic term by all sorts of contemporaries, disguises more than it reveals. Interestingly, Peter Earle has argued that it was 'quite often' used as 'a synonym for youth in general'.[193] More than this, it could have been a convenient catch-all to categorize an otherwise mixed bag of apprentices and other 'loose' groups including unpaid soldiers and sailors, vagrants, and the unemployed. This connection is much more explicit in those revealing references to apprentices and others in communications between the city and the crown. Interestingly, 'significant others' are attached to apprentices in other types of disturbance, and they will be discussed shortly. It is important to proceed beyond simple uncritical allusions to the safety-valve theory and the alleged tactical indulgence of magistrates when investigating the sacks because misrule (and Shrovetide) was many things to many people. The ritual misrule which marked that day seems to solely derive from the values, traditions, and expectations of the crowd, and perhaps moral codes associated with the apprentices in particular. They may have acted under cover of a penitential cloud which hovered over London with Lent so close at hand, though we may be chasing religious significances when it is inappropriate to do so. It is ultimately misleading to reduce layers of meaning to a single source, and catch the motives of governors, apprentices, vagrants, and unpaid sailors in the same explanatory framework. The Shrovetide crowd was an intricate thing composed of different faces, though apprentices clearly had a leading part. Nor did all of London's apprentices plunder playhouses and bawdy houses in Shrovetide. Where should we place John Woodstock, a grocer's apprentice and a regular caller at Black Luce's brothel? He was

---

[192] CLRO Rep. 27, fo. 171; BCB 5, fos. 92, 94ᵛ; CLRO Rep. 34. fo. 49; Lindley, 'Riot prevention and control', 110; J. C. Jeaffreson (ed.), *Middlesex County Records* (4 vols.; Middlesex County Record Society, 1886–92), ii. 49–50, 96–7.

[193] Peter Earle, *The Making of the English Middle Class: Business, Society and Family Life in London 1660–1730* (1989), 104.

taken to 'The Nosse Keyes' at Paul's Wharf by John Addis, his fellow apprentice, and told the Bridewell court that Addis 'brought him to Mrs Ripley who kept the howse on Shrove Tewesdaye . . . and he spent xiid and Addes vs'. How many other apprentices would have preferred to be inside a bawdy house with Woodstock and Addis rather than outside trying to pull it down?[194] Just as the Shrovetide crowd was not composed of identical parts, the apprentices were a multifarious group with a variety of attitudes, experiences, occupations, and social pedigrees, though they have also been interpreted (like the bawdy house sackers) as a distinct and homogeneous body.

6. *Apprentice Culture?*

Apprentice culture in urban society is one of the best-documented and widely researched aspects of early modern youth culture. In fact, it has been elevated to the pedestal of historical orthodoxy. Peter Burke (following Steven Smith) has suggested that London's apprentices inhabited 'a subculture with a strong sense of fraternity' and a long tradition of collective action, which was praised in song and print—tales of chivalry and heroism amongst apprentices fighting for King and country in distant lands, romance, morality, and social mobility (the inevitable Dick Whittington). We are told that a sense of solidarity could stretch across a city and gather apprentices together in a single sentiment or voice, which could break forth in political activity, in some other outbreak of collective disorder, or in more gentle form as shared recreation, including reading matter.[195] We could be best served going to urban records to hunt for traces of formal youth groups. That urban society presented opportunities to further social bonding among young men is beyond doubt. Alehouses, bawdy houses, and other leisure sites offered one interpretation of manhood. Yet youthful experiences in urban society and in particular collective forms like 'apprentice culture' (and the existence or otherwise of formal youth groups) require further investigation.

There is evidence that apprentices acted as a single group sparked

---

[194] BCB 3, fo. 228ᵛ. Cf. 3, fo. 2 July 1578. (The date of the case is given in the absence of pagination.)

[195] Burke, 'Popular culture in seventeenth-century London', 34; Smith, 'London apprentices'; Ann Yarborough, 'Apprentices as adolescents in sixteenth-century Bristol', *Journal of Social History*, 13 (1979); Bernard Capp, 'Popular literature', in Barry Reay (ed.), *Popular Culture in Seventeenth-Century England* (1985), esp. 200-1, 208-9.

by one strain of thought, though it is descriptive and often derived from the commentaries of magistrates and ministers. Civic orders, for example, and the rhetoric of moralists were directed at a group who are given the collective title, 'the apprentices', though it is an interpretative leap to produce these identifications as evidence of common sympathies circulating among actual apprentices. They were intended to draw attention to the particular target for prescriptive measures—youth; apprentices or servants residing in individual households. Again, Smith and others have suggested that the genre of apprentice literature assisted in creating a distinctive subculture.[196] Yet problems of contextualization are seldom considered. We possess little evidence of readership, and little trace of the spirit in which texts were read and digested.[197] That a text selects its audience and dwells on its pretended unity does not prove the reality of fraternal fidelities in everyday life, though it may satisfy an emotion or impulse, and flatter consumer taste with heroic tales of brotherhood, military organization, and the thrill of battle.

Beyond these scattered proclamations and narratives there are a few signals that some people thought of the apprentices as a corporate body in London. We are told that the cry of 'prentices and clubs' could quickly summon a crowd of young men.[198] This group-portrait entered the imagination and memory. In 1584 a gentleman announced that 'the prentizes were but the skumme of the worlde', and in 1627 rioting sailors warned that 'that they would join with the apprentices on Shrove Tuesday' and hatch a memorable rout.[199] This impression of unity was dispersed in print, news, and rumour, and conspirators and gossips outside London pinned their hopes on the help of the capital's apprentices. They included an Essex husbandman who was overheard by his parish clerk uttering 'certeine seditious wordes' in the churchyard in 1640, and Bartholomew Steer and his 'seditious' comrades who planned to march on London from Oxfordshire in 1596.[200]

We have also seen that many adult observers accused London's apprentices of sacking brothels in Shrovetide. Nevertheless, I have argued that identifications of the crowd must be treated with care;

---

[196] See esp. Smith, 'London apprentices'.

[197] However, David Cressy suggests that London's servants and apprentices were 'extraordinarily literate', *Literacy and the Social Order: Reading and Writing in Tudor and Stuart England* (Cambridge, 1980), 129.

[198] Valerie Pearl, *London and the Outbreak of the Puritan Revolution: City Government and National Politics, 1625–43* (Oxford, 1961), 107. Cf. PRO STAC 8, 178/2.

[199] T. Wright, *Queen Elizabeth and Her Times* (2 vols.; 1838), ii. 227; CSPV 1626–8, 125.

[200] PRO SP 16/454/37; 12/261/10–10ii; 12/262/4.

that they raise questions not only about the profile of the London crowd, but also processes of naming and reporting.[201] We need to dig deeper and discover what contemporaries had in mind when they used the title 'apprentices'. The descriptions of other serious disturbances (some of which have been closely if not wholly associated with the apprentices) provide further glimpses of the place of the apprentices in the crowd. 'Significant others' were present on other riotous occasions, though the language of description as it unfolds in different reports and over a few days is never entirely consistent. It is, in fact, fluid. The food riots in Southwark in 1595 provide just one example.[202] A further disturbance followed quickly on the heel of these riots. In June 1595 'a crowd of apprentices'[203] marched to Tower Hill meaning to plunder gunmakers' shops and, it was later reported, spoil the 'welthy and well disposed inhabitaunts', and pluck the sword of authority from governors.[204] Common Council gathered on the next day to still this protest, and was informed that 'divers and sundrie lewd and seditious apprentices and others' had contrived 'sundry tumultuous ryots and unlawful assemblies' to the 'greate disquietnes of the whole citie'. Aldermen were ordered to make 'speedy and diligent search' for 'persons that weare partakers in the riotts and tumults made by apprentices'. A stream of reports followed, and four days later Common Council noted attempts to snatch some rioters from 'publique officers', and made a further identification of the 'great assembly' which now consisted of 'multitudes of a popular sorte of base condition whereof some are prentices and servants to artificers'. The version of events had changed, and naming patterns had shifted considerably. The 'routs' were now revealed as being 'compounded of sundry sortes of base occupation and some others wanderinge idle persons of condition of rogues, vagabondes, and some colleringe their wanderinge by the name of souldiers returned from the warres'.[205]

Much the same sequence of shifting description can be followed

---

[201] See above, pp. 158–60.
[202] CLRO Jour. 24, fo. 22ᵛ. Cf. Archer, *Pursuit of Stability*, 1–2. See also CLRO Jours. 21, fo. 347ⁱ, 22, fo. 421, 24, fo. 26.
[203] The identification is Archer's, *Pursuit of Stability*, 1.
[204] Ibid.; see also R. B. Manning, 'The prosecution of Sir Michael Blount, Lieutenant of the Tower of London, 1595', *Bulletin of the Institute of Historical Research*, 57 (1984), 222.
[205] CLRO Jour. 24, fos. 25ᵛ, 29. The mayor of Newcastle informed the Privy Council that the vanguard of the crowd which gathered on the second day of the 1633 Shrovetide disturbances in the city was formed by at least sixty people, 'most of them being apprentices' who were supported by 400 'people of all sorts': PRO SP 16/233/60.1.

in other riots. In the Lambeth disturbances of 1640 the naming of the crowd, which in State Papers Domestic opens with instructions to the City, Westminster, and Middlesex justices to quickly set 'double watches' to check the movements of apprentices, servants, and vagrants, turns to more 'universal' descriptions of 'base people', 'idle and lewd persons', 'rebellious and insolent persons', or 'base and disorderly people' in the next few days.[206] Reports of the crowd in the 'December days' of 1641 first enter State Papers on 28 December, and we can trace the turns in naming over the following two days as news rushed around the city, fresh facts were incorporated, and a more complete picture emerged. Early commentaries do not closely inspect the crowd, they refer instead to 'great numbers of people'. But by 30 December Captain Robert Slingsby described how 'the prentices and baser sort of citizens, saylers, and watermen' gathered 'in greate numbers every day at Westminster armed with swords, halberds, [and] clubbes'. More significantly, both Thomas Walkley and Thomas Evans who were examined on 30 December gave information about '200 persons; who came from Westminster and '*went by the name of apprentices*'[207] [emphasis mine].

It is said that apprentices (or those calling themselves by that name) sported political colours in the Revolution, Restoration, and Exclusion Crisis, taking sides, expressing opinions, petitioning, demonstrating, and rioting.[208] They were treated as one constituency in the struggles between competing parties to tap support for their programme. These are striking intimations of mutuality and association, and reveal that young people in urban society in particular moments of political strife displayed a degree of political participation and consciousness which is seldom attributed to plebeians at this time. They may have brought a particular voice or set of priorities to these wider disorders. Nevertheless, we require further work on the social profile of crowds of alleged apprentices. Which trades did they belong to; were they older or younger youths?[209] The study of a few well-documented riots suggests that

[206] See PRO SP 16/453/16–19, 43, 61–3, 81–2; CLRO Remembrancia VIII, fos. 126–6ᵛ.

[207] PRO SP 16/486/99–114.

[208] See esp. Brian Manning, *The English People and the English Revolution* (1976), esp. ch. 4; Pearl, *London and the Outbreak of the Puritan Revolution*, esp. ch. 4; Harris, *London Crowds*, esp. ch. 7 and 41–50; Lindley, 'Riot prevention and control'.

[209] And were they all (*pace* our argument regarding brothel sacks) apprentices? Manning has produced evidence of the diverse nature of the London crowd in the early years of the Revolution, which shows artisans and 'masterless' people engaging in political activity alongside apprentices and others (*English People*, esp. 90–1). The significance of information about the ages and trades of apprentices also applies to other outbreaks of collective disturbance by people identified as being apprentices, including the periodic assaults on foreign

the title 'apprentices' must not be accepted at face value. We need to complicate the structure of this London crowd, explore its parts, and treat the apprentices as one potential layer. When this is done, it is not a simple step to produce collective disturbance as one segment of a much broader 'apprentice culture'.

The idea of 'apprentice culture' requires further examination. As we have seen historians tend to turn to contemporary texts targeting apprentices for evidence, or scattered episodes of disorder which have an illustrious place in the traditions of London life.[210] Yet we hear little about the more commonplace aspects of daily life, and we must fill in the intervals between these notable episodes to investigate the identities, enmities, and loyalties which were forged in the household, workplace, alehouse, and other recreational moments. It is perhaps misleading to relegate the body of apprentices to such tidy generalizations as 'apprentice culture'. If we explore experiences more closely a multitude of particular worlds come into view; rings of apprentices (and other youth) whose allegiances were structured by social class, for instance, age, wealth, occupation, neighbourhood, or religious belief. Godly apprentices distanced themselves from their reprobate peers. While older apprentices with greater prospects of getting money could participate in a different social round, and some tribute may have been paid to their senior status. Inequalities existed inside the household and outside its walls in the streets and markets where apprentices of lower-status trades rubbed shoulders with young people of higher social class.[211] These sentiments were not easily swallowed up by a sense of participating in a broader loyalty like 'apprentice culture'. Squabbles about precedence and demarcation scarred relations between the trades in London. They were sliced into two camps—the twelve worthy companies and the rest—and further dissected by more subtle distinctions within these two groups.[212] The related snobberies of status, wealth, and occupational prestige cut sharp vertical lines into the amorphous body of London apprentices.[213]

ambassadors and their retinues, the bawdy house sacks, and combat with other groups like foreigners and servingmen.

[210] See Burke, 'Popular culture in seventeenth-century London', 31

[211] Cf. Earle, *Making of the English Middle Class*, 105; and Chs. 4 and 6, below.

[212] The most impressive recent discussion of the significance (and limits) of community within guilds is in Archer, *Pursuit of Stability*, ch. 4, who also gives us a flavour of potential disputes between different companies, ibid. 146–7. Cf. Earle, *Making of the English Middle Class*, 105, who suggests that trade identities 'were much more important to the young men than the fact that they were all apprentices'.

[213] Cf. Vivien Brodsky Elliott, 'Marriage and Mobility in Pre-Industrial England . . .' (unpublished Ph.D thesis, University of Cambridge, 1978), esp. part 1, ch. 3.

Such occupational rivalries could explode, as Pepys reported, into pitched battles between the apprentices of rival companies. He tells the tale of a 'fray' between butchers' and weavers' apprentices in Moorfields ('between whom there hath been ever an old competition for mastery'). The butchers 'were soundly beaten out of the field, and some deeply wounded and bruised'. The young weavers left the field trumpeting their victory 'calling "A hundred pounds for a butcher"'.[214] Some young butchers also had sour relations with fishmongers. In 1599 Humphrey Homesley and Anthony Pennington, two fishmonger's apprentices, were charged with 'abusing and miscalling a butcher in the Stocks and giving very bad words against all the butchers there being a matter very like to make an uprore betweene the servants of both companies'. They admitted slapping the nose of a butcher's lad because he walked into the Stocks crying 'fougthe what stinking fishmongers be theis'. Homesley claimed that a butcher threw the first punch as he 'stept oute of his standinge', but another fishmonger grabbed him while Homesley 'stroke him divers blowes'. The fracas would have turned 'very dangerous [the court was told] if the other butchers in the Stocks had come and taken parte in it'.[215]

Young men of the same trade lived in the same neighbourhood or street; they moved in the same circles amongst peers and in the same spaces at the markets; and they shared free time drinking, gaming, and whoring. Even the fishmongers and butchers along the Shambles came together in less heated moments to plan fine suppers with hired fiddlers and whores.[216] In April 1630 the 'severall apprentices and servants' of eight weavers all dwelling along Grub Street were sent in to Bridewell 'for breaking the stocks newly set upp in Moorefields' and other 'misdemeanours'. Three weaver's apprentices were arrested in the following month 'for assembling themselves amongst a multitude of other apprentices and lewde persons beating upp the drum in a tumultuous manner in Little Moorefields'.[217] There are other reports of young people marching and trooping in military fashion in the streets. They may have watched the manœuvres of the trained bands with an admiring eye, pored over the tales of heroic apprentices, or they may have themselves been called to some type of martial training.[218] In 1615

---

[214] Pepys, *Diary*, v. 222–3.   [215] GL MS 5770/1, fos. 209–10.

[216] BCB 3, fos. 376ᵛ, 24 Sept. 1579, 26 Sept. 1579, 3 Oct. 1579. See also ibid. fos. 5 Oct. 1579, 14 Oct. 1579.

[217] CLRO Rep. 44, fos. 200–200ᵛ, 229.

[218] In March 1639, for example, fifty boys from Bridewell and Christ's Hospital were selected to train with drum and fife, CLRO Rep. 53, fos. 154–4ᵛ.

householders were instructed to 'cause their children and apprentices ymediately to surcease' from 'trooping and trayning' and striking drums in the streets. Eleven years later it was reported that 'much danger and hurt have happened amongste the boyes and youthes of this citty by their late meetinges and marchinges togeather with pikes, shotts, swords, and the like'. Sadly, these records leave no trace of what these marches were designed to evoke and represent, though the possibility of local or occupational colouring should not be lightly discarded.[219] As we have seen, the Bridewell apprentices were known as the 'Bridewell boys' or 'blewcoat boys', and they were distinguished from another group called the 'Roebuck mob'. In June 1620 some of the Bridewell 'boys' 'being abroad' were 'challenged by the lads of St Martin's parish to play at cudgells'. They were interrupted by a passing constable and 'a company of rogues with a bromestaff', who chased the Bridewell 'boys' through Blackfriars striking those they caught. The constable later claimed that their 'indecent carriage and striking att the doores and using terrible wordes put his wife being great with child into a great fright to the great indangering of her health'. A Bridewell artisan in turn accused him and the St Martin's boys of uneven and rough 'carriage'.[220]

These fragments permit us to trace the rough shape of some aspects of youthful identities in early modern London, which as in fourteenth-century Florence, late Renaissance Venice, or eighteenth-century Paris were shaped by membership of a certain trade, class, or neighbourhood.[221] Such narrow affiliations of occupation and locality make only sparse appearances in contemporary sources, and seem to raise little comment. They may have been momentary expressions of youthful camaraderie possessing no lasting place in metropolitan life. This seems rather improbable. It is far more likely that these silences imply a certain tacit tolerance towards the exploits of groups of youth on the part of both magistrates and people so long as they remained within well-defined limits and did not take to the streets on troublesome days, or create uproar which threatened to unsettle the city or the smooth course of socialization—late night conviviality, for instance, a Shrove Tuesday rout, raucous play, or some other type of brawl

---

[219] CLRO Jours. 29, fo. 314; 33, fo. 267. The role of youth in representing communal or neighbourhood identities has been well researched in Europe. See, for example, the recent discussion by Robert C. Davis, *The War of the Fists: Popular Culture and Public Violence in Late Renaissance Venice* (Oxford, 1994), esp. 58–9, 117–27.

[220] BCB 6, fos. 189–9ᵛ.

[221] Cf. Mitterauer, *History of Youth*, 196; David Garrioch, *Neighbourhood and Community in Paris, 1740–1790* (Cambridge, 1986), 58–9; Davis, *War of the Fists*.

Nor was apprenticeship the sole form of potential youthful solidarity in early modern London. The young men of the Inns, for example, or journeymen, could lay claim to a distinct interest.[222] They could share grudges or recreations,[223] and engage in periodic displays of solidarity against other groups of young men. Apprentices stirred squabbles and scuffles with foreigners, young men of the Inns of Court, servingmen, and the 'pages and lackeys attending' upon 'noble and honorable personages'.[224] In September 1590 Common Council moved quickly to quell a 'discord lately risen betwene the gentlemen of Lincolnes Inne' and certain servants, apprentices, and 'others'. It was reported that 'some apprentices and others being masterless and vagrant persons in and about the suburbs' attacked Lincoln's Inn 'breaking and spoyling' chambers. A royal proclamation imposed a curfew upon apprentices and further limitations on the movements of journeymen and others 'wandering abroad about the citie'. Common Council also made sure that 'good order' was 'taken with the said gentlemen by the auncyents and governors' of the Inn. In a much smaller fracas, Thomas Gent of the Middle Temple called an apprentice 'roague and base roague', and told him that 'he was a better man than he or anie prentice in London', prompting another apprentice to give him 'a box on ye eare with his fist'.[225]

Peter Earle writes that 'it is wrong to think of the [London] apprentices as a homogeneous group since, despite a superficially similar status and experience, they differed one from the other as much as adolescents as they were to do later when they had completed their terms'.[226] At present, this interpretation seems to have a firmer empirical footing than grander assertions of a neater (and more universal) unity, which are partly derived from the alleged persuasive narratives found in the 'apprentice literature' and evidence of collective disturbances hatched by apprentices. 'Apprentice culture' thus fragments into smaller clusters, and it is difficult to stretch a single consciousness across the territory of a town at any point in time. Yet the experience of youth in London and other towns did purchase some shared emotions and sympathies. Particular identities and interests could be subdued in certain moments of

---

[222] The most recent discussion of journeymen in early modern England is in Rappaport, *Worlds within Worlds*, 238–44. See also R. A. Houston, *Social Change in the Age of Enlightenment: Edinburgh 1660–1760* (Oxford, 1994), 93–101. Cf. Truant, *Rites of Labor*.

[223] See, for example, PRO SP 16/459/102; CLRO Rep. 16, fo. 107.

[224] See Archer, *Pursuit of Stability*, 3–4; CLRO Jour. 20(2), fo. 277.

[225] CLRO Jour. 22, fos. 417ᵛ, 421; PRO STAC 8, 156/1. See also GL MS 11,588/1, fo. 279.

[226] Earle, *Making of the English Middle Class*, 104–5.

political fervour and passion. It is far safer when sketching the rough idiom of apprentices in urban society to complicate their aspirations and round out their experiences. It is time to approach the notion of 'apprentice culture' and more universal categorizations like youth culture and youth groups with appropriate care, and with a string of qualifying remarks in our possession.

7. The Common Identity of Youth?

The common identity of youth has stirred much debate amongst historians who have searched for the forms of organization and unity of purpose which gave the youth a place in the structuring of past societies. It has been argued that misrule provides a context in which to explore the character and purpose of formal youth groups or abbeys in sixteenth-century France. These groups were highly organized with distinctive titles and positions, and served as a comic, moral voice of the community with special responsibility for marriage entry and the domestic and sexual mores of both the married and unmarried members of the community.[227] Formal groups of youth (though in towns they tended to be mixed groups of adults and young people) with much the same characteristics have been located in distant points of continental Europe spreading in a broad curve which connects France to Scandinavia and Romania, and returns to the Mediterranean in northern Italy.[228] But apart from a stray chapbook we have yet to discover an equivalent of these *formal* and *organized* groups in England, though Bernard Capp comments that *The Pinder of Wakefield* (1632) 'points at least to the strong probability, then or earlier, of organized adolescent groups with a measure of formal recognition acting as guardians of social morality'.[229] It is true that such texts can offer precious glimpses of cultural representations, but it is important to recover the form and meaning of vanished existences with the support of other sources. In fact, Natalie Davis comments that formal groups of youth 'perhaps' existed in England, and Mitterauer puzzles about their apparent absence in the English countryside. We are also told that 'nothing

[227] Natalie Zemon Davis, 'The reasons of misrule' in her *Society and Culture in Early Modern France* (Oxford, 1987); Robert Muchembled, *Popular Culture and Elite Culture in France 1400–1700*, trans. L. Cochrane (Baton Rouge, La., 1985), 95–7; Mitterauer, *History of Youth*, ch. 4.

[228] Davis, 'Reasons of misrule', 109; Mitterauer, *History of Youth*, 160.

[229] *The Pinder of Wakefield*, 1632, ed. E. A. Horsman (English Reprint Series, 12, Liverpool, 1956); Bernard Capp, 'English youth groups and *The Pinder of Wakefield*' in Paul Slack (ed.), *Rebellion, Popular Protest and the Social Order in Early Modern England* (Cambridge, 1984), 218.

so highly organized as the French abbeys of misrule' existed across the ocean in New England.[230]

There are naturally examples of young men in England participating in rough music, charivaris, and other forms of ritual ridicule, though unlike the French cases these events have not yet been proved to be age-specific or the particular tactic of the youth group.[231] Nevertheless, there are examples of young people acting as moral exemplar, pricking the conscience of older folk. Youth associations or confraternities existed in late medieval England. Duffy believes that they 'were clearly institutions giving some form of religious and social expression to peer groups within their communities'.[232] But they did not rouse the young to establish French style abbeys instituted by young men for the participation of young men. The nature of the sources which rarely record specific ages is unhelpful, but there are few examples of age-specific charivaris in early modern England. George Greene's young 'crue' in *The Pinder of Wakefield* launched a riding to repair Goodman Patience's household. He was married to a 'goodly gossip', 'a ranke scold that after honeymoon was past began to call him rogue and rascall instead of Lord and master'. A boy was dressed in 'apparell like the woman and a man like her husband', and they were put on a horse and carried 'throw the towne' to the tune of bagpipes, brass kettles, gridirons, tongs, and shovels. Greene's young gang marked the moral limits of the community, helping both to define and defend its integrity and territory. They challenged the servants of neighbouring wealthy

[230] Davis, 'Reasons of misrule', 109; Mitterauer, *History of Youth*, 176–7; Roger Thompson, *Sex in Middlesex: Popular Mores in a Massachusetts County, 1649–1699* (Amherst, Mass., 1986), 90. Bernard Capp argues that membership of a youth group was 'More often, probably . . . determined by a sense of local, occupational, or institutional identity rather than by ideological considerations' ('English youth groups', 213). Natalie Davis ('Reasons of misrule', 122), suggests that although what she calls 'the traditional youth group lasted for a very long time in the countryside and to some extent in smaller towns, the conditions of big city life were dissolving it by the sixteenth century, except in the colleges and the urban upper class, in favour of formal groupings based on profession or occupation or neighbourhood or class'. See also Mitterauer, *History of Youth*, esp. 154, 196.

[231] Martin Ingram, 'Ridings, rough music and the "reform" of popular culture in early modern England', *Past and Present*, 105 (1984), 104–9; E. P. Thompson, 'Rough music' in his *Customs in Common* (1991), esp. 468, 496, 511–12; Gillis, *For Better for Worse*, 81. See CUL EDR B/2/18, fos. 41, 175, 258ᵛ; Guilding, *Reading Records*, iii. 208. Cf. Mitterauer, *History of Youth*, 167, 'The unmarried youth are not always the only perpetrators for in England' others were involved. 'But the general association of these customs with the organized male youth groups is indisputable.'

[232] E. Duffy, *The Stripping of the Altars: Traditional Religion in England 1400–1580* (New Haven, 1992), 150 (see also 147–8, 151). Cf. Robert Whiting, *The Blind Devotion of the People: Popular Religion and the English Reformation* (Cambridge, 1989), 90, 105, 107, 111, 112; David Palliser, 'Civic mentality', 233.

clothiers, and tackled a host of local nuisances, including a litigious 'knave', 'a great lyer', a cutpurse, a Puritan barber, and a pack of robbers.[233] The noise and 'great wrong' of another 'young riding' interrupted the calm of the cloisters of Christ's Hospital in London during the night of Michaelmas Day 1630. It was reported that certain 'young fellowes . . . made a disordered and uncivill riding . . . in reproach' of the 'song scholemaster' and his wife. The 'chiefe instrument' of the riding was the teacher's maid who reported 'some difference' between her master and mistress to the other servants. The Hospital governors moved quickly to punish this 'mutinous revell' and 'disgracefull manner of riding'. The servants were ordered to confess their fault on their knees and beg for pardon. While the maid was instructed to submit to her master and mistress for uttering 'disgracefull speeches' and spreading rumours.[234]

Apart from a few scattered examples in dispersed archival and literary sources, the evidence for the existence of age-specific charivaris and formal youth groups in early modern England is wafer-thin. The Christ's Hospital incident is a rare case of a youth riding. Nor is there much evidence that gangs of young bachelors roamed the streets of towns after dark hunting women and organizing collective rapes as Jacques Rossiaud suggests young 'victims of boredom' often did in medieval and sixteenth-century France,[235] though there are of course many examples of groups of young men passing through dark streets *en route* to the alehouse or the bawdy house. Violence, whoring, eating, drinking, and gambling were all part of the rough male culture which acted as some sort of *rite de passage* for numerous sections of male youth.[236] There is also evidence that young people (especially young men) did organize feasts and drinkings which imparted a sense of age-differentials. The young men of Henry Newcome's town gathered at 'quarterly feasts' for 'all that are out of their time and unmarried'. These convivial congregations represented 'a linking of young men into good fellowship before they are entered into the world and must all be brothers

---

[233] *Pinder of Wakefield*, 7–10, 14–17, 35–9, 41–3, 44–8, 53–6; Capp, 'English youth groups', 215–16.

[234] GL MS 12,806/3, fos. 561–2.

[235] J. Rossiaud, *Medieval Prostitution*, trans. L. G. Cochrane (Oxford, 1988), ch. 2. In fact, the records that I have consulted suggest that rape was usually perpetrated by males acting alone in the domestic theatre. See, for example, BCB 1, fo. 79; 3, fos. 359, 363, 19 Aug. 1579; 4, fo. 437ᵛ; 5, fos. 3, 182ᵛ, 189ᵛ, 245ᵛ; CUL EDR 12/21, 1641–2; B/2/14, fo. 20ᵛ; B/2/28, fo. 86ᵛ; NRO NMC 9, fo. 77.

[236] See the many episodes recorded in this and subsequent chapters, and also BCB 2, fos. 161ᵛ–2, 164, 165, 167, 168ᵛ, 169, 171, 198ᵛ.

[Newcome further reports] and so cannot meet in the streets but must go together to drink'. Newcome's reproving tone colours every phrase. This 'combination' or 'confederacy of ye yong men to ye feasts and meetings [was] a sad omen to ye towne', and could only result in 'a sad succession' if 'yong men link on ys fashion'. Josiah Langdale was lured by his 'playfellows . . . to feasts where young men and women' gathered 'to be merry'. While in a much later period John Clare introduced his readers to a 'cottage' which 'was called the bachelors hall'. It was 'a sort of meeting house for the young fellows of the town', and here they would 'sing and drink the night away'.[237] Yet on these occasions and others under review in this chapter, there is only a faint glimmer of prior sophisticated organization of the sort we associate with formal youth groups. All of which provides extremely provoking glimpses of the nature of youthful existences in early modern England, and one possibility is that young people did not form single associations of youth in any remotely structured sense or ritual fashion either to expel or satisfy lust, or to keep a careful eye on the morals of local society. It could be argued that they were unlikely candidates for this regulatory role, and that it would be surprising if magistrates and moralists gave their consent given the chorus of outrage that usually descended on the age of youth from their pulpits, books, and courtrooms.

We have yet to discover in early modern England a formal youth group like the French societies made familiar by Natalie Davis with their close affiliations, separation of roles, titles, and ranks, and that mocking voice testing the community for whispers of moral or marital irregularity. There is not even a faint echo amongst the London apprentices.[238] We could in fact be hunting in the wrong place and time. Davis writes that 'the conditions of big city life were dissolving it ['the traditional youth group'] by the sixteenth century'. While Mitterauer comments that the early modern period 'saw the beginning of a general decline [in youth groups], although relics survived into the most recent past'. Both Protestants and Catholics, he continues, 'were strongly opposed to the rural youth fraternities', though Peter Burke argues that 'traditional festivities'

---

[237] *The Diary of the Reverend Henry Newcome From September 30 1661 to September 29 1663*, ed. T. Heywood (Chetham Society, 18, Manchester, 1849), 148, 155; FHL MS Box 10/10, 1–3, fo. 5; Clare is quoted by Ben-Amos, *Adolescence and Youth in Early Modern England*, 179.

[238] Cf. Rappaport, *Worlds within Worlds*, 9, 'there is little evidence that in sixteenth-century London the disorderly behaviour of young men was initiated by organised youth groups, occurring within the framework of ritual, or was functional in the sense elucidated by N. Z. Davis in her study of festive customs and organisations in early modern France'.

proved more enduring in the great cities of Catholic Europe—
Paris, Madrid, Naples, or Rome.[239] But even in the fields and villages of sixteenth-century England the formal youth group has left
no apparent trace, save for the niggling presence of *The Pinder of
Wakefield* teasing us with its credible representation of a French
abbey. However, we have not yet picked up a faint tremor of youth
misrule of this type sending a shudder through disordered households and the ranks of other neighbourhood reprobates in archival
materials.

Michael Mitterauer argues that the early spread of manufacturing
in the English countryside and high levels of mobility may have
been significant, reducing the scope for setting up youth groups,
which tended to prosper in more stable and traditional worlds.[240] It
has also been suggested that the quick rise of the alehouse as the
social hive of the local community also offered an interior focus for
social life, and pulled people away from the open spaces of fields
and churchyards, which had served as the chief location for communal sociability in earlier periods.[241] It may be that the significance of formal groups of youth in former centuries has been
predicated upon specious assumptions. Thus their steady decline
has been proposed as one precondition for the making of the
modern family.[242] More seriously, Mitterauer suggests that the rising availability of 'private space' for young people in more recent
times marks a meaningful break with earlier customs and structures
because it smoothed the path for the rise of what he calls 'informal'
youth groups with a bare minimum of organization, and 'no rituals
of eating and drinking, courting, and dancing'.[243] The poverty of
Shorter's account of a modern family bursting into first bloom at
some point in the eighteenth century has been demonstrated by
others. I also hope to show in this book that young people had a
great deal of 'private space' and creativity in early modern society.
Indeed, the neat partition of collective youth activity into 'formal'
and 'informal' associations at particular points in time is clearly
misleading as English materials offer many glimpses of this sort of
'informality' in the sixteenth and seventeenth centuries.

[239] Davis, 'Reasons of misrule', 122; Mitterauer, *History of Youth*, 187, 161 (see also 196);
Burke, 'Popular culture in seventeenth-century London', 38.
[240] Mitterauer, *History of Youth*, 176–7. Cf. Ben-Amos, *Adolescence and Youth in Early Modern
England*, 175–6, 205–6.
[241] See below, esp. pp. 200–1. Cf. Thomas Brennan, *Public Drinking and Popular Culture in
Eighteenth-century Paris* (Princeton, 1988), esp. 152–3.
[242] Thompson, *Sex in Middlesex*, 83, conveying Edward Shorter's ideas.
[243] Mitterauer, *History of Youth*, 226–7.

The nature of sources consulted raises a further point. The formal youth group clearly existed in one form at this time, in the printed page of chapbooks and other literary genres on both sides of the channel. But there are very few references in archival materials. Has the author of *The Pinder of Wakefield* been steering us along a false trail? Is the formal youth group only a paper image? The great majority of references in Natalie Davis's highly influential account of youth groups are in fact derived from creative literary sources. This does not reduce the significance of the quest; it is not a question of devaluing different types of sources, but of exploring the points of contact between them. Nevertheless, one objective for future work is to study the youth group as a literary representation or trope whose relationship with daily life remains a matter of dispute.

This discussion turns on how we define youth groups. We can puncture ideas about highly structured and polished associations, but what is left behind when we peel away these illusory tissues? We need to draw the distinction between formal youth groups with a political function, and more 'casual' associations who gathered to talk, play, drink, eat, gamble, and whore away their time, engaging in some of the bold posturing and subversive impudence which magistrates attributed to 'ill-advised and ill-nurtured youth'. This opposition is also that between Mitterauer's 'formal' and 'informal' groups, though he wrongly seeks to slice these forms of activity into separate epochs. I want to question interpretations of organized youth groups, but I am also very anxious to retain a sense of youth culture—of creative formative experiences of youth and peer association—in early modern society. The interpretation of youth culture is itself a contested issue, though it should not be confused with the existence (or otherwise) of formal groups of youth.

Young people did not need to be organized in these sorts of groups to share formative experiences, or to be perceived as an enduring problem in Tudor and Stuart society. In fact, the greater part of evidence for this third characterization of youth derives from situations of conflict—interventions to tame the rash temper of 'ill-advised and ill-nurtured youth'. In some respects youth was a series of 'contrary experiences', befitting an age which could be depicted as 'contested territory' in which good uneasily coexisted with bad. We discover young people in service, acquiring the requisite skill and capital to claim a place in adult society, and perhaps attending divine service, but these same youngsters could also seek other experiences of 'illicit' adventure, camaraderie, rough play, courtship, and the bachelor's social round at the alehouse and brothel (which is more fully discussed in the next chapter). We have already glimpsed the rough shape of the world of conviviality and play, which implicitly (and sometimes explicitly) challenged the controlling authority structure of householder, minister, and public magistrate, with its neat portrait of family life and orderly age-relations. The next chapter, which further explores particular aspects of this world and attempts by governors to control it, seeks to incorporate additional tales from the archives, not only to continue our discussion of formative experiences of youth, but also to help us to more fully reconstruct the contours of the problem of conflict and control in early modern age-relations.

4

The Church and the Alehouse

The problem of youth was firmly rooted in the minds of early modern magistrates and ministers—the distance between 'ill-advised and ill-nurtured youth' and the civil young hero of the conduct book was great indeed. How could young people be reduced to 'honest' citizens, or would the model characters of the sermon and text remain a mere paper image? It was hoped that young people would remain within the political compass of a 'fit' master's authority. Nevertheless, youth was not a passive experience. Young people responded in a variety of ways to the pressures of being socialized. They were obedient, indifferent, meek, resigned, keen, or 'mutinous'. They mingled aspects of conformity and opposition in the same progress to adulthood. The affection, company, and respect of other young people were key arbiters of behaviour and taste. This 'compound youth' blended elements of adult guidance like practical work skills, practical piety (e.g. church attendance and basic knowledge), and local lore with youthful conviviality and play. The cheer of the alehouse or games and other 'rough' pastimes were more exciting than the frugal and temperate existence anticipated by contemporary moralists. Young people were being presented with the conventional morality of early modern society, and they were able to accept or reject its sense of their future destiny.[1] They could also juggle priorities and strike a balance between their aspirations and the terms of formal authority structures. This middle territory is the best place to situate the experiences of early modern youth because it rejects polar points of conformity and opposition as final interpretations, while accepting both as key aspects of growing up.

The struggle by magistrates and ministers to exert control over the world of youthful conviviality and play is an inevitable tension in all societies which face the difficulties of managing the transition

[1] Cf. R. W. Scribner, 'Reformation, carnival and the world turned upside down', in his *Popular Culture and Popular Movements* (1987), 84–5.

from childhood to adulthood. Yet the problems arising from socializing young people have particular situations and meanings in different contexts. For this reason interpretations of socialization, for
example, juvenile delinquency, or youth itself are always shifting.
The problem of youth at this time was in large part an issue of a
person's relation with service—the expected experience of plebeian youth. It was felt that late-night conviviality, the perils of dancing,
or the temptations of whoredom could all be bridled by accom-
plished household discipline. This was how young people were
evaluated by those in authority. Moreover, the post-Reformation
era arguably introduced fresh or more urgent demands for the
regulation of the time (e.g. sabbatarianism and curfew), space (e.g.
the churchyard, street, and green), and mores of youth.

In this chapter which develops the theme of a youthful milieu
outside the 'safe' compass of structures of authority, we will approach familiar issues like religious commitment and recreation
from a youthful perspective to further explore peer association,
formative experiences, and issues of conformity and opposition.
The question of regulating youth is not only one of prescriptive
institutions and instruction, but also of *responses.* It will be clear by
now that the image of youth given in such repositories of dominant
ideologies and institutions as conduct books, civic or guild ordinances, and apprenticeship indentures was a pale reflection of daily
life. We must seek all sides of youthful experiences, conformity as
well as opposition, to construct a flexible interpretative model. We
will first explore one aspect of conformity by introducing some of
the godly youth of early modern England. These young 'mirrors of
piety' had a rough passage to religious conviction, and the stories
of their troubled youth are an indication of tensions in more general
depictions of youth—that essential ambiguity which was the subject
of the first chapter. Later sections will pick up the discussion of
religious commitment and the special role of the Church in shaping
the time and manners of youth.[2] We will go to divine service with
young people, and follow them to the alehouse and village green
to trace further expressions of identities which communicated the
difference of the ages in entertainment, dress, and hair-styles. These
distances also help us to spot changing styles or values within the
long age of youth. We will also be able to say something further
about the social construction of gender roles in youth, and to return to the question of other influences apart from the conceptions

[2] A discussion which commenced with the brief survey of catechizing in Ch. 2.

of authority which affected growing up. But we will first turn to a few success stories whom one contemporary christened the 'sons of wisdom'.

1. *The 'Sons of Wisdom'*

The Reformation, with its emphasis upon a return to original purity, mocked the traditions and familiar routine of a 'wicked' world with a range of symbols of lost innocence, regeneration, and youth. Each fresh wave of renewal clearly recognized the importance of the rising generation, and we are told that Protestants made a special appeal to the young, who were always willing to be rallied to a fresh cause.[3] In fact, Patrick Collinson has characterized the English Reformation as being partly 'a revolution of youth', and similar claims have been made for continental Reformations.[4] Susan Brigden has shown that some of London's apprentices, for example, gave the reformers' message a warm welcome.[5] In these whirlwind years of swift change and fast-altering allegiances older folk were said to be lost among their beads or images and 'out of date'.[6] But whether or not this early spark was prolonged throughout the sixteenth century and beyond is a matter of debate.[7] Above all, we should

---

[3] Cf. C. John Sommerville, *The Discovery of Childhood in Puritan England* (Athens, Ga., 1992), 22, and 79–80; Susan Brigden, 'Youth and the English Reformation', *Past and Present*, 95 (1982); Phillipa Tudor, 'Religious instruction for children and adolescents in the early English Reformation', *Journal of Ecclesiastical History*, 35 (1984), esp. 393; the remarks of Samuel Burrowes in *Good Instruction for All Young Men and Maids* (1642), 11; and the remarks of Richard Baxter regarding the special appeal of separatists for the 'young and raw sort' in *Reliquiae Baxterianae, Or Mr Richard Baxter's Narrative of the Most Memorable Passages of His Life and Times* (1696), 41. Erik Erikson writes that the age of youth 'finds expression in the movements of the day', in the 'riots of a local commotion' or in 'the parades and campaigns of major ideological forces'. Youth requires 'movement' and 'locomotion'. In turn, new movements always seek to 'harness youth in the service of their historical aims' ('Youth, fidelity and diversity', in Erikson (ed.), *Youth: Change and Challenge* (1963), 10). Cf. H. Moller, 'Youth as a force in the modern world', *Comparative Studies in Society and History*, 10 (1968).

[4] Patrick Collinson, *The Birthpangs of Protestant England: Religious and Cultural Change in the Sixteenth and Seventeenth Centuries* (Basingstoke, 1988), 36. Cf. Brigden, 'Youth and the English Reformation'; Stephen Ozment, *The Reformation in the Cities* (New Haven, 1975), esp. 123; Gerald Strauss, *Luther's House of Learning: The Indoctrination of the Young in the German Reformation* (1978), 299.

[5] Susan Brigden, *London and the Reformation* (Oxford, 1989), esp. 97–8, 119, 193, 329, 406, 419, 534, 598–600, and 604–20.

[6] See Keith Thomas, 'Age and authority in early modern England', *Proceedings of the British Academy*, 62 (1976), 45; John Stockwood, *A Sermon Preached at Paules Crosse on St Bartholomew's Day 24 August 1578* (1578), 55.

[7] A recent summary of research is Dairmaid MacCulloch, *The Later Reformation in England 1547–1603* (Basingstoke, 1990). Collinson has recently presented the 1580s as a 'moral and

perhaps stress the persisting *ambivalence* of the contribution of youth to the social history of the Reformation. On one side we can glimpse pious youth, but on the other we read narratives of irreverence and immorality. But more numerically significant are a large group of youth whose experiences cannot be fully represented in terms of either piety or profanity. They fall between these extremes in a middle ground which included elements of orthodoxy and the whims of youth in the same view of appropriate preparation for adulthood and salvation. What is very clear, however, is the intention of the godly to 'strike while the iron is hot', and to carry their message to young people—the hope of future years.[8]

While perceiving youth as a wild, lusty, and hot age, the godly were not unaware of the strategic necessity of proposing a counter-attraction to worldly pleasure—an appropriate outlet for youthful energy and passion. Contemporary accusations that pious people were grave and solitary killjoys inhabiting a cultural wasteland[9] were opposed in pulpit oratory and careful prose. Evangelical authors claimed that religion could be both fun and exhilarating. 'Do not think that religion is an enemy to your mirth, pleasure, and delight', Henry Hesketh told his young audience, 'it is no melancholy thing' for 'you may sing, rejoyce, and be merry [because] God envies you nothing but sin'. Religion, Hesketh declared, 'will make you truly cheerful.'[10] What was the nature of the alternative pious and sober culture recommended to young people?

Moralists did not, of course, oppose the idea of recreation, rather they reserved their hottest invective for profane and excessive leisure,[11] and placed firm limits upon the forms and purposes of youthful pastimes. Time was not to be squandered on unprofitable and by extension probably improper pursuits, and even free time was

cultural watershed' in which the Reformation broke with its recent past. As a result of this 'second Reformation' the reform largely lost its early youthful gloss. The fresh wind of change became stilled by a new establishment. Tactics also changed and reformers spurned popular songs and plays, for example, in favour of a sterner type of pedagogy—catechisms, sermons and psalms—with the result that Protestantism became less 'popular in character' (*Birthpangs*, esp. ch. 4; id., *From Iconoclasm to Iconophobia: The Cultural Impact of the Second English Reformation*, Stenton Lecture 1985 (University of Reading, 1986), esp. 4). Cf. Tessa Watt, *Cheap Print and Popular Piety, 1550–1640* (Cambridge, 1991), esp. 41–2, 134–9, and 324–5.

[7] See above, Ch. 1.

[9] See, for example, the insults Susan Kent hurled at her local 'proud puritans', quoted by Martin Ingram, *Church Courts, Sex and Marriage in England 1570–1640* (Cambridge, 1987), 120–1.

[10] Henry Hesketh, *The Importance of Religion to Young Persons* (1683), 27.

[11] For example, see *The Diary of the Reverend Henry Newcome from September 30 1661 to September 29 1663*, ed. T. Heywood (Chetham Society, 18, Manchester, 1849), 146. Cf. Christopher Hill, *Society and Puritanism in Pre-revolutionary England* (1964), 197 ff.

closely monitored. Dudley Fenner presented a typical commentary—
'christian recreation' was a 'necessary means to refresh either body
or mind that we may the better do the duties which pertain to us'.
William Perkins also cautioned that play should be 'moderate', 'lawful', and confined to 'days of labour'.[12] Moralists even recommended
'spiritual' dancing in which young men and women danced apart
as in Scripture, and 'not after our hoppings and leapings and inter-
minglings', but 'soberly, gravely, and matronly, moving scarce little
or nothing in their gestures' either 'in countenance or bodie'.[13]

Fun and diversion were poor justifications because recreation had
to be 'apt and fitting for our callings'. This was good use of time.[14]
Military activities like archery and wrestling were also deemed worthy for young men. Such martial sports were yet another expression
of manhood—they were 'manly sports'—the difference being that
they were recognized as legitimate pursuits by the authorities. As
such, they were controlled representations to be contrasted with
unregulated and violent expressions of developing masculinity at
the alehouse or on the street. Thus governors endorsed martial
training as appropriate exercise, a precaution for war, and a
worthwhile option to unlawful games and other spontaneous
expressions of manhood. In this martial plan 'every city and good
town' would 'have a common place appointed to the exercise of
youth, wherein they might at void (leisure) times exercise themselves'
in arms.[15] In London, the authorities issued orders in support of
the statute 'for the mayntenance and increase of archerye and the
abolyshinge of unlawfull games'.[16] An annual archery contest was
held at Finsbury Fields with trophies (including a golden arrow)
and an attendant 'honest trumpeter'.[17] Butts were also set up in
other places. In 1627 some of Derby's 'younger sort' agreed 'to
exercise themselves in martial discipline' rather than waste time in
alehouses and other 'unprofitable employments'.[18]

[12] Dudley Fenner, *A Short and Profitable Treatise of Lawfull and Unlawfull Recreations*
(Middelburg, 1590), unpaginated; *The Work of William Perkins*, ed. I. Breward (Courtenay
Library of Reformation Classics, 3, Appleford, 1970), 431, 471. Cf. John Downame, *A Guide
to Godlynesse, Or a Treatise of Christian Life* (1629), 269–75.
[13] John Northbrooke, *A Treatise wherein Dicing, Dauncing, Vaine Playes and Enterludes . . . Are
Reproved*, 1577? (facsimile, Garland Series: The English Stage: Attack and Defence 1577–
1730, New York, 1974), 142–3; Philip Stubbes, *An Anatomie of Abuses*, 1583, ed. A. Freeman
(Garland Series, The English Stage: Attack and Defence 1577–1730, New York, 1973), fo. N7.
[14] Downame, *Guide to Godlynesse*, 275.
[15] K. M. Burton (ed.), *A Dialogue between Reginald Pole and Thomas Lupset* (1948), 148.
[16] CLRO Reps. 16, fo. 394; 17, fo. 362ᵛ; Jours. 21, fos. 302, 448ᵛ; 22, fos. 27, 117–17ᵛ, 315.
[17] CLRO Reps. 14, fos. 54ᵛ, 522ᵛ; 15, fo. 110; Jours. 22, fo. 409ᵛ; 23, fo. 301; 24, fos. 49,
150, 229, 324; 25, fos. 86ᵛ, 191ᵛ, 286ᵛ. See also APC iii. 303–4.
[18] APC iii. 30. See also APC iv. 407; NRO NMC 7, fo. 318.

The godly also presented a culture of print and song for strong hearts and voices. Young people were invited to 'make merry in singing of psalmes and hymnes and spirituall songes'; to sing 'melodie to the Lorde in your heartes'.[19] Special sermons were arranged to persuade them to arise from worldly slumber and follow the true pious course.[20] Yet there seems to be no evidence that a religion associated with the family, individualism, and the crushing of spontaneous forms of traditional lay participation like fraternities and guilds encouraged formal groups of youth like the youth fraternities of catholic Florence studied by Richard Trexler.[21] Cotton Mather attempted to organize 'associations of young folks' across the ocean in Massachusetts.[22] But back in England the godly chose rather to contain collective worship within the close purview of a minister and householder. In his solitary hours after a long day of 'honest' work, the godly youth was expected to read such 'notable histories' as Foxe's *Book of Martyrs* and, above all, Scripture, pausing to meditate and dedicate himself to God, and always striving to 'deny ungodliness and worldly lusts' to render 'the entertainments of sense a mere trifle and a dream'.[23]

This pious life clearly engaged the enthusiasm of some young people,[24] though the minds of long-dead people are notoriously difficult to penetrate and we will never know the true extent of *committed* adherence. In his *Memoirs*, William Kiffin tells how in April 1633 when he was 17 years old, he came 'to be acquainted with several young men who diligently attended the means of grace'. They were all fellow London apprentices, doubtless living in neighbouring areas of the city and perhaps sharing trades. Their 'constant practice' each Sunday was 'to attend the morning lecture, which began at six o clock, both at Cornhill and Christchurch'. This ring

[19] Christopher Fetherstone, *A Dialogue Against Light . . . Lewde and Lascivious Dauncing*, 1582 (Scolar Press Facsimile edn., Ibstock, 1973), fos. D2ᵛ-3ʳ; Northbrooke, *Treatise*, 142-3.
[20] See Brigden, *London and the Reformation*, 444, 462, 492, 599-600; S. R. Smith, 'Religion and the conception of youth in seventeenth-century England', *History of Childhood Quarterly*, 2 (1975), 496-7; Collinson, *Birthpangs*, 102 ff; Sommerville, *Discovery of Childhood*, 33.
[21] See Richard Trexler, 'Ritual in Florence: adolescence and salvation in the Renaissance', and Natalie Davis, 'Some tasks and themes in the pursuit of popular religion', both of which can be found in C. Trinkaus and H. O. Oberman (eds.), *The Pursuit of Holiness in Late Medieval and Renaissance Religion* (Leiden, 1974).
[22] Roger Thompson, *Sex in Middlesex: Popular Mores in a Massachusetts County, 1649-1699* (Amherst, Mass., 1986), 93.
[23] Northbrooke, *Treatise*, 143; Caleb Trenchfield, *A Cap of Grey Hairs for a Green Head: Or the Father's Counsel to His Son an Apprentice* (1710), 4-5; Thomas Brooks, *Apples of Gold for All Young Men and Women and a Crown of Glory for Old Men and Women* (1662), 208-55; Hesketh, *Importance of Religion*, 19-20.
[24] See also Ilana Krausman Ben-Amos, *Adolescence and Youth in Early Modern England* (New Haven, 1994), 184-91.

of pious youth always gathered a full hour before the start of the service to pray and to tell each other 'what experience we had received from the Lord; or else to repeat some sermon which we had heard before'. Kiffin's friend, John Lilburne, followed a similar Sunday routine, and he read Cartwright, Perkins, Calvin, Beza, Luther, and, of course, Foxe, while he was an apprentice.[25] In his *History* (1706), John Crook described his years of service in early seventeenth-century London, and told how he 'came acquainted with those young people that frequented sermons and lectures so often as we had any liberty from our occasions being apprentices'. He fell in with a group of young men who gathered 'and prayed and conferred together about the things of God', and also planned regular 'private fasts and meetings'.[26]

Kiffin, Lilburne, Crook, and their pious companions were by no means unique, though one suspects that such rings of godly young men were a small minority of London's apprentices. However, the author of *The Prentise's Practise in Godlinesse* (1613) dedicated his improving tract to those 'religiously disposed and virtuous young men, the apprentices of the city of London'.[27] London's high concentration of youth and plentiful supply of preachers provided sympathetic conditions in which godly groups could prosper. Nevertheless, we also find kindred clusterings of youth outside the capital city in both urban and rural areas. In Roger Lowe's Lancashire village, for example, 'several young women and men . . . assembled together in fields' after morning service to 'hear repetition' of the day's sermon. Thomas Jolly noted how a group of 'young persons' in and around Manchester, 'set on foot . . . meetings to keep days of prayer together'. Young men and women met 'by themselves'. Across the border in Yorkshire, 14-year-old Oliver Heywood 'was entertained into the society of some godly Christians', who had been 'joyned together by the instigation of an ancient godly widow woman', and now numbered 'twenty young men and others'. The company had a fortnightly 'conference' at which they 'propounded necessary questions . . . and prayed our course'.[28]

---

[25] *Some Remarkable Passages in the Life of William Kiffin*, ed. W. Orme (1823), 11–12; John Lilburne, *The Legall, Fundamentall Liberties of the People of England* (1649), 19, 21.

[26] John Crook, *A Short History of the Life and Times of John Crook, Written by Himself* (3rd edn.; 1706), 6, 12, 8.

[27] W.P., *The Prentise's Practise in Godlinesse and His True Freedome* (1613). Cf. John Dunton, *The Life and Errors of John Dunton Late Citizen of London* (1705), 47; S. R. Smith, 'The London apprentices as seventeenth-century adolescents', in Slack (ed.), *Rebellion, Popular Protest and the Social Order*, 226.

[28] *The Diary of Roger Lowe of Ashton-in-Makerfield, Lancashire, 1663–1674*, ed. W. L. Sachse (1938), 5, 20, 49, 51; *The Notebook of the Reverend Thomas Jolly a.d. 1671–1693*, ed. H. Fishwick

Sadly, it is difficult to discover the degree to which these apparently spontaneous and informal groups were a durable aspect of the societies in which they first flourished. The entries in the literary sources are usually sparse, and tend to give a simple narrative of characters and events. They rarely extend in time beyond two or three years. But despite the fortunes of particular groups, the conditions in which they prospered (e.g. urban society with its concentration of youth) tended to be more enduring. There are also examples of people whose pious childhood and/or youth was recorded as an exemplar to prick the wavering conscience of their less virtuous older and younger peers. A succession of young prophets and saints who often displayed remarkable poise and resolution in the face of grim circumstances—which may raise our suspicions— had their stories circulated in sermons and print.[29] These paradigms of piety performed a useful rhetorical purpose, though at least one historian believes that they are sympathetic portraits.[30] The pious early life of other godly folk is recorded in biographies. It was claimed that George Trosse was a modest and civil youth, 'obedient to his parents and free from those youthful extravagances to which others of his age were addicted'; that 'the whole course' of Joseph Alleine's youth was 'an even spun thread of godly conversation'; and that John Shower 'very early discovered an inclination to the ministry and a suitable spirit and capacity for it'.[31]

George Trosse's admiring biographer provides the clue—these young saints were, of course, exceptional. They were elevated to the pedestal of godliness and civility. In his youth, William Gouge 'was more than ordinarily studious and industrious; for when other

(Chetham Society, 33, Manchester, 1895), 46, 102; Oliver Heywood, *Autobiography, Diaries, Anecdote and Event Books*, ed. J. Horsfal Turner (4 vols.; Brighouse, 1882), i. 156. Cf. Vavassor Powell, *The Life and Death of Mr Vavassor Powell* (1671), 5.

[29] For example, James Janeway, *A Token for Children Being an Exact Account of the Conversion, Holy and Exemplary Lives and Joyful Deaths of Several Young Children* (part 1, 1671, part 2, 1672); Henry Jessey, *A Looking-Glasse for Children Being a Narrative of God's Gracious Dealing with Some Little Children . . . Together with Some Sundry Seasonable Lessons and Instructions to Youth Calling Them Early to Remember Their Creator* (3rd edn., 1673); [Nathaniel Crouch], *Remarks upon the Lives of Several Excellent Young Persons of Both Sexes* (1678); Thomas White, *A Little Book for Little Children* (1660). See also Gillian Avery, 'The puritans and their heirs', in Avery and Julia Briggs (eds.), *Children and Their Books: A Celebration of the Work of Iona and Peter Opie* (Oxford 1989), 100 ff.; Sommerville, *Discovery of Childhood*, ch. 2; Alexandra Walsham, ' "Out of the mouths of babes and sucklings": prophecy, puritanism and childhood in Elizabethan Suffolk', in D. Wood (ed.), *The Church and Childhood* (Studies in Church History, 31, Oxford, 1994).

[30] Sommerville, *Discovery of Childhood*, ch. 2.

[31] Isaac Gilling, *The Life of George Trosse* (1715), 3; T. Alleine *et al.*, *The Life and Death of . . . Joseph Alleine*, appended to Alleine's *Christian Letters* (1671), 18–19; John Shower, *Some Memoirs of the Life of John Shower* (1716), 4.

scholars upon play-dayes took their liberty for their sports and pastimes, he would be at his study, wherein he took more delight than others could do at their recreations'. His cultural options settled in early life, young William was 'much grieved at the ordinary profanation' of the sabbath 'by publick sports and recreations'. Simon Forman claimed that whenever his master 'gave him leave to play, that was death or a greate punishment to him, for he would say play, play, there is nothing but play, I shall never be a good scholler'. When 'his fellowes went to playe', young Forman 'would goe to his booke, or into some secrett place to muse, meditate, or into church'.[32]

·These pious stories offer a profound sense of polarization and an early insight into the processes of social differentiation and cultural distancing, which gave the godly their particular identity and defined the large space between them and 'the great unjust rude rabble'.[33] Whether through choice, or gentle persuasion, godly young people declared their intention to withdraw from the dance and the convivial round which were the preferences of the young reprobates they left behind. Josiah Langdale, for example, recalled how he had sometimes 'withdrawn' from his friends and 'earnestly sought after the Lord'. One publisher praised a virtuous youth who sought refuge under hedges to pray in quiet solitude, while around his hedge other young people played happily. Young Vavassor Powell elected to 'leave off my old companions and to chuse others who professed religion'. Like John Crook, who 'reproved' his 'schoolfellows and companions' and walked alone with his private preoccupations while they were 'at play and pastime', he discovered comforting solitude in a 'secret place'. Calvin was remembered as 'a severe reprover of his schoolfellowes faults'. While Lancelot Andrewes, a future Bishop of Winchester, 'studied so hard when others played, that if his parents and masters had not forced him to play with them also' he would never have enjoyed a moment of leisure. 'His late studying by candle and early rising at four in the morning, procured him envie among his equals', who, however, were never able to match his pious example.[34]

[32] Thomas Gouge, *A Narrative of the Life and Death of Dr Gouge* (1665), fo. A1ʳ; Simon Forman, *The Autobiography and Personal Diary of Dr Simon Forman*, ed. J. O. Halliwell (1849), 11. It should be noted, however, that Forman's subsequent adult life was scarcely a pattern of piety. See also Crook, *Short History*, 5. Cf. Avery, 'Puritans and their heirs', 102.

[33] Cf. Patrick Collinson, *The Religion of Protestants: The Church in English Society 1559–1625* (Oxford, 1982), 190.

[34] FHL MS Box 10/10, 1–3, fo. 4; Sommerville, *Discovery of Childhood*, 60–1; Powell, *Life*, 5; Crook, *Short History*, 6; Sommerville, *Discovery of Childhood*, 58; [John Buckeridge], *A Sermon Preached at the Funeral of . . . Lancelot [Andrewes] the Lord Bishop of Winchester* (1629), 17.

Young people, therefore, were urged to seek godly company, and to shun the infectious lure of 'good fellowship', which was merely a 'specious pretence of young persons to meet and drink together'.[35] Thomas Brooks cautioned his audience that 'when your nearest friends and dearest relations stand in competition with Christ, or the things above, you must shake them off, you must turn your backs upon them'. Matthew Griffith simply commented that 'everyone is commonly like his or her company, good if good, bad if bad'.[36] Poor company contaminated pious youth and dangled the tempting bait of 'lewd' recreation and misspent time before them. We sometimes catch sight of a face at the window. The godly youth watching from behind the glass as his young peers danced on the green, or who listened with one ear to his father or master as he read from his Bible or catechism, the other ear catching the music and cheerful banter of the local dance.[37]

Yet this rather rigid representation of social and cultural distancing can be misleading. Some pious young people did venture outside their household to join the fun and laughter on the green. Even here, amongst the children of devout parents, the ebullient humour of youth could triumph over the sober disposition of 'withdrawn' and 'precise' youth; yet another sign of the ambiguity and fragility of that age. Richard Baxter recalled how as the village danced under the maypole until twilight and the sound of the tabor and pipe drifted through his father's house, he was 'many times . . . inclined to be among them and sometimes [he confessed] I broke loose from conscience and joyned with them: and the more I did it the more I was inclined to it'.[38] The authors of spiritual autobiography present their youth as a testing time of perpetual enticement and lapsing from spiritual comfort to gloomy depths of despair. Play was sorely tempting, but quick on its heels came a miserable time of sorrow and repentance. Samuel Ward kept an undergraduate diary in which he made careful note of his moments

---

[35] I am quoting Richard Burton, *The Apprentice's Companion* (1681), 80.

[36] Brooks, *Apples of Gold*, 312; Matthew Griffith, *Bethel, Or a Forme for Families* (1634), 266. See also John Dod and Richard Cleaver, *A Godlie Forme of Household Government* (1612), 66, 78; Burton, *Apprentice's Companion*, 64–5, 75–6; Trenchfield, *A Cap of Grey Hairs*, 47, 50–3, 56; William Gouge, *Of Domesticall Duties* (1622), 629; Abraham Jackson, *The Pious Prentice, Or the Prentise's Piety*, 1640 (facsimile, The English Experience, 746, Amsterdam, NJ, 1975), 82; William Martyn, *Youth's Instruction* (1612), 37, 38, 40, 44. Significantly, the majority of these works were written for masters and their apprentices and servants.

[37] Baxter, *Reliquiae Baxterianae*, 2–3.

[38] Ibid. Cf. FHL MS Box 10/10, 1–3; and the sporting exploits and remarks of Richard Conder quoted by Margaret Spufford, *Contrasting Communities: English Villagers in the Sixteenth and Seventeenth Centuries* (Cambridge, 1974), 231–2.

of remorse and youthful lapses in Cambridge—'my longing after damsons', 'my immoderate eating' of plums, cheese, walnuts, and pears, 'my immoderate laughter', 'my overmuch myrth at bowling', 'my goyng to the taverne with such lewde fellowes', and 'my adulterous dreame'. Ward's chapter of undergraduate transgressions reminds us of 'drunken' young William Perkins.[39]

These stories of godly young people, oscillating between the sober meditations of a heavy conscience and the exuberant temper of youth, provide a helpful point of entry to explore the circumstances by which pious people slowly disentangled themselves from their worldly neighbours. We can add a previously neglected age-aspect to the cultivation of religious commitment and the resulting processes of cultural differentiation.[40] Why did some young people follow a pious course of life? In many cases their early active piety appears to have been stirred by a godly relation or acquaintance who urged them to seek salvation.[41] Like Richard Baxter, the young saint was born into a pious family—a fertile breeding ground for strong commitment. William Gouge's father was 'a pious gentleman'. Thomas Hill was nurtured by 'godly parents', who dedicated their son 'unto God from his childhood'. A future Archbishop of Winchester was born 'of honest and godly parents', and 'his life was well composed and ordered even from his childhood'. While John Dunton's father took care to apprentice his son to 'a religious and just man', who was 'recommended' by a 'very intimate friend'.[42] Some people were first persuaded of the urgency of early turning to God by passionate preaching, by a chance meeting—Oliver Heywood with an 'ancient godly widow woman', and Josiah Langdale with a blind thresher—or by falling in with 'good company'—Kiffin and Crook's rings of godly apprentices.[43] While at Cambridge, John Shaw had the good fortune to be placed in Lancashire Chamber where he had 'good chamber fellowes' who shared their pious

---

[39] M. M. Knappen (ed.), *Two Elizabethan Puritan Diaries by Richard Greenham and Samuel Ward* (Chicago, 1933), 103–15. For some other examples see F. W. B. Bullock (ed.), *Evangelical Conversion in Great Britain 1516–1695* (St Leonard's-on-Sea, 1966), and above, Ch. 1.

[40] Cf. Ingram, *Church Courts*, 123.

[41] Cf. Ben-Amos, *Adolescence and Youth in Early Modern England*, 187–8.

[42] Samuel Clarke, *A Collection of the Lives of Ten Eminent Divines* (1662), 25, 85; Gouge, *Life and Death of Dr Gouge*, fo. A1ʳ; Dunton, *Life*, 33–4 (again, Dunton was not exactly a mirror of piety in later life); [Buckeridge], *Sermon*, 17. Further examples of this sort of influence can be found in Bullock, *Evangelical Conversion*, and W. K. Tweedie (ed.), *Select Biographies* (2 vols.; Wodrow Society, Edinburgh, 1845–7). Evangelical masters sometimes selected young evangelicals to be their apprentices, and some parents sought godly masters. See Brigden, *London and the Reformation*, esp. 419, and 97–8, 119, 193, 329.

[43] Heywood, *Autobiography*, 156; Barry Reay, 'Introduction: popular culture in early modern England', in Reay (ed.), *Popular Culture in Seventeenth-Century England* (1985), 3.

thoughts and virtuous ways. Roger Hough had a similar stroke of good luck. He was 'admitted of Jesus College where he fell in with the good young scholars'. *The Student's Prayer* required young people to crave the 'wisdom to make choice of the society of those [by] whose sobriety and gravity and good example I may be bettered', and to always seek 'to tread in their steps' and follow their good 'courses'.[44] Popular lecturers like Perkins at Cambridge ('who by his doctrine and life did much good to the youth of the university'), helped to prevent some young people falling prone to the 'sinnes of the university', which were listed as 'excess in apparell', 'excess in drinking', 'wicked company', and 'disobedience and contempt of authority in the younger sort'.[45]

The processes of social and cultural distancing, if only expressed as a yearning after godly company or the opportunity for solitary meditation pervade these stories of the early years of pious people. The godly frequently communicated their place in society in phrases which imply contempt, distance, and opposition.[46] They commented that godly youth were 'precious few' in number. Many young people were not *predisposed* by social or familial networks to follow a pious course. The rare qualities of that life—patience, restraint, and submissiveness—contradicted the image of 'headstrong and licentious youth' presented in the pulpit and print. The rash temper of youth provided strong opposition for moralists. 'But alas', Thomas Powell groaned, 'how few are the number of these young branches. How few are there of the sons of wisdom.' Richard Greenham believed that there were some young men, 'who notwithstanding the great prophaneness of the most . . . are so mightily preserved by the seed of grace, that they escape safely in a holy course of life'.[47] But this great escape was only made by a few young people.

Should we simply dismiss these cynical commentaries as a rhetorical trick, the trained reflexes of professional complainers, or were

---

[44] John Shaw, *The Life of Master John Shaw*, in *Yorkshire Diaries and Autobiographies of the Seventeenth and Eighteenth Centuries* (Surtees Society, 65, Durham, 1887), 123–4; *The Autobiography of Henry Newcome*, ed. R. Parkinson (2 vols., consecutively paginated; Chetham Society, 16–17, Manchester, 1852), i. 28; E. H. Emerson (ed.), *English Puritanism from John Hooper to John Milton* (Durham, NC, 1968), 185. See also William Hinde, *A Faithful Remonstrance of the Holy Life and Happy Death of John Bruen of Bruen Stapleford in the County of Chester* (1641), 20, Trosse, *Life*, 19.

[45] Knappen, *Two Elizabethan Diaries*, 130, 122; Emerson, *English Puritanism*, 185.

[46] Cf. Collinson, *Religion of Protestants*, 190–1.

[47] Thomas Powell, *The Beauty, Vigour and Strength of Youth Bespoke for God* (1676), 66; *The Workes of the Reverend and Faithful Servant of Jesus Christ Mr Richard Greenham*, ed. H[enry] H[olland] (1610), 90. Cf. Dod and Cleaver, *Godlie Forme*, 85, and the remarks of John Stock quoted by Emerson, *English Puritanism*, 194.

they grounded upon actual experiences? The sheer volume and regular tone of their evaluations may inspire scepticism, though it could also convey an authentic and perennial social concern—a problem that was never satisfactorily resolved. The regular stream of invective against youth may have issued forth from the pulpit and been written down in the seclusion of a cloistered study, but it was firmly grounded upon actual pastoral confrontations with festive and reprobate youth which are recorded in the records of ecclesiastical and secular courts.[48] In the first attempt to produce meaningful figures for the ages of offenders before the church courts, Robert von Friedeburg has discovered that the majority of culprits from the village of Earls Colne (Essex) were in fact young people who were in their teens or twenties.[49] The frequent complaints against youth in religious materials implies that there was an important age-aspect to the troubled relations between the godly and the multitude. The next section, therefore, will further explore aspects of the Church's sense of place and time as expressed in the drive to push profanity out of a newly fenced churchyard and the idea of the holy sabbath. We will look inside and outside parish churches on Sunday to see if young people were present at the service, and indeed, whether they attended in the spirit requested by the ecclesiastical authorities.

2. *Alternative Sundays?*

It has been argued that in the sixteenth and seventeenth centuries the alehouse fully emerged as the hub of popular sociability in place of the broader expanses of the churchyard and fields, which had provided the principal sites for the traditional communal culture.[50] Reformers dissected the familiar social round of communal ales, wakes, and revels, fencing off the churchyard to neatly distinguish between sacred and profane space.[51] Individuals who used sacred ground to tip rubbish or as a handy short-cut ran the risk of

[48] Cf. Eamon Duffy's remarks regarding the genesis of this literature of complaint in his 'The godly and the multitude in Stuart England', *The Seventeenth Century*, 1 (1986), esp. 32–5.

[49] Robert von Friedeburg, 'Reformation of manners and the social composition of offenders in an East Anglian clothing village: Earls Colne, Essex, 1531–1642', *Journal of British Studies*, 29 (1990), esp. 370, 373, 377–8.

[50] Peter Clark, 'The alehouse and the alternative society', in Donald Pennington and Keith Thomas (eds.), *Puritans and Revolutionaries: Essays in Seventeenth-Century History Presented to Christopher Hill* (Oxford, 1978), esp. 61–3. See also Felicity Heal, *Hospitality in Early Modern England* (Oxford, 1990), 358–60.

[51] See CUL EDR B/2/52, fo. 23ᵛ; D/2/52, fos. 8ᵛ, 24; B/9/10; B/9/12; B/9/15; B/9/52.

being presented at the ecclesiastical courts.[52] Officers were instructed to guard against 'the playeinge of children' and others in the churchyard, and to make sure that it remained free from the damage caused by profane 'playes, feastes, banquettes, drinkinges, or anie other games'.[53] The churchyard, however, provided a natural assembly point for the community every Sunday, and it was a site for gossip as well as brawls and quarrels sparked by local rivalries.[54] It was reported that the churchyard at Walden in Essex was 'profaned by the youth of the parish . . . fighting, wrestling, and [playing] other unlawfull sports'. The churchwardens of Harkness in York Diocese complained that their 'churchyard is abused with younge people for that they make it their common sporting place'. While in July 1618 the churchwardens of Stowe Maris (another Essex parish) were themselves presented 'for sufferinge the youth . . . to prophane the saboth by playeinge at unlawfull sports and games as raysinge the football in the churchyard and abusinge the name of God by most fearefull oathes, and in most rude manner playeinge at other sports', and 'abusinge themselves by fightinge'.[55]

This chapter of recorded incidents, and many more passed unnoticed or unreported, reveals a large number of sabbath day episodes. Sunday, a day of rest and a chance to escape the monotonous rhythm of everyday work for spiritual or worldly refreshment was eagerly anticipated. But it was a free day which was vigorously contested by the proponents of its proper use.[56] Sabbatarians like John Downame claimed the 'whole of the seventh day' for matters of faith and worship alone. God allocated six days 'for our own affaires' and 'imployments', and all he asked in return was a single day of

---

[52] For example, CUL EDR B/2/52, fos. 12, 24, 36, 47, 69; D/2/51, fos. 47ᵛ, 99; E. R. Brinkworth (ed.), *The Archdeacon's Court: Liber Actorum 1584* (2 vols. paginated consecutively; Oxfordshire Record Society, 23–4, 1942), 82; J. P. Earwaker, (ed.), *The Court Leet Records of the Manor of Manchester from 1552 to 1686* (6 vols.; Manchester, 1884) [hereafter *Manchester Court Leet Records*), i. 234; F. G. Emmison, *Elizabethan Life: Morals and the Church Courts* (Essex Record Office Publications, 63, Chelmsford, 1973), 267–73.

[53] See CUL EDR B/9/5; B/9/8; B/9/9; B/9/52.

[54] For example, CUL EDR B/2/21, fos. 27, 109, 113, 125ᵛ, 133ᵛ, 207ᵛ; B/2/28, fos. 89, 135ᵛ; BIHR CV/CB2, fos. 47, 56, 75; YV/CB2, fos. 29, 40ᵛ, 49; ERO D/ACA 30, fos. 75, 171ᵛ, 186; 44, fo. 34; PRO STAC 8, 96/8; 277/24.

[55] ERO D/ACA 52, fo. 207ᵛ; William J. Sheils (ed.), *Archbishop Grindal's Visitation, 1575: Comperta and Detecta Book* (Borthwick Texts and Calendars: Records of the Northern Province, 4, York, 1977), 86; W. Hale (ed.), *A Series of Precedents and Proceedings in Criminal Causes Extending from the Year 1475 to 1640: Extracts from the Act Books of the Ecclesiastical Courts in the Diocese of London*, 1847 (facsimile, Edinburgh, 1973) [hereafter, *Precedents and Proceedings*], 242. See also CUL EDR B/2/12, fos. 26ᵛ, 109–9ᵛ; B/2/18, fo. 24; B/2/35, fos. 50–50ᵛ; D/2/51, fo. 22; Brinkworth, *Archdeacon's Court*, 43, 54–5.

[56] See Hill, *Society and Puritanism*, ch. 5; Kenneth Parker, *The English Sabbath: A Study of Doctrine and Discipline from the Reformation to the Civil War* (Cambridge, 1988); Ronald Hutton, *The Rise and Fall of Merry England: The Ritual Year 1400–1700* (Oxford, 1994), esp. chs. 3–5.

'holy and religious exercises'.[57] Nevertheless, this was felt to be an unreasonable drain on free time by those like the fictional apprentice who politely enquired: 'I pray what day have we that be prentises to take our recreation in but this Sunday? For all the weeke we are kept so straight that we cannot so much as get out to speak with any friend.' The young purchased the right to play on the day of 'recreation' with their weekly sweat and toil.[58] This was, after all, a widely circulated justification for the Book of Sports (1633), which praised the virtues of 'lawful recreation' (e.g. archery, dancing, ales, and May games) after evening prayer on the sabbath. That book can serve as both symbol and symptom of the disagreement among Protestants of all shades about the suitable place of recreation on the seventh day. A painter stood on the market hill in Cambridge to inform passers-by that 'some scurvy popish bishop haith got a tolleration for boys to play uppon the sabboth day after evening prayer', and 'soe did dance and playe' before them.[59] Yet most people could agree about the value of worship, meditation, and moderate recreation on the seventh day.

The sabbath is a familiar issue, but previous historians have arguably not laid sufficient emphasis upon the extent to which the contest for the seventh day was in part a 'problem' of youth. The day of rest granted young people spare time and a degree of initiative which was in theory denied them on days of work, which had a different sense of time and obligation. Free time permitted creativity and was, therefore, suspicious and potentially subversive. In 1595, for example, a time of unease in London, governors reported that menacing and 'tumultuous stirres and uproares' were 'commonly plotted and enterprized upon sabbath dayes and holy dayes by reason of careles masters that badly govern their servants'. The tranquillity of the capital was rocked by young people who 'roamed idley abroad' meeting together outside their masters' regulatory reach, secretly 'whispering' and 'murmuring', and ridiculing the 'especiall' Sunday watch which was intended to keep a careful check upon their movements.[60] A number of towns also issued lengthy orders to further

[57] Downame, *Guide to Godlynesse*, 381–2.

[58] W.P., *Prentise's Practise*, fos. 65–5ᵛ, 64ᵛ; Fetherston, *Dialogue*, fo. A8ʳ; Burton, *Apprentice's Companion*, 154–5.

[59] PRO SP 16/293/97. The text of the Book of Sports can be consulted in J. P. Kenyon (ed.), *The Stuart Constitution 1603–1688: Documents and Commentary* (Cambridge, 1966), 99–103. See also Hill, *Society and Puritanism*, 193–201, 211; PRO SP16/265/14; 16/267/6; 16/267/90; STAC 8 180/11.

[60] CLRO Jours. 24, fos. 37, 11, 18ᵛ; 22, fo. 97. See also Ian W. Archer, *The Pursuit of Stability: Social Relations in Elizabethan London* (Cambridge, 1991), ch. 1.

'the holy keeping of the sabbath day' and elected special Sunday officers,[61] though the preamble to these ordinances painted a picture of people 'idelie sittinge at the doores in the streets and resorting unto alehowses . . . to the great grief of the godlie and better sorte of people'.[62]

Significantly perhaps, the principal penalties of the church courts —public penance and excommunication—had least impact upon the younger sections of the population and this stirred anxieties. Excommunication threatened exclusion from all local relations— sociability, commerce, and work. The particular impact of these punishments turned on the loss of credit and reputation in the public sphere, and young people, unlike householders and their wives, had little social or economic status. Established figures in local networks had more compelling reasons to safeguard their re- spectable public profile and reputation.[63] Young people (especially young men) were less sensitive to the snap judgements of gossip. In addition, the local community offered a far greater degree of tol- eration towards youthful conviviality and play,[64] and the young could also escape the attention of the authorities more easily, moving in and out of service and between different communities with appar- ent ease.[65] One Oxfordshire rector complained that servants 'are constantly shifting from place to place', and 'are likely to be always the most disorderly part of my parish'.[66] In this society, both mobil- ity and status were distinguished by considerations of age.

But did young people attend divine service on Sunday and other holy days? This question can be rephrased slightly to adjust its meaning; were the young expected to be at church? We can seek answers in ecclesiastical sources which attempted to establish a stand- ard for the population. The Elizabethan Acts of Uniformity and the Ecclesiastical Canons of 1604, for example, tell us that the Church expected those aged 14 years and above to be present at service every Sunday and holy day.[67] Nevertheless, we should not assume

[61] For example, CLRO Jours. 21, fos. 249^v, 371; 22, fo. 325^v; 23, fos. 303, 306; 25, fos. 190, 286^v; YCA B/32, fos. 5–5^v; B/33, fos. 2^v, 5–5^v, 70, 154^v, 290; B/34, fos. 29^v, 144, 215, 262; B/35, fos. 55–5^v.

[62] YCA B/32, fo. 2.

[63] Cf. J. A. Sharpe, *Defamation and Sexual Slander in Early Modern England: The Church Courts in York* (Borthwick Papers, 58, York, 1980); Ingram, *Church Courts*, ch. 10.

[64] See above, esp. pp. 117–20.

[65] Cf. Ingram, *Church Courts*, 354–7; Collinson, *Religion of Protestants*, 228–9.

[66] Quoted by Susan Wright, 'Confirmation, catechism and communion: the role of the young in the post-Reformation Church', in Wright (ed.), *Parish, Church and People: Local Studies in Lay Religion 1350–1750* (1988), 205–6. Cf. ERO D/ACA 46, fos. 106^v, 162^v.

[67] 1 Eliz I. c. 2; 35 Eliz I. c 1 & 2; Wright, 'Confirmation, catechism and communion', esp. 217.

that early modern people dutifully trooped to their church.[68] Martin Ingram believes that attendance was in many places 'primarily' the obligation of the householder—'servants and perhaps young people more generally were neither expected nor encouraged to attend regularly'.[69]

This is a difficult issue to resolve. Much of the evidence is necessarily inferential, and in the absence of registers of attendance we must turn to the observations of contemporaries and the records of the ecclesiastical courts which should be treated with caution. Official activity was not confined to periodic statements of intent. Visitation articles often infer that *every member* of the household should attend divine service, though they can also attach particular significance to the presence of householders. Grindal's 1571 Articles for York Diocese, for example, asked officials to inquire, 'Whether the people of your parish, especially householders, having no lawful excuse to be absent do faithfully and diligently endeavour themselves to resort with their children and servants to their parish church or chapel'.[70] Further evidence can be gleaned from other types of sources. The Dedham Classis, for example, instructed householders to 'carefully endevor' to 'frequent their owne churches . . . accompanied orderlie and soberly with their servants and whole family'. One of the few occasions in which the capital's apprentices could venture outside the household in time of curfew was to attend divine service 'in presence of their masters'. In April 1636 Common Council gave notice to all inhabitants to keep their servants and apprentices indoors except when they 'goe abroad . . . to there owne parishes to service and sermon'.[71] In 1610 Edward Wright appeared before the Colchester Archdeaconry Court 'for refusing to come to church with all his household', and there are other similar cases in contemporary sources.[72] Schoolmasters were also expected to bring their pupils to church 'upon all lecture dayes, holy days, and other tymes appointed by the Church'.[73]

[68] Cf. Donald A. Spaeth, 'Common prayer? Popular observance of the Anglican liturgy in Restoration Wiltshire', in Wright, *Parish, Church and People*, esp. 127, 140–1.

[69] Ingram, *Church Courts*, 106.

[70] W. H. Frere (ed.), *Visitation Articles and Injunctions of the Period of the Reformation 1536–1575* (3 vols.; Alcuin Club Collections, 14–16, 1910), iii. 266. Cf. ibid. 288, 307.

[71] R. B. Usher (ed.), *The Presbyterian Movement in the Reign of Queen Elizabeth as Illustrated by the Minute Book of the Dedham Classis, 1582–1589* (Camden Society Publications, 3rd ser., 8, 1905), 99; CLRO Jours. 24, fos. 28ᵛ, 141ᵛ; 37, fo. 173ᵛ. See also CLRO Jour. 24, fo. 18ᵛ.

[72] ERO D/ACA 32, fo. 251ᵛ. See also D/ACA 47, fo. 39; GL MSS 5770/2, fos. 71–2; 7090/2, fo. 45ᵛ; Emmison, *Elizabethan Life: Morals*, 86; Wright, 'Confirmation, catechism and communion', 208, 217–18.

[73] K. S. Martin (intro.), *Records of Maidstone Being Selections from Documents in the Possession of the Corporation* (Maidstone, 1926), 150. Cf. J. F. Williams (ed.), *Diocese of Norwich: Bishop*

One difficulty with using this material is that it rarely proceeds beyond age-titles to record precise ages, and so we are prevented from relating attendance patterns to spiritual adulthood (confirmation and the age of 'discretion' as implied by the Elizabethan Church), for example.[74] However, it appears that there was a widely held concern that children and servants should be present at divine service, if only expressed as its contrary—angry words levelled at young absentees.[75] In January 1624, for example, the Colchester Archdeaconry Court was informed that John Kent's maid had 'not beene' to church 'above twice or thrice' in twelve months. In 1618 20-year-old Robert Holcom, a churchwarden's son, admitted that he had 'never repayred' to his parish church 'in all his lyfe since he was baptised'. Thomas Ewell, a Norwich servant, was dispatched to prison by the Mayor's Court in 1615 for 'beinge asked yf he would goe to church to heare divine service [he] very obstinately answered that he wold not goe to church'. In York it was reported that 'the auncynter sorte' as well as 'yonge men neglected ther duetyes to God in not resortinge to devyne service'.[76] Young people may also have been expected to attend at certain points of the year like Easter, though prosecution for absenteeism occurs in all months of the year.

Some young people, then, never even began the walk to church, restrained by a popish master,[77] by a reprobate parent,[78] or by the pressure to work, which was more pressing at busy times in the agricultural calendar. Thus the rhythm of work sometimes contradicted the distinction between secular and sacred time. In 1617, for instance, the Ely Bishop's Court listened to the apologies of two servants, Henry and Simon Lane—that they 'in a caste of necessitye

Redman's Visitation 1597 (Norfolk Record Society, 18, Norwich, 1946) [hereafter *Bishop Redman's Visitation*], 38; John Latimer, *The Annals of Bristol in the Seventeenth Century* (Bristol, 1900), 284.

[74] Cf. Collinson, *Religion of Protestants*, 229–30.

[75] YCA City & Ainsty Quarter Sessions minute book, 1638–62, fo. 141; *The Diary of Ralph Josselin 1616–1683*, ed. Alan Macfarlane (British Academy Records of Social and Economic History, New Series, 3, 1976), 406, 454, 476–7, 547; Latimer, *Annals of Bristol*, 267. Cf. the remarks of Miles Hogarde quoted by J. W. Martin, *Religious Radicals in Tudor England* (1989), 96 (I must thank Bernard Capp for this reference).

[76] ERO D/ACA 44, fos. 9ᵛ; OUL EDR D/ᵃ/9C, fos. 40ᵛ; NRO NMC 19, fos. 9ᵛ; YCA D/ 33, fos. 2–2ᵛ, 55–5ᵛ. See also BCB 2, fo. 42ᵛ; GL MS 5770/2, fos. 71–2; ERO D/ACA 43, fo. 175ᵛ; 44, fo. 12ᵛ; 47, fo. 39; W. le Hardy (ed.), *Hertford County Records: Notes and Extracts from the Sessions Rolls 1581 to 1698* (9 vols.; Hertford, 1905–39), v. 5; *The Diary of Samuel Pepys*, ed. Robert Latham and William Matthews (11 vols.; 1970–83), iii. 194.

[77] ERO D/ACA 32, fo. 251ᵛ; Hale, *Precedents and Proceedings*, 228–9.

[78] CUL EDR B/2/36, fos. 200ᵛ–1; H. Johnstone (ed.), *Churchwarden's Presentments (Seventeenth Century) Part 2: Archdeaconry of Lewes* (Sussex Record Society, 50, Lewes, 1949) [hereafter *Lewes Churchwarden's Presentments*], 37–8.

laboured to heape a hoode of corne on ye sabbothe daye'. On 5 November 1607 Martin Foakes of Swaffham Bulbeck was duly present in church, though he had instructed his two servants to remain at home to plough his fields.[79] Other young people were kept behind to thresh and rake hay, plough, move barley, grind corn, cart, turn beer, and pluck hemp.[80] Again, governors cautioned against trading on the seventh day.[81] It was claimed that young people in the London parish of St Brides 'plotted' to stay away from church. In 1658 the vestry took 'into serious consideracon the great inconvenience of sufferinge prentices and other youth to frequent and make their meetinges in the belfrye disorderly janglinge the bells'. At these meetings 'they alsoe most impiously plott meetinges to walke abroad and neglect the church and service of God to ye spoile and distruccon of youth'.[82]

Despite many examples of voluntary and non-voluntary absenteeism from church, and the gloomy forecasts of godly authors, the often boisterous presence of young people is seen in reports of bad behaviour and some seating plans which allocated a section of the church to the subordinate young. Sunday worship was, of course, a public and social occasion too. Parishioners gathered in the churchyard, gossiping, negotiating, joking, casting aspersions, and reviewing the past week, perhaps raising their voices above a chorus of playing children.[83] Most of them made straight for their seat, though a few people loitered in the porch or churchyard. In 1661 there was 'much complaint' in St Bride's parish (London) 'of young fellowes that idle upp and downe in the churchyard and church porch dureing the time of divine service and sermon'.[84] Depending on how much space was available, some form of social partitioning sliced the church into pockets in which people were arranged according to social class, gender, and age. The young and poor as befitting their lowly status sat in the furthest reaches, though young

[79] CUL EDR B/2/36, fo. 122ᵛ; B/2/28, fo. 146. See also Spaeth, 'Common prayer?', 140–1; Archer, *Pursuit of Stability*, 89.

[80] For example, CUL EDR B/2/11, fos. 126, 164, 167ᵛ, 170, 179, 181, 190ᵛ, 191ᵛ, 192, 193ᵛ, 196ᵛ, 201, 203, 203ᵛ, 204ᵛ; ERO D/ACA 44, fo. 169; 47, fos.157, 206, 206ᵛ; 50, fo. 14ᵛ; 51, fo. 218; ORO PCBP 1626–36, fos. 3, 36, 46, 82, 89ᵛ; NRO Diocesan Records Vis 6/1; 7/1.

[81] GL MS 5770/1, fos. 342, 371.   [82] GL MS 6554/1, fo. 190.

[83] CUL EDR D/2/10, fo.14ᵛ.

[84] GL MS 6554/1, fo. 219. See also ORO PCBP 1626–36, fos. 37, 46; ERO D/ACA 32, fos. 6ᵛ, 145; 45, fo. 267; F. G. Emmison, 'Tithes, perambulations and sabbath-breach in Elizabethan Essex', in F. G. Emmison and R. Stephens (eds.), *Tribute to an Antiquary: Essays Presented to Mark Fitch by Some of His Friends* (1976), 199; id., *Elizabethan Life: Morals*, 118.

people may well have been further dissected into single-sex groups as a precaution against banter and horseplay.[85] In some churches officers brandishing 'white rods' were elected from the ranks 'of the most substantial and honest men of the parish . . . to see good order kept in the church'. In the London parish of St Margaret, New Fish St, the clerk was told to 'admonish' sleeping or talking servants, 'and with a wand to correct their stubbornnes'.[86]

Divine service was a lengthy affair, though the sermon and litany were often omitted from evening prayer. Lay spontaneity and participation were not much encouraged, with the result that worship was for many a highly monotonous and uncomfortable round of kneeling, standing, sitting, bowing, and repetition.[87] The courtbooks have their flaws and prejudices; they tend to reveal much more of the insolent and jocular aspects of daily life, and therefore tend to present the minister and 'better' or 'godly sort' struggling against an irreverent volley of jokes, gestures, laughs, and even shots—the eternal 'jangle and babble' from the middle and back benches.[88] Many instances of raucous conduct came before the ecclesiastical courts. In their records we discover parishioners sleeping and snoring,[89] drinking and vomiting,[90] brawling and quarrelling,[91] laughing and prating,[92] interrupting and 'misusing' the minister,[93] playing,[94] swearing,[95] climbing into the pulpit,[96] and bringing dogs and hawks

---

[85] See Dorothy Aston, 'Segregation in church', in W. J. Sheils and D. Wood (eds.), *Women in the Church* (Studies in Church History, 27, Oxford, 1990). This tidy model was naturally constructed to suit individual churches and local social structures. Again, the period under review was a time of transition in which the growing fashion for sitting in family pews cut into the far broader spaces which had previously catered for different social groups. See Aston, 'Segregation in church', 286 ff.

[86] Frere, *Visitation Articles*, iii. 168; CLRO Jour. 22, fos. 76ᵛ–7; GL MS 1175/1, fo. 40ᵛ. See also GL MSS 1175/1, fo. 51; 1431/2, fo. 187.

[87] Cf. Spaeth, 'Common prayer?', 142.

[88] Keith Thomas, *Religion and the Decline of Magic: Studies in Popular Beliefs in Sixteenth- and Seventeenth-Century England* (1971), 191–2; Frere, *Visitation Articles*, iii. 166.

[89] ERO D/ACA 32, fo. 47; 44, fo. 14; 48, fo. 34ᵛ; 50, fos. 171, 179ᵛ, 199; 51, fo. 182ᵛ; 52, fo. 235; 54, fos. 22, 22ᵛ, 89ᵛ, 141ᵛ; GL MS 1175/1, fo. 40ᵛ.

[90] ERO D/ACA 44, fo. 175; 45, fos. 87, 89; 47, fo. 112; 49, fo. 46ᵛ; 50, fos. 136ᵛ, 142, 194; 54, fo. 11ᵛ.

[91] ERO D/ACA 30, fo. 179ᵛ; 44, fos. 72ᵛ, 119; 45, fos. 17ᵛ, 33ᵛ, 54ᵛ, 165; 46, fo. 179; 47, fos. 58v, 84, 85, 158; 48, fos. 166ᵛ, 168; 49, fos. 6, 39ᵛ, 55ᵛ, 59; 50, fos. 174, 194ᵛ; 51, fo. 193; 52, fo. 226.

[92] ERO D/ACA 45, fos. 233ᵛ, 290ᵛ; 47, fo. 168; 48, fos. 110, 114, 158ᵛ; 49, fo. 99; 50, fos. 78, 132; 51, fos. 103, 112ᵛ, 140; 52, fo. 257; 55, fo. 119; NRO Diocesan Records Vis 6/1; 7/1.

[93] ERO D/ACA 30, fos. 60, 67; 45, fos. 173ᵛ, 248ᵛ, 276; 47, fos. 89, 154.

[94] ERO D/ACA 30, fo. 176ᵛ; 43, fo. 149ᵛ; 46, fos. 68ᵛ, 149, 166; 49, fos. 49, 63ᵛ, 136; 50, fos. 78, 170, 216; 54, fo. 89ᵛ.

[95] ERO D/ACA 45, fo. 95ᵛ.   [96] ERO D/ACA 45, fo. 163ᵛ.

into church.[97] This is not a balanced view of the Sunday congregation. Piety and conformity make few appearances in courtbooks, though their grip on some sections of parishioners is clearly implied in the filing of complaints at a sometimes distant court. Yet even if there was a moral majority in the congregation, many parishes encountered the comic and derisory antics of 'worldly professors', who were frequently drawn from the younger sections of the community.

There are reports of children playing and running up and down in church, 'trublinge the minister and other obedient hearers of God's word'. The sins of the children were often visited on their parents, some of whom were prosecuted 'for not guiding' their children in church.[98] One Essex minister complained in 1606 of the boisterous antics of servants who answered his sermon with a chorus of laughing, jeering, and jesting. In 1625 the churchwardens of Kingston in the Archdeaconry of Arundel (Sussex) presented a company of 'boys and servants' for 'striving and jostling and pinching one another for want of seats . . . to the offence of the congregacion and disturbance of divine service'. There was a 'final passage at the upper end' of the church at Hayes (Middlesex) 'in which many disordered boys did use to stand', who 'many times' interrupted the preacher by 'theire unrulie behavior'. Henry Machyn disapprovingly noted the 'gret uprore . . . showtyng' and 'herle borle' of 'yonge pepell' at Paul's Cross. William Rider of Maldon in Essex found himself before the church court 'for disturbing the congregacon causing the youth in the church to laugh in repeating the minister's words'. While Thomas Clark, another Essex youth, was presented for 'laughing in tyme of the sermon becawse the minister did tell the dutie of servants'.[99] We also see young people leaping onto the communion table and gesturing at the minister

---

[97] ERO D/ACA 46, fo. 122ᵛ; NRO Diocesan Records Vis 7/1.

[98] CUL EDR B/2/14, fo. 47ᵛ; B/2/28, fos. 108–9; B/2/30, fo. 44; ERO D/ACA 44, fo. 18ᵛ; 52, fo. 249; John Rushworth (ed.), *Historical Collections* (8 vols.; 1721), ii. 91.

[99] The North Ockenden case is cited in full by William Hunt, *The Puritan Moment: The Coming of Revolution in an English County* (Cambridge, Mass., 1983), 150; H. Johnstone (ed.), *Churchwarden's Presentments (Seventeenth Century) Part 1: Archdeaconry of Chichester* (Sussex Record Society, 42, Lewes, 1948) [hereafter, *Chichester Churchwarden's Presentments*], 101; PRO SP 16/288/72–3; *The Diary of Henry Machyn, Citizen and Merchant Taylor of London, 1550–1563*, ed. J. G. Nichols (Camden Society, Old Series, 42, 1848), 41; ERO D/ACA 54, fo. 89; 43, fos. 98, 107. See also BCB 7, fo. 377ᵛ; CH minute book 1558–81, fo. 239ᵛ; CUL EDR B/2/13, fo. 64ᵛ; B/2/18, fo. 192ᵛ; ERO D/ACA 46, fo. 163ᵛ; 55, fo. 40; NRO Diocesan Records Vis 7/1; PRO SP 16/75/87; GL MS 4415/1, fo. 13ᵛ; Hale, *Precedents and Proceedings*, 233; E. C. R. Brinkworth, *Shakespeare and the Bawdy Courts of Stratford* (1972), 150; David Underdown, *Fire from Heaven: Life in an English Town in the Seventeenth Century* (1992), 81.

and congregation; playing dice on the 'Lord's table'; 'villanously . . . defyling the pulpett'; 'casting things at the maides' and 'sticking feathers on a maides waistcoate'; tossing hats in the air; throwing bricks at a sleeping boy; and other acts of petty violence.[100]

Many other tales of irreverent behaviour in church wait in the records. Should we simply reduce them to mere youthful high spirits, posturing, and display? Such antics would seem to indicate that for many young people divine service was not a deeply spiritual experience. But beliefs are extremely difficult to pierce, and the glaring problem of typicality lingers. Where should we place the case of four young Essex men, who caused an uproar in divine service 'to the disturbance of the congregation and especially the other young people among whom they sat'?[101] The majority of moralists, however, tended to indict attendance as an unprofitable, habitual, and unspectacular performance, neither pious nor its opposite, complete indifference.[102] But some of their hottest invective was directed towards events outside the church on Sunday, and attention shifted to the alehouse or the fields, for example, where people danced the 'Devil's dance' and profaned the sabbath in their cups.

These counter-attractions to Sunday worship are often presented in terms of distant cultural and social polarities—the drinkers merry in their cups as others file past on their way to church, casting disapproving glances at the revellers who stayed away. Moralists presented such profane pastimes and the Church as direct rivals for the sympathies of parishioners. Visitation Articles sometimes enquired after 'common pastimes or plays . . . whereby the people or youth' are 'drawn away from their church at unlawful times, as hopping, dancing, singing, football, playing bowls, dicing, carding, stoolball, and scaylls'.[103] Many accusations are unequivocal, and there can be no doubt that an offence had been committed in the 'time of divine service' when Law commanded young and old parishioners to be at prayer. But other cases alert us to the significance of a rather neglected category of people—those who readily went to church (perhaps to morning prayer only), but who also enjoyed an

---

[100] ERO D/ACA 49, fo. 239ᵛ; 32, fo. 238; NRO NMC 7, fo. 520; Hale, *Precedents and Proceedings* 261–2; Emmison, *Elizabethan Life: Morals*, 118; ERO D/ACA 51, fo. 163ᵛ, C. II. Mayo (ed.), *The Municipal Records of the Borough of Dorchester, Dorset* (Exeter, 1908), 655, 669.
[101] Cited by Keith Wrightson, 'The Puritan Reformation of Manners with Special Reference to the Counties of Lancashire and Essex 1640–1660' (unpublished University of Cambridge Ph.D thesis, 1973), 176.
[102] Cf. Keith Wrightson, *English Society 1580–1680* (1982), 212.
[103] Collinson, *Religion of Protestants*, 24; Frere, *Visitation Articles*, iii. 343.

afternoon or evening of alcohol-spiced conviviality and play. Such people created what was in effect their 'alternative sabbath'.[104]

In a pessimistic moment, Ralph Josselin recorded some of his anxieties in his diary (27 November 1659). He wrote how Sunday was 'a day most wofully slighted especially by youth'. Josselin later related how he first 'heard and then saw the youth openly playing at catt on the green' on the sabbath. His feelings clearly stirred to a heated pitch, he 'routed' the playing youth, and to his great dismay discovered their fathers asleep 'in the chimney corner'. Josselin's cultural blast failed to reduce the sporting temper of his young parishioners, for on the next Sunday they returned to the streets to play 'cat', their slumbering parents again enjoying a fireside snooze. 'Oh how the sabbath is profaned', Josselin groaned, 'and persons hate to bee reformed, though officers endeavour the doing of it'.[105] Other parents in other places were presented 'for suffering' their 'children to playe on ye saboath daie'.[106] A miscellany of indoor and outdoor games lured the young away from church, and in the opinion of godly commentators, stained the purity of the sabbath. They appeared before the ecclesiastical authorities for playing stoolball, football, and bowls—the churchyard 'at service time' being one location.[107] One group of London apprentices declared that they would play 'in despight of whomsoever'.[108] Other young people were discovered dancing in time of divine service, perhaps following the call of a local piper or minstrel 'to the hindrance of godly exercise'.[109]

In his visitation of the Diocese of Rochester in 1572, Bishop Freke asked officials to inquire 'whether there be any that . . . receive

---

[104] The Book of Sports (1633), which of course had its precursor of 1617, permitted recreation on Sunday, but only after evening prayer. See James Tait, 'The declaration of sports for Lancashire (1617)', *English Historical Review*, 32 (1917); Collinson, *Birthpangs*, 137–8.

[105] Josselin, *Diary*, 454, 406, 476, 477, 547.   [106] NRO Diocesan Records, Vis 6/1.

[107] Emmison, 'Tithes and perambulations', 203–4; ERO D/ACA 32, fos. 2, 5, 124; 52, fo. 258; 54, fo. 137ᵛ; CUL EDR B/2/11, fo. 100ᵛ; B/2/12, fo. 26ᵛ; B/2/15, fo. 145; B/2/18, fo. 24; B/2/21, fos. 109–9; B/2/35, fo. 50ᵛ; B/2/36, fos. 102, 112, 169; YCA Proceedings of the Commonwealth Committee for York and Ainsty E/63, fo. 117; B/33, fos. 75ᵛ–6; Hale, *Precedents and Proceedings*, 242; Morris Marples, *A History of Football* (1954), ch. 5.

[108] GL MSS 5770/1, fo. 280; 7090/2, fo. 44; ERO D/ACA 25, fo. 73; CUL EDR B/2/15, fo. 143ᵛ; D/2/51, fo. 66; W. H. Stevenson *et al.* (eds.), *Records of the Borough of Nottingham* (9 vols.; Nottingham, 1882–1956) [hereafter *Nottingham Borough Records*], iv. 282.

[109] Williams, *Bishop Redman's Visitation*, 79; J. S. Purvis (ed.), *Tudor Parish Documents of the Diocese of York* (Cambridge, 1948), 39; Emmison, 'Tithes and perambulations', 222; CUL EDR B/2/21, fo. 81ᵛ. See also EDR B/2/10, fo. 6; B/2/11, fo. 174; B/2/15, fos. 54, 154; B/2/30, fo. 71ᵛ; B/2/35, fo. 28; ERO D/ACA 25, fos. 37ᵛ, 43; F. G. Emmison (ed.), *Elizabethan Life: Disorder* (Essex Record Office Publications, 56, Chelmsford, 1970), 210–11; Marples, *History of Football*, 59–60; Brinkworth, *Shakespeare and the Bawdy Court*, 151; Parker, *English Sabbath*, 137; Underdown, *Fire from Heaven*, 81.

into their houses . . . mens servants or children in the sermon or divine service time, or in the evening, or at any other unlawful time to eat, drink, hop, pipe, sing, dance, dice, card, or to use any other unlawful game or exercise'.[110] It would take up a great deal of space simply to sample cases of 'ryotting and tippling' and 'rioting and revelling', and also of people keeping 'evell rule', 'entertaining youth' to drink, eat, dance, and play away the precious time of the seventh day. A typical offender was Simon Wickins of Hayley (Oxfordshire), who was 'requested by the youth to brew some ale and thereby had lewd resort' and dancing to the tune of a minstrel, 'so that the youth did not repaire' to evening prayer.[111] These episodes supply strong evidence for the construction of an 'alternative sabbath' to that understood by the minister and moralist. Their elevated sense of the holy sabbath found young devotees, but stories of Sunday misrule show that young people and their adult companions could juggle and rescore seventh day priorities, and strike a different balance between play and worship. Despite the cautions of the law, many people treated Sunday as their time, and decided if and when they would go to church.

In 1599, for example, Stephen Fulston of Waterbeach in Cambridgeshire was presented 'for keping companye of yowthes in his howse drinking there in eveninge and prayer tyme'. Nine servants and sons were reported to have partaken of his ale, which 'sayd yowthes . . . did come (notwithstanding) to the church at the reading of the second lesson'. Four 'singlemen and women' slipped out of an Essex church during the sermon 'in the forenoone' and went to a nearby alehouse where they remained 'eatinge, drinkinge, and tiplinge' until evening prayer. John Strutt could not stand on his own two feet as they made their way to church, and he fell asleep in the fields and was left behind. His three comrades negotiated the journey, though Joan Goodman departed from church 'reelinge' and slept 'at the ende of the chancel . . . till the later ende of the sermon'. Richard Maul of Banbury 'departed' his parish church 'at

---

[110] Frere, *Visitation Articles*, iii. 344.

[111] Christopher Haigh, 'The Church of England, the Catholics and the people', in Haigh (ed.), *The Reign of Elizabeth I* (1984), 215. A single visitation of the Archdeaconries of Norwich and Sudbury in 1629, for example, reveals 33 cases of 'evil resort' to alehouses on the sabbath—NRO Diocesan Records Vis 6/1. Cf. CUL EDR B/2/15, fo. 29ᵛ; B/2/17, fo. 183; B/2/21, fos. 24, 121ᵛ; B/2/29, fos. 157, 167ᵛ; B/2/33, fo. 88ᵛ; BCB 5, fos. 119, 326ᵛ, 424; ERO D/ACA 30, fo. 44; 44, fo. 49; 45, fos. 92, 313; 54, fo. 23; GL MS 5770/1, fos. 494–5; CLRO Reps. 12, fo. 90ᵛ; 33, fo. 276; Brinkworth, *Shakespeare and the Bawdy Court*, 138; Willis Bund, *Worcestershire County Records*, 228; Wrightson, 'Puritan Reformation of Manners', 174; Williams, *Bishop Redman's Visitation*, 80; Emmison, *Elizabethan Life: Disorder*, 224; Johnstone, *Chichester Churchwarden's Presentments*, 128; Le Hardy, *Hertford County Records*, ii. 47, 173–4.

sermon and went to the alehouse giveinge very evill example to younger persons that there kept him company'.[112] Like Nicholas Cooke, the apprentice of a London pewterer, who 'mysorderly' left 'at his owne pleasure on the Sondaies and Holly Daies before servis was done withowt lycence of his master', the principal characters in all of these cases displayed an inordinate degree of initiative.[113] Significantly, each of them either walked out of church, or arrived in their own time and at their own pace. But at some point they did attend church, even if their presence was a mere formality and a gesture—an irreverent hour or two. These people simply shuffled the minister's script, and the resulting sabbath day was generously interpreted to include worship and recreation. It is sometimes misleading, therefore, to represent attitudes towards Sunday in distant polarities. There was a middle way, and it is wise to keep a few interpretative alternatives in sight. Some young people joined the ranks of excommunicates,[114] others kept a pious sabbath. Somewhere in between these two remote poles we should place the majority of early modern people, for whom the seventh day was a time of work, rest, and play.

3. *The Bachelor's Social Round*

The godly often observed that few young people were tempted away from the world of conviviality and play to follow an opposing pious culture, which included respect for Sunday observance. Worse still, martial pursuits sometimes failed to grip the imagination of young people, who much preferred their own 'lewd and evell exercises' like plays, football, dancing, and other 'unlawful games'.[115] A further source of anxiety was the growing popularity of the alehouse, which introduced far-reaching changes in the forms and sites of recreation. The rise in the number of alehouses at this time is well known.[116] Keith Wrightson has argued that this exodus to the

---

[112] CUL EDR B/2/17, fo. 183; Hale, *Precedents and Proceedings*, 153–4; S. A. Peyton (ed.), *The Churchwarden's Presentments in the Oxfordshire Peculiars of Dorchester, Thame and Banbury* (Oxfordshire Record Society, 10, Oxford, 1928), 23.

[113] GL MS 7090/2, fo. 44. See also GL MS 5770/1, fos. 149–50; BCB 2, fo. 62; ERO D/ACA 32, fo. 183; 48, fo. 196ᵛ; 49, fo. 23ᵛ; CUL EDR B/2/36, fos. 102, 169.

[114] Cf. Collinson, *Religion of Protestants*, 228–9; Baxter, *Reliquiae Baxterianae*, 85, 91–2.

[115] CLRO Jour. 21, fo. 448. See also CLRO Reps. 14, fo. 153; 16, fo. 442ᵛ; 17, fos. 236ᵛ, 404; Jours. 21, fos. 7, 127–7ᵛ, 190; 22, fo. 29; 23, fo. 232; 25, fos. 86ᵛ, 191ᵛ, 210–11, 286ᵛ.

[116] See Peter Clark, *The English Alehouse: A Social History 1200–1830* (1983), 50.

alehouse resulted in the fragmentation of traditional culture. It was adult males, in particular, who sat in their cups inside the alehouse, while outside its four walls the youth of the community still played in the fields and helped to perpetuate the customary outdoor culture.[117]

Yet rather than a tidy distinction between different age-groups, the alehouse and its threefold attractions of drink, gossip, and sport, had 'a prominent place in the social lives of servants and the young of both sexes'.[118] Countless words and pages poured outrage upon the alehouse. It was a den of disorder and vice, and governors promised swift reprisals against keepers who 'entertain apprentices'.[119] Nevertheless, the alehouse had a prominent place in the social life of the young, providing a focal point for the assignations and intrigues of courtship, and opportunities to further social bonding among young men in particular.[120] It has been said that the alehouse in eighteenth-century Paris cultivated 'corporate solidarities', playing host to groups of young men, especially journeymen.[121] The convivial ambience of the alehouse could act as a *rite de passage* for young men, providing a series of turning-points in which they forged alliances and constructed identities. Contemporary judicial sources in England provide many glimpses of young people inside alehouses.[122] A boisterous night of drink was sometimes rounded off with a volley of shouts and stones on the way home. The watch at Bootham Gate in York came across a group of servants in high spirits smashing windows 'at unlawfull times in the night' after a bout of heavy drinking. A 'company' of Norwich servants were presented in 1601 for breaking a wall and 'divers glasse windowes in the night' on their way home after several hours in an alehouse. While Henry Newcome had his sabbath eve sleep interrupted by 'ye villanous carriage of ye servants yt were all out at ye time of ye

---

[117] Wrightson, 'Puritan Reformation of Manners', 39–40. Cf. Clark, 'Alehouse and the alternative society', 63.

[118] Wrightson, 'Puritan Reformation of Manners', 95. Cf. Clark, *English Alehouse*, 127.

[119] YCA B/35, fo. 174ᵛ; NMC 12, fo. 193; Martin, *Records of Maidstone*, 19; Twemlow, *Liverpool Town Books*, i. 4, 31; J. S. W. Gibson and E. R. C. Brinkworth (eds.), *Banbury Corporation Records: Tudor and Stuart* (Banbury Historical Society, 15, Banbury, 1977), 40; R. Savage (ed.), *Minutes and Accounts of the Corporation of Stratford-upon-Avon, and Other Records 1553–1620* (Dugdale Society Publications, i, Oxford, 1921), 31.

[120] See the discussion of courtship in Ch. 5.

[121] See David Garrioch, *Neighbourhood and Community in Paris, 1740–1790* (Cambridge, 1986), 189; Thomas Brennan, *Public Drinking and Popular Culture in Eighteenth-Century Paris* (Princeton, 1988), 151–3, 242.

[122] For example, NRO NMC 7, fos. 269, 589; 9, fo. 429; 10, fos. 294, 756; 13, fo. 544; 14, fos. 103, 412ᵛ; 15, fos. 330ᵛ, 504; 16, fos. 82, 180ᵛ, 191,195, 240ᵛ, 245, 253, 385ᵛ; BCB 5, fos. 413ᵛ, 440, 457ᵛ.

night'.[123] Young 'drunkards' or 'common alehouse haunters' make regular appearances in contemporary sources.

Magistrates and ministers were certain that the lure of the alehouse intoxicated the young, and upset conventional patterns of authority, poisoning 'many towns, familyes, and persons'.[124] It was alleged that seditious and promiscuous words crossed paths in the alehouse creating an unwholesome climate, and it is not difficult to find supporting evidence in contemporary sources. Two 'incorrigible' London apprentices and 'frequenters of alehowses', for example, threatened 'to kill them that seek to call them into question for their lewd courses'.[125] Some young drinkers were also charged with other offences committed under the precarious influence of alcohol. These transgressions, especially domestic disorders, helped to perpetuate the image of the alehouse as a counter-influence to patriarchal values; a place to squander money, time, and wise counsel. Thomas Smart, for example, a servant and 'a common drunkard and blasphemer of God', was ordered to humble himself before his master and mistress, and to ask public forgiveness 'for intolerable abuses' offered to them and their children. John Baillie of Wapping, a baker's apprentice, and another notable 'drunkard', was presented for 'absentinge himselfe from his master's service night by night'. While Michael Kitchen, yet another young drunk, was charged with 'abusing his master manie wayes, offering him violence and beating him, and absentinge himselfe from his service'.[126]

Games bolstered the alehouses's reputation as a breeding ground for habits of profligacy and disobedience. Bowling alleys could be constructed in larger venues, though table games (e.g. backgammon, cards, and dicing) were staple fare and encouraged gambling, which naturally required money.[127] Preachers issued warnings against 'tables', one of them reminding his listeners that to play at cards

---

[123] YCA B/35, fo. 173ᵛ; NRO NMC 13, fo. 558 (irregular pagination); *The Diary of the Reverend Henry Newcome from September 30 1661, to September 29 1663*, ed. T. Heywood (Manchester, 1849), 19. See also BCB 5, fos. 177ᵛ, 282; NRO NMC 14, fos. 77, 184ᵛ; YCA B/34, fo. 83ᵛ.

[124] Wrightson, 'Puritan Reformation of Manners', 176–7; Clark, *English Alehouse*, 147–8. See also Willis Bund, *Worcestershire County Records*, 81, 136; J. S. Cockburn (ed.), *Western Circuit Assize Orders 1629–1648: A Calendar* (Publications of the Camden Society, 4th ser., 17, 1976), 238; F. A. Bailey (ed.), *A Selection from the Prescot Court Leet and Other Records, 1447–1600* (Lancashire and Cheshire Record Society, 89, Blackpool, 1937), 307.

[125] BCB 5, fo. 433.

[126] BCB 5, fos. 433, 203ᵛ, 377. See also ibid. fos. 167, 175, 196, 397, 424, 433, 433ᵛ; NRO NMC 11, fo. 143.

[127] See Clark, 'Alehouse and the alternative society', 63–4.

was to crucify Christ.[128] The young not only raided their master's purse or chest to obtain alcohol,[129] they also plundered his belongings to support dicing or tables. Some played for mere tokens (e.g. beer or apples),[130] though most of them required money to be admitted to the dicing table. Randolph Christopher, for example, who was 'neither to God, the Quene, nor his father obediente', was presented at London Bridewell for 'ryotouslie' spending 'his father's goodes, and consuming the same at dice and such like waies'. Another London apprentice was 'well whipped' in 1561 for 'disobedientlie misusing his master in wordes', despite having been 'commanded and divers tymes warned' by him 'not to play at dice' and waste his goods. It was reported that 'dyvers mens apprentices . . . bribed and picked from their masters' to 'maynteine play' with Symond Holland, 'a comon diceplayer'. John Davye acquired notoriety as 'a comon procurer and receiver of mens servants and prentyses . . . to play at dyse and lose their masters money and goodes'. While the bench of London Bridewell also heard the case of John Nayler, who had run away from his master 'above xx tymes', and had also 'sundrie tymes played away' his 'wares and money to the value of xxx pounds at dice' amongst 'cheating companie' at the alehouse.[131] There are many other young culprits in the sources, and they stole as much as £3, £7, £8, and £10 from their unlucky masters.[132]

The thrill of tables and the good fellowship of the alehouse frequently brought young people into conflict with religious and secular policies, including structured work, time, order, 'place', worship, and 'fit' recreation. The terms of service were quickly forgotten by young devotees of games and drink. They walked in the dark hours of night in 'suspicious' and 'unlawful' time, straying from their master's household (and the compass of his authority) and wasting time. Idle hours spent away from work or necessary rest blemished the collective spirit of work, and was harmful to a master's prosperity. The formal working day and the idea of 'unseasonable' time,

[128] C. H. Cooper and J. W. Cooper (eds.), *Annals of Cambridge* (5 vols.; 1842–1908), i. 334; ii. 429, 538; iii. 34. Cf. Machyn, *Diary*, 230.

[129] For example, GL MS 5770/1, fos. 420–1; BCB 1, fos. 184, 185; 5, fos. 65, 176, 185, 202, 300ᵛ; NRO NMC 15, fo. 289. See also below, pp. 334–7.

[130] For example, NRO NMC 12, fos. 165, 168; BCB 1, fo. 123ᵛ.

[131] BCB 2, fo. 113ᵛ; 1, fo. 180ᵛ; GL MS 3018/1, fo. 13; BCB 1, fo. 125; 5, fo. 377.

[132] For example, BCB 1, fos. 39, 47, 59–9ᵛ, 73, 123, 180ᵛ, 188, 196ᵛ, 199ᵛ, 211ᵛ; 2, fos. 23, 76ᵛ, 104ᵛ, 142ᵛ; 3, fo. 228; 4, fo. 374ᵛ; 5, fos. 97, 225ᵛ, 270, 392, 398ᵛ; GL MSS 3018/1, fos. 11ᵛ, 14ᵛ, 17ᵛ, 74ᵛ; 5770/1, fos. 589, 593; CH minute book 1558–81, fo. 179; NRO NMC 7, fos. 394, 405, 537; 8, fo. 560; 11, fos. 52, 101, 119; 12, fo. 168; 14, fos. 210, 342ᵛ, 416.

which was often heralded by the tolling of the curfew bell and the closing of gates (where appropriate), contributed a sense of structured time to the ordering of the community, and to the lives of young people, in particular. The working day began early (between 4 and 7 a.m., depending upon the season of the year), and for many its limits were marked by the rising and setting of the sun.[133] The day had a different duration and rhythm in early modern society, and the working population were expected to be resting indoors in the two or three hours before midnight, preparing for sleep and the 'lawful and necessary repose for recreation' of their 'tired and wearied' bodies for the next working day. In this 'dead tyme of the night' it was expected that 'all good subjects should be at quyet takinge theire naturall rest in theire bedds'. The authorities presented a contrast between the 'good and honest' citizens inside in their 'restful bed' and other 'lewd' and 'loose' people whose nocturnal movements stirred suspicions. Darkness was said to offer a cloak for nocturnal disorders. Young people who strayed outside the household after dusk were exposed to these accusations as well as to a politics which insisted that they remain safe inside with their master.[134] They returned home late from a night of drink and emerged the next morning unrested, fragile, and clumsy.

The patience of Lawrence Derry's master, for example, became finally exhausted and Derry was 'sente in' to London Bridewell for 'he had lyke to have spoyled his . . . hole brewing of beare by his negligence', and by his ceaseless running away and pilfering of money to spend 'lewdlye drinkinge and playinge'. In 1607 the Norwich Court of Mayoralty reminded George Cornwall of his obligations to the terms of his apprenticeship indenture and civic order—henceforth he was not to 'haunt innes, alehowses, or any other suspect howses or places, or use playeinge or gameynge', but 'keep his master's service and duely attend his busynes'.[135] An errand presented a golden opportunity. Issac Allingworth of London, 'a drunkard' who would 'not applie his busynes', was dispatched to Bridewell by his master, who informed the bench that 'he cannot send him abroade but he wold pilfer his napkins and other things . . . and ronne to the alehouse'. John Hampshire, 'a lewd and noughtie

---

[133] See Charles Phythian-Adams, *Desolation of a City: Coventry and the Urban Crisis of the Late Middle Ages* (Cambridge, 1979), 76; David Palliser, 'Civic mentality and the environment in Tudor York', in Jonathan Barry (ed.), *The Tudor and Stuart Town: A Reader in English Urban History 1530–1688* (Harlow, 1990), 215.

[134] PRO STAC 8, 152/22; 303/7.

[135] BCB 5, fo. 427ᵛ; NRO NMC 14, fo. 166. See also BCB 2, fos. 129, 131ᵛ.

boy', was 'well whipped' at the same place for 'loytering and playing at dyce' when he was sent by his master to fetch wood to 'dyvers
places'.[136]

Night-time like the hours of the sabbath was also 'spare time',
when the young could claim an inappropriate degree of freedom.
John Mandyke of Yorkshire was reported to have 'used and frequented evill company and lay forth' of his master's house or shop
'in the night and not behaved himselfe as a dutiful or careful servant ought to have done'.[137] Young people should have only ven-
tured outside on 'lawful busynes',[138] though contemporary sources
show them 'going abroad . . . at their own pleasure' or 'choosing'.[139]
In 1653, for example, Francis Martin of Leicester wrote to the
mayor to request him to send his 'ungodly sonne Edmund' to 'a fit
place' where he could repent 'for his wicked life and disobedience'.
The youth had been absent from his house for three nights and
'diverse other tymes this twelvemonth' returning 'at his pleasure'.
It was reported that the 'menservants' of Stoneleigh in Warwickshire
'gathered' to 'feast and banquet . . . uncivilly disordering themselves
by walking abroad in the night-time with uncivil songs of ribaldry'.
John Nash and William Holland of London, 'very dangerous
fellowes', were charged with 'dyvers tymes . . . goyng out of their
masters howses in the night' to waste time in 'alehowses and other
bad places' with 'lewde women'. It was reported that Nash had
'lyen out . . . at the least xl nights within this xii month'. While in
1607 the London Court of Aldermen disenfranchised a vintner
who managed The King's Head at Pie Corner, after hearing that he
had daily entertained apprentices and servants 'in disordered
manner' at 'unlawful houres' in the night. On one recent occasion,
'after manye admonitions and warnyngs . . . to keepe better order',
officers interrupted the revelries at 1 a.m. and discovered twenty-
seven 'apprentices and others' in various stages of drunkenness.[140]
Other young nocturnal trippers were found in alehouses, private
houses, and on the streets, playing cards, tables, and other games,

---

[136] BCB 3, fos. 223ᵛ, 225ᵛ; 1, fo. 180ᵛ. See also BCB 5, fos. 3ᵛ, 427.

[137] PRO E134 13 & 14, Charles I Hil. 15. Andy Wood kindly gave me this reference.

[138] For example Farwaker *Manchester Court Leet*, i, 159; Twemlow, *Liverpool Town Books*, i, 246.

[139] See also below, Chs. 6–7.

[140] Helen Stocks (ed.), *Records of the Borough of Leicester: Being a Series of Extracts from the Archives of the Corporation of Leicester 1603–1668* (Cambridge, 1923), 413; Nat Alcock, *Stoneleigh Villagers 1597–1650* (University of Warwick: Open Studies, 1975), 46 (I must thank Nat Alcock for this reference); GL MS 5770/2, fo. 99; CLRO Rep. 27, fo. 346ᵛ. See also BCB 5, fo. 84ᵛ.

drinking, banqueting, whoring, and dancing.[141] Again, governors were troubled by the ambivalent influences of peer association, and issued warnings about coarse company. Nevertheless, the sources reveal a host of young people tracing the steps of others who 'swaggered' to the alehouse or bawdy house. They included Jonas Bond, a London fishmonger's apprentice, and a 'comon dycer and player', who 'commonly resorted to a victualyng house in Walbroke drawing other mens apprentices unto the like'.[142]

Householders who entertained apprentices and servants at 'inconvenient' or 'unlawful hours' set an 'evel example' and merited swift justice.[143] They kept young people 'secret, denying them to their masters'.[144] Young offenders were likewise a blemish on domestic order and an 'evell example' to their peers.[145] The housebound ideology of the sermon, indenture, and ordinance imposed spatial and temporal constraints upon young people, though they could seek an alternative to the finely ordered hierarchies of household and social order in worlds of conviviality and play. They encouraged a number of counter-values to concerns with 'place', time, and 'honest' morality, including profligacy, vanity, independence, secrecy, vice, and free expression among sympathetic peers. But despite a formidable repertoire of checks and punishments, and the pessimistic verdicts of some recent historians, the young did meet in their own spaces with their equals, and some of them even charted a rival course of entry into the adult world.[146]

There is ample evidence in contemporary sources of the social significance of the alehouse, brothel, playhouse, and tables in the lives of young men.[147] Richard Christopher, a cook who sold apple

[141] For example, YCA B/35, fo. 173^v; City & Ainsty Quarter Sessions minute book 1638–62, fos. 33, 85; CUL EDR B/2/14, fo. 192; BCB 2, fo. 62^v; 5, fos. 203^v, 287^v, 324; GL MS 5770/1, fos. 140–1; CLRO Rep. 28, fo. 186^v; NRO NMC 7, fo. 269; 8, fos. 81, 186; Underdown, *Fire from Heaven*, 80–1; Clark, *English Alehouse*, esp. chs. 6–8.

[142] GL MS 5770/1, fo. 593.

[143] For a typical example see CUL EDR B/2/14, fo. 192.

[144] GL MS 3018/1, fo. 74.   [145] BCB 2, fo. 123; GL MS 3018/1, fo. 17^v.

[146] Cf. Clark, *English Alehouse*, 127, 148.

[147] The social world of the bawdy house is explored below, as part of a broader survey of apprenticeship clientage in London. Robert Ashton suggests that the majority of London apprentices would have been unable to pay the entrance fee to a theatre. Even the cheapest fees, he continues, were as much as six pence, 'which would automatically have excluded all but a small minority' (Robert Ashton, 'Popular entertainment and social control in late-Elizabethan and early-Stuart London', *London Journal*, 9 (1983), 4). However, the fees paid by apprentices to prostitutes would appear to indicate that they had rather more spare money than Ashton infers. Indeed, the apprentices have been recently identified as a key group of customers in the theatres (Andrew Gurr, *Playgoing in Shakespeare's London* (Cambridge, 1987), esp. ch. 3).

pies and tarts to 'apprentices to the distruccon of youth', was presented at London Bridewell in 1561 for 'suffering ... dyverse
prentises to resort unto his house and feast and banquet' on Sundays. Peter Smith, 'a lewd servant', was 'brought into' the same
court in 1560 for 'banquieting and eyetyng'. Dicing was another
favoured pursuit and we will discuss this particular pastime and its
consequences in a later chapter.[148] This bachelor's social round was
in one important respect not a competing progress to manhood
and adulthood because it was a route which many masters and
magistrates had followed themselves. Nevertheless, it was far removed from the sober image of public manhood drawn in conduct
books, guild rhetoric, and criminal codes.[149] This rough nocturnal
culture showed off the excessive and violent aspects of manhood
which poured forth in a volley of stones and insults, a flurry of fists,
a chorus of songs, or the discharge of urine, vomit, and sexual
electricity. It was in the male space of the street and the alehouse
that young men distanced themselves from the cosy domestic world
of childhood and their mother's care, and staked a claim for a
place in the ranks of adult men. If we turn to the image of manhood in the sources of civic or guild government, it is defined in
more 'serviceable' terms as work or military muscle—mustering,
marching, policing ceremony, archery, wrestling, or the quality of
skills and the finished product. Here lay the governors' dilemma—
male aggression was encouraged (though it was strictly channelled),
but when it broke forth in the alehouse or on the street it was flatly
condemned and prosecuted. It was a thin line and easy to cross.
Young men vigorously asserted the territory and identity of their
occupation or neighbourhood. They hurled punches and insults at
rival gangs, and paraded in the streets in military style beating drums
and brandishing weapons.[150] In so doing, they were sharing the
values of these geographical and occupational identities, and 'conforming to a widely accepted model of unmarried male behaviour'.
They 'had in common both youth and an errant life-style'.[151] Yet
drink and other expressions of male camaraderie and sexual vitality
still remained important aspects of manhood (and occupational
identities) in later life. The politics of age and the pressures of time
in youth provided one way of interpreting this stormy male culture.
Different ways of growing up were being contrasted—hard work,

[148] BCB 1, fos. 125, 90. See also below, Ch. 6.   [149] Cf. Roper, 'Blood and codpieces'.
[150] Cf. Robert C. Davis, *The War of the Fists: Popular Culture and Public Violence in Late
Renaissance Venice* (Oxford, 1994), esp. 109–12.
[151] I am quoting from Garrioch, *Neighbourhood and Community*, 203–4.

civility, sobriety, and piety with the rougher path of drink, violence, gambling, and sex—but there were uncomfortable points of contact between them, including expressions of aggression and convivial solidarity. Male youth would form the next generation of masters and magistrates. The London apprentices, for example, were called 'the hope of manhoode'.[152] But in contemporary sources there is much anxiety about social expressions of manhood, and the 'ill example' of the young drunk, pilferer, pugilist, gambler, 'whore-monger', banqueter, or runaway was constantly relayed in print media and legislation.

This bachelor's social round helped to plant male honour in young hearts. By contrast, notions of female honour played down this corporate dimension, and were more narrowly construed in terms of individual sexuality.[153] This rough nocturnal male culture provided a sharp contrast to the social lives of young women who are, however, less visible in the judicial sources at least. Neverthe-less, outside the courtship culture that was common to both sexes, the sources infer that women made scant use of the alehouse, which emerged as a place of male entertainment in the first instance, and that those women who did resort to the alehouse alone or in female company were exposed to a heavy load of suspicions and innuen-does.[154] Women appear in contemporary sources as customers of alehouses, though often in company with young men. George Blower of London was presented in 1575 for hosting 'divers bancketts and meetings' for apprentices and servants 'as well men and mayds', who 'most riotouslie consumed their master's goods'.[155] But then, as now, night-time was dangerous time, and ballads cautioned women to stay indoors after sunset.[156] Moreover, there could have been a seasonal aspect to female sociability, women stepping outside the household more often in summer months of late nights and max-imum light than in winter months of short days. Indeed, women who remained safe inside were distinguished from others who paced dark streets, entered 'suspect' houses, and (like men who stayed up late drinking) disturbed the structure of the male working day by

[152] Ester Sowerman is quoted by Ben-Amos, *Adolescence and Youth in Early Modern England*, 23.
[153] Cf. Roper, 'Blood and codpieces', 109.
[154] Cf. Brennan, *Public Drinking and Popular Culture*, esp. 148, and 60–5.
[155] BCB 2, fos. 167, 171ᵛ.
[156] For example, 'The Silver Age, Or the World Turned Backward', ' Newes from Tower Hill, Or a Gentle Warning to Peg and Kate to Walke No More Abroad So Late', and 'The Two Welsh Lovers', all of which are reprinted in W. C. Day (ed.), *The Pepys Ballads* (Cam-bridge, 1987), 154, 266–7, 270–1.

serving as a dubious nocturnal temptation. Women walked along the streets after nightfall at the risk of violence, mockery, and/or being confused with alleged 'fallen' women and attracting a pliable label like 'nightwalker' or 'whore' which criminalized their late movements.[157]

Women who entered alehouses alone or in company with each other were prone to the same insults, taunts, and suspicions about reputation and cleanliness. In March 1605, for example, Robert Cowell and George Starkey, two apprentices, fell in with 'a couple of young women' at a London alehouse, who were described as 'dishonest persons'. Interestingly, Cowell advised caution, telling Starkey 'to bee carefull what he did for hee thought if hee would have th'use of either of them he might happen to catch some disease'. The two apprentices 'parted without further words', providing a rare glimpse of the range of expectations young men carried to the alehouse.[158] Women present on such occasions were treated as 'fallen' and 'dishonest' persons by the courts. Some of these stories should probably be situated at the lower rungs of prostitution. In February 1579 one Flood, the tapster at The Bear in Wood Street, was presented at London Bridewell in company with eight named women, who were all 'comen gests' at his alehouse staying there 'all daie long', and 'as men come into the house to drinke they will go to them, and eate and drinke with them and keep them companie'.[159] Men could not walk the same streets and enter alehouses in a wholly carefree air. Their nocturnal culture also raised suspicions, and the alehouse, after all, was a public and suspect place which was associated with sedition, immorality, criminality, and the marginal fringe.[160] Nevertheless, women had less freedom to walk the streets at night, and we are more likely to see young men in the sources associating in single-sex groups, dodging the curfew and the watch, drinking, playing, eating, spending money, and purchasing sex.[161]

There are few glimpses in the sources I have consulted of female sociability after dark other than these arguably untypical situations in which women only become visible because they appeared before a court. They called on friends and relatives, but these types of hospitality usually belonged to the kitchen, parlour, or bed-chamber,

---

[157] I hope to publish an article exploring the labelling of nocturnal criminality which further explores these and related issues.

[158] BCB 5, fo. 20ᵛ.   [159] BCB 3, fo. 367. Cf BCB 5, fo. 1ᵛ.

[160] See CLRO Reps. 27, fos. 137–7ᵛ, 142, 149, 152, 160; 30, fos. 13ᵛ–14, 40ᵛ–1ᵛ; 33, fo. 191; 34, fo. 180ᵛ; 43, fos. 261–1ᵛ, 159ᵛ; Brennan, *Public Drinking and Popular Culture*, esp. 297.

[161] Cf. Brennan, *Public Drinking and Popular Culture*, 148.

though it was no less important for that reason. The quantitative and qualitative evidence for single-sex conviviality is far richer for males, and many of our glimpses of women are restricted to day-light hours. One fruitful point of entry is the archival narratives in cases of defamation, scolding, and witchcraft, which at their most helpful give striking references to female work and leisure.[162] A more tested route to female experiences has been literary sources, which often show that the working day provided opportunities for women to meet in the workplace, street, washing-place, and market-place. Agricultural tasks like raking, reaping, sowing, milking, dairy-ing, and caring for animals were often allocated to women.[163] The distinction between work and sociability was not rigid. Samuel Pepys was walking with his father to Portholme where he came across a group of maids milking, 'and to see', he declared, 'with what mirth they came all home together in pomp with their milk, and some-times they have musique go before them'. Dorothy Osborne spent 'the heat of the day' reading and working in her Bedfordshire home, 'and about six or seven o' clock' she walked to 'a common that lies hard by the house, where a great many young wenches keep sheep and cows, and sit in the shade singing of ballads'. Osborne sat and talked to the young women, and decided 'that they want nothing to make them the happiest people in the world but the knowledge that they are so . . .'[164]

Women worked at home in pairs or larger groups, perhaps wash-ing or spinning or some other task which was easily performed indoors. They also performed work at night and this offered one forum for female sociability at all ages. Interestingly, in his *Remaines of Gentilisme and Judaisme,* John Aubrey spends a few lines discussing the German spinning bee or sewing circle, a society of female work and discourse—'at night in the wintertime all the mayds of the village met together, and brought with them along their spinning-wheel, or distaff, and spun very late in the night, where then the young men were not far off'. He wrongly concluded that this custom 'now [1686–7] is quite abolished by reason of the great exorbitances

[162] See, for example, Laura Gowing, 'Gender and the language of insult in early modern London', *History Workshop Journal,* 35 (1993); Bernard Capp, 'Separate domains: women and authority in early modern England', in Paul Griffiths, Adam Fox, and Steve Hindle (eds.), *The Experience of Authority in Early Modern England* (Basingstoke, 1996).

[163] Cf. Michael Roberts, 'Sickles and scythes: women's work and men's work at harvest time', *History Workshop Journal,* 7 (1979); Ann Kussmaul, *Servants in Husbandry in Early Modern England* (Cambridge, 1981), esp. 34.

[164] Pepys, *Diary,* iii. 221; *The Letters of Dorothy Osborne to Sir William Temple 1652–54,* ed. Kingsley Hart (Oxford, 1968), 68–9.

they committed', though it is perhaps significant that Aubrey, a repository of his country's customs, makes no reference to an English equivalent.[165] Nevertheless, other sources, including judicial records and the pages of moralists and balladeers, refer to groups of female gossips, and Aubrey himself provided examples of sports played by 'mayds' and 'young wenches', often after supper, most of which were intended to match one of their number with a young and desirable bachelor.[166] However, we should be cautious about producing polarities between patterns of female sociability characterized by gossip on the one hand, and the rough male culture on the other. Gossip was not a female privilege, and gossip groups were frequently *representations* of female experiences. Males gathered in the alehouse and other places to discuss their hopes and fears, they joked, laughed, swapped news, and cast aspersions from out of which a 'fame' or libel could spring.

We can trace the rough shape of female lives from narratives in the archives and the chance observations of elite contemporaries recorded in literary sources, though conviviality and sociability among young women in early modern England remains a decidedly unreconstructed experience. This frequent silence is deeply ambiguous. Did a darker cloud of suspicion hang over the bachelor's social round, so that they were more likely to appear before a court and therefore enter the historical record with greater frequency? This seems unlikely. Above all, there was a difference in the character and location of single-sex conviviality, and in the nature of assumptions about appropriate male and female conduct. Money was a further prohibitive factor. Young men tended to have earlier and more regular access to money wages to spend in convivial moments. Some women may have had to wait to be *invited* to the alehouse, while others chose to remain inside the household at night, talking, working, and drinking. There were often several servants under a single roof, and friends were close at hand in a nearby street. Other 'snapshots' from the archives show women working away from home and having to walk alone at a late hour only to bump into the watch to whom they had to tell their stories. Mary Fosame, for example, 'a pyewoman's girle', went in to a London

---

[165] John Aubrey, *Remaines of Gentilisme and Judaisme 1686–1687*, ed. James Britten (Folklore Society, 4, 1881), 46. See also Hans Medick, 'Village spinning bees: sexual culture and free time among rural youths in early modern Germany', in Medick and David Sabean (eds.), *Interest and Emotion: Essays on the Study of Family Life and Kinship* (Cambridge, 1984).

[166] Aubrey, *Remaines*, esp. 24–5, 44–5, 65. See also Capp, 'Separate domains'; Ralph Houlbrooke, 'Women's social life and common action in England from the fifteenth century to the eve of the Civil War', *Continuity and Change*, 1 (1986), esp. 173.

alehouse—to sell pies?—with one of her mistress's pies which was eaten by 'some company', and she 'durst not go home'. Agnes Russell said that 'she was going home from one of her mistresse's with whom she had bene washinge'. While Katherine Duncombe told officers that 'she was going to watch with a woman'.[167] Other women who were discovered walking after nightfall said that they were carrying work or on some business, they said that they were searching for a midwife, going to the carriers, or that their master had turned them out. A few were found asleep,[168] others hid from the watch rather than run the risk of being confused with prostitutes and labelled accordingly.[169]

Nocturnal conviviality presents a situation where it is often appropriate to distinguish male and female experiences. The rough bachelor's social round, which was itself the preference of only certain sections of male youth when money and morals permitted, contributed a particularly masculine form of social and sexual maturity to preparation for adulthood. Moreover, women who featured in stories of male conviviality tended to appear as *providers* of a dubious service—selling drink or sex, for example—or they were discovered in male company, or out late at night, which stirred suspicions. They were, therefore, prosecuted as bawds, prostitutes, nightwalkers, or charged with being 'lewd', 'light', or 'loose'. Young men more regularly feature as *clients* or *customers* in these events, 'drincking and swaggeringe' in alehouses.[170] They were prosecuted as drunkards or patrons of other shady institutions. Young men who participated in this bachelor's round were encouraged to see sexual prowess as part of the meaning of manhood. The geographical pattern of this sort of camaraderie is uncertain. In small communities there are traces of the significance of alehouses and feasts. Quaife has reminded us of the place of the 'semi-amateur prostitute' and 'village whore' in rural society.[171] In larger towns the brothel did exercise a pull over the lives of some young men. A reading of literary sources has persuaded Lawrence Stone, for example, that 'prostitutes congregated in London . . . partly to supply the needs of the twenty to thirty thousand bachelor apprentices in the city'.[172] Not every young man was tempted by the invitation to commercial sex.

---

[167] BCB 8, fo. 127^v; 7, fo. 36; 6, fo. 141.

[168] For example, BCB 6, fos. 65, 107^v, 240, 245^v, 293^v, 362; 7, fos. 28^v, 59; 8, fos. 16, 41^v, 46^v, 63, 100^v, 125, 187, 308^v.

[169] For example, BCB 7, fo. 44; 8, fo. 379^v.   [170] BCB 5, fo. 1^v.

[171] G. R. Quaife, *Wanton Wenches and Wayward Wives: Peasants and Illicit Sex in Early Seventeenth-Century England* (1979), 146–52, 246–7.

[172] Stone, *Family, Sex and Marriage*, 616.

Nevertheless, the records of London Bridewell offer colourful confirmation of the significance of the alehouse and bawdy house as an expression of male sexual vitality, which overlapped with other items of male consumption, offering drink, food, gossip, tables, and further affirmation of manhood.[173]

4. *London's Apprentices and the Bawdy Houses*

On 24 September 1579 Jarrett Asherby, a butcher's apprentice who lived in the Shambles, was presented at London Bridewell 'for haunting tavernes with lewd persons'. His story takes us inside some of the places which were a familiar part of the bachelor's social round. He visited one Good's alehouse, The King's Head at 'Powles Cheyne' in company with four fishmonger's apprentices, and five or six fellow butcher's apprentices, though John Wood, a brewer's son, was the first to arrive, and he brought along three prostitutes. The party sat down to a fine supper—'a quarter of lambe, a shoulder and a loyne of veyle, 3 shoulders of mutton, [and] a capon'. The supper paid for—eight shillings—and a minstrel—five shillings —they 'contynewed dancyinge and playeinge till 4'o clocke in the morninge'.

Another nocturnal revel was arranged by the same apprentices at The Bell in Newgate Street a month later. Eleven apprentices sat down to supper with two women who 'tarried till th'ende', though it seems that the dancing came to a close at an earlier hour—the minstrel departed with his fiddle at midnight. Bartholomew Robinson, another apprentice from the Shambles, who had previously been found in a field with a prostitute, and who had also appeared before the same court six months earlier for calling at 'divers brothel houses in Long Lane, Gilding Lane, and Seocle Lane in company of harlotts' with his fellow apprentice Roger Meredick,[174] informed the bench that Asherbye and Anthony Brooke persuaded the keeper of The Bell to allow them to remain there until dawn. It was reported that Robinson and Asherbye 'had to doe with the 2 women', and 'then Brooke abused Joane and George Clarke the other'. Then it was the 'turn' of two fishmonger's apprentices, Thomas Walker and Thomas Bell. A smaller party was

---

[173] Cf. Lyndal Roper, *The Holy Household: Women and Morals in Reformation Augsburg* (Oxford, 1989), 91–3; Jacques Rossiaud, *Medieval Prostitution*, trans. L. G. Cochrane (Oxford, 1988), esp. 38–9 and ch. 8.
[174] BCB 3, fo. 376[v].

held a few days later at an alehouse in Aldersgate Street, though on this occasion only four apprentices turned up—Asherbye, Brooke, and the Clarke brothers—and they were joined by one Dale's wife and her sister. Henry Boden, 'inholder of Newgate Market', was also presented at Bridewell, and charged with 'receyvinge and lodginge' apprentices and prostitutes. While Katherine Dale was charged with 'kepynge company with th'apprentices'.[175]

This was a colourful episode in the bachelor's social round, gathering apprentices of two trades in the same neighbourhood at parties in several alehouses. The same names resurface. While the substantial banquet and the presence of the fiddler and women implies a measure of organization and a common purse. There were also other more unremarkable meetings between young men and prostitutes. Many more apprentices walked to one of London's bawdy houses, though their passage was plagued with potential hazards like the watch.[176] It was reported that one of the capital's more notorious keepers, William Blunt, was host to 'dyvers prentyses', who spent time with 'three noughtie women' who lodged in his house. One Bridewell deponent claimed that 'divers prentices dwelling in Chepesyde and other places' were regular callers at Mistress Cotton's and Joyner's bawdy houses. John Shaw had a constant stream of visitors at his five brothels, and they included 'dyvers younge men'. While another Bridewell witness claimed that 'divers younge women and men have gotten their deseases and burned their bodies in Long Lane'.[177]

Many young men like John Madammer, a feltmaker's apprentice 'who haunteth harlotts', made return trips to bawdy houses.[178] In February 1578 Edward Pew, the apprentice of one Mr Elleway who was probably free of the Merchant Tailors, was examined by the Bridewell governors. He told them 'that he twise had th'use of the bodye of a wife that dwelleth in a vittelinge house in Lambeth' giving her 'vid at one tyme and iiiid at another tyme'. Pew also admitted having 'th'use of another woman' in Southwark at one Foxe's alehouse, which was well known to be 'a comon bawdye'. It was a tailor's apprentice who told him about Foxe's house, and he 'had to doe with that Susan also'. Pew later confessed that 'he had

---

[175] BCB 3, fos. 24 Sept. 1579, 26 Sept. 1579, 3 Oct. 1579.

[176] The organization, location, and dimension of prostitution in Elizabethan London is more fully discussed in my 'The Structure of prostitution in Elizabethan London', *Continuity and Change*, 8 (1993), esp. 44–56.

[177] BCB 3, fos. 14ᵛ, 48ᵛ, 20 June 1579. Cf BCB 4, fo. 16 Aug. 1598.

[178] BCB 2, fo. 107ᵛ. Cf. BCB 4, fo. 49.

th'use of' Margery Gold of Hosier Lane 'in the middle of the lane'. Thomas Flood, a clothworker's apprentice, 'delt first with her'. A few days later one Edward Borrowhead escorted Pew and another apprentice 'to a vittelinge house in Chancery Lane'. He told the pair that Betts the landlord (and a tailor by day) 'had ii or iii pretty wenches'. Pew also had sex with the 'wiffe' of a 'lewde house' in St Katherine's, and 'aboute halfe a year sens he toke a wench [whom he met in the street] into his master's shopp, and ther had th'use of her bodye and turned her out agayne' giving her four pence. His recorded trips to the capital's bawdy houses closed with a visit to one 'Frances at Carter's house in Long Lane'.[179]

Pew's deposition gives us a clear impression of the map of prostitution—we see him walking around the city, drifting into the out-parishes, and crossing the river into Southwark. He visited the bawdy houses with other apprentices, and his tale conveys the convivial spirit which was a further attraction of such places. Many of London's bawdy houses masqueraded as alehouses and food, drink, tables, dancing, and gossip all helped to set the tone of camaraderie which was forged in the alehouse. Roland Bradshaw, another apprentice, was a regular caller at The White Lion, 'a very bawdye house' in East Smithfield where goodwife Jane Fuller kept the door. He also purchased sex at the Bee along Wood Street, another 'very comon brothel house', where he had regularly seen 'divers companyons of servingmen and prentises with harlotts'.[180] In October 1579 Robert Skerry, a stationer's apprentice, told the Bridewell governors how he had taken advantage of his master's absence 'out of towne', to visit a bawdy house in Cock Alley in St Martin's with four friends including another stationer's apprentice, Hugh Rawlyns. They remained 'for 3 howres in bed'. Later in the same evening, after shaking off a prying constable, 'Rawlyns knocked at the certen houses which had evell names . . . intending to have founde some harlots as he wente in the strete which they should abuse'. Summoned before the court, Rawlyns admitted that he had knocked at the door of a house in Thames Street, a notorious spot, and 'a house at Tower Hill nere the galloes for the like intente'. Thomas Scant, one of the four apprentices who joined Rawlyns that night, told the bench that Rawlyns fetched 'a whore from The Crosse Keyes at Powles Wharff to The Blew Boare, and ther Rawlyns and she were above together'.[181]

---

[179] BCB 3, fos. 287^v-8.   [180] BCB 3, fo. 274.
[181] Ibid. fos. 5 Oct. 1579, 14 Oct. 1579.

Hugh Rawlyns was familiar with London's shadier quarters. He knew the names and locations of the 'evell' houses, having been told about the bawdy house in Thames Street by a servingman and the 'house at Tower Hill nere the galloes' by Thomas Holme of Soper Street. Other apprentices also claimed that they had been introduced into the society of keepers and pimps by their fellows and friends. In 1600, for example, Richard Collingham was charged at Bridewell with fetching a number of 'lewd women' to his master's house where his fellow waited. John Woodstock's guide to 'The Nosse Keyes' at Paul's Wharf was his fellow, John Addis. While Henry Bennet was introduced to Anne Smith by George Wheatly, an apothecary's apprentice.[182] The locations of bawdy houses were well known, and there were characters in the bachelor's social round who could pass on news by word of mouth from one apprentice to another, or in the communications of pimps and other go-betweens like alehouse-keepers and tapsters. We have seen how Pew and his fellow were 'carried' to Betts's bawdy house. Edward Borrowhead, a tapster, told the Bridewell bench that 'he went to Browne's in Shove Lane at vii starres and ther caused to be lodged one night' two apprentices. In November 1607 John Crew was presented 'for frequentinge bawdie houses and intysinge mens apprentices to the like wickednes'.[183] Pimps were always seeking to build contacts with London's apprentices. They had a mental map of shady London peppered with dots fixing the locations of the bawdy houses and the likely places to target new clients. We can follow pimps in the sources as they 'carry' clients who are variously described as being 'young', 'apprentices', or 'servants' to bawdy houses. John Shaw, a keeper himself, claimed that John Byllard was 'a pander and carryer', and that he was closely 'acquainted with very many young men in London', fetching them 'to lewde howses and to the company of lewde and naughtie women who he is very well acquaynted withal'.[184] Contacts of this type were often informal; they were fashioned according to the rhythms of everyday life in the household, workshop, and alehouse, by a friend's invitation or a tapster's suggestion.

Even if prostitutes did not place themselves exclusively in a 'youth market', they could certainly hope to find a regular source of income among the capital's apprentices. One prostitute told the Bridewell court that she was 'acquaynted with iii prentises' in Thames

---

[182] BCB 4, fo. 177ᵛ; 3, fos. 228ᵛ–9, 355, 287ᵛ–8, See also BCB 3, fo. 2 Jan. 1577; 4, fo. 16 Aug. 1579; 5, fo. 356; GL MS 5770/2, fo. 99.

[183] BCB 3, fo. 288; 5, fo. 231. See also BCB 4, fo. 187.

[184] BCB 3, fo. 2 Jan. 1577.

Street, three of whom had 'th'use of her body', and two of them in The Bell at Shoreditch, 'one after another'. Her pimp, 'one that speaketh all languages', kept up a steady stream of apprentices. On two other occasions, three apprentices, Thomas Jackson (alias Taylor), Thomas Bridge, and Richard (Mr Sempar's man 'called fatt dick') 'had all three of them th'use of her bodye one after another at one tyme, and they gave her xiid a piece'. She also told the court about another meeting with three more apprentices at Goodwife Lett's house. In February 1576 Margery Brownwell admitted that she 'most filthilie hathe entised Richard Pennington and other mens prentises to have the use of hir bodie'. The 'divers immodest, lascivious, and shamelesse women' of Saffron Hill, who were nothing but 'common whores' lodging at 'divers houses for base filthy lucre sake', conducted their trade 'to the great corruption of youth'. While there are a number of cases in which apprentices were the targets of the provocations of nightwalkers who attempted 'to incite' them 'to lewdness'.[185] These narratives should be treated with care. Bawds, pimps, and prostitutes turned informant before the authorities, and supplied information which cast their fellows in a dark light to shift blame. The language which was used by young men (and the clerk) to relate events also attempted to allocate greater blame to prostitutes by speaking of enchantment and corruption. Like widows, wives, and dames who were charged with corrupting young men,[186] it was said that prostitutes tantalized apprentices. Thus Frances Baker was accused by a constable 'to be a comon enticer of mens apprentices' having been 'heretofore carted for a bawde'. Other prostitutes were rounded up 'enticing' young men in Cheapside, grabbing, seizing, and nestling up to them.[187]

A large number of other cases wait in the records; many visits to bawdy houses went unpunished and unrecorded. John Parmyter, for example, confessed that he had 'often resorted' to Alice Barlow before he finally attracted the attention of the authorities. Robert Ratcliffe claimed that he 'had th'use of' a 'very hansom younge woman' at Mistress Neale's bawdy house 'so often as he knoweth

---

[185] BCB 3, fos. 240ʳ, 7ᵛ, 1, fos. 113, 166; J. C. Jeaffreson (ed.), *Middlesex County Records* (Middlesex County Record Society, 4 vols.; 1886–92), ii. 171–2; BCB, 6, fos. 25ᵛ, 26ᵛ. It was said that the closure of the Southwark Stews was justified because 'youth is provoked, enticed and allowed to execute the fleshly lusts' (quoted by Archer, *Pursuit of Stability*, 332).

[186] See below, pp. 278–81.

[187] BCB 8, fo. 214. See also BCB 6, fos. 25, 26ᵛ, 185ᵛ, 252, 327, 336ᵛ, 348ᵛ, 417, 430ᵛ; 7, fos. 26ᵛ, 40ᵛ, 64, 66, 68, 95, 101ᵛ, 102, 147, 150, 161ᵛ, 280, 332, 359ᵛ, 360; 8, fos. 8ᵛ, 9, 10, 28ᵛ, 97, 130, 149ᵛ, 161, 170ᵛ, 192, 206, 206ᵛ, 234ᵛ, 236ᵛ, 239, 240ᵛ, 245ᵛ, 268, 281; 9, fo. 7.

not'; while two pimps reported that men resorted to bawdy houses 'and have harlotts as redely and commenly as men have vittels'. Other statements of daily resort ranged from six or seven clients to fifteen 'and lx or lxxx men in one daie'.[188] Despite problems raised by recording misdemeanours, we have presented sufficient archival evidence to bolster Stone's less well-supported argument that London's apprentices were an important clientage group. In fact, sources like the Bridewell courtbooks should be of interest to demographic historians, as they show that some young men could not contain their libidos in the interval between the first stirrings of puberty and the pattern of late marriage in early modern society. Yet London, after all, was a spacious city with alehouses clustered along its bustling thoroughfares and maze of alleys and courts. The records of smaller towns and rural districts also mention 'bawdy houses', 'bawds', 'whores', and many cases of 'lewd resort'. Yet we should not assume that such words offer reliable evidence of commercial sex. They also belonged to a far broader vocabulary of moral meaning in élite and popular discourse which labelled people who either tolerated or encouraged illicit sex; a look-out at a door, for instance, or a harbourer of pregnant women.[189] Our picture of provincial and rural prostitution before 1700, however, is far from complete. In fact, the sources I have consulted outside London rarely record payments to prostitutes, though we can sometimes infer forms of commercial sex from the scattered entries in these courtbooks and even the occasional telling sign of a bawdy house.[190]

Not only does the example of London raise questions of typicality, the sample obtained from the London sources may itself be unrepresentative. The number of prosecutions in the records is, after all, a pale reflection of the absolute number of apprentices in

[188] BCB 3, fos. 114, 339^v, 318, 147, 20 June 1579; 4, fo. 261^v.

[189] Cf. Ingram, *Church Courts*, 282; Archer, *Pursuit of Stability*, 211.

[190] The following references provide scattered examples of bawdy houses, fees and tales of illicit activity that seem to be the provincial counterpart of the many examples in the London sources. See, for example, ERO D/ACA 25, fo. 172^v; 30, fo. 215; 50, fos. 113, 117; ORO PCBP 1626–36, fos. 123^v, 134; CUL EDR B/2/13, fo. 76; B/2/14, fos. 7, 17; B/2/15, fo. 131; B/2/17, fo. 6^v; NRO NMC 7, fo. 211; 8, fos. 582, 632; 9, fos. 272, 311, 425; 10, fos. 482, 557, 576; 12, fos. 121, 178, 225, 429, 563; 13, fo. 473; 14, fos. 37, 165, 237, 258^v, 314^v; 15, fo. 40; 16, fo. 58; 20, fo. 443^v; NCQS 'The Sessions Booke 1630–38', fo. 24; YCA B/33, fos. 65, 304^v; 34, fos. 3, 9^v, 20^v; City and Ainsty Quarter Sessions minute book, 1638–62, fos. 73, 183, 187; BIHR YV/CB2, fo. 20^v; Wis/1 (unpaginated); W. Hale (ed.), *A Series of Precedents and Proceedings in Criminal Causes Extending from the Year 1475 to 1640: Extracts from the Act Books of the Ecclesiastical Courts in the Diocese of London*, 1847 (facsimile, Edinburgh, 1973), 201; H. E. Salter (ed.), *Oxford Council Acts 1563–1625* (Oxford Historical Society, 87, Oxford, 1928), 172; Cooper and Cooper, *Annals of Cambridge*, ii. 19, 167, 496; iii. 15–16; Stone, *Family, Sex and Marriage*, 616.

the capital. Did all of London's apprentices visit bawdy houses, or, indeed, participate in the bachelor's social round, and were young clients drawn from certain sections of apprentices? It will be clear by now that it is misleading to relegate the body of apprentices to tidy terms like 'apprentice culture', which disguise stark inequalities of wealth and status.[191] A trip to a brothel required some money. Was it therefore the case that only certain groups of apprentices could pay the fee charged by prostitutes? Contemporary authors fill the brothels with young sparks, gallants, fops, 'rough roaring roysters', and captains. The fop was a prominent character in moral commentaries treating the iniquities of prostitution.[192] The image of the spark suggests wealth and status. Nevertheless, the Bridewell records convey the real impression that apprentices of all trades purchased sex. The clerk did not always note a master's occupation, but from those occasions when he did we can draw a reasonable image of the pattern of clientage. No single trade is notably prominent. But the apprentices of goldsmiths, butchers, fishmongers, merchants, haberdashers, dyers, and servants of the upper ranks head the Bridewell sample. One prostitute could not remember the names of her clients, but she could confirm that 'they were of all trades'.[193]

Apprentices are also well represented in the broader survey of the social status of all clients or 'gessts' as they were more politely known to keepers, prostitutes, and pimps. In a small sample of 219 clients whose status can be positively identified,[194] apprentices/servants form the largest group (39.3 per cent), followed by a mixed bag of craftsmen and tradesmen (12.3 per cent),[195] ambassadors' retinues (7.8 per cent), the servants of bishops and the upper ranks (5 per cent), and young men of the Inns of Court (3.2 per cent).[196]

---

[191] See above, Ch. 3.

[192] For example, Thomas Dekker, *Northward Ho*, in Thomas Bowers (ed.), *The Dramatic Works of Thomas Dekker* (4 vols.; Cambridge, 1955–61), 4. 3. 74–5; and in the same edition see *Westward Ho*, 2. 2. 236; 4. 1. 10; and *Honest Whore, Part 2*, 2. 2. 5–9. See also *Amanda, Or the Reformed Whore*, 1635, facsimile, ed. F. Ouvry (1869), 35; John Dunton, *The Night-Walker, Or Evening Rambles in Search of Lewd Women*, 1696, ed. R. Trumbach (Garland Series: Marriage, Sex and the Family in England 1660–1800, 19, 1985), Feb., 11, 19.

[193] BCB 3, fo. 280.

[194] This sample has the problem of identifying groups of clients as one individual: i.e. 'divers stillyard men' or 'divers prentises' are reduced to a single entry in these particular cases 'foreign merchant' and 'apprentice'. This sample, therefore, clearly underrepresents the true extent of clientage for a number of groups, most frequently apprentices.

[195] For the sake of clarity this group unfortunately includes a wide range of trades, from a goldsmith to a bricklayer.

[196] Other major groups in the sample include servants and the sons of civic officials, members of the aristocracy and the military (2.3 per cent each), and attorneys and pimps (1.4 per cent).

The bawd's best customers in Dekker's *Northward Ho* (1607) were apprentices and tailors.[197] One problem with using Bridewell records is that because the bench targeted the brothels rather than the streets, they provide a window to the higher echelons of the structure of prostitution, so that the level of fees they reveal or the social profile of clientage is likely to be unrepresentative. Ian Archer has also argued that wealthier clients may have enjoyed some immunity from prosecution, though Bridewell's examiners 'often stirred muddy waters near the centre of power'.[198] Keepers opened their doors to some well-connected individuals;[199] some of them established links with foreign merchants;[200] still others played host to the capital's apprentices, who were numerically far more significant.

Fees might cast further light on clientage patterns. We lack an estimate of the average fee in Tudor and Stuart London. My sample of 111 payments, however, is sufficient to convey a first impression.[201] The average fee was 4s. 3d., though clear distinctions emerge between the average paid by apprentices (1s. 10d.), and that paid by a rather amorphous and untidy group—the non-apprentices— where the one rule for inclusion is that they cannot be positively identified as apprentices (5s. 8d.). Twenty-two apprentices paid twelve pence or less for sex (53.6 per cent),[202] but only 27.1 per cent of the non-apprentices paid two shillings or less. The highest recorded fee paid by an apprentice was ten shillings, though 96.7 per cent of them paid five shillings or less. As many as 27.2 per cent of the non-apprentices paid over five shillings for their trip to a brothel. A rough indication of what apprentices were able to pay is provided by John Madammer, the feltmaker's apprentice who 'haunted harlotts'. He was paid 'iiiis a weke being great wages'.[203] Ages and wages were sensitive variables. Apprentices were more likely to be paid towards the end of their term; they had greater purchasing power in years five–seven of their service.[204] There may also be a number of apprentices hidden among the non-apprentices, who

---

[197] Dekker, *Northward Ho*, 4. 3. 84, 86 (but cf. 4. 3. 74–5). See also Dekker's *Honest Whore, Part 2*, 2. 2. 5–9; 4. 3. 75; *Amanda*, 37; Thomas Nashe, *Christ's Tears over Jerusalem*, 1593 (Scolar Press facsimile, Menston, 1970), fo. 77.

[198] Archer, *Pursuit of Stability*, 231–2.

[199] They included one of Sir Christopher Hatton's servingmen, 'a steward to my Lord Catlyn', a 'gent to my Lord of Warwicke or my Lord of Leicester', 'my Lord of Oxford's man', one of Essex's servants, and Sir Owen Hoxton's second son.

[200] Most of the clients that Mother or Melcher Perse or Pelse 'carried' across London were merchants who could 'speak no Englishe' (BCB 3, fos. 109ᵛ, 112).

[201] The sample consists of forty-one apprentices and seventy non-apprentices.

[202] 2d. × 1, 4d. × 2, 6d. × 6, and 12d. × 13.   [203] BCB 2, fo. 107ᵛ.

[204] Cf. Ben-Amos, *Adolescence and Youth in Early Modern England*, 128–9.

would have reduced the differential between the two groups. The lower fee paid by apprentices is difficult to interpret. A more sophisticated survey would compare the status of the client's trade with the fee; young men of high-status trades may have had more money to spend. Apprentices may have spent money in the lower quarters of metropolitan prostitution—in the low-grade bawdy houses, or the maze of alleys and streets. My sample of fees, however, is too small for this next step.

Some apprentices, therefore, not only had the opportunity to visit the capital's bawdy houses, but also the means to purchase sex. Fees were quite generous. Nor were 'pocket-money' from home or money wages the only sources of income. Money could be obtained in other ways, and the Bridewell governors were often concerned to locate sources of funding. They asked Hugh Rawlyns 'where he had the monye he spent' during his tour of the bawdy houses. He told them 'that when his master sent him to sell wares he solde sometymes iiiid or vid over his master's price and that he kept to himselfe'. Edmund Ingelthorpe topped up his meagre payments with gifts of stockings stolen from his master. He explained that when he fetched stockings from suppliers 'he would sett upp two payres for one payre in the book'. Thomas Wilson pilfered candles and apples, and he also confessed that 'sometymes he sould some of his master's householde hearbes'. Other apprentices raided their master's household or shop, stealing a wide range of items—including beef, cheese, bread, and fine materials to make aprons or hats—which they used to pay for sex in kind, or to top up the money in their pockets. A master's purse was another source of funds. The amounts stolen varied greatly, but they could be as high as six or ten pounds.[205] Small wonder then, that a near proverbial wisdom held that 'whoring is succeeded by robbery'.[206]

5. 'Outward Conformity'

Prompted by a deep concern with socialization and images of moral corruption, the authorities launched periodic campaigns to tame

[205] BCB 3, fo. 5 Oct. 1579; 4, fos. 178" (irregular pagination), 23 May 1590. See also BCB 3, fos. 31ᵛ, 34ᵛ, 57, 228ᵛ–9, 231, 289ᵛ, 293ᵛ, 349; 4, fos. 179, 462; 5, fos. 251, 328.

[206] Saunders Welch, *A Proposal to Render Effectual a Plan to Remove the Nuisance of Common Prostitutes from the Streets of the Metropolis*, 1758, facsimile, ed. R. Trumbach in *Prostitution Reform: Four Documents* (Garland Series: Marriage, Sex and the Family in England 1660–1800, 22, 1985), 14. See also Nashe, *Christ's Tears*, fos. 77–7ᵛ; Dunton, *The Night-Walker*, Feb., Epistle Dedicatory; *Amanda*, 74; Robert Greene, *A Disputation between a He Cony-Catcher and a She Cony Catcher*, 1592, reprinted in A. V. Judges (ed.), *The Elizabethan Underworld* (1965), 223, 224–5.

this rough male culture targeting alehouses, bawdy houses, gaming houses, and playhouses.[207] In January 1611, for example, London Common Council claimed that

apprentices do in these daies live more riotouslie and at their pleasures in spending their times in daunsing scholes, dycing houses, tennys courtes, bowling allies, brothell houses, and other exercises unfitt for their degrees and callings to the high displeasure of almightie God, wastinge of their master's substances, and utter overthrowe of themselves.

Apprentices were forbidden to 'have anie chest, presse, truncke, deske, or other place to laie upp or keepe anie apparrell or goods, saving onelie in his master's house or by his master's license'.[208] Magistrates and moralists also associated fine clothes with wayward, promiscuous youth. The hunger for fashion to parade in the bachelor's social round also produced young spendthrifts and pilferers. The style of clothes and accessories like swords or codpieces were further emblems of youth and developing manhood.[209] Worse still, these examples of inordinate pride upset social order, including age-relations.[210] The public demonstration of social order was not only an issue of choreographed rituals like processions and church seating plans, individual appearance, especially clothing and hairstyles, was also subject to the critical gaze of magistrates. As each teenage year passed by, the desire to catch the eye of a potential sweetheart or to strike a pose among fellows by wearing dashing clothes and sporting fashionable hair-styles became stronger. In this sense, the taste for fashion was a further distinguishing mark between age-groups and stages in the long age of youth. Clothing provided another way of expressing the difference of the ages of man, and provoked generational squabbles because many young people, especially middle and upper class youth with money to spare, attached significance to striking clothing.

Writing in 1629, Edmund Bolton commented that apprentices had 'drunke and sacrificed too deeply to their new godesse, Saint Fashion'. Even godly John Crook derived great satisfaction from his fine clothing.[211] The principal purpose of the London Common Council Act of 1611 which regulated access to institutions in the bachelor's social round was in fact the 'reformacon of abuses in

[207] For example, CLRO Reps. 13, fo. 86ᵛ; 14, fo. 378; Jours. 21, fo. 68; 23, fo. 38; 25, fo. 345.

[208] CLRO Jour. 28, 161–2ᵛ.   [209] Cf. Roper, 'Blood and codpieces', esp. 117–19.

[210] Cf. Margaret Pelling, 'Apprenticeship, health and social cohesion in early modern London', *History Workshop Journal*, 37 (1994), 43, and above, Ch. 2, and below Ch. 6.

[211] Bolton, *Cities Advocate*, 40; Crook, *Short History*, 7.

apparrell in apprentices and mayden and women servants'. The preamble drew attention to 'abuses growinge by reason of excesse and strange fashion of apparrell used by manie apprentices'. Other young men set a shining example; they were 'contented with such decent apparrell as is fittinge and their masters well able to afford'. But this taste for fashion had caused 'many inconveniences'.[212] The sight of a mere 'servant' parading in fine clothes in the public theatre of a bustling street provided a visual proof of how youthful pride could subvert social order. They crossed valued social categories which preserved distinctions of 'place', and merited swift public redress. In November 1570, for example, Thomas Bradshaw, a merchant tailor's apprentice was spotted 'contrary to good order' strolling along a London street in 'a payre of monstrous great hose' lavishly decorated with 'stuffinge and lyninge'. The Court of Aldermen ordered 'that he be put into his [plain] doblet and hose, and so lead home through the streates into his master's howse'. Before his master's door and an audience of neighbours, 'the lyninge and stuffinge' of the offensive hose 'were cut and pulled out' as a ritual affirmation of the close correspondence between clothing and the politics of age. In 1575 seven apprentices were 'sett up on a scaffold in Cheapsyde for that they being apprentices . . . did buye certyn apparell not being decent for any apprentys to weare'. They remained in full public view for one hour 'havinge the same apparell on their backs', and 'afterwards' were strapped to a cart and whipped through the streets.[213]

Historians have tended to interpret early modern dress with regard to class and the condition of English textiles hitherto,[214] though contemporary magistrates and moralists also assumed that clothes would serve as a further visual validation of the social distance between youth and age (what Edmund Bolton called 'outward conformity').[215] William Gouge reminded young people that their clothes 'must be so fashioned and ordered as . . . may declare them

---

[212] CLRO Jour. 28, fos. 161–2ᵛ.

[213] CLRO Reps. 17, fo. 78ᵛ; 18, fo. 456. See also CH minute book 1558–81, fo. 220ᵛ; CLRO Rep. 15, fos. 78, 411ᵛ.

[214] For example, Joan Thirsk, 'The fantastical folly of fashion: the English stocking knitting industry 1500–1700', in N. B. Harte and F. C. Ponting (eds.), *Textile History and Economic History: Essays in Honour of Miss Julia de Mann* (Manchester, 1973); N. B. Harte, 'State control of dress and social change in pre-industrial England', in D. C. Coleman and A. H. John (eds.), *Trade, Government and Economy in Pre-Industrial England: Essays Presented to F. J. Fisher* (1976); R. A. Houston, *Social Change in the Age of Enlightenment: Edinburgh 1660–1760* (Oxford, 1994), esp. 56–8; Daniel Roche, *The Culture of Clothing: Dress and Fashion in the Ancien Regime*, trans. Jean Birrell (Cambridge, 1994), esp. 39, 511–13.

[215] Bolton, *Cities Advocate*, 40.

to be servants and under their masters'.[216] Magistrates made connections between appearance and behaviour, and in so doing attempted to distinguish stable boundaries between young and old,
and appropriate conduct for young men and women. Particular
concern was expressed about apprentices.[217] It was hoped that 'substantial' citizens and future governors would emerge from their
ranks. So, the proper distance between these custodians of future
prosperity and mere 'ruffians' and women was one measure of an
ordered society. Thus Edmund Bolton described a distinctive apprentice uniform. In 1634 the governors of London Bridewell complained about apprentices for not wearing standard hospital dress,
'but altering the same' and 'dying their hatts blacke'.[218] There is
other evidence that early modern people associated inferior dress
with the low status of youth. In an answer to a charge filed at Star
Chamber, John Gent reported that Thomas Greenwood walked into
an alehouse 'without a gown . . . apparrelled more like an apprentice than a gentleman, his hose being untrust and his bosom opened,
his doublett being unbuttoned and his shirte out it seemed by the
bosome verie fowle and slabbered'. Richard Flood confirmed that
Greenwood 'was apparelled in a slubbered suite of clothes like an
apprentice without a gowne'.[219] In this case, the appearance of
youth was associated with the way in which clothes were put on—
open shirts and trailing garments.

The choice of outer garments was a means of communicating
distinctions of age and social pedigree. Sumptuary legislation reserved fine materials and decorations as 'a special and laudable
marke' for the upper classes and high ranking officials. Yet a regular lament was that a taste for fashion blurred social categories.
Arthur Dent's Pilagathos declared, 'nowa-dayes . . . fewe will keep
within compass, fewe will knowe their places . . . and thus we see in
this matter of apparrell how all is out of joynt'.[220] Sumptuary laws

---

[216] Gouge, *Domesticall Duties*, 456, 622.

[217] Cf. Catherine Kovesi Killerby, 'Practical problems in the enforcement of Italian sumptuary law, 1200–1500', in Trevor Dean and K. J. P. Lowe (eds.), *Crime, Society and the Law
in Renaissance Italy* (Cambridge, 1994), 115, who writes that in Florence at that time 'Not a
single prosecution has been found concerning men'. She considers this to be unsurprising
'if one considers that the overwhelming majority of sumptuary laws were directed at women's
clothing and ornaments'. Diane Owen Hughes also relates sumptuary measures in Renaissance Italy to a concern with women ('Sumptuary law and social relations in Renaissance
Italy', in John Bossy (ed.), *Disputes and Settlements: Law and Human Relations in the West*
(Cambridge, 1983), esp. 82–4). Young men were more often the subjects of rhetoric and the
few prosecutions which I have discovered in English materials.

[218] Bolton, *Cities Advocate*, 39; BCB 7, fo. 377ᵛ.   [219] PRO STAC 8, 156/1.

[220] CLRO Jour. 22, fo. 164; Arthur Dent, *The Plaine-Mans Path-way to Heaven*, 1601 (facsimile, The English Experience, 652, Amsterdam, NJ, 1974), 58–9.

were repealed in 1604.[221] Nevertheless, the connection between class, morality, theft, and appropriate dress was perpetuated in courts and institutions which were still prepared to prosecute young people who paraded in unseemly clothing. Young apprentices received clothing at the start and finish of their terms, though some of them clearly craved other styles of dress and expression. There are examples of apprentices pilfering from their master to purchase fashionable clothes. In 1598 Robert Saker of London was presented 'for purloyning' his mistresse's goods to buy 'a hose and doblett laid out with satten, a payre of jersey stockings, a payre of Spanish leather shoes, a payre of silke stockings, and change of clothes and other apparrell'. William Atkinson, who called at 'tavernes dyvers tymes with dyvers companyes of prentyses', admitted stealing ten pounds in money and goods from his master, and spending 'as he thinks', £4 or £5 upon fresh clothes. A woodmonger's apprentice was presented for 'violentlye . . . spending his master's moneyes and goods to the value of £7', drinking and dicing at an alehouse in Charing Cross. He also 'brought a paire of hose' worth 6s. 8d., 'and a dublett' priced at eight shillings.[222] Tailors who cut and measured clothes for young people did so at the risk of prosecution.[223]

The ambitious purpose of this drive to reform dress habits was to procure 'uniforme order . . . touching apprentices apparell',[224] to describe a standard code of dress for apprentices, which would advertise their subordinate status to all passers-by. 'Conformitie' was also the objective of the aforementioned Act of January 1611. An earlier Common Council Act of 1582 preached the virtues of 'uniformitie'. The preamble to this particular drive for conformity tells the familiar story about fashion-conscious young people dressing above their status and calling, 'haunting . . . inconvenient places and exercyses', and elevating pride and irreverence above honest thrift and toil. The following articles stripped apprentices of all 'stitching', 'cuttinge', 'edginge', 'garnishing', ruffs, frills, girdles,

---

[221] But not because of any reduction in the significance of the visual properties of clothing. The lack of success in enforcing the legislation is a more likely reason for its removal from the statute book.

[222] BCB 4, fo. 53ᵛ; 3, fo. 114ᵛ; 1, fo. 184. See also CLRO Jours. 17, fo. 324ᵛ; 21, fo. 296ᵛ. For examples of attempts to enforce sumptuary laws in Norwich see NRO NMC 7, fos. 550, 554, 613; 8, fo. 184; 9, fo. 469.

[223] For example, BCB 2, fo. 164; NRO NMC 12, fo. 380. In 1575 the Bridewell governors were instructed to 'take order with certayne taylors' producing clothes for apprentices 'beinge not decente or seamely for apprentyses to weare', CLRO Rep. 19, fo. 4; while in 1577 the Court of Aldermen inquired about people 'harboring cloathes in comon ines or other places', ibid. fo. 267.

[224] CLRO Rep. 17, fo. 389.

and garters, and proposed a plain alternative—a 'most plaine' pair of breeches, a plain shirt, doublet, coat, cloak, and a woollen cap, all made from the poorest cloth and held together by 'plaine stringes' and 'plain white seame'. Again, the point was made as simply as possible; to counter theft, irreverence, and immorality, young people should be confined to clothes provided by their master. Nor were they to wear 'any sword, dagger . . . or other weapon' save for a 'convenient' meat knife, on their travels about the capital.[225] The Act of 1611 went into even finer detail, closely checking each turn and fold of clothing, traversing the body from hat to shoe, and proposing limits to the length of various items of dress and expenditure. Hats should be 'no broader' than three inches, and no more than five shillings should be spent on them. Ruffs and bans were not to exceed three yards. Collars were to be 'close and comelie'. Silk doublets, breeches, and stockings were forbidden, and legs were to be dressed only in 'cloth, kersey, fustian, sackcloth, canvas, English leather and Englishe stuff not exceeding 2s/6d,' and woollen stockings. No more than twelve pence should be spent on gloves, and Spanish leather shoes were clearly out of step with plain uniformity. If young people could not cast off fine materials and decorations they were to be committed to the Little Ease prison for eighteen hours.[226]

This preoccupation with the subversive potential of dress is well documented in London in the stream of correspondence flowing between central and metropolitan authorities, and in a number of orders and acts of Common Council. The 'matter of apparell' was in large part a problem of youth. It prompted gloomy forecasts about respect for social order, and was one aspect of a far broader perception of criminality which associated theft and immorality with the servant class. In 1559 the Privy Council instructed masters to keep a regular check on their servants' boxes, chests, and wardrobes, and to throw out any unsavoury items.[227] Thirteen years later the Court of Aldermen set up a special committee to 'devise some good advise for reformacon of that great disorder nowe as used by prentises in there excesse and monstrousness in apparell'.[228] Guidelines were circulated to the livery companies 'to be openly redd unto the whole companie'. Watches were appointed at strategic spots to arrest young people dressed in 'monstrous' clothing, and

---

[225] CLRO Jours. fos. 28, 161–2ᵛ; 21, fos. 206ᵛ–7ᵛ. The public wearing of daggers was prohibited in other towns like Stratford-upon-Avon (Savage, *Stratford-upon-Avon Minutes*, 72, 83, 126).

[226] CLRO 28, fos. 161–2ᵛ.   [227] Harte, 'State control of dress', 145–6.

[228] CLRO Rep. 17, fos. 353–3ᵛ, 389, 454ᵛ. Cf. Rep. 14, fo. 252ᵛ.

aldermen were cautioned 'to have a vigilant eye'. Special searches and watches had been a regular feature of the drive to contain 'the wearing of great hose or long swordes and daggers'.[229] Nevertheless, the problem of dress in London resurfaced with alarming regularity. A Common Council Act was passed in 1582. Another Act of 1588 lamented the 'inordinate excesse in apparell . . . to the confusion of degrees and all estates', and gave this problem its customary age-aspect declaring that 'this infection was seene to have made entrie amongst the youth'.[230]

The 1582 Act, which was reissued in 1588 and 1597,[231] appears to have met with little success. Further 'committees for excesses of apparell' were created in 1584. Nevertheless, in 1597 fine garments and embellishments still stood out like bright beacons in the crowd, and Common Council announced that 'no reformacon at all hath followed . . . sundrie proclamacons'.[232] Thirteen years later complaints flooded in to governors from 'divers grave and worthy citizens', who declared that 'the excessive and inordinate pride used by apprentices and mayden servants of this citty in their apparell' was 'evident to the view of all men'. The taste for fresh styles had even gathered pace, 'so much that there is not almost any fashion used att the court' but is quickly followed by apprentices who squandered their master's possessions. Another committee was established.[233] There were many hurdles in the way of metropolitan orders and royal proclamations regulating dress.[234] But one piece of evidence suggests that rumours about an imminent act resulted in a careful pause in the retailing of fine clothing. In November 1616 Nathaniel Brent wrote that 'every houre we expect a proclamation about wearing of clothe, which because it hath bin long talked of hath made a great number of people forbear to buy stuffes and silks, and hath caused a deadnesse of merchandise in Cheapside as yt may protest there was not a greater in ye time of ye greatest plague'.[235] But there is far more evidence to suggest that the drive to force 'uniformity' in dress on the youth of London despite numerous acts, watches, wards, and committees was a miserable failure. The final committee which is mentioned in pre-Revolution

[229] See CLRO Jours. 21, fos. 210ᵛ, 428; 22, fos. 164ᵛ–5ᵛ; 24, fos. 227, 237ᵛ; Reps. 14, fo. 332ᵛ; 15, fos. 77, 86; 16, fo. 48ᵛ; CH minute book 1558–81, fos. 9, 16ᵛ, 70, 70ᵛ, 90, 167, 170, 208; GL MS 11,588/1, fos. 46, 48, 128.
[230] CLRO Jours. 21, fos. 206ᵛ–7ᵛ; 22, fos. 164–4ᵛ.
[231] CLRO Jours. 22, fos. 164ᵛ–5ᵛ; 24, fos. 227–8.
[232] CLRO Jours. 21, fo. 399ᵛ; 24, fo. 227; Rep. 21, fo. 26ᵛ.
[233] CLRO Rep. 29, fos. 277ᵛ–8.   [234] Cf. Killerby, 'Practical problems'.
[235] PRO SP 14/89/55.

records of city government was set up in November 1638 to 'advise and consider' the dangerous freedom claimed by apprentices in their extravagant clothes.[236]

Plain and 'severe habit' was also requested by the Merchant Adventurers of Newcastle. The company wished to dress its apprentices in a 'coarse side-coat, close-hose [and] clothe-stockings', and to trim all 'great ruffes', velvet, lace, or silk. A number of acts were issued 'for the apperell of apryntyses' and every youth was handed a copy of the 1554 Act. Young people who continued to wear forbidden garments were dispatched to a 'special' apprentices' 'gaoll or prison'. Interestingly, this mistrust of decoration was one aspect of a wider concern with the morals of youth, which also included the closer policing of dancing, dicing, and mumming.[237] In London too, the scrutiny of personal appearance was part of a broader moral thrust, which was in large part stirred by anxieties about distinctions of age and the socializing process. The Court of Aldermen made the connection between 'the reformacon of apparell' and the purge of alehouses. While a final clause in the Common Council Act of 1582 banned the capital's apprentices from dancing and fencing schools. It will be remembered that the Act of 1611 also marked off 'daunsing scholes, dycing houses, tennys courtes, bowling allies, [and] brothell houses' as forbidden territory for youth.[238] It was not only young men who came under the microscope of this concern with appropriate dress. Nevertheless, the greater part of élite commentaries targeted apprentices who pilfered to purchase clothes, and others who may well have had the money already in their pockets; young men of wealthier trades and backgrounds. The 'swaggering' fop, spark, or gallant may well have been a principal quarry for these drives to reform the manners of youth.[239] He was also the object of heated invective in works treating the iniquities of prostitution and playhouses.[240] But relatively humble apprentices also visited brothels and paraded in fine clothes.

Another expression of the ages of man and good morals was hair, the visual accomplice of clothing crowning, as it did, outward

[236] CLRO Jours. 28, fos. 161–2ᵛ; 38, fo. 173ᵛ.
[237] J. R. Boyle and F. W. Dendy (eds.), *Extracts from the Records of the Merchant Adventurers of Newcastle-upon-Tyne* [hereafter, *Newcastle Merchant Adventurers Records*] (2 vols.; Surtees Society, 93, 101, Durham, 1895, 1899) i. 20–1, 22–3.
[238] CLRO Rep. 14, fo. 245; Jours. 21, fos. 206ᵛ–7ᵛ; 28, fos. 161–2ᵛ.
[239] Cf. Christopher Brooks, 'Apprenticeship, social mobility and the middling sort 1550–1800', in Jonathan Barry and Brooks (eds.), *The Middling Sort of People: Culture, Society and Politics in England, 1550–1800* (Basingstoke, 1994), 80.
[240] See above, p. 219.

appearances. Indeed, the Common Council Act of 1611 coupled clothing and hair in the same stern reprimand. No apprentice was to 'weare his haire with any tuft or lock but cut short in decent and comelie manner'. The threat of eighteen hours in prison again hung over young offenders. The 1638 committee set up to invest-igate opulent dress also discussed a suitable curb on the 'libertie [taken by apprentices] in wearing of long haire'.[241] Improper hair-cuts elicited sharp responses from moralists. They dwelled upon the dreadful portents of long hair in male youth, which was appar-ently becoming popular towards the close of the sixteenth cen-tury.[242] In his *The Loathsomenesse of Long Haire* (1654), however, Thomas Hall wrote that long hair, 'a most loathsome and horrible disease', was 'unheard of in former times', and John Aubrey, writ-ing in the 1680s, reported that 'the cropping short of ye appren-tices haire' was 'now out of fashion'.[243] Hall claimed to have tracked the origins of this 'disease' to Poland. He quoted no less an author-ity than William Perkins—'the wearing of long haire in the younger sort is an abuse of it, it hath been among the aged [but] now it is become a trick of youth'.[244] Some contemporaries felt concerned if they were confused with such styles (and their association with youth and effete fashion). Two yeomen and an attorney plotted 'not onely to defame, disgrace, and discreditt' Gervase Markham, a Notting-hamshire justice, but also to 'withdraw good opinion of him'. They were alleged to have circulated libels 'in divers and sundry places', claiming that Markham 'kept noe house nor hospitality, that he was a great swearer, a great quarreller', who seldom went to church and plundered illicit spoils from his position on the bench, and 'that he did wayre his hayre verye longe'.[245]

Nor was it simply a question of the politics of age. Long hair in male youth was considered to be untidy, unbecoming, and a reli-able intimation of immorality, but it also blurred distinctions be-tween appropriate male and female appearances (and conduct). Thomas Hall commented that long hair was 'proper to women', so that it was a 'shamelesse thing for women to poll their heads'. Indeed, William Prynne thought that it was 'the very badge and character of their subjection both to God and men'.[246] In this case,

---

[241] CLRO Jours. 28, fos. 161–2ᵛ; 38, fo. 173ᵛ.
[242] V. A. La Mar, 'English dress in the age of Shakespeare', in L. B. Wright and La Mar (eds.), *Life and Letters in Tudor and Stuart England* (Ithaca, NY, 1962), 398.
[243] Thomas Hall, *The Loathsomenesse of Long Haire* (1654), Preface; Aubrey, *Remaines*, 37.
[244] Hall, *Loathsomenesse of Long Haire*, 1. [245] PRO STAC 8 208/31.
[246] Hall, *Loathsomenesse of Long Haire*, 26; William Prynne, *The Unlovelinesse of Lovelockes* (1628), fo. A3ʳ.

as in others in which women 'contrary to all honestye of womanhood
. . . wente abroade in the streats' dressed in 'manes clothinge',[247] it
was felt that outward appearance was an emblem of inner character. Again, Prynne refers to the 'unnatural [and] whorish cutting'
of female hair, which should fall in a gentle cascade over the shoulders. He reminded his audience that women who cut their hair
high above the collar were 'brazen-faced, shamelesse (if not unchast
and whorish) English hermophrodites or man-woman monsters',
who cried 'battel and defiance unto Heaven itself'.[248] Young men
who sported 'frizzles' and 'lovelocks' were wholly 'degenerated and
metamorphosed into women', effeminate, unkempt, and unmanly.
Prynne typically stated that hair 'of a moderate, ordinary, grave,
and decent length' was 'most suitable' for 'the most noble race'.[249]

It was vital to differentiate sex roles at an early stage, so that
young men could be adequately prepared to employ and govern
others. Apprentices, therefore, were told to wear their hair 'close
cut'. In 1603 the Newcastle Merchant Adventurers ordered apprentices not to 'weare their haire longe, nor lockes at their eares like
a ruffian'. Observing that of late young men in London had allowed their hair to fall 'unseemly long more like ruffians than to
citizens apprentices', the Ironmongers' Court refused to grant any
apprentice his freedom unless he had first 'orderly cutt and barbed
his hayre' (1638). Two years later, the Court of Aldermen ruled
that no apprentice would be made free of the city unless 'he shall
present himself at that time with the hair of his head cut in decent
and comely manner'.[250] On occasion, courts ordered that the hair
of vagrants, thieves, and other offenders should be 'clipped' in
open court or some anteroom, though long hair alone was sufficient
to warrant punishment.[251] 'Long curled locks' had been banned at
Cambridge in 1595, but in his 1636 visitation, Laud enquired after
'long frizled hair upon ye head' of undergraduates.[252] It was a

---

[247] For example, CLRO Reps. 18, fo. 372; 19, fos. 93, 137.

[248] Prynne, *Unlovelinesse of Lovelockes*, 40 (irregular pagination).

[249] Ibid. fos. A3^{r-v}, 34.

[250] Bolton, *Cities Advocate*, 39; Boyle and Dendy, *Newcastle Merchant Adventurers Records*, i. 23; Dunlop and Denman, *English Apprenticeship*, 192; Smith, 'London apprentices', 221. Cf. S. R. G. Gardiner (ed.), *Reports of Cases in the Courts of Star Chamber and High Commission* (Camden Society, New Series, 39, Westminster, 1886), 114.

[251] For example, NRO NMC 15, fos. 32, 120^v, 294; NCQS minute book 1629–36, fo. 80; BCB 4, fo. 425; 6, fos. 47^v, 318, 318^v, 319, 363, 367^v, 390^v, 393^v, 394^v, 407^v, 408, 412^v, 426^v, 430, 433^v, 436^v, 442; 7, fos. 31, 35^v, 44, 86, 89^v, 107, 127, 132, 150^v, 162^v, 171, 178^v, 201, 216, 222, 229, 252^v, 289^v, 316^v; 8, fo. 117^v; CH minute book 1581–1605, fo. 213; Dunlop and Denman, *English Apprenticeship*, 192.

[252] Cooper and Cooper, *Annals of Cambridge*, ii. 538; iii. 280.

happier story from Oxford. In 1634 the warden of All Souls wrote 'an answere' to Laud 'concerning . . . reformation in haire and apparell', telling the archbishop 'that there is a good conformity' both in clothing and hair.[253]

Nehemiah Wallington purchased his copy of *The Loathsomenesse of Long Haire* in the topsy-turvy years of the English Revolution. He also sent a copy to London's Chamberlain with a covering letter pressing him 'to do what lies in his power to suppress this sin of long hair in youth and apprentices'.[254] In these years the foundations of social order appeared to shake and gloomy soothsayers saw moral chaos in every corner. It was said that young people turned authority upside down, and savoured 'liberty of vice without reprehension or restraint'.[255] Thomas Edwards claimed that toleration would admit all 'allowance and practises of long hair [and] all kindes of fashions in apparell'.[256] The concern with long hair at this time was not restricted to the printed page. In October 1649 the Newcastle Merchant Adventurers passed an Act 'for the better regulating of apprentices in their hayre, apparell, and behaver' (the large province of the Act, incorporating both appearance and conduct is again striking). Each apprentice was instructed to cut his hair 'from the crowne of the heade', and to 'keepe his forelocke bare'. He was also told that his locks should not 'reach below the lap of his eare, and that the same length [was] to be observed behynd'. Additional clauses urged apprentices to show greater obedience to their masters.

Four apprentices were presented at the company court in the following month, 'and there were desired to conforme, but shewing themselves disobedient and very obstinate [and] not in the least yielding to that wholesome acte, [they] were first in courte made exemplary by shortning their hayre, and taking from their clothes superflous ribbining, and after for their wilfull obstinacy' were committed to prison. Seven other apprentices agreed to conform, and they were ordered to return to the court four days later, so that the authorities could check that that their hair and decorations had been trimmed. They duly turned up in court, though three of them, 'being not cut suitable to the said act', were immediately referred

---

[253] PRO SP 16/278/74.

[254] Paul Seaver, *Wallington's World: A Puritan Artisan in Stuart England* (Stanford, Calif., 1985), 175.

[255] Here I am quoting Edward Hyde, Earl of Clarendon, *The Life of Edward Hyde, Earl of Clarendon* (3 vols.; Oxford, 1827), i. 358–9.

[256] Thomas Edwards, *The First and Second Parts of Gangreana* (1646), 69–70.

to Hall the barber, 'to be better trimmed'. Further prosecutions swiftly followed, including that of Thomas Swan, a freeman, who 'was complayned on for jerying some of the apprentices whose haire was cutt according to the companye's acte, calling them the company's coved tupps'. Early in the new year the company admitted that the 'irregularity is not curbed', laying the blame squarely upon stubborn young people, who treasured their effete styles, and their 'severall masters slownes'. Indeed, the company had encountered nothing but 'continual trouble' in pressing 'conformity by correcting some apprentices superfluityes of hayre and apparell'. A thinly disguised recognition of defeat followed, and the Act was repealed on 24 January 1650,[257] though prosecutions still continued. The company beadle was sent a list of nonconformists in February, and a week later ten apprentices were summoned before the court. Six of them were ordered to be 'clipped'. A further twenty-one young men were presented in April and May of the same year. Long hair was being prosecuted as late as 1655. Significantly, these sumptuary measures were again one aspect of a far broader crusade to bring apprentices to general order, which also included the closer policing of fornication, religious nonconformity, and youthful irreverence.[258]

This particular coupling of visual expression with proper conduct is yet another manifestation of the age of youth as 'contested territory' in early modern society. A number of different representations of youth derived from disparate sources portrayed competing conceptions of the characteristics acquired in preparation for adulthood. Opposing progresses to full maturity were proposed in which piety and civility stood at polar points to profanity and impurity; and 'regulated' expressions of femininity and manhood were contrasted with 'wanton' women and the rough male culture, and with each other. Nevertheless, they existed in meaningful tension because 'ill-advised and ill-nurtured' youth were evaluated according to their pious and civil obverse. Serious and sober youth dressed in tidy if plain clothes, and they closely followed the rhythms of structured work and time. This process of comparison is clearly visible in prosecutions, apprenticeship indentures, texts, sermons,

---

[257] However, it was also ordered 'That every master shall regulate his own apprentices according to the forementioned acte, before the first of February next', though cases were brought after the spring of 1650 and beyond. Cf. Dunlop and Denman, *English Apprenticeship*, 24–5.

[258] Boyle and Dendy, *Newcastle Merchant Adventurers Records*, i. 23–5, 27–9, 154–5, 161–2, 185.

and catechisms. But even a godly youth like Richard Baxter could fall short and stumble into a middle territory between profanity and piety. Governors and moralists thought of youth as a struggle, and within this stage of life there was plenty of scope for the articulation of discrete attitudes towards different social groups, including young women, who were often differentiated according to dress, hair, and patterns of conviviality and sociability.

The convergence of a striking array of intellectual, physical, cultural, and socio-economic factors convinced contemporary magistrates and ministers that youth presented an unrivalled opportunity to introduce people to fresh habits of work, leisure, time, and piety.[259] The pious life engaged the passions of some young devotees. Yet there was considerable distance between such young saints and the profane youth whom they left behind as they 'withdrew' into a virtuous course of life. The construction of polarities is a risky enterprise; they can often exaggerate distinctions and sharply dissect a complex reality into two camps. This was how the godly often defined their place in society. Descriptions of youth, therefore, tended to follow unhelpful generalizations like 'ill-advised and ill-nurtured youth', which caught all sorts of youth in the same hostile image. Yet there was a large gap between these opposite poles of utter profanity and piety—an extensive middle territory in which people blended orthodoxy with their own assumptions about authority, piety, work, time, youth, conviviality, and play. A point to which we will return.

One important aspect of growing up which often took young people outside the household and sometimes stirred conflict with authority structures was courtship. The place of sentiment and sex in young lives in early modern society has created storms amongst later generations of historians as well as contemporaries. As we have seen, moralists characteristically introduced the problem of youth in a vivid and heated language of passion, lust, and excess. Patrick Collinson has suggested that uppermost in the minds of moralists as they issued cautions about recreation and filed prosecutions against 'corrupt' pastimes was 'the irrepressible sexuality of the young'. David Underdown comments that this alleged disposition towards play, fun, flirting, and sex was 'a constant worry to older people'.[260] Worse still, these youth spaces provided a congenial climate for immorality to prosper. These glum forecasts of moral

[259] See above, Ch. 1.
[260] Collinson, *Religion of Protestants*, 225; Underdown, *Fire from Heaven*, 82.

confusion may appear extravagant, incoherent, and furious, but they mattered because they were the perceptions of people in places of authority and sparked urgent calls to regulate the time of youth. Young people grew up with these suspicions hanging over their heads. Physical desire and sentiment raised potential problems; the first stirrings of attraction and affection blossomed both inside and outside the household, and resulted in joy, sorrow, and cruelty. Contemporary sources reveal a host of unfortunate or odious characters; philanderers, the love-sick, the seduced, the abandoned, and figures of authority who exploited their positions to obtain sexual favours. They will be the subject of the next chapter, which discusses courtship and the range of sexual options open to young people. Narratives of abuse, desire, and pleasure reveal both the gloomy and happy sides of growing up in Tudor and Stuart England.

5

Courtship, Sexual Behaviour, and Moral Order

In May 1598 Thomas Wilson, a London apprentice, was presented at Bridewell for fornicating with his fellow servant, Alice Gray. His 'lewdness' had in fact been the occasion of earlier complaints in his master's household, and they show how jests and pranks could contain darker shades of insult and outrage for their intended audience. Wilson told the Bridewell governors 'that one night' the maids 'called him up to their chamber and willed him to fetch a candell, and when he brought upp the candell to them he began to jest with them whereuppon they complained to his master'. Interestingly, on this occasion the master appears as an arbitrator and was invited to still a storm which broke forth in his servants quarters. Wilson also admitted that 'he laye twyse with Goodwyfe Claxton, a washer', and 'jested with many others but he had to do with none but with one Goodwife Moore of whome he had th'use of her body at two severall tymes'. 'Jested' was a nebulous term which drew attention to a broad spectrum of behaviour ranging from joking and flirting to kissing and heavy petting. It implied a sense of fun and casual opportunity. Wilson also claimed that he 'jested with one goodwife Page and kissed her when she was going forth of doores', but 'he never had to do with any other saving once' when he put his hands under the apron of one of his master's maids. He denied a further charge of 'medling' with his master's children, but in the course of his examination it emerged that Goodwife Page was not in fact his final encounter, and Wilson confessed to having 'th'use and carnal knowledge of the body of Goodwfye Harrison three tymes', Dorothy Barnett twice in his master's household, one Whitelocke's daughter once, and 'also severall tymes' with 'one Barett's wife at her own house'.[1]

Thomas Wilson's case-history may have been exceptional; he lived

[1] BCB 4, fo. 15 Sept. 1598 (the date of the case is given in the event of irregular or absent pagination).

in London and in a large household with several male and female servants who possessed few private spaces. However, we will see the circumstances of his sexual encounters repeated in other episodes, and discover that the words he chose to use to describe them were spoken by others and were common currency. One peculiarity of this case may be that it is recorded and is therefore available for us to consult because it was brought before a court. Nevertheless, Wilson's experience is one pattern of behaviour which it is difficult to place in the model of sexual relations described by Peter Laslett, Lawrence Stone, Edward Shorter, and others. They share a number of assumptions about sexual behaviour in the long interval between the first stirrings of sexual maturity and marriage which remain unproven and open to question. Youth is seen as a tense time of restraint in which the young internalized sexual desire.[2] The chaste young figures of these accounts closely resemble the pious heroes of the conduct book and apprenticeship indenture, which should raise our suspicions. Again, one problem in the study of early modern youth hitherto has been the tendency to pass generalizations from a few sources, which arbitrarily confine discussion to 'ideal types' or particular social groups.

We may in fact discover that the progress from childhood to adulthood is far more complicated than is suggested by this tidy image of youthful temperance. As we have seen contemporary magistrates and moralists painted a different portrait of youth as a 'licentious' age and viewed particular youth spaces with deep suspicion. This literature of complaint was not mere rhetoric, though the connection between conviviality and vice does place youth at one extreme of promiscuity (which has also found its historian)[3] at an opposite point to the abstinent youth of the ordered household. We need to traverse the spacious terrain from chastity to promiscuity, and consider evidence about sexual behaviour from petting to full intercourse, and from consent to abuse. The history of youth must be contextualized in terms of dominant adult ideologies and institutions, but also in terms of rather more private moments of peer association and courtship. Nor should we forget the availability of commercial sex.[4] Narratives of sexual encounters must be

[2] Peter Laslett, *The World We Have Lost: Further Explored* (1983); Lawrence Stone, *The Family, Sex and Marriage in England 1500–1800* (1977); Edward Shorter, *The Making of the Modern Family* (1976).

[3] G. R. Quaife, *Wanton Wenches and Wayward Wives: Peasants and Illicit Sex in Early Seventeenth-Century England* (1979).

[4] See above, Ch. 4.

read closely to spot the potentially savage or subtle pressures of conventional patterns of social relations, and the sentiments of each partner. Later sections of this chapter, therefore, will discuss courtship and household life. But we will begin with the historiography, and more closely explore existing interpretations of sexual behaviour and mentalities (which naturally have important consequences for the way we view the nature of youth and maturity). A number of problems raised by procedure and the nature of the available sources means that it is very difficult to offer persuasive accounts of representative experiences. The young, as ever, defy generalization. This lack of unity is one theme in the study of sexual relations (and youth), and it can be a source of deep frustration for scholars who prefer straightforward and polished answers. But in this case there is no tidy and absolute answer. To be sure, we can present cases of chastity or promiscuity, but neither extreme can ever be a final interpretation. What I want to establish, for reasons which will become apparent, is that the tale of celibate youth rests upon very shaky methodological roots; that insufficient attention has been paid to forms of sexual pleasure which fall short of full intercourse; and that our incomplete knowledge of birth control at this time as well as the random survival of sources and the 'dark figure' of unprosecuted crime obscures our view of this aspect of the past. The silences in contemporary sources cannot always be treated as evidence of abstinence.

1. *A Celibate Youth?*

It must be said that there is a temptation to write the history of sexual behaviour in terms of distant polarities of chastity and immorality. The nature of the sources is one provocation because they tend to represent sexual experience in terms of utter immorality (e.g. elements of the literature of complaint or the judicial record), or commendable moderation. We should never stray along these false trails. The methodological points of entry proposed by previous historians have also raised a few problems. On the one hand we can relate stories in the archives with little care, and in a jocular and shocking fashion present a society in which people snatch the chance of sexual pleasure at the drop of a hat.[5] On the other hand, some historians have used demographic measures and rates of

[5] See below, p. 241.

prosecution of sexual crime to recover in their words representative experiences. The important work of Stone and Shorter, for instance, is blemished by a tendency to anchor cavalier generalizations about the nature of sexual behaviour and mentalities upon series of figures of registered sexual crime across two or three centuries. Bare numbers are deemed sufficient to allow sweeping inferences about the feelings of long dead people. Thus Shorter, in a typically extravagant gesture, comments that the quantitative method permits us to recover 'the representative experience of the average person'. In similar fashion, Stone claims that the rate of prosecution of bridal pregnancy is 'as good a guide to the realities of premarital sexual behaviour as the historian is likely to find'.[6]

On the basis of this strategy of passing emphatic assessments of commonplace experiences from recorded misdemeanours and demographic patterns, both Stone and Shorter argue that the low rate of illegitimacy before 1750 (a few percentage points) and the late age at first marriage suggests that youth in Tudor and Stuart society was a taxing time of involuntary abstinence. Stone comments 'that during the sixteenth and seventeenth centuries, most men must have exercised extraordinary self-control during the first twelve to fourteen years of optimum male potency'. Shorter is 'obliged to conclude that men and women abstained from intercourse for ten to fifteen years or more after puberty'. In one of those cavalier generalizations which have often scarred the history of youth, he comments that before 1750 'the lives of most young people were resolutely unerotic'. After 1750, then, moderation was forgotten; the dams of self-restraint began to crumble, and the libido was given free rein to wander and seek pleasure. And if we require some further confirmation of this more regular discharge of sexual electricity we can turn to the rising tide of illegitimacy towards the close of the eighteenth century.[7]

We may accept that sentiments slowly change as centuries roll by, though any shift will be largely imperceptible and will leave no firm imprint in the sources left behind by a few decades. Yet some scholars are fascinated by the 'discovery' of a 'new world'[8] at some point in the eighteenth century when family structures and feelings irrevocably changed into something we can recognize today.[9] The

---

[6] Shorter, *Making of the Modern Family*, 79; Stone, *Family, Sex and Marriage*, 608.
[7] Stone, *Family, Sex and Marriage*, 615; Shorter, *Making of the Modern Family*, 98–9.
[8] I am adapting the ideas of J. H. Plumb, 'The new world of children in eighteenth-century England', *Past and Present*, 67 (1975).
[9] See above, esp. pp. 2–4.

period 1560–1640 seems suddenly foreign and remote; a time of vanished beliefs and practises. Nevertheless, these arguments often rest upon thin foundations; inferences about past behaviour and mentalities. Thus Laslett suggests that the libido was checked by strict 'personal discipline' in early modern society, which was boosted by a deep sense of Christian ethics, but more obviously by harsh demographic realities at a time when daily life was often a sorry struggle for mere survival. He also consigns a large share of illegitimacy to a small 'bastardy prone sub-society' (though this clustering of illegitimate births in a narrow band of 'repeaters' has been questioned by subsequent work).[10] Stone also produces optimistic evaluations of the ability of the reformed ministry to plant new sentiments and matching patterns of conduct. He suggests that decades of patient evangelism reaped reward in 'the successful internalization of ideas about chastity and virginity'. Early modern people grew up in a 'remarkably chaste society' of 'largely virgin brides', who swapped marital vows with young men who had resisted the lure of the flesh.[11] These ideas have sometimes been uncritically accepted by other scholars, including John Gillis, who treat them as near orthodoxies. Gillis comments that early modern youth were 'steadfastly celibate'; the years of growing up were 'celibate years'.[12]

This interpretation of the sexuality of young people prior to a dramatic series of turning-points in the long eighteenth century provides the context for Shorter's bold pronouncement that 'the central fact in the history of courtship over the last two centuries has been the enormous increase in sexual activity before marriage'. He turns to the rise in the *recorded incidence* of bridal pregnancy and illegitimacy since 1700 for numerical testimony of this startling 'sexual revolution'.[13] We must labour this point, for it proposes that

[10] Peter Laslett, 'The bastardy prone sub-society' in Laslett, Karla Oosterveen, and Richard M. Smith (eds.), *Bastardy and its Comparative History* (1980); id., *Family Life and Illicit Love in Earlier Generations* (Cambridge, 1977), ch. 3. Cf. Keith Wrightson and David Levine, 'The social context of illegitimacy in early modern England', in P. Laslett *et al.* (eds.), *Bastardy and its Comparative History* (1980); Richard Llewelyn Adair, 'Regional Variations in Illegitimacy and Courtship Behaviour in England 1538–1754' (Unpublished University of Cambridge Ph.D thesis, 1992), esp. 112.

[11] Stone, *Family, Sex and Marriage*, 645, 623–5. Stone still clings to these views. See his *Road to Divorce: England 1530–1987* (Oxford, 1990), 60: 'England in the seventeenth century was sexually an extraordinarily restrained society. Inhibiting factors were the fear of pregnancy ... the moral and religious teaching of the Puritan ministers about sin ... and the strong disapproval of neighbours and kin.'

[12] J. R. Gillis, *For Better for Worse: British Marriages 1600 to the Present* (Oxford, 1985), 11, 15. For a careful summary see Martin Ingram, *Church Courts, Sex and Marriage in England 1570–1640* (Cambridge, 1987), 159–63.

[13] Shorter, *Making of the Modern Family*, 165–6, 80.

there were distinctive social, psychological, and physical experiences of youth, which can be traced by tracking quantifiable trends in the judicial records. In Tudor and Stuart England, therefore, seriously intended young couples were less likely to have full intercourse. They met and fell in love, but only within the compass of close ecclesiastical, communal, and familial regulation, which touched all aspects of their first years together. Stone attributes the subsequent rise of illegitimacy and bridal pregnancy to an alleged 'relaxation in the external controls on sexual behaviour'.[14]

We will shortly review the evidence for adult regulation of youthful romance and desire. In certain circumstances sections of the community clearly felt concerned about youthful conviviality and play, and discussed the growing tide of immorality and the cost of supporting illegitimates who would surely spring from these casual meetings of young people. Yet we have already argued that such informal modes of communal regulation as gossip, publicity, and reputation, which also provided a compelling social aspect to the penalties of the church courts, only lightly touched the concerns of people who were still negotiating the transition to full membership of society. In addition, despite some expressions of concern with youthful licence in particular quarters, others were more prepared to turn a blind eye to the antics of the young.[15] Keith Wrightson has commented that there was 'a high degree of tolerance of certain kinds of offence, most notably of premarital fornication and bridal pregnancy' in plebeian culture. William Stout of Lancaster complained at the turn of the eighteenth century about 'what's too common with not only youth but also married men and women with each other'; namely 'to entertain each in a bantering way in such terms as could only tend to beget evil thoughts and excite to lewdness'. A casual code of morality which Stout thought was 'inconsistent with true christianity'.[16] The timorous model of sexual development proposed by Stone, Laslett, and Shorter offered one pattern of behaviour. Nevertheless, narratives of youthful spontaneity and creativity in contemporary sources caution us against relegating glimpses of the 'inner self' to seething suppression and internalized desire.

[14] Stone, Family, Sex and Marriage, 628; Shorter, Making of the Modern Family, 167.

[15] See above, pp. 117–20.

[16] Keith Wrightson, 'The nadir of English illegitimacy in the seventeenth century', in Laslett et al., Bastardy and its Comparative History, 178 (see also in the same volume Alan Macfarlane, 'Illegitimacy and illegitimates in English history', 75–6); The Autobiography of William Stout of Lancaster 1665–1752, ed. J. D. Marshall (Chetham Society, 3rd ser., 14, Manchester, 1967), 104.

Yet selective sampling in judicial records can also raise issues of typicality and sensationalism, and has moulded another interpretation of sexual behaviour which is a million miles away from 're- markable chastity'. With a sharp eye for a comical and salacious tale, John Addy and Geoffrey Quaife have mined the deposits of the Cheshire and Somerset church courts (respectively) to gather evidence of the rich varieties of sex at this time.[17] Shorter's 'unerotic youth' are distant figures in this largely anecdotal sketch of promiscuous 'peasants' drawn from scattered episodes. Quaife takes us through the Somerset countryside along lanes and into fields and households, where 'sex was not a moral issue', except for the daughters and wives of yeomen and gentlemen. The rest of this 'amoral' community, including young people of the lower classes, frolicked whenever opportunity beckoned. It is possible to write a persuasive account by mingling colourful stories in a single narrative. But Addy and Quaife misrepresent contemporary sentiment by treating interesting materials as an unambiguous statement about the nature of plebeian practices. It is, after all, helpful to consider how mentalities may alter in changing social and economic conditions.[18] Wrightson, for instance, has placed the greater part of premarital sexual misdemeanours in the context not of promiscuity, but of ideas regarding courtship and the shattering of marriage plans in tight socio-economic circumstances.[19] To complicate matters still further, different age-groups may on occasion possess distinct attitudes. Young and old, for example.

And so we greet two polarities—chastity and promiscuity, or involuntary restraint and voluntary licence—with their striking evidential and methodological faults and little common ground. This middle territory has recently been claimed by Martin Ingram, however, and in his *Church Courts, Sex and Marriage* (1987) he shows how early modern youth could hope to grow up free from disabling interference, especially in courtship. There were a host of opportunities for casual meetings, match-making, talking, petting, and sex. Yet the interpretative leap from prospect to 'amorality' is highly

[17] Quaife, *Wanton Wenches*; John Addy, *Sin and Society in Seventeenth-century England* (1989).
[18] Cf. Ingram, *Church Courts*, esp. 166, 278–81; id., 'Religious communities and moral discipline in late-sixteenth and early-seventeenth-century England: case studies', in Kaspar von Greyerz (ed.), *Religion and Society in Early Modern Europe* (1984); Keith Wrightson, *English Society 1580–1680* (1982), ch. 7; Wrightson and David Levine, *Poverty and Piety in an English Village: Terling 1525–1700* (1979), 126–33, and chs. 4–5.
[19] Wrightson, *English Society*, 84–6; id., 'The Puritan Reformation of Manners with Special Reference to the Counties of Lancashire and Essex 1640–1660' (unpublished University of Cambridge Ph.D. thesis, 1973), 63.

speculative, and lacks close sympathy with the multitude of customs which characterize this complex society.[20] So, we should never
assume that the young were the casual wantons of Quaife's interpretation. It is quite easy to discover a case of apparent promiscuity
in a selected source. In the Ely church court records, for example,
we find Margery Grezedye of St Trinity parish in Ely, who was presented for 'unhonestly dishonering hirself naked from the gyrdle
downward before vi boyes and maydes sayeinge yt was no synne to
lye with any man yt woulde lye with her and offered hirselfe to lye
with any man yt wolde for iid or iiid'.[21] There are also women who
gave birth to more than one illegitimate child, though we must not
infer promiscuity in any of their cases.[22] It is very misleading to
characterize young people by one pattern of behaviour because the
question of typicality is always lurking. Some young men participated in a bachelor's social round in which the alehouse and brothel
had a prominent place.[23] But William Kiffin and other godly youth
would doubtless have consigned drunkards, pimps, prostitutes, and
their young clients to an eternity of suffering in hell-fire, or
counselled them to seek the virtuous path to salvation. How typical
was the London apprentice who told his master 'that he would not
tarry with him for he kept a whore in his house', or the Essex youth
who returned the invitation to purchase sex with frosty words, saying
'that God would never give a blessinge' to such dubious proceedings.[24] But then we have to consider the opinions of young people
like Thomas Wilson whose story began this chapter, and another
apprentice Robert Cowell. After an evening spent in the company
of one Anne Kitchen at a London alehouse, Cowell called at the
house of his friend George Starkey, a servant, who asked him 'if hee
ever had the use of . . . Anne Kitchen's bodie, to which he answered
yea what els, what els'.[25]

There are many hurdles to recovering even remotely representative experiences from the puzzling range of situations in the sources,
which are further complicated by differences in the range of sexual
options available in town and country, access to money, class, and
gender. Even more difficult to recover are forms of sexual pleasure
falling short of full intercourse. In fact, the reputed 'internalization

---

[20] Ingram, *Church Courts*, esp. ch. 4.
[21] CUL EDR D/2/9, fo. 152ᵛ. See also B/2/17, fo. 142.
[22] For example, BCB 4, fos. 208ᵛ, 256, 285; 5, fos. 1ᵛ, 13, 28, 146, 227ᵛ, 231, 235, 288ᵛ,
334, 350ᵛ, 351, 355, 367.
[23] See above, Ch. 4.
[24] BCB 5, fo. 113; Wrightson, 'Nadir of English illegitimacy', 117.
[25] BCB 5, fos. 20ᵛ–1ᵛ.

of desire' would appear to have been largely confined to full inter-course between consenting, single heterosexuals. So, we find Shorter pondering about the appeal of other forms of sexual stimulation, and commenting that 'even if young adults did not have plain old straight-up-and-down sex before marriage, perhaps they found other ways of relieving their sexual longing and giving life to their sexual fantasies'. He proposes that masturbation, prostitution, petting, homosexuality, or bestiality may have provided an alternative route to sexual pleasure. (Stone also believes that 'sexual frustration' was soothed for those in the towns who had access to a brothel.)[26] Yet Shorter remains reluctant to recast significantly his image of chaste youth, and with little regard for problems raised by the sources (and their absence) comments that heavy petting was not a familiar aspect of courtship before 1700. Partners kept their distance, there was 'an absolute minimum of actively erotic contact'. Young people could experience crushing sensations of love and passion, but they did not consider sex to be 'an object of joy and delight'. Again, the experiences of urban and rural folk may have differed. In the small town or village, which is called 'the heartland of traditional society', commercial sex was a rare option, and 'the local lads . . . remained in purity for a long time'. Shorter even claims that there was little resort to the largely private act of masturbation before the middle decades of the eighteenth century when complaints first began to appear in conduct books.[27]

The limitations of this particular source for the recovery of ple-beian mentalities and practices have long been familiar to histor-ians. It is true that contemporary sources of all types rarely mention masturbation, although we sometimes discover a single episode which may cast light on a greater truth, which is largely obscured from us by feelings of guilt and shame, or discretion. One day in 1696, for example, 12-year-old John Cannon of Somerset 'took a ramble to the river' with his schoolfellows. At the riverside an older youth who is mysteriously called 'the elder of the Scraces then about 17 [years old] after some aquarian diversions took an occa-sion to show the rest what he could do if he had a female in place, and withal took his privy member in his hand rubbing it up and down till it was erected and in short followed emission, the same as

---

[26] Shorter, *Making of the Modern Family*, 99. See also 98–109; J. F. Flandrin, 'Repression and change in the sexual life of young people in medieval and early modern times', in R. Wheaton and T. K. Hareven (eds.), *Family and Sexuality in French History* (1980); Stone, *Family, Sex and Marriage*, 615–20.

[27] Shorter, *Making of the Modern Family*, 98–108.

he said in copulation'. This 'elder of the Scraces' then 'advised more of the boys to do the same, telling them that although the first act would be attended with pain yet by frequent use they could find a deal of pleasure, on which [Cannon reported] several attempted and found as he said indeed'. Cannon confided in his *Memoirs* that he was one of the elder's 'pupils'.[28]

Cannon's riverside story offers a rare glimpse of masturbation in early modern society, which for him began at age 12. Such solitary tales as this have value, but the relative absence of comparative tales makes it difficult to pronounce on the typicality of this group of Somerset boys. We would require work on the cultural and social attitudes of early modern people towards masturbation (which may prove to be an elusive quarry). One early eighteenth-century commentator thought that 'self-pollution' was a 'frequent . . . offence, especially among the male youth', though one of his 'correspondents' informed him that 'it is now become almost as frequent amongst girls'.[29] Young people shared rooms and beds,[30] and it would not be unreasonable to assume that pairs or larger groups may have freely swapped ideas about techniques (and beliefs/ superstitions?) of masturbation. The author of *Onania; Or the Heinous Sin of Self-Pollution* produced a series of letters in which people told the tale of their fall into this 'unnatural practice', and in many of these brief confessions the penitents explained how they were guided by an elder or a member of their peer group—a fellow servant or scholar.[31] Significant silences in contemporary sources often have many causes, and in this particular case a thick cloak of secrecy may have covered the 'wicked thoughts' of 'thousands of young people of both sexes'.[32]

Recording sexual misdemeanours is naturally an important task and a vital first step in the history of sexual behaviour and its regulation. Nevertheless, the 'dark figure' of unrecorded crime is a notorious variable which perplexes attempts to trace the true rate of illegitimacy, for example, and to rely on figures alone to infer sexual activity and implicit mentalities is a risky interpretative

---

[28] SRO DD/SAS/C/1193. I must thank David Cressy for this reference.

[29] Anon., *Onania; Or the Heinous Sin of Self-Pollution*, 8th edn., 1723, ed. R. Trumbach (facsimile; Garland Series: Marriage, Sex and the Family in England 1660–1800, New York, 1986), fos. A2^r, A3^v.

[30] See below, pp. 269–71.

[31] *Onania*, 64, 145, 159, 163. See also ibid. fo. A3^r, and in the same Garland edition, *A Supplement to the Onania*, 90, 152.

[32] *Onania*, 10–11, 2, 80.

enterprise.[33] After all, we are left with fragments; the prosecuted record. The scale of unreported sexual lapses was surely colossal, and even greater in relatively 'tranquil' periods when the authorities were less interested in the morals of the multitude. Clearly we should not leap to the conclusion that silence in the sources means abstinence, or a youth of simmering frustration. The sexual crime in the records also contains whispers and sometimes shrill cries of sexual activity that escaped the attention of the courts. In February 1606, for example, Alice Coverton and Edward Payner were presented at London Bridewell for having sex 'as often as he and she pleased [to] doe as they might conveniently be together'. While Elizabeth Hall and her young lover had sex 'many tymes' over a period of four years in her master's house 'in the night-tyme upon everie his . . . watch nighte (which came everie tenth night)'—on perhaps as many as 150 separate occasions if Hall's memory is to be trusted. Other cases also reveal past histories of sexual behaviour, and it was reported that sex had occurred 'often', 'many tymes', 'at his pleasure', or 'as often as he pleases'.[34] In forty-seven cases which came before the Salisbury Episcopal Court in the period 1615–21, eleven defendants claimed that they had sex on a single occasion, another eleven told the authorities that sex had occurred on only two or three occasions, while a further twenty-five could not be specific, the memory of past couplings had faded or they were too frequent to recount, and they resorted to catch-alls like 'many', or 'divers and sondry'.[35] In many of these cases pregnancy often attracted the unwelcome intervention of the courts, and gave these people an unexpected place in the historical record. But how did they avoid pregnancy on former occasions—with luck by running the risk of conception, contraception, *coitus interruptus*, or perhaps by turning to the painful course of abortion? And how many other couples were able to escape the attention of the courts altogether? We can see opportunities for sexual pleasure in contemporary sources, but a far greater number must have passed unnoticed and unrecorded, and we are left to guess at the nature of the silences and gaps in the records.

The sexual experiences of early modern people are further obscured by the gaps in our knowledge of conception, contraception,

[33] Cf. J. A. Sharpe, *Crime in Early Modern England 1550–1750* (1984), 142, 147–8.

[34] BCB 5, fos. 87, 360ᵛ. See also CUL EDR B/2/28, fo. 28; BCB 2, fo. 95ᵛ; 3, fos. 26 Sept. 1579, 93ᵛ, 154; 4, fos. 229, 232, 257ᵛ, 376, 412, 424ᵛ, 438; 5, fos. 5ᵛ, 23ᵛ, 38, 46ᵛ.

[35] Ingram, *Church Courts*, 260.

and abortion.[36] Laslett argues that the number 'of baptised births may well have to be multiplied by fifty, seventy, or even a hundred times and more in order to guess at the number of sexual lapses which lay behind them'.[37] There are few glimpses in the records I have consulted of the actual use of contraception in this period, although contemporaries discussed a number of magical and herbal contraceptives, and the condom according to Angus McLaren was 'the only new and presumably the most effective contraception produced in the early modern period'. Contemporaries also mention sponges and tampons—'more obvious female contraceptives'— and refer to a wide range of oral (e.g. vomits and laxatives) and mechanical (e.g. bloodletting, genital baths, and pessaries) contraceptives in cook books, herbals, and discussions of birth control.[38] But it is difficult to know whether condoms were widely available in their gestation period (McLaren's examples are drawn from literary quarters, the upper classes, and the specialist services of the bawdy house), and they may have been chiefly used as a guard against venereal disease.[39] *Coitus interruptus* was practised, and was the target of bitter remarks by some moralists.[40]

Abortion or attempted abortion may have been relatively common.[41] The picture is rather complicated by the troubled distinctions between abortion, miscarriage, infanticide, and still birth in contemporary sources. A high rate of still births, for example, like that traced in Hawkshead in Lancashire (fluctuating in each decade of the seventeenth century between twenty-nine and ninety-six per thousand live births) has been read as evidence that an unknown

[36] Cf. E. A. Wrigley, 'Family limitation in pre-industrial England', in his *People, Cities and Wealth* (Oxford, 1987), 265–6.

[37] Laslett, *World We Have Lost*, 163. Cf. Ingram, *Church Courts*, 159.

[38] Angus McLaren, *A History of Contraception: From Antiquity to the Present Day* (Oxford, 1990), 157; Robert V. Schnucker, 'Elizabethan birth control and puritan attitudes', *Journal of Interdisciplinary History*, 5 (1975), 656–7. Keith Thomas has noted the 'relative rarity of charms to prevent conception', and suggests that abortion and *coitus interruptus* were more widely practised (*Religion and the Decline of Magic: Studies in Popular Beliefs in Sixteenth- and Seventeenth-Century England* (1971), 223).

[39] McLaren comments that 'the discussions of magical and herbal contraceptives declined' between the sixteenth and eighteenth centuries (*History of Contraception*, 154). Cf. Merry E. Wiesner, *Women and Gender in Early Modern Europe* (Cambridge, 1993), 70.

[40] Wrigley, 'Family limitation', 266; McLaren, *History of Contraception*, 154–7; Quaife, *Wanton Wenches*, 133–4, 171–2; Ingram, *Church Courts*, 158–9; Ralph Houlbrooke, *The English Family 1450–1700* (1984), 128. Cf. Wiesner, *Women and Gender*, 70.

[41] Ingram, *Church Courts*, 159; McLaren, *History of Contraception*, 159–62, 124–6. Quaife concludes 'that attempted abortions were widespread and often successful, but they were resisted by many girls for fear of their physical safety in this world rather than fear of eternal damnation'. He finds that 'One in five of the men who tried to conceal the pregnancy of their sexual partners suggested it [abortion] to the girl concerned' (*Wanton Wenches*, 120, 118).

number of miscarriages were in fact abortions, though the poor quality of many diets and the rigours of hard work may tell a different story in some cases.[42] Nevertheless, some contemporary books described various ways of prompting abortions including leaping, dancing, riding, vomiting, and a number of oral abortifacients.[43] Indeed, the abortifacient qualities of various herbs, including, savin, rew, bearsfoot, and 'raisons of the sun', are reported in a number of judicial sources, which also mention prominent figures who passed on recipes and herbs, including local wise women and apothecaries.[44] The dealings of a minister's wife from Cardiganshire came to the attention of London's recorder, who told her story to Lord Burghley. She admitted 'that she was greatlie sought unto by young women . . . when they were gotten with childe', and 'confessed that she gave them saven'.[45]

A scandal rocked the community of Barnes (Middlesex) in 1616. It was reported at Star Chamber that Christopher Davies, a servant of George Digby esq., had 'most lewdlie in secrett manner' resorted to the house of his master's neighbour, Francis Beale esq., 'and begotten with childe one Anne Alden', Beale's maidservant. To avoid the cost and shame of exposure, Davies 'confederated' with two other men to collect the 'money and meanes to make the birth she went with abortive'. Davies 'persuaded' Alden 'to buy and procure some drugs, simples, or medicines, and to take and drinck the same therewith to destroy the childe in her wombe whereby the same might become abortive'. He gave her six shillings, and Alden duly purchased the drugs, though her means of supply is sadly not recorded. But 'the same not sorting according to the expectacon and desires of the confederates' (the prescribed drugs may not have worked), they were forced to seek other means of concealing Davies's paternity. Steps had already been taken to prepare his

---

[42] R. S. Schofield, 'Perinatal mortality in Hawkshead, Lancashire, 1581–1710', *Local Population Studies*, 4 (1970). Cf. Houlbrooke, *English Family*, 128, who mentions John Graunt's conclusion that the rate of miscarriage in London *c.*1662 was fifty per thousand live births. Alan Macfarlane comments that the timing of Jane Josselin's miscarriages 'coincided almost exactly with the earliest point at which . . . [she] could have known [that] she was pregnant', and could indicate that she 'used some form of abortion' (*The Family Life of Ralph Josselin, a Seventeenth-Century Clergyman: An Essay in Historical Anthropology* (Cambridge, 1970), 201).

[43] Schnucker, 'Elizabethan birth control', 658–9.

[44] For some examples see Quaife, *Wanton Wenches*, 118–20; F. G. Emmison, *Elizabethan Life: Morals and the Church Courts* (Essex Record Office Publications, 63, Chelmsford, 1973), 41. Cf. Wiesner, *Women and Gender*, 51, 70.

[45] T. Wright (ed.), *Queen Elizabeth and Her Times* (2 vols.; 1838), ii. 242–3. Cf. Rosalind Mitchison and Leah Leneman, *Sexuality and Social Control: Scotland 1660–1780* (Oxford, 1989), 209–10.

'secret departure' to a neighbouring county. The three 'conspirators' also tried to 'defraud' the course of justice by coaxing bogus
witnesses to testify that Beale had fathered his maid's illegitimate
child, and there is strong reason to suppose that they offered bribes
to a local justice to distil the rumour of Davies's paternity, and pass
responsibility for the cost of maintaining the child to the parish.[46]
These cases, like those concerning *coitus interruptus* and contraceptives, only alert us to the measure of familiarity some early modern
people had with such forms of birth control. They are scattered
episodes from dispersed locations and do not permit us to establish
persuasive trends; the quality of extant evidence and methodology
casts a dark cloud (or figure) over attempts to write histories of
sexual mentalities and behaviour. All that we can safely do is to
report their existence, which is well-documented in certain cases
which comment on the use of abortifacients (though there is also
evidence of uncertainty and unease)[47] and local channels of supply.

This well-documented resort to birth control and abortion provides yet another reason to pause before turning to the recorded
sexual crimes of a tiny minority as a good guide to actual or representative experiences. These puzzles will probably remain unresolved. Nevertheless, accounts of 'unerotic' and 'celibate' youth are
still retold, and the history of youthful sexuality in the period 1500–
1800 has been written as an uninterrupted progress from unblemished chastity to eroticism and pleasure. Such grand theories possess
value, they usually contain glimmers of truth and prompt responses
and further work. The alleged 'sexual revolution' of the eighteenth
century, however, which draws the greater part of its support from
shaky roots (the rising rate of illegitimacy and dubious claims for
the strong hold of ecclesiastical authorities over the young), probably
never occurred. It is tempting (though too simple) to match a rising
tide of illegitimacy with a greater frequency of sexual intercourse.
But other explanations have recently been proposed, and the question is still unresolved.[48] The experience of youth before 1700
was clearly not 'resolutely unerotic'. This was one possible route
to adulthood. By contrast, we can trace the rough contours of the
world of youthful conviviality and play, and see young people playing, drinking, talking, walking, working, courting, whoring, and so

[46] PRO STAC 8 20/10. See also STAC 8 49/3.

[47] See, for example, the cases quoted by Quaife, *Wanton Wenches*, 119–20.

[48] See, for example, Adair, 'Regional Variations in Illegitimacy and Courtship Behaviour',
who argues that the decline in the custom of spousals, especially towards the close of the
seventeenth century, may have had a decisive impact upon the rate of illegitimacy.

on. It should also be remembered that some moralists recognized that youthful sexuality could not always be contained by late marriage, and recommended early marriage as 'a necessary remedy to keep us from plunging into unbridled lust'. 'If they cannot abstaine', Matthew Griffith declared, 'they must marrie.'[49]

For some young people, especially young men, the progress to sexual maturity in youth was in fact an important aspect of the shift to adulthood; it helped to define masculinity itself in company with other elements of the bachelor's social round. It was not recommended by moralists, but this 'unsavoury' addition to the spiritual, political, and economic adulthood envisaged by magistrates, employers, and pious authors was accepted by many early modern people as a dimension of growing up. Roger Ascham complained that when people 'cum to lust and youthful days' older folk give them 'licence to live as they lust'.[50] This point of tension is one example of how plebeian mentalities could clash with ideas about proper conduct and morality held by ministers and magistrates, who preferred to confine sex to the marital bed. A number of historians, including Laslett, Shorter, and Stone, agree in identifying the pivotal point at which the curbs on self-restraint began to slacken and young people had sexual intercourse more freely. It is argued that a spousal (betrothal or marriage contract) offered a customary endorsement of sexual relations. At this point in the muddle about the meaning of legitimate marriage, sexual intercourse was more likely to occur. Shorter, for instance, comments that 'in Europe before 1800, people seldom had sexual intercourse before it was absolutely certain they would marry'.[51] It would also be misleading to enclose premarital sex within the boundaries of the spousal.[52] Yet this association between the verbal pledge of the spousal and the first flowering of sexual relations requires further

---

[49] John Calvin, *Institutes of the Christian Religion.* ed. J. T. McNeill (2 vols.; Library of Christian Classics, 20–1, 1961), i. 405; Matthew Griffith, *Bethel, Or a Forme for Families* (1634), 18. See also *Homilies*, 322; William Gouge, *Of Domesticall Duties* (1622), 218–24; John Dod and Robert Cleaver, *A Godlie Forme of Household Government* (1612), 136, 156; *The Works of the Reverend and Faithful Servant of Jesus Christ Mr Richard Greenham*, ed. H[enry] H[olland] (1601), 261–4.

[50] Roger Ascham, *The Scholemaster*, in *English Works*, ed. W. Wright (1970), 204. See also Wrightson, 'Puritan Reformation of Manners', 46.

[51] Shorter, *Making of the Modern Family*, 165–6.

[52] Cf. the remarks of Richard Adair: 'The fact that premarital sex was common can hardly be denied, but the extent to which a spousal was held to sanction it is more controversial' ('Regional Variations in Illegitimacy and Courtship Behaviour', 188). See also Martin Ingram, 'The reform of popular culture? Sex and marriage in early modern England', in Barry Reay (ed.), *Popular Culture in Seventeenth-century England* (1985), 147.

discussion. Having explored some of the interpretative and meth-odological flaws which have scarred discussions of the nature of premarital sexual relations hitherto, we will now turn to courtship to further explore the character of the world of youthful conviviality and play. Did courtship encourage the creation of particular youth spaces and places? And did serious courting couples have sexual relations?

2. *Courtship and Spousals*

We have been encouraged to think about marriage formation in this period as a process; a series of stepping-stones from the first meeting, the blossoming of love, the exchange of spousals and finally, solemnization in a church, though the exact relationship between spousals and solemnization is sometimes obscure.[53] Ingram suggests that in the period 1560–1640 'the essential requisite for a legally binding union was not the formal solemnization of marriage in church but a contract—called in popular usage, "spousals", "making sure", or "handfasting"—by which the couple took each other as husband and wife using words of the present tense'. This public promise of mutual consent was usually sealed with gifts.[54] It is said that for most people the betrothal marked 'the real begin-ning of marriage'.[55] However, the church had been struggling for a number of centuries to convince the population of the desirabil-ity of publicly formalizing nuptials by calling banns and solemniz-ing marriages in church. This crusade gradually changed the marital traditions of the majority of the people,[56] though customs die hard and Richard Adair has argued that the meaning of full solemniza-tion was accepted in lowland regions of England by the close of the sixteenth century, but in highland districts the first clear signs of the unmistakable decay of spousals came as late as the early decades of the seventeenth century.[57] Adair suggests that there were 'two

[53] See Adair, 'Regional Variations in Illegitimacy and Courtship Behaviour', esp. 184.

[54] Ingram, *Church Courts*, 189–90. For a fuller discussion of spousals see ibid., ch. 4; Alan Macfarlane, *Marriage and Love in England: Modes of Reproduction 1300–1840* (Oxford, 1986), 297–305; Stone, *Road to Divorce*, ch. 3; Laslett, *World We Have Lost*, 169–72.

[55] Gillis, *For Better for Worse*, 21.

[56] Ingram, *Church Courts*, 205–9; Stone, *Road to Divorce*, 67–79.

[57] Adair, 'Regional Variations in Illegitimacy and Courtship Behaviour', 213. Adair's highly interesting ideas about 'courtship behaviour' rely heavily on the close link between spousals and sexual intercourse, for he passes comments about the relative popularity of spousals from figures of prosecuted bridal pregnancy and illegitimacy—the 'regional distribution of illegitimate baptisms' (ibid. 209). He comments that 'every piece of evidence forthcoming

essentially separate courtship regimes' in sixteenth- and seventeenth-century England. They did share 'a spectrum of broadly similar responses', but were in fact 'culturally distinct' from each other; a cultural contrast which was sharpened by greater unemployment and land-shortages in highland districts.[58] This intriguing 'first step'[59] in tracing regional aspects of courtship and sexual behaviour requires further work. But its principal success (and perhaps its most controversial aspect) is to contextualize tender experiences of first love and passion, which for most people were first felt in youth.

The exchange of spousals has been widely interpreted as being the point at which sexual relations often began; a flagrant challenge to the Church's endeavours to contain sexual intercourse within an orderly solemnized marriage.[60] William Gouge in a well-known passage commented that betrothed couples were cast adrift in an uncertain space, neither satisfactorily married nor thoroughly single, yet 'tak[ing the] liberty after a contract to know their spouse as if they were married'.[61] Roger Thompson has advised us to pursue 'the shotgun wedding theory . . . that betrothal followed pregnancy rather than *vice versa*'. He claims that it is 'almost impossible to choose between the two', though his empirical footing is rather slender, and more careful study of the social context of sexual misdemeanours in early modern society certainly shows that Gouge

from the analyses of bastardy and bridal pregnancy statistics points away from any developed system of spousals being in operation in the lowlands during the sixteenth and seventeenth centuries'. Exchanging spousals was 'a minority activity . . . signifying serious courtship', which fully accepted the desirability of solemnization in church'. The betrothal was considered to be 'the lesser ceremony', and Adair suggests that 'there is no evidence that they were made at any time other than shortly before the publishing of the banns, and between couples who were confident of their ability to set up an independent household immediately' (ibid. 204–5, 202, 201). By contrast, Adair identifies two distinct forms of courtship behaviour in the highlands. Some couples exchanged spousals, had sex, but were forced to delay marriage, though they recognized the value of solemnization in church. Others felt that the spousal 'was wholly sufficient in itself', and if they ever proceeded to the altar it was a few years later, though many of them had 'no immediate prospect of setting-up an independent household' (ibid. 205, 209, 211). It would in fact be interesting to discover if there was a regional pattern in charges of sexual misdemeanours in which defendants pleaded that a prior betrothal offered a form of customary sanction for their actions. This would cast further light on regional distinctions. Evidence from well-dispersed lowland locations *c.*1560–1640 shows that plea being used by a reasonably large number of defendants.

[58] Ibid. 268.
[59] Ibid. 267. Adair modestly says that his model of courtship behaviour should be treated as 'a coherent but provisional hypothesis'—'a theoretical net thrown over a mass of disparate data' (ibid. 214).
[60] Ingram, *Church Courts*, 228–9; Macfarlane, *Marriage and Love*, 305; Wrightson, 'Nadir of English illegitimacy', 188–9.
[61] Quoted by Laslett, *World We Have Lost*, 171–2. Cf. the remarks of Henry Swinburne quoted by Wrightson, 'Nadir of English illegitimacy', 178.

had very good reason to make the connection between a promise of marriage and sexual intercourse.[62] A number of contemporary ballads have much to say about courtship behaviour, and one recurring piece of advice was that 'a promise of marriage gave adequate security for intercourse'.[63]

Further evidence can be gleaned from cases of illegitimacy and fornication in which one or both defendants deposed that a heartfelt pledge of love with the clear understanding that marriage would follow conferred customary approval on sexual relations.[64] Helen Anderson of Grantchester on the western fringes of Cambridge, for example, told the Ely Episcopal Court that William Mann 'had the use of her bodye' pleading in mitigation of her 'indiscretion' that 'he did promise her marriage one fortnight before the first acte'. Grace Sayer of Fordham in Essex attempted to defend herself by telling how Rudolph Leech 'promised [that] if she would let him lye with her he would marry her'. In 1585 Margaret Sellers, 'singlewoman and servant' of Norwich confessed at the Mayor's Court that Thomas Bell had 'carnall copulacon with her' in her master's house. Bell did not contradict her story, but he did inform the mayor and aldermen 'that he is persuaded in his conscyence that he hath passed a speech for maryage with her'. While Alice Clarke and Gabriel Browne, who were charged with fornication at the court of London Bridewell in 1601, told the bench that 'they are disposed to marry' and had in fact taken the step of procuring 'a license for the effecting thereof'.[65]

A grim catalogue of misery, misuse, and misfortune is revealed in many of these cases. Anne Bowland was pardoned and transported 'for murdering a smalle bastard childe born of her body' in 1637. A midwife who 'searched her testified that she was convinced the childe was borne dead'. 'Dyvers' others reported 'that she had beene well educated' and well behaved, 'and that she was promised marryage by him that got the childe whoe [subsequently] decyved her'. Elizabeth Staple of St Giles-in-the-Fields petitioned Laud for

[62] Roger Thompson, *Women in Stuart England and America* (1974), 245.

[63] Margaret Spufford, *Small Books and Pleasant Histories: Popular Fiction and Its Readership in Seventeenth-century England* (Cambridge, 1981), 158, 176–7.

[64] Adair has also consulted the records of Ely Diocese, and he concludes that 'it is surprisingly rare for a promise [of marriage] to be imputed in cases of fornication' ('Regional Variations in Illegitimacy and Courtship Behaviour', 197). In their study of Scotland *c.*1660–1780, Mitchison and Leneman uncovered only one case in which a couple who were 'cited for scandalous carriage (sex not leading to illegitimacy), tried to claim courtship as a valid reason for their actions' (*Sexuality and Social Control*, 180–1).

[65] CUL EDR B/2/12, fo. 81ᵛ; ERO D/ACA 43, fo. 82ᵛ; NRO NMC 11, fo. 515; BCB 4, fo. 261.

her discharge from prison in 1638, telling him that her 'fellow servant' George Harris, 'being [an] earnest suiter . . . in the way of marriage did contract himselfe' to her 'and afterwardes by his importunitye', she 'being a weake and younge woman and giveing creditt to his deepe protestacons did yeeld unto his unlawfull desires since which tyme' he 'refused to performe his faithfull promise . . . to marry her according to their mutuall contract, and now hideth himself in obscure and secret places about London', and plans to go 'beyond seas' to her 'utter undoing'.[66] Many of these cases strongly suggest that it was the woman who exploited the alleged customary consent of sex with marriage in mind, perhaps because her reputation was more closely evaluated by sexual conduct. They manipulated conventional opinion regarding the alleged frailties of women by representing themselves as 'weake' in order to pass the larger portion of blame to their absent partner. Such defences were lodged in the expectation that they would spark sympathy among magistrates and lighten their judgment of the defendant's conduct and the impending sentence. Both rural and hitherto less well-explored urban records reveal a significant number of people putting forward these justifications, and this must cast some light upon sexual behaviour. One young woman told the governors of Christ's Hospital in London that before her lover 'abused hir he gave hir a ring of golde and promised hir marriage'.[67]

As Elizabeth Staple discovered to her cost, some of these passionate pledges of undying love were a cruel trick to swindle a partner into having sexual intercourse. Young men were the principal culprits. In 1589 Sir Anthony Thorold wrote to Burghley from Marston in Somerset to tell him of a

mischeif (which is horrible) of late years which is wonderfully increased and one common in every towne, village, or hamlet in these partes, and (as I heare), is lykewise in other countreys. Young able fellowes do wickedly allure foolish lewd young women to folly, promysing them marryage, and when they are perceived to be with child, the men runne awaye into unknown places in farre countreys.[68]

[66] PRO SP 16/361/63; 16/401/68.

[67] GL MS 12,806/2, fo. 149. For some other examples see ibid. fos. 101ᵛ, 124, 126, 128, 138, 149, 162, 166, 170, 183ᵛ, 184ᵛ; BCB 5, fos. 10, 26, 46ᵛ, 76, 82ᵛ, 171ᵛ, 224, 243ᵛ, 257, 318ᵛ, 350ᵛ, 357, 359ᵛ, 381, 386, 407; ERO D/ACA 25, fo. 68; 30, fo. 175ᵛ; 43, fos. 82ᵛ, 161; 45, fo. 300; 47, fos. 70ᵛ, 195; 51, fos. 33, 62ᵛ; 52, fo. 234ᵛ; CUL EDR B/2/10, fo. 106; B/2/29, fo. 151; D/2/26, fo. 54; D/2/35, fo. 25; D/2/41, fo. 98.

[68] Wright, *Queen Elizabeth and Her Times*, ii. 407. See also Ingram, *Church Courts*, 229.

Other contemporaries were suspicious of the haste in which some young people rushed into verbal pledges. Dr Thomas Iles, for example, grumbled that 'in Oxon if a yong man and mayd meete by chance at a friend's howse, within a day or two they shall bee contracted if not marryed'.[69] Thorold's concern was no fiction. In 1575, for example, Thomas Metcalfe and Margaret Apiner, two London servants, were presented at Bridewell for illegitimacy. We can learn much from proceedings in their case because we can follow the governors trying to discover exactly how far their relationship had progressed. Apiner was asked—'what words or promys was made there betwene you and him?' She told the bench that Metcalfe 'required good will of her, and that she wolde consente to him and he wolde marrie hir', though the future did not look entirely bright. Apiner asked him—'how maie wee live for I am a poor maide and have nothinge?' Metcalfe replied with reassuring words, telling her that his 'unkle will give me two or three howses and some substance besydes, and I shall have to live well on', announcing, 'I will never breake promise but will marrie you'. Persuaded, Apiner returned declarations of love, 'and thereuppon [they] delte together those two tymes'. But only the pain of broken promises followed, and the bench was told that 'she is [still] waiting for him to mary her'.[70] It was alleged that a Wiltshire labourer, Henry Hatchet, plotted to get the marriage portion of Edith Eastman of Downton. He engineered a meeting, and a short time later the couple swapped spoken promises and became betrothed without the 'privitie' of parents. Hatchet then joined her in her father's house by becoming a household servant, 'by collar of which assurance' he 'unlawfullie abused the companie' of his master's daughter, 'and deflowered her and hath openly in the presence of good testimonie promised to marrye her'. The couple had even 'appointed and prefixed the day and tyme certayne' for the solemnization of their marriage. But Hatchet's subterfuge had a final twist. He had indeed applied for the Bishop's licence, but he had 'lewdly concluded and unchristianly solemnized a marriage' with one Christabel Mowdy, and now 'loytereth and lurketh in corners and places unknowne', leaving Eastman pregnant and 'her reputacon incurable'.[71]

This was not an isolated episode. There are other cases in which calculating folk contracted themselves to two partners at the same time. We can also trace other dubious situations in contemporary sources, including the stories of young men who 'meaneth to marrye'

[69] PRO SP 16/401/20.   [70] BCB 2, fo. 79ᵛ.   [71] PRO STAC 8, 138/11.

their stepmother or mistress.[72] The marriage portion was also the sole object of other conjured romances or 'pretended' unions in which it was reported that a 'secret or subtill devise', 'flattery', 'trifeling gifts', 'stronge drinke', 'feigned and fayer speeches', and questionable ministers and licences were used to trick young women into giving up their 'goods and chattels' to a counterfeit suitor.[73] One manœuvre open to apprentices who only wanted sexual pleasure was to tell their partner that in keeping with the stern conditions of their indenture they could not marry until they had completed their term. Guild and civic ethics both preached the virtues of chastity, and apprentices who could not resist the lure of the flesh, or who married in service, risked losing the right to citizenship. In Norwich, young culprits could be asked to 'duble their yeares'.[74] Elizabeth Morley, a maidservant, was presented at London Bridewell for illegitimacy with Richard Morgan, an apprentice. She told the bench that Morgan 'gave her nothinge but promised to marrie hir when he was forth of his tyme'. Joan Crane (another maidservant) was presented at the same court in 1605. She was accused of fornicating with Thomas Burt, a bricklayer's apprentice, 'for this fowre yeares space as often as he pleased'. Crane lodged a familiar appeal for a sympathetic hearing, telling the bench that 'he promised hir marriage and [that] she stayed for him untill hee had served his apprenticeshood'. But Burt had stirred a whisper of doubt and she had cautioned him—'Thomas if ye will not marry me when ye come out of your tyme I will make ye lose your freedom'. Her warning did not draw the hoped-for response, and she explained that 'now he is a freeman he denieth her'.[75]

These cases and similar episodes uncovered by other historians reveal some of the darker aspects of courtship behaviour in early modern society. The feelings of well-meaning partners could be manipulated by more artful characters for sexual pleasure or pecuniary advantage. In these unhappy events we can trace some of the expectations, hopes, and fears of people who were seeking someone to love and marry. Like those defendants who produced evidence of a prior betrothal to reduce the enormity of sexual misdemeanours, these 'false' lovers took advantage of well-established cultural benchmarks. Many people fully endorsed sexual intercourse between couples who hoped one day to set up home together. It is significant that in some well-dispersed locations people charged with sexual

---

[72] For example, BCB 2, fos. 95ᵛ, 129; 3, fos. 15 Aug. 1579, 330ᵛ; 4, fo. 10 May 1598.
[73] For example, PRO STAC 8, 228/7; 300/6.
[74] NRO NMC 7, fos. 592–3.   [75] BCB 5, fos. 20, 46ᵛ.

crimes endeavoured to stir the sympathies of the authorities by telling them the tragic tale of their bogus courtship, and how sex was a common step for two people who fell in love. They tried to salvage the fragments of their reputation by urging that what they had done was not utterly unexceptional. They must have expected that their remarks would purchase some pity and perhaps even understanding. Equally instructive are those occasions when the line of questioning probed the issue of spoken promises—'what words or promys was made there betwene you and him?'

The relatively high rate of bridal pregnancy is one indication that the majority of 'contracted' couples duly proceeded to church.[76] But a picture of courtship which is in large part drawn from judicial records is in some respects tarnished because our source usually limits discussion to the fortunes of couples against whom a charge of sexual impropriety was filed at a court. One repercussion of this is that sexual misdemeanours and spousals have arguably had a disproportionate prominence in interpretations of sexual behaviour hitherto. Again, it would be unwise to enclose all premarital sex within the tidy limits of the spousal; there are plenty of cases in which for reasons which are often lost to us this defence was not lodged, and still others in which different circumstances spawned sexual relationships—abuse, for example, or a casual encounter. Yet for many early modern people the customary bond connecting sex and serious courtship certainly held deep meaning.[77] One vital aspect of this issue of youth sexuality (and culture) is the extent to which the young were able to form social relationships and spaces of their own choosing. A strong flavour of freedom has become a near orthodoxy in recent historiography. Ingram comments that 'courting couples were customarily allowed a good deal of freedom'. Wrightson and Levine believe that courtship 'must frequently have been informal and relatively unsupervised' in the lower reaches of early modern society. While Stone suggests that 'Among the propertyless poor, who comprised perhaps the bottom third of

---

[76] The rate of bridal pregnancy in sixteenth- and seventeenth-century England was roughly 20 per cent, though there were regional variations; a point which has been recently powerfully restated by Richard Adair, who comments that 'Regionally the highlands of England show a far greater tendency towards early term bridal pregnancy before 1650 than the lowlands, a pattern which largely evens out as illegitimacy falls' ('Regional Variations in Illegitimacy and Courtship Behaviour', 136). See also P. E. H. Hair, 'Bridal pregnancy in rural England in earlier centuries', *Population Studies*, 20 (1966); id., 'Bridal pregnancy in earlier rural England further examined', *Population Studies*, 24 (1970); Ingram, *Church Courts*, 219–20.

[77] Cf. Adair, 'Regional Variations in Illegitimacy and Courtship Behaviour', 189.

the population, young people's freedom of courting was almost absolute'.[78]

In the upper ranks and prosperous middling belt marriage could often involve the exchange of significant parcels of property, and even provide a good opportunity to further political unions and boost family status. In these lofty echelons, therefore, parents could pressure their offspring to marry an 'appropriate partner'. This was not always the case in the lower reaches of society, though even here property often changed hands. Nevertheless, young people could mingle freely and the initial attraction formed by a chance encounter could develop into a life-long partnership. Ralph Josselin, who, of course, belonged to the more substantial quarter of village society, wrote in his diary about his first glimpse of his wife—'my eye fixed with love upon a mayde; and hers upon mee: who afterwards proved my wife'.[79] To complicate matters still further, there are also a broad spectrum of additional possibilities to explore. Perhaps one or both parents were in fact dead. How healthy was the economic climate in the period under review? Was there a substantial godly presence in the community? Did the young couple live in the countryside or town, in service or otherwise, or at some distance from their parental home?[80] Young migrants in London, for example, may have had greater freedom than the sons and daughters of established residents.[81]

This striking range of potential circumstances makes it difficult to generalize about plebeian courtship. Nevertheless, we can say that there was a good deal of free contact between the sexes; an impression which is confirmed in contemporary cheap print, and in those children's games which provided a cultural model by parodying experiences of courtship and marriage.[82] Young men and women did not grow up apart; although distinctive gendered experiences

---

[78] Ingram, *Church Courts*, 225–6; Stone, *Road to Divorce*, 62; Wrightson and Levine, *Poverty and Piety*, 131. See also Adair, 'Regional Variations in Illegitimacy and Courtship Behaviour', esp. 178–9, 193.

[79] *The Diary of Ralph Josselin 1616–1683*, ed. Alan Macfarlane (British Academy Records of Social and Economic History, New Series, 3, 1976), 7.

[80] Helpful summaries of factors affecting courtship in all classes can be found in Keith Wrightson, *English Society 1580–1680* (1982), 71–88; Stone, *Road to Divorce*, 59–64; Ingram, *Church Courts*, 134–40.

[81] Vivien Brodsky Elliott, 'Single women in the London marriage market: age, status and mobility, 1598–1619', in R. B. Outhwaite (ed.), *Marriage and Society: Studies in the Social History of Marriage* (1981), esp. 97.

[82] Spufford, *Small Books and Pleasant Histories*, 162; Alice Bertha Gomme, *The Traditional Games of England, Scotland and Ireland* (2 vols.; 1894, 1898), ii. 461–2; Gillis, *For Better for Worse*, 38 ff.

did, of course, exist. They discovered ample time and space to meet, talk, play, jest, flirt, and fall in love at alehouses, dances, revels, wakes, hiring fairs, church, fields, greens, and other open spaces.[83] John Aubrey gives a brief account of events at revels or wakes, and tells how 'the jornemen of every handycraft' walk to the fields 'where the tradesman's daughters and maids are not very far off, which they take and dance very civilly till they are weary'. The alehouse featured prominently in young Roger Lowe's social round. He met 'wenches' there, and it was in an alehouse during Ashton wakes that he first plucked up the courage to talk with Emm Potter his future wife.[84]

Some moralists also treated courtship as a good chance to unravel a partner's 'dispositions' and 'qualities'. Dod and Cleaver, for instance, advised young couples 'before either be married to the other . . . to see the one the other eating and walking, working and playing, talking and laughing, and chiding too', though they imposed firm limits upon any further intimacies. The image of licentious youth was still uppermost. 'Let us remember', John Northbrooke cautioned his readers, 'that although honest matrimonies are sometimes brought to passe by dancing, yea much more often are adulteries and fornications wont to follow these daunces'. Mixed dancing attracted howls of outrage. 'What clipping, what culling', asked Philip Stubbes, 'what kissing and bussing, what smouching and slabbering one of another, what filthie groping and uncleane handling is not practised everywhere in these dancings?'[85] But the matching of young couples was doubtless an important function of youthful conviviality and play as it is today. Rumours and speculations about courtship must have been one staple commodity of young people's conversation; the current string of relationships and the pool of eligible single folk in their home communities would have been well known to them. The bitter-sweet experiences of courtship were retold in

[83] Cf. Wrightson, *English Society*, 74–6; R. W. Malcolmson, *Popular Recreations in English Society 1700–1850* (Cambridge, 1973), 53–5; Adair, 'Regional Variations in Illegitimacy and Courtship Behaviour', esp. 178–9.

[84] John Aubrey, *Remaines of Gentilisme and Judaisme 1686–1687*, ed. James Britten (Folklore Society, 4, 1881), 46; *The Diary of Roger Lowe of Ashton-in-Makerfield, Lancashire 1663–1674*, ed. W. L. Sachse (1938), 26, 68, 79, 97.

[85] Dod and Cleaver, *Godlie Forme*, 109; John Northbrooke, *A Treatise Wherein Dicing, Dauncing, Vaine Playes and Enterludes . . . Are Reproved* 1577? (facsimile; Garland Series: The English Stage: Attack and Defence 1577–1730, New York, 1974), 126; Philip Stubbes, *An Anatomie of Abuses*, 1583, ed. A. Freeman (Garland Series: The English Stage: Attack and Defence 1577–1730, New York, 1973), fos. M8^r–v. See also Patrick Collinson, *The Religion of Protestants: The Church in English Society 1559–1625* (Oxford, 1982), 225–6; Gillis, *For Better for Worse*, 47–8, 52.

cheap print. Ballads and chapbooks also carried hints about spells and other simple methods to discover the identity of a future spouse, some of which were collected by Aubrey.[86]

Young couples could spend plenty of time alone, taking long walks together, joining in the conviviality of the alehouse or green, or perhaps 'sitting up' at night. The custom of 'night visiting' was a common aspect of courtship in most districts, even though it had many different names and guises; 'sitting up' in the North, for example, 'nights of watching' in Wales.[87] On his way home from Bamfurlong, Roger Lowe 'cald att Roger Naylor's' and 'stayd awhile' talking in the shop, though the chief purpose of his visit was to 'sit up' with Mary Naylor. He tells how he 'privatly ingaged to Mary to sit up awhile to let us discourse'. The couple 'agreed' that 'because we lived seaverally that we would not act soe publickely as others, that we might live privately and love firmely'. Lowe wrote in his diary—'This was the first night that ever I stayed up a wooing ere in my life'. It was reported that Walter Appleyard of Dullingham in Ely Diocese regularly visited Margaret Thurall at her mother's house and 'manie tymes stayed there all night and manie time a great part of the nighte, and would not suffer her to goe to bed and sometimes a maide sate up with them and sometimes no bodie at all'.[88]

In the records of London Bridewell there are a number of cases in which a young couple were found in 'suspicious' circumstances in alehouses or the houses of widows or goodwives, and they raise the possibility that courting couples could go to such places and hire a room to spend some precious time alone (though there are also examples of young servants from two different households having sex in a master's house).[89] In 1602, for example, Abraham Martin, a silkweaver's apprentice, admitted 'having th'use and carnal knowledge of Margaret Baker' at 'one Goodwife Maye's house in Petticoat Lane'. He reassured the governors that he would 'marye her and take her to [be his] wife'. The records are rather unhelpful, the clerk often enters only the bare matter of the offence, though a fee may have been paid for the use of the room.[90] Nevertheless,

---

[86] W. C. Day (ed.), *The Pepys Ballads* (Cambridge, 1987), 224–5, 228–9, 264–5, 278–9, 280–1, Margaret Spufford, *Small Books and Pleasant Histories*, 61.

[87] Gillis, *For Better for Worse*, 30–1.

[88] *The Diary of Roger Lowe*, 20 (see also ibid. 26); CUL EDR D/2/46, fo. 52.

[89] For example, BCB 4, fos. 162, 255, 257ᵛ, 283ᵛ, 322, 345; 5, fos. 99, 126ᵛ, 360ᵛ.

[90] BCB 4, fo. 321. See also ibid. fo. 450ᵛ; 5, fos. 25ᵛ, 27, 44; GL MS 12,806/2, fos. 125ᵛ, 126ᵛ, 137ᵛ, 161ᵛ. However, some of these cases could in fact be meetings between prostitutes and their clients, although none of the female partners mentioned in these cases can be positively identified as being keepers or prostitutes.

it should be clear by now that intimate physical contact was often accepted as a particular stage in the progress of a serious courtship; kissing and fondling were just one part of a far wider process of 'discovering' a partner, though there was less agreement about full intercourse. It has been suggested that the ritual of 'bundling', in which a young couple spent the night together—sometimes in the company of friends—involved 'most other forms of sexual gratification' than intercourse. Courtship, we are told, 'normally involved the habit' of 'bundling'.[91] But the national picture is far from complete, and evidence is thin. An incident which appears in the records of Ely Diocese, however, bears strong traces of this ritual. Thomas Dale and Margaret Bird were found together at a late hour in the night. It was reported that 'he laye' in Bird's bed 'in the night tyme ii or iii houres, which is suspicious . . .'. Dale attempted to put an end to these charges by explaining that 'there were companye by all the while'.[92]

It worried the Ely Diocesan officials that Dale and Bird were discovered together in the early hours of the morning; though many layfolk may not have shared their deep concern. Indeed, the 'almost absolute' freedom permitted young couples is in close keeping with the 'mood of tolerance' which I have argued often characterized lay attitudes towards the world of youthful conviviality and play. But there are some differences. Again, we must always remember the striking array of potential circumstances—the absence of a parent, distance away from the parental home, the zeal (or otherwise) of a master or neighbours, the significance of property, and so on.[93] But there is reason to suspect that courtship behaviour was a regular item of communal gossip which stirred comment in some places, and on occasion the attention of parents, masters, other householders—and ratepayers—young friends, or local officers. These 'observers' may have interfered for a number of reasons— because it was thought that a wrong choice had been made, for example, a concern with immorality and the parish rate, or the curbs of service. In June 1575 Agnes Bayly was presented at London Bridewell for 'resorting' to Abraham Neale, an apprentice, 'to whome she saith she is suer'. Civic policy was duly observed and the bench told her not to 'resort anymore' into his 'companie . . . until he be out of his yeres' when 'he maie lawfullie marrie her'. In 1594 Robert Bussell of Triplow (Cambridgeshire) was charged with 'misbehaving

---

[91] Stone, *Road to Divorce*, 61–2.   [92] CUL EDR D/2/10a, fo. 138.
[93] See above, p. 257.

himself' in calling for a maid 'at unlawfull houres of the nighte beinge oute of his master's house'.[94]

It is clear that in most plebeian courtships it was the young couple who took the first steps to become acquainted. But there is evidence that in some cases this 'absolute' freedom could drain away as the relationship progressed and neighbours and parents became aware of its existence. Parents were often consulted, and their approval was 'a deeply desirable commodity'.[95] Marriage entry has been characterized as a deft compromise between the hopes and fears of both parents and their offspring.[96] The courtship narratives of Leonard Wheatcroft and Roger Lowe reveal not only the significance of the alehouse as a place to hatch romance, but also of the desirability of warm familiarity within the wider circle of a partner's family and friends. Lowe went to the alehouse with Emm Potter's brothers. Ralph Josselin's daughters brought their future husbands to stay with their father for a few days. Josselin recorded how he 'had good society' with two young 'wellwishers to my virgin daughters'.[97] Even 'sitting up' was not entirely free from potential parental interruption. After all, the room in which the couple 'discoursed' was in the house of (usually) the woman's parent(s); Roger Lowe, Thomas Appleyard, and Thomas Dale all visited their partners at home. Henry Best, a Yorkshire yeoman, wrote an account of the sequential stages of courtship. Significantly, parents and a broader element of public scrutiny feature at every turn. After a period of 'visiting'—perhaps as long as six months— it was customary for the two families to negotiate the financial aspects of the match, and make other preparations for the wedding day. 'Private' vows were often celebrated in public, and the banns were called before a congregation who would joke, tease, mock, and express their good will or regret.[98] These well-known literary narratives were written by yeomen and ministers and should not, therefore, be treated as entirely representative. In some cases the moderate wealth and reputation of the two families (although Lowe was an orphaned apprentice) probably exaggerates parental

[94] BCB 2, fo. 114; CUL EDR B/2/13, fo. 93^v.
[95] Adair, 'Regional Variations in Illegitimacy and Courtship Behaviour', 179.
[96] For example by Wrightson, *English Society*, 77.
[97] *The Courtship Narrative of Leonard Wheatcroft, Derbyshire Yeoman*, ed. G. Parfitt and R. Houlbrooke (Reading, 1986); *The Diary of Roger Lowe*, 52, 70; Josselin, *Diary*, 641. Despite this interesting element of parental scrutiny, Alan Macfarlane suggests that the choice of a partner 'still lay in the hands' of Josselin's children, who 'clearly initiated the process themselves' (*The Family Life of Ralph Josselin*, 95–6).
[98] Best's account can be followed in Gillis, *For Better for Worse*, 47–8, 52–4.

involvement. Yet they show some aspects of marriage entry in the lower quarters of early modern society, the process of negotiation between parents and children, and the interest taken in romances by the community, which could quickly blossom and become a sharp commentary—a public 'fame'.

The public 'fame' or 'report' is an instructive guide to aspects of opinion in local societies in early modern England because it can reveal not only how knowledge of a particular courtship could travel to the furthest points of the community and become the staple fare of local news, but also some of the assumptions which spice the retelling of these tales. Thus Ralph Freeman and Elizabeth Wilkinson of Cambridgeshire were presented in 1599 'for dwellinge and (as comon fame goeth) lying together they being unmaryed'.[99] The intrusion of a public 'fame' which kept gossip hovering over the movements of targeted couples resulted in other charges of 'incontinent living', for example, before ecclesiastical authorities.[100] This form of 'public news' can serve as a topical and informal guide to local rumour, extending beyond reported cohabitation to pass comment on fornication, illegitimacy, incest, rape, married couples 'living asunder', the neighbourhood bawdy house, and so on. In fact, the 'fame' by catching the morality of self-styled 'honest' neighbours and anxieties about the risks and charges of pregnancy, firmly articulates the limits to the toleration of courtship and premarital sexual behaviour in some quarters.

This is well demonstrated in a Star Chamber case of 1620, in which it was alleged that William and Margaret Simons, who 'pretended themselves to be brother and sister' and had recently set up home together in Burton-on-Trent, were in fact unrelated and unmarried. Rumours swiftly travelled around the town. 'Lusty yonge men' and others had been seen calling at the Simonses' house; people remarked that Margaret 'suspiciously behaved herselfe'. Fragments of gossip were woven into substantial narratives, and speculations turned into firm charges. The couple 'grew to be generally defamed and ill reported of through the towne'. Darker

---

[99] CUL EDR B/2/15, fo. 89. See also B/2/14, fo. 23.

[100] The following examples are taken from just two of the act books of the Archdeaconry of Colchester, and only include cases of 'living incontinently' before marriage in which a 'fame' is actually recorded in the sources, and excludes a large number of other cases in which it is not, and still others in which there is no specific mention of marriage—ERO D/ACA 50, fos. 3, 14, 15ᵛ, 23ᵛ, 69ᵛ, 73ᵛ, 89, 102ᵛ, 108, 109ᵛ, 110, 114ᵛ, 115 (two cases), 116 (two cases), 117ᵛ, 118ᵛ, 124ᵛ, 129ᵛ, 130 (two cases), 136, 137 (two cases), 143, 163ᵛ, 164, 167, 170, 174, 179ᵛ, 182, 192, 193; 51, fos. 7, 14ᵛ, 15, 23ᵛ, 39ᵛ, 66, 103, 107, 125ᵛ (two cases), 129, 141, 150, 165ᵛ, 168ᵛ.

suspicions developed in other corners; were this brother and sister in fact having incestuous sex—'there grew suspicion of incontinencye'. One neighbour 'gave them knowledge of that suspition . . . and tould them [that] if they did not amend their course some publick punishment by carting or the like must be inflicted on them'. The Simonses attempted to still suspicions; they told their doubting neighbours that they were indeed brother and sister. But this did nothing to cool the heated rumours, and the same neighbour was 'pressed' by other townsfolk to search the house and 'ringe them with basons through the towne . . . as by auncient usage and custom of longe and very auncient tyme' had been done in Burton in similar cases. The couple were indeed found in bed and carried through the town to the stocks.[101]

Nor was this communal curiosity merely confined to passing on second-hand news about local celebrities. It could clearly matter in certain circumstances. If a range of customs and rituals did indeed help to create a recognized passage to full sexual maturity in which kissing and fondling were an approved introduction to sexual intercourse in the later stages of courtship (and possibly after a betrothal), then we may expect to hear the occasional expression of concern about the length of a courtship which had not yet proceeded to full solemnization. The later stages of courtship were more closely monitored than its early weeks/months when the first seeds of love and passion were sown. After all, the customary backing for sex between couples who had swapped promises of marriage was not accepted by all. Thomas and Katherine Brooks of Bassingbourn in Cambridgeshire, for example, were presented in November 1577 for 'laying together before they were married to the offence of the congregation'.[102] This concern could have sharpened towards the turn of the seventeenth century in those districts in which the more successful inculcation of stricter standards of behaviour coupled with rising administrative and financial pressures on the Poor Law made some neighbours more acutely sensitive towards the conduct of courtship and sexual relations.[103]

In some places there is firm evidence that there was a clearly understood idea of the 'decent interval' between a spoken promise of marriage and solemnization in church. Once again time emerges as an issue in the socialization of young people; in this case the

---

[101] PRO STAC 8, 104/20.
[102] CUL EDR D/2/10, fo. 86ᵛ. See also Ingram, *Church Courts*, 227–8; Wrightson, 'Nadir of English illegitimacy', 188.
[103] See the studies cited above, n. 18.

Church was attempting to move couples along a sequence of formal steps (betrothal, banns, and solemnization), and concern about the pace of this progress was to some extent elevated by the suspicion that sexual relations would become both emotional and physical aspects of courtship as months (and years) passed by. In 1601, for example, the parish authorities of Taversham in Cambridgeshire were clearly concerned about the time that Thomasine Chambers and William Wrench had spent together; 'they have been a longe tyme courted together in marage and . . . they doe defer to marrye together'. Another Cambridgeshire couple were reported to the ecclesiastical authorities at Ely because it was well known that they 'have courted . . . together', yet 'doe defer to marye'.[104] In such cases, local pressure was brought to bear in the hope that an extended courtship could be put on a more 'regular course'. Contemporary sources reveal a number of situations in which banns had been duly 'thrise called', but there was no apparent rush to the altar, only ominous lethargy. Couples were, therefore, prosecuted 'for companyeng and continewing together without marriage'. In 1622 Jane Crackbone of Braxted Magna in Essex was charged with 'living incontinently with one Peter Halrutton' after being 'thrise asked'. She told the court that they fully 'purposed to marry' but 'are hindered by the parishioners'. In other cases couples explained their inactivity by describing their economic inadequacy—'the wante and lacke of things necessarye', and 'want of ability'; a familiar tale also in cases of illegitimacy. Still other couples blamed the cold response of their families to the news of the match (a further insight into the value attached to multilateral consent).[105] Some of these stories were true, though an unknown number could have disguised another idea of customary marriage (cohabitation, for example, or spousals) which challenged that held by the ecclesiastical authorities.

One would expect to discover a complex mixture of ideas and few settled issues in those communities in which ministers and pious layfolk struggled to persuade the rest of the parishioners to accept their 'higher standards' of morality, including full solemnization of marriage. And while disputes remained unresolved, the politics of these parishes were contested and provisional; an uneven texture which was partly the product of quarrels about customary modes of courtship and marriage. The rough shapes of these distant skirmishes can be traced in the records. A 'comon fame' sparked stormy

---

[104] CUL EDR B/2/18, fos. 93^v, 105^v.
[105] CUL EDR D/2/42, fo. 110^v; ERO D/ACA 43, fo. 104^v. See also CUL EDR B/2/21, fo. 64; B/2/46, fo. 86; D/2/10, fos. 39, 50; D/2/18, fo. 42; LA/3, fo. 10^v; BCB 2, fo. 232^v; 3, fo. 330^v.

comments in a Colchester parish in 1623 from where it was reported that one couple had 'lived together to the great offence and scandal of the congregation'. Another Essex couple were accused 'of longe tyme lyving incontinentlye and slandrously to the offence of their neighbours'.[106] We do not know if on these occasions the views of the 'neighbours' and 'the congregation' represented a single outpouring of public opinion which descended upon a wholly marginalized couple. They may in fact be the commentaries of the 'godly' or 'better sort' of the community. But a dispute was in motion, and two parties had opposing interpretations about where the border between respectability and immorality was to be fixed; cohabitation, in one view, was perfectly reasonable. Interestingly, Adair has argued that many people were not upset by cohabitation, but that a reluctance to proceed to full marriage could trigger heated discussion (Wrightson, it will be remembered, has also remarked that plebeian culture widely tolerated premarital sex).[107] Ingram, however, argues that 'actual cohabitation' was 'rare' and that 'prosecutions were correspondingly few'.[108] There is, of course, a risk in drawing portraits of plebeian life from rates of prosecution. A further complication is the range of socio-economic conditions in more than 9,000 parishes. But some districts and parishes experienced moderately high numbers of prosecutions for 'incontinent living'. Thus in a single visitation of the Archdeaconry of Norwich, Sudbury, and Suffolk (1629), sixty-eight couples were discovered living together.[109] In these cases suspicions were easily stirred; prosecutors were concerned about time and solemnization and that romance should unfold in public space and the parental home, and not in the far too private seclusion of a shared house. It was for such reasons that George Tewson and Joanne Lovett found themselves before the Ely church courts in 1634, 'for that after theire banes, 3 tymes published in the church, and after they had lived some tyme together', they still seemed in no hurry to 'proceede' to 'the solemnization of their marriage'; that Elizabeth Garner and John Johnson of Ely were presented in 1594 for 'keping together suspitiouslye not beinge married'; and that Francis de Garden and Joanne Goulding were charged at Colchester in 1636 with 'suspicion of living incontinently . . . and meeting together in suspitious places as the fame goeth'.[110]

[106] ERO D/ACA 45, fo. 89ᵛ; 25, fo. 51ᵛ.

[107] Adair, 'Regional Variations in Illegitimacy and Courtship Behaviour', 199.

[108] Ingram, *Church Courts*, 224.   [109] NRO Diocesan Records Vis 6/1.

[110] CUL EDR B/2/46, fo. 75; B/2/14, fo. 57; ERO D/ACA 51, fo. 184. See also CUL EDR B/2/14, fo. 60ᵛ; B/2/18, fo. 106ᵛ.

Friends, parents, masters, and neighbours could on occasion interfere with the smooth course of a courtship and bring it to an abrupt halt, or launch a prosecution to push the relationship to the next stage of the Church's sequence of formal steps, or—far more often—to act their part in the process of negotiation between elders and their young offspring. It is arguably misleading to suggest that even among the lower ranks of 'propertyless poor . . . young people's freedom of courting was almost absolute'.[111] There are too many qualifications for this to remain an untroubled orthodoxy. It should be clear that there was no single attitude towards courtship. Opinions moved in time with the progress of the relationship, and more generally we can locate at least two potential layers of adult opinion, which were in turn affected by the facts of each case. The first of these is represented by those people who took it upon themselves to pressure their neighbours to forsake their traditional customs and pastimes, and follow a more 'pious' way of life to save themselves from a terrible fall into hell and the parish from the cost of maintaining their offspring. The propertyless poor were more frequent targets of suspicions and prosecutions, and it was their courtships and marriages which often came under the critical gaze of 'honest' neighbours; some of them were rudely halted.[112] The world of conviviality and play in which people often first met and fell in love was closely monitored. This frame of mind is more easily uncovered in contemporary sources; in the angry outbursts of moralists, and in cautions and prosecutions.

But customary attitudes which held that sexual intercourse and/or cohabitation were appropriate behaviour in long-term relationships were more sympathetic, and it is likely that such sympathy still remained even after the long campaign to convince early modern people that they should solemnize their marriages. There was an uneasy coexistence between these positions and a grim economic climate could turn consent into repression. Nevertheless, youthful conviviality and play were thought to be less menacing than magistrates and moralists imagined, and the alehouse, green, and other open spaces were generally watched with far more approval than suspicion, even if parents and neighbours still retained the right to pass comment on proposed nuptials.[113] Again, the simple age/youth polarity disguises an uneven, contested, and contradictory situation, and there is still the timeless question of typicality. Our knowledge

---

[111] See above, pp. 256–7.   [112] Ingram, *Church Courts*, esp. 131, 141, 212–15, 234.
[113] See above, esp. pp. 116–21.

of attitudes towards premarital sex, for example, cohabitation, or the cultural meaning of promises which took the place of spousals is far from complete. We should also be cautious about producing ideas which could not possibly be stretched to cover all young people in their cities, towns, villages, neighbourhoods or families, or young orphans, paupers, migrants, criminals, labourers, servants, or apprentices. Much of what we can reconstruct with confidence is taken from more 'settled' communities or households. Yet each parish had its own socio-economic character, and each household had its individual personalities. It is now time to reduce our focus and to turn to individual households and, in particular, to explore some aspects of the master/servant relation. Some masters took a close interest in the marriage plans of their apprentices and servants. Others may have been less concerned, though in theory civic institutions regulated the progress from youth to marriage and full adulthood. Nevertheless, as the apprentices Robert Bussell and Abraham Neale discovered to their cost,[114] the ideology of the household (and the pressures of socialization) could upset the romantic plans of young couples. All sorts of dramas were enacted behind the closed doors of households—tales of abuse, affection, chastisement, mutual pleasure, prohibition, and rejection; an aspect of the history of courtship and sexual behaviour which has been arguably insufficiently explored by historians hitherto.

3. *Inside the Household*

In many respects the hierarchy of authority in the 'imagined household' of the conduct book, sermon, and civic ordinance proposed an ideal solution to youthful disorder, and indeed the household was one key institution in the process of turning the young into good citizens and Christians.[115] Conduct books counselled masters to prevent 'all filthy speech, words, and actions' by their servants who were in turn urged to 'abstaine from fleshly lusts which fight against the soule'. The periodic reading of *The Homily against Whoredom and Uncleanness* repeated the warning to masters 'to provide that no whoredom, nor any point of uncleanness be used among their servants', while reminding their young charges that 'whoredom was an enemy to the pleasant flower of youth'. The author of *The*

---

[114] See above, pp. 260–1.
[115] For a fuller discussion of the significance of the household and service see above, Ch. 2.

Office of Christian Parents was only expressing a conventional wisdom
in the circles of magistrates and moralists when he told his readers
that the tight boundaries of service would help still 'the lusts and
temptations of youth'.[116] Nevertheless, household life was often very
different to the well-ordered existence envisaged by these finely
graded hierarchies. The household was a complex social situation
and in a large number of well-documented incidents we can observe
it being rocked by daily tensions and personality politics. The 'lewd
couplings' of servants in their master's household were interpreted as
a dark blemish on authority structures. In March 1601, for example,
Grace Jenks was presented at London Bridewell 'for abusinge . . . her
master's house, and lyveinge lewdlie and committing fornicacon'
with a fellow servant.[117]

The family group was held together not only by close emotional
ties, respect, and inclusion, but also by distance; by vertical patterns
of authority deriving from differences of age, for example, gender,
and the unequal distribution of economic power. The early modern household cannot be characterized as being 'well-ordered',
'godly', 'tranquil', 'disordered', 'gloomy', or 'tense' (though there
are many households and situations in contemporary sources in
which one or more of these epithets is entirely appropriate). Above
all, it was a deeply ambivalent institution.[118] Such a household was
a fertile ground for amours, temptations, suspicions, and jealousies;
all those emotions which follow reciprocal or unrequited love. Some
servants fell in love; others plotted and intrigued. Some masters
declared their love for their servants; others practised deceit and
abuse. Household order was not always immediate; it often had to
be gained. In many families, therefore, the distribution of authority
was in some respects provisional; proper order had to be pursued
by cautioning disorderly servants and uncaring or lovesick masters.
In April 1634 Sara Wentcrosse appeared before the Colchester
Archdeaconry court. Her story demonstrates how private and secret
moments could be rare in the small society of the household, and
how rumour could circulate, become confirmed, and shatter the
peace of family life. She told the court that she was put 'out of
doors' by her mistress 'because she being in her master's chamber

---

[116] Abraham Jackson, *The Pious Prentice, Or the Prentise's Piety*, 1640 (facsimile, The English
Experience, 746, Amsterdam, NJ, 1975), 49, 51; *Homilies*, 132, 125; anon., *The Office of
Christian Parents* (Cambridge, 1616), 161, and 74–5. See also Edmund Bolton, *The Cities
Advocate*, 1629 (facsimile, The English Experience, 175, Amsterdam, NJ, 1975), 51; Jackson,
Pious Prentice, 57; John Bunyan, *The Life and Death of Mr Badman* (1928), 172.
[117] BCB 5, fo. 420ᵛ.   [118] This point is more fully explored in Ch. 6.

one night to carry up his slippers, he sayd unto her the more he loved her the more she slighted him'. But her mistress overheard their conversation, 'being in the next chamber', and interpreted it by casting the blame on the servant who was turned out.[119] Other such examples could be multiplied. Samuel Pepys's diary is a store-house of lechery, intrigue, and suspicion. Pepys recorded his fondling and 'dallying' with his maids, and his wife's doubts, jealousies, and rage.[120] Indeed, inequalities of power placed a young outsider—a servant or apprentice—in a position of some potential physical and sexual vulnerability.[121] (These same vulnerabilities could also be exploited to gain favour, a share of influence, and simple material gain.) It has been shown that some young people could not come to terms with the mental scars left behind by exploitation, and they took their own lives.[122] No incest taboo covered sexual relations as it would have done in the parental home.[123] To extend potential unwelcome attention further still, a master's household could also be a key arena in his social relations, granting frequent access to a host of his friends, trading associates, and relatives.

For some young people, therefore, service in another household offered a rather precarious existence. It will be clear by now that they could construct their own spaces and places outside its four walls, though more checks were placed upon the movements of young women, especially after dark.[124] Inside the household, young people often lived at close quarters with their master, his family, and their fellow servants, sharing both living and working spaces. Opportunities for private space and time were governed not only by the pressures of the working day, but also by the architecture of the household, the number of rooms, and the uses to which they were put. The layout of individual households is rarely presented in con-temporary sources, though we sometimes discover passing references

[119] ERO D/ACA 51, fo. 68.

[120] *The Diary of Samuel Pepys*, ed. Robert Latham and William Matthews (11 vols.; 1970–83), iv. 122, 165, 180; v. 274; vi. 205, 206; vii. 60, 175, 176; ix. 439, 440–1, 481.

[121] Wrightson, 'Nadir of English illegitimacy', 187; David Garrioch, *Neighbourhood and Community in Paris 1740–1790* (Cambridge, 1986), 137; Marjorie Keniston McIntosh, *A Community Transformed: The Manor and Liberty of Havering, 1500–1620* (Cambridge, 1991), 70–1; Sandra Lauderdale Graham, *House and Street: The Domestic World of Servants and Masters in Nineteenth Century Rio de Janeiro* (Austin, 1992), 40; Wiesner, *Women and Gender* 50

[122] S. J. Stevenson, 'Social and economic contributions to the pattern of "suicide" in south-east England, 1530–1590', *Continuity and Change*, 2 (1987), 249. See also Michael Macdonald and Terence R. Murphy, *Sleepless Souls: Suicide in Early Modern England* (Oxford, 1990), 254–5; and the case of Elizabeth Godwell discussed by Wrightson, 'Infanticide', 13.

[123] Michael Mitterauer, 'Servants and youth', *Continuity and Change*, 5, (1990), 32; Mitchison and Leneman, *Sexuality and Social Control*, 184.

[124] See above, Ch. 4.

to particular rooms or sleeping arrangements. In some households there was an 'apprentices chamber', a 'maids chamber', or garret. Other young people slept in the workshop. Thomas Bradshaw, a joiner's apprentice from High Holborn in London, described how he 'and foure other apprentices did lodge together in two severall bedds' in the shop.[125]

In many households, therefore, young men and women slept apart in rooms which must also have been places for more private communication. Nevertheless, there are many examples of young people trespassing onto forbidden space, so that simply placing doors and walls between lovers offered no guarantee of restraint. In 1603 Mary Field was charged at London Bridewell with illegitimacy with her fellow servant, Gavin Clark. She explained to the court 'that she could not goe into the garrett nor into any other place but . . . [he] would followe after her'. 'In houses where the masters have set battlements on the roof', one contemporary noted, young people 'have leap'd over into the ditch'.[126] In other households no such barriers were constructed and they had some quite dubious sleeping arrangements which left young people at potential risk. William Sutton of Norwich, for example, was discovered in bed with his two maids, 'the one of them on the one syde of hym, and the other on [the] other'. He admitted that he 'used to lye with thym . . . at other tymes'. Alice Barband of London told the Bridewell bench 'that her mistress is a harlot and comytted whoredom [with her fellow apprentice] in hir own sight' in the bed where she lay.[127] John and Alice Rix of Whitford in Cambridgeshire lodged their 'men and maidservants together in one bedd by the space of fower yeares'. One of the maidservants had often left the bed to sleep on the floorboards. While Stanton Bateman and Judith Snow of London 'were commanded by there master and dame to lye in one bedd together'. Illegitimacy proceedings followed in both of these cases.[128] A number of masters and mistresses offered poverty or the small size of their house as a defence of such irregular sleeping plans. In 1616, for example, William Massey of Wiltshire pressured

---

[125] PRO SP 16/222/47. See also GL MS 12,806/2, fo. 65ᵛ; BCB 3, fos. 55–5ᵛ, 182, 235, 361ᵛ–2; 4, fos. 19 May 1598, 23 Sept. 1598, 171ᵛ; 5, fo. 232; Pepys, *Diary*, ii. 213; McIntosh, *A Community Transformed*, 68.

[126] BCB 4, fo. 354. Richard Mayo is quoted by Ann Kussmaul, *Servants in Husbandry in Early Modern England* (Cambridge, 1981), 44.

[127] NRO NMC 12, fo. 673; BCB 1, fos. 83ᵛ–4. Cf. BCB 4, fo. 29 July 1598; Mitchison and Leneman, *Sexuality and Social Control*, 185.

[128] CUL EDR B/2/14, fo. 138ᵛ; BCB 5, fo. 204ᵛ. See also BCB 2, fo. 100; 4, fo. 27 May 1598.

his maidservant to have sex, and claimed that a lack of space and furniture had resulted in the two of them sharing a bed for six years; Massey's wife had slept in between them for all that time.[129]

Alan Bray has plausibly argued that such sleeping arrangements may have encouraged homosexuality, although his evidence is wafer-thin, perhaps because attraction and affection blossomed in a private chamber. In fact, on the few occasions when this 'sodometicall synne not mete to be wryten' (the implications of this wording are themselves significant) was presented at London Bridewell the couple were more likely to be discovered outside in an alley or field.[130] There are few examples of masters having sex with their male servants. Thomas Woodford was sent to gaol in November 1606 for 'being accused to have committed sodomie with William Wood his servant, a boye of xiii yeares'. This is the bare information in the courtbook, and we are left to wonder whether this was a case of mutual consent, abuse, or malicious prosecution.[131] In some respects a position of authority exposed a master to charges of abuse, or perhaps improper association with young people who, like other subordinates, should have been kept at a distance. Nor was it only relations between masters and servants which stirred these suspicions. In 1638 Laud was informed that a number of fellows of an Oxford college 'have lately frequented ye companye of ye bachelors and scholars making them bedfellowes in their chambers and in ye towne in innes and alehouses, an abuse [it was reported, which was] unheard of in recent yeares'. Worse still, Laud's correspondent informed him that 'they still offend secretly'. Indeed, a bachelor and master had recently been 'taken together' by a proctor 'in a drinking schoole on a Sunday morninge in sermon tyme'.[132]

A faint impression of the pressures which could unsettle young lives can be drawn from the relative significance of a master's household as a location for sex among its resident male and female servants. The following comments and figures are drawn from cases of fornication and illegitimacy which came before the Court of London Bridewell in the years 1559–62, 1574–9, and 1597–9, and Norwich's Court of Mayoralty in the period 1555–1610 in which apprentices, maids, and servants can be identified as defendants—a final sample of 230 young women and 193 young men.[133] Some

---

[129] Ingram, *Church Courts*, 266.

[130] Alan Bray, *Homosexuality in Renaissance England* (1982), 48. For some examples of cases in the Bridewell courtbooks see BCB 1, fos. 128ᵛ, 130; 2, fo. 200; 3, fo. 19 July 1579; 4, fo. 237.

[131] CLRO Rep. 27, fo. 319ᵛ.   [132] PRO SP 16/397/18.

[133] The sources consulted are BCB 1–4 and NRO NMC 7–14.

clear patterns emerge. Female experiences of sexual intercourse were more likely to be contained within a master's household; in 193 cases women reported that sex took place there (83.9 per cent). The figure is somewhat lower for the young men in the sample; 125 of them told the bench that they had sexual intercourse in their master's household (64.8 per cent). In all of these cases young people informed the court that sex occurred in their master's household, though their partners were drawn from a range of social relationships. They included a master or mistress, their children, friends, and relations, fellow servants, or other people who were introduced to the household by a servant—a friend, for example, or a casual or more serious partner. We can narrow the focus of the 'household' to discover the number of cases in which servants had sexual intercourse with their master/mistress or their resident family. Fifty-one of the 120 female servants who were charged with illegitimacy accused their master or one of his close relatives of fathering their child (42.5 per cent). There is a solitary case in which an apprentice was alleged to have fathered an illegitimate child upon his mistress. Twenty-seven young women were charged with fornicating with their master or his close relative (24.5 per cent, 27/110). While only ten young men (8.6 per cent, 10/116) told the London or Norwich courts that they had sexual relations with their mistress or her daughter.[134]

We cannot treat these figures as a simple index of sexual abuse.[135] One obvious concern is that the actual dimensions of this problem will never be known; fear, awe, and helplessness conspired to place a servant in a weak position, and ensured that in many cases abuse was covered up and remained a household secret. One also suspects that some cases of abuse have entered the historical record as charges of fornication or illegitimacy.[136] Nevertheless, the geography of illicit sexuality shows that even in cases of mutual consent the aspirations and choices of young women who feature in this sample (which in turn is highly selective—it is derived from the narratives of servants who were living in a London or Norwich household) were either more narrowly centred upon the people who moved in

[134] It should be remembered that this brief survey excludes cases in which it was alleged that young men had sexual intercourse with prostitutes. If those cases had in fact been included the impression that women were more likely to have sex inside their master's household would have been much stronger.

[135] Cf. Adair, 'Regional Variations in Illegitimacy and Courtship Behaviour', 95.

[136] J. M. Beattie, *Crime and the Courts in England 1660–1800* (Oxford, 1986), 124; N. Bashar, 'Rape in England between 1500 and 1700', in London Feminist Group, *The Sexual Dynamics of History: Men's Power, Women's Resistance* (1983), 28, 36.

the social world of their master's household, or in other cases, that his home was a place to take their partners. Young men had more freedom to roam outside the household after dusk, and the bachelor's social round offered some of them a widely accepted introduction to drink, commercial sex, gaming, and male camaraderie. Sexual relations were more acceptable for male youth outside the boundaries of courtship or marriage. The reputation of young women was more closely measured by sexual behaviour; by chastity in youth and restraint in marriage.[137] Thus we find one young maid 'upon her knees' in a field begging her partner 'to marrie her for that she was with child by him or else to kill her'.[138] In fact, it could be argued that purity and prudence were more sensitive issues for women poised on the border of adulthood.[139] An unblemished youth, therefore, was one important yardstick of femininity; a bustling social life and progress to full sexual maturity were arguably more regular aspects of the acquisition of masculinity, and this found expression in the conversation and meaning of the bachelor's social round.

Yet the geography of these sexual encounters is also one sign of the greater vulnerability of female servants inside the household. We have been encouraged to picture the social context of illegitimacy as a 'compound phenomenon'. In most studies, however, the greater part of cases resulted from sex between people living side-by-side in the same household. Keith Wrightson has convincingly interpreted illegitimacy as being to a large extent a 'problem of household discipline'.[140] Martin Ingram has commented that 'the great majority of women' who appear as mothers of illegitimates in the records of the Bishop of Salisbury's Court were unmarried. 'Many were in fact domestic servants—perhaps as many as 70 per cent in the 1580s.'[141] Less well-explored urban sources tell a similar tale. The social status of 174 mothers is recorded in charges of illegitimacy filed at the courts of London Bridewell in the period 1605–9 and

---

[137] Cf. Laura Gowing, 'Gender and the language of insult in early modern London', *History Workshop Journal*, 35 (1993); J. A. Sharpe, *Defamation and Sexual Slander in Early Modern England: The Church Courts at York* (Borthwick Papers, 58, York, 1980).

[138] BCB 4, fo. 161.

[139] See above, Ch. 1.

[140] Wrightson, 'The Puritan Reformation of Manners', 57, 60–1; id., 'Nadir of English illegitimacy', 187; Wrightson and Levine, 'Social context of illegitimacy', 163–9; Quaife, *Wanton Wenches*, ch. 4. Again, Richard Adair has reminded us of the possibility of regional variations in both the extent and context of illegitimacy. He in fact suggests that illegitimacy was less likely to be a problem of household discipline in highland districts ('Regional Variations in Illegitimacy and Courtship Behaviour', 96).

[141] Ingram, *Church Courts*, 264.

Christ's Hospital, London, in the period 1592–6. The greater part of these defendants are identified as servants in the courtbooks (114, 65.5 per cent); a further four appear as the daughter of a householder (2.2 per cent). Another forty mothers belonged to London's vagrant or marginal quarter (22.9 per cent), and we would expect to find casual servants and others who had been turned out by their master among their ranks.[142] Scattered contemporary remarks help cast further light on this darker side of the household. In August 1624 London's Common Council reported that 'of late divers and sundry women have secretly been delivered of bastard children' and had left them in many places about the city to the 'great charge' of the parish. 'The greatest nomber', it was claimed, go 'under the name of maide servants', and officers were instructed to apprehend 'maidservants and others that go under that name and doe lye out of service that cannot give accompt of their living'.[143]

It is certainly not my intention to present an unpleasant image of the master as a coarse tyrant who viewed his female servants as 'easy prey'. Yet there is a great deal of evidence in contemporary sources which shows the limited usefulness of another highly idealized general character; Laslett's 'superbly satisfactory master figure'.[144] Except for the occasional twinge of remorse, Samuel Pepys thought that his molestation of female servants was but a mere 'dalliance'; he was only 'playing the fool'.[145] The master's broad discretionary powers of instruction and discipline could be corrupted, misinterpreted, or rescored. Their 'sovereign' status in much contemporary advice and teaching, together with the abject position of servants, could have encouraged some masters to view their servants as an item; a piece of property. In April 1605 Robert Parker, a London cook, was charged at Bridewell with illegitimacy with his maid Alice Ashemore. The bench was informed that he 'had th'use and carnall knowledge of hir bodie for the space of a twelvemonth and somewhat more at his pleasure . . . [whenever] he could find her alone'. But Parker had told Ashemore that this was his privilege as her master; it was another one of her duties—'thowe art my servant and

---

[142] The sources consulted are BCB 5 and GL MS 12,806/2. Only four of the 174 defendants can be positively identified as being married. The sample is completed by eleven widows and one woman whom we can only identify as the sister of an apprentice's master. There are a further 142 charges of illegitimacy filed at London Bridewell in the period 1605–9 in which I have been unable to produce positive identifications of the mother's status.

[143] CLRO Jour. 32, fo. 319. Cf. CLRO Rep. 34, fo. 288.

[144] Laslett, *World We Have Lost*, 5–6.

[145] Pepys, *Diary*, iii. 152, 157; vii. 104, 172; viii. 276, 280, 293, 315; ix. 188, 307. Cf. Josselin, *Diary*, 403.

I may doe with thee what I please'. In 1610 Sara Evans told the same court how 'one day when her mistress was from home... her master called her into his chamber and tooke her and cast her upon the bedd and toke up her clothes, and put his hand into her bodie'. He later 'called her into the kitchen and told her [that] he had heard she was with child, and therefore would see saeing masters and mistresses might see anye things of the servant'. One Suffolk apprentice was sharply aware that his master 'could enforce' his will 'being under him as his apprentice to bring him to doe any acte'.[146]

Young women sometimes fell victim to forceful or honey-tongued masters whose blunt aggression or false charm was a reversal of their responsibilities. Elizabeth Evans served Jesus Scarborough the parson of St Gregory's in Botolph Lane (London) for ten weeks, and in all that time he 'laboured to have her consent that he might use her body, which he prosecuted till he had obtained'. She left his service only to fall in with another hard-hearted master, one goodman Dennys. He seemed to be a reasonable employer, 'alledging nothing but her service'. However, this was only a mask of good faith. After she moved into his house Evans told the court that Dennys told her 'that if she wolde yelde her body than he woulde place her well' in another household. In 1604 Elizabeth Green admitted having sexual intercourse with her master, James Powell (a tailor) 'in her owne bedd' and in the hall chamber. She had turned to her mistress for help, telling her that her master had 'put her in feare, and [that] she would not dwell theare'. Her dame's cool response carried a strong hint of a recent history of similar experiences and conversations in Powell's household—'what is he fallen to his old wont to follow whores'.[147] The language in these cases is revealing. Parson Scarborough seeks to 'use' his maidservant, who is treated as a mere item much like his other household possessions; Powell's wife seeks to shift a large part of the blame onto her servant girl; the 'whore'.[148]

Such cases provide striking glimpses of masters who manipulated conventional rhetoric which elevated their position; they put to one side curbs upon their arbitrary powers. This was just one aspect of household relations, but it was a regular item in the business of the

---

[146] BCB 5, fos. 23ᵛ, 411; PRO STAC 8, 291/28.
[147] BCB 4, fos. 439, 459. See also BCB 1, fo. 122; 3, fos. 36, 294ᵛ, 347ᵛ; 4, fos. 77ᵛ, 147, 439; 5, fo. 17ᵛ.
[148] Although it should, of course, be remembered that 'had the use of' was used to describe sexual intercourse between couples in many situations other than that between superiors and their subordinates.

courts, which attracted much contemporary comment. The cases of
Alice Ashemore and Sara Evans are by no means peculiar. There
are many examples of masters having 'th'use and carnall knowledge' of their female servants; some 'dyvers and sundry tymes' with
one young woman, others with two or more servants.[149] In a number
of cases sexual relations began in the first few days or weeks of the
arrival of a new maid. 'The first tyme' that Richard Bradshaw 'had
th'use of' Elizabeth Foldes 'was the first day she came to him'.[150]
Other masters bided their time perhaps waiting until their wife
made a long trip 'out of town', or was otherwise detained. The first
occasion that Margaret Jolly had sexual intercourse with her master, the keeper of Newgate, was at Christmas 1575 when 'his wyfe
was prisoner in the White Lyon'. William Athey, a London tailor,
'had th'use' of his maidservant while his wife was away at Graves-
end, promising that 'she should never want but that he would
provide for her, and that he would repaire to her whoesoever she
was'.[151] Still other masters first turned to their female servant when
their wife was in bed pregnant or sick. Joanne Young of London
told the Bridewell bench that 'the first tyme' her master 'abused'
her was when his wife 'lay last in childbedde, the second tyme three
wekes after she was churched'. A London glazier 'had th'use and
carnall knowledge' of his maid while his wife lay in 'childbed'.[152]

Some households earned notorious reputations and were targeted
by neighbourly gossip. Alice Foreman of London, for example, was
'charged by fower honest men of the lane wherein she dwelleth to
be a very bad woman', and her neighbours reported how all of her
servants 'hadd children or els the desease'. One London servant
who was charged with illegitimacy at Bridewell in 1575 alleged 'that
iiii or v have gone out of . . . [her master's] howse with child'.[153]
Some of these ill-famed households were probably bawdy houses.
A familiar narrative in the judicial sources is that of the 'honest'
maidservant who was 'enticed' from her true master, only to fall
into the world of prostitution by the procurer's trick. One May's

---

[149] There are hundreds of similar cases involving masters and maids in the records I have
consulted. For some examples from just two courtbooks see BCB 4, fos. 4 Oct. 1598, 285^v,
320^v, 323^v, 329^v, 374, 376, 381, 389^v, 412, 419, 424, 431, 435^v, 439, 445^v, 457, 459; 5, fos.
9–9^v, 11, 17^v, 23^v, 55^v, 70, 100, 110, 128, 130^v, 146, 147, 148^v, 160^v, 170, 197, 239^v, 248^v,
253.

[150] GL MS 12,806/2, fo. 134^v. See also BCB 4, fos. 254^v, 376; 5, fos. 55^v, 197.

[151] GL MS 12,806/2, fo. 167^v; BCB 4, fo. 320^v. See also BCB 4, fos. 187, 329^v, 459;
Ingram, *Church Courts*, 266.

[152] BCB 3, fo. 315^v; 4, fo. 187^v.

[153] BCB 5, fo. 142; GL MS 12,806/2, fo. 132^v. See also ERO D/ACA 50, fo. 97; CUL EDR
B/2/15, fo. 57.

wife of The Three Tonnes in London kept 'a lewd bawdy house for all that come'. The court was told that she often 'recruited' her prostitutes from the stream of young women pouring into the capital, doubtless taking advantage of the highly unstable nature of the milieu of service. 'She hireth maidservants', one witness alleged, 'and sayeth she hired them, but keepeth them to play the harlot.' Elizabeth Wilkinson claimed that she was 'entysed' by her mistress 'to playe the whore with northern men'. While it was reported that John Cowe's wife, 'a bad lyver', had 'kept bawdry a long tyme and hath procured hir servants'.[154]

Yet not all such cases can be explained by abuse, deception, or guile. In the courtroom a maidservant is given an opportunity to give her version of events, and this is what we see in the records. She could tailor her narrative to pander to the expectations and sentiments of the male bench, and present herself as the helpless young victim of male fury and cunning. We must read their 'stories' with care. Some testimonies may be laced with significant words or turns of phrase to squeeze the sympathies of the bench. Nevertheless, it is likely that in the majority of depositions we encounter authentic situations of persecution. We sometimes see maidservants in dire circumstances trying to defend themselves against their master, as some items of cheap print urged them to do,[155] spurning his unwanted advances, and 'praying to God to keep her honest'.[156] Other young women clearly conveyed a deep sense of their vulnerability. Joan Lane of London, for example, 'lyked not the resort of such as come to [her master's] house for that they wold be using evell speeche and dede towards her'.[157] In such cases the master is clearly presented in court as a domestic despot and seducer who corrupted the meaning of patriarchal obligation and instruction. A variety of pressures and inducements can be found in contemporary sources. Sex may have been an onerous aspect of a disagreeable

---

[154] BCB 3, fos. 228ᵛ, 161ᵛ–2; 5, fo. 158ᵛ. See also BCB 1, fos. 4–5, 5ᵛ, 10ᵛ, 16; 2, fos. 107, 188; 3, fos. 70ᵛ, 156ᵛ–7, 277, 299ᵛ, 364ᵛ–5, 20 June 1579, 20 Aug. 1579; 4, fos. 49, 64, 66ᵛ, 69ᵛ, 139, 248ᵛ, 389, 4 Mar. 1598, 27 Sept. 1598, 4 Oct. 1598, 22 Nov. 1598; 5, fos. 26ᵛ, 158ᵛ, 161ᵛ, 397ᵛ; GL MS 12,806/2, fo. 134ᵛ. Cf. Paul Griffiths, 'The structure of prostitution in Elizabethan London', *Continuity and Change*, 8 (1993), esp. 49–52.

[155] See Charles P. Lord, 'Image and Reality: The Chapbook Perspective on Women in Early Modern Britain' (unpublished University of St Andrews M.Phil. dissertation, 1988), 53–4.

[156] For example, NRO NMC 12, fo. 300; BCB 3, fo. 269; Quaife, *Wanton Wenches*, 70.

[157] BCB 3, fos. 353–3ᵛ. For some examples of female servants being accused of having sex with their master's friends, lodgers, and relatives see BCB 4, fos. 53, 152, 285, 385ᵛ; 5, fos. 47, 91ᵛ, 115ᵛ, 119ᵛ, 134, 223, 1 Apr. 1598, 9 Apr. 1598; GL MS 12,806/2, fos. 53, 79; ORO PCBP 1626–36, fo. 75; ERO D/ACA 44, fo. 143; 47, fo. 39.

situation in which the male possessed complete authority; a form of 'terrible resignation'. By contrast, some young women viewed friendship and sexual relations with their master as a golden opportunity for material benefit and even worldly progress. A number of masters tempted their maidservants with the beguiling though obscure promise of 'great reward'.[158] On occasion, the motives of master and servant seem muddled or unclear. The courts often listened to the maid's story (in many cases in the Bridewell courtbooks, for example, it is from her narrative that we have to reconstruct the circumstances of the charge), although in the sources I have consulted the master's testimony (if it was entered) is rarely recorded. In some cases the awarding of blame seems reasonably straightforward; the master shrinking from the shame and slur of public exposure threatened, bullied, bribed, and beat his pregnant servant. But in many others a cloud of ambiguity hovered over the sexual act; who was to blame—the reprobate master, the maidservant (who could have appeared in a number of guises, as conniving, luckless, pragmatic, or lusty), or both?

In some respects sexual relations between a mistress and her/her husband's apprentice were treated with the same regard for authority and moral order by the courts. A mistress, after all, held a position of responsibility which was frequently institutionalized and discussed by contemporary moralists. Young males too, could present themselves before the court as harassed subordinates. In February 1574 Hercules Anthom, a London apprentice, told the Bridewell court that his mistress, Mrs Gold, 'hath alwaies sought to have the use of his bodie'. Gold admitted 'that Hercules her man hathe come to hir bed and that she once wente' to his bed. In December 1575 John Orred and Thomas Llewellyn, the apprentices of Richard Carter, filed complaints at the same court. Orred told the governors that his mistress 'hath divers tymes come unto the bedd where he and one Thomas Cape did lye and ther hath used suche allurements and evocations of incontynense' that in order to evade her provocative gestures the pair 'have bene fayne to forfeit their bedd and to go out of their chamber'. On another occasion, they 'were sittinge at dynner' while their mistress sat 'by the fyer in the hall where they dyned'. Orred claimed that she rose to her feet, and turning towards the table where they sat drinking and eating 'lifted upp all her clothes above the naville and showed hirselfe naked unto them . . . and clapped hirselfe on the bare buttocke saeinge look my masters here are neither scabbes nor seales'. Mrs

---

[158] Quaife, *Wanton Wenches*, 70; NRO NMC 12, fo. 300; BCB 3, fo. 269.

Carter then pulled down her clothes only to raise them up again a few minutes later, 'verie shamefullie showinge hir privities contrarie [it was reported] to all womanhood and honestie'.[159] Again, we should treat these narratives with care. Charges and insinuations could spring from a melting-pot of jealousy, craving, resentment, vengeance, or unrequited love. But it is interesting that Anthom described his sexual encounters with his mistress in much the same language as that used by Elizabeth Evans when she put into words the abuse of the parson Jesus Scarborough.[160] It should be remembered that a freeman's widow offered young men the comforting prospect of a secure economic footing. Yet such a romance was also a delight for gossips, another opportunity to recycle the tale of the lusty widow. William Lilly's account of his marriage to his late master's widow reveals a strong flavour of public disapproval. Lilly reported that when their match became public news, 'some people blamed her for it'. However, his wife was not the sole target of scorn. Lilly also reported neighbourly concerns that he would not make a 'good husband'. In fact, the couple had taken steps to stop news of their marriage leaking out. They were 'very careful to keep all things secret', and were able to hide the truth about their nuptials for as long as two years.[161]

One Bristol preacher thought fit to caution apprentices about the temptations of a master's wife or daughter.[162] A few households were dens of sexual entanglement. Helen Read of London was 'charged that her menservants hath laine with her continuallye', though she told the court that she only had sex with William Stevens at 'two severall tymes'. Richard Fell, a pewterer's apprentice, confessed to having 'the use and carnall knowledge of the bodye of Alice Good', his late master's wife, 'divers and sondrye tymes' (a second witness, a maid living in the same household, confirmed his story), though in a moment of pious reflection Fell reminded the court that 'it was better to repent in this world than in the world to come'.[163] Nevertheless, the number of recorded sexual encounters

---

[159] BCB 2, fos. 66ᵛ, 188ᵛ–9ᵛ.   [160] See above, p. 275.

[161] William Lilly, *William Lilly's History of His Life and Times* (1822), 50–2. Cf. Lord, 'Image and Reality', 158 ff.; Vivien Brodsky Elliott, 'Widows in late Elizabethan London: remarriage, economic opportunity and family orientations', in L. Bonfield *et al.* (eds.), *The World We Have Gained: Histories of Population and Social Structure Presented to Peter Laslett* (Oxford, 1986); Wiesner, *Women and Gender*, 75.

[162] The minister is quoted in A. Yarborough, 'Apprentices as adolescents in sixteenth-century Bristol', *Journal of Social History*, 13 (1979), 30.

[163] BCB 4, fos. 29 July 1598, 22 Apr. 1598. See also CUL EDR B/2/21, fo. 27ᵛ; D/2/23, fo. 35; ERO D/ACA 43, fo. 34ᵛ; NRO NMC 12, fo. 97; 15, fo. 60; GL MS 7090/2, fo. 229ᵛ; BCB 1, fos. 83–4ᵛ, 200; 3, fos. 55–5ᵛ; 5, fos. 211ᵛ, 516. There are also examples of male

between male servants and their mistress was far fewer than that between masters and maidservants. This may be a reflection of the greater vulnerability felt by a young woman inside the household, or perhaps the deeper sense of reputation felt by older women. The character of the mistress is being closely examined in these proceedings. On the one part she is a figure of authority, but on the other she is an older woman who is accused of having sexual intercourse with a young apprentice, who is expected to make the progress from youth to full adulthood and prominent status in the community. The flower of youth is plucked in an unequal encounter with a vulgar elder, who steers young aspirants away from the virtuous path to economic and political responsibility.

In these cases the principal female character plays the part of the tainted temptress; a familiar figure in contemporary moral commentaries. The language used to communicate the meaning of these encounters, therefore, is often that of enchantment, corruption, and seduction. The coupling of the promise of youth with domestic and civic order is made explicit in other cases in which it was reported that older women had 'spoiled' young men. In August 1609, for example, Anne Ellis of London was charged with 'playeinge the queane' with John Walden, 'a verie boy and spoyling him'. Symond Martin, another apprentice, was 'spoyled' by a woman he met on the highway. While Arthur Morey was 'spoyled' by a 'wicked woman'.[164] Elizabeth Holgate found that even as her reputation was being closely reviewed by the court, the concern with civic and household order worked to her advantage. She was charged with fornicating with John Haydock, an apprentice who lived in the same London street. An earlier charge of 'ill resort' by suspected men to her house was brought to the attention of the court. Worse still, her 'late servant' told the bench that she had 'lett in' Haydock to the house at 'aboute iiii of the clock in the morninge', and left him 'in the hall with her mistress, the bed being there'. However, Holgate was spared further punishment because as the Bridewell bench explained, 'she is a man's wyffe . . . [and we] are lothe to break householdes'—a very interesting footnote to the near symmetry between domestic and social order.[165] Yet it must be remembered that

apprentices having sex with their master's female relatives and lodgers: e.g. BCB 4, fos. 82, 96, 404; 5, fos. 2, 85ᵛ, 110, 155ᵛ, 409.

[164] BCB 5, fo. 374; 4, fos. 69ᵛ, 213. See also NRO NMC 8, fo. 621; 9, fos. 74, 425; 11, fos. 541, 603; 12, fo. 779; 13, fo. 259ᵛ; 14, fo. 44; CUL EDR B/2/10, fo. 2ᵛ; B/2/52, fo. 138; BCB 2, fos. 89, 205; 3, fos. 311ᵛ, 329; 4, fos. 52, 69, 78, 80ᵛ, 83, 147, 179, 179ᵛ, 205, 215, 341ᵛ, 374, 415ᵛ, 423ᵛ, 426, 1 Feb. 1598, 22 Oct. 1598; 5, fos. 16ᵛ, 33ᵛ, 186ᵛ, 208ᵛ.

[165] BCB 2, fos. 141–3ᵛ. Cf. ibid. fo. 230.

young men could also turn such anxieties to their own favour in court, and reiterate their partner's faults when in some cases they may have been bending the truth or telling tales. More generally, the dame often appears as a careless mistress who has stained her authority by swooping upon her inexperienced apprentice, who may in turn receive a share of the blame, but who is on occasion treated as a victim.

Contemporary sources reveal a still higher level of sexual activity between fellow servants, which may reflect a mere maid's reluctance to report the abuses of her master.[166] In 204 charges of sexual crime filed at London Bridewell in the periods 1574–6 and 1597–1610, 125 (61.2 per cent) alleged sexual relations between fellow servants, and seventy-nine between masters and their female servant.[167] Richard Baxter recognized the possible harm in placing young people of both sexes in the limited space of the household. In his *Christian Directory* (1673), Baxter cautioned servants to beware of 'immodest familiarity', which lured 'those of different sexes into a snare'. He claimed that an 'abundance of sin and misery have followed such tempting familiarity of men and maids that were fellow servants. Their nearness gave them opportunity so the devil provoketh them to take their opportunity.' Richard Mayo issued a similar warning twenty years after Baxter. He commented that 'undue familiarity between servants of different sexes in a family has had tragic and fatal effects'. He posed the question, 'how often has opportunity and privacy exposed men and maids that live together to the Devil's temptations?'[168]

Nor should these be dismissed as the ill-conceived suspicions of a few moralists. Maids and apprentices who first met in a master's household fell in love, making passionate declarations to each other, and swapping promises of marriage. It should also be clear that household life presented opportunities for treachery, trickery, and more casual sexual relations. John Robinson of London 'had the use and carnal knowledge' of Sara Bradford 'the first night she lay' in his master's house. While Joseph Tanner discovered his fellow William Rose 'in naked bed' with Joanne Angel, the maidservant, 'and that all night', their 'master beinge in the countrey'. The next night Rose 'perswaded' Tanner 'to lie in naked bedd' with Angel, and he told the Bridewell governors that 'he had th'use and carnall

---

[166] Cf. Adair, 'Regional Variations in Illegitimacy and Courtship Behaviour', 95.
[167] BCB 3 and 4.
[168] Richard Baxter, *A Christian Directory, Or a Sum of Practical Theologie and Cases of Conscience* (1673), 561. Mayo is quoted in Kussmaul, *Servants in Husbandry*, 44.

knowledge of her bodye' but 'repentinge of his fault he rose from the bed' and left the room.[169] In these cases the dominant issue was not that of institutional authority, the 'proper' distance between those in places of authority and their subordinates had not been diminished. Instead, household order had been stained by sexual relations between resident underlings. In some respects blame and shame could have been allocated in equal measure. Yet it was sometimes clear that young men had planted well-planned traps to deceive and abuse maidservants. Some male servants probably understood the strategic value in shifting the initiative to their partners by masquerading as a victim to soften the responses of the bench. Again, the male can introduce female seduction and temptation as the pivotal point on which the discussions of the court could turn. Casting aspersions on a sexual partner was a useful strategy in the courtroom. This at least provides one way of reading these narratives and the assumptions of the court. Thus in 1610 Jane Calten was presented at London Bridewell for 'enticing her fellow servants and apprentices to lewdness, and suffered them as also others that came to bringe worke [to her master's house] to have the use and carnall knowledge of her bodie'. In other cases male servants told the court that they were 'invited' to have sexual intercourse by the maidservant who 'came' to their bed.[170]

How did these abuses come to the notice of the court? It often proved difficult to conceal the signs of romance, seduction, or abuse from other members of the household. In a number of cases it was fellow residents who passed on information to a constable or a neighbour, or went directly to the court. Such tell-tale signs as a creaking bed or a tired and yawning servant or master could quickly become an item of household gossip.[171] Stories and rumours rarely remained within the walls of the household. Local social relations provided corridors of communication, turning domestic murmuring into public news from which an 'ill report' or 'fame' could spring.[172] Suspicions quickly travelled around the community when

---

[169] BCB 5, fo. 47; 4, fo. 436^v. For a small selection of illegitimacy cases involving servants in the same household in just one courtbook of London Bridewell see BCB 5, fos. 2^v, 6, 17, 18, 31^v, 41^v, 77^v, 89^v, 104, 130^v, 150^v, 167, 206, 224, 226, 257^v, 283^v, 336^v, 350^v, 374^v, 389^v. And for some cases of fornication between servants in the same courtbook, see ibid., fos. 7, 24, 38, 47, 50, 84, 87, 385^v, 420^v.

[170] BCB 5, fo. 441; BCB 4, fos. 1 July 1598, 23 Sept. 1598, 381^v, 436^v; 5, fos. 2, 18, 269^v, 441.

[171] For example, NRO NMC 9, fo. 690; CUL EDR B/2/52, fo. 125; B/2/35, fo. 192; BCB 3, fos. 27 May 1579, 356.

[172] For example, ERO D/ACA 32, fo. 232; 44, fo. 119^v; 47, fo. 12; 50, fos. 113, 138^v; 51, fo. 113; 52, fo. 158.

it was reported that a master and his maid were 'living incontinently' together.[173] In some cases distressed young women confided in their mistress, but they did so at the risk of being misunderstood and turned out of doors, the sorry victim of marital jealousy and intrigue, or of desperate measures to safeguard the 'credit' of their master and his household. We find Robert Wheatley of London on his knees before his wife begging her 'to appease the matter' of his sexual indiscretion with their maidservant.[174] In fact, wives rarely brought their husband's misdemeanours to the attention of the courts in the records I have consulted. They often supported their husband. In 1599 Alice Skinner of London told the Bridewell governors that 'she was conceyved with child' by James Lacey, a cutler. She had in fact charged another man with fathering her child, but claimed that this was 'for feare' of Lacey's wife. Another wife urged her pregnant maidservant 'to saie that a servant of thers got her with childe who is gone overseas'.[175]

It was more likely that young victims of exploitation would turn to a friend or relative for help. Miriam Heath had served one Mr Hesterlind of Colchester for eighteen months in August 1634, 'and in that tyme [she told the Colchester Church Courts, he] . . . had oftentymes the carnall use of her body'. Again, it was the fear of pregnancy which resulted in her experiences becoming registered in the historical record. Heath told her sister and then her mother of Hesterlind's 'carnall use of her body'—'she fearing herselfe to be with childe'. Interestingly, the mother first called at Hesterlind's house 'and privately told him of it'. He did not deny the truth of the matter, and 'did acknowledge for that he had wronged her daughter'. What followed next is unclear, but the records indicate that it was not strictly the mother's endeavours but the force of the 'fame' which resulted in a charge being filed at the church courts. The story was 'spread abroade in the town', and Heath was instructed to appear before a local justice who 'told her that the court would punish . . . Hesterlind for his sayd offence and let her goe'.[176]

Heath did have one stroke of good luck, she was not pregnant after all. The fate of the pregnant single woman was often a sorry tale of cruelty and bureaucratic indifference. She was caught between the concern of her master with his public face, and that of the parish to keep a careful check on the poor rate and the moral

[173] See ERO D/ACA 44, fo. 106; 46, fo. 161; 47, fos. 37, 60; 49, fo. 214ᵛ; 50, fo. 113; 52, fo. 167; 54, fo. 75ᵛ.

[174] GL MS 12,806/2, fo. 68ᵛ.   [175] BCB 4, fo. 65; GL MS 12,806/2, fo. 71.

[176] ERO D/ACA 50, fo. 68.

lapses which threatened to raise contributions.[177] Even Pepys felt 'shame' as he fondled his maidservants, and a far greater concern that one of them would 'refuse and then tell my wife'.[178] The potential injury in having their private lives exposed for public comment was too great for some masters, and they volunteered large sums to the poor rate to escape the 'great disgrace' of public penance. In February 1568 Jerome Lambert fell 'upon his knees' before the Court of Christ's Hospital in London to beg 'God's mercie' after being charged with illegitimacy with his servant, though his pleas fell on deaf ears and he was ordered to enter sureties and sent in to Bridewell.[179]

This sense of shame could force the fathers of illegitimates to take radical steps to silence their partners to stop their misdemeanours from becoming public news. Some of them issued threats and offered money to pressure the mothers of their illegitimate child to depart the parish or to lay the blame on another man. Some fathers, and they included masters as well as apprentices, did in fact marry their accusers even if they had to be persuaded by a higher authority.[180] But far more commonly in the sources we discover charges of abuse, neglect, and menacing words. One pregnant woman confronted the father of her child who 'threatened her that if she wolde not clere him' and 'denye' it 'he woulde troble her and never leve it of while he lived', and promised her 'that if she wolde clere him she shoulde have x^{li}, a peticote and a kassock'. Jasper Cooke of the Middle Temple 'confessed that he gave thirtye pounds' to Katherine Cuffe's master 'upon condicon' that she 'should not exclayme agaynst him . . . nor charge him to be the father of her child'. Agnes Melkirk who served in the Swan in Shoreditch claimed that William Davis, her fellow servant, was the father of her illegitimate child. He had 'promised hir faithfully maryage', but she later received news that he had married another woman. Davis took steps to prevent rumours of his alleged paternity spreading in the neighbourhood. He found Melkirk washing her master's clothes in the kitchen, 'and saide yf thou be with child beware thou do not . . . [say it was] at my hand'. Davis urged her to 'say it was gotten in the

[177] Cf. Quaife, *Wanton Wenches*, chs. 4 and 9; Lord, 'Image and Reality', 55; Wiesner, *Women and Gender*, 51–2.

[178] Pepys, *Diary*, iii. 152, 157; viii. 276.

[179] GL MS 12,806/2, fo. 34; ERO D/ACA 46, fo. 154.

[180] For example, NRO NMC 10, fo. 563; BCB 2, fo. 75; 3, fos. 72^v, 271, 7 Aug. 1579; 4, fos. 57, 24 Mar. 1598, 16 Aug. 1598.

fields by a person unknown', and promised her money if she kept his paternity a secret. Agnes Strange also claimed that her fellow servant was the father of her child, though it later emerged that one Mr Issack had first offered her fifteen shillings to return to Salisbury, and on another occasion a further twenty shillings 'if she would father her child on some other man and not charge his man Henry Haskett'. In 'the greatest payne of her labor' Strange told the midwife who cautioned her that she would have to answer 'at the dreadfull day of judgment', that Haskett was the father of her child. Other masters took similar steps to shield their apprentice from such accusations.[181]

There are also examples of young women being smuggled out of their master's household, and in these cases knowledge was clearly passed on giving details of residents who were prepared to 'receive' pregnant young women for a fee. These 'harbourers' offered shelter until after the birth of the child, and it seems that at least some of them were 'irregular' midwives.[182] Other young women were turned out by their master or mistress when news of their pregnancy came to light or its visible signs could be disguised no longer.[183] Still others left their child outside the house of a well-known citizen, on the steps of a church, or in some other public place in the hope that they would be better provided for. In London there are examples of people being paid to lay new-born children at strategic points about the city, and this may have been one well-known method of discarding the offspring of the bawdy houses and other illegitimate children.[184]

The courts were anxious to establish paternity and ensure that the child did not fall into the care of the parish, though a strong

---

[181] BCB 3, fos. 259, 58, 61; GL MS 12,806/2, fo. 140; 4, fos. 61ᵛ, 77ᵛ. See also ERO D/ACA 32, fo. 22ᵛ; GL MS 12,806/2, fos. 42, 68ᵛ, 71, 117, 140ᵛ; BCB 3, fos. 180ᵛ, 259, 315ᵛ, 370–1, 26 Sept. 1579; 4, fos. 58, 65, 78ᵛ, 135ᵛ, 145ᵛ, 187, 192, 374, 376; 5, fos. 23ᵛ, 110, 147.

[182] For example, ERO D/ACA 30, fos. 76, 162ᵛ, 260ᵛ, 267ᵛ; 32, fos. 59, 121ᵛ; 43, fo. 140; 44, fos. 75, 141ᵛ; 52, fos. 189, 241; NRO NMC 15, fos. 220ᵛ, 466ᵛ; 16, fo. 9ᵛ; 20, fos. 238ᵛ, 275ᵛ; BCB 2, fos. 1 Oct. 1575, 154, 199, 208; 3, fos. 27, 288, 288ᵛ, 310, 346, 26 Sept. 1579; 4, fos. 51, 83, 192, 207, 258ᵛ, 260, 375, 376. In a couple of these London cases we can firmly identify the house in which the pregnant woman served as a bawdy house. Putting pregnant women out to irregular midwives could have been one way of managing pregnancy in an institution such as this.

[183] For example, NRO NMC 15, fos. 1ᵛ, 171ᵛ; ERO D/ACA 51, fo. 68; 52, fo. 180ᵛ; GL MS 12,806/2, fo. 117; BCB 2, fo. 250ᵛ; 3, fos. 112ᵛ, 180ᵛ, 265, 327; 4, fos. 232, 258ᵛ, 285.

[184] For example, BCB 4, fo. 51; 6, fos. 349ᵛ, 364ᵛ; 7, fo. 58; 8, fos. 24ᵛ, 92ᵛ; GL MSS 12,806/1, fos. 5, 6, 10ᵛ, 11, 171ᵛ, 28ᵛ, 30ᵛ, 41ᵛ, 45ᵛ, 50, 51, 54ᵛ; 12,806/2, fos. 14, 15, 28, 34, 57ᵛ, 94ᵛ, 116ᵛ, 117, 130, 151ᵛ, 174, 186ᵛ, 200, 217.

flavour of moral disapproval is also implied in those cases in which prosecutions continued even though the child had been still-born.[185] Even though both father and mother were likely to be blamed for this moral outrage and potential financial burden, methods of punishment imply that responsibility and shame were rarely allocated in equal measure. If the father of the child was apprehended the judgments of the court often turned on his ability to provide solid assurances to enter sureties. Nor did masters escape responsibility for the errors of their servants. They could be required to file similar guarantees if one of their male servants fathered an illegitimate child,[186] and they risked prosecution if he managed to evade his financial obligations.[187] The image of the father in these proceedings is that of the provider; it is the woman who is more likely to be punished by a spell in a House of Correction, whipping, or both.[188] If the name of the father remained a mystery or a matter of controversy the court could place further pressure on the mother, who it was thought carried the secret of paternity in her heart. In some cases pregnant women were 'strictly examined' by a midwife and several 'honest women' of the parish 'concerning the father of her childe'. As she lay in 'extreame paynes' and was told that she was 'in great daunger of death', the mother was cautioned 'for so moche as her lyfe was in God's hands and unknowne to herself or to them whether she should lyve or dye', to reveal the name of the father and save the parish from future cost.[189] Women who were not resident in the parish in which they were arrested were usually handed a pass and returned to their last place of settlement. They

[185] For example, BCB 3, fo. 72ᵛ; 4, fos. 56ᵛ, 65, 277, 419, 1 July 1598; 5, fos. 1ᵛ, 26, 61ᵛ, 66, 77ᵛ, 104ᵛ, 106ᵛ, 113, 259, 281ᵛ, 350ᵛ.

[186] For example, NRO NMC 11, fo. 423; 15, fos. 61ᵛ, 171ᵛ, 289ᵛ; 16, fos. 9ᵛ, 75, 83, 292ᵛ; BCB 2, fo. 170; 3, fos. 73ᵛ, 6 May 1579, 24 July 1579. Illegitimate children were sometimes put out to wet-nurses by the authorities (e.g. NRO NMC 10, fo. 594; 16, fo. 280). Cf. Valerie Fildes, *Wet Nursing: A History from Antiquity to the Present* (Oxford, 1988), 79. Guardians could also be asked to maintain illegitimate children until they reached 7 years of age when they would be put into service.

[187] For example, ERO D/ACA 25, fo. 73ᵛ; 30, fo. 150ᵛ; 45, fo. 307; 50, fo. 73ᵛ; 51, fo. 2; 52, fo. 12.

[188] Quaife comments that 'The punishment provisions of most orders were directed solely against the woman. Punishment of the male was rare. Of several hundred orders investigated only eight imposed corporal punishment on the man and all of these involved a second offence . . . Eleven in every twelve men suffered no punishment at all.' He also discovers that in Somerset 'Whipping as the sole punishment was replaced after 1630 by confinement in the House of Correction as the normal method of punishment' (*Wanton Wenches*, 216, 217–18). See also NRO NMC 15, fos. 1, 3ᵛ, 10ᵛ, 49ᵛ, 123, 235ᵛ, 522; 16, fos. 230ᵛ, 249ᵛ, 347ᵛ, 359, 431, 439ᵛ, 479ᵛ.

[189] The quotations are taken from two cases, ORO PCBP, 1626–36, fo. 72; NRO NMC 12, fos. 679–80.

became victims of disputes between parishes, and were tossed about by rival authorities anxious to transfer financial care elsewhere.[190] We find some of them in dire straits, joining the ranks of rootless vagrants, giving birth on a street, or in other grim conditions.[191]

It was for considerations of this nature that the risks of premarital sex even after earnest promises of marriage had been exchanged were far greater for young women. Knowledge about abortion and contraceptive techniques, the social value of reputation, and the potentially grave repercussions of pregnancy, prompted some women to delay sexual relations until the later stages of courtship, and many of them would have expected firm tokens of love, loyalty, and support. We must be cautious because the sequence of events usually has to be reconstructed from the woman's testimony. Nevertheless, in the great majority of cases it is the woman who seeks a firm pledge of marriage, and the male who forgets his spoken promises and deserts his partner. It also seems that young men were more likely to have sexual relations outside their master's household. They probably had more opportunities for casual sex outside its four walls, and in some well-documented encounters we catch them meeting with prostitutes, wives, and widows. For such people sexual prowess was one dimension of the meaning of manhood. Yet this is not recognized in the excessively sterile image of early modern youth presented in the work of Stone, Shorter, Laslett, and others.

In their pages Tudor and Stuart youth are impeccably restrained, 'unerotic', and seething with pent-up frustration. A ground-swell of inner turmoil festered and hampered self-expression. At about the same time parental affection was guarded, discipline was uppermost, and religious zeal set the moral tone.[192] Each detail of this picture was redrawn in the eighteenth century as family structures altered, religious tempers sagged, and structures of control slackened. It was then that shackled youth shed their inhibitions, and embarked on a voyage of self-discovery, finding pleasure, self-expression, and themselves. My account of the work of Stone, Shorter, and others is inevitably truncated, but it conveys the basic elements of a story of free sexual expression and release of emotion which is often recycled. We turn to the period before say 1700 and

[190] For example, NRO NMC 9, fo. 447; 11, fos. 519, 599; BCB 3, fos. 368^v-9; 4, fos. 33^v, 161.

[191] There are many examples of pregnant female vagrants in the records I have consulted in Norwich and London. For some typical cases see BCB 2, fos. 227^v, 23 Mar. 1579, 20 Oct. 1579.

[192] See esp. Stone, *Family, Sex and Marriage*, chs. 1, 5, and 9.

find frustration in the lust-expelling antics of the Shrovetide bawdy house sackers, low illegitimacy rates, and the long interval between the first stirrings of puberty and marriage. Higher rates of illegitimacy in the eighteenth century could indicate soaring levels of sexual intercourse. Nevertheless, we must recall the limitations of sources. We know little about birth control in early modern society, or the popularity of sexual activity short of full intercourse. How many sexual encounters passed undetected and unrecorded? Nor is there much evidence in contemporary sources of itching sexual frustration.

One exasperating feature of the debate about sexual behaviour at this time is the virtual impossibility of delivering a straightforward answer, a final interpretation, or a smooth linear progress. It seems entirely appropriate to close on an uneven and fragmentary note, and simply to draw attention to the many potential options and reservations. Forthright ideas about earlier 'simmering frustration' and later 'sexual revolution' can appear persuasive precisely because they brush aside such awkward complications. Yet one way forward is to tread more deeply into context and, rather than count prosecutions of sexual misdemeanours in order to pass doubtful speculations about the resort to sexual intercourse, we could look more closely at how particular personality politics inside households, types of work, communities, changing socio-economic conditions, and the attitudes of families, friends (if they were still living or living nearby), and parish authorities affected sexual behaviour. We could draw up a multitude of variables within which to study sexual relations in the past. There were points of tension but they cannot be relegated to age/youth polarities, though on occasion the precepts of service dampened passion and romance, or squabbles about the choice of a partner rocked families, especially when the transfer of parcels of property was at issue. Customary ideas about courtship and sexual behaviour which all parts of the community could share if they so wished, granted young people freedom as part of a far broader toleration of youthful conviviality and play in plebeian society. Yet there were well-defined boundaries to this licence. In times of scarce resources and deeper unemployment attitudes could sharpen, especially in the ranks of parish government. The later stages of courtship stirred anxieties as it was more likely that a couple would have sealed their love with full intercourse. One concern was the duration of a courtship, and its 'private' or 'public' nature, and a more 'precise' religious temper could turn indulgence into repression. These possible contexts of ideology, work, place, and time are vital aspects of a more complex yet more accurate portrait of sexual behaviour at this time. They certainly did not exclude the expectation of sexual relations, indeed some of them operated on that very assumption.

Most of the young people who appeared in this chapter were apprentices or servants. They had left home to live in another household for a single year or more. Their position and status placed them in a situation of tutored restraint in which the danger of abuse and negligence always lurked, but it did not stop warm feelings blossoming between some masters and their servants. Stories of sexual behaviour and courtship in Tudor and Stuart society reveal scenes of intense emotion, deceit, despair, exhilaration, passion, and pleasure. We have encountered happy and sad people, and others who were caught out by the authorities. Passion and romance have always been turbulent aspects of growing up. They can shatter people, but also households and relations between masters and servants. There was a great deal of contemporary comment on this theme, and suspicions circulated about promiscuous and poor domestic relations. The 'disorderly' servant and 'disorderly' master were regular objects of sharp denunciation. The next chapter will probe more deeply into the state of households in Tudor and Stuart society, and seeks to further our understanding of the relationship between the happy and positive aspects of domestic life and their unhappy and negative opposites, by exploring the provenance, progress, and resolution of household disorders.

6

The Disordered Household

Peter Laslett's *The World We Have Lost* is a storehouse of images of
early modern society, but perhaps one of the most familiar and
enduring is introduced in the first few pages, the description of a
patriarchal household—a baker's shop in which 'everyone had his
or her circle of affection', and every 'relationship' was 'seen as a
love relationship'. Outside the four walls of the household in the
'hurly burly' of daily life, lurked danger, fear, and uncertainty, but
inside life was far more pleasant and constant. People moved 'in a
circle of loved familiar faces', and 'known and fondled objects'.[1]
This tidy and cloistered domestic circle is the 'imagined community' of the conduct books, sermons, and catechisms which helped
to define conventional patterns of authority in early modern England. Laslett draws upon a number of sources for his representation
of the baker's dwelling, but they are overwhelmingly secondary and
prescriptive in nature. In fact, daily experiences contradicted this
patriarchal vision. We lose sight of its finely graded hierarchies and
baggage of duties and obligations in the more mercurial theatre of
everyday life. We have already encountered a number of situations
in which young people did not play the part in which they were cast
by the politics of age and 'place'. These youthful lapses corrupted
not only the robust image of the domestic patriarch, but also the
metaphor of age and authority. Familial disorder and inversions of
age-relations troubled the social hierarchy and the ideology from
which it derived legitimacy. In *Eastward Ho*, Touchstone tells his
wayward apprentice Quicksilver that 'I will no longer dishonest my
house, nor endanger my stock with your licence'.[2]

The principal aim of this chapter is rather modest. It is certainly
not to juxtapose an alternative view of the early modern household to
the ordered godly community of the text—presenting a bleak view
of disorder and misery. I simply wish to add to our understanding

[1] Peter Laslett, *The World We Have Lost: Further Explored* (1983), 5, 21, 5–6, and 1–6.
[2] George Chapman *et al.*, *Eastward Ho*, 1605 (Tudor Facsimile Texts, New York, 1970), fo.
B3ᵛ.

of a further dimension of this complex situation, which catches both the broad spectrum of emotions inside its four walls, and also the ways in which people could move between different postures ranging from conformity to opposition, and incorporating 'intermediate' stances like resignation or indifference. The multiple identity of subordinates and their tactical use of different modes of behaviour deserves further exploration. In fact, the potential for dispute was anxiously noted by contemporaries, and we can follow their deep pessimism about the household and age-relations more generally in the sources. Their concern is a sensitive index of the fragile ambiguity of domestic relations. Yet it has been to some extent passed over in histories of the life-course, and also in accounts which emphasize the significance of the household for the pursuit of sound religion and social order. Above all, it will be clear by now that domestic order was not always immediate; the authorities often had to *pursue* stability.

This chapter will present fresh evidence for the forms of dispute between the members of households, and the methods by which the authorities attempted to still unquiet households. It is a limited study because I have chiefly consulted manuscript sources from the two largest cities at this time—London and Norwich. The countryside is not touched on here.[3] Servants are also lumped together with apprentices as subordinate youths,[4] though I draw attention to some of the ways in which their separate statuses led to different experiences in the settlement of domestic disputes when it is appropriate. This account of disordered households is also in many respects a 'stationary' tale. I have explored social relations in motion in terms of the exchanges between masters and their servants, but not over an extended period of time. Yet in different times and places problems emerged which further complicated domestic relations. In 1564, for example, the London Grocers complained 'that divers younge men of this companye being apprentices lacketh masters'. In 1628 the Farriers claimed that the 'most apparent causes' of their recently 'decayed' state was the 'late heavie visitacon of sicknes', which 'swept awaye most of the ablest and most expertest' in their 'arte and trade'.[5] Particular climates which raised such

---

[3] But see Ann Kussmaul, *Servants in Husbandry in Early Modern England* (Cambridge, 1981), esp. part ii; Ilana Krausman Ben-Amos, *Adolescence and Youth in Early Modern England* (New Haven, 1994), ch. 3.

[4] Cf. Barbara Hanawalt, *Growing up in Medieval London: The Experience of Childhood in History* (New York, 1993), chs. 8–10.

[5] GL MS 11,588/1, fo. 130ᵛ; CLRO Rep. 42, fos. 106–6ᵛ.

difficulties would be aspects of a more rounded discussion. The terms and conditions of service also altered as centuries slipped by, and this might provide a useful point of entry for future work.

However, the principal themes of this chapter were chosen in the light of present research, and it is hoped that they will provide suggestions for future work. We will observe courts and guilds entering this 'private' sphere to arbitrate in skirmishes between masters and servants, and to arrest the rude and disorderly servant, or the negligent and violent master in support of the 'imagined' ordered household.[6] These institutions used familial rhetoric not only to articulate an abiding sense of unity and purpose, but also to cultivate a mood of inclusion to lighten the sense of differentiation and distance upon which their authority depended. They much preferred to settle differences between masters and servants within the household, or if this was not possible, guild or civic structures, so that 'outside' bodies did not have to be invited into their domain or 'society'. The potential ambiguity of age-relations is revealed not only in the occasion of disputes, but also in the forms of arbitration, intervention, and decision-making. The terms of order were being continually disputed and redefined. Later sections of this chapter, therefore, will examine the character of household disorders. Close attention will be given to the language and contexts of these squabbles, and the measured responses of the guilds and courts. But first we must return to the current discussion of the nature of service in this period to sketch our conceptual point of entry to these disordered households.

1. *The Disordered Household?*

In contrast to the angry words of contemporary moralists who despaired of the lazy householder and his upstart servant, some recent historians have given us a rather optimistic account of the early modern household as an agency of discipline and socialization. It was at least a qualified success. Service turned young people into adults; families reproduced, generation succeeded generation, and

---

[6] A very similar case could also be made for the forms of disputes (and their resolution) between parents and children, though contemporaries did distinguish between the two relationships and often advised householders to treat these two forms of subordination in different ways. However, I have chosen to focus upon master/servant relations because I believe that service in another household was a more common experience for young people of the lower and middle classes in their teens and early twenties, and, after all, it is a pivotal point of the life-cyclical definition of youth.

the world continued to turn.[7] Some historians reduce the dynamics of domestic experiences to a paragraph or two, in which the household rightly emerges as the principal rock of social order.[8] Yet many of these accounts simply describe the ideology and forms of domestic order, and rarely proceed to ask how effective was the household as a guarantor of order. Did service successfully prepare young people for entry into the world created by their elders, or did some of them grow up in different ways to the image of temperate youth which dominates prescriptive attitudes informing authority structures?[9] Such questions are often left unanswered, or they are put to one side, which is partly understandable for they would seem to defy attempts at quantification. Any single interpretation is likely to trace the prejudices of a chosen source or line of enquiry. Even after each avenue is explored one imposing hurdle still stands before us—how is it possible to characterize such a complex and changeable institution as the early modern household?

We can at least proceed by exploring its parts and functions. Ilana Krausman Ben-Amos and Steve Rappaport describe the processes by which young people were socialized and departed the dependence of service (and youth) for the full independence of economic and political citizenship.[10] The records of guilds, for example, permit us to map movement along the life-cycle from the first stumbling steps of enrolment to freedom and the dawn of adulthood. At the close of his term of service the capable apprentice, one 'of honest behaviour and good workmenship' and able to teach his 'servants their occupacion sufficiently', was admitted as a householder. Thus in March 1637 Vincent White who had recently completed his term, petitioned the governors of London Bridewell for a room in which to follow his occupation. They were informed that he was 'a very honest man and one that is very like to discharge

[7] See, for example, Ralph Houlbrooke, *The English Family 1450-1700* (1984); Ilana Krausman Ben-Amos, 'Service and the coming of age of young men in seventeenth-century England', *Continuity and Change*, 3 (1988); Steve Rappaport, *Worlds within Worlds: Structures of Life in Sixteenth-century London* (Cambridge, 1989), esp. 234-7.

[8] See, for example, the 'Introduction' in Anthony Fletcher and John Stevenson (eds.), *Order and Disorder in Early Modern England* (Cambridge, 1985), 31-2; Martin Ingram, *Church Courts, Sex and Marriage in England 1570-1640* (Cambridge, 1987), 125. Other historians spend a chapter discussing the 'godly household'. See John Morgan, *Godly Learning. Puritan Attitudes towards Reason, Learning and Education* (Cambridge, 1986), ch. 8; Patrick Collinson, *The Birthpangs of Protestant England: Religious and Cultural Change in the Sixteenth and Seventeenth Centuries* (Basingstoke, 1988), ch. 3.

[9] Cf. Ian W. Archer, *The Pursuit of Stability: Social Relations in Elizabethan London* (Cambridge, 1991), 216-17.

[10] Ben-Amos, *Adolescence and Youth in Early Modern England*, esp. chs. 5, 9; Rappaport, *Worlds within Worlds*, 232-8.

a good conscience towards those that the governors shall hereafter appoint unto him in the bringing them up in the feare of God and well instructing them in their trades'.[11] White was a successful product of service; a virtuous citizen, and he was not alone. The greater number of master/servant relations may have been fairly cordial and polite. We should at least recognize that social distance implies a measure of respect as well as inequality and authority, and that hands of affection could join across this divide. Apprentices, after all, had a golden chance to ascend civic and guild hierarchies. It must also be remembered that some young people were placed with other members of their family, or their father's trusted trading partners or friends.[12] We have evidence of warm regard, compassion, and trust. Some old servants called in to see their former masters, and some masters left money or other items like tools to their servants in their will. A number of servants still worked on their master's behalf as their executor even after he had drawn his final breath.[13] Others joined forces with their masters to defend their household from attack, or to menace or assault their adversaries.[14]

Nevertheless, it was still felt necessary that the authorities should police the unfolding of the life-cycle. They took steps to prevent apprentices from marrying, and arrested others who took a short-cut to adulthood by setting up shop before the close of their terms. It was claimed that early economic independence inflated self-images and stirred illusions of grandeur (though as we shall see some young people acquired skills, fell in love, and had difficulty reconciling this 'maturity' to their dependent status). Such young

[11] CH minute book 1558–81, fo. 92ᵛ; BCB 8, fo. 107ᵛ. See also CLRO Jour. 25, fo. 255.

[12] See Vivien Brodsky Elliott, 'Single women in the London marriage market: age, status and mobility, 1598–1619', in R. B. Outhwaite (ed.), *Marriage and Society: Studies in the Social History of Marriage* (1981), 93; Kussmaul, *Servants in Husbandry*, 59; P. J. P. Goldberg, *Women, Work and Life-Cycle in a Medieval Economy: Women in York and Yorkshire c.1300–1520* (Oxford, 1992), 177–80; Christopher Brooks, 'Apprenticeship, social mobility and the middling sort, 1550–1800', in Jonathan Barry and C. Brooks (eds.), *The Middling Sort of People: Culture, Society and Politics in England, 1550–1800* (Basingstoke, 1994), 74.

[13] For example, CLRO Reps. 38, fos. 44–4ᵛ; 45, fo. 213; 51, fos. 295–5ᵛ; Ben-Amos, *Adolescence and Youth in Early Modern England*, 173–5; Marjorie Keniston McIntosh, *A Community Transformed: The Manor and Liberty of Havering, 1500–1620* (Cambridge, 1991); Susan Brigden, 'Youth and the English Reformation', *Past and Present*, 95 (1982), 49; Graham Mayhew, 'Life-cycle, service and the family unit in early modern Rye', *Continuity and Change*, 6 (1991), 221; Robert Whiting, *The Blind Devotion of the People: Popular Religion and the English Reformation* (Cambridge, 1989), 70; Goldberg, *Women, Work and Life-Cycle*, 182–3; Hanawalt, *Growing up in Medieval London*, 147, 170–1; David Garrioch, *Neighbourhood and Community in Paris, 1740–1790* (Cambridge, 1986), 134–7; Roger Thompson, *Sex in Middlesex: Popular Mores in a Massachusetts County, 1649–1699* (Amherst, Mass., 1986), 163. Both Ralph Josselin and Samuel Pepys were visited by their former servants.

[14] For example, PRO STAC 8 112/1; 165/17; 246/9.

people became 'not only hawtie mynded, highe stomoked, and wanton condycyoned', but also 'less obedyent and serviceable to theyr masters'.[15] In 1612 both Amos Locke of London and Henry Pierson his former apprentice were disenfranchised. Pierson had married before his term began, and 'in the tyme of his apprenticeship was a housekeeper and executed the office of a constable'. Locke had sealed a false oath to allow Pierson to enter the freedom. In 1631 the Coopers company filed a complaint at the Court of Aldermen against Samuel Eagles and Richard Johnson his 'sometyme apprentice'. It emerged that Johnson with his master's 'leave and sufferance . . . did trade for himselfe within the terme of his apprenticeship' and had married 'contrary to the custome' of the city. The court had good grounds to suspect that Eagles 'did knowe' that his apprentice was 'married at the tyme he made him a freeman' because he had been invited to his wedding. In other cases masters put their apprentices in charge of a shop and allowed them to draw a portion of the profits; one apprentice married at the Savoy under a cloak of secrecy; others set up shop under a false name, 'being not free nor yett of age to be made free'. It was the duty of a master in such cases to track his apprentice's deeds, and to bring them to the attention of the authorities, or risk losing his place in the freedom.[16] In other cases young people were made free by redemption, by 'especiall favour' of the court before the close of their term because their master was approaching the end of his working life and wished to turn over his trade to them, or he had in fact died, and his widow requested that the shop be 'put over'.[17]

From these cases (and many others wait in the records) it is possible to see how the authorities monitored progress along the life-cycle. Yet the evidence for daily life in the household is ambiguous and difficult to interpret.[18] This equivocal note is a common thread in some recent work in which we encounter not only affection and respect, but also the possibility of abuse, neglect, and conflict

---

[15] J. R. Boyle and F. W. Dendy (eds.), *Extracts from the Records of the Merchant Adventurers of Newcastle-upon-Tyne* (2 vols.; Surtees Society, 93, 101, Durham, 1895, 1899), i. 6–7.

[16] CLRO Reps. 31(1), fos. 18–18'; 45, fos. 205–5 . See also CLRO Reps. 28, fos. 53 , 224; 29, fo. 73'; 30, fo. 22'; 31(2), fos. 343'-4, 396; 39, fo. 223'; 41, fo. 155'; 47, fos. 116–16'; GL MS 5770/2, fo. 489; GCL minute book O2, fo. 283; GL MS 8200/1, fo. 447'.

[17] For example, CLRO Reps. 33, fos. 168', 349–9', 358', 363; 34, fos. 400–0', 471'; 40, fo. 287; 41, fos. 93–3', 137–8.

[18] Cf. Archer, *Pursuit of Stability*, 217; A. L. Beier, 'Social problems in Elizabethan London', in Jonathan Barry (ed.), *The Tudor and Stuart Town: A Reader in English Urban History, 1530–1688* (Harlow, 1990), 132–7; Garrioch, *Neighbourhood and Community*, esp. 134–7.

between people living side-by-side in the same household.[19] The nature of domestic relations has been further obscured by unhelpful polarities in work which treats the subject either sensationally or impressionistically—one reproducing the tidy household of the conduct book,[20] the other telling a shocking story in which a master preys upon his servant who is sorely abused and alone.[21] It has been argued that the high proportion of young suicides is partly explained by 'the emotional life and legal situation of the servant'. Michael MacDonald and Terence Murphy present a bleak image of 'terrified and brutalized boys and girls' who 'had nowhere to turn', and who 'killed themselves to escape their elders' wrath'.[22] We can find evidence of acute distress. John Jewell, a vagrant on the run from his master, 'who putt a halter in his pockett wherewith in prison he would have hanged himselfe', was only kept alive by his 'fellowe prisoner callinge for help in the night'. In June 1618 London's chamberlain after 'a great deal of pains' working on the case, ordered that Thomas Jolles should be discharged from the service of Thomas Draper. Uppermost in his mind were 'some desperate speeches' by Jolles—'that he would rather make himselfe away then returne to his master's service'. It was said that 'this appeareth not to be in wordes onely', but that he 'would have performed as much in deedes'. Draper was cautioned for his 'much severity of correction', and instructed to free his apprentice 'for quietnes sake'.[23]

In *Sleepless Souls*, however, Macdonald and Murphy draw a far too pessimistic picture of the position of the servant. There is no place in their account for the mediating efforts of family, 'friends', and the courts, for example.[24] Yet they rightly emphasize the potential

[19] For example, S. R. Smith, 'The ideal and the reality: apprentice–master relationships in seventeenth-century England', *History of Education Quarterly*, 21 (1981); Keith Wrightson, *English Society 1580–1680* (1982), ch. 4; Keith Thomas, 'Age and authority in early modern England', *Proceedings of the British Academy*, 62 (1976); Archer, *Pursuit of Stability*, 216–18. This chapter opened with Laslett's description of an ideal patriarchal household yet he also refers to 'incessant and unrelieved' tension in the domestic sphere (*World We Have Lost*, 6).

[20] For example, Richard Greaves, *Society and Religion in Elizabethan England* (Minneapolis, 1981), ch. 7.

[21] For example, Michael Macdonald and Terence R. Murphy, *Sleepless Souls: Suicide in Early Modern England* (Oxford, 1990), 252–5.

[22] S. J. Stevenson, 'Social and economic contributions to the pattern of "suicide" in southeast England, 1530–1590', *Continuity and Change*, 2 (1987), 229; Macdonald and Murphy, *Sleepless Souls*, 252–3; Terence R. Murphy, '"Woful childe of parents rage": suicide of children and adolescents in early modern England', *Sixteenth Century Journal*, 17 (1986), 265, 270.

[23] BCB 5, fo. 292ᵛ; CLRO Rep. 33, fos. 328–8ᵛ.

[24] For a typical case see BCB 4, fo. 423. A great deal of further evidence is presented below. See also Margaret Pelling, 'Apprenticeship, health and social cohesion in early modern London', *History Workshop Journal*, 37 (1994); Hanawalt, *Growing up in Medieval London*, 159, 184–5.

for conflict in the household.[25] A menacing threat, a choice slander, or a punch could shatter master/servant relations. The lives of fellow servants could also be marked by a sense of hierarchy and distance, which sometimes spilled over into bickering and even violence, though few young people followed the example of William Purvis of Norwich who was charged in 1574 with 'putting a hot iron upon one of his fellows willingly'.[26] It is by no means uncommon, however, to find servants described as 'common fighters' or 'brawlers' with their fellows.[27] We know that some of them went to the alehouse and brothel together, swapped news, and joined forces to oppose a fierce master or fellow. Nevertheless, minor and major skirmishes also rocked the servants' quarters.

There was a 'pecking order' in some households. Older servants usually expected some sort of tribute, and believed that menial tasks rightfully belonged to their juniors.[28] Apprentices and older servants were handed greater responsibilities; they instructed children and younger servants; managed a part of their master's business; or even traded in their own right.[29] Some apprentices also seem to have rated their work more highly than the routine chores of servants.[30] In *Jack of Newbury* the apprentices are shocked that Jack, an older youth, is handed 'many menial tasks . . . for they are far below the tasks that senior apprentices usually do'. Simon Forman recalled that when he was 'the youngest apprentice of four' he was put to 'all the worst' tasks and 'everyone did triumph over me'.[31] Again, John Nicholson, a London clothworker's apprentice, was charged with 'mysbehaviour, stubbornness, and disobedience' for insisting upon seniority. Asked to brush his master's cloak one Sunday morning, he 'made answer that it was as fytt for the mayde servant and the younger apprentice as fir hymself to brush it, and therefore refused to doe it'. A few hours later, 'beinge comanded

---

[25] They comment that service 'permitted a wide latitude for abuse' (*Sleepless Souls*, 253). An interesting comparison can be made with James C. Scott's description of master/slave relations on the plantation in his *Domination and the Arts of Resistance: Hidden Transcripts* (New Haven, 1990), 21.

[26] NRO NMC 9, fo. 469.

[27] For example, NRO NMC 8, fos. 432, 441; GL MS 5770/1, fos. 149–50; CH minute book 1558–81, fo. 179; BCB 2, fo. 39; 5, fos. 324, 439ᵛ.

[28] Cf. Peter Earle, *The Making of the English Middle Class: Business, Society and Family Life in London 1660–1730* (1989), 101–2, 105.

[29] Ben-Amos, *Adolescence and Youth in Early Modern England*, esp. 93, 224–5, 237.

[30] Cf. Hanawalt, *Growing up in Medieval London*, 160.

[31] Laura Caroline Stevenson, *Praise and Paradox: Merchants and Craftsmen in Elizabethan Popular Literature* (Cambridge, 1984), 195; Simon Forman, *The Autobiography and Personal Diary of Dr Simon Forman*, ed. J. O. Halliwell (1849), 6. Cf. Chapman *et al.*, *Eastward Ho*, fo. G3ʳ.

to fetch a cloth', he again refused 'sayinge that there were younger apprentices which might be sent for as well as hee'. Nicholson clearly felt that his years of service set him apart from the younger servants and merited appropriate consideration.[32]

Armed with the cautionary tale that the judicial sources can tell us very little about the happy and stable side of life, we can tease out some of the ambiguities of household life from the dramas related in these records. The master/servant relation generated a great deal of litigation. Yet we will never know the true extent of domestic disorder. Some masters chose to punish their servants without seeking arbitration or going to court.[33] Many secrets of the household lie buried in the past, covered by a range of anxieties and emotions—fear, trust, resignation—they escaped the attention of neighbours, officers, and the courts.[34] We are left with the records of prosecution, an arguably unrepresentative slice of domestic life. Happy households existed, and it would be unwise to place excessive weight upon judicial sources.[35] Nevertheless, we can learn much about rhetorics of order and contemporary conceptualizations of household relations from such evidence. We can feel the ambiguity of authority structures. In fact, patriarchal ideologies and structures were sufficiently flexible to contain most disputes, even though domestic peace sometimes turned on the intervention of a third party or outside tribunal. Far from being a guarantor of youthful subordination, however, the master/servant relation was on occasion inherently unstable.

Even if such disputes were the exception rather than the rule, a momentary blemish which was quickly smoothed over, they possessed ideological significance above that of mere numbers. The servant who hurled punches, threats, or slanders at his master was placed on the margins of the community. Indeed, he was in real danger of being perpetually excluded, though this was usually a final resort. A wound had opened in the civic body and it required healing. We find the authorities making reluctant gestures, conciliations, and concessions to reintegrate the young misfit or his unsatisfactory master. The forms of mediation and punishment by which contemporaries struggled to restore domestic tranquillity exposed the frail ambiguities of the 'ordered' household—the weak master,

---

[32] CH minute book 1605–23, fo. 211. Cf. Forman, *Autobiography*, 6–8.

[33] Cf. Cynthia Herrup, *The Common Peace: Participation and the Criminal Law in Seventeenth-century England* (Cambridge, 1987), 83; Archer, *Pursuit of Stability*, 215–17.

[34] Cf. J. M. Beattie, *Crime and the Courts in England 1660–1800* (Oxford, 1986), esp. 124.

[35] Cf. Goldberg, *Women, Work and Life-Cycle*, 184.

the lusty servant; the fierce master, the suffering servant. The terms of the indenture of apprenticeship may have been written down as a strict code of behaviour, but everyday life was rarely quite as straightforward as that.

2. *The Politics of Service (i)*

The apprenticeship indenture, signed and witnessed by the master, servant, and members of the family and company, set out in clear and certain terms an idea of 'honest' relations and behaviour, thereby creating mental images of the perfect master and servant— the one authoritative but just, the other busy, obedient, and virtuous.[36] Thus young people could be accused of 'denying' their indentures.[37] A master's ultimate sanction was, of course, force, though he was usually reminded that his 'correction' was to be fair and reasonable. If 'moderate' punishment failed to tame the servant, then a master could turn to the guilds or courts for a solution, and he could send his servant to a House of Correction if there was one nearby.[38] Servants were to be given clothes, fed, and kept clean in sickness and in health.[39] Regulations and prosecutions also helped to fix an idea of how a servant 'ought to be used'.[40] This understanding of legal obligations which attempted to strike a balance between the interests of masters and servants was well known. It was yet another dimension of popular legal consciousness, and stirred anxious relatives, neighbours, and the courts to keep a check on stormy households. Prosecutions could spring from this concern. Different groups had particular preoccupations—a child's welfare, for example, or a company's reputation—but all could agree that a servant should obey a worthy master, and that a master should 'fairly' provide for and caution a diligent servant.

The terms of service possessed political meaning. The apprenticeship indenture, for example, established a working relationship, but it was also a moral contract and had symbolic significance. It attempted to set the tone of apprentice/master relations, communicated

---

[36] Cf. Rappaport, *Worlds within Worlds*, 234, 317–19; Arlette Farge, *Fragile Lives: Violence, Power and Solidarity in Eighteenth-Century Paris*, trans. Carol Shelton (Oxford, 1993), 117; Hanawalt, *Growing up in Medieval London*, 139–40.

[37] For example, BCB 6, fo. 267.

[38] Cf. Robert B. Shoemaker, *Prosecution and Punishment: Petty Crime and the Law in London and Rural Middlesex c.1660–1725* (Cambridge, 1991), 174.

[39] See Pelling, 'Apprenticeship, health and social cohesion'.

[40] See NRO NMC 12, fo. 517.

the grounds for complaint on both sides, and opened a door to political citizenship. Young people could step inside, behave themselves, work hard, learn a trade, and hope one day to participate fully in the politics of the community. The indenture was, therefore, a very political document, which offered legitimacy and confirmation. Citizenship was one sign of good 'credit'. To establish the great distance between him and his accuser, one London citizen informed the Star Chamber that his opponent was 'a sleight fellowe of little or noe credit', but he was 'a householder of staid condicon and one of the liverie of his companie'.[41] But the progress to political maturity was also measured in terms of moral behaviour, and some 'lewd' young people were 'barred' from entering the freedom of the city.[42]

The indenture could prove to be a ticket to privileges which were highly valued, though it was also a piece of paper which could be spoiled, rewritten, or forged. In 1634, for example, a London tailor was charged with 'procuring many apprentices and others by false indentures and other indirect meanes to be made freemen'. While in 1615 it was reported that William Barrow, who had served six of his seven years with a London carpenter, 'fraudulently procured one indenture of apprenticeshipp to be made and forged . . . to the end he might be made free' of the Skinners. He had even 'procured and suborned' a witness to testify that he had 'truly served' with a skinner.[43] A master could also rewrite the terms of service to his advantage. It was alleged at Star Chamber that one Suffolk master who had been appointed guardian to his orphaned apprentice 'fraudulentlie and cunninglie' forged a new indenture to prolong his term. The bill of complaint claimed that his sole purpose was to extract rents and timber from his servant's lands.[44] The authorities often attempted to monitor the drafting of indentures by insisting that documents should be drawn up in the company hall. In 1629 London's Court of Aldermen was 'informed that many apprentices have their indentures made at scriveners shopps' and other 'private places', which complicated the processes of enrolment and entry into the freedom. It was ordered that 'from henceforth' only apprentices who could show that their indentures were drafted by the clerk of the company in the hall were to be enrolled.[45]

If an indenture was reported lost or stolen considerable confusion could ensue, the precise position of the servant was in doubt,

[41] PRO STAC 8, 121/6.
[42] For example, CLRO Reps. 29, fos. 302–2ᵛ; 30, fos. 75ᵛ–6.
[43] CLRO Reps. 48, fo. 359; 32, fos. 90ᵛ–1.   [44] PRO STAC 8, 291/28.
[45] CLRO Rep. 43, fo. 269ᵛ. See also CLRO Reps. 33, fo. 416ᵛ; 46, fo. 206.

and steps had to be taken so that their privileges and anticipations of future political maturity could be restored.[46] A number of young people stole or spoiled their indentures; an act which ripped their masters' authority into tiny pieces of paper. In 1596, for example, John Rawson of Cambridge, who was apprenticed to the stationer John James, ran away from his master 'and did playne take [his indenture] out of the cubbard' pulling off the seal and taking it 'out of ye possession of ye said James'. There was a solitary sighting at Stourbridge Fair, but Rawson and his indentures had vanished. In 1560 the governors of London Bridewell were informed that Walter Smith, 'a forward' and 'naughty boye', had 'denyed his servyce' and 'hathe rent in peeces his indentures of prentishood'. On this occasion the fragments of the indenture (and the master/ servant relationship) were pieced back together. The master forgave his servant who returned with appropriate humility.[47]

Some young people who had completed their term and were poised on the border of adulthood were plunged into uncertainty as they reported their indentures missing. The future was in doubt, but one option was to search in the registers for a record of enrolment. Another was to produce a 'credible' witness who confirmed the apprentice's story. In 1622, for example, it was reported that William Felday of London, a cook's apprentice, had lost his indentures. Worse still, his master had fallen victim to plague. The case was referred to the chamberlain and witnesses lodged their reports. One of them was able to confirm that Felday had served his master for eight years, though no 'presentment' could be found at the Cooks hall. This gap in the records was blamed on the neglect of the master and the clerk, and Felday was permitted to enter the freedom by service at the 'special favour' of the Court of Aldermen. Negligence was by no means rare. There are other cases in which a master was reported to be dead. In these circumstances the usual course was to investigate the apprentice's story, and to permit them to proceed to the freedom by service in the company so long as any lingering doubts were stilled.[48]

Being received into the civic body through service had clear political meaning because it preserved a relation with a company and imparted a sense of belonging in civic and trade structures.

---

[46] Cf. Hanawalt, *Growing up in Medieval London*, 158.

[47] CUL VC Ct. III/6–26; BCB 1, fo. 76. See also NRO NMC 8, fos. 569, 666; 10, fo. 13; 12, fo. 845; 15, fo. 334; 20, fo. 334ᵛ; BCB 3, fo. 15.

[48] CLRO Rep. 36, fos. 38ᵛ, 41ᵛ–2. See also CLRO Reps. 33, fo. 98; 35, fos. 272ᵛ–3; 36, fos. 198–8ᵛ; 45, fos. 484, 485–5ᵛ, 505–5ᵛ; 51, fo. 309ᵛ.

One further aspect of this sense of community which has some interesting implications for the resolution of household disputes must be emphasized. Individual trades and corporations were always seeking to preserve a mask of unity and inclusion by using a rhetoric of community which expressed corporate mutuality. Livery companies tried to disguise inequalities and distance by harmonizing their different parts and members in a single 'fellowship', 'body', 'society', 'fraternity', or 'brotherhood'. Individual members were brothers, and the trade was 'one corporate body' turning in 'perpetual succession'.[49] This useful rhetoric helped to heal or disguise disputes, and on occasion could itself be the subject of controversy.[50] Nevertheless, it provided one justification for containing disputes within the household, workshop, guild, or town. The role of the law in the settlement of disputes in early modern communities is well known, and we possess work which discusses how it was often thought best that they resolve disputes and stop up their source without recourse to formal law.[51] Less well explored have been the ways in which considerations of this nature also affected the politics of service and the settlement of domestic disorders. Here too an exercise of 'damage limitation' to preserve the fabric of 'fellowship' was often felt to be appropriate. Masters were expected to punish disorderly servants inside their household. If not, it was hoped that tensions would be calmed within the 'society' of the trade by seeking settlement, arbitration, or punishment within its regulatory structures. In Bristol, 'every merchant adventurer was forbidden to "vex, trouble or sue" any of his brethren in any court before first bringing the "maiter hangyng in variaunce" to the master and wardens'.[52] Richard Fisher was one of many unlucky London residents exposed to full public gaze by 'false and slanderous' libels. These 'false' phrases clearly touched a sensitive nerve, and one of them alleged that Fisher was 'a very obstynate, perverse, and

---

[49] For example, CLRO Reps. 35, fos. 164–5; 36, fos. 79, 111, 257; 37, fos. 26ᵛ–7, 183ᵛ; 38, fo. 59ᵛ; 42, fo. 27; 43, fo. 24; 45, fos. 18, 212ᵛ, 563ᵛ; 46, fos. 32ᵛ–3, 61ᵛ; 47, fo. 20; 48, fos. 241ᵛ, 284; 49, fos. 2ᵛ, 123, 250ᵛ; 50, fo. 168; 51, fos. 287, 333ᵛ; 52, fos. 184, 185, 226ᵛ–7ᵛ, 237, 286–8; 55, fo. 219ᵛ. Cf. Brooks, 'Apprenticeship', 77.

[50] These issues are part of my present work on seventeenth-century London.

[51] The more influential contributions include Keith Wrightson, 'Two concepts of order: justices, constables and jurymen in seventeenth-century England', in John Brewer and John Styles (eds.), *An Ungovernable People: The English and Their Law in the Seventeenth and Eighteenth Centuries* (1980); J. A. Sharpe, ' "Such disagreement betwyx neighbours": litigation and human relations in early modern England', in John Bossy (ed.), *Disputes and Settlements: Law and Human Relations in the West* (Cambridge, 1983).

[52] David Harris Sacks, *The Widening Gate: Bristol and the Atlantic Economy, 1450–1700* (Berkeley, 1991), 90–1.

troublesome fellowe amongste the company of Plaisterers whereof he is free, not conforminge himselfe to any orderly government but worketh and begetteth many troublesome suites and contencons amonge' his fellow craftsmen.[53]

Going to the great trouble of formal prosecution at quarter sessions or borough courts was in certain cases a reluctant step; it introduced an 'outside' tribunal into the affairs of the 'society' and could in fact be interpreted as a sign of weakness or division. But in the case of servants who were not formally apprenticed they were often courts of first resort. The sequence of steps often turned on the nature of the offence, the source of the complaint (e.g. whether it was filed by a master or his servant), and the local legal structure (e.g. borough jurisdictions, including quarter sessions, or company courts). The complete picture resembled a set of connected, overlapping circles which represented particular jurisdictions and identities. The household was the source of quarrels, but when young people unsettled good order it was also the first agency of prevention and resolution. In many cases healing words (arbitration) from magistrates or company officials offered a far smoother path to domestic tranquillity than formal prosecution. If mediation failed to soothe domestic tensions or was felt to be inappropriate, it was still politically important to contain disputes within the 'society' of the trade or community.

In the winter of 1616 the household of Walter Hopton, a London drugster, was rocked by a dispute which threatened to shatter relations between Hopton and his apprentice, George Christmas. Steps were taken to reconcile master and servant. But in April 1617 Christmas complained to the Court of Aldermen about Hopton's reluctance to come to terms, and to strike a balance between their competing interpretations of the squabble. The case was referred to the chamberlain. After hearing 'both sides', the court decided that Hopton was indeed 'very obstinate and would not bee drawne to any quiett end . . . *but rather desired extremitie of law*' (emphasis mine) against his apprentice, even though Christmas had 'humbled himself uppon his knees' before him 'desiring pardon for any offence' he had committed. Hopton was told to return £15 of the £25 he received with his apprentice and to set him over to another master 'for the staying of all suits and the end of all controversies'. But he agreed to take his apprentice back, a change of heart 'which the bench well liked', and which it was hoped contact with the courts

---

[53] PRO STAC 8, 145/6.

would encourage.[54] A firm push in the direction of reconciliation without prosecution was evidence of a sense of unity and purpose. In 1620 Richard Taylor of Norwich complained 'of some ill use gyven by his master', prompting the Mayor's Court to instruct two aldermen 'to call both parties before them and to heare and to ende the same yf they can'.[55] On occasion, the steady resolve of the master or servant (or both) proved to be a formidable hurdle, and one option here was to discharge the apprentice. In July 1623, for example, there seemed to be little prospect of healing the dispute between Aliezer Robinson and his master who was charged with 'hard usage' of his apprentice. The chamberlain could make no progress in the case, and Robinson was finally released to seek another service, so that 'there [could] be noe prosecucon of suits by either partie against one another'.[56]

Christmas and Taylor's cases offer striking illustrations of the value attached to the arbitration of master/servant conflict. They also show how the authorities were prepared to take the side of a servant if it was felt that a master had blocked attempts to settle the dispute. In 1636 the London stationer and future collector of Civil War pamphlets, George Thomason, was cautioned for refusing to 'accept' his apprentice according to the order of the Court of Aldermen. However, Henry Fetherstone told the bench that Thomason's apprentice had 'of late abused and wronged' his master 'in words and gesture'. Another committee was appointed to 'examine all matters' between the two and to 'reconcile the same if they can'. In 1632 the same court reported that it had 'endeavoured as much as we could' to persuade William Rich to take his apprentice back into his service after a dispute. But despite his apprentice's submission Rich remained firmly unco-operative. The court decided to 'leave him to take his choyse either to receive' his apprentice or to return £20, so that he could be 'set over' to another master.[57]

In such circumstances if 'earnest moving'[58] had worked no alteration a master could easily become the villain of the piece. George Beck, a London brewer, proved to be one such nuisance. In October 1614 the Court of Aldermen was told that he had 'put away' his two apprentices 'upon some conceived displeasure', and refused to take them back again even though they 'did seeke to submitt themselves unto him and earnestly desired his favour'. This disordered

[54] CLRO Rep. 33, fos. 89–9ᵛ.   [55] NRO NMC 15, fo. 276.
[56] CLRO Rep. 37, fo. 224ᵛ.   [57] CLRO Reps. 50, fos. 184ᵛ–5; 47, fos. 81ᵛ–2.
[58] GL MS 11,588/1, fo. 121.

household was summoned before the court, and after 'a full hearing' it was decided that Beck 'could not shew or prove any further cause of putting away his apprentices then only some smale matters of misdemeanours'. The bench used 'much entreatie and perswacons' to encourage him to seek reconciliation. The apprentices were asked to 'acknowledge their offences' a second time, and they again fell on their knees and 'expressed their harty sorrowe' with 'all submission'. But Beck 'obstinately refused to accept of them or to consent that they should be turned over' to another master. So, the apprentices, 'destitute both of master and meanes', were turned over by order of the court.[59] In 1620 a Lincolnshire father petitioned the same court to complain about Hugh Ingram of Cheapside, who 'utterlie refused' to take his son back into his service for 'some disorder in behaviour through drinke' despite being requested to forgive and forget. Ingram was 'convented' to appear at the court and 'was here heard at large'. But it was clear that he 'did not allege anything material' against his apprentice 'more than what hath bene confessed . . . nor made it appeare that he had received any losse'. Yet Ingram could 'not be perswaded to receive him'. His 'obstinacy' and 'hard and unconsciable dealinge' was the stumbling block in this case. Moreover, the court was aware of 'the frequent complaint against masters . . . who onelie for the lucre of money take apprentices and afterwards care not howe soone and upon what slight occasion they put them awaye to make a benefit to themselves'. It was one 'cause of the utter ruin of apprentices'. Ingram was ordered to return the bond, indenture, clothing, and £25 to his apprentice, 'unles' he would agree to allow him 'to serve out the residue of his tearme'.[60]

Youthful misdemeanours required stern reprimands, but attention could quickly shift to the 'obstinate' master if he rejected a strategic compromise after 'hearinge and mediatinge'. It was hoped that both sides would 'yield to reason'. Courts were prepared to introduce the threat of disenfranchising quarrelsome masters. One London master was sent to Newgate for refusing to comply with an order; another was put in prison to stay further suits.[61] A grocer who was told to turn over his apprentice 'flatly refused' telling company officials 'he is my apprentice and I will kepe him sale what please you, I will deliver no indenture do evin what you will'. He was also sent to prison. Another grocer who gave his apprentice

[59] CLRO Rep. 31(2), fo. 432.
[60] CLRO Rep. 34, fos. 438–9. See also CLRO Rep. 54, fos. 193^v–4, 327^v–8.
[61] CLRO Reps. 35, fos. 132^v–3, 260^v; 34, fo. 52; 45, fos. 126^v–7.

'unlawfull correction', informed the same officials 'that he would exhibit a byll of complainte into the chancery against them'.[62] The image of each party before the authorities could change if they continued to put their case in the face of doubt, suspicion, and critically, mediation. At this poirŧt the initial complaint itself became the source of irritation. Thus in 1640 the London Court of Aldermen decided that a mercer was a stubborn nuisance because he would not accept their calculated mediations—he 'would not charge' his apprentice 'with any dishonesty nor allege more than his absence'. Other masters who provided no other reason for their resistance to compromise 'then only some smale matters of misdemeanours' were in danger of losing their place in the 'brotherhood'. They had persisted in their original course beyond what was considered to be acceptable to the charitable morality of the 'society'.[63] Nevertheless, in other cases it was apprentices who fell short in their testimonies, and their complaints were declared to be 'untrue and false', 'without just occasion', and 'without cause and contrarie in all respectes'.[64]

On such occasions the authorities liked to portray themselves as the arbiter of domestic justice. They ordered and ended disputes 'for quytnes sake' and the 'quiet composing' of the household. It was their role to 'arbitrate and end disputes', so that 'all matters of controversie . . . from the begynnung of the world until this daie shall cease and be cleared'.[65] They, therefore, preached universal maxims—'equitie and indifferencye', proof and truth—and said that their task was to 'lawfully advise and determyne'. Both sides had to show 'just cause' or 'occasion'.[66] The authorities who regulated access to the courts and the healing process of arbitration claimed

---

[62] GL MS 11,588/1, fo. 249ᵛ. Cf. ibid., fo. 321; GCL minute books O2, fo. 174; O3, fo. 487; P1, fos. 79, 79ᵛ.

[63] CLRO Reps. 54, fos. 193ᵛ–4, 327ᵛ–8; 31(2), fo. 432; 45, fos. 168ᵛ–9.

[64] CH minute books 1558–81, fo. 43; 1581–1605, fo. 134; 1558–81, fos. 136, 137ᵛ. See also GL MS 7090/3, fo. 127; CH minute books 1558–81, fos. 78, 186ᵛ; 1581–1605, fo. 125ᵛ; CLRO Reps. 35, fos. 179–9ᵛ, 246ᵛ–7.

[65] GL MSS 5770/1, fo. 58; 7090/3, fo. 18ᵛ; 7090/4, fos. 216, 83ᵛ; 5602/1, fo. 79. For some examples of arbitration which do not appear in the following account see CH minute books 1558–81, fos. 63ᵛ, 182ᵛ, 226, 249ᵛ; 1581–1605, fos. 8, 99, 112ᵛ; GL MSS 5770/1, fos. 58, 302, 577; 5770/2, fo. 154; 7090/2, fos. 36, 51; 7090/4, fos. 83ᵛ, 173ᵛ, 216; NRO NMC 15, fos. 109, 122ᵛ; 16, fos. 26, 479; 20, fo. 327ᵛ. In London, sensitive cases were referred to the chamberlain and/or aldermen who could draw on the advice of other officials. See also Pelling, 'Apprenticeship, health and social cohesion', esp. 42, and CLRO Rep. 33, fos. 108, 120ᵛ, 130ᵛ; CLRO Reps. 32, fos. 267ᵛ, 274; 33, fos. 320ᵛ, 328–8ᵛ; 35, fos. 60–60ᵛ; 37, fos. 32–2ᵛ; 43, fo. 241ᵛ; 46, fos. 244ᵛ–5; 48, fos. 299ᵛ–300; Earle, *Making of the English Middle Class*, 104.

[66] CH minute book 1581–1605, fos. 69ᵛ, 72ᵛ. Cf. 5 Eliz. I c. 4, servants with 'just cause to complaine' were instructed to report abuses to a justice.

that ideas of equality and justice were uppermost in their minds. They listened patiently to 'both sides' of the story.[67] It was often recorded that their inquiries probed every twist and turn of the plot. Cases were 'indifferentlye heard', 'throwghly heard', and 'throwghly examined'. All 'matters' were examined, and decisions were only reached after 'large' and 'long debate', 'longe conference', 'due examanacon', and after 'full and mature consideration'.[68] Charges of 'immoderate correccion' by a master, for instance, were usually taken seriously, and victims were stripped to search for cuts and bruises. Surgeons were occasionally asked to examine injuries and to provide a certificate. It was agreed, for example, that Lawrence Littleboy 'greeved with such a rupture' which had been occasioned by hard labour.[69] Neighbours, parents, and friends were also asked to give evidence on 'both sides',[70] and officers visited disordered households. In February 1631, for example, the London Fishmongers' Court instructed two company officials 'to confer with Mistris Coles aboute her servante and to compose the difference [between them] . . . or els to certify the courte where the fault lyeth'.[71]

In a number of cases we can see how legal standards of universality, proof, and equity were observed despite the social distance between householders and their dependants. In some respects these maxims could serve as a neutral counterpoise to theories of authority. To be sure, hierarchical relations between masters and servants were expressed in the rhetoric and forms of legal procedure besides the countless words and pages which poured forth from moralists. As we have seen, masters could use their position to advantage; they could exploit their servants, and we have much more to say on this matter. But in this situation, as in many others, legal procedure had particular qualities and rhetorics which were treated, on occasion, as a safeguard of the rights and welfare of underlings. The courts and the mediating interventions of officials offered one protection against the abuse of power, though as we shall shortly see legal procedure was not always the great bulwark

[67] For example, NRO NCQS minute book 1629–36, fo. 22; CLRO Reps. 32, fo. 130; 33, fos. 89–9ᵛ; 48, fos. 299ᵛ–300; 55, fos. 82ᵛ–3.

[68] See, for example, CH minute book 1580–81, fos. 30, 43, 171ᵛ, 102ᵛ, 106ᵛ, 246, 291ᵛ; GL MSS 5770/1, fo. 181; 7090/4, fo. 3ᵛ; 11,588/1, fos. 196, 240, 240ᵛ; CLRO Reps. 31(2), fo. 432; 47, fos. 81ᵛ–2; 50, fos. 184ᵛ–5.

[69] See CH minute book 1558–81, fo. 132; CLRO Reps. 46, fos. 294ᵛ–5; 31(2), fos. 267, 274; 33, fo. 331.

[70] For example, CH minute books 1558–81, fos. 105, 208; 1581–1605, fo. 2.

[71] GL MS 5770/2, fo. 881. See also GL MSS 5770/1, fos. 254, 346; 7090/4, fos. 3ᵛ, 346; BCB 4, fo. 423; 5, fos. 62, 306, 424ᵛ, 440; CH minute book 1558–81, fo. 68ᵛ.

that has been presented here. We have to consider the relative strengths and weaknesses of young people who were formally serving by indenture of apprenticeship and others who served by annual contract, or who were sent into service by parish authorities because they had been raised in poor families. Company officials and magistrates did not always manage disputes competently, and one might ask how many domestic disorders remained a household secret. Nor could abuse ever be stamped out. Nevertheless, legal procedure provided one medium for the settlement of household disorders, giving them an ordered (and theatrical) dimension because they were expressed in the presence of officials and usually in the forms of law. That law, however, was not as uniform as rhetorics of equity and universality would appear to suggest. The guilds wrote their own regulations, though generally with the consent and guidance of civic authorities. The laws of the trade, town, and State all contained provisions for regulating disordered households.[72] This interpretation of the law is generalized. There were many potential arrangements between masters and servants, and (of course) many urban and rural districts. Nevertheless, respect for justice and equity seems to have been a regular aspect of proceedings. Partiality disfigured the forms of 'brotherhood' and 'unity' which legitimized the authority of institutions and communities. In theory at least, the rural servant could file a complaint at quarter sessions; the apprentice could turn to his company or other officials. They could act alone or with the help of friends and relatives (a point to which we will return). We might question access to and control of legal procedure, and also note the funds of power and wealth in the hands of householders. But in some well-documented cases it is clear that legal standards were introduced into disordered households, which tamed the dispute if only for a brief period, treated its rival interpretations with the same regard for equity, and helped the authorities to reach a decision.

The treatment of 'proof' in some squabbles provides a way of understanding the significance of legal procedure as in some respects a 'neutral' territory. In 1598 the London fishmonger Arthur Mouse filed a complaint at the company court against his servant, Richard Goldsmith, who, he alleged, was 'of very bad behaviour and very unjust in his service'. He was 'verily persuaded' that Goldsmith had stolen £20 from him, and had also kept the cloth

---

[72] Cf. James Casey, 'Household disputes and the law in early modern Andalusia', in Bossy (ed.), *Disputes and Settlements*, esp. 217.

which he had given him £30 to buy from a passing chapman. The servant 'utterly denyed' these charges. Mouse produced a piece of cloth and 'a paire of sweet gloves' that Goldsmith 'bought to give a wench' as corroborative evidence. But his servant told the court that the money to buy the gloves had come from his 'friends' and cast doubt not only on Mouse's integrity, but also on his role as a master. The testimony presented, the bench retired to debate the merits on each side. On this occasion they decided in favour of the servant. Mouse had tabled 'no proof . . . but onelie his own words of any mispendinge of his goods'. He chose to free Goldsmith so that he could find another fishmonger to serve with rather than retain him and enter promises of future good conduct.[73]

In this case judicial procedure was followed, proof was not established, and the authorities ruled against the divinely legitimized master whose very words were suspicious. If only for a brief moment legal procedure suspended the hierarchy in a single disordered household, casting a legal eye over its affairs, and exposing some of the ambiguities of conventional social relations. The master may have retained his authority, but his household government was under review. In 1639 Anthony Draper of London, a merchant tailor, claimed that his apprentice 'had imbezelled and wasted his goods'. The Court of Aldermen ordered officers to examine the case, and it was decided that Draper's 'suggestion' was 'only upon surmise and suspicion without proofe'. In 1610 Thomas Allen, 'a long suter for his freedome', was 'objected against' by his master Leonard Townson, another London fishmonger, who told the company that 'he hath made him dyvers debts during his apprenticeship without his knowledge or consent'. Townson asked that his servant 'answere those debts before he be made free'. Again, officials examined the facts of the case. They concluded that the master 'maketh no manner of proof thereof but [only] his owne affirmacon', and Allen duly proceeded to the freedom.[74]

The final verdict in these cases turned on issues of proof—the culture of the law. Thus one master alleged that he had 'pregnant proofes' of his servant's 'lewde life and vile practises'.[75] In other

---

[73] GL MS 5770/1, fo. 101.

[74] CLRO Rep. 53, fo. 255; GL MS 5770/1, fo. 577. Townson also argued that earlier offences of stubbornness and running away should prejudice Allen's petition for admission to the freedom. However, the company decided that these matters were in fact 'ended' because the servant had been punished at the time for these offences, and Townson had taken him back into his service.

[75] PRO SP 16/274/55. See also NRO NMC 15, fos. 12, 108; NCQS minute book 1629–36, fo. 22; GL MS 5770/1, fos. 227–8; CH minute books 1558–81, fos. 80, 116, 117, 208;

cases charges of 'misuse' 'appeared very likely to be true', or were 'proved trewe'. In London the Clothworkers' Court agreed that Francis Bolton's master was 'in some fawlte'; that William Kettle's beating of his servant with two rods and a bedstaff 'did evydently appeare to be unreasonable'; and that Edward Body's eight apprentices had 'good cawse to compleyn' about him.[76] The Court of Aldermen was satisfied that a scrivener's apprentice had 'proved' that his master 'had at sundrye tymes' given him 'unreasonable correction in verye evell manner', and that evidence had been offered in another case of 'severe and cruell usage . . . provinge that' a master 'did throw a pressinge iron' at his apprentice 'and cruelly beate him and kickt him under his short ribbs'.[77]

These cases also show that some young people had more than a passing familiarity with legal procedure, company regulations, and civic customs. It should be no surprise that householders often appeared to be very comfortable with the meaning and fine detail of legal procedure. They were, after all, one voice in the 'society' of the trade and community. But their young underlings also filed petitions, gave evidence before officials, exploited legal devices, and tailored their strategies to suit the twists and turns in proceedings. In many cases friends and relatives offered support. Some of them told officials that it was their 'ignorance' of procedure and custom which was the root of their predicament, though on occasion this may have been a deliberate strategy to squeeze some sympathy. In November 1629, for example, Timothy Blackstone of London was disenfranchised because he had served with four masters in different occupations 'by severall indentures of apprenticehood'. Yet he was able to use his alleged unfamiliarity with the law to draw understanding from the Court of Aldermen, telling the bench that he was 'ignorant of the custome of this cittie', and that he had been 'seduced' by his first master who entered a 'false oath' before 'Mr Chamberlain'. Blackstone asked for some 'compassion', he was 'poore and lame of one of his hands'. He was allowed to proceed to the freedom by redemption, so long as he served the rest of his term with a leatherseller—his first occupation.[78] Other freemen lodged similar defences, telling the courts that they were 'ignorant' of the fact that they were not permitted to serve with foreigners, or

1581–1605, fos. 2, 39ᵛ; CLRO Reps. 28, fo. 283ᵛ; 30, fo. 87ᵛ; 31(1), fos. 144–4ᵛ; 35, fo. 260ᵛ; 31(2), fo. 432.

[76] CH minute books 1558–81, fos. 116, 108ᵛ; 1581–1605, fos. 27, 16, 82ᵛ; 1558–81, fo. 130.

[77] CLRO Reps. 28, fo. 283ᵛ; 30, fo. 87ᵛ.   [78] CLRO Rep. 44, fos. 30ᵛ–1ᵛ.

that they had to enter their enrolment with the civic authorities. Some of them drew attention to their present poverty; others claimed that the fault lay with their careless master. Clearly these 'counsels of ignorance' were sometimes strategies pursued by young men who had left service before the close of their term because their master was poor, dead, inept, or they believed that four or five years was time enough in which to learn their trade.[79]

Servants may have sometimes spun webs of deceit, or issued vexatious suits to seek revenge against a master, for example, or to gain admission to the freedom ahead of time. Some of them were 'ignorant' of law and custom; many others could demonstrate considerable understanding of both. The petitions of some London apprentices show that they clearly understood that they should not have been bound before 14 years of age; that their masters' shops should have been within the liberties of the city; that there was a firm conception of 'unreasonable punishment' which placed limits on their masters' right of correction; and that some of them were resourceful players who knew when to appear contrite or submissive.[80] One advantage of young people who were formally apprenticed is that they were in possession of an indenture which communicated knowledge of the rights and obligations of both master and servant. They had an appreciation of proper conduct which was in some cases sharpened by high social origins and the premium paid by their parents.[81] One further piece of protection for young people who were formally bound was provided by the bond sealed by some masters in which they pledged themselves to raise their servants 'honestly' and 'faithfully', or risk losing the sum of the bond.[82] Older servants were also in a stronger position, which resulted from a few years of association with their master, wages, and the acquisition of skills. In some respects the balance of power

[79] See CLRO Reps. 31(2), fos. 382-2ᵛ; 34, fo. 587; 38, fos. 145-5ᵛ, 190ᵛ; 41, fo. 75ᵛ; 44, fos. 172, 182; 47, fos. 318ᵛ-19.

[80] For example, CLRO Reps. 34, fo. 180ᵛ; 35, fos. 179-9ᵛ, 246ᵛ-7; 40, fo. 366ᵛ; 42, fo. 27ᵛ; 43, fos. 266ᵛ-7; 47, fos. 210ᵛ-11; 53, fo. 249ᵛ. In 1638 it was reported that one 'poore boy . . . goeth about by suite . . . to make voyd of the indenture' alleging that he was bound at the age of 12. The Court of Aldermen commented that 'these kinde of suites doe much concerne many whoe at their charitye for the ease and benefitt of poore parents, parishes, and hospitells doe take poore children very young'. They 'much hindered charity'. This particular petition failed, and the apprentice was instructed to serve out his time (CLRO Rep. 52, fos. 185ᵛ-6, 221ᵛ). The knowledge of young people and their friends and relatives in legal matters is revealed in many other cases which are examined in this chapter.

[81] Premiums are discussed by Ben-Amos, *Adolescence and Youth in Early Modern England*, 87-8.

[82] See ibid. 103.

inside the household tipped slightly towards young people who had served four or five years or more and were themselves highly able workers. The subordination of the young which was vital to order coexisted uneasily with this sense of ability, accomplishment, and seniority. In such circumstances the politics of age could be renegotiated, revised, or even contested.

It should be clear by now that young people were not always 'friendless', mute, or cast adrift in some patriarchal void in which happiness and safety solely depended upon their master.[83] They could on occasion exploit this feeling of isolation in evidence before courts.[84] Nevertheless, in the records of quarter sessions, guilds, or borough courts, for instance, there are reported interventions by parents, relatives, friends, and officials on behalf of young people, who also on occasion brought their masters' abuses to the attention of the authorities. Neighbours also passed comments on disordered households and tipped off officials.[85] In 111 petitions drawing attention to a master's abuse, seventy-six mention only the name of the servant (68.5 per cent), twenty-four were filed by one or both parents (21.6 per cent), while a further eleven were lodged with the support of 'friends' (9.9 per cent).[86] Much depended on judicial facilities, the particular position of the servant (e.g. social origins, gender, age, and period of service), and (critically) whether they were formally apprenticed as a junior member of a guild.

The arbitrations, prosecutions, and punishments of individuals and institutions charged with the resolution of these household disorders offered safeguards. A master was to 'use his servants honestly as an honest man ought to do'.[87] But offences had to come to light, and when they did servants could be discharged, 'turned over' to another master, or returned to their master on the understanding that another complaint would be treated with grave concern.[88] Final sanctions included disenfranchisement, or prosecution at criminal law. But depending on the specific nature of the offence, arbitration was a desirable first step. Significantly, the form of these disputes shows that the 'politics of service' was often sufficiently flexible to contain them within the trade or the community. Nevertheless, these proceedings raise a further problem which has been little explored hitherto—the large number of apprentices

---

[83] Cf. Hanawalt, *Growing up in Medieval London*, 159.
[84] For example, PRO STAC 8, 291/28.   [85] For example, CLRO Rep. 28, fo. 283ᵛ.
[86] The sample is drawn from the records of Norwich's Mayor's Court, the London Court of Aldermen, and the London guilds.
[87] CH minute book 1558–81, fo. 146.   [88] See below, pp. 321–4.

who were 'turned over' from their first master. The authorities issued many such orders, though the sources rarely permit us to trace the sequence of events which brought the matter to their attention. But as well as abuse and neglect, young people were turned over because their masters breached regulations covering the registration or taking of apprentices;[89] other masters fell into ill-health,[90] or poverty;[91] still others were reported to have simply fled.[92] Some apprentices were turned over on more than one occasion. A number of them were passed on many times and this must have been unsettling.[93] The 'turnover rate' of apprentices would repay further work. It at least suggests that for some young people the passage to adulthood was not entirely smooth; they were uprooted and sent to serve in a new household.

Yet it should be emphasized that this 'interruption' on the progress to adulthood was usually managed within the structures of the company or community. In fact, the more general settlement of disputes within the 'fellowship' of the guild or civic jurisdiction was a further confirmation of their unity and legitimacy. There is evidence that in certain cases equity, proof, and discretion 'monitored' the uneven distribution of authority. Yet we must not be too optimistic. This distribution of power was highly uneven, and the records of prosecution only scratch the surface of the true extent of disordered households. It is time to explore these domestic disorders more closely, and to explore further the principal characteristics of the politics of service. It is with the 'disorderly master' that we will begin.

3. *The 'Disorderly Master'*

Formal complaints of cruel treatment, poor instruction, and neglect were issued in a fraction of master/servant relationships. In

---

[89] For example, GL MSS 15,842/1, fos. 17ᵛ, 30ᵛ, 72ᵛ; 5602/1, fos. 33ᵛ, 41; 7090/4, fos. 42ᵛ, 62, 102ᵛ, 106ᵛ, 181ᵛ, 230, 240ᵛ, 246ᵛ, 259, 288; 3295/1, fos. 4 Aug. 1607, 10 Apr. 1611, 16 June 1612, 11 Nov. 1614, 24 Oct. 1615, 18 May 1616; CH minute book 1558–81, fos. 88ᵛ, 104, 211, 211ᵛ, 212ᵛ, 213ᵛ, 214, 215.

[90] For example, CH minute books 1558–81 fos. 17, 59, 63ᵛ, 101, 153, 177ᵛ, 219ᵛ, 233ᵛ; 357, 514, 516; 7090/2, fos. 96ᵛ, 136ᵛ, 158, 189ᵛ, 208ᵛ; 7090/3, fos. 38ᵛ, 189ᵛ, 191, 195; 7090/4, fos. 3, 15; 15,842/1, fo. 71.

[91] For example, GL MSS 5770/1, fos. 221, 341, 346; 5770/2, fos. 129, 261, 493; 7090/2, fo. 237; 7090/3, fos. 52, 111ᵛ; 7090/4, fos. 19, 243ᵛ; CH minute book 1581–1605, fo. 169.

[92] For example, NRO NMC 14, fos. 326ᵛ, 337, 340, 423; 16, fo. 404ᵛ; 20, fo. 184ᵛ; CH minute book 1581–1605, fo. 122.

[93] See CH minute book 1581–1605, fos. 76ᵛ, 169ᵛ.

some courts they were a staple item of business. But in others we can turn over the pages of their records and months, years, and even decades pass by before we discover a single reference to the filing of a complaint by a servant or concerned friends and relatives. This silence is ambiguous and should not be treated as an index of domestic tranquillity. But it is clearly meaningful. Servants (and their confederates), however, petitioned about a broad spectrum of abuses, including poor instruction, debt, being 'turned out of doors', calculated manœuvres to stop them from entering the freedom, and verbal and physical violence.[94] While magistrates and officials 'debated' and 'examyned' suspicion hung over the disordered household, and the words and actions of its principal characters. Drawing on the same vocabulary (and morality) of 'honest' household relations, masters and servants put their case before officials. Their testimony was shaped by this conception of order, which was more clearly communicated by indentures of apprenticeship. Rival interpretations disputed the meaning of obligation, punishment, or authority, and on occasion introduced points about company, civic, or legal procedure. A domestic dispute was in motion. These tales of abuse and dissent capture the dark side of the household; the very worst aspects of the politics of age.

In 1630, for example, Richard Playford, a Norwich apprentice, filed a petition at the city's Quarter Sessions in which he alleged that his master, John Furrys, 'had most unreasonably and without any just cause abused and evill intreated him'. As in other cases, magistrates treated the underling's evidence with respect, and fully examined 'both sides' of the case. After 'a full and deliberate hearing of the said cause, and of both the said parties, and of the proofs on eyther parties produced', they concluded that Furrys had indeed 'much abused' Playford 'with unreasonable stripes and correction for small or no cause'. Uppermost in their thoughts was the conviction that the apprentice had 'carryed himselfe well and dutifully'

---

[94] We can identify the particular source of complaint in ninety-four petitions. There were forty-two complaints of physical violence (44.7 per cent), thirteen each of poor instruction or a master's inability to continue instructing his servant, and a refusal to admit an apprentice to the freedom (13.8 per cent), ten of neglect (10.6 per cent), seven of being 'turned-out' (7.4 per cent), four of beating and neglect (4.2 per cent), three of debt (3.2 per cent), and 1 each of not being enrolled, neglect and debt, and neglect and poor instruction. Violence was an aspect of forty-six complaints (48.9 per cent), neglect of sixteen (17.0 per cent), and poor instruction of fourteen (14.9 per cent). These petitions and others are the main subject of this present discussion. Sexual abuse is studied in Ch. 5. An interesting comparison with what I have to say about master/servant relations is Marcus Rediker's study of relations between captain and crew in the 'wooden world' of the ship, *Between the Devil and the Deep Blue Sea: Merchant Seamen, Pirates and the Anglo-American Maritime World 1700–1750* (Cambridge, 1987).

towards his master. Yet his poor return, and the reciprocal nature of the relationship was often a vital aspect of the 'examynacon', was 'grevious and hard use'. The justices decided that this disordered household was in this instance beyond repair, and they ordered that Playford's 'abode' with his master 'cannot be contynwed without great perill' to his 'life or lymmes'. The apprentice was therefore discharged to seek another service.[95]

Playford chose his words carefully. 'Unreasonable', 'just', 'misuse', and 'evill' were emotional terms, but they were directly derived from conceptions of domestic order and, in effect, cast aspersions on his master's commitment to the 'moral compact' of service. An idea of 'reasonable' and 'lawful' correction which was rarely defined except in terms of its opposite—'unlawful', 'overmuch', 'overviolent', 'extraordinary', or 'extreme'—informs many complaints.[96] It helped young victims or their friends and relatives to frame their responses. In fact, certain weapons were sometimes thought to be 'unlawful'. In 1577 Thomas Garth of London 'complayned' about his master 'for beatinge hym with unlawfull weapons viz. with a staffe and a beotle [bottle]'.[97] A variety of household and workshop items were picked up to beat servants, including pots, rods, chains, knives, broomstaffs, keys, sticks, chairs, rope, and, of course, fists, arms, legs, and teeth.[98] Because the meaning of 'unreasonable' harm was neither specific nor written down, the issue of punishment remained deeply controversial, and gave free rein to a variety of interpretations. 'It appeared' to the Court of Aldermen in London that a draper who was 'using correction . . . which ought to have been moderately done' had in fact 'immeasurably and cruely beaten' his apprentice with 'a cord and rodes in unmercifull manner'. Again, the apprentice was discharged. It also 'appeared' to the same court that another draper had 'in very unreasonable manner beaten, thrown downe, and trodden uppon William Compton his apprentice under color of giving him reasonable correction'.[99] But in what circumstances was

[95] NRO NCQS minute book, 1629–36, fo. 22.

[96] And not just those complaints brought against masters. The beadles of Christ's Hospital in London were accused of giving 'unreasonable correction' to young inmates (GL MS 12,806/2, fos. 40, 45).

[97] CH minute book 1558–81, fo. 208. Cf. NRO NMC 10, fo. 232.

[98] For example, NRO NMC 9, fos. 117, 145; 10, fo. 690; 11, fos. 327, 549; 12, fos. 474, 911; 13, fo. 543; 15, fos. 8, 107ᵛ, 109, 123ᵛ, 269; NCQS 'The Sessions Booke 1630–38', fos. 66ᵛ, 74ᵛ; BCB 1, fo. 75; 3, fo. 236; GL MSS 4655/1, fo. 66; 5770/1, fos. 58, 199, 426; 7090/2, fo. 207ᵛ; 7090/3, fo. 165; CH minute books 1536–58, fos. 206ᵛ, 222ᵛ; 1558–81, fos. 75ᵛ, 77ᵛ, 130, 132, 135, 171ᵛ; 1581–1605, fos. 35ᵛ, 81ᵛ, 82ᵛ, 134.

[99] CLRO Rep. 28, fos. 239ᵛ–40, 316ᵛ.

punishment 'reasonable', and where was the border to be situated? Juries were prepared to pass guilty verdicts in cases of manslaughter or murder if a master's correction was deemed to be 'immoderate'. But they reserved the right to acquit defendants if they were satisfied that his blows were delivered in 'just cause' and were in fact 'moderate'.[100] Titus Oates of Norwich was instructed to give his apprentice 'eight stripes upon the buttocks' with a rod, and told 'that from henceforth' he 'shall have liberty to correct' him 'with a rod so as he give not above eight stripes at any one time'. Another master thought it reasonable to give his servant 'onely one blow' with his staff 'over the backe and noe more'.[101] It was hoped that masters would 'reasonably' correct with 'just cause' whenever occasion required, and we catch glimpses of them doing this in contemporary materials. In 1596, for example, William Mere of London appears giving his apprentice 'reasonable correccon' for his 'bad speeches' and scratches. In February 1554 Richard Usher refused 'to take reasonable correccyon . . . but did vyiolently stryke' his master and mistress.[102] But much more frequent in the courtbooks are the complaints of young people like Richard Playford who received punishment that was considered to be 'unreasonable'.

They included Bartholomew Clifford, a London pewterer's apprentice. In 1591 his master was 'found fawlty' by the company's warden and assistants 'in abuse of his apprentys . . . burnyng his face with a hot irone and other abuses'. Clifford was 'set over'. In October 1577 Ellen Bolintout, 'a mayde of xiiii or xv yeres of age', who was in service with a Norwich tailor, told the Mayor's Court how she had 'bene greatly abused' by her master's wife, who had given her 'not only correccon with a stycke in beting her bowte the showlders and armes tyll she was black and blewe but also in tearyng her skynne and fleshe with a woolcarde and casting salte upon her body' to her 'greate grefe'. Again, the servant was discharged. John Wise, a joiner, was charged at the same court in 1569 with 'very evelly entreating and using' Thomas Cordy, his apprentice. Wise 'cut' Cordy 'in the face with an edge tole, and further threatened hym that he will geve hym a mark that he shall remember so long as he lyve'. Cordy was released from his service and invited to 'chose one other honest master'.[103]

[100] Beattie, *Crime and the Courts*, 86.
[101] NRO NMC 15, fo. 125ᵛ; CH minute book 1558–81, fo. 208.
[102] CH minute book 1581–1605, fo. 158ᵛ; CLRO Rep. 13, fo. 127. Cf. BCB 5, fo. 326ᵛ; GL MS 5770/1, fos. 209–10, 494–5, 594–5; NRO NMC 12, fo. 911; 15, fo. 230ᵛ; PRO STAC 8, 96/8.
[103] GL MS 5770/3, fo. 28ᵛ; NRO NMC 10, fo. 177; 9, fo. 23.

The motives behind such cruel treatment were as varied as the range of potential weapons which a master had close at hand. The majority of masters probably played the part of a guardian, instructor, and companion.[104] Others did not. Money was the root of abuse in a large number of cases. When Faithful Vaughan entered his service, Robert Burrowe, a London barber surgeon, received £10 and a bond for his 'true and faithfull service'. Shortly afterwards, however, he was offered £20 to take another apprentice, and his thoughts quickly turned to ways of putting Vaughan from his service. Burrowe's first idea was to tell the company clerk 'that he had a stubborne and carelesse apprentice'. A few stumbling blocks emerged, and he was forced to confide in the clerk, 'confessing . . . that he could have twenty pounds with another apprentice and was loth to keepe two'. It seems that the two hatched a plot because Vaughan's parents were told to appear before the clerk. But Burrowe had also set his sights on the bond, and he informed the mother 'that his mynde was altered and he would keepe her son'—a trick 'to worke matter out of his own apprentice by his owne confession' to claim the entire bond. He set his plan in motion one morning at 5 a.m., pulling Vaughan out of his bed and 'tying him to the bedpost with one of his garters', and 'very cruelly whipped him' with 'a birching wand . . . to make his apprentice confesse that he had cosened and deceived him' of money which he spent on his brothers. The apprentice, however, remained firm and refused to comply. A second whipping was necessary, and Vaughan was beaten 'very sorely almost an houre'. Yet he 'refused to confesse any matter of deceipt'. Burrowe 'pursued his violent and tyrannous handling of him', and at some point this disordered household was brought to the attention of the Court of Aldermen, who considered that the abuse was 'proved' by testimony and the 'often complaints' of Vaughan's mother: The court 'earnestly wished' Burrowe to return the bond and free his apprentice, but he 'contynually refused' to comply with their orders. 'How the government of this citty is greatly scandalized by the cruell and evell dealings of such freemen who use these practises to take money with apprentices', the bench lamented, 'and then by imoderate correccon and hard usage to drive them from them and by devices to steale the forfeiturer and bondr given them for the truth of theire apprentices.' Firm steps had to be taken, and the bench handed out a 'condign punishment . . . that other delinquents in the same kinde might learne by his example'.

[104] Cf. Thompson, *Sex in Middlesex*, 164.

Vaughan was disenfranchised, and the windows of his shop were shut up.[105]

Vaughan's 'tyranous handling' of Burrowe was not an isolated case; the concern of the authorities is a testimony of that fact.[106] One master who 'unreasonably' punished his apprentice also put him 'to base services, thereby to drive him away and soe to gaine the money and in the end indeavoured to send him to Virginia'. The court was told that 'he hath used divers other apprentices in the like order making it a common trade to take money with apprentices and by such unnatural usage to cause them to goe awaye to the great disgrace of the freemen'. The master was disenfranchised 'to the example of others'.[107] The opportunity to gain a few pounds was exploited on other occasions. Some masters attempted to avoid paying the enrolment fee by not presenting their apprentice for registration before the authorities, though simple ignorance was pleaded in a few cases.[108] The master's purse was also expected to be produced at the close of a term. A final wage might be outstanding; the apprentice expected a suit of clothes. A number of masters drew attention to a fault on the part of their apprentice; an outstanding debt, or a history of disorder. Again, some of these complaints may have been pure invention. In 1620, for example, Edward Silvester told the Court of Aldermen that 'about a fortnight before the end' of his term his master had 'occasion to search' his trunk and discovered £23 'and other things' which belonged to him (the petitioner). He explained that his master 'not onlye deteyned' his possessions, 'but alsoe denyeth' to make him free, despite the intervention of company officials.[109] The authorities were prepared to punish persistent young offenders (to set an 'example' to other servants) by withdrawing the right to full citizenship.[110] It is not always clear that discipline was the principal issue in other cases in which impatient young people felt aggrieved that their path to the freedom had been blocked at this last moment. On

[105] CLRO Rep. 31(1), fos. 144–4ᵛ.

[106] Cf. CLRO Reps. 24, fo. 265; 25, fo. 74ᵛ; 26(2), fo. 378ᵛ; 30, fo. 87ᵛ; 31(1), fos. 82ᵛ, 183ᵛ; 31(2), fo. 241; 32, fos. 91ᵛ, 219ᵛ, 267ᵛ, 274; 33, fos. 228–8ᵛ; 37, fo. 224ᵛ; 41, fo. 32ᵛ; 44, fo. 244; 48, fos. 339–9ᵛ; Farge, *Fragile Lives*, 118–19; Hanawalt, *Growing up in Medieval London*, 159.

[107] CLRO Rep. 29, fo. 52. See also Rep. 43, fo. 241ᵛ.

[108] For example, GL MSS 5770/1, fos. 51, 490; 5770/2, fos. 107, 622, 826; 7090/2, fos. 61ᵛ, 93, 96, 129 (four cases), 136, 140, 211; 7090/3, fos. 12, 88, 90, 137, 150; 7090/4, fo. 263; 5602/1, fos. 61ᵛ, 65ᵛ, 82; CH minute books 1536–58, fo. 230; 1558–81, fos. 68ᵛ, 89, 134ᵛ, 150ᵛ, 251ᵛ; 1581–1605, fos. 27, 77, 80ᵛ–1; GCL minute books O2, fos. 242, 376; P1, fos. 54, 68.

[109] CLRO Rep. 34, fos. 395–5ᵛ.   [110] See above, p. 300.

occasion, it is difficult to disentangle financial considerations from a simple reluctance to release an 'unruly' apprentice to duly proceed along the life-cycle.[111] Other petitions for admission to the freedom were granted by the authorities despite a master's strong objections, one master crying that he 'wolde rather tear his indenture in a thowsand peces'.[112]

The descriptions of the principal characters in these cases communicated a strong sense of outrage at the master's evident rejection of the politics of service. The 'disorderly master' was 'unnatural', 'inhumane', 'monstrous', 'cruel', 'strange', and 'tyrannical'. He 'corrected' in 'extraordinary' rather than 'lawful' fashion; the opportunity to reap some money or revenge was elevated above true compassion and concern. Poor provision and instruction also contradicted the terms of service and were the subject of other complaints. An apprentice had hopes of mastering a craft; a servant expected reasonable wages, treatment, and the chance to acquire skills. A number of young people complained that promised wages had failed to materialize, some of them sued for debt.[113] Others protested that they were 'not instructed and tawghte' in their chosen occupation; they were put to 'base services instead'. One apprentice accused his master 'for imploying' him 'only in drawing of beare as a victualler'. He was set over. A grocer's apprentice claimed that he had 'onely bin kept to goe to markett and upon erands and not ymployed or instructed in his trade'. His master alleged that he had 'absented himselfe out of his service', and had 'wronged him in his estate to the value' of £14. The bench listened to both sides and turned the apprentice over to another grocer.[114]

Other servants protested that they had been 'turned out of doors'; some of them were in fact ill and of no use to their master for a short interval. One London servant who was 'full of the tokens' of

[111] For example, GL MSS 5770/1, fos. 234, 254, 255, 577; 5770/2, fos. 496, 504; 7090/2, fo. 8ᵛ; CH minute books 1558–81, fo. 117ᵛ; 1581–1605, fo. 16ᵛ; CLRO Reps. 29, fo. 58ᵛ; 43, fos. 23, 322.

[112] See, for example, CH minute books 1558–81, fos. 80, 116, 117, 208; 1581–1605, fos. 2, 39; GL MS 5770/1, fos. 227–8; CLRO Reps. 29, fo. 170ᵛ; 30, fos. 319ᵛ, 320, 320ᵛ; 33, fo. 221; 34, fo. 323.

[113] For example, NRO NMC 15, fos. 97, 118; GL MSS 7090/2, fos. 80ᵛ, 180ᵛ, 171ᵛ; 7090/3, fo. 28; 4329/2, fo. 15; CH minute book 1581–1605, fo. 79. Cf. Garrioch, *Neighbourhood and Community*, 137.

[114] CLRO Reps. 29, fo. 52; 46, fo. 430; 44, fos. 307ᵛ–8, 314ᵛ–15. See also NRO NMC 15, fo. 108ᵛ; GL MSS 5602/1, fo. 29; 11,588/1, fo. 249ᵛ; CH minute books 1558–81, fos. 43, 46ᵛ; 1581–1605, fo. 27; CLRO Reps. 35, fos. 179–9ᵛ; 36, fos. 210–10ᵛ; 43, fos. 323–3ᵛ; GCL minute books O2, fo. 172; P1, fo. 76ᵛ; Q2, fo. 153; S1, fo. 20ᵛ; Earle, *Making of the English Middle Class*, 97; Hanawalt, *Growing up in Medieval London*, 157–8.

plague was 'put out' by her master 'and died the next day' at her mother's house.[115] Neglect was not uncommon. In May 1603 William Rogers, whose son was apprenticed to one Levett, a London fishmonger, complained, 'as he hath oftentymes heretofore done', of 'the evil usage' of his son. A warden was directed to investigate the complaint. Another household was being reviewed. A few days later he reported 'that he hath bene at Levett's house and seene the boy and viewed the lodging'. He uncovered a sorry situation. Rogers was 'lodged without sheets and without sufficient clothes, and by reason of cold and evill usage the fleshe of his legg' was 'rotten off'. He was in a 'very pittifull case' and 'like to perishe if he be not speedily looked unto and succored'. The company court told Rogers to return home with his father to be 'cured', and then he would be set over to another master 'by the good liking of this house and to the liking of his father'. In 1584 Thomas Godward told the Norwich Mayor's Court how he had been 'abused' by his master 'as well in pynching him of victuells as for want of good lodging and apparell whereby...' he was 'extremely eaten with lice'. The eight apprentices of a London clothier complained 'of there... maister for mysusinge them in corecon as also for wante of meate, drink and apparrell'. One clothworker's apprentice told the company court that he was 'daily misused'.[116] Other unfortunate young people filed petitions against their master 'for want of apparell and things necessarye'; for 'lacke of meate, and drinke and clothes'. Others were found 'destitute of meanes of imployment and maintenance'; 'full of vermine'; 'not kepte clene but... full of lyse'; and suffered 'to runne full of vermen'.[117]

Clearly all was not always well inside the early modern household, and we should not assume that order was immediate and consensual. Some households were 'dens of disorder'; the majority were probably not, though we will never know where the true balance lies. Much depended upon how a master viewed his servant; as cheap labour, a nuisance, an employee, a colleague, or friend. That impression could also change as the years rolled by. But what

---

[115] PRO SP 16/164/35. See also NRO NMC 13, fo. 17ᵛ; NCQS 'The Sessions Booke 1630–38', fo. 115ᵛ; CH minute book 1558–81, fos. 47ᵛ, 55ᵛ; BCB 5, fos. 114, 165, 396ᵛ; 6, fos. 1, 1ᵛ, 17; GL MSS 5770/2, fo. 881; 11,588/1, fos. 240, 240ᵛ, 248; CLRO Rep. 26(2), fo. 361; GCL minute book O2, fo. 196.

[116] GL MS 5770/1, fo. 346; NRO NMC 11, fo. 321; CH minute books 1581–1605, fo. 16; 1558–81, fo. 144.

[117] NRO NCQS 'The Sessions Booke 1630–38', fos. 34ᵛ, 35; NMC 7, fo. 500; 9, fos. 91, 117; 11, fos. 14, 131, 178, 311 (irregular pagination), 533; 12, fo. 517; 13, fo. 543; 14, fos. 216ᵛ, 333, 364ᵛ, 365ᵛ, 445; 15, fos. 8, 321, 334; GL MS 5770/1, fo. 221; 5770/2, fo. 128; CH minute books 1558–81, fos. 43, 55ᵛ, 68ᵛ, 108ᵛ, 109, 116ᵛ; 1581–1605, fos. 2, 14, 16ᵛ, 134.

actions did the authorities take; what considerations guided their interventions? Were they keen to punish or reconcile; to keep the household together and heal its wounds; or to break up its parts, and in one stroke dismantle a political institution and relationship? In some cases the fragments of the household were pieced back together, but in others the damage was beyond repair. As we have seen, regard for proof and equity in some respects provided a counterpoise to the full rigours of authority.[118] But another anxiety was the political function of service, as revealed in the concern with the stability of the particular relation before the court. In some cases it is clear that ill-treated young people were turned over with reluctance. The authorities did not enter disordered households with the sole intention of rescuing persecuted young people. They often tried to strike a balance between the interpretations of the master and his servant, and to arbitrate on these terms. They had 'power and authoritie by an Act of Parliament . . . to discharge any apprentice of his apprentishood that shall at any tyme be abused or misused by his master',[119] though we have evidence that 'setting over' was often reserved for a second offence.

We can trace the fate of forty-eight of the seventy-six young people who filed a complaint without, it seems, any additional support. Forty-four of them were the victims of proven physical abuse or neglect.[120] Sixteen were 'set over' to another master (36.4 per cent); twenty-eight were returned to their master who was cautioned to treat them as a servant 'ought to be used'—a few masters were bound to good behaviour (63.6 per cent).[121] Many ill-treated young people were returned to their master with the slender comfort that they would be 'turned over' if they presented 'just occasion' or 'cause' of further abuse.[122] Some harsh masters were whipped;[123] a

---

[118] See above, pp. 306–10.   [119] NRO NMC 10, fos. 22–3.

[120] The remaining four all complained of poor instruction. Three of them were returned to their masters who were cautioned by officials. One apprentice was turned over to another master (GL MS 5602/1, fo. 29; CH minute books 1558–81, fos. 46ᵛ, 65ᵛ; 1581–1605, fo. 27).

[121] See NRO NMC 9, fo. 23; 10, fos. 177, 690, 752; 11, fos. 14, 131, 178, 311, 321, 533; 12, fos. 474, 517; 13, fo. 186; 15, fos. 8, 114ᵛ, 123ᵛ, 142, 197ᵛ, 269, 272ᵛ, 359, 482ᵛ; NCQS minute book 1629–36, fo. 22; 'The Sessions Booke 1630–38', fos. 34ᵛ, 110ᵛ; CH minute books 1558–81, fos. 47ᵛ, 55, 109, 132, 136, 138ᵛ; 1581–1605, fos. 16, 31ᵛ; GL MSS 5770/ 1, fos. 193, 221, 346; 5770/2, fo. 129; 7090/2, fos. 125, 157; 7090/3, fo. 28ᵛ; 7090/4, fo. 173ᵛ; CLRO Reps. 30, fo. 87ᵛ; 31(1), fo. 82ᵛ; 44, fos. 307ᵛ–8, 314ᵛ–15; 48, fos. 339–9ᵛ.

[122] For example, NRO NMC 14, fo. 333; 15, fos. 180, 238ᵛ, 281ᵛ; CH minute books 1558– 81, fos. 65ᵛ, 75ᵛ, 77ᵛ, 100ᵛ, 106ᵛ, 108ᵛ, 130, 144, 173ᵛ, 182ᵛ; 1581–1605, fo. 14; GL MS 5770/ 1, fo. 58v. Cf. cases in which officials decided that young people had 'no lawfull cause' to be turned over to another master (for example CH minute book 1581–1605, fos. 13ᵛ, 122ᵛ).

[123] For example, NRO NMC 10, fo. 17; 11, fos. 321, 327, 549; 12, fos. 474, 517; 14, fo. 233; 15, fo. 8.

few were sent to prison.[124] But most of them were just asked to promise that they would 'use' their apprentice 'as is fitting for an apprentice to be used'; to make good amends for past abuses, become 'new' masters, and provide wholesome food, instruction, and clothing.[125] On occasion, the apprentice who filed a complaint was also asked to 'serve trewely', which implied that in these cases the authorities placed a degree of blame on both sides.[126]

This strategy of attempting to heal the rift between the 'disorderly master' and his servant was followed in all types of ill-treatment. A judgment had to be made; could the particular relation under review be restored? In September 1587, for example, William Quyney of London, a clothworker's apprentice, complained that his master William Standish had given him 'unreasonable correccon . . . and therefore [he] desired to be freed' and turned over to another master. Company officials carefully examined this disordered household and reported back to the court. They agreed that Standish was 'not . . . of good government towardes his servauntes as he ought to be'. Yet they decided not to turn Quyney over, preferring instead to return him to Standish, who was ordered 'to use' him 'in better sort hereafter . . . to use reasonable correction towardes him, and not to be over furious for every little faulte'.[127] Other masters were warned to be more 'moderate' and 'gentle', to punish reasonably and with 'just cause' as 'just occasion shall serve'. A master's promise was considered to be sufficient,[128] though the authorities rarely bothered to define the meaning of 'reasonable'.[129] In a few cases, however, they removed the authority to punish. In 1577 the London Clothworkers ordered that Richard Lycett, who had punished his apprentice with 'unlawfull weapons', should 'not correcte hym neither for this or anie other . . . offence therafter upon the comittinge thereof, and they to judge of the fault and of his correction'. John Clere of Norwich was told 'not henceforth to correct' his servant 'without the consent of the aldermen of the ward or one of them'. While a London apothecary was warned not to 'strike' his apprentice 'hereafter, but [to] make his faults knowne . . . and the

[124] For example, CLRO Reps. 25, fo. 74ᵛ; 31(2), fo. 241.
[125] NRO NMC 7, fo. 500; 9, fo. 121; 14, fos. 333, 364ᵛ, 365ᵛ; GL MSS 5770/1, fos. 199, 202; 5770/2, fo. 128; 7090/2, fo. 207ᵛ; CH minute books 1558–81, fos. 5ᵛ, 46ᵛ, 65ᵛ, 68, 100ᵛ, 106ᵛ, 109, 146, 173ᵛ, 251; 1581–1605, fos. 14, 16ᵛ, 27.
[126] CH minute books, 1558–81, fos. 108ᵛ, 116ᵛ, 171ᵛ, 175ᵛ; 1581–1605, fos. 14, 16ᵛ, 39ᵛ, 81ᵛ.
[127] CH minute book 1581–1605, fo. 81ᵛ.
[128] NRO NMC 15, fos. 123ᵛ, 269; GL MSS 5770/1, fo. 199; 7090/2, fo. 207ᵛ; 7090/3, fo. 165ᵛ; CH minute books 1536–58, fo. 206ᵛ; 1581–1605, fos. 82ᵛ, 108ᵛ.
[129] See above, p. 315.

company will punish him'.[130] On occasion, we see the authorities in their chambers debating 'if ever' a master 'shall come to have another apprentice'.[131]

We can often only guess what followed the return of an ill-treated servant. The authorities spoke soft words of reconciliation, though resorting to an alternative coercive vocabulary when it was felt to be appropriate. The master and servant went home with mutual pledges and forgiveness ringing in their ears. But back in the household the strains of tension may have lingered, creating an uneasy climate; the master smarting after his rebuke, the servant moody at the failure of his request to serve elsewhere. Some masters quickly returned to former courses. In 1594 the Fishmongers' Court in London 'ordered and ended' the 'controversie' which had flared up between Henry Hemming and his apprentice, who was 'sent home with his master'. Hemming shut the door behind them, and 'fell upon his apprentice and beate him most extremely'. He was sent to prison for his 'bad abuses and vile wordes', and refused permission to take another apprentice.[132] A number of young people also forgot their pledges to the authorities. Thomas Swan had served Alice Fox, a London widow, for six years 'in which tyme', it was reported, 'he performed ill service to her and purloyned and misspent' her goods. He 'freely and voluntariely acknowledged and confessed' his 'negligent and untrue service', and 'uppon his humble submission' and promise 'to perform better service' the authorities persuaded widow Fox to take him back into her service. An air of composure descended upon this household, but it was illusory. A 'short tyme after' their return home, Swan 'did unlawfully departe out' of Fox's service. His history of disobedience stretched back over the whole of his term, and as Swan made his application for the freedom of the city he was roundly rebuffed, the authorities ruling that 'a precedent of this kinde might be dangerous and a meanes to enboulden and incourage apprentices against their masters and to goe and come at their pleasure'.[133]

Nevertheless, some young people had to file several petitions before they were finally turned over from their turbulent master, though in the case of the Wells brothers of London three proofs were still deemed insufficient by the Clothworkers' Court.[134] We

---

[130] CH minute book 1558–81, fo. 208; NRO NMC 15, fo. 155; GL MS 8200/1, fo. 408. See also CH minute book 1558–81, fo. 173ᵛ.

[131] For example, GL MSS 5770/1, fos. 58, 165, 255; 7090/2, fos. 89ᵛ, 125.

[132] GL MS 5770/1, fo. 58.   [133] CLRO Rep. 35, fos. 60–0ᵛ.

[134] CH minute book 1581–1605, fo. 14. Cf. minute books 1558–81, fos. 132, 182ᵛ; 1581–1605, fo. 16; NRO NMC 13, fo. 543; GL MS 5770/1, fo. 58ᵛ.

also come across some masters who persecuted their servants, and in some cases different servants, for a number of years. We can trace the stormy history of John Garland's relations with his apprentices and the hierarchy of the London Clothworkers for at least twenty-five years in the company records (May 1567–September 1592). Garland's unsavoury career was sharply condemned by the company, but he was still allowed to enrol four apprentices in that time, and have others turned over to his service. In 1600 the London Fishmongers complained that Arthur Mouse 'taketh many apprentizes and bringeth them upp very few or none to any purpose'.[135] Yet in many cases a single appearance before the authorities (and in the historical record) was sufficient to restore domestic tranquillity; the master was cautioned and gestures of forgiveness were offered on all sides, though in some cases the safest course was to discharge the servant. Nevertheless, so far we have only seen one part of the potential sources of tension—the 'monstrous' and 'unnatural' disorderly master. It will be remembered that the authorities often investigated 'both sides' of a dispute. They recognized that there could be two sides to the same story, and two principal origins of household quarrels. It is now time to turn to the 'disorderly servant'.

4. The 'Disorderly Servant'

Most young people recognized the value of gaining skills and money in their youth to take into marriage and employment. This technical competence often stirred aspirations and pride, and was itself a potential point of tension; it was difficult to square with dependent status and an unknown number of young people departed service for marriage, or to set up for themselves. They had outgrown service and compliance only hampered further progress.[136] Few young people questioned the institution of service while they picked up fresh skills, though it is difficult to disentangle squabbles with their masters—the immediate representative of the politics of age in the household—from expressions of discontent with dependent status.[137] Domestic disorders are usually entered in the sources as protests

---

[135] For Garland see CH minute books 1558–81, fos. 67, 106ᵛ, 137, 154ᵛ, 171ᵛ, 175ᵛ, 182ᵛ, 187ᵛ, 241ᵛ, 243; 1581–1605, fos. 54, 72ᵛ, 79ᵛ, 89ᵛ, 101, 128. And for Mouse, GL MS 5770/1, fo. 255.

[136] See below, pp. 330–1.   [137] Cf. Hanawalt, *Growing up in Medieval London*, 163.

about the qualities of a particular master. Thus in August 1575 Thomas Harris told a friend that 'his master was his mortall enemie'.[138] Young people could be disobedient, stubborn, lewd, and refuse to serve, or they could run from their masters, steal from them, insult them, threaten them, hit them, or scatter abroad a scurrilous slander putting his name in disrepute.

We have also seen that youthful conviviality and play often collided with the conceptions of work, time, and order held by the authorities. The politics of age were on occasion uneven, reinterpreted, and disputed. To this extent it was a precarious politics. Many young people slipped outside the compass of their master's authority in free or 'unlawful' time.[139] They departed 'without his leave' or knowledge raising the spectre of independence which haunted the darkest thoughts of moralists and magistrates, and caused them to pass grim forecasts about crime rates, or the progress of sound religion and work discipline. In 1628 the London Court of Aldermen was told that William Whitley, a merchant tailor's apprentice, 'had often absented himselfe day and night from his master's service without his consent'. The fishmonger's apprentice Thomas Parry, who was 'very unjust and untrue', was charged with going 'often . . . abroad at his owne pleasure'. While it was claimed that John Moras, a 'stout' and 'stubborn' carpenter's apprentice, 'lieth out of his [master's] house when [it] pleaseth him'.[140] To make matters worse, some young people remained outside the household until dawn;[141] a number of them stayed away from their master's household for 'divers nights'.[142] These young people were often simply expressing a wish for conviviality and an opposition to being kept safe inside after dark. Their choices were 'natural', deriving as they did from the taste for play and companionship. Thomas Harris of London, a tailor's apprentice, was presented at Bridewell in 1610 'for absentinge himselfe day and night from his master's service and often lyeinge out'. The bench complained that he 'will work when he list and play when he list'.[143]

Inside the walls of the household we discover many examples of

---

[138] BCB 2, fo. 146.

[139] See above; Chs 4 and also BCB 9, fos. 10, 00, 104", 120", 109", 103", 193, 196, 230", 281, 287ᵛ, 317, 322ᵛ, 336ᵛ, 397, 416ᵛ, 424, 433, 435, 437ᵛ.

[140] CLRO Rep. 43, fos. 6–7; GL MS 5770/1, fo. 9; BCB 1, fo. 194ᵛ. Cf. NRO NMC 14, fo. 283ᵛ.

[141] For example, NRO NMC 10, fo. 387; 14, fo. 132ᵛ; BCB 4, fos. 334ᵛ, 337ᵛ; 5, fos. 72, 75ᵛ, 84ᵛ, 126, 203, 208ᵛ; 8, fo. 246ᵛ; CH minute books 1581–1605, fo. 101; 1605–23, fo. 211.

[142] For example, BCB 5, fos. 84ᵛ, 326ᵛ; CH minute book 1581–1605, fo. 1ᵛ.

[143] BCB 5, fo. 423. See also BCB 5, fo. 3ᵛ; GL MS 7090/2, fo. 180.

'disobedient',[144] 'stubborn', and 'obstinate' young people.[145] They included Anthony Harrington who 'verye negligentlye and disobedientlye behaved himself towards his master and mistress' and 'groweth worse to worse'.[146] A vague term like 'misdemeanour', 'abuse', 'unruliness', 'misbehaviour', or 'lewdness' was often used to portray these forms of juvenile delinquency. This pliable vocabulary masked all sorts of offences. Such domestic disorders were 'outragious', 'lewd', 'intollerable', 'horrible', and 'odious to God and the Prince'.[147] In some cases young culprits were clearly intoxicated by drink,[148] but in many others their words were more than mere beer-talk and expressed anger and contempt. A number of servants and apprentices simply refused to work or to serve their master.[149] John Hamlyn, a haberdasher's apprentice, was presented 'for withstandyng and resystyng of his master and mistress'. Martin Roberts of London was described in court as 'a vagrant that is a lewd fellowe . . . rebellious to his master and ronneth from him'. While another young offender was called 'an unruly fellowe and a drunkard', and charged with 'abusing his mistress . . . a widowe-woman of good worth', and with being 'mutinous amongste his fellowe servants'.[150] Nor were they alone. Other young people were presented for spurning 'due obedyence', or 'obstinately refusing to be ruled'.[151] In some cases it was admitted that a servant could 'not be ruled'.[152] One of the anti-heroes of the conduct literature, the upstart youth who treasured liberty and mocked restraint, makes regular appearances in the judicial sources, ensuring that the vision

[144] For example, NRO NMC 9, fos. 252, 543; 14, fos. 183, 342ᵛ; 15, fos. 235ᵛ, 266ᵛ; GL MSS 7090/2, fo. 176ᵛ; 7090/3, fos. 64ᵛ, 75ᵛ; 7090/4, fos. 83ᵛ, 197; CH minute book 1558–81, fos. 70ᵛ, 78ᵛ, 79, 133, 207; BCB 5, fos. 6ᵛ, 32ᵛ, 37, 66ᵛ, 71ᵛ, 75, 100ᵛ, 102, 104ᵛ, 119, 133, 160, 161ᵛ, 164ᵛ, 165ᵛ, 167, 167ᵛ, 174, 196, 255ᵛ, 261, 275, 344.

[145] For example, NRO NMC 11, fos. 307, 633; GL MSS 5770/1, fos. 149–50, 577; 5770/2, fo. 536; BCB 1, fos. 5ᵛ, 6, 74, 92, 201ᵛ; 2, fos. 33, 107ᵛ, 126ᵛ, 129, 224ᵛ; 4, fos. 283ᵛ, 347, 349, 382ᵛ, 405; 5, fos. 146, 159, 279, 324, 336, 362ᵛ, 371, 405ᵛ, 423; 6, fos. 23, 46; CH minute book 1581–1605, fos. 101, 139.

[146] GL MS 5770/1, fos. 140–1.

[147] The number of such cases in contemporary sources is enormous. For some typical examples from Norwich records see NRO NMC 7, fos. 583, 615; 9, fo. 702; 10, fos. 26, 151; 11, fos. 302, 406; 12, fos. 110, 261, 273, 407, 429, 864; 13, fos. 473, 598, 691; 14, fos. 70ᵛ, 414ᵛ; 15, fo. 250; 16, fos. 166ᵛ, 325; 20, fos. 106, 381.

[148] For example, BCB 5, fos. 7, 43, 161, 195, 292, 329ᵛ, 377ᵛ, 404.

[149] For example, NRO NMC 8, fos. 16, 156, 573, 583; 13, fo. 572; 14, fos. 298, 426ᵛ; 20, fos. 97, 230ᵛ; GL MS 4329/2, fo. 72; BCB 2, fo. 34ᵛ; 4, fo. 11 Nov. 1598; 5, fos. 314ᵛ, 344.

[150] BCB 1, fo. 50ᵛ; 6, fos. 80ᵛ, 201.

[151] BCB 1, fos. 16ᵛ, 50ᵛ; 5, fo. 341ᵛ. Cf. BCB 5, fos. 82ᵛ, 107ᵛ; GCL minute book O2, fo. 89.

[152] For example, BCB 1, fo. 106; 2, fo. 69; 3, fos. 84ᵛ, 86ᵛ, 199, 203ᵛ; 5, fo. 380; 6, fos. 2ᵛ, 11, 20ᵛ, 25, 26, 103, 126ᵛ, 131, 131ᵛ, 198ᵛ, 366ᵛ.

of a finely ordered domestic existence remained a paper image in many households.

If the entries in the records are a rough guide to the concerns of the authorities or the frequency of types of offence, then the most persistent nuisance were young runaways. The sources are littered with simple two or three line entries—'Thomas Gytton . . . a wandreing person up and downe the streets . . . being an apprentice with Edward Parker a smith from whom he ran away and refuse to stay anie longer'.[153] A high proportion of young offenders ran away on more than one occasion. William Comber, a 'houseboy' of London Bridewell, ran away 'above 30 times'; John Naylor ran away 'above xxtye tymes'; Nicholas Penley, another Bridewell 'houseboy', left his master '20 tymes', and was finally 'sent to sea'; Alice Carter absconded on fourteen occasions; Elizabeth Carter 'nine tymes since Bartholomewtide last' (she was picked up in November 1609); John Baker, John Norman, Josiah Jenks, and John Hillyard ran away seven times; William Scarlet is recorded slipping away from his master's household on six occasions; while James Bowver ran away 'four times in one week'.[154] A large number of young people ran away 'several', 'divers', or 'sundry tymes'.[155] The authorities complained that young runaways would not 'tarry' or 'stay' in service; they would 'stay nowhere'.[156] They ran away 'often', 'oftentimes', 'commonly', and 'continually'.[157] It was reported that Christopher Moore of Norwich took off 'continually'. Richard Wells of the same city 'often' ran away, and 'as yet contineweth running'. It was said that John Baldwin of London did 'nothing but runn away'. While

---

[153] BCB 5, fo. 329. Again, the number of cases is enormous. Runaways presented difficulties for urban authorities in particular. See Beier, 'Social problems in Elizabethan London'; Archer, *Pursuit of Stability*, 204–10. If we turn to just one courtbook of London Bridewell, volume 5, which covers the period November 1604–July 1610, we discover at least 357 *reported* cases of young people running away from a master. This figure is likely to underestimate greatly the number of offenders in London at this time. These are only the recorded examples; young runaways were also presented in other courts; they received summary treatment in Bridewell; while I have not included cases of reported absence from a master's household, or the number of previous offences in cases of 'multiple running'.

[154] BCB 8, fo. 114; 5, fo. 377; 8, fos. 357, 139^v; 5, fos. 394, 375^v, 419; 7, fo. 131; 8, fo. 145; 6, fo. 203; 7, fo. 188.

[155] For example, PRO SP16/109/77; BCB 4, fos. 26 June 1598, 156, 177, 187^v, 209^v, 315^v, 157, 6, for 70^v, 101, 101, 160, 160^v, 267^v, 811^v, 881, 811^v, 856^v, 880, 809, 110^v; 6, for 16^v, 163, 222^v, 244^v, 259, 282, 333^v; 7, fos. 32, 46, 78^v, 80, 121^v, 132^v, 145, 202^v, 217^v, 275, 282; 8, fos. 16^v, 184, 286, 303^v, 308, 331, 3 Nov. 1641; CH minute books 1536–58, fo. 226; 1558–81, fo. 246; 1581–1605, fo. 101.

[156] For example, BCB 6, fos. 2^v (two cases), 26^v, 48, 101, 103, 114^v, 126^v, 131, 131^v, 164^v, 174^v, 198^v, 222^v, 263^v, 301, 441^v; 7, fos. 63^v, 64^v, 79^v, 100^v, 147, 148, 153^v, 177, 204^v, 215^v, 216, 224, 244^v, 247^v, 260^v, 275^v, 287^v; 8, fos. 16^v, 46^v.

[157] BCB 6, fos. 324^v, 366^v; 7, fos. 56, 57, 62, 64^v, 103^v, 190, 220, 220^v, 288^v, 304; 8, fos. 3, 4, 212^v, 217^v, 220, 220^v, 279^v, 283 (two cases), 297^v, 376 (two cases), 391, 28 July 1641.

Sara Staynes was sent to London Bridewell 'for running away from her master,' even though she carried 'a locke on her leg' which had been fixed because she had 'often' run away before.[158] Runaways left in all years of their terms, they left alone and in pairs, though rarely in larger groups.[159]

The decision to run away was not to be taken lightly for it invited an encounter with the watch, the courts, the whip, hard labour, and the unpleasant prospect of an awkward return to a master. As they left the house and sank into the crowd or dark shadows young people must have felt many emotions—fear, relief, guilt, or satisfaction. Running away was a gesture of sorts, though it must not be assumed that it represented a rejection of the structures of service. Many young runaways were fleeing the personal rule of their master. We are rarely helped by the records which often simply note a name, status, and give a bare statement of offence, ensuring that context and experience is often a matter of guesswork.

Young people ran away for many reasons, though on occasion it was said that they had 'no occasion' or 'no great cause'.[160] Some of them planned ahead, stealing and storing possessions in anticipation of the fateful day when they would run away.[161] Some 'ronnegates' were seeking refuge from 'over correccion' or 'hard usage'. Mary Taylor alleged that her mistress 'thrust hir out of dores and beate her'. William Vincent ran away nine or ten times 'within a yeare', though he was able to offer an explanation—his master had 'almost beaten out his eye and much misused him', he was 'a careles man who neglecteth his trade . . . and misuseth his apprentice'.[162] Others left because they had the fear of punishment hanging over them for another offence.[163] Still others wanted to join their sweethearts.[164] One apprentice explained that he had 'no mynde to serve' as a bookbinder.[165] A master reported that two of

---

[158] NRO NMC 14, fo. 543; 13, fo. 597; BCB 8, fo. 17; 7, fo. 78ᵛ.

[159] NRO NMC 7, fo. 578; 8, fo. 321; 9, fo. 681; BCB 1, fo. 129ᵛ; 3, fos. 80ᵛ, 93; 4, fos. 57ᵛ, 166; 5, fos. 355ᵛ, 416ᵛ.

[160] For example, BCB 5, fos. 354, 394; CH minute books 1558–81, fo. 129; 1581–1605, fo. 125.

[161] For example, NRO NMC 8, fos. 266, 405; 10, fos. 580, 677, 726; 11, fo. 86; 13, fos. 598, 706; 14, fo. 143; BCB 4, fos. 20 May 1598, 5 July 1598, 52ᵛ, 53, 57ᵛ, 69, 333ᵛ, 382, 383ᵛ; GL MSS 5770/1, fos. 483, 593–4; 7090/2, fo. 82; 7090/3, fo. 211ᵛ; PRO SP 16/216/78.

[162] BCB 6, fos. 10, 105ᵛ. See also BCB 3, fo. 177ᵛ; 5, fos. 33ᵛ, 264ᵛ, 270, 392; GL MS 5770/ 2, fo. 430; CLRO Rep. 48, fos. 299ᵛ–300.

[163] For example, BCB 3, fo. 177ᵛ; 5, fos. 33ᵛ, 264ᵛ, 270, 392; GL MS 5770/2, fo. 430.

[164] For example, NRO NMC 13, fo. 763; 14, fo. 200ᵛ; BCB 3, fo. 294ᵛ; 5, fo. 149ᵛ; CH minute book 1581–1605, fo. 112.

[165] BCB 6, fo. 302ᵛ. Cf. ibid., fo. 421ᵛ.

his apprentices 'ran away from him and gott themselves into a ship in his majesties service' on three occasions, remaining at sea for four months, six months, and 'aboute a yeare and a quarter'. In 1632 a group of London masters informed the Privy Council that their apprentices 'have unlawfully departed' from their service, 'and have taken entertainment within the precinct of St Katherine's . . . under certayne captaines and officers' to 'serve under the King of Swethland in the wars voluntarely'.[166] The authorities must have felt some sympathy with Joanna Pale, 'who took her boxe' and left her master's house after finding 'divers pictures of crucifixes and beades with crosses on them'.[167] While John Stock of London, a haber-dasher's apprentice, demonstrated a passing familiarity with com-pany law and the custom of the city, telling the Bridewell governors that he was perfectly entitled to leave his master because 'he was not indentured and therefore might lawfullye go away from him'. In fact, he had not yet served a full year, and the bench reminded him that his master could present him for formal enrolment 'at anye time within the first yeare of his terme'.[168]

Some young 'ronnegates' were quickly picked up on the very first day of their flight, hiding under a stall, sheltering inside a church, cellar, hayloft, or another sheltered place, or lying at the edge of a street. Others were discovered after a few days, still wandering the streets near their master's home. A smaller number were recorded missing for two weeks, three weeks, one month, six weeks, seven weeks, eleven weeks, three months, six months, seven or eight months, one year, two years, four years, six or seven years, seven years, and eight years.[169] We even have a cockney Arnaud du Tilh,[170] Thomas Kinder *alias* Richard Appleyard, who fled from London to Yorkshire and assumed the identity of a dead man. He succeeded in convincing his 'new' mother and sister that he was in fact their lost son/brother, and settled into family life. Nevertheless, the memory of his previous existence lingered, and he later returned to the capital 'moved in conscyence to confess the trewth lest he should now deny his owne father and mother'.[171]

[166] PRO SP 16/109/77; 16/216/78.   [167] BCB 5, fo. 109.

[168] BCB 4, fo. 6 May 1558. Cf. BCB 5, fo. 381.

[169] CH minute books 1536–58, fo. 200; 1558–81, fos. 75ᵛ, 137ᵛ, 230ᵛ; BCB 5, fos. 164, 199ᵛ, 362ᵛ, 381, 394; 6, fos. 123ᵛ, 149ᵛ (two cases); 7, fos. 92ᵛ, 105ᵛ, 108ᵛ, 116, 120, 149ᵛ; 8, fos. 2ᵛ, 17, 46, 49ᵛ, 80ᵛ, 122ᵛ, 200, 201ᵛ, 212, 262, 263ᵛ, 275, 283, 297ᵛ, 309, 396, 22 Oct. 1641; GL MSS 5770/1, fo. 588; 7090/2, fo. 66.

[170] Arnaud du Tilh was of course the imposter, 'the new Martin', in the tale of the return of Martin Guerre (Natalie Zemon Davis, *The Return of Martin Guerre* (1983)).

[171] BCB 5, fos. 185ᵛ, 194, 258ᵛ.

One important numerical indication, the high drop-out rate of apprentices in most English towns studied hitherto, should make us pause before we elevate the early modern household to the pedestal of order and stability. A high proportion of young people did not complete their terms, and they failed to integrate into urban society, though the question of motivation is hampered by poor documentation.[172] A bare fact obscures a multitude of tensions, fears, and aspirations. Some young people, however, went to an early grave (it has been estimated that as many as 10 per cent of London apprentices died in the course of their term).[173] Rappaport has argued that after picking up the essentials of the trade in the first few years of training, many young people returned home with fresh skills to 'set up' in work rather than waste their talents in a place where freeman status was not sufficient temptation to persuade them to remain as part of a pool of cheap labour until they finished their terms.[174] Ben-Amos has argued that Bristol's 'drop-outs' had a few options. They could have joined the ranks of the unskilled or the wave of emigration across the ocean. Other options included setting up as independent craftsmen in the nearby countryside or in another town. The freedom of the city was only one alternative. Ben-Amos also consults contemporary autobiography (which demonstrates the value of familial advice and material help in setting up) to sketch a broader canvas, but the evidence for Bristol is rather slim, and the argument seems to turn on a number of explanatory hypotheses and coincidences which leave the case as yet open.[175]

The journey home to take up work, however, was one option.

[172] The drop-out rate in sixteenth-century London was roughly 60 per cent, Rappaport, *Worlds within Worlds*, 311–12; 75 per cent in Norwich *c.*1500–*c.*1700, 83 per cent in sixteenth-century Bristol, and 79 per cent in Salisbury *c.*1610–20—A. Yarborough, 'Apprentices as adolescents in sixteenth-century Bristol', *Journal of Social History*, 13 (1979), 80; Peter Clark, 'Migrants in the city: the process of social adaptation in English towns 1500–1800', in Peter Clark and David Souden (eds.), *Migration and Society in Early Modern England* (1987), 269–70. Cf. Ben-Amos, *Adolescence and Youth in Early Modern England*, 130.

[173] Rappaport, *Worlds within Worlds*, 313. Cf. Ben-Amos, *Adolescence and Youth in Early Modern England*, 119–24.

[174] Rappaport, *Worlds within Worlds*, 314.

[175] Ilana Krausman Ben-Amos, 'Failure to become freemen: urban apprentices in early modern England', *Social History*, 16 (1991); ead., *Adolescence and Youth in Early Modern England*, esp. 129–31. Cf. Hanawalt, *Growing up in Medieval London*, 138, 164; Brooks, 'Apprenticeship', 74–5; R. A. Houston, *Social Change in the Age of Enlightenment: Edinburgh 1660–1760* (Oxford, 1994), 93. To establish her point Ben-Amos relates the cycle of employment opportunities in Bristol (and freedom admissions in particular trades) to the occupational structure of the nearby countryside and towns; reviews the secondary literature emphasizing the defensive mentality of those in employment and the resulting pool of journeymen; and considers the ever growing emigration to the New World. Though the evidence from Bristol sources is rather thin.

Ben-Amos remarks that 'many' motives prompted young people to leave before the close of their term, 'but what was common to all was a reluctance to continue work for their masters when they could use their skills to pursue their own ends'.[176] We know that some young 'ronnegates' returned home, others found lodgings. Three or four years was probably sufficient time to master most skills, though in some cases training was more complex and drawn out.[177] A number of apprentices were discharged after a few years, and there is no record of them being turned over. Some travelled home to resume work; others continued to work for a wage in the place in which they served, or even as independent craftsmen at the risk of prosecution.[178] In London, there is evidence that a number of young people who applied for freedom through redemption were in fact seeking another route to full citizenship because they had left service after a few years, though in many cases a firm reason was produced—a master had given up his trade, or fallen into 'decay' or poor health. We must approach these petitions with caution. Some of them may have disguised past strategies by constructing stories to explain their premature exit from formal training. But a majority of petitioners departed service in years three–six, and this offers further support for the idea that they became impatient with the prospect of further dependence at a time when they were fully skilled.[179] Another source of frustration was the check on passions and emotions; marriage was prohibited, and in other petitions for freedom by redemption we find former apprentices who had married before the end of their term seeking to recover their right to full citizenship. Some young people chose to marry and work for themselves rather than stay in formal service.[180]

There is also evidence that some householders 'poached' apprentices from others who had taught them skills. In fact, craftsmen

[176] Ben-Amos, *Adolescence and Youth in Early Modern England*, 130.
[177] Ibid. 119–24.   [178] See above, pp. 294–5.
[179] For some London examples see CLRO Reps. 31(2), fos. 402, 421ᵛ; 32, fos. 201–1ᵛ, 212ᵛ; 34, fos. 323ᵛ–4, 346ᵛ; 37, fos. 83ᵛ–4; 38, fo. 212ᵛ; 41, fos. 27ᵛ, 125ᵛ, 356ᵛ–7; 42, fo. 123; 43, fos. 197–7ᵛ; 44, fos. 80, 107ᵛ, 207ᵛ, 306; 45, fos. 120–20ᵛ, 184ᵛ–5, 236–6ᵛ, 445ᵛ, 501, 501ᵛ, 557ᵛ; 47, fo. 150ᵛ; 46, fos. 218–18ᵛ, 434ᵛ; 48, fos. 62ᵛ, 78ᵛ–9, 452–2ᵛ; 51, fos. 336, 361ᵛ, 368; 52, fos. 26ᵛ, 193ᵛ–4, 214ᵛ–15,
[180] For example, CLRO Reps. 32, fos. 25, 345–5ᵛ, 363ᵛ; 36, fos. 104, 195ᵛ, 208–8ᵛ; 39, fos. 141, 167ᵛ, 188ᵛ; 41, fos. 171ᵛ, 255–5ᵛ; 42, fo. 178ᵛ; 43, fos. 29–9ᵛ, 57ᵛ–8, 58, 60, 84, 97, 117ᵛ, 251–1ᵛ; 44, fos. 3ᵛ–4, 171ᵛ–2, 172–2ᵛ; 45, fos. 189ᵛ–90, 260, 377, 445, 446ᵛ, 493ᵛ–4, 506–6ᵛ, 537ᵛ–8; 46, fos. 3–3ᵛ, 233ᵛ, 234–4ᵛ, 249ᵛ, 321–1ᵛ; 47, fos. 107, 256ᵛ, 372ᵛ, 424ᵛ–5; 48, fos. 9ᵛ, 37–7ᵛ, 117–17ᵛ, 243, 247, 349, 425ᵛ, 618; 49, fos. 65ᵛ, 73, 122, 164, 286, 315ᵛ; 50, fos. 171ᵛ–2, 172ᵛ, 266ᵛ; 51, fos. 180ᵛ–1, 284–4ᵛ, 291ᵛ; 52, fos. 22ᵛ–3, 72ᵛ, 151; 54, fos. 25ᵛ, 47, 90ᵛ–1, 153, 222ᵛ–3, 250ᵛ, 255; 55, fos. 68ᵛ, 109.

were often accused of 'enticing' young people away from their masters. In 1606 'divers freemen' of London gave information to the Court of Aldermen about a fishmonger who 'unlawfully and very lewdly hath persuaded and inticed' their apprentices and 'divers' others who served dyers and fustian dressers 'into bonds' to 'depart from their masters' and 'goe into France there to work and sett up' in their trade 'and instruct others there in the skill'. One year later it was a merchant tailor who was charged in the same court with 'inticing sondrye fustian dyers and fustian dressers apprentices from their masters' to cross the channel and 'use' their skills 'to the decay of their masters and hurt of the commonwealth'. He was sent to prison.[181] There are other cases of masters 'selling' the years of their apprentice.[182] In these cases as in others in which young people set up by themselves ahead of time, mere underlings were bypassing the long route to adulthood. But their maturity was 'narrowly construed' in terms of economic competence, and it did not fully reflect the virtuous adulthood contemplated by moralists. It was dangerous to pass responsibility to rash underlings, that transition was to be managed carefully. To complicate matters still further, the authorities (including masters) sometimes gave young people permission to set up in full employment. Others were hired out by their masters.[183] In 1630, for example, the London Coopers filed a complaint against 'divers of the inferior sorte' of the company who 'take apprentices and after a smale tyme of service with them for a peece of money sell their tyme unto merchants, brewers, and others to worke on ships at sea, brewhouses, and elsewhere'. One consequence was a lack of work for 'many poore freemen' coopers. Another, was that 'at the expiracon of theire apprenticeships' these young coopers were 'verie imperfect in their trade'.[184]

Other young people were pressed into military service, they ran away to sea or to join a military expedition. Again, there are petitions for entering the freedom by redemption from apprentices who served in the wars.[185] Concern was expressed in many quarters that it would be difficult to 'reduce' servants who took sides in the English Revolution to their former dependent status upon their return from armed conflict. This anxiety was by no means new; nor

---

[181] CLRO Reps. 27, fos. 251–1ᵛ, 262; 28, fo. 52.
[182] For example, GL MSS 4329/2, fo. 8; 5770/1, fos. 214–15, 269; 7090/2, fos. 95, 156ᵛ; 7090/4, fo. 246ᵛ.
[183] See Ben-Amos, *Adolescence and Youth in Early Modern England*, chs. 5 and 9.
[184] CLRO Rep. 44, fo. 173ᵛ.
[185] For example, CLRO Reps. 32, fo. 328; 42, fos. 227, 242ᵛ–3; 43, fos. 157ᵛ–8.

was it without justification. In 1625 Thomas Price of Pembrokeshire told the Court of Aldermen in London of the fate of his son. He had been apprenticed to one Walton, a merchant, who at some point accused young Price of stealing 'a good some of money' without, it seems, 'just provocacon'. The apprentice, however, 'departed from his master's service' to 'become a souldier in forraine parts beyond the seas', and now having returned to England with the help of his father he took steps to tidy up his position with his master. The authorities discharged him, and their reasons for following this course are interesting. They reported that 'wee conceave it not to bee in the power of the father to reduce his sonne againe to his maister, nor in the will of the youth to be replaced as an apprentice'.[186]

The pull of independent work, marriage, war, and the sea drew some young people away from formal training, and gave them opportunities to express the technical and social competence picked up during three to six years of service. An unknown number of young 'drop-outs', however, simply vanished from view; they can no longer be traced in the records of the place in which they served. It might be possible to follow them to their home community and see if they appear in its sources as workers, employers, ratepayers, parents, or officers. It would be no surprise if they did, and this sort of record-linkage offers one potentially fruitful direction for further work. Other 'ronnegates' can be tracked in the records of the place in which they served, not only working, but also inhabiting a shady quarter, drifting in and out of service, stealing, begging, loitering, and moving in 'lewd company'. The larger towns offered greater opportunities for this 'vagring life', and its rough shape can be traced in the records of Norwich and especially London.[187] Young people were 'enticed' to join this urban basement.[188] In London, we find runaways picking pockets,[189] pilfering,[190] cutting purses,[191] cozening,[192] begging,[193] and frequenting 'lewd company'.[194] They

---

[186] CLRO Rep. 39, fos. 76–7.

[187] Cf. Beier, 'Social problems in Elizabethan London', 132–4; Ben-Amos, *Adolescence and Youth in Early Modern England*, 130.

[188] For example, NRO NMC 8, fo. 690; 9, fos. 47, 348; 11, fo. 399; 12, fo. 74; BCB 2, fos. 222ᵛ–3; 5, fos. 255ᵛ, 416ᵛ; 6, fo. 3; 7, fo. 226; 8, fos. 140ᵛ, 28 July 1641; CLRO Jour. 25, fo. 216ᵛ; GL MS 5770/1, fos. 420–1. Much of the evidence from Norwich materials is used in the following chapter.

[189] BCB 6, fo. 289ᵛ.

[190] BCB 6, fos. 15ᵛ, 45, 101, 144, 164ᵛ, 174ᵛ, 327, 378 (two cases), 27 May 1625; 7, fos. 32, 177ᵛ, 213ᵛ, 218ᵛ, 226ᵛ (two cases), 253ᵛ; 8, fos. 27, 51, 99, 100, 108, 174ᵛ, 212ᵛ, 217ᵛ, 316.

[191] BCB 7, fo. 38.   [192] BCB 6, fo. 431.

[193] BCB 7, fos. 22ᵛ, 208, 219ᵛ; 8, fo. 99.   [194] BCB 6, fos. 19, 177, 244ᵛ; 7, fo. 60ᵛ.

included Christopher Losher, 'a vagrant boy' and a 'dayly pickpockett in the marketts', who ran away from one Mr Dawson and was finally transported across the ocean to Virginia; Elias Huntingdon, 'a vagrant' and former Bridewell apprentice, 'that liveth ydlie and will not followe his trade'; and Toby Clark, 'a vagrant boy' who would 'not stay' in service 'but liveth pilfering aboute the streetes'.[195] Other runaways followed a 'vagring life'; they were found loitering, vagrant, and 'out of service'.[196]

A number of runaways followed the alternative rhythm of the 'vagring life', but for many it was a brief interval; they returned to their master, or left for home. Some were persistent offenders. In January 1622, for example, a constable found Thomas Taylor, 'a lewde vagrant', pacing the streets and carried him to Bridewell. He had been placed in service by the Bridewell authorities, but raided his master's possessions, and was 'whipped att a cart's tayle', given a passport to return home, 'yet loitereth about the towne'. Taylor was handed another pass.[197] In this time of growing up when great strides should have been taken towards maturity, a number of young people had been tarnished by 'lewd courses'. They included John Lowe and Robert Tunton, the former apprentices of a fustian weaver who were 'made free' of London, but chose to spend their days 'lyving idely in the marketts'; Arthur Felday, a 'baker by trade and hath served seven yeares apprenticeshippe in Foster Lane', who followed the 'vagring life'; John Usher, 'a vagrant that havinge a good trade will not worke but inticeth and keepeth company with other mens apprentices and causeth them to spend their masters goods'; William Newsan, who completed his term as a Bridewell apprentice but 'now loytereth up and downe the towne and will take no course to live'; and William Offley of London, an alderman's son, who petitioned the Court of Aldermen in 1624 promising 'to amend his former course of life intendinge now to goe over amongst others prest for service of the Kinge'.[198]

The working day also presented opportunities for theft. Servants could stroll through most parts of their master's shop and household, all sorts of domestic and working materials were within easy reach. Young people traded on behalf of their master; took care of the shop; fetched provisions; mingled with his associates and friends; and stayed behind when their master travelled 'abroad'. There are

[195] BCB 8, fo. 60; 6, fo. 97ᵛ; 7, fo. 63ᵛ.
[196] BCB 6, fos. 4, 31ᵛ, 41ᵛ, 43ᵛ, 130, 149, 367, 410ᵛ; 7, fos. 220ᵛ, 282; 8, fos. 13ᵛ, 58ᵛ, 82ᵛ, 251ᵛ, 279ᵛ, 286, 314ᵛ, 22 Sept. 1641.
[197] BCB 6, fo. 265ᵛ.   [198] BCB 6, fos. 63, 144, 130, 65; CLRO Rep. 39, fo. 29.

examples of young people adjusting the books or selling goods above their master's price to pocket the profits.[199] The chance to top up wages and fund conviviality and play was a strong temptation. Pepys reported that gossip in coffee houses often turned to pilfering servants, who were 'very common nowadays' (1664).[200] It was not a new problem. The Court of Aldermen in London appointed a committee in 1601 to 'consider what course is fitt to be taken touching bankrupt mens servants and apprentices which deceave their masters'.[201] Theft was a steady drain on some master's resources.

Contemporary sources show servants raiding their master's pantry, cupboard, store, chest, and purse. They 'pilfered', 'cozened', 'misspent', and 'wasted' apples, aprons, beakers, beef, beer, bottles, brass, bread, candles, candlesticks, cheeses, cloth, clocks, fish, hats, herbs, napkins, plates, rope, sheets, shoes, spoons, spices, stirrups, stockings, sugar, tools, and yarn. Money also went missing from purses and chests. The sums stolen ranged from a trivial few pence to a considerable slice of a master's wealth. Some servants displayed cunning and tried to cover their tracks. Others helped themselves to a fraction of a larger pile of money. Grace Jones was 'indicted and arraigned' at London Sessions 'for taking six pounds out of a bagg of fiftie pounds' from her master who made the mistake of 'leavinge open his closet dore'.[202] Most stolen goods were 'small' and 'petty things', or 'trifles'.[203] Some young people stole over a period of weeks, months, or years. While others picked up a bunch of items in one fell swoop.[204] Young thieves fenced stolen goods; others ran away with their ill-gotten gains; still others stashed them in their trunk. Even the goods of high ranking officials were at risk. In January 1626 the mayor of London set up a 'search in all suspected places and howses for the apprehencon of one Katherine Griffith', a 22-year-old maidservant of 'full face' and 'haire of a sadd color who this last weeke beinge entertayned into my house by my skouringe women to wash plates and doe like busines hath as is vehemently suspected stolen away' four silver plates and spoons, 'and is theire uppon fledd'.[205]

One youth complained 'that it was a hard matter if an apprentice

[199] For example, CH minute book, fo. 248; GL MS 5770/1, fos. 9, 140–1, 274; BCB 4, fo. 321; 5, fo. 406.
[200] *The Diary of Samuel Pepys*, ed. R. Latham and W. Matthews (11 vols.; 1970–83), v. 294.
[201] CLRO Rep. 25, fo. 295.   [202] PRO SP 16/111/15.
[203] See BCB 5, fos. 140, 314; 6, fo. 3.
[204] For example, NRO NMC 13, fo. 414; BCB 4, fos. 52, 20 May 1598; 5, fo. 207.
[205] CLRO Jour. 33, fo. 198.

could not in the tyme of his yeares get some money'.[206] Uppermost in the minds of young pilferers were lack of money, play, conviviality, courtship, and sex. They lavished gifts on their partners. Francis Baldwin, of London, for example, a pewterer's apprentice, raided his master's goods on several occasions, taking 'viii[li] of brasse, a candlestick and two castinge bottells . . . iii[li] in money . . . viiid in money . . . a peece of mettall', and 'a stone dishe, the which was paynted, and gave it to kepe to Joane the cobler's maide'.[207] Other young people pilfered to fund a trip to the playhouse, alehouse, or bawdy house, to buy clothes, and to support dicing or tables. Some were 'enticed' to steal by friends, receivers, or fences.[208] In December 1622 Jane Robinson of London, 'a comon nipp', was accused of being 'a notorious queane and inveigher of apprentices to robb their masters and receiver of their goods'. It was alleged that Margaret Whittingham 'threw things out of her master's house in the night to [Alice] Dibbes who inticyeth her thereto'. Alice Merriday was transported to Barbados because she 'combined with a girl that her master's back dore should be left open in the night'. While in 1640 Anne Bromage confessed at London Bridewell that Martha Jackson 'came and perswaded her to open her masters dores, and then she came and opened a cupboard in her master's house and tooke there 5[li] in money and a golde ringe'.[209] One contemporary perception made the connection between rising levels of theft, vagrancy, shifting youth, and pilfering servants, and it has recently been argued that this concern played a major part in the making of some pieces of the 'Bloody Code' c.1689–1718,[210] though it was a familiar anxiety for earlier generations of magistrates too. In 1600 London's governors took steps to police 'many idle, loose, vagrant, and evill disposed persons' of 'the worst and basest condicon and manners', who under 'color and pretence of buyinge, gatheringe' and raking 'cuttings of paper . . . cards, ragges, old ropes, cords', and 'paynted clothes', walked in the streets 'having frequent access to the houses of good citizens'. Some of them persuaded young

[206] GL MS 5770/1, fo. 274.   [207] GL MS 7090/2, fo. 82.

[208] For example, NRO NMC 10, fos. 143, 321; 12, fos. 184, 317, 318, 471; 13, fos. 395, 605; 14, fos. 234, 377; 15, fo. 308[v]; BCB 5, fos. 332, 334; 6, fos. 14, 55, 173[v], 220[v], 263[v], 278, 287[v], 301[v], 318[v], 374[v]; 7, fos. 28[v], 53, 56, 72[v], 82, 110, 121[v], 126, 131, 139[v], 194, 226[v], 229, 231[v], 239, 260[v]; 8, fos. 89[v], 253[v], 284, 294, 379, 387, 391[v]; CLRO Rep. 25, fo. 418; PRO STAC 8, 151/15.

[209] BCB 6, fo. 313; 7, fos. 232, 311; 8, fo. 298.

[210] John Beattie, 'London and the making of the "Bloody Code", 1689–1718', in L. Davison et al. (eds.), *Stilling the Grumbling Hive: The Response to Social and Economic Problems in England, 1689–1750* (Stroud, 1992), esp. 54, 61, 64, 68–70.

people 'to depart from theire masters . . . alluring and enticing them to loose and vicious course of life, and some others animatinge and encouraginge them to robbe and spoile theire masters'.[211]

Nor should we forget that theft not only purchased alcohol and a place at the dicing table, it also cut into a master's funds and affected his fortunes. On occasion, young pilferers hatched their crime to harm their master. In 1573 Robert Coles, a London apprentice, 'was openly ponished' in the Clothworkers' hall 'before diverse and sundrie householders and apprentices for certen misdemanours and evill facts by hym practised against his . . . master'. He was charged with pilfering his cloth, and 'confederating with his fellowe to go about to cutt broade clothes and carseys beinge brought to his master's house to tacke, thinkinge by that meanes to make his master banckroupte'.[212] Sadly, the sources seldom permit us to connect theft with open animosity, even if it was a drain on masters' funds. Physical and verbal violence—'speeches and blowes', 'wordes and deedes'—provides a clearer indication of resentment. Again, in a few cases alcohol peeled off inhibitions.[213] Nevertheless, angry words or blows were more often an expression of festering tensions. A choice slander or blow could shatter the tranquillity of the household. A carefully chosen phrase could touch a sensitive nerve. Many early modern people composed cruel jibes and shrill libels. Young people also knew the harmful qualities of particular words. Some of them wounded their masters with 'unfitting wordes', 'slanderous speeches', 'hard speeches', 'vile and lewd wordes', and 'indecent and uncomelie speeches not to be suffered in any apprentice or servant'.[214] 'Vile words' were also mingled with punches.[215] On occasion, masters and servants traded insults, passing 'some speeches of myslikinge on both sides'.[216] Young people also hurled insults and slanders at higher authorities. One fishmonger's apprentice told the master and wardens of his company 'that he wold see them hanged before he wold come at them'.[217] But the greater part of their stinging phrases were levelled at masters, who were said to be liars and cowards, lacking 'credit', in shameful debt, and 'laide of the french poxe'. It was claimed

[211] CLRO Jour. 95, fos. 221 a. [212] CH minute book 1558–81, fo. 177.
[213] For example, BCB 5, fos. 66ᵛ, 153, 249ᵛ; 6, fo. 55.
[214] See CH minute books 1558–81, fos. 30, 54ᵛ, 80, 93, 245; 1581–1605, fos. 7ᵛ, 57ᵛ; BCB 1, fo. 6; 5, fos. 165ᵛ, 416ᵛ; GL MS 7090/3, fo. 91ᵛ.
[215] For example, CH minute book 1558–81, fos. 30, 158ᵛ, 220ᵛ, 245; BCB 1, fo. 93.
[216] CH minute book 1581–1605, fos. 2, 13ᵛ.
[217] GL MS 5770/2, fo. 99. See also ibid. fo. 780; GL MSS 7090/2, fo. 33ᵛ; 11,588/2, fo. 49ᵛ.

that mistresses were 'barren scoldes', 'drunkards', and bawdy house keepers.[218]

In 1592 John Robinson of London filed a complaint at the Fishmongers' Court on behalf of James Plug to complain about his friend's apprentice—Thomas Parry—'for giving' his master 'very vile and lewde wordes and speeches seeking utterly to discredite and overthrowe him, saying that he was not able to pay his debts, and if every man were paid hee was not worth a groate'. On another occasion Robinson was talking with a friend when Parry stepped out of the shadows 'with his cleaving knife and offered and said he would cleave his head and further gave report that' he 'could not have credit for a barrel of fish'. Plug also alleged that Parry 'oftentimes [hurled] most vile wordes, saying hee will spytt in his face and such like'.[219] Moving in the circles of commerce, exchange, and credit networks, in which character and 'credit' were synonymous, masters were sensitive to circulated smears about poverty, unreliability, and false promises. The servants of a silkman 'went to his creditors and reported' that their master 'was broken or woulde breake shortly'. Another master alleged that his apprentices 'secretly' met together to 'devise and frame diverse false wicked libellouse and scandalous notes in wrytinge', spreading rumours that he 'most wickedly and ungodly defrauded and deceyved his customers by false weights and measures and secret devises by wyre to hold his scales', and false accounting. He also claimed that they 'repaired' to his customers in Buckinghamshire, Epping, Braintree, Hertford, Brentwood, Ongar, and other places, to inform them that they had been sorely 'wronged and abused'.[220]

Other libels exposed the condition of a master's marriage and household to public view. In 1589, for example, Mabel Atkinson of Kirkby Kendal (Cumbria) 'forgetting her duty to Almighty God' and 'that servile regard' which was the true posture of the young underling, 'by the instigation of our mortal enemy the Devil, the author of all falsehood and lying . . . most maliciously . . . devised, framed and brought a very horrible, unjust, and feigned slander and misreport' of her master and mistress. Her verses sent a rumour around the town 'tending to the dishonest and unchaste life' of her master 'and the defiling of the wedded bed'. Atkinson was ordered to be 'openly called forth of prison to the bar in the Mootehall', and 'in very penitent, humble, and sorrowful manner . . . upon

---

[218] BCB 5, fos. 38, 271ᵛ-2, 311ᵛ, 409ᵛ; GL MSS 5770/1, fos. 494–5; 4329/2, fo. 35; 7090/4, fo. 222; CH minute books 1558–81, fos. 7ᵛ, 179, 245; 1581–1605, fo. 161ᵛ.
[219] GL MS 5770/1, fo. 161ᵛ.   [220] PRO SP 16/274/55; STAC 8, 222/6.

her knees in the presence of all people then and there assembled',
to 'ask and crave at God his hands mercy and forgiveness for her
. . . false and untrue report and slander'. She was also instructed to
seek the 'pardon' of her master and mistress, so that the audience
(and public opinion) may 'be fully satisfied and resolved'.[221] Edward
Attaborne of London, the servant of Andros Rodrigues, went to even
greater lengths and to some of the highest circles in the city to
scatter his 'untrothes of his master'. He 'complained to the aldermen deputy of the ward, the sheriffe, and also the lord mayor'
telling them 'untrothes' to get his master in 'trouble'. Attaborne
was weaving an elaborate fiction—that his master was plotting to
take his life. He told officials that he had found an empty grave in
his master's house; it had been freshly dug, and it was clear that it
was soon to be filled. It was only during his third examination that
Attaborne 'admitted that he made it'. He also told the authorities
that 'he ment to take a rope and to putt yt aboute his necke and
to have made an outcrye onelye to dryve into mens heddes that his
master went aboute to murder him', to 'bring his master to displeasure and trouble', and also to compel him to 'forfeite' £50 'wherein
he stode bound for the good usage of himselfe' towards his servant.
There was a history of disorder in this household. On this occasion,
however, it was the servant who was reprimanded by the authorities.
He was whipped and returned to his master, 'promisinge and
byndinge hymselfe in twentye poundes' to the mayor and Bridewell
governors, that he would serve 'well, diligentlie, and obedientlye',
and obey his master and mistress 'according to the tenor, form,
effect, and true meaning' of his indentures.[222]

The sources also reveal young people beating, striking, stabbing,
and scratching their masters.[223] They used a variety of weapons
in their 'contemptuous usage' of their masters, including pots, daggers, a cowlestaff, crockery, furniture, and 'a grene pokinge stick',
though most of them relied on their fists and legs. John Dixon of
London 'stabbed his master in the brest with a knife', one of many
'intollerable abuses'. Other young people pulled their master by
the beard or 'broke' his head.[224] Mistresses were also the target of

---

[221] R. S. Ferguson (ed.), *The Boke of Recorde of Kirkbie Kendall* (Cumberland and Westmorland
Antiquarian and Archaeological Society, extra series, 4, Kendal, 1892), 146–8.

[222] BCB 1, fos. 220ᵛ–1.

[223] For example, NRO NMC 7, fo. 550; 9, fos. 297, 462, 628; 11, fo. 191; 12, fo. 812; 14,
fo. 360ᵛ; 16, fo. 666; 20, fo. 143; BCB 1, fo. 93; 2, fo. 69; 4, fos. 2 Oct. 1598, 55, 58, 187ᵛ,
334ᵛ; 5, fos. 46ᵛ, 72, 89, 137, 155ᵛ, 249ᵛ, 272ᵛ, 328, 355ᵛ, 409ᵛ, 413, 417, 433; 6, fo. 6ᵛ; GL
MS 7090/2, fo. 132ᵛ.

[224] See BCB 5, fo. 417; 1, fo. 193.

assaults; one woman was pregnant at the time. Another, mistress Clacott, a grocer's wife, was stabbed in the face 'an inche and a halfe deepe'.[225] Some masters were left in great fear of their lives.[226] Others were plunged into deep fright by fierce threats. Thomas Evans 'threatened to stab' his master 'in the harte', and also 'abused' his mistress.[227] Daggers were drawn and a few servants made threatening gestures in the air.[228] Were Evans and the rest acting in earnest? There are in fact several examples of attempted murder; the most usual method was poisoning.[229]

Why did young people hurl threats and punches? The risks were high, the murder of a master was judged petty treason. Our evidence is thin, but suggestive. A few servants were themselves the victims of abuse. Mary Spencer, who put 'a kinde of salve which is tempered with poison into her master and dame's pottage', suffered from their 'hard usage'. Margaret Austin purchased a 'pennyworth of quicksilver' and 'mingled the same in a messe of [her mistress's] milke' because 'her mistris did misuse her hardly'.[230] Romance blossomed in one case in which an apprentice threatened 'to runne' his master 'through with a knife'. He informed the Bridewell governors that after the task was finished 'hee would marrie his mistris'.[231]

In other cases young people were resisting 'just punishment'. John Edwards was 'reasonably correcting' his servant William Mere 'for his faulte in rejecting a pair of nether stockes provided for hym', when Mere with 'bad speeches' began 'resisting' him, 'and threw him downe and scratched bothe his necke and handes'. We have already met Thomas Awdley, 'a comon fighter and brawler in his master's howse', and 'a great swearer and blasphemer of God', who preferred the alehouse to church. He also resisted his master with threats, and on one occasion his master, 'goyng about to correct him', grabbed a 'bromestaff to fight with him'.[232] In some disordered households authority was faint and fragile. Awdley's master admitted that his apprentice was 'so stubborne and devilish that he dare not correct him as he should'. In 1610 John Robinson

---

[225] NRO NMC 12, fo. 812; BCB 2, fos. 39, 69; 4, fo. 347.
[226] BCB 1, fos. 59–9ᵛ.
[227] BCB 4, fo. 173ᵛ. See also ibid., fos. 16 Aug. 1598, 214; 5, fos. 163ᵛ, 169ᵛ, 193, 424, 436.
[228] For example, NRO NMC 7, fo. 461; BCB 5, fos. 212, 289ᵛ, 419, 439ᵛ.
[229] For example, NRO NMC 8, fo. 430; BCB 1, fo. 77; 4, fo. 74ᵛ; 5, fos. 63, 275; GCL O3, fo. 538.
[230] BCB 5, fo. 63; 4, fo. 74ᵛ. See also BCB 5, fo. 404ᵛ.   [231] BCB 4, fo. 345ᵛ.
[232] CH minute book 1581–1605, fo. 158ᵛ; GL MS 5770/1, fos. 149–50. Cf. BCB 5, fos. 153, 326.

told the London Fishmongers that he 'doth not dare correct' Jonas Bond, 'a comon dycer and player', who often spoke 'vile words'. Pepys disapprovingly noted the state of affairs in his brother's household, where authority seemed to have vanished—the master 'hath not command over his two men, but they do what they list and care not for his commands'.[233]

Were young men more likely to challenge a master openly, and did women follow different tactics to demonstrate opposition and indifference? The various acts of disobedience have been put in seven categories—running away (including reported absences from the household), misdemeanours (including 'abuse' and 'misuse'), disobedience (including refusals to serve), violence (including threats), attempted murder, slander, and theft—and samples have been taken from the first five courtbooks of London Bridewell to discover the number of offences committed by either sex.[234] Young men were in a majority in all categories except for slander and attempted murder. Their proportionate representation in cases of running away was 85.8 per cent (617/719), misdemeanours 95 per cent (57/60), violence 98.4 per cent (62/63), theft 71.6 per cent (86/120), and disobedience 96.3 per cent (104/108). An equal number of men and women hurled 'vile wordes' at their master or mistress.[235] All six attempts to murder heads of household (or their partner) were made by a young woman; poison was the chosen method in every case. These figures are only suggestive. It must be remembered that this is not an exhaustive list of possible sources or strategies. They suggest that young women were more likely to express hostility in words alone.[236] We would certainly expect to find far more young men formally indentured, and this printed code conveyed knowledge of their rights. They were more likely to bring rough treatment to the attention of relatives, friends, and the authorities.

5. 'For Examples Sake'

It was not expected that mere underlings would redress a grievance, or strike a note of discord without the intervention of the

---

[233] GL MS 5770/1, fo. 593; Pepys, *Diary*, iii. 194. See also BCB 3, fo. 199; 5, fo. 324; NRO NMC fo. 387; GL MS 4329/2, fo. 11ᵛ.

[234] I have included cases of running away from NRO NMC 15–16 and 20.

[235] Nor does there appear to be any distinctive gendered pattern in the cases I have consulted. It appears that a maidservant was equally likely to slander her master; and a male servant equally likely to slander his mistress.

[236] In fact, the one act of violence committed by a female servant was against her mistress.

authorities. They could not take the law into their own hands, but were encouraged to turn to formal channels to seek assistance. It was hoped that young people would not stray outside their 'place'. For this reason the authorities were especially concerned with 'example' and public display to communicate their interpretation of upright youth. 'Disorderly' servants set a bad example. It was claimed that John Richards 'most lewdly and arrogantly resisted' his master and 'gave him a blow on the face to the lewd example of all his household'. While Robert Oates 'very undutifully and in outrageous manner abused his master to the evill example of other servants'. He was committed to prison and instructed to 'acknowledge his offence and humble himself to his master'.[237] Some young people built up a long list of offences, and became notorious figures in their companies, households, and neighbourhoods.[238] One concern was that they might encourage others to follow their 'lewd courses'.[239] It was hoped that young strays would be put on the path to virtuous adulthood. Steps were taken to preserve the relationship which they put in doubt when they threw punches or uttered stinging phrases. Again, the formal collapse of the relationship was an option for a later offence.[240] Thus the language of the authorities was often that of reconciliation, friendship, forgiveness, amendment, and submission, though on occasion these strategies had a much sharper edge—stern words, whipping, or public punishment.

The question of who was to punish the 'disorderly servant' was a sensitive issue. Masters were expected to 'reasonably correct' their servants. The Court of London Bridewell, for example, sometimes referred cases back to the master or company for punishment. Companies had a range of options which were neatly stated in the case of James Johnson of London, a fishmonger's apprentice. He was presented in 1617 for speaking 'very vile and lewde speeches' to one of the assistant's wives. It appeared that the company had three options; to punish Johnson 'openly in the howse [the company's hall], at Bridewell, or by the apprentice's master in his owne howse'. They chose the third course, thereby containing the dispute within their close quarters.[241] More generally the authorities followed a strategy of 'damage limitation' to ensure that the household

---

[237] BCB 1, fo. 28ᵛ; CLRO Rep. 28, fo. 128ᵛ. See also GL MS 5770/1, fos. 420–1; CH minute book 1558–81, fo. 239ᵛ.

[238] For example, CH minute books 1581–1605, fo. 13ᵛ; 1605–23, fo. 211; GL MSS 5770/1, fos. 140–1, 149–50, 396, 593; 5770/2, fos. 99, 408; BCB 5, fos. 336ᵛ, 341ᵛ, 371, 433.

[239] Cf. BCB 4, fos. 399ᵛ, 438ᵛ.

[240] For some typical examples see GL MS 11,588/1, fo. 84; CLRO Rep. 43, fos. 6–7.

[241] GL MS 5770/1, fos. 494–5.

emerged intact from the mess of interpersonal conflict. Thus 'disorderly' servants were whipped and warned, and returned to their master.[242] Many of them were imprisoned and put to work.[243] Some offenders were ordered to serve an additional period at the close of their term 'yn full recompence' for their mischief.[244]

The principal actors, however, did not always follow the script. It was hoped that masters would 'gentlye receave' their 'disorderly' servants,[245] but in some cases they refused to take them back, or to turn them over to another householder. In such circumstances the authorities often resorted to firm 'perswaycons', pressing reluctant masters 'to consider of the matter'. A Norwich blacksmith was won over with a loan; a London haberdasher refused to be moved by 'perswaycons', 'except he may have a pott of money geven him'. If appeals fell on deaf ears, the authorities could discharge a servant, turn them over to another master, or refer the case to other officials like justices, aldermen, or the parish.[246] A number of young people also had to be persuaded to 'bringe' themselves 'to unitye and to be reconcyled' with their master.[247] Persistent offenders could expect harsh treatment. A pair of pothooks or an iron ring was sometimes fixed to the body of regular runaways in Norwich. In 1561, for example, it was ordered that William Bannock, who had run away three times, should 'have a rynge aboute his necke according to the statute'.[248] A final option was banishment from the guild and the possibility at that time of obtaining full political citizenship.[249]

Bannock's shackles, which were a visual validation of the politics of age, can help us to locate two principal themes of punishment—submission and example.[250] A suitably chastened youth was expected

[242] There are many examples in the sources. For a selection of cases from Norwich materials see NRO NMC 8, fos. 108, 321, 428, 624, 695, 701; 9, fo. 185; 10, fos. 92, 620; 14, fo. 360ᵛ; 15, fo. 419.

[243] For example, NRO NMC 7, fos. 485, 578, 670; 8, fo. 25; 9, fo. 43; 10, fo. 13; 11, fo. 399.

[244] For example, CH minute book 1558–81, fos. 61ᵛ, 115, 118ᵛ, 222, 242ᵛ.

[245] GL MS 11,588/1, fo. 119ᵛ.

[246] See, for example, GL MSS 5770/1, fos. 58, 151, 181; 7090/2, fo. 240ᵛ; 7090/4, fo. 3ᵛ; 15,842/1, fos. 18, 53; CH minute book 1581–1605, fos. 41, 103, 128; BCB 5, fos. 2ᵛ, 66ᵛ, 68, 154, 339ᵛ, 367, 422ᵛ; NRO NCOS 'The Sessions Booke 1630–38', fos. 53ᵛ, 58ᵛ, 115; NMC 16, fo. 411; 20, fo. 310.

[247] For example, CH minute book 1581–1605, fos. 2 (two cases), 27.

[248] NRO NMC 8, fo. 236. See also NMC 7, fo. 550; 8, fo. 605; 9, fos. 191, 194; 10, fo. 677; 14, fo. 421ᵛ; 15, fos. 189ᵛ, 275, 489ᵛ.

[249] For example, GL MSS 7090/2, fos. 52, 157ᵛ, 215, 229ᵛ; 7090/3, fos. 24ᵛ, 91ᵛ.

[250] The most convenient survey of punishment in early modern England is J. A. Sharpe, *Judicial Punishment in England* (1990), ch. 2. For the significance of 'example' in enforcing

to submit to authority, ask forgiveness, and promise future amendment.[251] Thus in 1609 John Baker, who was presented at London
Bridewell for running seven times from his master and 'frequentinge
lewde houses and companie . . . submitted himselfe to his master
present promising to become a newe man . . . doe good service and
wynne againe his master's love'.[252] Young offenders were urged to
serve 'trewly and faithfully as an apprentice ought to doe'.[253] A regular part of these proceedings, therefore, was a staged and scripted
acceptance of legitimate authority. Thus William Fitton, who abused
his master 'with speeches and blowes . . . did with teares upon his
knees aske his master's' and the court's 'forgyveness'. Other 'disorderly' servants said that they 'were sorye and craved mercy',
and promised 'never to comytt the like offence agayne'. They were
instructed to 'submitt', and 'crave the friendshipp and good will of
their master'.[254]

The theme of reconciliation touched even the very worst cases.
A volley of abuse poured forth in Francis Leech's household; the
apprentice issuing a chilling threat, the master returning scornful
words. Was this a lost cause, a lost household? Leech agreed to
follow the verdict of the Clothworkers' Court. But his apprentice,
Robert Fenrutter, remained resolutely unhelpful, and 'wold in no
wyse yeald'. The bench 'used many perswaycons to . . . bring him to
unitye and to be reconcyled', and when a glimmer of hope beckoned they sent the pair to the company garden to settle the issue.
'After longe talke' they came back inside 'contented of theire owne
accordes to become lovers and friends'. Another disordered household was returned to order, and 'in token of friendship' the pair
'shook hands and protested to renounce and forgeve all olde injurys,
evill speeches and mysdemeanours comytted on eyther parte, and
to become lovers from the bottom of their harte'.[255]

The image of the penitent youth seeking forgiveness on his knees
communicates the political and theatrical nature of the settlement

conventional ideas about authority see P. Spierenburg, *The Spectacle of Suffering: Executions and
the Evolution of Repression from a Pre-industrial Metropolis to the European Experience* (Cambridge,
1984), esp. 53–4; Scott, *Domination and the Arts of Resistance*, 45, 197.

[251] Cf. Scott, *Domination and the Arts of Resistance*, 57–8; Hanawalt, *Growing up in Medieval
London*, 184.

[252] BCB 5, fo. 375^v.

[253] For example, CH minute book 1558–81, fos. 50^v, 54^v, 69^v, 125, 173^v, 175^v; GL MS
5770/1, fo. 594.

[254] CH minute book 1581–1605, fos. 158^v, 101; BCB 3, fo. 15; NRO NMC 9, fo. 543; GL
MS 5770/1, fos. 594–5.

[255] CH minute book 1581–1605, fo. 2. See also ibid., fo. 13^v.

of household disorders. John Deane, a London grocer's servant, who 'unreverently behaved hymself' towards his master and mistress 'as well in worde and deede', was ordered to 'humblie' kneel down 'in open courte' and beg the 'good will' of the 'assistants and of his master', and to promise 'by the grace of God never soe to use hymself in the like evill as heretofore he hath done'. Deane was also told to 'go to his master's house and their kneele downe uppon his knees in the shopp' before the apprentices 'and ask his master's forgiveness'.[256] As the circle of abuse extended to a master's friends or family punishment was often tailored to suit the public nature of the offence. Thus Richard Barnes of London, who 'slanderouslye reported unto sondrie persons' that his master had refused to settle a debt of £20, was ordered to go with his master to those who heard his 'report', and to 'denie the same words by him before spoken'. Richard Harrison, who gave his master 'slanderous speeches' and spread scurrilous reports about him to his 'friends', was ordered to 'reconcyle hymselfe towardes' his master and to 'confesse his fault . . . kneele down and aske his forgiveness'. Yet this could only satisfy the domestic aspect of his offence; the public shame remained. Harrison was therefore told to go with the company beadle to his master's 'friends' and 'creditors', and 'others to whome he had uttered such slanderous speeches', and to 'confess his offence and desyre them to forgeve hym'.[257]

In certain cases a servant's submission was bolstered by his master's 'earnest entreaty' or 'request' for mercy. His special pleading was perfectly consistent with the politics of age because events set in motion the very best side of paternalism—the compassionate master, the benevolent magistrate, and the obedient servant. Yet this form of 'entreaty' or 'gentle submission' could not guarantee an escape from the whip.[258] Punishment was selective, adaptable, and political. Uppermost in the minds of the authorities was the correct representation of the politics of age. This is dramatically witnessed in the forms of 'open' and 'public' punishment in which the distribution of domestic authority was visually affirmed. The scene of these displays was chosen with communal or work identities

[256] CJ MS 11,588/1, fo. 8 1 See also BCB 3, fo. 166'; CH minute books 1558-81, fos. 30, 45, 136, 226; 1581-1605, fos. 4', 110', 112, 134; GL MSS 5770/1, fo. 9; 5770/2, fo. 780; 7090/4, fos. 83', 222; 11,588/1, fo. 119'; GCL minute book O3, fo. 35'.

[257] GL MS 4329/2, fo. 35; CH minute book 1581-1605, fo. 57'. See also CH minute books 1558-81, fos. 50', 129; 1581-1605, fos. 150, 248'. Cf. Scott, *Domination and the Arts of Resistance*, 113.

[258] For example, BCB 5, fo. 375'; 6, fo. 13'; GL MS 5770/1, fos. 149-50, 594-5; NRO NMC 20, fos. 89', 117'; CH minute books 1558-81, fos. 54', 81; 1581-1605, fos. 162', 184'.

in mind; the civic space of the market-place, the busy streets in the heart of the community, the Guildhall, or the company hall. The distinction between 'public' and 'private' punishment was well understood. The two possessed discrete meaning and the authorities proposed particular penalties in individual cases. In February 1610, for example, London's Court of Aldermen ordered that John Dixon should be 'brought to the Guildhall' for his 'great and intollerable abuses', and 'tyed at a cart's taile and from thence ... whipped through the publique streetes' to his master's house. Dixon's punishment was 'stayed' because of his master's 'earnest suite' for some 'consyderation'—his apprentice was a gentlewoman's son, and was 'very penitent and sorrowfull for his falte'. Dixon's master claimed that he 'never expected [that] any such publique punishment should be inflicted upon him'. It was therefore 'agreed that he should be punished in private' behind Bridewell's walls rather than in full public gaze.[259]

The form and meaning of 'open' punishment is well demonstrated in the responses of the London Fishmongers to 'the dyvers great abuses and misdemeanours' committed by 'dyvers apprentices' in the market in 1610.[260] The company court instructed that a 'mynister [i.e. administor]' was to be 'ready for the purpose masked' and the offenders were 'stripped to the girdle' before 'as many boyes and apprentizes of the company ... as could be gotten hither to see there punishment for examples sake'. They were whipped '*in terrorem* ... and all there warned to take example by them and avoyd the like'. The young audience were 'streightly charged never to speak word to anyone whosoever of the matter, nor once to mock or cast in the teeth of them that is punished'. The occasion was intended to be solemn, educative, and strictly a company matter. The culprits were 'exhorted to take a new course of liff', and 'to serve the rest of there apprentishood faithfully, honestly, and diligently'.[261]

Such 'open' punishments were staged 'for ensample to other apprentices to avoid the like abuses'; for 'examples sake *in terrorem* of the rest'; 'for the example of others of the like condicon'; and 'for example of all such lyke offenders'.[262] Young offenders were

---

[259] CLRO Rep. 29, fo. 184ᵛ.

[260] Some of the details of these 'misdemeanours' are described above, pp. 130–1.

[261] GL MS 5770/1, fos. 594–5.

[262] CLRO Rep. 13, fo. 127. See also GL MSS 5770/1, fos. 140–1, 149–50, 420–1; 5770/2, fo. 99; 7090/2, fo. 56ᵛ; 7090/3, fo. 211ᵛ; 11,588/1, fo. 168ᵛ; CH minute book 1558–81, fos. 177, 207. The governors of Christ's Hospital in London also staged 'open' punishments for the benefit of the Hospital's children. In December 1576, for example, John Stockdale

expected to follow the script and make good public show of remorse. There are few recorded outbursts like that of James Townsett, who 'protested' that 'he would never submitt nor make anie such acknowledgemente while he lived'.[263] One advantage of gathering a chosen audience to witness a whipping in the formal setting of the company hall or Guildhall was the creation of an opportune moment (as in the case of funeral sermons)[264] to call young people to obedience. They could serve a particular purpose in a period of unrest in the company.[265] But it was not only young people who were paraded in public, the symbolic representation of the politics of age was also ordered in cases of ill-treatment. The 'unnaturall and cruell dealinges' of David and Ann Evans towards their servant, Anne Hawkins, was punished in full public gaze in April 1582. The pair were 'stripped . . . naked from the gyrdle upwards and tyed to a cart's tayle' at Newgate, and whipped through the streets, stopping for maximum publicity at busy spots like Newgate Market, Cheapside, and Leadenhall. Hawkins was 'borne before them in a man's armes to th'end the people may see howe unreasonablye she hath bynne dealt withall', and proclamations were published at principal locations in the city ('and before theyre own dwelling house') 'declaringe thyre monstrous, cruell, and unnaturall dealings'. Both husband and wife were refused permission to 'keep any more apprentices', and Thomas Pigott was removed from their service 'for ever'.[266]

6. *The Pursuit of Household Stability*

The lessons of order were regularly articulated. In some cases it is clear that the authorities had to take firm steps to steady disordered households. Ian Archer has recently reminded us that London's governors had to *pursue* stability,[267] and one further scene of this drive for conformity was the household. Governors developed strategies to quash disorder in the many parts from which the political community was constructed; the household, the source of the neighbourhood, village, town, county, and civil society, and the nursery

who was 12 years of age and a hospital apprentice, ran away from his master and was found 'lying in the streates'. He was 'readmitted' to Christ's, but 'punished to th'example of the other children of this howse' (GL MS 12,806/2, fo. 165).

[263] GL MS 8200/1, fo. 25.   [264] See above, p. 45.
[265] See, for example, GL MS 5770/1, fos. 149–50; CH minute book 1558–81, fo. 133.
[266] CLRO Rep. 20, fo. 315.   [267] Archer, *Pursuit of Stability.*

of future generations. There was, therefore, a vital, formative age and domestic aspect to piety and politics. The politics of age was a domestic politics in meaning and setting. This is one reason why it is arguably a misrepresentation of contemporary mentalities and patterns of authority to dismiss household disorders as yet another 'trick of youth', or insignificant because they were few in number. Counting prosecutions is rather inappropriate in this particular case. The authorities produced well-defined strategies to counter domestic unrest; particular rhetorics and forms of intervention, arbitration, prosecution, and punishment. The forms of 'open' punishment were carefully scripted; the audience was not a random company, it was selected for a political purpose. None of these strategies belonged exclusively to the settlement of domestic disputes. But their character and form was often tailored to comply with the politics of age. We should not doubt that these disordered households mattered to contemporaries.

Nevertheless, we should also not exaggerate the extent of domestic strain, and produce these squabbles between masters and servants as typical experiences. It is risky to propose generalizations of this sort from judicial sources alone. Indeed, Graham Mayhew has recently reminded us that in early modern Rye 'relations between apprentices and their masters and mistresses seem to have been good'. Apprentices lived in 'a normal family'; only seven of them were dismissed at their master's request throughout Elizabeth's long reign, and there is only a single case of ill-treatment by a master in pre-1660 materials.[268] John Lilburne also spent his youth in a peaceful household in which he served Thomas Hewson 'as faithfully about six years as ever [an] apprentice served' a master. He recorded how 'many thousands of pounds' passed 'through my hands driving a large wholesale trade; yet directly or indirectly', he recalls

I cannot remember that ever I wronged him of a groat . . . or that ever all the time I was with him, I was ever branded or taxed with one base visible action; or that I ever gave or took a boxe on the eare, or anything like it, or ever quarelled with any flesh alive all the time I was there (although I had then as much mettle, life and spirit as most young men in London . . .)[269]

But how typical were Rye's stable master/servant relations and Lilburne's rosy account of his youth, which was written in later life for the sake of example and moralizing? The early modern

[268] Mayhew, 'Life-cycle, service and the family unit', 220–1.
[269] John Lilburne, *The Legall, Fundamentall Liberties of the People of England* (1649), 20–1.

household, as ever, resists simple generalization and characterization. But we can at least cast some light on its myriad complexities.

It has not been the sole purpose of this chapter to present the household as a disordered institution, but rather to illuminate the threat of disorder, its meaning, and context, and the responses of the authorities who valued the stable household as one starting-point for good order. There were a number of strategies for settling domestic disputes, and they could be modified to suit particular cases. Above all, it was a flexible system for easing household tensions; the principal authority figures had a degree of choice when proceeding against 'disorderly' servants and masters. They could arbitrate, apply pressure by threatening to remove both political and economic benefits, discharge servants without bringing a formal prosecution by breaking the contract with the master, or file a prosecution. Masters or servants (and their friends and relatives) could petition the authorities, they could even file complaints at the great equity courts. In the event of competing interpretations, the authorities often claimed to 'debate' and 'examine' both sides. In this sense proof and equity could suspend the natural hierarchy in disordered households while the dispute was in motion. But the authorities were often anxious to settle disputes within the structures of the guild or the community through arbitration or by cancelling the contract; formal prosecution at criminal law was often reserved for thoroughly outrageous abuses, or the unilateral tactics of a servant or master. But the authorities were reluctant to cancel indentures without first seeking to heal the wound by persuasion, entreaty, or menacing threats if necessary. In some well-documented cases it is clear that warring servants and masters were given time to seek common ground. It was usually persistent offenders who were ostracized, and in irreparable situations that young people were turned over to another master, or simply discharged. Uppermost in the minds of the authorities was the respectable identity and unity of the community and particular trades. It was hoped that disputes would be settled in local 'fraternities'; that the community would consist of well-ordered households; and that young people would be turned into worthy householders. For these reasons the failure of the authorities to soothe domestic tensions was a sign of weakness.

Yet in disorders which came to light the authorities often managed to preserve the contract between master and servant, or they concluded one relation to allow a servant to make a fresh start with a new master. But there was a potential for domestic tension which was noted by early modern people. Again, the authorities had often to pursue stability. A few historians reduce the significance of these troubled households in their hurry to attend to the routine aspects of the life-course and 'inevitable socialization'. One casualty of these institutional histories is the age of youth itself, which often loses agency. Young people did not always consent to the politics of age. The 'subversive' disobedience of the 'disorderly' young and the sense of time and sociability held by many of them provide windows to the 'double consciousness' of subordinates, who could mingle elements of conformity with opposition.[270] Alongside the happy tales of life-cyclical progress and social mobility (the Tudor Dick Whittingtons who parade through Rappaport's pages, for example), we must consider contemporary preoccupations, the high drop-out rate of apprentices, informal training, and these disordered households. The settlement of domestic disputes produced some interesting interpretations of authority. On occasion, the authorities took the side of the young underling; some young people testified against their master.[271]

Above all, it should be remembered that young people could carry some of their own preferences into adulthood, and also make their own judgements about the timing of maturity. A large number of them made a premature departure from service (and the process of socialization) to set up households and workshops. They clearly found it difficult to square confidence in their social and economic maturity with the inferior status of mere underlings. Other young plebeians also had a distant relationship with structures of service. They followed casual work, informal training, or made choices about when and where to enter service. It is now time to introduce a fourth characterization of early modern youth: 'masterless young people.' That is, young people who perhaps by choice, force of circumstance, or the arbitrary concerns and definitions of magistrates, were perceived to have contradicted conventional theories of work, time, and order by drifting in and out of service, remaining at home but 'out of service', wandering, or taking chambers on their own. The 'masterless' young often crossed the vague border which distinguished so-called conventional society from its attendant marginal fringe. They are the subject of the next chapter, which further explores the relations of young people with the world of formal service.

[270] The phrase is James C. Scott's (*Domination and the Arts of Resistance*, esp. p. 44).
[271] For example, NRO NMC 15, fos. 26ᵛ, 516ᵛ; 16, fo. 244ᵛ; CLRO Rep. 33, fos. 386–6ᵛ; GL MS 5770/2, fo. 148; BCB 3, fo. 13 Aug. 1578; 5, fos. 207ᵛ, 310ᵛ.

7

Masterless Young People

In June 1623 Jane Sellars was discovered idle on the streets of Norwich and promptly dispatched to the town's Bridewell to be put to work 'till she be reteyned in service'. This was the first in a long string of offences which was to give Sellars the rather dubious distinction of being one of the most prosecuted individuals in late Jacobean and early Caroline Norwich.[1] In April 1624 she was again found 'livinge idely' in the city. In Michaelmas 1625 Thomas Robinson of Yarmouth retained her for one year, but she broke her covenant and ran back to Norwich where the beadles discovered her 'vagrant' in April 1626. After the statutory whipping, the bench issued a pass and told her to return to Robinson, but Sellars never left Norwich and was back in Bridewell a few days later. At her discharge in August she was allowed two days to leave the city. Typically Sellars ignored the order, and was discovered 'vagrant and out of service' in October 1626, and was once again committed to Bridewell 'till she be reteyned in service'. She was probably discharged without such employment, however, for she was picked up idle in November 1626, and confined in Bridewell 'till further order'. In 1627 she ran away from two different masters, and in October found herself back inside the now familiar walls of Norwich Bridewell, where she also celebrated Christmas 1628. In November 1629 Sellars was whipped for 'ill rule' and 'michery' (petty theft)[2]—her first recorded theft. Her first appearance at City Quarter Sessions was in April 1630, when she was charged with stealing sundry items, including six pairs of stockings. By now she had an illegitimate child who was 'put' to a wife of St Swithin's parish in the following month. Eight months later Sellars was 'punished at the post' for 'lewdness and ill rule', and again prosecuted for 'ill rule' at the close of the same month. In April 1631 she was acquitted of petty larceny, and in August was returned

---

[1] This comment is based upon evidence from the surviving records of Norwich City Quarter Sessions and the Mayor's Court.

[2] A form of petty theft.

to Bridewell with Blanch Fryer (another regular young offender)[3] for begging. A few days later Sellars was branded for 'felony under x shillings'. She was discharged in October and promised the court that she would go 'forthwith to Yarmouth to gett... a service'. An entry in the Quarter Sessions minute book for December 1631 simply states, 'Jane Sellars to be executed'. This could refer to an outstanding action, or it may be a reference to a verdict reached elsewhere. Sellars makes no further appearances in any later Norwich city records. Perhaps she chose to remain in Yarmouth, or perhaps the limited patience of the civic magistrates had finally been exhausted, and the hangman's noose provided the final twist in an eight-year long tale in which Jane Sellars had proved to be a sharp thorn in the side of Norwich's civic body.[4]

Jane Sellars belonged to one of early modern England's marginal groups—the 'masterless' young. That is, young people who were *perceived* by those in places of authority to have stepped outside the well-marked boundaries of the normative socializing process by not being under the charge of an older householder, and who endured the perils of being labelled by governors as part of a definitional process of criminal regulation, which was intended to publish and punish their nonconformity with the politics of age. They were, therefore, masterless by definition, though occasionally by choice. The stigmatization of deviance is of course a common preoccupation of magistrates, and Howard Becker has commented that 'the attack of hierarchy begins with an attack of labels and conventional conceptions' of inclusion and exclusion.[5] Early modern people, for example, were expected to follow conventional patterns of authority, and to comply with a series of connected roles which were allocated according to age, gender, class, and work.[6] Marginality can be defined as a lack of participation, and the selected labelling of groups represents a collision between those in places of authority and the values of alleged deviants.[7] In this case, it appeared that some young people did not fully participate in formal service. By

---

[3] For Fryer see NRO NMC 16, fos. 118ᵛ, 153ᵛ, 188, 194, 218, 357ᵛ.

[4] Sellars's case history can be followed in NRO NMC 15, fos. 428ᵛ, 524; 16, fos. 88ᵛ, 89, 109, 115ᵛ, 120ᵛ, 137, 166, 221, 264ᵛ, 266, 280, 315ᵛ, 316, 357ᵛ, 363; NCQS 'The Sessions Booke 1630–38', fo. 55; minute book 1629–36, fos. 38ᵛ, 42ᵛ, 53.

[5] Howard Becker is quoted by Richard V. Ericson, *Criminal Reactions: The Labelling Perspective* (Farnborough, 1975), 112.

[6] Cf. Gino Germani, *Marginality* (New Brunswick, NJ, 1990), 50.

[7] Ibid. 54, 64–5; Daniel L. Potter and Julian B. Roebuck, 'The labelling approach re-examined: interactionism and the components of deviance', *Deviant Behaviour*, 9 (1988), 23–4, 27, 29; David Downes and Paul Rock, *Understanding Deviance: A Guide to the Sociology of Crime and Law Breaking* (2nd edn.; Oxford, 1988), 178–9; Paul Rock, 'The sociology of crime, symbolic interactionism and some problematic qualities of radical criminology', in

naming, publishing, and prosecuting deviance, governors seek to clarify the shape of the social order and its ordering principles, including age.[8] Contemporary governors were resolute nomenclators, and they disseminated an intimidating array of labels, which placed people who corrupted their ideas of law and order on the margins of society. Their opening stratagem was frequently to label unsavoury groups with a badge like 'lewd', 'idle', or 'vagrant', which advertised their conceptualizations and suspicions. The study of certain labels can tell us a great deal about the nature of age-relations in early modern society.

This chapter will explore the history of two labels, being 'out of service' and 'at their own hand', in a single city (Norwich) in the period 1560–1645. It seeks to explain what governors had in mind when they used such epithets to communicate their understanding of experiences which stirred suspicions. This social language drew attention to young people who appeared to have few points of contact with formal service. We must consider why suspicions were first aroused, and upon whom they fell. The first section of this chapter, therefore, attempts to construct an explanatory model for the study of 'masterless' young people, which incorporates the symbolic meaning of service—the typical experience of plebeian youth. Anxieties tend to fluctuate, they seldom proceed at a stream over a long period of time, but rise and fall in cycles which hamper linear readings. The timing of prosecutions for being 'out of service' and 'at their own hand' will be related to Norwich's changing socio-economic fortunes. Having introduced a problem and recovered a trend, later sections will explore the social milieu of 'masterless' young people, including gender, criminality, patterns of residence, and sociability, and finally, the responses of authority at a time of lingering socio-economic difficulty. But it is with the politics of service that we will begin.

1. *The Politics of Service (ii)*

Youth has been identified as a principal characteristic of marginal groups in former centuries as in our own.[9] Indeed, youth itself is in

---

David Downes and Paul Rock (eds.), *Deviant Interpretations* (Oxford, 1979), 69–70; Ericson, *Criminal Reactions*, 34, 38, 83, 95–6; Peter Burke, *Sociology and History* (1980), 58.

[8] Downes and Rock, *Understanding Deviance*, 150; Stephen Box, *Deviance, Reality and Society* (1971), 31, 39–41, 49.

[9] For example, by Bronislaw Geremek, *The Margins of Society in Late Medieval Paris*, trans. J. Birrell (Cambridge, 1987), esp. 121, 286, 288.

some respects a marginal stage of life, an age in which people were being prepared for participation in adult society; a 'dark' age which had to be steered towards a virtuous course.[10] Parental responsibility, full participation in a trade, and the growth of wisdom and maturity provided a series of stages by which people passed into full independent adulthood from the 'wilderness' years of youth.[11] It will be clear by now that the age of youth was a stage of life in which it was hoped that people would adjust to fresh rhythms of time and work. But the unpredictable temper of youth often upset the politics of age, and induced a series of generational collisions which were sometimes referred to the courtroom.

Squabbles about time, work, and order helped to raise the spectre of 'masterless' young people. Perceptions of youthful independence naturally derived from contemporary notions of what young people were thought to be evading. Most of them spent the greater part of their youth in some form of service. The urge to craft good citizens and Christians in this time of service was one political impulse of a society in which age was a further principle of authority. Young people, therefore, were pushed into service. Structured work (and time) promised one solution to the threat of youthful disorder. It was claimed that 'the bringing up of apprentices of both sexes' was 'very profitable in the commonwealth and acceptable and pleasing to almightie God'. The smooth running of service would reduce the number of executions and the 'multitude of enormities' and sins.[12] The idea that structured work could be provided both by service and bridewells was given a statutory footing in 1576, so that 'youth may be accustomed and brought up in labour and work, and then not like to grow to be idle rogues'.[13] It was hoped that these two institutions would tame the natural energy of youth and channel it towards productive purposes. Thus residents of Norwich who were prosecuted as vagrants, scolds, or filchers,[14] or who were discovered 'out of service' or 'idle', were sometimes presented with the option of a spell in Bridewell or entering service.[15] Magistrates naturally related service to tranquillity and good order. In their reply to the Privy Council's inquiry about the impact of the Book of Orders

---

[10] See above, Chs. 1–2.   [11] Cf. Box, *Deviance*, 146.

[12] 7 Jac. I c. 3; John Rushworth (ed.), *Historical Collections* (8 vols.; 1721), ii. 358.

[13] 18 Eliz. I c. 3. Cf. Tim Hitchcock, 'Paupers and preachers: the SPCK and the parochial workhouse movement', in L. Davison *et al.* (eds.), *Stilling the Grumbling Hive: The Response to Social and Economic Problems in England 1689–1750* (Stroud, 1992).

[14] Another form of petty theft.

[15] For example, NRO NMC 7, fo. 510; 8, fo. 503; 9, fos. 3, 41, 43, 94, 211; 10, fo. 534; 11, fos. 19, 127, 181; 13, fos. 167ᵛ, 568–9.

(1631), the Essex justices reported that pressuring young people to enter service 'doth exceedingly prevent both disorders and poverty'.[16] Thus the failure to implement effectively a policy of regular service was often felt to be a principal source of disorder. In a petition of the 1630s the Sheffield gentry argued that the meaning of the Poor Law of 1601 'was not for the education of boys in arts but for charity to keep ym and relieve ym from turning to roguery and idleness'.[17] Governors in turn aspired to keep a careful check on the quality of masters. In Norwich, it was ordered that nobody was to take people into service, 'unles he or she bee able and shall kcpc and bring upp' servants 'honestly without begging'.[18] This concern with order held that outside the regulatory reach of competent adults, young people easily if not naturally slipped into disorder and began the fatal descent to the hanging tree.

The language coined by contemporaries to label youthful independence expressed the disciplinary aspects of service. Young people who strayed outside the political compass of adult regulation were said to be 'masterless', sometimes 'vagrant', 'out of service', or 'at their own hand'.[19] Such titles had a strategically vague character; a spectrum of possible meaning to satisfy magisterial sentiment, individual biography, occasion, and circumstance. They belonged to a highly manipulative vocabulary which articulated in clear and easy terms suspicions which were the very nerve-end of conventional theories of authority. This social language should be approached with care because it is age-related rather than age-specific. In fact, service could imply any form of work and was not the exclusive property of youth, so that being 'out of service' could simply mean being 'out of work'.[20] In the Norwich Census of the Poor (1570), however, the language used to depict 129 cases of adult unemployment does not feature service—the preferred terms being 'work' in 115 cases (89.2 per cent), and 'occupation' in thirteen others.[21] In

[16] Quoted by William Hunt, *The Puritan Moment: The Coming of Revolution in an English County* (Cambridge, Mass., 1983), 250.

[17] Quoted by I. Pinchbeck and M. Hewitt, *Children in English Society*, i: *From Tudor Times to the Eighteenth Century* (1969), 235.

[18] NRO NAM iv, fo. 139ᵛ. Cf. E. M. Leonard, *The Early History of English Poor Relief* (1965), 244.

[19] In Italy young female migrants were described as being 'out of place'. See Sherrill Cohen, *The Evolution of Women's Asylums since 1500: From Refuges for Ex-prostitutes to Shelters for Battered Wives* (New York, 1992), 62, 79.

[20] Cf. K. S. Martin (introd.), *Records of Maidstone Being Selections from Documents in the Possession of the Corporation* (Maidstone, 1926), 23.

[21] The source is J. F. Pound (ed.), *The Norwich Census of the Poor 1570* (Norfolk Record Society, 40, Norwich, 1971).

contrast, when the clerk of the Mayor's Court bothered to record ages in cases of being 'out of service' or 'at their own hand' they all fell within the 14–26 age-range. On a further sixty-five occasions offenders were given a significant age-title, and they all infer youth— 'servant', 'singlewoman', 'daughter', 'son', 'wench', 'lad', and 'maid'. Service was not age-specific, though it was clearly age-related in this period.[22]

In resorting to such language contemporaries had in mind a good deal more than the regulation of labour-supply and wages which has received most coverage in discussions of the legislation governing service.[23] William Hunt has commented that cases of 'being out of service' in Essex were brought by parishes concerned to push young people into service to produce a steady stream of labour, and to help in the task of 'fairly allocating scarce employment'.[24] The governors of Norwich also pursued such strategies, but to contain interpretation within an economic straitjacket is to seriously misread contemporary mentalities. It should be remembered that the Statute of Artificers of 1563, which remained on the statute books until 1814, was also intended to curb the 'licentious manner of youth'.[25] Political and economic concerns were woven in an explanatory framework. Parishes were concerned that young people 'out of service' would prove 'burdensome' *and* 'dangerous'. They would only be raised in 'idleness and disordered kynde of lyfe to their utter overthrow and to the great prejudice of the whole commonwealth'.[26] Work was a moral as well as an occupational category, and governors treated limited participation in service as

[22] The ages of offenders are as follows: age 15/1 example, 16/2, 17/1, 18/1, 19/3, 21/1, 24/1, 26/1. Cf. Michael Roberts, ' "Words they are women and deeds they are men": images of work and gender in early modern England', and Susan Wright, ' "Churmaids, huswyfes and hucksters": the employment of women in Tudor and Stuart Salisbury', both of which can be found in Lindsey Charles and Lorna Duffin (eds.), *Women and Work in Pre-industrial England* (1985), esp. 157–8, The distribution of significant age-titles in the Norwich records is as follows—daughter, 34 cases; single woman, 17; wench, 4; servant, 3; young woman and son, 2 each; maid, lad, servingman, 1 each.

[23] For example, Donald Woodward, 'The background to the statute of artificers: the genesis of labour policy 1558–1563', *Economic History Review*, 2nd ser., 33 (1980).

[24] Hunt, *Puritan Moment*, 65.

[25] See R. Tawney and E. Power (eds.), *Tudor Economic Documents* (3 vols.; 1924), iii. 363, 345, 356.

[26] 7 Jac. I c. 3; B. H. Cunnington (ed.), *Some Annals of the Borough of Devizes* (Devizes, 1925), 83. Cf. the fears expressed by the Wiltshire bench in 1655, discussed by Anthony Fletcher in his *Reform in the Provinces: The Government of Stuart England* (1986), 220. Joanna Innes comments that cases of being 'out of service' were part of a dual concern 'to keep wages down' and to assert patriarchal authority ('Prisons for the poor: English bridewells 1555–1800', in Francis Snyder and Douglas Hay (eds.), *Labour, Law and Crime: A Historical Perspective* (1987), 48).

evidence of immorality and even resistance. A young life spent drifting in and out of service, therefore, was interpreted not only as an absence of subordination to appointed authority, but also as a competing form of socialization; a shocking opportunity to claim independence and display invention.[27]

'At their own hand' is also a term with several meanings, but the common thread is again political and economic independence, which permits us to treat both terms in the same interpretation. (Maidstone's élite related the policing of 'out of service' and 'at their own hand' to 'good government'.[28]) It implied working alone outside the reach of regulatory institutions,[29] and a freedom to impose ideas about the quality of product and fair wages.[30] But on occasion it certainly meant much more than this. 'At their own hand' also incorporated a chosen course of life; gaining a living in an untutored and by extension probably improper way. Most offenders in the Norwich records are said to be *living* rather than working 'at their own hand', though the two meanings naturally inform each other. Consider this episode from Manchester in April 1584 when the Leet Jury complained that

whereas gret unconvenyence ys in this town in that senglewomen being unmarried be at ther owne hands and doe bake and brewe and use other trades to the great hurte of the poore inhabitants havinge wieffe and children. As also in abusing themselves with younge men and others *havinge not anny man to controle them* to the gret dishonor of God and evell ensample of others. In consideraccon whereof [the jury ordered] ... that noe senglewomen unmaried shalbe at ther owne hands, or keepe any house or chamber within this towne [emphasis mine].

This order was reissued in 1589 and on at least one other later date.[31] Dubious conduct was tied to the fair allocation of scarce structured work, and common to both was the uneasy state of independence. In London, women who were discovered 'out of service' and suspicious were sometimes 'searched' by the matron of Bridewell to check if they were a 'maid' or 'noe maid', 'light' or

[27] Including the opportunity to pursue 'alternative sources of income' (Roberts, '"Words they are women"', 157).

[28] Martin, *Records of Maidstone*, 123, 72.

[29] Moll Flanders is described as being 'at her fingers ends' (Roberts, '"Words they are women"', 157).

[30] Cf. NRO NAM iv, fo. 139.

[31] J. P. Earwaker (ed.), *The Court Leet Records of the Manor of Manchester from 1552 to 1686* (6 vols.; Manchester, 1884–90), i. 241; ii. 37, 43.

'otherwise', yet another indication of the coupling of work and 'honest' behaviour in early modern minds.[32]

Work, then, was a moral category. It was, however, gendered also,[33] and one further dimension of these cases must be emphasized. While they were not gender-specific they were certainly gender-related. Of the 263 cases of being 'out of service', 212 involved women (80 per cent). Cases of being 'at their own hand' were entirely gender-specific before as late as 1632 when the only male was prosecuted. Sixty-one of the sixty-two cases concerned women (98.4 per cent). We have a series of arrests which are clearly related to issues of gender. In 84 per cent of prosecutions it was women who appeared before the Mayor's Court. This gender bias was less sharp before 1600,[34] though it was striking in the 1600s, and most visible in periods which witnessed peaks in the number of arrests like 1609–11 when fifty-one of fifty-six cases involved women. It sprang from ideas which closely associated structured work with order, purity, and honesty, and casual work or unemployment with their opposites, confusion, corruption, and pollution.

This contrast affected the lives of both sexes but not in equal measure, and in Norwich *c.*1560–1645 it was singlewomen and female servants who suffered the accusations of the authorities in far greater numbers. They attracted a great deal of speculation about their reputation and character.[35] Merry Wiesner has recently argued that the figure of the independent woman was a potent symbol of disorder at a time when religious reformers were placing much greater emphasis upon the authority of husbands, parents, and masters, and describing marriage as a 'natural' state for women. Moreover, 'the early modern period was a time of increasing suspicion of masterless persons', and 'the most mistrusted' group were 'unmarried women working and living on their own'. Wiesner also suggests that such problems were more visible in the towns.[36] Cases of being 'out of service' and 'at their own hand' in Norwich clearly imply that the problem of youth in urban society had particular

---

[32] For example, BCB 4, fos. 348ᵛ, 349, 356, 386ᵛ; 5, fos. 118, 130, 385ᵛ.

[33] Cf. Michael Roberts, 'Women and work in sixteenth-century English towns', in P. J. Corfield and D. Keene (eds.), *Work in Towns 850–1850* (1990).

[34] In this period eight of the twenty-three cases (23.8 per cent) involved males.

[35] Cf. Geremek, *Margins of Society*, 221 (singlewomen of the 'popular and plebeian classes' who lived 'outside the context of the family' were often suspected of immorality); E. P. Thompson, 'Rough music', in his *Customs in Common* (1991), esp. 501; P. J. P. Goldberg, *Women, Work and Life-Cycle in a Medieval Economy: Women in York and Yorkshire c.1300–1520* (Oxford, 1992), esp. 299–300; Cohen, *Evolution of Women's Asylums*, 62, 79.

[36] Merry E. Wiesner, *Women and Gender in Early Modern Europe* (Cambridge, 1993), 62, 23, 99, 62, 89. Cf. Goldberg, *Women, Work and Life-Cycle*, 299.

gendered aspects regarding conceptualizations of work, character, and criminality.

These epithets were usually reserved for young *residents* of Norwich; *outsiders* were more likely to be punished as vagrants, though this was not a completely tidy distinction. Young outsiders, however, were an imported problem, and the responsibility for their reintegration belonged to another community. They were, therefore, whipped and handed a pass to send them on their homeward passage.[37] Yet both residents and outsiders were suspect because of their 'masterless' condition. They belonged to a subgroup of youth which was felt to present a distinctive problem. The social language of being 'out of service' and 'at their own hand' belonged to a pliable vocabulary of social discipline which was coined to conceptualize a number of social situations in which the principal characters were characteristically young. Moving with apparent ease across the border dividing Norwich from the nearby countryside and conventional society from its marginal fringe, 'masterless' young people inhabited a shady quarter of urban society which has been little penetrated by historians hitherto. We will follow this group in the records of the Mayor's Court (the principal court for the regulation of daily life and petty disorders in Norwich),[38] and try to sketch the rough contours of their world. We will also follow them through time, and the next section will trace the rate of prosecution of cases of being 'out of service' and 'at their own hand'.

2. *Masterless Young People, 1560–1645*

Young people living 'out of service', 'at their own hand', or 'vagrant' were a perennial source of concern in the period 1500–1700, but these problems were sharper in particular years and places. One interesting aspect of the rate of prosecution in Norwich is its changing frequency. Prosecutions proceeded at a trickle, but

[37] However, there are some examples of outsiders being presented. The residential pattern in 325 cases is as follows—285 offenders can be positively identified as Norwich residents (87.7 per cent), twenty-five were outsiders (7.6 per cent), while a further fifteen cannot be positively placed. In turn the resident young were sometimes labelled as 'vagrants': for example, NRO NMC 13, fo. 387; 14, fos. 46, 183, 268ᵛ.

[38] The operation and character of the Mayor's Court is examined in greater detail in J. F. Pound, *Tudor and Stuart Norwich* (Chichester, 1988), ch. 9; John T. Evans, *Seventeenth-Century Norwich: Politics, Religion and Government 1620–1690* (Oxford, 1979), esp. 58–9, 85. The City Quarter Sessions were used less frequently for these sort of petty disorders, though as we shall see a few 'masterless' youth were prosecuted there.

gathered pace and became a stream in certain periods. The timing
of cases is one guide to the falling and rising concern with 'masterless' youth in governing circles. There were periods of relative tranquillity and greater tolerance, and other more anxious moments
when unease was elevated to a pitch which could only be resolved
by arrests. Attaching labels to alleged crime is not a casual or mercurial exercise, but a calculated process of monitoring with specific
contexts and concerns. We can trace the fortunes of Norwich to
examine the situations in which the problems raised by 'masterless'
young people became more visible in the sources.

The turn of the seventeenth century was a time of socio-economic
difficulty, one highly visible consequence of which was a rising tide
of vagrants, most of whom were young people in their teens and
twenties.[39] Service was as vulnerable as any other institution (including the family) to the harmful effects of rising population,
unemployment, inflation, land shortages, deeper poverty, and the
keen instinct to safeguard present employment. Justices in early
seventeenth-century Wiltshire, for example, 'expressed alarm at the
growing number of masters . . . who refused to take apprentices
bound to them by the parish authorities', or who 'abandoned . . .
apprentices in the midst of training'. Debt and poverty had a prominent part to play in the economy of service.[40] Two principal, potential problems interfered with the smooth running of service at this
time. First, it was more difficult to gain entry into service. Second,
master/servant relations were rather more fragile. Peter Clark has
commented that masters were 'unable to cope in periods of rising
population and mounting unemployment'.[41] Young people who
encountered difficulties in obtaining a foothold in service raised
problems for the authorities. The age-structure of the population
in this period tipped towards the young, and Beier has suggested
that a result of the coincidence of this demographic condition with
socio-economic strain, despite high levels of infant and child

---

[39] See A. L. Beier, 'Vagrants and the social order in Elizabethan England', *Past and Present*,
64 (1974), esp. 9–10; Paul Slack, 'Vagrants and vagrancy in England 1589–1664', in Peter
Clark and David Souden (eds.), *Migration and Society in Early Modern England* (1987), esp. 54;
Ilana Krausman Ben-Amos, *Adolescence and Youth in Early Modern England* (New Haven, 1994),
chs. 2–4. Cf. Goldberg, *Women, Work and Life-Cycle*, esp. 282, 292, 294.

[40] A. Salerno, 'The social background of seventeenth-century emigration to America',
Journal of British Studies, 19 (1979), esp. 38. The difficulties in placing parish apprentices can
be partly followed in State Papers. See, for example, PRO SP 16/239/6; 16/240/35; 16/
250/2; 16/250/10; 16/259/15; 16/266/72. See also Paul Slack, *Poverty and Policy in Tudor
and Stuart England* (1988), 142; T. G. Barnes, *Somerset 1625–1640: A County's Government
during the 'Personal Rule'* (1961), esp. 200; Fletcher, *Reform in the Provinces*, 216.

[41] Peter Clark, *The English Alehouse: A Social History, 1200–1830* (1983), 139.

mortality, was that 'the problem of great numbers of unproductive youngsters was greatly intensified'.[42] One response to a lack of opportunity at home was to move in search of service. Indeed, Salerno has discovered that many Wiltshire people who crossed the ocean to the New World were recently 'out of service'. More generally, a majority of emigrants were male, single, and young.[43] However, most displaced young people kept their feet on English soil, and they joined in the drift to the towns and wood-pasture regions.

All of this may have resulted in problems of absorption in some English towns.[44] A number of historians and criminologists tell us that most 'complex' societies possess marginal fringes inhabited by shadowy figures such as vagrants, alleged criminals, casual workers, and others who were drawn to the towns.[45] Tudor and Stuart England was no exception, though historians have been rather reluctant to descend to these urban basements hitherto, and explore patterns of work and criminality in the less penetrable quarters of teeming towns like London or Norwich. The nature of urban society at this time is, of course, a much debated question. The impact of high levels of in-migration upon order and criminality, for example, has stirred a great deal of discussion.[46] Much recent scholarship has stressed the basic stability of urban society,[47] though some contributions draw attention to the strategies by which civic rulers vigorously pursued stability.[48] A number of these studies have arguably relied too much on evidence relating to the more stable and integrated

[42] A. L. Beier, *Masterless Men: The Vagrancy Problem in England 1560–1640* (1985), 20. See also the complaints from thirteen Norfolk hundreds and the market towns of Hertfordshire in 1638 which are quoted ibid. 47, 55.

[43] Salerno, 'Social background of seventeenth-century emigration', esp. 38. Cf. David Souden, 'Rogues, whores and vagabonds? Indentured servant emigration to North America, and the case of mid-seventeenth-century Bristol', *Social History*, 3 (1978), esp. 27; Beier, *Masterless Men*, 161–3; David Cressy, *Coming Over: Migration and Communication between England and New England in the Seventeenth Century* (Cambridge, 1987), 63, 68.

[44] Cf. Beier, *Masterless Men*, 39–40.

[45] For example, Geremek, *Margins of Society*, 6; Germani, *Marginality*; Howard Becker, *Outsiders: Studies in the Sociology of Deviance* (New York, 1973); Gervase Rosser, *Medieval Westminster 1200–1540* (Oxford, 1989), esp. 217–21; Beier, *Masterless Men*, esp. ch. 3.

[46] The best recent summary of research is in D. M. Palliser, *The Age of Elizabeth: England under the Late Tudors 1547–1603* (2nd edn.; 1992), ch. 7. See also Jonathan Barry, 'Introduction', in Barry (ed.), *The Tudor and Stuart Town: A Reader in English Urban History, 1530–1688* (Harlow, 1990).

[47] For example, Valerie Pearl, 'Change and stability in seventeenth-century London', in Barry (ed.), *The Tudor and Stuart Town*; Steve Rappaport, *Worlds within Worlds: Structures of Life in Sixteenth-Century London* (Cambridge, 1989); Jeremy Boulton, *Neighbourhood and Society: A London Suburb in the Seventeenth Century* (Cambridge, 1987).

[48] See Ian W. Archer, *The Pursuit of Stability: Social Relations in Elizabethan London* (Cambridge, 1991); Peter Clark, 'A crisis contained? The condition of English towns in the 1590s', in Clark (ed.), *The European Crisis of the 1590s* (1985).

sections of urban life, thereby focusing disproportionately upon more functional aspects of urban experiences, including social mobility, poor relief, neighbourhood, guilds, office-holding, and the life-course.

Yet a surface gloss of stability should not disguise 'dysfunctional' aspects of urban society. A more 'rounded' interpretation would investigate the social milieux of 'criminal' groups and their points of contact with more 'orthodox' occupational, political, and residential structures. Much can be gleaned about rhetorics of civic order in encounters between élite typecasters and labelled criminals. This study does not seek to elevate disorder at the expense of institutions and officers charged with the task of pursuing stability. I simply hope to draw attention to a neglected dimension of urban society—'masterless' youth—which is difficult to accommodate within the tidy interpretative models proposed by Pearl and Rappaport, for example, in which alleged social equalizers such as poor relief or social mobility rendered the majority of urban residents patient and even content in the slender comfort of present relief or the contemplation of future aspirations. A more complete view of urban society would incorporate such fatalism and dreaming, but also other people and groups who whether by choice or force of circumstance found themselves, if only for a short time, at the margins of society.

In addition, the drift to the towns where subordinate groups may have had greater freedom[49] was in large part a movement of youth.[50] Poverty and crime were more clustered (and visible) in the bustling townscape, and a contemporary perception made the connection between rising levels of theft and troops of 'idle and suspicious' vagrants.[51] As we have seen, the problems raised by petty crime were often attributed to shifting youth and pilfering servants.[52] Some historians have noted the over-representation of young people among those accused of property offences.[53] Young migrants would

[49] Cf. J. M. Beattie, *Crime and the Courts in England 1660–1800* (Oxford 1986), 242; Mary Elizabeth Perry, *Crime and Society in Early Modern Seville* (Hanover, NH, 1980), esp. 166, 190, 194, 203.

[50] The high number of young people amongst those prosecuted for vagrancy in Norwich is discussed in the following paragraphs.

[51] For some London examples see CLRO Jours. 25, fos. 139–40, 201–2; 26, fos. 266ᵛ, 297ᵛ; 27, fos. 19, 212ᵛ.

[52] See above, esp. pp. 335–6.

[53] See esp. Beattie, *Crime and the Courts*, 243–7; Peter King, 'Decision makers and decision making in the English criminal law 1750–1800', *Historical Journal* (1984), esp. 34–42; Arlette Farge, *Fragile Lives: Violence, Power and Solidarity in Eighteenth-century Paris*, trans. Carol Shelton (Oxford, 1993), 144–5.

have found greater opportunities for both lawful and illicit spoils in urban society, and a greater concentration of youth. Not only did service create problems of household discipline,[54] the 'pull' of service also mustered a wave of migrants, some of whom were less successfully integrated into the urban economy and political structure.

A 75 per cent rise in Norwich's population in the period 1580–1620 is directly attributable to the quickening pace of in-migration.[55] John Patten has commented that 'the years between 1500 and 1700 were a time of great stability for East Anglian towns'. There were 'no major social disruptions' and 'no urban disasters'.[56] It is true that despite the best efforts of Robert Kett the city's walls never came tumbling down, but Patten's interpretation of urban disorder —disasters and major disruptions—is misleading and exaggerated because it neglects more commonplace aspects of the problem of order, including petty crime, which were a persistent nuisance. Norwich's rulers had to wrestle daily with questions of law and order, and we can also identify periods when stability appeared to be under greater threat.

Historians of urban 'crisis' tend to channel their energies into the 1590s. Norwich had its problems in that decade, though one sensitive indication of urban anxieties, vagrancy prosecutions, draws attention to the period 1615–30 as a time of strain. Figure 7.1 presents figures for the number of vagrants brought before the Mayor's Court in the period 1581–1645 who were *not* residents of the city. The timing of prosecutions is marked by peaks in 1600–1, 1609–11, 1615–17, and 1622–3. The fall in numbers after 1623 is still distinguished by notable increases in 1630–1 and 1634–6. In Norwich, as elsewhere, vagrants were characteristically young. In the period 1595–1609 72 per cent of arrested vagrants were under 21, and 52 per cent were under 16 years of age.[57] Young people took to the road for many reasons, though in most cases the principal concern was that they had fled from a master or parent. The chance to find a service, to beg, hide, or steal, carried young East Anglians to their regional capital. Either on the road or at large in the city, they were perceived to be beyond the political compass of appointed authority.

[54] See above, Ch. 6.
[55] Penelope Corfield, 'A provincial capital in the late seventeenth century: the case of Norwich', in Peter Clark and Paul Slack (eds.), *Crisis and Order in English Towns 1500–1700: Essays in Urban History* (1972), esp. 132; Evans, *Seventeenth-Century Norwich*, 4–5.
[56] John Patten, *English Towns 1500–1700* (Folkestone, 1978), 294–5.
[57] Beier, *Masterless Men*, 54.

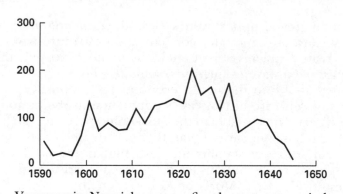

FIG. 7.1   Vagrancy in Norwich, 1590–1645 by two-year periods

Note: The sources are NRO NMC 11–16, and 20. I have excluded people who were expelled without being prosecuted for vagrancy. Banishment was imposed upon residents, but we can be sure that an unknown number of outsiders are within their ranks. However, the trends presented here would remain the same if we included the banished people.

This first group of *immigrant* 'masterless' young people were joined by a second, consisting of young *residents* of Norwich who were discovered vagrant, being 'out of service', or 'at their own hand'. Here the accusation of independence turned on the correspondence between service and the control of work and youth. Three groups of residents were targeted by governors—children or servants who ran away from a parent or master; others who remained at home, but 'out of service' with a master (a contemporary perception related idleness to young people who chose to remain at home rather than enter service);[58] and young people who had independently taken lodgings. These groups of migrant and resident 'masterless' youth converged in time. Cases of being 'out of service' and 'at their own hand' among residents peak in much the same years that witnessed rises in vagrancy prosecutions. The combined totals for the first two offences are presented in Figure 7.2. Prosecutions peak in the 1630s, though the timing of cases is again distinguished by prominent clustering. The problem of independence among young residents was most acute in years of rising vagrancy like 1609–11, 1630–1, and 1634–6, when 134 of the 313 recorded cases of

[58] See William Gouge, *Of Domesticall Duties* (1622), 535; Hugh Cunningham, 'The employment and unemployment of children in England *c.*1680–1851', *Past and Present*, 126 (1990), esp. 126. Merry Wiesner has commented that 'Authorities at times even tried to prevent grown daughters from continuing to live with their parents, arguing that parents gave them too much freedom which caused "nothing but shame, immodesty, wantonness and immorality", with their idleness leading to "tearing hedges, robbing orchards, beggaring their fathers"' (*Women and Gender in Early Modern Europe*, 99).

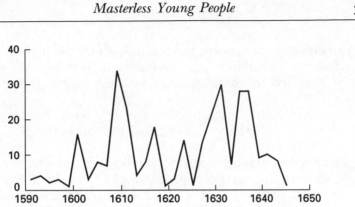

FIG. 7.2 'Out of service' and 'at their own hand' in Norwich, 1590–1645 by two-year periods

Note: The sources are NRO NMC 12–16 and 20. In total, 313 cases were prosecuted—cases of being 'at their own hand' number 61, and 'out of service' 252. The timing of prosecutions of both offences follows the same pattern. See Paul Griffiths, 'Some Aspects of the Social History of Youth in Early Modern England' (University of Cambridge Ph.D thesis, 1992), 353, table 6.3.

being 'out of service' and 'at their own hand' in the period 1590–1645 (42.8 per cent) were prosecuted.[59] Lesser peaks in 1600, 1617, 1623, 1626, and 1628 also coincided with rises in the numbers of vagrants arrested in the city.

Cases of being 'out of service' and 'at their own hand' were not confined to the years after 1590. There were eleven prosecutions in the period 1560–89. This language was by no means chronologically specific, though it was rarely heard before 1600. There were six more cases in the single year 1609 than in the forty-year period 1560–99. In contrast, the expression 'at their own hand' belonged to the turn of the century. The first case in the city sources was in December 1599.[60] The turn of the century witnessed a sharp intensification of the gender bias, and the appearance of a language of social discipline which was age-related and first coined to describe an exclusively female social situation—'at their own hand'. These expressions were not the exclusive property of Norwich's élite. They were heard at different times in different places.[61] But in this East

[59] The distribution of cases in these periods is as follows—1600–11, 56; 1630–1, 30; and 1634–6, 48.
[60] NRO NMC 13, fo. 387.
[61] For example, at the parish vestries of Finchingfield and Braintree in Essex, F. G. Emmison (ed.), *Early Essex Town Meetings: Braintree 1619–1636, Finchingfield 1626–1634* (Chichester, 1970), esp. 9, 15, 23–4, 46, 57–8, 63, 65, 78, 92, 115–16, 22, 126; in Maidstone, Martin, *Records of Maidstone*, 23, 72; Dorchester, David Underdown, *Fire from Heaven: Life in an English Town in the Seventeenth Century* (1992), 82; Bedworth in Warwickshire, S. C. Ratcliff and H.

Anglian city the 1600s mark the point at which the problems raised by youthful independence and especially female independence could only be resolved by going to court with much greater regularity.

3. Policy, Policing, and Punishment

Life in early seventeenth-century Norwich was punctuated by campaigns against 'masterless' young people, part of a far broader concern with morality and social discipline, which included the policing of alehouses, deeper poverty, begging, and inmates.[62] The Mayor's Court steered these drives against unshackled youth. It was here that strategies were discussed, beadles and marshals were appointed, and powers of search granted to aldermen in their wards. Policy usually took the form of round-ups of pairs or small groups of 'masterless' youth, who were either discovered pacing the streets with no particular place to go, or at home 'out of service'. In March/May 1601, for example, searches turned up a pack of young residents who were found begging on the streets, and they were sent in to Bridewell at much the same time as the Mayor's Court expelled a number of young vagrants who had tramped to the city.[63] We know that migrants were usually whipped and returned home. In some cases the authorities ordered that a beadle,[64] parent, or

C. Johnson (eds.), *Warwick County Records* (9 vols.; Warwick, 1935–64), v. 212, 217; Manchester, see above, p. 357; and London—for example, BCB 4, fos. 153, 186, 278, 312ᵛ, 320, 348ᵛ, 349, 356, 363, 370, 374; 5, fos. 61ᵛ, 80, 111, 118, 130, 168ᵛ, 308ᵛ; CLRO Jours. 29, fo. 20ᵛ; 32, fo. 319; Rep. 34, fo. 288. Cf. Roberts, ' "Words they are women" ', 157 ff.; Roger Thompson, *Sex in Middlesex: Popular Mores in a Massachusetts County, 1649–1699* (Amherst, Mass., 1986), 89, 91–2; id., 'Adolescent culture in colonial Massachusetts', *Journal of Family History*, 9 (1984), 127–44, esp. 134. Interestingly, the gender bias is equally pronounced in these dispersed locations. Forty-one of the fifty-three Bedworth cases (77.4 per cent), and twenty-six of the thirty-four Braintree and Finchingfield cases (76.5 per cent) involved women. At the court of London Bridewell 87.7 per cent of offenders in the period 1617–42 were women. The tensions under review here also affected late medieval towns. See M. D. Harris (ed.), *The Coventry Leet Book* (Early English Text Society, numbered in original series 134–5, 138, 146, 1907–13), 545, 568. The court did not refer directly to being 'at their own hand' or 'out of service', but a 1492 order ruled that 'no senglewomen . . . within the age of l yeres' should keep a house or chambers by themselves or lodge with 'eny other persones', but that they 'go to service till they be married'. In 1495 the order was significantly amended, and single-women were allowed to take chambers with 'honest persones' who were prepared to answer for their lodgers' 'good demeasnyng', or else they would be put in service.

[62] See NRO NMC 13, fo. 177; 14, fos. 256ᵛ–7ᵛ, 257–9; 16, fos. 291, 314ᵛ, 316, 317; 20, fos. 9, 11–11ᵛ, 32–2ᵛ, 132.

[63] For example, NRO NMC 13, fos. 568–71, 572–82. For other examples of action against the 'masterless' young see NMC 14, fos. 246–50ᵛ, 256ᵛ–7ᵛ, 257–9, 268–8ᵛ, 278–82ᵛ; 16, fos. 278, 287ᵛ, 301ᵛ, 316ᵛ; 20, fos. 17ᵛ–18, 118, 133–3ᵛ.

[64] For example, NRO NMC 15, fos. 293ᵛ, 409, 450ᵛ; 16, fos. 275, 276ᵛ, 294ᵛ.

master,[65] should escort them. Edward Burges was returned to Yarmouth by a craftsman 'who hath occasion to goe to Yarmouth'.[66] One London master tracked his apprentice to Norwich, though he is a solitary example of an amateur sleuth.[67] Young residents were invited to choose between a spell in Bridewell or a fixed period in which to find a service. In these cases magistrates hoped that the fear of Bridewell with its dark cells and tough labour discipline would be sufficient to frighten them into finding a master. In thirty-seven of the seventy-eight cases for which we possess information (47.4 per cent), the time allowed to find a place in service was two weeks, in thirty-two others it was one week (41 per cent). Other young people were permitted ten days (two cases), three weeks (two cases), one month (four cases), and two months (a single case).[68]

The records reveal very little about how these young people were expected to find work in service, and the few snapshots we possess disappointingly identify the individual rather than the precise method. In a few cases responsibility rested with a parent—the mother in eight cases[69] and father in four.[70] Nor was the bench slow to introduce the threat of committal proceedings against wavering parents.[71] But in the majority of cases in which young people were not ferried to Bridewell, the records simply report that the court ordered them to find a place in service.[72] Overseers and justices occasionally intervened, though their role is again obscured by the bare information recorded in the courtbooks. In 1634, for example, Cecily Robinson being 'out of service', was told either to stay in Bridewell 'or be reteyned in service before some justice of the peace of this citty', and in November 1600 one Frances Key was ordered to be 'put to service by the overseers'.[73]

In most cases, however, offenders were not permitted the liberty of remaining at home to obtain employment, and rather than rely upon mere fear the court issued a committal order. The typical sequence of events in these proceedings, as in the case of Martha Johnson, who was alleged to be of 'lewde life' and was found

---

[65] For example, NRO NMC 15, fos. 32ᵛ, 250ᵛ; 16, fos. 188, 193ᵛ, 407ᵛ; 20, fo. 138.
[66] NRO NMC 15, fo. 247ᵛ.   [67] NRO NMC 15, fo. 332.
[68] Cf. Innes, 'Prisons for the poor', esp. 105–6.
[69] NRO NMC 8, fo. 193; 15, fo. 22ᵛ; 16, fo. 211; 20, fos. 9ᵛ, 17ᵛ, 22, 279ᵛ, 488.
[70] NRO NMC 15, fos. 84, 489; 20, fos. 12ᵛ, 322.
[71] For example, NRO NMC 20, fos. 17ᵛ, 22.
[72] For example, NRO NMC 13, fos. 516, 523, 533, 582, 589; 14, fo. 179ᵛ; 15, fos. 80, 312ᵛ, 324ᵛ, 351; 20, fos. 279ᵛ, 359 (two cases), 370ᵛ.
[73] NRO NMC 20, fo. 12ᵛ; 13, fo. 307. See also NMC 13, fos. 523, 533.

'wandring abroad idely', was that offenders were 'set on worke in the howse of correccon' until they 'be reteyned in service'.[74] They were given a short and sharp introduction to the world of tutored work to tame their wandering spirits, and usually held in Bridewell for days, weeks, or less often, months.[75] The records are again unhelpful. Some offenders were confined 'till further order' but make no further appearances. We can make informed guesses in a few cases. We know that Ann Hyndes had been in Bridewell for at least six months in April 1629, but we cannot be certain of the exact length of her stay there.[76] She is a rare recorded example of somebody who was detained for more than two months. A real exception was Robert Marcon, 'an idle boy', who was committed for petty theft in February 1635 and returned to his grandfather in November 1636, 'having longe continued in Bridewell'.[77] Five other young people who we know spent more than five months in Bridewell were all well-known members of the resident 'masterless' group— Ann Hyndes, William Curson, Richard Dynnes, Alice Robinson, and Joanne Weeting.[78]

We tend to lose sight of young people once they were inside Bridewell, and the methods by which they were expected to find a master are largely lost to us. In a few cases the authorities issued a committal order with a master in mind.[79] Other evidence implies that they sometimes attempted to find a service, but we cannot be sure whether this was routine or a final resort. Anne Saffrey, for example, who was 'not settled in a good service', was set on work 'till she shalbe provided of a master'. In another case an artisan acted as job-hunter. John Hallawaye was told 'to remayne in Bridewell till Mr Maior can send William Morris a taylor . . . to see if he can gett him a mayster'.[80] We can also assume that there was some talk with Bridewell craftsmen, and that family, friends, and neighbours would have helped some young people to be placed in service.

[74] NRO NMC 20, fo. 210. There were 144 cases in which young people were confined in this way. This is nearly double the number of cases in which offenders were first sent home and given a fixed period to find a master—78.

[75] Cf. Innes, 'Prisons for the poor', 54, 57, 76; Beattie, *Crime and the Courts*, 562, table 10.6.

[76] NRO NMC 16, fos. 219, 233.   [77] NRO NMC 20, fos. 44ᵛ, 133.

[78] See NRO NMC 16, fos. 187ᵛ, 219, 233, 238, 251, 270ᵛ, 271; NCQS minute book 1629–36, fos. 53, 60ᵛ, 64 (Hyndes); NMC 16, fos. 131, 154, 156, 194, 215, 266; NCQS minute book 1629–36, fo. 42ᵛ (Curson); NMC 16, fos. 293, 293ᵛ, 297, 297ᵛ, 324, 387, 401ᵛ, 489 (Dynnes); NMC 15, fo. 494; 16, fos. 35ᵛ, 49, 56, 61ᵛ, 87, 113, 131 (Robinson). For Weeting see below, pp. 370–1.

[79] For example, NRO NMC 14, fos. 207, 258.

[80] NRO NMC 15, fo. 429; 20, fo. 276ᵛ.

The gaps in the sources mean that any impression of success or failure can only be at best preliminary. We know that some young people were retained,[81] and that others were accepted for a trial period upon a 'liking',[82] though potential masters may have been less co-operative in periods of strain when arrests increase. Still others who make a single appearance in the records had a brief historical moment, a fleeting taste of marginality, only to sink without trace into the anonymity of daily life upon their return to conventional structures of socialization. In contrast, we also know of some young people who were discovered 'at their own hand' or 'out of service' and suspect on more than one occasion.[83] Their case-histories provide a sign of the enduring nature of this urban marginal fringe. The timing of cases also shows that this 'unsavoury' addition to urban life was more closely scrutinized in certain periods. The regular coincidence of peaks in prosecutions with a rising tide of vagrancy was a sober thought for the authorities who associated youthful independence with disorder. Nor were such anxieties without good foundation. Patten stresses the basic stability of urban society, but he also writes that in a town like Norwich the poor must have 'collected in great number, regulated and sometimes supported by better-off citizens. Pickpockets, thieves, and prostitutes', he continues, 'must have flourished in urban society.'[84] We may wish to dispute his association of poverty and criminality, but marginal groups tend to grow and prosper in towns.[85]

In Norwich vagrants who were typically young begged[86] and stole[87] their way along the streets, always trying to keep one step ahead of officers. They were found drunk and playing unlawful games,[88]

---

[81] For example, NRO NMC 15, fos. 114, 501; 16, fos. 219, 225; 20, fos. 17ᵛ, 309, 347.

[82] See NRO NMC 16, fo. 255ᵛ; 20, fo. 347.

[83] They include Susan Starkey, NRO NMC 16, fos. 178, 214; Bonny Peck, NMC 16, fo. 254ᵛ; 20, fo. 280; Alice Bensley, NMC 16, fos. 224ᵛ, 311ᵛ; 20, fo. 17ᵛ; Pleasance Moore, NMC 20, fos. 18, 22; Elizabeth Cotton, NMC 20, fos. 83, 131ᵛ, 133ᵛ; Avelina Hott, NMC 16, fo. 468; 20, fo. 103ᵛ; Mary Prince, NMC 20, fos. 261, 263ᵛ; Judith Chest, NMC 20, fos. 18, 359, 475; Mary Mason, NMC 16, fos. 278, 367ᵛ; Thomasin Lockwood, NMC 16, fo. 278ᵛ; 20, fo. 189.

[84] Patten, *English Towns*, 265.   [85] Cf. Geremek, *Margins of Society*, 7.

[86] For example, NRO NMC 12, fo. 502; 13, fo. 23; 14, fos. 110, 138, 231, 234, 239, 374; 15, fos. 13ᵛ, 18ᵛ (two cases), 25, 42, 69ᵛ, 79, 95, 98ᵛ, 110 (three cases), 170ᵛ, 194ᵛ, 233ᵛ, 237ᵛ, 238ᵛ, 369, 372 (two cases), 465ᵛ, 492 (two cases); 16, fos. 37, 94ᵛ, 125, 137ᵛ, 177, 180 (two cases), 207, 261, 281, 293, 329ᵛ, 330ᵛ, 331, 366, 369, 378ᵛ, 379ᵛ, 436ᵛ; 20, fos. 129, 132, 140ᵛ, 146, 192ᵛ, 215ᵛ, 227ᵛ, 243ᵛ, 253ᵛ (two cases), 297 (three cases), 325, 330.

[87] For example, NRO NMC 12, fos. 74, 619, 772; 13, fos. 28, 216, 311, 637, 662; 14, fos. 122ᵛ (two cases), 146, 163, 230ᵛ, 306ᵛ, 308ᵛ; 15, fos. 2, 9ᵛ, 70, 112, 469, 526, 560ᵛ; 16, fos. 78ᵛ, 87ᵛ (two cases), 118ᵛ, 363ᵛ, 364, 387ᵛ; 20, fos. 106ᵛ, 207, 265.

[88] For example, NRO NMC 15, fos. 218ᵛ, 255ᵛ, 490, 506ᵛ, 516 (two cases); 16, fos. 91, 315, 401; 20, fo. 252ᵛ.

having illicit sex,[89] extending 'ill rule',[90] and committing other
uncertain offences, which were gathered under some vague catch-
all like 'misdemeanour', 'misbehaviour', 'lewd', 'idle', 'dangerous',
or 'suspicious'.[91] These migrants only added to the problems raised
by those clearly resident, who smashed windows, robbed orchards,
abused those in authority, enjoyed sex, and stole anything they
could get their hands on (e.g. clothes, money, food, lambs, ducks,
dogs, horses, and hens).[92] The changing fortunes of urban economies as well as domestic tensions provided a steady procession of
new recruits into the 'masterless' group, and helped to create a
distinctive problem of youth in the towns. Young Norwich folk joined
the migrants on the streets, gathering at markets and fairs, and
adding to the cast of misfits, begging here, stealing there, who
exercised the wits of officers. They included Dorothy Sadlington,
who was noted for 'commonly begging in the streets'; John Foster,
apprentice with Whinney the tailor, who was picked up 'living idely
about the city'; and Edward Bushel, a boy, who was sent in to
Bridewell and 'would be carefully looked unto [for] he ys a very
bad one'.[93]

Crime among the 'masterless' young tended to be opportunistic—
petty theft and begging to get food and drink. The sources convey
a very real sense that they were an enduring subgroup in Norwich,
though in number and personnel they were fluid. One problem is
the silence of the sources in periods of few or no arrests. Is this
apparent calm an illusion springing from a reduction in anxieties
in periods of greater stability, or does it represent a fall in numbers
of 'masterless' and 'vagrant' youth? I shall return to these questions
shortly. Despite this there emerge some individuals who spent the
greater part of their youth moving in and out of this urban basement. We first catch sight of Joanne Weeting, for instance, in March
1630 when she was 'branded for felony' at Quarter Sessions, given
a pass, and told to return to her master, John Thaxter of Hanworth.
But it seems that she never left the city. In August she was

---

[89] For example, NRO NMC 15, fos. 37ᵛ, 64ᵛ (irregular pagination), 112, 152ᵛ, 176, 378,
444; 16, fos. 79, 84ᵛ, 87, 103; 20, fos. 334ᵛ, 455.

[90] For example, NRO NMC 15, fos. 24, 27, 27ᵛ, 34ᵛ, 39ᵛ, 69ᵛ, 93, 132, 150, 472 (two cases);
16, fos. 10ᵛ, 274, 364.

[91] For example, NRO NMC 12, fos. 109, 204, 341, 624; 13, fo. 81ᵛ; 15, fos. 242, 246, 259,
299ᵛ, 369, 483ᵛ; 16, fo. 71ᵛ; 20, fos. 10ᵛ, 49, 99, 119ᵛ, 192, 210, 338, 352.

[92] For full archival references see P. Griffiths, 'Some Aspects of the Social History of Youth
in Early Modern England, with Particular Reference to the Period *c*.1560-*c*.1640' (unpublished University of Cambridge Ph.D thesis, 1992), 367.

[93] NRO NMC 16, fo. 414ᵛ; 14, fos. 344, 246. Again, full references to crimes committed
by runaways are in Griffiths, 'Social History of Youth', 368.

discharged from Bridewell, being 'nowe desirous to goe to Holland'. However, Weeting did not venture outside the gates of the city, preferring her present life to foreign travel. In September 1630 she was convicted of petty larceny with Dennis Powell, another doyen of the 'masterless' group,[94] and ordered to be 'whipped about the markett' and confined until she could be returned to her master. Back on the streets she was quickly rearrested for ripping up the pass 'signed by Mr Maior and Mr Jermy'. A second pass was issued for 'conduccon of her' to Hanworth, but she was discovered in Norwich at the close of the same month and returned to Bridewell. In January 1631 Weeting was ordered to remain there 'till she be reteyned in service'. Further confining orders were issued in April, May, and June. We then lose sight of her until July 1632 when she was again sent in to Bridewell 'till she shall be reteyned in service', though she was probably set free without such employment. At large in the city she returned to theft and was whipped in December 1632 for petty larceny and set on work once again; Weeting was also pregnant with an illegitimate child at this time, as she was back in Bridewell in May 1634 'for havinge a bastard'. Yet she did not serve the statutory year, for the bench was satisfied with 'her affirmacon that she shall goe overseas to Holland'. Weeting had fooled the court with the same promise four years earlier, and on this occasion also her feet remained firmly on English soil. In fact, she never left the city, and in September 1634 we find her committed to Bridewell for 'ill rule' with one Butters of Norwich, her final appearance in civic materials.[95]

Weeting displays many of the attributes of the 'masterless' group which upset the authorities—slipping in and out of Norwich, disregarding the magistracy almost as a matter of course, committing petty crime, and refusing to play the part in which they were cast by patriarchal ideologies. Like Jane Sellars, who began this story, she drifted with apparent ease along East Anglia's roads. Similar case-histories can be traced for other young people who ran to Norwich. In June 1604 William Jackson and Robert Mayer, 'two boyes', were sent in to Bridewell for 'cuttinge of purses'. A few days later Jackson was ordered 'to retorne to Colston in Norfolk where he was borne'. Mayer was discovered vagrant in August 1605 when he was 16 years of age, whipped, and given a pass to return to his

---

[94] For Powell see NRO NMC 16, fos. 272, 300, 304, 325ᵛ, 326ᵛ, 331ᵛ, 362ᵛ, 462; NCQS minute book 1629–36, fos. 30, 113ᵛ, 117.

[95] NRO NMC 16, fos. 298ᵛ, 303ᵛ, 305, 316, 331ᵛ, 337ᵛ, 347, 400ᵛ, 479ᵛ; 20, fos. 3, 14, 21; NCQS minute book 1629–36, fos. 21ᵛ, 30, 74; 'The Sessions Booke 1630–38', fos. 1ᵛ, 30.

village, Forncett in Norfolk. However, he was wandering in Norwich two months later, when he was again whipped and handed a pass. Mayer chose to taunt the authority of the court as he was picked up 'roging and begging' in November with Robert Simpson of Lincolnshire aged 12. The pair were whipped and expelled, though Mayer was at large in Norwich in January 1606, and he was whipped for a fifth time in March for 'myching' with Peter Lynes, another boy. April saw the return of Jackson who was whipped and given a pass. He was found 'roginge' in September, when he was 12 years old.[96] James Goldsmith, a 'boy aged xiii years [was] taken begging' in January 1608, whipped, and sent home. Nevertheless, he was picked up begging in February 1609 and twice more in October 1610. Robert and Margery Gedg were presented in November 'for receiving Gouldsmith and Webb, two leawd boyes, and giving them almost a weeks lodging'. They asked the pair to steal fowls for them. A few days later Goldsmith was whipped for vagrancy. But the whip was clearly no deterrent in his case, for he was again discovered vagrant in January 1611.[97]

In Norwich, therefore, the correspondence between 'masterless' young people and petty crime is well-established. The sources sometimes show that they wandered, stole, and begged in small groups and pairs.[98] There were a number of assembly points in Norwich—public sermons, fairs, and the market places attracted the pilferers, pickpockets, and cutpurses who were active in the city.[99] It was also thought that sanctuary could be found in the cathedral grounds. In January 1600 the beadles complained 'that rogishe boyes and beggars escape from them [and] runne into the liberties of Christe's Churche where they are harbored and not punished, and in the evenings they goe abroad in the citie begging'. In October 1632 a baker was presented 'for counsellinge the apprentices in London that run from their masters to fly to Christ Church being a priviledged place that they might not be followed'.[100] A number of alehouses and lodging-houses also offered a room and refreshment. Robert Morgan, for example, was prosecuted for 'lodging and harboring young and ydel vagrants', and told that he would lose an

---

[96] NRO NMC 14, fos. 38ᵛ, 39, 101ᵛ, 108, 110, 115ᵛ, 123ᵛ, 125ᵛ, 127ᵛ, 148.

[97] NRO NMC 14, fos. 231ᵛ, 234, 304, 304ᵛ, 306, 306ᵛ, 313.

[98] As well as some of the evidence presented here see NRO NMC 14, fos. 38ᵛ, 110, 123ᵛ, 206ᵛ; 16, fos. 424ᵛ, 430; 20, fos. 123, 156ᵛ; NCQS minute book 1629–36, fos. 38ᵛ, 71, 87ᵛ, 113ᵛ, 117ᵛ.

[99] See NRO NMC 12, fos. 488, 595, 745, 820; 13, fos. 132, 133, 139 (two cases), 387, 674 (three cases); 14, fo. 38ᵛ; 16, fo. 19; NCQS 'The Sessions Booke 1630–38', fo. 27.

[100] NRO NMC 13, fo. 399; NCQS 'The Sessions Booke 1630–38', fo. 27.

ear if he sheltered any other young strays. While John More was arrested for lodging 'cutpurses and other lewd persons' 'from tyme to tyme'.[101] The White Horse, The Cardinal's Hat, and a few other alehouses were safe ports of call for 'masterless' young people.[102] Others less fortunate who could not afford a few pence to get a room for the night were forced to sleep as best they could 'in the streets', barns, and cellar windows.[103]

A steady stream of young people tripped in and out of Norwich and across the nearby countryside. Some of them ignored the wishes of governors as a matter of course, and they provide a clue to the structural inadequacies of a system of law enforcement which relied upon the good faith and participation of 'masterless' youth and their families. Some parents refused to co-operate with the court. In September 1634, for example, the Mayor's Court received word that widow Moore's daughter, who had been told to find a service a month earlier, had not yet been 'retayned' because her mother persuaded her to ignore their order.[104] A number of young migrants drifted in and out of Norwich with little concern for the threats of the magistrates. William Miller, for instance, 'a boye of xii years of age' from Seething in Norfolk, was picked up 'roginge and begging' in 1596, having been 'divers tymes heretofore commaunded oute of the citie'. While Margaret Utting was ferried to Bridewell in 1598 'to dwell and remayne for ever', though this did not stop her from embarking upon a decade of vagrancy and theft.[105] It is as if we are witnessing a theatre of rehearsed responses, a clandestine return follows quickly on the heels of an involuntary removal. But despite the perhaps inevitable flaws in civic strategies, the city preserved an orderly image. Yet beneath this surface gloss of managed order the 'masterless seam' cut deep, and was laying strong roots in a period of rising in-migration. However, the timing of cases of being 'out of service' and 'at their own hand' is decidedly uneven, and we must try to explain why anxieties sharpened in certain periods —in particular, we must explore the 'peaks' of 1609–11, 1630–1, and 1634–6.

[101] NRO NMC 7, fo. 588; 14, fo. 359.
[102] NRO NMC 13, fos. 508, 524. See also NMC 8, fo. 571; 9, fo. 485; 12, fos. 368, 528, 619, 840, 960; 13, fos. 467, 551; 14, fos. 264, 306; 16, fos. 138, 176ᵛ, 360, 468; 20, fos. 79ᵛ, 96ᵛ, 205ᵛ, 287; NCQS 'The Sessions Booke 1630–38', fo. 32.
[103] For example, NRO NMC 13, fo. 17ᵛ; 20, fos. 156ᵛ, 215.
[104] NRO NMC 20, fos. 18, 22. Cf. Roberts, '"Words they are women"', 159–60; Cunningham, 'Employment and unemployment of children', 106.
[105] NRO NMC 13, fos. 23, 182. The limitations of space prevent us from adding to our gallery of 'masterless' youth. Others feature in my thesis; still others wait in the records.

4. *The 'Commonweal Tune'*

The cycle of cases closely shadowed the timing of dearth, plague, and deeper poverty when visible death and distress elevated concern with rhetorics of inclusion and exclusion. Severe plague cast a shadow over the city in 1603–4 and 1625–6,[106] and cases of vagrancy and being 'out of service' increased. Yet the more prominent peaks occurred a few years after these grave epidemics as fresh reports of plague coincided with deeper poverty, higher in-migration in the wake of chronic plague (the jobs of the dead had to be filled, and Norwich's population quickly regained its pre-plague levels)[107] and, in 1630, bitter dearth. In 1609–10 there was a fresh crop of infections which were more than an echo of 1603–4.[108] This helped to raise fears which were still strong in recent memory. Poverty cut deeper. In January 1608 the Mayor's Court was passing orders 'in regard of the hardness of the tymes'.[109] In 1610 a rumour travelled around the city that 100 apprentices in the textiles trades planned to strike until all non-apprenticed labour was dismissed.[110] Thus the light plague of 1609–10 played its part in bringing anxieties into sharper focus, with the result that rulers were left brooding about the grim coincidence of plague, deeper poverty, and rising vagrancy.

Much the same sequence of events can be traced in the next peak of arrests in 1630–1, and rising concern with 'masterless' young people should be contextualized against a social canvas of lingering plague, dearth, deeper poverty, and problems in local textiles, including unemployment. The severe plague of 1625–6 was followed by further infections in 1630–1. The court noted fresh plague cases in April 1630, and appointed a 'searcher for the infected' and watchmen at the pesthouses.[111] There was a notable rise in vagrancy in 1630 when 111 individuals were arrested—the second highest annual total in the period 1581–1646. A marshal was appointed 'for the taking up of rogues and idle persons' in June, and two 'able and sufficient men' were appointed in each ward in July 1631 to check rogues, beggars, and other disordered persons. The 'very miserable' state of the poor was attributed to the present 'scarcity and dearth of all manner of victualls', and the 'want of worke' and

---

[106] The chronology of plague in Norwich can be followed in Paul Slack, *The Impact of Plague in Tudor and Stuart England* (paperback edn., Oxford, 1990), 126–43.

[107] Cf. ibid., esp. 126–43, and ch. 7.

[108] Ibid. 131.   [109] NRO NMC 14, fo. 196.   [110] CSPD 1603–10, 611.

[111] NRO NMC 16, fos. 280, 290ᵛ–1, 332, 334, 337ᵛ. The light plague of 1630–1 and socio-economic difficulties at that time are discussed in Slack, *Impact of Plague*, 132–3, 194.

'all things necessary for the maintenance of life'.[112] There were a steady procession of measures on behalf of the poor in 1630–1, including the fair allocation of grain, reassessments of contributions to the poor rate, and orders to put the resident poor to work. Further cases of plague were reported in April 1631 at the same time as grumbling about unemployment and the shortage of work in some parts of the textiles trades reached the ears of magistrates.[113] Dearth and disease seem to have retreated in 1632–3, but concern with 'masterless' young people again sharpened in 1634 at much the same time as orders regarding poor relief, begging, inmates, alehouses, and further complaints about unemployment were entered in the sources.[114] 'Country journeymen' who 'filled' the city were the subject of 'dayly' complaints from 'out of worke' resident journeymen to 'Mr Maior' in 1634. They also arranged a meeting at The Unicorn under cover of choosing '4 feastmakers' to 'consent how they might draw their . . . masters to give greater wages'.[115] A slight lull in magisterial activity in 1635 was followed by further plague measures and detailed orders for the poor in 1636.[116]

John Walter has demonstrated that in dearth years magistrates attempted to strike up a rallying communal tune; a powerful sense of what he calls 'the myth of the community'. They followed their paternal role with vigour, distributing relief to protect the poor from hunger and to still the threat of disorder which hung over the community.[117] By playing the 'commonweal tune',[118] the authorities restated civic identity, thereby casting outsiders in a darker and even more suspicious hue. Plague also assisted in the framing of policies of exclusion (and inclusion) and a rhetoric of community. It was ordered that the infected should be shut up and prohibited any communication with the healthy civic body. A watch was set at the approaches to the city to turn back suspicious characters.[119] Vagrants were popularly believed to carry plague, leaving behind a

---

[112] NRO NMC 16, fos. 291, 351; NCQS minute book 1629–36, fo. 35.

[113] See NRO NMC 16, fos. 290ᵛ, 314ᵛ, 317, 320ᵛ-1, 322-2ᵛ, 325-6ᵛ, 326-6ᵛ, 327-8, 329-9ᵛ, 348ᵛ, 351ᵛ-2, 366ᵛ; NCQS minute book 1629–36, fos. 27-7ᵛ, 30ᵛ-1, 35, 53; 'The Sessions Booke 1630–38', fo. 16; NAM vi, fo. 91.

[114] NRO NMC 16, fos. 470ᵛ, 475ᵛ; 20, fos. 9, 11-11ᵛ.

[115] NRO NMC 16, fo. 470ᵛ; NCQS 'The Sessions Booke 1630–38', fo. 60

[116] Slack, *Impact of Plague*, 278; NRO NMC 20, fos. 128, 132.

[117] John Walter, 'The social economy of dearth in early modern England', in John Walter and Roger Schofield (eds.), *Famine, Disease and the Social Order in Early Modern Society* (Cambridge, 1989), esp. 126-8. Cf. Slack, *Impact of Plague*, chs. 10–11; id., *Poverty and Policy*, 143-5; Pound, *Tudor and Stuart Norwich*, 116, 122.

[118] The phrase is Paul Slack's, *Poverty and Policy*, 145.

[119] See Slack, *Impact of Plague*, chs. 2, 8–10.

trail of misery as they drifted across the land. In fact, marginal groups—and young people—suffered high death-rates.[120] The reintegration of young misfits and the expulsion of risky outsiders had a close correlation with cycles of socio-economic difficulty. In these grim times greater pressure was applied to push young people into formal service.[121] The cycle of cases traced the twists and turns in Norwich's fortunes. In years of relative calm like 1632–3 the number of cases dipped. The next three years were a virtual barometer of civic activity—a rise in 1634, a fall in 1635, and a further increase in 1636. We can also identify difficult months like June 1630, January 1632, July–August 1634, and the autumn of 1636, when poverty, plague, or dearth accompanied the highest monthly totals of prosecutions in a single year.[122]

Nevertheless, the coincidence of two peaks of arrests for vagrancy and youthful independence in times of dearth, plague, and deeper poverty, and the fall into crime of some 'masterless' young people (which partly confirmed élite labelling) will not explain the striking gendering of cases of being 'out of service' and 'at their own hand'. We can recover an ideological context to discuss anxieties; that wise age, for example, should tame the rash temper of youth. Yet the usual sequence of events placed a young woman in a male-dominated courtroom. Perhaps the rulers of Norwich were spurred on by a concern with the place of women in their city?

In 1985 David Underdown alerted us to the possibility of a 'crisis' in gender relations in England *c.*1560–1640. His argument turns on the alleged convergence in time of three gender-related offences—witchcraft, being 'out of service', and scolding.[123] Norwich had its cucking-stool by 1562, though that usual barometer of gender tensions, cases of scolding, remained steady hovering at one, two,

---

[120] Ibid. 181–4, 188; R. S. Schofield and E. A. Wrigley, 'Infant and child mortality in England in the late Tudor and early Stuart period', in Charles Webster (ed.), *Health, Medicine and Mortality in the Sixteenth Century* (Cambridge, 1979). Cf. CLRO Jour. 26, fo. 172.

[121] Cf. Pamela Sharpe, 'Poor children as apprentices in Colyton 1598–1830', *Continuity and Change*, 6 (1991), esp. 259–60, who finds 'large rises' in the number of pauper apprentices in times of 'specific distress' like dearth, high prices, the Dutch Wars and related trade depression. In Colyton the year of the highest number of apprenticeships, 1647, was a year of plague and high prices.

[122] See NRO NMC 16, fos. 280, 290ᵛ, 291, 317, 320ᵛ–1, 322–2ᵛ; 20, fos. 9, 11–11ᵛ, 128, 132.

[123] David Underdown, 'The taming of the scold: the enforcement of patriarchal authority in early modern England', in Anthony Fletcher and John Stevenson (eds.), *Order and Disorder in Early Modern England* (Cambridge, 1985). Sadly, Underdown confines his thoughts about being 'out of service' to a single sentence (ibid. 119). Further, he simply assumes that these cases are gender specific without investigating the sex-ratio of offenders, or indeed, the precise tensions which lay behind them.

or three prosecutions each year. In fact, there were no cases in seventeen years of the period 1581–1640. If there was a gender 'crisis' in Norwich it was not a crisis of tongues.[124] At first sight the tempting timing of cases of being 'out of service' and 'at their own hand' would appear to offer support for Underdown's gender 'crisis'. Yet we have seen that these offences are gender-related rather than gender-specific. While the concept of 'crisis' with its strong connotations of a rapid fall into confusion may not provide the most helpful way of depicting gender relations at this time. We need to know, for example, what levels of magisterial activity represented more 'ordinary' and 'routine' periods. The idea of 'routine' also raises complications. The study of one part of Underdown's threefold interpretation in a single city suggests that we must distinguish more tense moments within his alleged 'crisis' period. In fact, it is more helpful to interpret a heightened sensation of gender as part of a broader concern with order. Nevertheless, in Norwich the generalized concern with fetching young people within the regulatory reach of service was to become more narrowly focused on issues of gender as investigations turned up a greater number of women living independently. We can precisely fix a turning-point in the wave of arrests in 1609–11. In June 1609 the Mayor's Court ordered overseers to search for 'maydes and singlewoman' who 'lyve at their owne handes'.[125] As the gender bias intensified, the gendering of prosecutions may have become a near self-fulfilling prophecy.

There is no simple answer to this question of the prominent role of gender in the drive to push young people into formal service. We in fact require a complicated explanatory model with several strands to explain both the timing and gendering of prosecutions. Conditions in Norwich provide one part of the model for the timing of arrests, but as we shall see the activities of central government also had a part to play. The issue of gender is one of work, residence, and the suspicions hanging over the independent woman. It may also be a question of numbers. We are told that larger towns had 'a disproportionately high number of women', one reason being the pull of domestic service.[126] I have consulted the registers of

---

[124] Ibid. 123–4. However, my figures are only drawn from civic judicial sources. They reveal a total of ninety-five prosecuted scolds in the period 1581–1640. Interestingly, the only period in which there was a regular run of cases at about three or four each year was the troubled period 1629–32.

[125] NRO NMC 14, fo. 250ᵛ.

[126] J. A. Sharpe, *Early Modern England: A Social History 1550–1750* (1987), 80.

seven 'poor' and four 'medium' wealthy Norwich parishes to compare sex-ratios of births and burials in two decades, 1610–20 and
1710–20.[127] Following the usual ratio of 104 male to 100 female
baptisms, there was a slight preponderance of women in the earlier
period when the sex-ratio of baptisms was 103.6 and burials 102.3.
It seems that growing numbers of women were making journeys to
Norwich in the seventeenth century because the sex-ratio of baptisms in 1710–20 hovered at 104.0, while the burial-ratio clearly
tipped towards women, 96.6.[128] The population of early Stuart
Norwich was in this respect more 'balanced', though further work
may well uncover a more difficult situation towards the close of the
seventeenth century if the pace of female in-migration was rising as
fast as burial figures would seem to indicate. Yet in Norwich numbers
alone are not an adequate explanation.

Being 'out of service' and 'at their own hand' in Norwich, however, were chiefly perceived and prosecuted as the transgressions of
independent young women.[129] One answer may be that young men
were more likely to travel in search of work or service. Another, is
that they had a greater prospect of being in service in their home
community, formally apprenticed or otherwise. One might expect
to discover a higher number of women living and working at home,
perhaps being taught skills by a relative.[130] This twilight world of
casual work and informal training in which young women boosted
the family economy of widows[131] or unemployed men[132] was more

[127] I am following the categorization of 'poor' and 'medium' parishes given in Slack,
Impact of Plague, esp. tables 5.4 and 5.5. The parishes studied are the 'poor' parishes of All
Saints, St Julian, St James, St Augustine, St Margaret, St Benedict and St Peter Parmentergate,
and the 'medium' parishes of St Gregory, St Giles, St Lawrence, and St John Timberhill.

[128] I have followed the discussion of sex-ratios in Wrigley and Schofield, *Population History*,
224–6. Cf. D. Souden, 'Migrants and the population structure of late seventeenth-century
provincial cities and market towns', in P. Clark (ed.), *The Transformation of English Provincial
Towns 1660–1800* (1984); Pound, *Norwich Census of the Poor*, appendix 1, who presents figures
for the age, marital and sex structure of the population aged 16 and above; and appendix
2, which presents figures for the age and sex of children under 16 years of age in the census.
There was a slight majority of females, which primarily reflects the higher number of young
women below 16 years of age.

[129] Interestingly, the proportion of males among the small number of prosecuted migrants
was higher than their 16 per cent participation rate in the *overall* sample of 313 cases—nine
of the twenty migrants were males.

[130] Cf. Ben-Amos, *Adolescence and Youth in Early Modern England*, ch. 6; ead., 'Women
apprentices in the trades and crafts of early modern Bristol', *Continuity and Change*, 6 (1991);
Sharpe, 'Poor children as apprentices', 259; Roberts, 'Women and work', 91.

[131] For example, Pound, *Norwich Census of the Poor*, 39, 42, 44, 49, 51, 54, 56, 57, 59, 60,
62, 64.

[132] For example, ibid. 33, 34–5, 38, 41, 43, 45, 50, 55, 57. The informal training of young
women in this period is more fully explored in Ben-Amos, *Adolescence and Youth in Early
Modern England*, 145–50.

egalitarian than the ordinance-ridden world of the guilds.[133] But it is an aspect of Norwich life which is seldom mentioned in the records I have consulted. The Census of the Poor of 1570, however, offers one window, and in its 'tour' of poor households we can observe women working at home, usually assisting in the manufacture of textiles.[134] It is well known that women had no public or formal role in the guilds, widows being the exception, and that ideas about occupational careers were largely confined to young men. Casual work took opportunities away from apprenticed labour and householders, who in theory earned a wage to provide for their families and keep them from turning to poor relief. The allocation of work was prioritized in favour of resident males, especially in times of unemployment and work shortages. A further concern was that women should have been at work in formal service, earning wages which were considered to be appropriate by the authorities.

Michael Roberts has recently argued that the nature of women's work in urban society was changing c.1570–1650, 'sharing [to a limited extent] in that general proliferation of occupational roles with which these later years [of the sixteenth century] have been identified'. Growing opportunities for female work 'of all kinds' uneasily coexisted with the unequal share of freedom given to men and women in political and occupational spheres, especially in stressful times when competition sharpened. So, Roberts has also argued that 'what might almost be called a late sixteenth-century urban "crisis of gender"' offered a 'significant challenge' to civic rulers.[135] Again, 'crisis' infers a leap into severe instability and may be inappropriate here. But Roberts has identified structural changes in patterns of work, and if he is correct they may help to explain the timing of cases. Thus rising numbers of arrests may have resulted from attempts to regulate the greater participation of women in work at a time when female independence was viewed with suspicion. In tough conditions like those in 1609–10 and 1630–6, élites intervened to help secure the life-chances of householders by more closely regulating wages and labour-supply. Outsiders of all sorts were one target.[136] Another were resident women like Rose

[133] Cf. Wright, ' "Churmaids, huswyfes and hucksters" ', 104–5.

[134] In a total of ninety-three girls and young women aged between 5 and 27 years of age who can be observed in the Census, eighty-two were engaged in the manufacture of textiles (87.2 per cent). Twelve of the thirty-nine young men who can be clearly observed were working in textiles (30.8 per cent). Fourteen boys attended school. See Griffiths, 'Social History of Youth', 396, esp. table 6.5; Pound, *Norwich Census of the Poor*, appendix 4.

[135] Roberts, 'Women and work', esp. 91, 93–4, 95.

[136] See NRO NMC 16, fos. 279–9ᵛ, 334ᵛ–5, 335, 337, 338–40, 341ᵛ, 364ᵛ–5, 366, 379; 20, fos. 30, 96ᵛ; NCQS 'The Sessions Booke 1630–38', fo. 8.

Nelson, a singlewoman who was presented for 'not [being] in service for wages', and who like Joanne Norton a 'singlewoman lyveing wholly at her own handes', was free to plot her own course.[137] These cases belonged to the same concern which spurred on the would-be strikers in 1610 and 1634—marginal and foreign workers—the difference being that they resulted from the responses of governors. To the concern with reintegrating 'masterless' youth in times of dearth, plague, and economic difficulty, we can add the prioritizing of work in favour of resident men in the same conditions.

For work was a moral category. Young women like Martha Johnson, one of 'lewde life', who was found 'wanderinge abroade idely' and confined in Bridewell 'till she be reteyned in service'; Jane Humeston, who was picked up 'roginge about the towne and not abyding in any service', living 'very suspiciously and disorderly in lewdnes of her body'; Katherine Prostwick, 'one who keepeth at her owne hande', and who had committed 'filthines'; and Jane Palsy, 'a yonge wench of 24 yeares goeinge at hir owne hand and frequentinge the alehouse', provided some confirmation of the connection between untutored time and immorality.[138] A significant number of 'masterless' young women were also charged with suspected or actual sexual offences.[139] A singlewoman taking private chambers stirred suspicions. It is clear that youth was seen as a troublesome stage of life. 'Masterless' young people raised anxieties, but a particular gendered discourse elevated suspicions about independent young women.[140] In May 1605, for instance, Grace Kerrison, a 'singlewoman' and 'one who lyved very suspiciously' at Stephen Warnfrey's alehouse, was expelled for 'ill rule'. In the same year Grace Sketch was ordered to depart the city 'unlesse she shall be retained in service with some honest man not beinge an inholder'. While Margaret Thackwell and her companion, 'beyng young women . . . out of service', were sent to Bridewell for 'taking chambers' in March 1592.[141]

These half-expressed suspicions connecting alehouses, immorality, freedom, and private work can help us to conceptualize the magistrates' responses. Patriarchy looms large over these events. In

---

[137] NRO NMC 14, fos. 257ᵛ, 235. Cf. ibid., fos. 24, 102ᵛ, 175.

[138] NRO NMC 12, fos. 910, 918; 20, fo. 210; 14, fo. 175; 16, fo. 211.

[139] For example, NRO NMC 14, fos. 121ᵛ, 426; 15, fo. 63; 16, fos. 271, 379; 20, fos. 6ᵛ, 9ᵛ, 184.

[140] Cf. above, esp. pp. 358–9.

[141] NRO NMC 14, fos. 83, 46; 12, fo. 640. Cf. NMC 14, fo. 235; 16, fos. 360, 468; 20, fos. 53, 165, 205ᵛ. Cf. R. A. Houston, *Social Change in the Age of Enlightenment: Edinburgh 1660–1760* (Oxford, 1994), 80, 139, 81–2.

1561, for example, Margaret Watt was punished for 'ill rule' and told 'not to dwell in the town unless she shall fortune to marry some honest man'. While Elizabeth Claxton was given two weeks to find a service 'with some sufficient man'.[142] 'Honest' and 'sufficient' clearly implied correct morals, hard work, and the ability to provide; yet another sign of the correspondence between issues of economics and morality. In these cases 'masterless' young women were to be disciplined by marriage and the regulated rhythm of work with 'sufficient' men. Significantly, the chances of a woman being presented for a habit of independence alone without being charged with an additional offence were higher—79.4 per cent of women were only labelled with a title like being 'out of service'; the figure for men was 59.6 per cent. Singlewomen raised anxieties, and like their Manchester cousins many of them had 'not anny man to controle them', which raises issues of family structure, and in particular the presence of a male householder.

We can partly reconstruct the households of thirty women who were discovered at home 'out of service', and ten others who were 'at their own hand'.[143] There was no visible pattern in cases of being 'out of service'. Nine women were living with their widowed mother at the time of the search, and five others with their mother who may have been widowed. But sixteen others were reported to be living with their father when they attracted the magistrates' attention. Not one of these fathers was deemed unfit to keep his daughter. In contrast, Alice Stubbs was judged to be an incompetent tutor and provider; she was 'not fit' to care for her daughter. While widow Bensley was considered 'not able to keepe' her daughter who was found 'out of service' in December 1628 and December 1630, and 'at her own hand' in 1634. Widow Bensley herself had been presented for 'lewdnes and ill rule', 'for frequenting the companye of the bearers of the infected', and for lodging 'masterless' people.[144] Cases of being 'at their own hand' reveal a clearer pattern, and the potentially tenuous position of female heads of

---

[142] NRO NMC 7, fo. 494; 20, fo. 148.

[143] Sadly, we only possess information about two males who were both found 'out of service': John Furrys, the 'sonne of Furrys the dummer', who finally took him into his service; and William Palsy, 'a boy' of eighteen years of age, who was living at home with his mother in the parish of St Martin's-in-the-Palace. NRO NMC 20, fos. 64–4ᵛ, 66ᵛ; 16, fo. 211.

[144] NRO NMC 16, fos. 31ᵛ, 224ᵛ, 311ᵛ, 338ᵛ, 359; 20, fos. 9, 17ᵛ. In Finchingfield (Essex) the family background of young people who were told to find employment in service also shows a significant number of households which were headed by widows (see above, n. 61). Cf. Merry E. Wiesner, *Working Women in Renaissance Germany* (New Brunswick, NJ, 1986), esp. 88–9.

household is more apparent. Only one daughter was living at home with her father at the time of her arrest, while another eight households were headed by women (three of whom can be positively identified as widows). One other woman was living with her sister at the time of the search.[145]

5. *'The 'Ordinarie and Dailie Mode of Lief'*

The ambiguous position of widows returns us to the question of chronology and the cyclical pattern of arrests. Widows were fully responsible for ninety-four families in the Census of the Poor, and it was recorded that those households contained at least 171 young people.[146] It is quite likely that prosecutions for being 'out of service' would have swiftly followed such revelations in early Stuart Norwich, but a paltry two cases were brought in the period 1570–5. An order was issued by the Norwich Assembly in 1577 to apply the Statute of Artificers—'that no maydes [being able to serve] maye hyer chambers' or 'be harbored in eny mans howse'. Young women 'refusing to serve' were to be promptly dispatched to 'prison or bridewell'.[147] Yet no wave of arrests followed this decree. There is only significant silence in the records. In addition, a number of severe plagues swept through the city in 1579,[148] 1584–5, and 1589–92, and a light plague, sufficient to cause scares and many deaths, was reported in 1597–9.[149] The 1590s were a bleak time of dearth. Nor did the cycle of economic difficulty which left a blemish on the city's fortunes leave any notable trace upon the timing of prosecutions before the turn of the seventeenth century. Nevertheless, these were the very conditions which raised the spectre of 'masterless' young people in subsequent decades. In fact, there was a greater or equal number of cases of being 'out of service' or 'at their own hand' in each of nine single years in the period 1600–36 than in that whole 'crisis' decade of 1590–9. Yet this social language was part of civic vocabulary well before 1600, though it was not widely used. We can find it in Norwich materials, but a single mention is sometimes followed by years of silence.

[145] The combined total for both offences is forty. A male householder was resident in seventeen cases (42.5 per cent). Twenty-three households were headed by women, and twelve of them can be positively identified as widows.

[146] Pound, *Norwich Census of the Poor*, 18, table 7.   [147] NRO NAM iv, fo. 139.

[148] The 1579 plague was 'the greatest mortality in the town's history after the black death' (Slack, *Impact of Plague*, 129).

[149] This 'light' plague may partly explain the rise in prosecutions in 1600–1.

Thus the first years of the seventeenth century seem to mark the point at which either the various tensions contained in this social language cut deeper into the fabric of Norwich life, or civic anxieties had been elevated to a pitch resulting in a sequence of clampdowns. The cycle of cases is related to the close correspondence between these two explanations; between perceptions and realities, ideology and the material environment. But there is in fact a third layer of explanation which has the value of directing attention to the period when cases were rising fast. The Poor Laws of 1598 and 1601 did not provide the occasion to launch prosecutions, but they contributed a legislative means to pursue 'masterless' young people, giving a further statutory stamp to forced service, and drawing more attention to outsiders who charted an alternative course of life. A firm identification of the marginal fringe was made in the 1601 Act—it was ordered that people who 'use no ordinarie and dailie mode of lief to get their livinge by' should be put to work. A later Act of 1610 'for erecting and buylding of howses of correccion' and punishing vagrancy, encouraged an institutional solution to the problems raised by the 'idle and wandring life', and offered another statutory justification for issuing manipulative labels by drawing attention to strategically pliable categories like 'rogue', 'vagabond', 'disorderly', and 'idle'.[150] The Assembly order of 1577 had little impact on the rate of prosecution, which proceeded at a faint trickle. However, the Assembly issued a further set of articles in 1600 'to be inquired upon by the churchwardens and overseers' of every parish, which asked the question 'what maids or singlewomen keepe chambers by themselves beynge under the age of xl years and goe to their owne hands', as part of a broader moral thrust which also included the closer regulation of inmates, 'naughty packs' with child, suspected houses, unlawful games, country journeymen, and vagrant and idle folk, as well as ordering that 'pore folkes children' should be placed in service at age 14 for boys and 15 for girls.[151] This drive ushered in the first peak of prosecutions in 1600–1.

This significant sequence of central and civic legislation not only encouraged a particular interpretation of marginal groups, but also proposed clear strategies for tackling these apparent nonconformists, which if not entirely new were gathered under a single statutory seal. It should also be remembered that the Act of 1610 articulated a far harsher line on illegitimacy, while the Infanticide

[150] 43 Eliz. I c. 2; 7 Jac. I c. 4. Cf. Robert B. Shoemaker, *Prosecution and Punishment: Petty Crime and the Law in London and Rural Middlesex c.1660–1725* (Cambridge, 1991), 168–70.
[151] NRO NAM v, fo. 45.

Act of 1624 bitterly condemned the activities of 'lewd women'. The background to this interpretative climate which articulated concern with marginal groups and female sexuality in the corridors of power is beyond the scope of this chapter, though it requires serious attention. It is true that none of these perceptions or problems belonged exclusively to the early seventeenth century, but their statutory form at that time is surely significant.

A more complete picture of the mental world of Norwich's governors would also explore other lines of communication between the city and central government, including the registers of Privy Council.[152] Another line of enquiry is offered by the beliefs of the officials who sat on the bench of the Mayor's Court. Does the shift in the rate of prosecutions reflect the advance or retreat of godliness among the civic élite, or perhaps new policing strategies?[153] Are we witnessing yet another wave of reforming manners which have been discussed by Martin Ingram and others, and which he in fact partly relates to the preoccupation with educating youth?[154] Yet these fruitful lines of enquiry will probably only contribute a further dimension to the idea that 'masterless' youth were more tightly policed in certain conditions. A heightened sensation of godliness, however, could be a neglected aspect here. Magistrates and ministers tended to dwell on sin in plague sermons and orders, and they also 'mistrusted' singlewomen.[155]

In fact, magistracy and ministry had a long association in Norwich which can be traced as far back as the 1570s.[156] Interestingly, it has been suggested that the 'Puritan movement in Norwich exhibited considerable strength in the 1620s and 1630s', and that in the same period 'city government decisively committed itself to the protection of the godly cause'. New figures emerged in civic politics and some of them were 'imbued with strong religious ideals'.[157] It

---

[152] Cf. Evans, *Seventeenth-Century Norwich*, 63–4.

[153] Ian Archer has traced rising godliness on the bench of the court of London Bridewell and related this to significant changes in the pattern of prosecuting immorality (*Pursuit of Stability*, esp. 248–54).

[154] Martin Ingram, 'Reformation of manners in early modern England', in Paul Griffiths, Adam Fox, and Steve Hindle (eds.), *The Experience of Authority in Early Modern England* (Basingstoke, 1996).

[155] See, for example, Slack, *Impact of Plague*, esp. ch. 2; Margaret Healy, 'Discourses of the plague in early modern London', in J. A. I. Champion (ed.), *Epidemic Disease in London* (Centre for Metropolitan History Working Papers Series, 1993).

[156] See Evans, *Seventeenth-Century Norwich*, esp. 84–6, 96–7; Pound, *Tudor and Stuart Norwich*, 87; Patrick Collinson, *The Religion of Protestants: The Church in English Society 1559–1625* (Oxford, 1982), 141–5; Slack, *Poverty and Policy*, 119.

[157] Evans, *Seventeenth-Century Norwich*, 96; Pound, *Tudor and Stuart Norwich*, 85. The emergence of new groups is fully examined in Evans, *Seventeenth-Century Norwich*, chs. 2–3; and

appears that Puritans 'were always in the minority', though the corporation was sympathetic, and 'was of great utility in sponsoring puritan lectureships, and in enacting and enforcing local ordinances regulating the desired moral and social behaviour'. The Mayor's Court played a prominent part.[158] Yet the social rhetoric being studied here is not often associated with elevated piety and reforming manners. Moreover, Norwich was an early reformed city, and we still need to explain the puzzling reluctance to use this language before 1600. Nevertheless, active piety is one potential layer of a much broader explanation, which must also explore how the interpretative climate of the early seventeenth century and socio-economic conditions in Norwich sharpened concern with 'masterless' youth, work, and gender. The social language and tensions under review here were not created by central and civic legislation after 1600, but more and clearer strategies and identifications were certainly being proposed, and they could be treated as one sign of elevated concern with their principal subjects.

Yet these acts can only explain the pursuit of the *resident* young.[159] To pursue coincidences we can turn to the as yet little explored problems regarding entry into service in this difficult period, and the growing number of people coming to Norwich at the close of the sixteenth century. Rising in-migration contributed to the city's population explosion, but it also had some unpleasant side-effects elevating poverty, economic competition, and the threat of disorder. In-migration at this rate could have altered the 'shape of service as a form of work', and caused a multiplication of casual work.[160] This may partly explain why arrests increased after 1600. The articles of that year, therefore, were a response to alterations in the fabric of the city resulting from rising in-migration and changes in

---

Pound, *Tudor and Stuart Norwich*, 78–82. One indication of this shift in the distribution of influence in municipal politics was the number of disputed elections in this period: Evans, *Seventeenth Century Norwich*, 66–79. Another was the controversy about the appointment of lecturers: Evans, *Seventeenth-Century Norwich*, 84–96; Pound, *Tudor and Stuart Norwich*, 88–90; Peter King, 'Bishop Wren and the suppression of the Norwich lecturers', *Historical Journal*, 11 (1968). Evans comments that 'By the 1620s Puritanism was a socially respectable movement with deep roots and its leaders were among the town's elite' (*Seventeenth-Century Norwich*, 102).

[158] Evans, *Seventeenth-Century Norwich*, 97, 102. Evans has argued that the Puritans were 'only a determined hard-core minority in the Court of Aldermen', but that they were 'supported by an overwhelming number in the Common Council' (ibid. 103). Both he and Pound call the Mayor's Court a 'moral policeman' (ibid. 85; *Tudor and Stuart Norwich*, 88).

[159] That is, if I am correct in suggesting that residents and migrants were treated differently, the first being more likely to be labelled as being 'out of service' and 'at their own hand', and the second, simply punished and expelled for vagrancy.

[160] Roberts, 'Women and work', esp. 92.

occupational structures.[161] Thereafter, the cycle of cases reveals a sequence of prominent clusterings, abruptly punctuated by a few sudden falls; the timing of arrests being one sign of how concern with civic order, unshackled youth, gender, and work peaked in particular conditions. The problems raised by 'masterless' youth were not created in these circumstances; they do not lie dormant for a number of years and then spring into life when summoned. It is unlikely that casual work, the preference for living and working at home, or drifting in and out of service were the product of difficult times alone. Vagrancy increased, and perhaps theft in time of need. One key to 'clustered prosecutions' is élite perceptions, which may have been already finely tuned by the interpretative climate of the early seventeenth century and the rise in the size of the city. Suspicions about 'masterless' youth and the regulation of work became more clearly articulated and prosecuted in 1609–10, for example, 1630–1, and 1634–6.

There were also some relatively tranquil periods when troubles apparently eased and a semblance of tolerance settled on Norwich. Casual and domestic work or the connection between female independence and disorder did not cease to operate in less stressful times. Yet we could argue that magisterial concern (as revealed in the historical record) was dampened. The courtbooks, therefore, do not disclose the true extent of the problems raised by 'masterless' young people; tensions festered and then broke forth in a fresh crop of arrests. This clustering of prosecutions possesses ideological significance above that of mere numbers. Gender and youth are timeless problems which touch all societies in some form. Yet

---

[161] We require much further work on aspects of urban history and migration before structural changes in urban occupational structures *c*.1570–1650 are fully established, and then related to the type of problems discussed in this chapter. First, we require closer study of the character and extent of in-migration to the towns in this period, and in particular, sex-ratios should prove significant. Secondly, the timing of prosecutions for the sort of offences under review here requires further study in other towns. The concerns behind labelling (and the histories of other labels) need to be established. Thirdly, we need to explore further the policing of casual labour and employment more generally in times of stress. It would also be of great value to relate prosecutions for being 'out of service' and 'at their own hand' to occupational structures by gleaning more evidence about the occupational histories of offenders than the Norwich sources I have consulted so far have permitted. The home parish (when appropriate) of offenders would also help us to build up a picture of the provenance of labels. Finally, one missing (and important) dimension in this chapter has been the socio-economic conditions in the countryside and the study of 'push' factors in migration patterns. I have tended to assume that many of the reasons for in-migration can be related to the demand for labour in the towns and other attractions the town could offer, though the possible correspondence between the demands of the town and problems in its hinterland may be significant (cf. Goldberg, *Women, Work and Life-Cycle*, 291).

no principle of order is ever experienced as a historical constant; ideologies are redefined or reanimated, and anxieties can sharpen. In early Stuart Norwich a number of factors isolated one conspicuous group—singlewomen. The wounds that they inflicted upon patriarchal feelings were expressed in a label which was also age-related —'at their own hand'. Another term, 'out of service', which before 1600 revealed no striking gender trend, was to become primarily a badge of female independence in the new century.

The provenance and meaning of such labels has received little attention hitherto. Yet they were a dynamic aspect of the articulation of authority and process of law enforcement, and caught a multitude of 'suspicious' situations and characters within the wide circumference of their supple meaning. The social language being studied here captured a spectrum of tensions, but uppermost in the minds of governors as they applied their labels was the concern that the young should remain within the compass of a master's authority in tutored work (and time). This concern took on a gendered character which was in large part derived from particular suspicions about female independence and enterprise. 'Masterless' young people appeared free and restless. Some of them worked at home in casual labour or informal training, and became more visible in difficult periods. Others followed an 'idle and wandring life', taking lodgings, and drifting from service or home. They shared the common thread of *perceived freedom* and had a tenuous and sometimes distant relationship with formal structures of authority and work.

Slipping in and out of service, Jane Sellars, Joanne Weeting, Robert Mayer, and others moved between competing statuses of 'masterless' and 'servant', thereby blurring the fine distinction between socialization and the impulses of youth, which defined conformity and opposition in strategic polarities. They did not follow the 'ordinarie and dailie mode of lief'. In fact, they interpreted the implications of their appointed inferiority in different ways to the image of virtuous youth which was defended in courtroom prosecutions, and further communicated in apprenticeship indentures, government decrees, sermons, conduct books, and catechisms. Moreover, with the steady decline of apprenticeship and service in later centuries,[162] and the growth in the size of towns, the proletariat,

[162] Though this decline was gradual and more rapid in certain trades; others retained tight control over entry through service. See C. Brooks, 'Apprenticeship, social mobility and the middling sort 1550–1800', in Jonathan Barry and Christopher Brooks (eds.), *The Middling Sort of People: Culture, Society and Politics in England, 1550–1800* (Basingstoke, 1994), esp. 54–63. Cf. Keith Snell, *Annals of the Labouring Poor: Social Change and Agrarian England, 1660–*

and casual labour, the difficulties raised by the control of youth may have sharpened. Tutored work and time became more contested issues.[163] Adam Smith mourned the gradual loss of indoor apprenticeship in which young people were in theory confined within the compass of their master's authority.[164] In the first decade of the nineteenth century the master clothiers and workers in the west of England thought that the proposed repeal of the Statute of Artificers was 'one of the most awful propositions ever submitted to the legislature'. They argued that apprenticeship was 'both a moral and political institution' and 'a custom which has prevailed time out of mind'.[165] Opposing the repeal of the Statute in 1814, one MP drew upon an age-old concern with dissolute youth, declaring that its loss would be 'ruinous to the morals of youth'. His was not a lone voice, and he was joined in the House by Mr Searjant Best, who argued that 'it was much better that young people should not be left without some controle'.[166] Thus the concern with 'masterless' youth stretches across centuries, and already Adam Smith could sit at his desk in the second half of the eighteenth century, and glance back to a fading 'golden age' when it appeared that young people were tightly bound to their master's household.

It would be unfair to lay the blame for the misinterpretations of some later historians with Adam Smith. He had a very optimistic impression of the disciplinary potential of service, and that rosy image may have become a fond memory and 'a lesson from the past' as structures of authority and patterns of work irrevocably changed. The long decline of service and the rise of wage-labour raised problems for authority structures, and the process of socializing young people.[167] Some historians have argued that the problem of juvenile delinquency surfaces towards the close of the eighteenth century or even after. We may dispute both the timing and definition of this interpretation (and the resulting impression of early modern

1900 (Cambridge, 1985), chs. 2 and 5; Ann Kussmaul, *Servants in Husbandry in Early Modern England* (Cambridge, 1981), chs. 2 and 6–7.

[163] Cf. E. P. Thompson, 'Time, work-discipline and industrial capitalism', in his *Customs in Common* (1991).

[164] See Harry Hendrick, *Images of Youth: Age, Class and the Male Youth Problem, 1820–1920* (Oxford, 1990), 15–16.

[165] Quoted by Adrian Randall, *Before the Luddites: Custom, Community and Machinery in the English Woollen Industry 1776–1809* (Cambridge, 1991), 243.

[166] *Hansard* 1813–14, 879, 892–3.

[167] Cf. E. P. Thompson, 'The patricians and the plebs', in his *Customs in Common*, esp. 36–42; John Rule, 'Employment and authority: masters and men in eighteenth-century manufacturing', in Griffiths *et al.* (eds.), *The Experience of Authority in Early Modern England*; Wiener, *Reconstructing the Criminal*, 17–19, 51.

youth),[168] yet still recognize rising concern with youth in the later period.[169] This heated debate about youth (a common aspect of most societies) stirred regret at the passing of the Statute of Artificers, and may even have helped to construct a myth of shackled youth in former centuries. Again, each society is convinced that its youth are the very worst youth.[170] Memory, nostalgia, and present preoccupations can distort the past. The 'great enclosure' of early modern youth or the tight grip of authority structures, therefore, were not the inventions of a few twentieth-century historians. They were an aspect of social commentary in late eighteenth-century England and beyond which was one expression of the problem of youth at that time. More recently, some historians have felt unable to detach early modern youth from authority structures. But as we consult different types of sources, new problems and experiences come into view—the little explored worlds of informal training, domestic work, youth criminality, and the tension between the competing statuses of 'servant' and 'masterless' all require further work. None of these problems were new in the long eighteenth century or after, though they may have presented more formidable hurdles for magistrates as they managed the slow transition from a system of youthful subordination which depended upon living-in service. The ways of growing up may have changed and even expanded in the two or three centuries after 1640. Nevertheless, there were clearly different ways of growing up in Tudor and Stuart England when many young people exercised a measure of autonomy and choice even within existing authority structures.

[168] See above, Ch. 3.
[169] Cf. Peter King and Joan Noel, 'The origins of "the problem of juvenile delinquency": the growth of juvenile prosecutions in London in the late eighteenth and early nineteenth centuries', *Criminal Justice History*, 14 (1993), 17.
[170] See above, esp. p. 111.

CONCLUSION

Different Ways of Growing Up

1. 'The Making or the Marring of the World'

It was often repeated that the progress of civil society and sound religion turned on a 'continuall and perpetual succession of all kinds of callings', which was felt to be 'a necessity of all necessities'.[1] Respectable parents who raised upright youth were a blessing not only for the present generation, but also for later generations who profited from their virtuous offspring. It was hoped that parents and masters would help to safeguard households, villages, towns, and the kingdom. They were 'either the making or the marring of the world'.[2] But the poor quality of domestic governors was a persistent grievance, and throughout this period (and after) those in places of authority identified a perennial structural problem of generational succession, censuring casual parents, and passing pessimistic forecasts about the rising generation of 'lost' youth. 'Oh what a lamentable case have ungodly parents brought the world into', Richard Baxter groaned, 'wicked education hath unmade the world'. The sorry cycle of generational corruption repeated itself, so that young people were 'posses[sed] . . . with the same dislike from generation to generation'.[3] Baxter knew all about the 'tricks of youth'. He remembered how the infectious sound of play pierced the walls of his father's pious household pulling him away from his devotions, and we also find him in later life slicing his Kidderminster congregation into twelve degrees of religious commitment, ranging from the seriously 'precise' to the strictly indifferent. This 'lamentable' state of affairs resulted from cycles of 'generational corruption'. Many ministers may have in fact accepted that a 'middle

---

[1] I am quoting William Gouge, *Of Domesticall Duties* (1622), 560; and anon., *The Office of Christian Parents* (Cambridge, 1616), 10.

[2] John Dod and Robert Cleaver, *A Godlie Forme of Household Government* (1612), 336.

[3] Richard Baxter, *A Christian Directory, Or a Sum of Practical Theologie and Cases of Conscience* (1673), 519, 544.

territory' between conformity and opposition was the best that they could ever achieve.[4]

This may be belligerent rhetoric, but it should not be dismissed lightly. It is true that authors nearly always sketched an uphill struggle with no certain downward slope. Nevertheless, it would be unwise to conveniently file these complaints under a derogatory category such as 'mission rhetoric' or 'propaganda', and so deny them historical authenticity.[5] One purpose of this 'missionary language' was to sketch the task which lay ahead, and we know that ministers and magistrates provided institutions and advice to turn young people into responsible adults. But we should never assume that householders actively consented to follow this task in the ways demanded by the authorities. Nor should we evaluate their constant 'interferences' in the process of generational succession by the standards of moralists, and sift through the sources in pursuit of the collapse of the family and social order, or an irresistible tide of immorality. Families reproduced and generations continued to turn. Young people grew up to become employers, parents, husbands, wives, constables, and so on. They discovered new tasks and priorities, including parental and institutional responsibilities. Yet a near proverbial wisdom held that what was sown in youth was reaped in adulthood, and ideas about sex, conviviality, play, and religious commitment could as moralists feared be carried into later life.

In fact, the social history of youth provides an excellent illustration of the deep ambiguity of conventional patterns of authority in early modern society. Moralists and magistrates had a clear set of expectations, though most young people grew up in very different ways to the image of temperate and chaste youth recycled in the conduct literature and indenture of apprenticeship. In our progress from the representations of the prescriptive literature to the archival record, a number of different characterizations and experiences of youth have come into view. Image and reality are often blurred, and ambiguity lingers even in the very definition of youth.[6] Of

---

[4] For Baxter's divisions see Eamon Duffy, 'The godly and the multitude in Stuart England', *Seventeenth Century*, 1 (1986), 39–40.

[5] As Eamon Duffy, amongst others, is inclined to do. See his 'The godly and the multitude', esp. 37.

[6] For example, magistrates and ministers on occasion offered competing conceptions of youth. Full membership of the Church and spiritual adulthood was in theory bestowed at confirmation and first communion, while the Church also urged the tactical ploy of early marriage in the eternal combat with the flesh. Yet guilds and town corporations, for instance (supported it must be said by the authors of conduct texts), prolonged the ideal duration

much greater significance to the codes of the authorities was the independence and creativity of early modern youth. Youth was rarely (if at all) an inevitable or passive experience; a procession of ideal types and paper figures. Above all, the performance is more important than the script, and the limitations of the conduct literature are plain to see. Young people actively contributed to their maturation, seeking formative experiences and peer association, and in so doing (with Aries's ideas of 'lost youth' in mind) they helped to make their own history. Jane Sellars, who moved in and out of service; Thomas Parry, who hurled 'very vile and lewde wordes' at his master; Bartholomew Robinson, who hunted after prostitutes in the fields; Joanne English, who insulted her 'elders and betters'; Joanne Goodman, who visited the alehouse as well as the church on Sunday; Randal Christopher, the dicer; Robert Coles, the thief; Richard Wells, the runaway; and the host of young players, drinkers, runaways, and irreverent young people, experienced youth as an uneasy compromise between the demands of governors and their own preferences. Young people were presented with choices, piety or profanity, obedience or irreverence, idleness or hard work, or restraint or liberty. But most of them lived their youth in a 'middle territory' somewhere between these opposites, even though others were more firmly attached to one pole or the other.

This spacious middle way was a source of confusion for contemporary moralists because they tended to classify youth in terms of conspicuous 'absolutes' of good and bad; there was a right and wrong route to adulthood. Youth was the 'choosing time'. But young people could freely move between the rival statuses of conformity and opposition. They entered full adulthood as 'composite characters', and most of them bore only a passing resemblance to 'the sons of wisdom'. In so doing, they blurred the neat and indisputable distinction between right and wrong, and complicated their relationship with authority structures. The enforcement of authority was rarely immediate or absolute; subordinates were seldom entirely tame or passive, though that remained one possible pattern of behaviour. The progress to adulthood rarely proceeded on an even trajectory; there was in fact a great deal of 'zigzaggery'. Some young people drifted in and out of service; unknown numbers received informal training and engaged in casual work.

of 'secular' youth until 24 years of age and after for men (marriage and full participation in a trade), and 21 or earlier for women (marriage or the close of service). In theory at least, therefore, women could enter adulthood at an earlier age, though gender is, of course, only one potential distinctive experience.

Ministers and magistrates competed for the ears and hearts of youth, who acquired knowledge and skills from many sources— parents, brothers, sisters, other relations, neighbours, and friends. Peer association and formative experiences of youth were highly valued. Nor must we forget the stories, legends, and advice of local lore and proverbial wisdom, which were spoken and sung from generation to generation. One significance of children's games, for example, is that they communicated ways of thinking about marriage and other aspects of the life-cycle which were frequently passed on by the young. Each household had its own set of characters and story. We can turn the pages of contemporary sources and find clear traces of the rough male culture, the 'alternative sabbath', casual work, informal training, games, and young people making choices about the work they would like to do, for example, or the person they would like to marry.[7]

The 'great enclosure' of Tudor and Stuart youth inside the household never took place. Nevertheless, we are still told that the household and socialization were daunting twin towers hovering over the lives of early modern youth, stretching out their oppressive grips and pulling young people back within the 'safe compass' of authority structures. They touched all aspects of daily life, but we must cross the threshold of the house, as early modern youth so often did, and enter the world of conviviality and play. This vital step allows us to sketch formative experiences and distinctive youthful identities, which help us not only to define the age of youth itself, but also to feel the ambiguities, the happy, passive, and gloomy aspects of household life and age-relations. Youth was experienced outside the household in a range of social and cultural possibilities, which gave the young a greater degree of autonomy than that permitted by the restrictive ethos of the politics of age and 'place'. Young people understood the practical value of worldly progress, and youth provided an opportunity to obtain requisite skills and save up money. Yet they also injected their own values into the socializing process. The significance that they attached to conviviality, courtship, and play not only affected their attitudes towards authority, but also shaped formative experiences in the long interval between childhood and adulthood.

In fact, moralists and magistrates were deeply troubled by the ambivalent influences of peer association in youth, and issued stern

---

[7] Cf. Ilana Krausman Ben-Amos, *Adolescence and Youth in Early Modern England* (New Haven, 1994), esp. chs. 4–7 and 9.

cautions against 'loose' company both inside and outside the household. These formative experiences in which the young came together to drink, play, dance, walk, and talk are the best place to seek experiences of youth in early modern society. They may seem mundane, ordinary, and perhaps a trifle dull. Yet one quality of these commonplace experiences is their familiarity, for it represents a degree of historical activity and identity which has been denied to early modern youth by a number of highly influential historians. Their significance lies in their existence. The 'middle territory', therefore, was also an arena for accommodation; young people could create their own spaces and places in Tudor and Stuart society within existing structures of authority.

Their experience of 'accommodation' was one important aspect of age-relations because the 'middle territory' was also a place for consent and even toleration. As we have seen, adults appear in the sources as participators, providers, planners, and spectators. These 'shamelesse adult bawds' were objects of contempt in the pulpit, study, and courtroom, but they were also influential mediators of authority. They offered a measure of clemency and toleration to youth which was considered inappropriate in a stage of life when good and evil wrestled for possession of souls. After all, the portrait of shackled youth closely closeted within the household depends upon the consent and participation of adults. This can help us to understand how young people clarified their inferiority in early modern society; the adult 'bawd' mitigated the stern tone and ordered existence of the politics of age. The nature of experiences inside regulatory institutions like the household or service was often a pale reflection of the comprehensive subordination envisaged by moralists. Ultimately, the 'adult bawd' shows how the meaning of patriarchy was interpreted in different ways. The authorities may not have agreed with them, but many householders saw little harm in allowing young people a large slice of freedom so long as the significance of work and time was not entirely forgotten. The memory of their youth had not yet faded and they, after all, had grown up in much the same way. Again, the rough age/youth polarity is too simple. Young and old found themselves on the same side in conflicts with the clerical authorities, for example, about religious commitment and popular culture in which many of the principal actors were typically young.

Nevertheless, the household was not always a place of harmony and order. Discordant notes were sounded, and domestic tranquillity was often shattered by a menacing threat, a choice slander, a firm blow, light fingered servants who stole from their masters, and others who ran away. There were many ambiguous notes in constructions of authority—the grooming of male aggression in martial training, for example, or images of the age of youth itself. In fact, there were fine limits to the 'tricks' of youth in the small households and workshops in which young people lived and worked. The smooth passage of the working day, profit, and efficiency were of great concern to masters and guilds, and such interests shaped their ideas about youthful conviviality. One potential point of tension in the socialization of youth, therefore, was tutored work and time. Masters and magistrates agreed about the value of an ordered working day, though a large number of householders were less concerned with producing virtuous and pious youth, and rather more prepared to grant their young charges freedom for pastimes which were considered suspicious by moralists. One suspects that even some of the latter wearied of the task, and ritually bleated the time-honoured slogans and paroxysms of those for whom the ideal figures of virtuous youth were a desperate necessity. They bleated in a regular and predictable manner because they were professional complainers, but also because the nature of experiences of youth was more creative than the politics of age could possibly allow.

There are still an intimidating number of questions to answer, so many aspects of the lives of early modern youth to uncover, and other sources to investigate. Some parts of the story are only lightly touched on here like potential parental control of their offspring through inheritance and the transfer of property, or the position of journeymen—young wage labourers who were poised at the border between youth and adulthood. Journeymen formed a distinct interest group, who on occasion felt that their life-chances were being squeezed by the entry of an excessive number of apprentices into their trade, for example, or by a rising tide of foreigners.[8] Their position over time as pools of wage labour expanded in the towns requires further work. Still other aspects of youth are difficult to recover, obscured by the nature or uneven survival of the sources. One problem in the use of courtbooks is that dissent plays the leading part, and conformity and orthodoxy can appear remote. The visibility of dissident youth is a temptation, but it is risky to draw impressions of youth from such sources alone. Nevertheless, the meaning of conformity or opposition raises further questions.

[8] See Steve Rappaport, *Worlds within Worlds: Structures of Life in Sixteenth-century London* (Cambridge, 1989), 238–44.

The interpretations of moralists, magistrates, and householders were rarely consistent, and there were interesting quarrels about the significance of work, instruction, free time, and toleration.[9] The status of conformity, therefore, was one point of dispute. So much so, that even godliness provoked squabbles and opened up distances between godly youth and their family and friends. The 'sons of wisdom' found consolation and inner strength in their commitment; a confidence which not only gave them a sense of purpose, but also a desire to 'withdraw' from the 'wicked' company of wanton friends and, on occasion, their profane family.[10] The pressure to raise pious youth was not accepted in every quarter, and the resulting impression of conformity is inevitably confused. Further work on the character of these ambiguities, the meaning of conformity, and the concessions and compromises made on all sides, will help us to sketch a more complete (and complicated) picture of age-relations. One possible next step is to reduce our focus and explore experiences of youth in particular occupations, communities, and manufacturing and agricultural districts.

Despite these calls for closer understanding of historical contexts of place and work, this introduction to issues of youth and authority has often tended of necessity to treat youth in a rather general fashion. Yet we would require many shades of colour to draw distinctions of regional patterns of work, economies, and structures on a national map. Early modern society was a 'patterned' society. Is there, therefore, an ecological interpretation of age and authority? Was the problem of youth more visible in the scattered settlements of wood-pasture regions, or in the closer-knit arable communities?[11] The form and availability of work was naturally of great importance, and a more complete picture would only emerge after close study of employment in cities, towns, coastal, industrial, and agrarian communities. It is arguably unhelpful to treat life in town and country as being thoroughly different. Nevertheless, a few lines of enquiry require further work. Natalie Davis and others have argued that formal youth groups crumbled in urban society and that they had a longer life-span in the countryside.[12] The nature of cultural

---

[9] See above, esp. Chs. 3–4 and 6–7.

[10] The ideas of Philip Greven communicated by Roger Thompson, *Sex in Middlesex: Popular Mores in a Massachusetts County, 1649–1699* (Amherst, Mass., 1986).

[11] Cf. David Underdown, *Revel, Riot and Rebellion: Popular Politics and Culture in England 1603–1660* (Oxford, 1985); id., 'Regional cultures Local variation in popular culture during the early modern period', in Tim Harris (ed.) *Popular Culture in England, c.1500–1850* (Basingstoke, 1995).

[12] See above, Ch. 3.

experiences in rural districts could be further investigated. Territorial affiliations energized by perambulations provided a source of identification for young people, who expressed the pedigree of their birthplace in rivalry with the youth of neighbouring communities. The hunt for organized youth groups should continue. But the role of young people in patrolling local mores has been exaggerated, and looser affiliations of youth which were none the less formative experiences take us closer to the nature of youth culture. The principal aspects of service in husbandry are well known,[13] though the role of family and the courts in regulating disordered households in the countryside has been little explored. The images of youth and expectations of socialization regulating rural servants, parish apprentices, and urban apprentices and servants all require further work.

2. *The 'Magnification of Distance'*

Another ordering historical context is time. This book has explored the years of youth—a time in the life-course—in a particular period, *c.*1560–*c.*1640. It has argued that the history of youth is neither static nor predictable. Some aspects of change were touched on in the Introduction, and more fully explored in the discussion of 'masterless' young people. They include shifting demographic structures, changes in patterns of work, cycles of unemployment, and periodic scares like plague and dearth. Contexts change and shape the history of youth. But they also require further study over a few centuries to sketch general explanations of the changing nature of collective experiences, juvenile delinquency, and definitions of youth as a particular subgroup. None of these things remained to be invented or discovered after 1750. It is now time for any future general interpretation of youth in history to trace the history of youth in England not simply from the now much diminished 'watershed' of the eighteenth century, but from a distant point like 1400 to more recent times. One side of the story would be changes in experiences and contexts, though another no less vital point of entry is that formative experiences of youth existed in former centuries. This is one reason why protests about 'ill-advised and ill-nurtured youth' were a perennial lament. The substance of the

---

[13] Ann Kussmaul, *Servants in Husbandry in Early Modern England* (Cambridge, 1981); Keith Snell, *Annals of the Labouring Poor: Social Change and Agrarian England, 1660–1900* (Cambridge, 1985); Ben-Amos, *Adolescence and Youth in Early Modern England,* ch. 3.

complaint clearly altered. In early modern society (but not only then) the problem of youth was most commonly expressed in the limitations of service. The incidence of service fluctuated, more people earned a wage, and more servants lived outside the household.[14] In time factories dotted the landscape and the classroom became a further arena for instruction (and peer association). But the idea of youth as a distinctive problem or subgroup was firmly rooted well before the dawn of 'modernity'. We discover descriptions of problems associated with youth, and fears about socialization in the records of Tudor and Stuart England. They send a shudder across the centuries. The rhetoric and structures of authority change in time, but the particular identity of youth raised problems for each new generation of magistrates, compelling them to propose precise solutions to ensure the regular turning of the life-cycle.

So, the question of time is also that of comparisons across different centuries; the distances or resemblances between traditional, pre-industrial, early modern youth, and their modern, industrial, and post-industrial successors. It will be clear by now that I feel that peculiarities have been inflated. This magnification of distance has also distorted our impression of the nature of youth in early modern society. There are, however, some glaring contrasts. As time passed it was much less likely that young people would work in service or be apprenticed. Other forms of work and education replaced the institution of service as primary arenas for socializing the young. Few young people now depart home in early teens, many of them remain there for most of their teenage years. Authority structures have changed, even if the form of instruction is in some respects remarkably similar. The catechism and sermon are no longer principal tools of persuasion; that element of compulsion has been lifted for most people. The schoolteacher has replaced the master. The duration of youth has also been trimmed as opportunities for earning a wage in youth have soared, and age at first marriage has fallen. The interval between the first stirrings of puberty and full employment and marriage has been considerably cut back in the last two hundred years, even if puberty now begins at an earlier point.[15] A shorter youth affects the assimilation of new experiences and feelings. It is evident that the scale of paid work in youth has risen; that a corresponding change in opportunities to

[14] See Kussmaul, *Servants in Husbandry*, chs. 2 and 6–7; Snell, *Annals of the Labouring Poor*, chs. 2 and 5.

[15] See Peter Laslett, 'Age at sexual maturity in Europe since the Middle Ages', in his *Family Life and Illicit Love in Earlier Generations: Essays in Historical Sociology* (Cambridge, 1977).

follow and express independent styles and positions has occurred; that these sentiments and countenances of youth are widely disseminated in sophisticated and popular print and audio-visual media; and that schools, youth clubs, bars, and discothèques, for example, provide a growing number of venues for peer-association and the articulation of youthful identities.

Nevertheless, the scale of this independence, expression, and creativity in recent times should not eclipse similar (though less visible) affiliations and sentiments in early modern society. Material and cultural circumstances have unquestionably altered. A larger stock of money, news, ideas, and images are in circulation. The forms of outward expression continue to change at a dazzling pace. But what about inward feeling—emotions? Has the changeable and restless material environment touched youthful emotions, rewriting sensitivities at it continues its forward march? We have already seen too many connections over four or five centuries to present any period as being entirely remote. Much feels quite familiar in early modern England. We do not have to search too hard in contemporary records to discover disruptive, posturing, and disobedient youth; blossoming physical attraction, and young people falling in love; and emotional and social solidarities forged by conviviality and play. Tudor and Stuart youth experienced puberty, they treasured self-expression, and delighted in novelty. They even had their equivalents of denim, hair gel, violent skirmishes, and rock and roll. Youthful clothing, hair-styles, violence, and dancing provoked a chorus of outrage as moralists struggled to communicate their images of upright youth, including 'outward' appearances. The taste for striking clothing and long hair, especially among apprentices, was a highly public representation of youthful preferences and competition with the authorities.

The quarrel about 'outward conformity' between young people and older moralists has a long history; it draws from a deep well of common emotions which connect distant centuries. But not everything can be the same. Structures and forms have changed, and feelings have been renewed, revised, or released. It seems reasonable to argue that there has been a lifting of some sources of frustration in the past two centuries. The conflict between extended youth and independence, dependency, and self-expression, is not as sharp. The prolonged youth which was common in early modern society was itself a source of impatience for some young people who took short-cuts to adulthood and married or set up in trade before the close of their term of service. The earlier entry into marriage or full employment in recent times raises other types of problems, but it has softened the simmering frustration which some early modern youth felt as they saw their years of service stretching ahead of them. This partial erosion of dependency, especially in late teens and early twenties, has fostered a more confident, earlier expression of independence, which is further cemented by the wider circulation of images and ideas, and earlier frequent access to money. (Yet even these ubiquitous channels of communication are double-edged because the numerous images which are flashed before today's young people are so often fictional representations of youth drawn by commercial and regulatory interests.) Whether a more regular discharge of hitherto dammed-up sexual electricity has helped to soothe inner stresses depends on how we characterize the nature of youth in former centuries. But it is not possible to call the young people of Tudor and Stuart England 'resolutely unerotic';[16] too much contrary evidence and too many prudent reservations have been presented. Let us simply say that potential checks like late marriage and a long spell in service have ceased to operate as they did in early modern society. A more widely dispersed and spirited sense of youthful independence is as likely a consequence of these life-cyclical adjustments as a great escape of sexual energy.

The changing form and scale of problems of youth has encouraged recent generations to think of their fresh crop of youth as a highly visible, troublesome, noisy, and distinctive contemporary problem. The anxieties and aspirations of older generations are projected onto the rising youth, who will be principal participants in the unpredictable yet imminent future. There is always hope of improvement. It is a necessary theme, and a 'positive' image of diligent and good-natured youth is a strategic symbol. Upright young people will be found to inform their less worthy peers; pictures and stories will be circulated. But there will also be a negative and pessimistic rhetoric. The struggle between good and bad morals is always enacted in miniature in competing representations of youth, and given further age-aspects by references to generational tension, or youth as an emblem of renewal—the hope of the future. This two-sided representation of youth as 'contested territory' is a basic component of rhetorics of authority at any time. To be sure, 'orthodox' and 'dissident' youth will be found at each pole. But the most useful purpose of the idea of 'contested territory' is to present alternatives; to play one off against the other; to encourage conformity

---

[16] See above, Ch. 5.

and, ultimately, a fluent cycle of generational succession, producing upright youth. It tends to discount the middle territory between outright conformity and dissent—the juggling of the two, choice, and experimentation. But this was where most young people have grown up in the past, and still continue to grow. That much has remained constant. It is true that the ways of growing up have expanded or changed since say 1700. New institutions, communications, and structures of authority have emerged, but few of the positions and postures of youth have in fact altered. If we 'stop' history at any point in time between 1560 and the present day, we will discover an extensive range of experiences—passivity, resignation, indifference, conformity, resistance, creativity, and autonomy. Young people will always retain the skill to move between these statuses. In recent times they may have done so with increasing perception and competence. New styles and habits are highly visualized, at each turn we encounter the latest fashion, the most recent drug, or current juvenile crime. They have become public property. This means that the scale of juvenile delinquency, for example, can seem crushing. But the problem itself is not making its first appearance. It is a question of scale and publicity; of historical context. That is the great observable difference across time.

Nevertheless, while recognizing the existence of youth in early modern England, recent interpretations have presented the nature of experiences of youth at this time in rather negative and colourless terms.[17] One closes some studies with a sense of wonder; in their pages young people in early modern society seem so distant. They were quiet conformists, it seems, and had little time or liberty for formative experiences. This sort of common participation and feeling is missing. It makes the youth that we know (and had) seem very different. Were young people in early modern society really that foreign? To be sure, they have their unique qualities, but the social and emotional bond of youth flowed through them. So long as the householder looms large over them and quashes their energy and enterprise; so long as we abbreviate formative experiences by denying them their own space and time, early modern youth will always seem remote and exotic creatures. But the 'enclosure' of youth was never complete. This early modern youth was not a shackled youth. It was busy, creative, resourceful, but also complex and enigmatic. Friedrich Nietzsche once said that the history of punishment 'has finally crystallized into a kind of complex which it is

---

[17] I have in mind the recent monograph by Ilana Krausman Ben-Amos.

difficult to break down and quite impossible to define'.[18] The social history of youth is equally composed of many parts. This complication of interpretation may appear to be a sheltering place from a single resolute line of explanation, or an exhilarating linear progress. But it is itself a shrewd interpretative position. Yet this misty ambiguity cannot conceal the creativity of youth, which bursts through on so many occasions, giving early modern youth a presence, an identity, and, above all, historical agency.

[18] Quoted in David Garland, *Punishment and Modern Society: A Study in Social Theory* (Oxford, 1990), 17.

BIBLIOGRAPHY

1. MANUSCRIPT SOURCES

Borthwick Institute of Historical Research, York

CV/CB1 Archdeaconry of Cleveland, Visitation Book, 1632.
CV/CB2 Archdeaconry of Cleveland, Visitation Book, 1634.
CV/CB3 Archdeaconry of Cleveland, Visitation Book, 1641.
YV/CB1 Archdeaconry of York, Visitation Book, 1598.
YV/CB2 Archdeaconry of York, Visitation Book, 1613.
Wis/1 Prebendal visitation of Wistow (articles); petitions and responses regarding a pew dispute in Wistow church, 1663.
D/C CP. 1640–2 Disputes about pew rights in Wistow parish.

Cambridge University Library

(a) *Ely Diocesan Records*

B/2/10 'A Book of Actes upon Presentments within the Deaneries of Ely and Wisbech, 1581'; Comperta and Proceedings, 1581–3.
B/2/11 Liber Visitationis 1590; Comperta and Proceedings, 1590–2.
B/2/12 Liber Compertorum ... 1592; Comperta and Proceedings, 1592–3.
B/2/13 Liber Compertorum ... 1593; Comperta and Proceedings, 1593–6.
B/2/14 Pro Decanatu Ely; Comperta and Proceedings, April 1593.
B/2/15 Pro Decanatu Wisbech; Comperta and Proceedings, 1593–1600.
B/2/16 Visitatio Archiepiscopi Cant Sede Episcopalie Eliens Vacante, 1596; Comperta in Eadem Visitatione, 1596; Comperta and Proceedings, 1596–9.
B/2/17 Visitatio Archiepiscopi Cant, 1599; Comperta in Eadem Visitatione; Comperta and Proceedings, 1599–1600.
B/2/18 Visitation Book; Comperta and Proceedings, 1601.
B/2/20 Consistory Court Office Act Book, Wisbech Deanery, 1600–6.
B/2/21 Consistory Court Office Act Book, Ely Deanery, 1600–6.
B/2/22 Visitation Book, Comperta and Proceedings, 1602–3, 1603–4.
B/2/24 Consistory Court Office Act Book, Ely Deanery, 1606–7.
B/2/25 Archdeaconry Visitation of Barton, Camps and Chesterton Deaneries; Comperta and Proceedings, 1605.
B/2/26 Consistory Court Office Act Book, Wisbech Deanery, 1606–8.
B/2/27 Consistory Court Office Act Book, Wisbech Deanery, 1608–11.

B/2/28 Consistory Court Office Act Book, County only, 1609.

B/2/29 Metropolitan Visitation, 1608; Comperta and Proceedings, County only; Comperta and Proceedings, Isle of Ely.

B/2/30 Consistory Court Office Act Book, Ely Deanery, 1609–10.

B/2/31 Visitatio Reverendi . . . Lancelotti . . . 1610, 1615, 1616; Comperta and Proceedings, Ely and Wisbech Deaneries, 1610; County only 1610–11.

B/2/32 Visitation Book; Comperta and Proceedings, County only, 1622–3.

B/2/33 Metropolitan Visitation, 1615; Comperta and Proceedings, County only, 1615–16; Ely Deanery, 1615.

B/2/34 Consistory Court Office Act Book, Wisbech Deanery, 1614–18.

B/2/35 Consistory Court Office Act Book, Ely Deanery, 1614–18.

B/2/36 Consistory Court Office Act Book, County only, 1617–18.

B/2/37 Visitation Book, 1617; Comperta and Proceedings, County and Isle, 1619.

B/2/38 Consistory Court Office Act Book, Wisbech Deanery, 1618–23.

B/2/39 Consistory Court Office Act Book, Ely Deanery, 1618–22.

B/2/40 Consistory Court Office Act Book, County only, 1624.

B/2/46 Assignation Book etc., Isle only, 1633–5.

B/2/52 Consistory Court Office Act Book, County only, 1639; Ely Deanery, March 1639; Wisbech Deanery, 1639.

B/2/53 Consistory Court Office Act Book, Ely Deanery, April 1639; Wisbech Deanery, April 1639.

B/9/1 Barton-in-Whitwell Churchwardens' Presentments, 1582.

B/9/5 St Edward's Passage, Cambridge, Churchwardens' Presentments, 1639.

B/9/8 Chesterton Churchwardens' Presentments, 1662.

B/9/9 Ungry Hattley Churchwardens' Presentments, 1662.

B/9/10 Maddingley Churchwardens' Presentments, 1662.

B/9/12 Histon Churchwardens' Presentments, 1662.

B/9/15 Dry Drayton Churchwardens' Presentments, 1662.

B/9/52 Impington Churchwardens' Presentments, 1666.

C/10/1 Wisbech Barton Court Rolls, 1609–11; Wisbech Court Leet Presentments, May 1607.

D/2/9 Presentments before the Commissary, Isle of Ely, 1572–7.

D/2/10 Visitation Books, 1576, 1579; Act Book of Office Causes, County only, 1577–9; Comperta and Proceedings, County only, 1579.

D/2/10a Presentment Book, Isle only, 1633–5.

D/2/18 Consistory Court Instance Act Book, 1588–92.

D/2/23 Consistory Court Office Act Book, County only, 1604–5.

D/2/25 Consistory Court Office Act Book, County only, 1605–6.

D/2/26 Consistory Court Office Act Book, Wisbech Deanery, 1606–8.

D/2/29 Act Book of Causes, Ely Diocese and Wisbech Deanery, 1608.

D/2/32 Consistory Court Office Act Book, County only, 1613.

D/2/35 Consistory Court Office Act Book, County only, 1616–17.
D/2/41 Consistory Court Assignations in Office Causes, County only, 1625–7; Occasional Notes of Presentments.
D/2/42 Consistory Court Assignation Book, Instance Causes, 1628–9.
D/2/46 Consistory Court Assignation Book; Presentments; County only, 1634–5.
D/2/51 Consistory Court Office Act Book, Isle only, January 1639; Comperta and Proceedings of 3 Visitations, Midsummer, Michaelmas, and Metropolitan, 1638.
D/5/40 Matthew Wren's Visitation Articles, 1638.
LA/3 Archdeaconry of Ely Act Book, 1622–3.
LA/4 Archdeaconry of Ely Comperta Book, 1624.
LA/5a Archdeaconry of Ely Comperta and Proceedings, 1626.
12/21, 1641–2 Deposition

(*b*) *Vice-Chancellor's Court*

Exhibita:
   VC Ct. III/1, 1540–95.
   VC Ct. III/2, 1586–96.
   VC Ct. III/3, 1593–4.
   VC Ct. III/4, 1594–5.
   VC Ct. III/5, 1595–6.
   VC Ct. III/6, 1596–7.
   VC Ct. III/7, 1597–8.
   VC Ct. III/8, 1597–1600.

(*c*) *Cambridge University Registry*

37.7, Town.
Collect Admin. 8, Tabor's book.

Canterbury Cathedral Library and Archives

MS X.17 Visitation Act Book, Comperta and Detecta, 1565.

Clothworkers' Hall, London

Company Minute Books:
   1536–58.
   1558–81.
   1581–1605.
   1605–23.

Corporation of London Record Office

Journals of London Common Council:
   Jours. 12–39, 1518/19–1640.
Remembrancia Books:
   II 1593–1609.
   III 1610–14.

IV 1616–18.
V 1618–22.
VI 1622–9.
VII 1629–37.
VIII 1618–40.

Repertories of the Court of Aldermen, London:
Reps. 12–55, 1548–1641.

Miscellaneous Files:
PD Series.

Essex Record Office

Act Books of the Archdeaconry of Colchester (I have consulted microfilm
copies of the original manuscripts in the possession of Keith Wrightson):
D/ACA 25, 1598–1602.
D/ACA 30, 1605–9.
D/ACA 32, 1608–11.
D/ACA 43, 1621–3.
D/ACA 44, 1623–5.
D/ACA 45, 1624–7.
D/ACA 46, 1627–9.
D/ACA 47, 1629–31.
D/ACA 48, 1631–2.
D/ACA 49, 1632–4.
D/ACA 50, 1634–5.
D/ACA 51, 1635–7.
D/ACA 52, 1637–8.
D/ACA 54, 1638–41.
D/ACA 55, 1663–6.

Friends' House Library, London

MS Box 10/10, 1–3, Josiah Langdale, *Some Account of the Birth, Education
and Religious Exercise and Visitation of God to That Faithful Servant and
Minister of Christ Josiah Langdale* (1723) (I have consulted a copy of this
document in the possession of Margaret Spufford)

Goldsmiths' Company Library, London

Court Minute Books:
O2 1599–1604.
O3 1604–11.
P1 1611–17.
P2 1617–24.
Q1 1624–9.
Q2 1629–30.
R1 1630–1.
R2 1631–4.

S1 1634–5.
S2 1635–7.
T 1637–9.
V 1639–42.
W 1642–5.

Guildhall Library, London

MS 6 *Memoires Historical Relating to the 5 Principall Hospitals in London viz of St Bartholomews, Bethlem, Bridewell, St Thomas'* (1681).
MS 1175/1 St Margaret's, New Fish St, Vestry Minute Book, 1578–1789.
MS 1431/2 St Alphage, London Wall, Vestry Minute Book, 1608–1711.
MS 1454 St Botolph Aldersgate, Churchwarden's Accounts.
MS 3016/1 St Dunstan's-in-the-West Vestry Minute Book, 1588–1663.
MS 3018/1 St Dunstan's-in-the-West Wardmote Inquest Book.
MS 3295/1 Turners Company Minute Book, 1605–33.
MS 3570/1 St Mary's, Aldermanbury, Vestry Minute Book, 1569–1609.
MS 3570/2 St Mary's, Aldermanbury, Vestry Minute Book, 1610–1763.
MS 4069/1 Cornhill Wardmote Inquest Book.
MS 4165/1 St Peter-upon-Cornhill Vestry Minute Book, 1570–1717.
MS 4214/1 St Benet, Gracechurch, Vestry Minute Book, 1607–1758.
MS 4329/2 Carpenters Company Wardens Account Book, 1573–94.
MS 4415/1 St Olave Jewry, Vestry Minute Book, 1574–1680.
MS 4655/1 Weavers Company Minute Book, 1610–42.
MS 5602/1 Coopers Company Minute Book, 1567–96.
MS 5770/1 Fishmongers Company Minute Book, 1593–1610.
MS 5770/2 Fishmongers Company Minute Book, 1610–31.
MS 6122/1 Plasterers Company Minute Book, 1571–1634.
MS 6554/1 St Bride's, Fleet St, Vestry Minute Book, 1645–65.
MS 7090/2 Pewterers Company Minute Book, 1561–89.
MS 7090/3 Pewterers Company Minute Book, 1589–1611.
MS 7090/4 Pewterers Company Minute Book, 1611–46.
MS 8200/1 Apothecaries Company Minute Book, 1617–51.
MS 11,588/1 Grocers Company Minute Book, 1556–91.
MS 11,588/2 Grocers Company Minute Book, 1591–1616.
MS 11,588/3 Grocers Company Minute Book, 1616–39.
MS 12,806/1 Christ's Hospital Minute Book, 1556–63.
MS 12,806/2 Christ's Hospital Minute Book, 1562–92.
MS 12,806/3 Christ's Hospital Minute Book, 1592–1632.
MS 15,842/1 Haberdashers Company Minute Book, 1582–1652.

Bridewell Hospital records (consulted on microfilm):
BCB 1 Courtbook, 1559–62.
BCB 2 Courtbook, 1574–6.
BCB 3 Courtbook, 1576–9.
BCB 4 Courtbook, 1597–1604.
BCB 5 Courtbook, 1604–10.

BCB 6 Courtbook, 1617–26.
BCB 7 Courtbook, 1627–34.
BCB 8 Courtbook, 1634–42.

Norwich and Norfolk Record Office, Norwich

(*a*) *Corporation Records*

Minute Books of the Norwich Court of Mayoralty:
    NMC 7 1555–62.
    NMC 8 1562–69.
    NMC 9 1569–76.
    NMC 10 1576–81.
    NMC 11 1582–87.
    NMC 12 1587–95.
    NMC 13 1595–1603.
    NMC 14 1603–15.
    NMC 15 1615–24.
    NMC 16 1625–34.
    NMC 20 1634–46.

Assembly Minute Books vols iv and v.

City of Norwich Quarter Sessions Minute Book, 1629–36.
'The Sessions Booke 1630–38'.

(*b*) *Diocesan Records*

Vis 6/1 Visitation Book, Archdeaconries of Norwich, Sudbury and Suffolk,
    1629.
Vis 7/1 Visitation Book, Archdeaconry of Norfolk, 1626.

Oxfordshire Record Office, Oxford

MSS Oxfordshire Diocesan Papers, Proceedings of the Court of the Offi-
    cial of Banbury Peculiar, 1626–36.

Public Record Office, Chancery Lane

E134 Exchequer Depositions by Commission.
SP 12 State Papers Domestic, Elizabeth I.
SP 14 State Papers Domestic, James I.
SP 16 State Papers Domestic, Charles I.
STAC 8 Star Chamber proceedings, James I.

Somerset Record Office

DD/SAS/C/1193 Memoirs of John Cannon.

York City Archives

City Housebooks:
    B/32 1598–1605.
    B/33 1605–12.

B/34 1613–25.
B/35 1625–37.
B/36 1638–50.
E/63 Proceedings of the Commonwealth committee for York and Ainsty.
City and Ainsty Quarter Sessions minute book, 1638–62.

2. EARLY PRINTED BOOKS

ANON., *A Catechisme or Brief Instruction in the Principles of Christian Religion* (1617).
—— *The Office of Christian Parents* (Cambridge, 1616).
—— *A Short Catechisme for Householders with Praiers to the Same Adioyning* (1614).
—— *A Two-Fold Treatise, the One Decyphering the Worth of Speculation, the Other Containing a Discoverie of Youth and Age* (Oxford, 1612).
—— *A Warning to Young Men, Or a Man of Blood* (1680).
ABBOT, R., *A Christian Family Builded by God* (1653).
ALLEINE, J., *Christian Letters Full of Spiritual Instruction* (1671).
ALLEINE, R., *A Briefe Explanation of the Common Catechisme* (1630).
ALLEINE, T., et al., *The Life and Death of . . . Joseph Alleine* (appended to T. Alleine's *Christian Letters*, 1671).
ALLEN, E., *A Catechisme, That is to Say a Christian Instruction of the Principall Points of Christian Religion* (1551).
[ALLESTREE, R.], *The Whole Duty of Man* (1658).
AMES, W., *Conscience with the Powers and Cases thereof* (1639).
BABBINGTON, G., *A Very Fruitfull Exposition of the Ten Commandments* (1596).
BAILEY, N., *An Universal Etymological English Dictionary* (1721).
—— *Dictionarium Britannicum* (1736).
BALL, J., *A Short Treatise Contayning All the Principall Grounds of Christian Religion by Way of Questions and Answers* (1633).
—— *Short Questions and Answers Explaining the Common Catechism in the Book of Common Prayer* (1655).
BARGRAVE, I., *A Sermon Preached before King Charles . . . [on] March 27, 1627* (1627).
BARKER, P., *A Learned and Familiar Exposition upon the Ten Commandments* (1633).
BARNES, T., *The Wise-Man's Forecast against the Evill Time* (1624).
BAXTER, R., *A Christian Directory, Or a Sum of Practical Theologie and Cases of Conscience* (1673).
—— *The Poor Man's Family Book* (1674).
—— *Compassionate Counsel to All Young Men* (1681).
—— *The Catechizing of Families: A Teacher of Householders How to Teach Their Households* (1683).
—— *Reliquiae Baxterianae, Or Mr Richard Baxter's Narrative of the Most Memorable Passages of His Life and Times* (1696).

BAYLY, L., *The Practice of Piety* (30th edn., 1632).

BEARD, T., *The Theatre of God's Judgment* (1631).

BERNARD, R., *Two Twinnes or Two Parts of One Portion of Scripture* (1613).

—— *A Double Catechisme* (Cambridge, 1607).

BILLINGHAM, F., *Christian Oeconomy or Household Government* (1609).

—— *The Young Man's Scripture* (1609).

The Book of Common Prayer (1620).

BOWNDE, N., *The Doctrine of the Sabbath Plainly Layde Forth* (1595).

BRADFORD, J., *Godlie Meditations upon the Lordes Prayer, the Beliefe and Ten Commandments* (1652).

BROOKS, T., *Apples of Gold for All Young Men and Women and a Crown of Glory for Old Men and Women* (1662).

[BUCKERIDGE, J.], *A Sermon Preached at the Funeral of . . . Lancelot [Andrewes] the Lord Bishop of Winchester* (1629).

BURROWES, S., *Good Instruction for All Young Men and Maids* (1642).

BURTON, R., *The Apprentice's Companion* (1681).

CALVIN, J., *The Catechisme or Manner to Teache Children the Christian Religion* (1598).

CARPENTER, J., *The Plaine-Man's Spiritual Plough* (1607).

The Case of the Army Soberly Discussed (1647).

CAWDREY, D., *Family Reformation Promoted* (1656).

CAWDREY, R., *A Short and Fruitfull Treatise of the Profite and Necessitie of Catechising* (1580).

CHARRON, P., *Of Wisdome, Three Bookes*, trans. S. Lennard (1630).

CHEYNELL, F., *A Plea for the Good of Posterity* (1646).

CLARKE, S., *A Collection of the Lives of Ten Eminent Divines* (1662).

COTTON, J., *Milk for Babes* (1646).

CROFTON, Z., *Catechizing God's Ordinance* (1656).

CROOK, J., *A Short History of the Life and Times of John Crook, Written by Himself* (3rd edn., 1706).

CROOKE, S., *Brief Direction to True Happinesse* (1643).

CROSSMAN, S., *The Young Man's Calling, Or the Whole Duty of Youth* (1678).

[CROUCH, N.,] *Remarks upon the Lives of Several Excellent Young Persons of Both Sexes* (1678).

CUFFE, H., *The Difference of the Ages of a Man's Life* (1607).

DIGGES, D., *The Unlawfulnesse of Subjects Taking up Arms against Their Sovereign* (Oxford, 1643).

DOD, J., *A Plaine and Familiar Exposition of the Ten Commandments* (1606).

—— and CLEAVER, R., *A Godlie Forme of Household Government* (1612).

DOWNAME, J., *A Guide to Godlynesse, Or a Treatise of Christian Life* (1629).

DUNTON, J., *The Life and Errors of John Dunton Late Citizen of London* (1705).

EDWARDS, T., *The First and Second Parts of Gangreana* (1646).

ELTON, E., *A Forme of Catechizing* (1620).

ELYOT, Sir T., *The Castel of Health* (1541).

ESTYE, G., *A Most Sweete and Comfortable Exposition uppon the Ten Commandments* (1602).

FARINDON, A., *The Sermons of the Reverend Anthony Farindon* (4 vols.; 1849).

FENNER, D., *A Short and Profitable Treatise of Lawfull and Unlawfull Recreations* (Middelburg, 1590).

FLOYD, T., *The Picture of a Perfit Commonwealth* (1600).

FORTESCUE, T., *The Forest, Or Collection of Historyes* (1576).

FULLER, F., *Words to Give the Young Man Knowledge and Discretion* (1653).

GIFFORD, G., *A Catechisme Containing the Summe of Christian Religion* (1583).

GILLING, I., *The Life of George Trosse* (1715).

GOODMAN, G., *The Fall of Man, Or the Corruption of Nature Proved by the Light of Our Natural Reason* (1616).

GORE, J., *The Poor Man's Hope* (1646).

GOUGE, T., *A Narrative of the Life and Death of Dr Gouge* (1665).

GOUGE, W., *Of Domesticall Duties* (1622).

GRANGER, T., *The Tree of Good and Evil: Or a Profitable and Familiar Exposition of the Commandments* (1616).

GREENHAM, R., *The Works of the Reverend and Faithful Servant of Jesus Christ Mr Richard Greenham*, ed. H[enry] H[olland] (1601).

GRIFFITH, M., *Bethel, Or a Forme for Families* (1634).

GUILD, W., *A Young Man's Inquisition or Trial* (1608).

HALL, T., *The Loathsomenesse of Long Haire* (1654).

—— *Funebria Florae: The Downfall of May Games* (1661).

HARRINGTON, J., *Seven Models of a Commonwealth Ancient and Modern* (1659).

HARRISON, W., *The Difference of Hearers: Or an Exposition of Certayne Sermons* (1614).

HESKETH, H., *The Importance of Religion to Young Persons* (1683).

HEYWOOD, T., *The Foure Apprentices of London* (1600?).

HINDE, W., *A Faithfull Remonstrance of the Holy Life and Happy Death of John Bruen of Bruen Stapleford in the County of Chester* (1641).

The Humble Advice of the Assembly of Divines . . . Concerning i a Confession of Faith ii A Larger Catechism iii A Shorter Catechism (1648).

HYDE, E., *The Life of Edward Hyde, Earl of Clarendon* (3 vols.; Oxford, 1827).

INGELHARD, T., *A Pretie and Mery Enterlude Called the Disobedient Child* (1569).

JANEWAY, J., *Death Unstung: A Sermon Preached at the Funeral of Thomas Mowsley* (1669).

—— *A Token for Children Being an Exact Account of the Conversion, Holy and Exemplary Lives and Joyful Deaths of Several Young Children* (part 1, 1671, part 2, 1672).

JESSEY, H., *A Looking-Glasse for Children Being a Narrative of God's Gracious Dealing with Some Little Children . . . Together with Some Sundry Seasonable Lessons and Instructions to Youth Calling Them Early to Remember Their Creator* (3rd edn., 1673).

JONES, W., *Briefe Exhortation to All Men to Set Their Houses in Good Order* (1631).

KEACH, B., *War with the Devil, Or the Young Man's Conflict with the Powers of Darkness* (1684).

LAMBARDE, W., *The Duties of Constables, Borholders . . .* (1602).

LENTON, F., *The Young Gallant's Whirligigg, Or Youth's Reakes* (1629).

LILBURNE, J., *The Legall, Fundamentall Liberties of the People of England* (1649).

LILLY, W., *William Lilly's History of His Life and Times* (1822).

LOVELL, T., *A Dialogue between Custom and Veritie Concerning Dancing and Minstrelsie* (1581).

MAINWARING, R., *Religion and Allegiance; In Two Sermons Preached before the King's Majestie . . . [on] 4 July 1627* (1627).

MARTYN, W., *Youth's Instruction* (1612).

MAYER, J., *The English Catechism Explained, Or a Commentarie Set Forth in the Booke of Common Prayer* (1623).

MULCASTER, R., *Positions Wherein Those Primitive Circumstances be Examined Which are Necessarie for the Training up of Children* (1581).

The New Catechisme According to the Form of the Kirk of Scotland Very Profitable and Useful for Instructing of Children and Youth (1644).

NICHOLES, M., *A Catechisme Composed According to the Order of the Catechisme in the Common Prayer Book* (1642).

NICHOLLS, J., *An Order of Household Instruction* (1596).

NOWELL, A., *A Catechism or First Instruction and Learning of Christian Religion*, trans. T. Norton (1570).

OPENSHAW, R., *Short Questions and Answers, Conteyning the Summe of Christian Religion* (1614).

P., W., *The Prentise's Practise in Godlinesse and His True Freedome* (1613).

PAGITT, E., *Heresiography, Or a Description of the Hereticks and Sectaries of These Latter Times* (4th edn., 1647).

PARKER, H., *Vox Populi, Or a Discourse Wherein Clear Satisfaction is Given, as Well Concerning the Right of Subjects as the Right of Princes* (1644).

POWELL, T., *The Beauty, Vigour and Strength of Youth Bespoke for God* (1676).

POWELL, V., *The Life and Death of Mr Vavassor Powell* (1671).

PRICE, S., *The Two Twins of Birth and Death* (1624).

PRYNNE, W., *The Unlovelinesse of Lovelockes* (1628).

—— *Minors no Senators* (1646).

R., F., *A Collection of English Proverbs* (Cambridge, 1670).

RALEIGH, W., *The History of the World in Five Books* (1614).

SHELFORD, R., *Lectures or Readings upon the 6 Verse of the 22 Chapter of Proverbs Concerning the Vertuous Education of Youth* (1606).

SHOWER, J., *Seasonable Advice to Youth* (1692).

—— *Some Memoirs of the Life of John Shower* (1716).

SMITH, J., *The Pourtract of Old Age* (1676).

SPARKE, T., *A Treatise to Prove that Ministers Publickely and Householders Privately are Bound to Catechize Their Parishioners and Families* (Oxford, 1588).

STAFFORD, A., *Meditations and Resolutions, Moral, Divine, Political, Written for the Instruction and Bettering of Youth* (1612).

STALLHAM, J., *A Catechisme for Children in Yeeres and Children in Understanding* (1644).

STEELE, R., *A Discourse Concerning Old Age* (1688).

STOCKWOOD, J., *A Sermon Preached at Paules Crosse on St Bartholomew's Day 29 August 1578* (1578).

STRYPE, J., *Lessons Moral and Christian for Youth and Old Age* (1699).

—— *Annals of the Reformation and Establishment of Religion* (4 vols.; 1725–31).

SWAN, J., *Redde Debitum: Or a Discourse in Defence of Three Chief Fatherhoods* (1640).

TAYLOR, J., *A Bawd, a Vertuous Bawd*, in his *Works* (2 vols.; 1630).

TAYLOR, T., *The Works of the Faithfull Servant of Jesus Christ, Dr Thomas Taylor* (1653).

TRENCHFIELD, C., *A Cap of Grey Hairs for a Green Head: Or the Father's Counsel to His Son an Apprentice* (1710).

TURNER, R., *Youth Know Thyself* (1624).

VAUGHAN, W., *The Golden-Grove* (1600).

—— *Directions for Health* (1626).

VINCENT, T., *Words of Advice to Young Men* (1688).

VOWELL [HOOKER], J., *Orders Enacted for Orphans and for Their Portions within the Citie of Exeter* (1575).

WHITE, T., *A Little Book for Little Children* (1660).

WIDLEY, G., *The Doctrine of the Sabbath* (1604).

3. EDITIONS OF EARLY BOOKS AND MANUSCRIPTS

A Supplement to the Onania, 1723 ed. R. Trumbach (facsimile, Garland Series: Marriage, Sex and the Family in England 1660–1800, New York, 1986).

Amanda, Or the Reformed Whore, 1635, ed. F. Ouvry (1869).

Aristotle's Compleat Masterpiece in Three Parts Displaying the Secrets of Nature in the Generation of Man, 23rd edn., 1749, ed. R. Trumbach (Garland Series: Marriage, Sex and the Family in England 1660–1800, 11, 1986).

Aristotle's Book of Problems, 13th edn., 1775, ed. R. Trumbach (Garland Series: Marriage, Sex and the Family in England 1660–1800, 11, 1986).

ASCHAM, R., *The Scholemaster*, in *English Works*, ed. W. A. Wright (Cambridge, 1970).

ATKINSON, J. C. (ed.), *North Riding Quarter Sessions* (9 vols.; North Riding Record Society, 1–9, 1884–92).

AUBREY, J., *Remaines of Gentilisme and Judaisme 1686–1687*, ed. James Britten (Folklore Society, 4, 1881).

BAILEY, F. A. (ed.), *A Selection from the Prescot Court Leet and Other Records 1447–1600* (Lancashire and Cheshire Record Society, 89, Blackpool, 1937).

BARMBY, J. (ed.), *Churchwarden's Accounts of Pittington and Other Parishes in the Diocese of Durham from A.D. 1580–1700* (Surtees Society, 84, Durham, 1888).

BARNES, R.,*The Injunctions and Other Ecclesiastical Proceedings of Richard Barnes* (Surtees Society, 22, Durham, 1850).

BECON, T., *A New Catechism Set Forth Dialogue Wise* (Parker Society, 13, Cambridge, 1864).

BLUNDELL, M. (ed.), *Blundell's Diary and Letter Book 1702–1728* (Liverpool, 1952).

BLUNDELL, N., *The Great Diurnall of Nicholas Blundell of Little Crosby*, ed. J. J. Bagley (3 vols.; Lancashire and Cheshire Record Society, 110, 112, 114, Preston, 1968–72).

BLUNDELL, W., *Crosby Records: A Cavalier's Notebook*, ed. T. Ellison Gibson (Liverpool, 1952).

BOLTON, E., *The Cities Advocate*, 1629 (facsimile, The English Experience, 175, Amsterdam, NJ, 1975).

BOYLE, J. R., and Dendy F. W. (eds.), *Extracts from the Records of the Merchant Adventurers of Newcastle-upon-Tyne* (2 vols.; Surtees Society, 93, 101, Durham, 1895, 1899).

BRAND, J., *Observations on the Popular Antiquities of Great Britain*, rev. Harry Ellis (3 vols.; Bohns Antiquarian Library, 8–10, 1849).

BRINKWORTH, E. R. (ed.), *The Archdeacon's Court: Liber Actorum 1584* (2 vols.; Oxfordshire Record Society, 23–4, 1942).

—— (ed.), *Shakespeare and the Bawdy Courts of Stratford* (1972).

BROWN, R., *et al.* (eds.), *Calendar of the State Papers and Manuscripts Relating to English Affairs, Existing in the Archives and Collections of Venice* (40 vols.; 1864–1947).

BULLOCK, F. W. B. (ed.), *Evangelical Conversion in Great Britain 1516–1695* (St Leonard's-on-Sea, 1966).

BUNYAN, J., *Grace Abounding to the Chief of Sinners* and *The Life and Death of Mr Badman* (Everyman edn., 1928).

BURTON, K. M. (ed.), *A Dialogue between Reginald Pole and Thomas Lupset* (1948).

CALVIN, J., *Institutes of the Christian Religion*, ed. J. T. McNeill (2 vols.; Library of Christian Classics, 20–1, 1961).

CARDWELL, E. (ed.), *Synodolla: A Collection of Articles of Religion, Canons and Proceedings of Convocation in the Province of Canterbury* (2 vols.; Oxford, 1966).

CHAMBERS, R. (ed.), *The Book of Days: A Miscellany of Popular Antiquities* (2 vols.; 1859).

CHAPMAN, G., *et al.*, *Eastward Ho*, 1605 (Tudor Facsimile Texts, New York, 1970).

CHAPPELL, W. (ed.), *The Roxburghe Ballads* (Ballad Society, 14 vols.; London, 1869–95).

COCKBURN, J. S. (ed.), *Western Circuit Assize Orders 1629–1648: A Calendar* (Publications of the Camden Society, 4th ser., 17, 1976).

COOPER, C. H., and COOPER, J. W. (eds.), *Annals of Cambridge* (5 vols.; 1842–1908).

Cox, J. C. (ed.), *Churchwarden's Accounts from the Fourteenth Century to the Close of the Seventeenth Century* (1913).

Cranmer, T., *Miscellaneous Writings and Letters*, ed. J. E. Cox (Parker Society, Cambridge, 1846).

Crosse, H., *Vertue's Commonwealth*, 1603, ed. A. B. Grossart (Edinburgh, 1878).

Cunnington, B. H. (ed.), *Some Annals of the Borough of Devizes* (Devizes, 1925).

Dasent, J. R., *et al.* (eds.), *Acts of the Privy Council* (46 vols., 1890–1964).

Day, W. C. (ed.), *The Pepys Ballads* (Cambridge, 1987).

Dekker, T., *The Dramatic Works of Thomas Dekker*, ed. T. Bowers (4 vols.; Cambridge, 1955–61).

Dent, A., *The Plaine-Man's Path-way to Heaven*, 1601 (facsimile, The English Experience, 652, Amsterdam, NJ, 1974).

Dunton, J., *The Night-Walker, Or Evening Rambles in Search of Lewd Women*, 1696, ed. R. Trumbach (Garland Series: Marriage, Sex and the Family in England 1660–1800, 19, 1985).

Earwaker, J. P. (ed.), *The Court Leet Records of the Manor of Manchester from 1552 to 1686* (6 vols.; Manchester, 1884–90).

Eliot, J., *Christian Commonwealth*, 1659 (facsimile, Research Library of Colonial Americana, New York, 1972).

Elyot, Sir T., *Dictionary*, 1538 (Scolar Press Facsimile, Menston, 1970).

Emerson, E. H. (ed.), *English Puritanism from John Hooper to John Milton* (Durham, NC, 1968).

Emmison, F. G., *Early Essex Town Meetings: Braintree 1619–1636, Finchingfield 1626–1634* (Chichester, 1970).

Ferguson, R. S. (ed.), *Some Municipal Records of the City of Carlisle* (Cumberland and Westmorland Antiquarian and Archaeological Society, 4, Kendal, 1887).

—— (ed.), *The Boke of Recorde of Kirkbie Kendall* (Cumberland and Westmorland Antiquarian and Archaeological Society, Extra Series, 4, Kendal, 1892).

Fetherstone, C., *A Dialogue against Light . . . Lewde and Lascivious Dauncing*, 1582 (Scolar Press Facsimile, Ibstock, 1973).

Forman, S., *The Autobiography and Personal Diary of Dr Simon Forman*, ed. J. O. Halliwell (1849).

Frere, W. H. (ed.), *Visitation Articles and Injunctions of the Period of the Reformation 1536–1575* (3 vols.; Alcuin Club Collections, 14–16, 1910).

Freshfield, E. (ed.), *The Vestry Minute Book of the Parish of St Margaret Lothbury in the City of London 1571–1677* (1887).

—— (ed.), *The Vestry Minute Book of the Parish of St Bartholomew-by-the-Exchange in the City of London 1567–1676* (1890).

Gardiner, S. R. G. (ed.), *Reports of Cases in the Courts of Star Chamber and High Commission* (Camden Society Publications, New Series, 39, Westminster, 1886).

GASCOIGNE, G., *The Glass of Government*, 1575 (Tudor Facsimile Texts, New York, 1970).

GIBBS, A. E. (ed.), *The Corporation Records of St Albans* (St Albans, 1890).

GIBSON, J. S. W., and BRINKWORTH, E. R. C. (eds.), *Banbury Corporation Records: Tudor and Stuart* (Banbury Historical Society, 15, Banbury, 1977).

GOOMBRIDGE, M. J. (ed.), *Calendar of the Chester City Council Minutes* (Lancashire and Cheshire Record Society, 106, Blackpool, 1956).

GOUGH, R., *The History of Myddle*, ed. David Hey (Harmondsworth, 1981).

GREENE, R., *A Disputation between a He Cony-Catcher and a She Cony-Catcher*, 1592, repr. in A. V. Judges (ed.), *The Elizabethan Underworld* (1965).

GUILDING, J. M. (ed.), *Reading Records: Diary of the Corporation* (4 vols.; Reading, 1886).

[GWILLIM, J.], *The London Bawd with Her Character and Life*, 4th edn., 1711, ed. R. Trumbach (Garland Series: Marriage, Sex and the Family in England 1660–1800, 17, 1985).

HALE, W. (ed.), *A Series of Precedents and Proceedings in Criminal Causes Extending from the Year 1457 to 1640: Extracts from the Act Books of the Ecclesiastical Courts in the Diocese of London*, 1847 (facsimile, Edinburgh, 1973).

HARRIS, M. D. (ed.), *The Coventry Leet Book* (Early English Text Society, numbered in original series 134–5, 138, 146, 1907–13).

HERBERT, G., *The Works of George Herbert in Prose and Verse* (2 vols.; 1859).

HEYWOOD, O., *Autobiography, Diaries, Anecdote and Event Books*, ed. J. Horsfal Turner (4 vols.; Brighouse, 1882).

—— *The Life of John Angier of Denton* (Chetham Society, 97, Manchester, 1937).

HOBSON, M. G., and SALTER, H. E. (eds.), *Oxford Council Acts 1626–1665* (Oxford Historical Society, 95, Oxford, 1933).

JACKSON, A., *The Pious Prentice, Or the Prentise's Piety*, 1640 (facsimile, The English Experience, 746, Amsterdam, NJ, 1975).

JAFFRAY, A., *The Diary of Alexander Jaffray*, ed. J. Barclay (1833).

JEAFFRESON, J. C. (ed.), *Middlesex County Records* (Middlesex County Record Society, 4 vols.; 1886–92).

JOHNSTONE, H. (ed.), *Churchwarden's Presentments (Seventeenth Century), Part 1, Archdeaconry of Chichester* (Sussex Record Society, 42, Lewes, 1948).

—— (ed.), *Churchwarden's Presentments (Seventeenth Century), Part 2, Archdeaconry of Lewes* (Sussex Record Society, 50, Lewes, 1949).

JOLLY, T., *The Notebook of the Reverend Thomas Jolly a.d. 1671–1693*, ed. H. Fishwick (Chetham Society, 33, Manchester, 1895).

JOSSELIN, R., *The Diary of Ralph Josselin 1616–1683*, ed. Alan Macfarlane (British Academy Records of Social and Economic History, New Series, 3, 1976).

KENYON, J. P. (ed.), *The Stuart Constitution 1603–1688: Documents and Commentary* (Cambridge, 1966).

KIFFIN, W., *Some Remarkable Passages in the Life of William Kiffin*, ed. W. Orme (1823).

KNAPPEN, M. M. (ed.), *Two Elizabethan Puritan Diaries by Richard Greenham and Samuel Ward* (Chicago, 1933).

LANCASHIRE, I. (ed.), *Two Tudor Interludes* (Manchester, 1980).

LATIMER, J., *The Annals of Bristol in the Seventeenth Century* (Bristol, 1900).

LE HARDY, W. (ed.), *Hertford County Records: Notes and Extracts from the Sessions Rolls 1581 to 1698* (9 vols.; Hertford, 1905–39).

LOWE, R., *The Diary of Roger Lowe of Ashton-in-Makerfield, Lancashire, 1663–1674*, ed. W. L. Sachse (1938).

MACHYN, H., *The Diary of Henry Machyn, Citizen and Merchant Taylor of London, 1550–1563*, ed. J. G. Nichols (Camden Society, Old Series, 42, 1848).

MACKAY, C. (ed.), *A Collection of Songs and Ballads Relative to the London Prentices and Trades* (Percy Society, 1, 1841).

MARTIN, K. S. (introd.), *Records of Maidstone Being Selections from Documents in the Possession of the Corporation* (Maidstone, 1926).

MARTINDALE, A., *The Life of Adam Martindale Written by Himself*, ed. R. Parkinson (Chetham Society, 4, Manchester, 1845).

MAYO, C. H. (ed.), *The Municipal Records of the Borough of Dorchester, Dorset* (Exeter, 1908).

MILTON, J., *Of Education*, in *Prose Works*, ed. K. M. Burton (1958).

MITCHELL, A. F., and STRUTHERS, J. (eds.), *Minutes of the Sessions of the Westminster Assembly of Divines* (1874).

NASHE, T., *Christ's Tears over Jerusalem*, 1593 (Scolar Press Facsimile, Menston, 1970).

NEWCOME, H., *The Diary of the Reverend Henry Newcome from September 30 1661 to September 29 1663*, ed. T. Heywood (Chetham Society, 18, Manchester, 1849).

—— *The Autobiography of Henry Newcome*, ed. R. Parkinson (2 vols.; Chetham Society, 16–17, Manchester, 1852).

NORTH, R., *The Autobiography of the Hon. Roger North*, in R. North, *The Lives of the Right Hon. Francis North, Baron Guildford . . . Together with the Autobiography of the Author*, ed. A. Jessop (3 vols.; 1890).

NORTHBROOKE, J., *A Treatise wherein Dicing, Dauncing, Vaine Playes and Enterludes . . . Are Reproved*, 1577? (facsimile, Garland Series: The English Stage: Attack and Defence 1577–1730, New York, 1974).

Onania; Or the Heinous Sin of Self-Pollution, 8th edn., 1723, ed. R. Trumbach (Garland Series: Marriage, Sex and the Family in England 1660–1800, New York, 1986).

OSBORNE, D., *The Letters of Dorothy Osborne to Sir William Temple 1652–54*, ed. K. Hart (Oxford, 1968).

PEPYS, S., *The Diary of Samuel Pepys*, ed. R. Latham and W. Matthews (11 vols.; 1970–83).

PERKINS, W., *The Work of William Perkins*, ed. I. Breward (Courtenay Library of Reformation Classics, 3, Appleford, 1970).

PEYTON, S. A. (ed.), *The Churchwarden's Presentments in the Oxfordshire Peculiars of Dorchester, Thame and Banbury* (Oxfordshire Record Society, 10, Oxford, 1928).

POUND, J. F. (ed.), *The Norwich Census of the Poor 1570* (Norfolk Record Society, 40, Norwich, 1971).

PURVIS, J. S. (ed.), *Tudor Parish Documents of the Diocese of York* (Cambridge, 1948).

RATCLIFF, S. C., and Johnson, H. C. (eds.), *Warwick County Records* (9 vols.; Warwick, 1935–64).

RAWLINGS, P., *Drunks, Whores and Idle Apprentices: Criminal Biographies of the Eighteenth Century* (1992).

READ, C. (ed.), *William Lambarde and Local Government* (Ithaca, NY, 1962).

RUSHWORTH, J. (ed.), *Historical Collections* (8 vols.; 1721).

SALTER, H. E. (ed.), *Oxford Council Acts 1583–1625* (Oxford Historical Society, 87, 1928).

SAVAGE, R. (ed.), *Minutes and Accounts of the Corporation of Stratford-upon-Avon and Other Records 1553–1620* (Dugdale Society Publications, 1, Oxford, 1921).

SELLERS, M. (ed.), *The Acts and Ordinances of the Eastland Company* (Camden Society Publications, 3rd ser., 11, 1906).

SENG, P. J. (ed.), *Tudor Songs and Ballads from MS Cotton Vespasian A-25* (Cambridge, Mass., 1978).

SEYMOUR-SMITH, M. (ed.), *The English Sermon: An Anthology*, i: *1550–1650* (Cheadle, 1976).

SHARPE FRANCIS, R. (ed.), *Ormskirk Sessions Order Books*, in *A Lancashire Miscellany* (Lancashire and Cheshire Record Society, 120, Blackpool, 1965).

SHAW, J., *The Life of Master John Shaw*, in *Yorkshire Diaries and Autobiographies of the Seventeenth and Eighteenth Centuries* (Surtees Society, 65, Durham, 1887).

SHEILS, W. J. (ed.), *Archbishop Grindal's Visitation, 1575: Comperta et Detecta Book* (Borthwick Texts and Calendars: Records of the Northern Province, 4, York, 1977).

SIBBES, R., *Works*, ed. A. B. Grossart (Edinburgh, 1973).

SMITH, Sir T., *De Republica Anglorum: A Discourse on the Commonwealth of England*, ed. L. Alston (Cambridge, 1906).

STEVENSON, W. H., *et al.* (eds.), *Records of the Borough of Nottingham* (9 vols.; Nottingham, 1882–1956).

STOCKS, H. (ed.), *Records of the Borough of Leicester Being a Series of Extracts from the Archives of the Corporation of Leicester 1603–1688* (Cambridge, 1923).

STOUT, W., *The Autobiography of William Stout of Lancaster 1665–1752*, ed. J. D. Marshall (Chetham Society, 3rd ser., 14, Manchester, 1967).

STRUTT, J., *The Sports and Pastimes of the People of England*, ed. J. C. Cox (1903).

STUBBES, P., *An Anatomie of Abuses*, 1583, ed. A. Freeman (Garland Series: The English Stage: Attack and Defence 1577–1730, New York, 1973).

TAWNEY, R., and POWER, E. (eds.), *Tudor Economic Documents* (3 vols.; 1924).

TENNENHOUSE, L. (ed.), *Two Tudor Interludes: Nice Wanton and Impatient Poverty* (The Renaissance Imagination, 10, New York, 1984).

The Pinder of Wakefield, 1632, ed. E. A. Horsman (English Reprint Series, 12, Liverpool, 1956).

TIBBUT, H. G. (ed.), *The Minutes of the First Independent Church (Now Bunyan's Meeting) at Bedford 1656–1766* (Bedfordshire Historical Society, 55, Bedford, 1976).

TROSSE, G., *The Life of the Reverend Mr George Trosse Written by Himself and Published Posthumously According to his Order in 1714*, 1714, ed. A. W. Brink (Montreal, 1974).

TWEEDIE, W. K. (ed.), *Select Biographies* (Wodrow Society, 2 vols.; Edinburgh, 1845–7).

TWEMLOW, J. A. (ed.), *Liverpool Town Books: Proceedings of Assemblies, Common Councils, Portmoot Courts 1550–1603* (2 vols.; Liverpool, 1918, 1935).

The Two Books of Homilies Appointed to be Read in Churches, ed. J. Griffiths (Oxford, 1849).

USHER, R. B. (ed.), *The Presbyterian Movement in the Reign of Queen Elizabeth as Illustrated by the Minute Book of the Dedham Classis, 1582–1589* (Camden Society Publications, 3rd ser., 8, 1905).

WEAVER, F. W., and CLARK, G. N. (eds.), *Churchwarden's Accounts of Marston, Spelsbury, Pyrton* (Oxfordshire Record Society, 6, Oxford, 1925).

WELCH, S., *A Proposal to Render Effectual a Plan to Remove the Nuisance of Common Prostitutes from the Streets of the Metropolis*, 1758, ed. R. Trumbach in *Prostitution Reform: Four Documents* (Garland Series: Marriage, Sex and the Family in England 1660–1800, 22, 1985).

WHEATCROFT, L., *The Courtship Narrative of Leonard Wheatcroft, Derbyshire Yeoman*, ed. G. Parfitt and R. Houlbrooke (Reading, 1986).

WHITGIFT, J., *Works*, ed. Revd J. Ayre (3 vols.; Cambridge, 1851–3).

WILLIAMS, J. F. (ed.), *Diocese of Norwich: Bishop Redman's Visitation 1597* (Norfolk Record Society, 18, Norwich, 1946).

WILLIS BUND, J. W. (ed.), *Worcestershire County Records: Division 1, Documents Relating to Quarter Sessions; Calendar of the Quarter Sessions Papers*, i: *1591–1643* (Worcester, 1900).

WRIGHT, A. R., *British Calendar Customs*, ed. T. E. Lones (3 vols.; 1936–40).

WRIGHT, T., *Queen Elizabeth and her Times* (2 vols.; 1838).

4. SECONDARY SOURCES

ADDY, J., *Sin and Society in Seventeenth-Century England* (1989).

ALCOCK, N., *Stoneleigh Villagers 1597–1650* (University of Warwick: Open Studies, 1975).

ALLDRIDGE, N., 'Loyalty and identity in Chester parishes 1540–1640', in

S. Wright (ed.), *Parish, Church and People: Local Studies in Lay Religion 1350–1750* (1988), 85–124.

AMUSSEN, S. D., *An Ordered Society: Gender and Class in Early Modern England* (Oxford, 1988).

ARCHER, I. W., *The Pursuit of Stability: Social Relations in Elizabethan London* (Cambridge, 1991).

ARIES, P., *Centuries of Childhood: A Social History of Family Life*, trans. R. Baldick (New York, 1962).

ASHTON, R., 'Popular entertainment and social control in later Elizabethan and early Stuart London', *London Journal*, 9 (1983), 1–19.

ASTON, M., 'Segregation in church', in W. J. Sheils and D. Wood (eds.), *Women in the Church* (Studies in Church History, 27, Oxford, 1990), 237–94.

AVERY, G., 'The puritans and their heirs', in G. Avery and Julia Briggs (eds.), *Children and Their Books: A Celebration of the Work of Iona and Peter Opie* (Oxford, 1989), 95–118.

BARNES, T. G., *Somerset 1625–1640: A County's Government during the 'Personal Rule'* (1961).

BARRY, J., 'Popular culture in seventeenth-century Bristol', in B. Reay (ed.), *Popular Culture in Seventeenth-Century England* (1985), 59–90.

—— 'Introduction', in J. Barry (ed.), *The Tudor and Stuart Town: A Reader in English Urban History, 1530–1688* (Harlow, 1990), 1–34.

BASHAR, N., 'Rape in England between 1500 and 1700', in London Feminist Group, *The Sexual Dynamics of History: Men's Power and Women's Resistance* (1983).

BEATTIE, J. M., *Crime and the Courts in England 1660–1800* (Oxford, 1986).

—— 'London and the making of the "Bloody Code", 1689–1718', in L. Davison *et al.* (eds.), *Stilling the Grumbling Hive: The Response to Social and Economic Problems in England, 1689–1750* (Stroud, 1992), 49–76.

BECKER, H., *Outsiders: Studies in the Sociology of Deviance* (New York, 1963).

BEIER, A. L., *Masterless Men: The Vagrancy Problem in England 1560–1640* (1985).

—— 'Vagrants and the social order in Elizabethan England', *Past and Present*, 64 (1974), 3–29.

—— 'Social problems in Elizabethan London', in J. Barry (ed.), *The Tudor and Stuart Town: A Reader in English Urban History 1530–1688* (Harlow, 1990), 121–38.

BEN-AMOS, I. K., *Adolescence and Youth in Early Modern England* (New Haven, 1994).

—— 'Service and the coming of age of young men in seventeenth-century England', *Continuity and Change*, 3 (1988), 41–64.

—— 'Failure to become freemen: urban apprentices in early modern England', *Social History*, 16 (1991), 157–92.

—— 'Women apprentices in the trades and crafts of early modern Bristol', *Continuity and Change*, 6 (1991), 227–52.

BOULTON, J., *Neighbourhood and Society: A London Suburb in the Seventeenth Century* (Cambridge, 1987).

BOX, S., *Deviance, Reality and Society* (1971).

BRACKETT, J. K., *Criminal Justice and Crime in Late Renaissance Florence, 1537–1609* (Cambridge, 1992).

BRAY, A., *Homosexuality in Renaissance England* (1982).

BRENNAN, T., *Public Drinking and Popular Culture in Eighteenth-Century Paris* (Princeton, 1988).

BRIGDEN, S., *London and the Reformation* (Oxford, 1989).

—— 'Youth and the English Reformation', *Past and Present*, 95 (1982), 37–67.

BRODSKY ELLIOTT, V., 'Single women in the London marriage market: age, status and mobility, 1598–1619', in R. B. Outhwaite (ed.), *Marriage and Society: Studies in the Social History of Marriage* (1981), 81–100.

—— 'Widows in late Elizabethan London: remarriage, economic opportunity and family orientations', in L. Bonfield *et al.* (eds.), *The World We Have Gained: Histories of Population and Social Structure Presented to Peter Laslett* (Oxford, 1986), 122–54.

BROOKS, C., 'Apprenticeship, social mobility and the middling sort 1550–1800', in J. Barry and C. Brooks (eds.), *The Middling Sort of People: Culture, Society and Politics in England, 1550–1800* (Basingstoke, 1994), 52–83.

BURKE, P., *Popular Culture in Early Modern Europe* (1978).

—— *Sociology and History* (1980).

—— 'Popular culture in seventeenth-century London', in B. Reay (ed.), *Popular Culture in Seventeenth-Century England* (1985), 31–58.

BURROW, J. A., *The Ages of Man: A Study in Medieval Writing and Thought* (Oxford, 1986).

BURTON, A., 'Looking forward from Aries? Pictorial and material evidence for the history of childhood and family life', *Continuity and Change*, 4 (1989), 203–29.

BUSHAWAY, B., *By Rite: Custom, Ceremony and Community in England 1700–1880* (1982).

CAMP, C. W., *The Artisan in Elizabethan Literature* (New York, 1923).

CAPP, B., 'English youth groups and *The Pinder of Wakefield*', in P. Slack (ed.), *Rebellion, Popular Protest and the Social Order in Early Modern England* (Cambridge, 1984), 212–18 (1st pub. in *Past and Present*, 76 (1977)).

—— 'Popular literature', in B. Reay (ed.), *Popular Culture in Seventeenth-Century England* (1985), 198–243.

—— 'Separate domains: women and authority in early modern England', in P. Griffiths, A. Fox, and S. Hindle (eds.), *The Experience of Authority in Early Modern England* (Basingstoke, 1996), 117–47.

CASEY, J., 'Household disputes and the law in early modern Andalusia', in J. Bossy (ed.), *Disputes and Settlements: Law and Human Relations in the West* (Cambridge, 1983), 189–217.

CHEW, S. C., *The Pilgrimage of Life* (New York, 1973).

CLARK, P., *The English Alehouse: A Social History, 1200–1830* (1983).

—— 'The alehouse and the alternative society', in D. Pennington and K. Thomas (eds.), *Puritans and Revolutionaries: Essays in Seventeenth-Century History Presented to Christopher Hill* (Oxford, 1978), 47–72.

—— 'A crisis contained? The condition of English towns in the 1590s', in P. Clark (ed.), *The European Crisis of the 1590s* (1985), 44–66.

—— 'Migrants in the city: the process of social adaptation in English towns 1500–1800', in P. Clark and D. Souden (eds.), *Migration and Society in Early Modern England* (1987), 267–91.

CLARK, S., 'Inversion, misrule and the meaning of witchcraft', *Past and Present*, 87 (1980), 98–127.

COHEN, S., *The Evolution of Women's Asylums since 1500: From Refuges for Ex-prostitutes to Shelters for Battered Wives* (New York, 1992).

COLLINSON, P., *The Religion of Protestants: The Church in English Society 1559–1625* (Oxford, 1982).

—— *The Birthpangs of Protestant England: Religious and Cultural Change in the Sixteenth and Seventeenth Centuries* (Basingstoke, 1988).

—— *From Iconoclasm to Iconophobia: The Cultural Impact of the Second English Reformation*, University of Reading Stenton Lecture 1985 (Reading, 1986).

—— 'Shepherds, sheepdogs, and hirelings: the pastoral ministry in post-Reformation England', in W. J. Sheils and D. Wood (eds.), *The Ministry: Clerical and Lay* (Studies in Church History, 26, Oxford, 1989), 185–220.

CORFIELD, P., 'A provincial capital in the late seventeenth century: the case of Norwich', in P. Clark and P. Slack (eds.), *Crisis and Order in English Towns 1500–1700: Essays in Urban History* (1972), 236–310.

—— 'Class by name and number in eighteenth-century Britain', in P. Corfield (ed.), *Language, History and Class* (Oxford, 1991), 101–30 (1st pub. in *History*, 72 (1987)).

CRAWFORD, P., 'Public duty, conscience, and women in early modern England', in J. Morrill, P. Slack, and D. Woolf (eds.), *Public Duty and Private Conscience in Seventeenth-Century England: Essays Presented to G. E. Aylmer* (Oxford, 1993), 57–76.

CRESSY, D., *Literacy and the Social Order: Reading and Writing in Tudor and Stuart England* (Cambridge, 1980).

—— *Coming Over: Migration and Communication between England and New England in the Seventeenth Century* (Cambridge, 1987).

—— *Bonfires and Bells: National Memory and the Protestant Calendar in Elizabethan and Stuart England* (1989).

—— 'Describing the social order of Elizabethan England', *Literature and History*, 3 (1976), 29–44.

CROSS, C., 'A man of conscience in seventeenth-century urban politics: Alderman Hoyle of York', in J. Morrill, P. Slack, and D. Woolf (eds.), *Public Duty and Private Conscience in Seventeenth-Century England: Essays Presented to G. E. Aylmer* (Oxford, 1993), 205–24.

CUNNINGHAM, H., 'The employment and unemployment of children in England *c.*1680–1851', *Past and Present*, 126 (1990), 115–50.

DAVIS, J. C., *Fear, Myth and History: The Ranters and the Historians* (Cambridge, 1986).

DAVIS, N. Z., *The Return of Martin Guerre* (1983).

—— 'Some tasks and themes in the pursuit of popular religion', in C. Trinkaus and H. O. Oberman (eds.), *The Pursuit of Holiness in Late Medieval and Renaissance Religion* (Leiden, 1974), 307–36.

—— 'The reasons of misrule', in her *Society and Culture in Early Modern France* (Oxford, 1987), 97–123 (1st pub. as 'The reasons of misrule: youth groups and charivaris in sixteenth-century France', in *Past and Present*, 50 (1971)).

DAVIS, R. C., *The War of the Fists: Popular Culture and Public Violence in Late Renaissance Venice* (Oxford, 1994).

DITCHFIELD, P. H., *Old English Customs* (1901).

DOWNES, D., and ROCK, P., *Understanding Deviance: A Guide to the Sociology of Crime and Law Breaking* (2nd edn., Oxford, 1988).

DUFFY, E., *The Stripping of the Altars: Traditional Religion in England 1400–1580* (New Haven, 1992).

—— 'The godly and the multitude in Stuart England', *The Seventeenth Century*, 1 (1986), 31–55.

DUNLOP, J., and DENMAN, R. D., *English Apprenticeship and Child Labour: A History* (1912).

DURSTON, C., *The Family and the English Revolution* (Oxford, 1989).

DYMOND, D., 'A lost social institution: the camping close', *Rural History*, 1 (1990), 165–92.

EARLE, P., *The Making of the English Middle Class: Business, Society and Family Life in London 1660–1730* (1989).

EGMOND, F., *Underworlds: Organised Crime in the Netherlands, 1650–1800* (Oxford, 1993).

EISENSTADT, S. N., 'Archetypal patterns of youth', in E. Erikson (ed.), *Youth, Change and Challenge* (1963), 24–42.

EMMISON, F. G., 'Tithes, perambulations and sabbath-breach in Elizabethan Essex', in F. G. Emmison and R. Stephens (eds.), *Tribute to an Antiquary: Essays Presented to Marc Fitch by Some of his Friends* (1976), 177–215.

—— *Elizabethan Life: Disorder* (Essex Record Office Publications, 56, Chelmsford, 1970).

—— *Elizabethan Life: Morals and the Church Courts* (Essex Record Office Publications, 63, Chelmsford, 1973).

ERICSON, R. V., *Criminal Reactions: The Labelling Perspective* (Farnborough, 1975).

ERIKSON, E., 'Youth, fidelity and diversity', in E. Erikson (ed.), *Youth, Change and Challenge* (1963), 1–23.

EVANS, J. T., *Seventeenth-Century Norwich: Politics, Religion and Government 1620–1690* (Oxford, 1979).

FALLER, L. B., *Turned to Account: The Forms and Functions of Criminal Biography in Late Seventeenth- and Early Eighteenth-Century England* (Cambridge, 1987).

FARGE, A., *Fragile Lives: Violence, Power and Solidarity in Eighteenth-Century Paris* (1st pub. in France in 1986), trans. C. Shelton (Oxford, 1993).

FILDES, V., *Wet Nursing: A History from Antiquity to the Present* (Oxford, 1988).

FINCHAM, K., *Prelate as Pastor: The Episcopate of James I* (Oxford, 1990).

FISH, S., *The Living Temple: George Herbert and Catechizing* (1978).

FLANDRIN, J. F., 'Repression and change in the sexual life of young people in medieval and early modern times', in R. Wheaton and T. K. Hareven (eds.), *Family and Sexuality in French History* (1980), 27–48.

FLETCHER, A., *Reform in the Provinces: The Government of Stuart England* (1986).

—— and STEVENSON, J., 'Introduction', in A. Fletcher and J. Stevenson (eds.), *Order and Disorder in Early Modern England* (Cambridge, 1985), 1–40.

FOX, V. C., 'Is adolescence a phenomenon of modern times?', *Journal of Psycho-History*, 5 (1977), 271–90.

GARLAND, D., *Punishment and Modern Society: A Study in Social Theory* (Oxford, 1990).

GARLAND, R., *The Greek Way of Life* (1990).

GARRIOCH, D., *Neighbourhood and Community in Paris, 1740–1790* (Cambridge, 1986).

—— 'Verbal insults in eighteenth-century Paris', in P. Burke and R. Porter (eds.), *The Social History of Language* (Cambridge, 1987), 104–19.

GAVITT, P., *Charity and Children in Renaissance Florence: The Ospedale Degli Innocenti, 1410–1536* (Ann Arbor, 1990).

GENTLES, I., 'The struggle for London in the second civil war', *Historical Journal*, 26 (1983), 277–305.

GEREMEK, B., *The Margins of Society in Late Medieval Paris* (1st pub. in Polish in 1971), trans. J. Birrell (Cambridge, 1987).

GERMANI, G., *Marginality* (New Brunswick, NJ, 1990).

GILLIS, J., *Youth and History: Tradition and Change in European Age-Relations 1770 to the Present* (1981).

—— *For Better for Worse: British Marriages 1600 to the Present* (Oxford, 1985).

—— 'The evolution of juvenile delinquency in England 1890–1914', *Past and Present*, 67 (1975), 96–126.

GOLDBERG, P. J. P., *Women, Work and Life-Cycle in a Medieval Economy: Women in York and Yorkshire c.1300–1520* (Oxford, 1992).

GOMME, A. B., *The Traditional Games of England, Scotland and Ireland* (2 vols.; 1894, 1898).

GORING, J., *Godly Exercises or the Devil's Dance: Puritanism and Popular Culture in Pre-Civil War England*, Friends of Dr William's Library, 37th lecture (1983).

GOWING, L., 'Gender and the language of insult in early modern London', *History Workshop Journal*, 35 (1993), 1–21.

GRAHAM, S. L., *House and Street: The Domestic World of Servants and Masters in Nineteenth-Century Rio de Janeiro* (Austin, Tex., 1992).

GREAVES, R., *Society and Religion in Elizabethan England* (Minneapolis, 1981).

GREEN, I., ' "For children in yeeres and children in understanding": the emergence of the English catechism under Elizabeth and the early Stuarts', *Journal of Ecclesiastical History*, 37 (1986), 397–425.

—— 'Reformed pastors and *bon cures*: the changing role of the parish clergy in early modern Europe', in W. J. Sheils and D. Wood (eds.), *The Ministry: Clerical and Lay* (Studies in Church History, 26, Oxford, 1989), 249–86.

GRIFFITHS, P., 'The Structure of prostitution in Elizabethan London', *Continuity and Change*, 8 (1993), 39–63.

GURR, A., *Playgoing in Shakespeare's London* (Cambridge, 1987).

HAIGH, C., 'The Church of England, the Catholics and the people', in C. Haigh (ed.), *The Reign of Elizabeth I* (1984), 195–219.

HAIR, P. E. H., 'Bridal pregnancy in rural England in earlier centuries', *Population Studies*, 20 (1966), 233–43.

—— 'Bridal pregnancy in earlier rural England further examined', *Population Studies*, 24 (1970), 59–70.

HANAWALT, B. A., *Growing up in Medieval London: The Experience of Childhood in History* (New York, 1993).

HARRIS, T., *London Crowds in the Reign of Charles II: Propaganda and Politics from the Restoration until the Exclusion Crisis* (Cambridge, 1987).

—— 'The bawdy house riots of 1668', *Historical Journal*, 29 (1986), 537–66.

—— 'Problematising popular culture', in T. Harris (ed.), *Popular Culture in England, c.1500–1850* (Basingstoke, 1995), 1–27.

HARTE, N. B., 'State control of dress and social change in pre-industrial England', in D. C. Coleman and A. H. John (eds.), *Trade, Government and Economy in Pre-industrial England: Essays Presented to F. J. Fisher* (1976), 132–65.

HEAL, F., *Hospitality in Early Modern England* (Oxford, 1990).

HEALY, M., 'Discourses of the plague in early modern London', in J. A. I. Champion (ed.), *Epidemic Disease in London* (Centre for Metropolitan History Working Papers Series, 1993), 19–34.

HENDRICK, H., *Images of Youth: Age, Class and the Male Youth Problem, 1820–1920* (Oxford, 1990).

HERRUP, C., *The Common Peace: Participation and the Criminal Law in Seventeenth-Century England* (Cambridge, 1987).

HILL, C., *Society and Puritanism in Pre-revolutionary England* (1964).

—— *The World Turned upside down: Radical Ideas during the English Revolution* (1st pub. 1972) (Harmondsworth, 1975).

HITCHCOCK, T., 'Paupers and preachers: the SPCK and the parochial workhouse movement', in L. Davison *et al.* (eds.), *Stilling the Grumbling Hive: The Response to Social and Economic Problems in England 1689–1750* (Stroud, 1992), 145–66.

HOBSBAWM, E., and RANGER, T. (eds), *The Invention of Tradition* (Cambridge, 1983).

HOULBROOKE, R., *The English Family 1450–1700* (1984).
—— 'Women's social life and common action in England from the fifteenth century to the eve of the Civil War', *Continuity and Change*, 1 (1986), 171–89.
HOUSTON, R. A., *Social Change in the Age of Enlightenment: Edinburgh 1660–1760* (Oxford, 1994).
HUGHES, D. O., 'Sumptuary law and social relations in Renaissance Italy', in J. Bossy (ed.), *Disputes and Settlements: Law and Human Relations in the West* (Cambridge, 1983), 69–99.
HULL, S., *Chaste, Silent and Obedient: English Books for Women 1475–1640* (San Marino, Calif., 1982).
HUMPHRIES, S., *Hooligans or Rebels? An Oral History of Working Class Childhood and Youth 1889–1939* (Oxford, 1981).
HUNT, W., *The Puritan Moment: The Coming of Revolution in an English County* (Cambridge, Mass., 1983).
HUTTON, R., *The Rise and Fall of Merry England: The Ritual Year 1400–1700* (Oxford, 1994).
INGRAM, M., *Church Courts, Sex and Marriage in England 1570–1640* (Cambridge, 1987).
—— 'Religious communities and moral discipline in late-sixteenth and early-seventeenth century England: case studies', in Kaspar von Greyerz (ed.), *Religion and Society in Early Modern Europe* (1984), 177–93.
—— 'Ridings, rough music and the "reform" of popular culture in early modern England', *Past and Present*, 105 (1984), 79–113.
—— 'The reform of popular culture? Sex and marriage in early modern England', in B. Reay (ed.), *Popular Culture in Seventeenth-Century England* (1985), 129–65.
—— 'Reformation of manners in early modern England', in P. Griffiths, A. Fox, and S. Hindle (eds.), *The Experience of Authority in Early Modern England* (Basingstoke, 1996), 47–88.
INNES, J., 'Prisons for the poor: English bridewells 1555–1800', in F. Snyder and D. Hay (eds.), *Labour, Law and Crime: A Historical Perspective* (1987), 42–122.
JAMES, M., 'Ritual drama and the social body in the late medieval English town', in his *Society, Politics and Culture: Studies in Early Modern England* (Cambridge, 1986), 16–47 (1st pub. in *Past and Present*, 98 (1983)).
JORDANOVA, L., 'New worlds for children in the eighteenth century: problems of historical interpretation', *History of the Human Sciences*, 3 (1990), 69–83.
KILLERBY, C. K., 'Practical problems in the enforcement of Italian sumptuary law, 1200–1500', in T. Dean and K. J. P. Lowe (eds.), *Crime, Society and the Law in Renaissance Italy* (Cambridge, 1994), 99–120.
KING, P., 'Decision makers and decision making in the English criminal law 1750–1800', *Historical Journal* (1984), 25–58.
—— and NOEL, J., 'The origins of "the problem of juvenile delinquency": the growth of juvenile prosecutions in London in the late eighteenth

and early nineteenth centuries', *Criminal Justice History*, 14 (1993), 17–41.

KING, P., 'Bishop Wren and the suppression of the Norwich lecturers', *Historical Journal*, 11 (1968), 237–54.

KLEIJWEGT, M., *Ancient Youth: The Ambiguity of Youth and the Absence of Adolescence in Greco-Roman Society* (Amsterdam, 1991).

KUSSMAUL, A., *Servants in Husbandry in Early Modern England* (Cambridge, 1981).

LA MAR, V. A., 'English dress in the age of Shakespeare', in L. B. Wright and V. A. La Mar (eds.), *Life and Letters in Tudor and Stuart England* (Ithaca, NY, 1962), 385–401.

LAROQUE, F., *Shakespeare's Festive World: Elizabethan Seasonal Entertainment and the Professional Stage* (1st pub. in France in 1988), trans. Janet Lloyd (Cambridge, 1993).

LASLETT, P., *Family Life and Illicit Love in Earlier Generations: Essays in Historical Sociology* (Cambridge, 1977).

—— *The World We Have Lost: Further Explored* (1983).

—— 'The bastardy prone sub-society', in P. Laslett, K. Oosterveen, and R. M. Smith (eds.), *Bastardy and its Comparative History* (1980), 217–39.

—— 'Age at sexual maturity in Europe since the Middle Ages', in his *Family Life and Illicit Love in Earlier Generations: Essays in Historical Sociology* (Cambridge, 1977), 214–32.

—— and WALL, R. (eds.), *Household and Family in Past Time* (Cambridge, 1972).

LEONARD, E. M., *The Early History of English Poor Relief* (1965).

LINDLEY, K., 'Riot prevention and control in early Stuart London', *Transactions of the Royal Historical Society*, 5th ser., 33 (1983), 109–26.

MACCULLOCH, D., *The Later Reformation in England 1547–1603* (Basingstoke, 1990).

MACDONALD, M., *Mystical Bedlam: Madness, Anxiety and Healing in Seventeenth-Century England* (Cambridge, 1981).

—— and MURPHY, TERENCE R., *Sleepless Souls: Suicide in Early Modern England* (Oxford, 1990).

MACFARLANE, A., *The Family Life of Ralph Josselin, a Seventeenth-Century Clergyman: An Essay in Historical Anthropology* (Cambridge, 1970).

—— *The Origins of English Individualism: The Family, Property and Social Transition* (Oxford, 1979).

—— *Marriage and Love in England: Modes of Reproduction 1300–1840* (Oxford, 1986).

—— review of Lawrence Stone, *The Family, Sex and Marriage*, in *History and Theory*, 18 (1979), 103–26.

—— 'Illegitimacy and illegitimates in English history', in P. Laslett, K. M. Oosterveen, and R. M. Smith (eds.), *Bastardy and its Comparative History* (1980), 71–85.

MCINTOSH, M. K., *A Community Transformed: The Manor and Liberty of Havering, 1500–1620* (Cambridge, 1991).

McLaren, A., *A History of Contraception: From Antiquity to the Present Day* (Oxford, 1990).

Malcolmson, R. W., *Popular Recreations in English Society 1700–1850* (Cambridge, 1973).

Manning, B., *The English People and the English Revolution* (1976).

Manning, R. B., *Village Revolts: Social Protest and Popular Disturbances in England 1509–1640* (Oxford, 1988).

—— *Hunters and Poachers: A Cultural and Social History of Unlawful Hunting in England 1485–1640* (Oxford, 1993).

—— 'The prosecution of Sir Michael Blount, Lieutenant of the Tower of London, 1595', *Bulletin of the Institute of Historical Research*, 57 (1984), 216–24.

Margery, S., 'The invention of juvenile delinquency in early nineteenth-century England', *Labour History*, 34 (1978), 11–25.

Marples, M., *A History of Football* (1954).

Marsh, C., *The Family of Love in English Society, 1550–1630* (Cambridge, 1994).

Martin, J. W., *Religious Radicals in Tudor England* (1989).

May, M., 'Innocence and experience: the evolution of the concept of juvenile delinquency in the mid-nineteenth century', *Victorian Studies*, 17 (1973), 7–29.

Mayhew, G., 'Life-cycle, service and the family unit in early modern Rye', *Continuity and Change*, 6 (1991), 201–26.

Medick, H., 'Village spinning bees: sexual culture and free time among rural youths in early modern Germany', in H. Medick and D. Sabean (eds.), *Interest and Emotion: Essays on the Study of Family Life and Kinship* (Cambridge, 1984), 317–39.

Mitchison, R., and Leneman, L., *Sexuality and Social Control: Scotland 1660–1780* (Oxford, 1989).

Mitterauer, M., *A History of Youth*, trans. Graeme Dunphy (Oxford, 1992).

—— 'Servants and youth', *Continuity and Change*, 5 (1990), 11–38.

Moller, H., 'Youth as a force in the modern world', *Comparative Studies in Society and History*, 10 (1968), 237–60.

Morgan, E., *The Puritan Family: Essays on Religion and Domestic Relations in Seventeenth Century New England* (Boston, 1944).

Morgan, J., *Godly Learning: Puritan Attitudes towards Reason, Learning and Education* (Cambridge, 1986).

Muchembled, R., *Popular Culture and Elite Culture in France 1400–1700*, trans. L. Cochrane (Baton Rouge, La., 1985).

Muir, E., *Civic Ritual in Renaissance Venice* (Princeton, 1981).

Murphy, T. R., '"Woful childe of parents rage": suicide of children and adolescents in early modern England', *Sixteenth Century Journal*, 17 (1986), 259–70.

Neeson, J. M., *Commoners: Common Right, Enclosure and Social Change in England 1700–1820* (Cambridge, 1993).

O'DAY, R., *Education and Society: The Social Foundations of Education in Early Modern Britain* (1982).

O'DONOGHUE, E. G., *Bridewell Hospital, Palace, Prison and School from the Death of Elizabeth to Modern Times* (1929).

OGELVIE, S., 'Coming of age in a corporate society: capitalism, pietism and family authority in rural Wurtemburg 1590–1740', *Continuity and Change*, 1 (1986), 279–331.

OZMENT, S., *The Reformation in the Cities* (New Haven, 1975).

PALLISER, D. M., *The Age of Elizabeth: England under the Late Tudors 1547–1603* (2nd edn., 1992).

—— 'Civic mentality and the environment in Tudor York', in J. Barry (ed.), *The Tudor and Stuart Town: A Reader in English Urban History 1530–1688* (Harlow, 1990), 206–43 (1st pub. in *Northern History*, 18 (1982)).

PARKER, K., *The English Sabbath: A Study of Doctrine and Discipline from the Reformation to the Civil War* (Cambridge, 1988).

PATTEN, J., *English Towns 1500–1700* (Folkestone, 1978).

PEARL, V., *London and the Outbreak of the Puritan Revolution: City Government and National Politics, 1625–43* (Oxford, 1961).

—— 'Change and stability in seventeenth-century London', in J. Barry (ed.), *The Tudor and Stuart Town: A Reader in English Urban History 1530–1688* (Harlow, 1990), 139–65 (1st pub. in *London Journal*, 5 (1979)).

PEARSON, G., *Hooligan: A History of Respectable Fears* (Basingstoke, 1983).

PELLING, MARGARET, 'Apprenticeship, health and social cohesion in early modern London', *History Workshop Journal*, 37 (1994), 33–56.

PERRY, M. E., *Crime and Society in Early Modern Seville* (Hanover, NH, 1980).

PETTIGREE, A., *Foreign Protestant Communities in Sixteenth-century London* (Oxford, 1986).

PHYTHIAN-ADAMS, C., *Local History and Folklore: A New Framework* (1975).

—— *Desolation of a City: Coventry and the Urban Crisis of the Late Middle Ages* (Cambridge, 1979).

—— 'Ceremony and the citizen: the communal year at Coventry 1450–1550', in Peter Clark and Paul Slack (eds.), *Crisis and Order in English Towns 1500–1700: Essays in Urban History* (1972), 57–85.

PINCHBECK, I., and HEWITT, M., *Children in English Society*, i: *from Tudor Times to the Eighteenth Century* (1969).

PLUMB, J. H., 'The new world of children in eighteenth-century England', *Past and Present*, 67 (1975), 64–93.

POLLOCK, L., *Forgotten Children: Parent–Child Relations from 1500 to 1900* (Cambridge, 1983).

—— ' "Teach her to live under obedience": the making of women in the upper ranks of early modern England', *Continuity and Change*, 4 (1989), 231–58.

POTTER, D. L., and ROEBUCK, J. B., 'The labelling approach re-examined: interactionism and the components of deviance', *Deviant Behaviour*, 9 (1988), 19–32.

POUND, J. F., *Tudor and Stuart Norwich* (Chichester, 1988).

PRUETT, J., *The Parish Clergy under the Later Stuarts: The Leicestershire Experience* (1978).

QUAIFE, G. R., *Wanton Wenches and Wayward Wives: Peasants and Illicit Sex in Early Seventeenth-century England* (1979).

RANDALL, A., *Before the Luddites: Custom, Community and Machinery in the English Woollen Industry 1776–1809* (Cambridge, 1991).

RAPPAPORT, S., *Worlds within Worlds: Structures of Life in Sixteenth-century London* (Cambridge, 1989).

REAY, B., 'Introduction: popular culture in early modern England', in B. Reay (ed.), *Popular Culture in Seventeenth-century England* (1985), 1–30.

REDIKER, M., *Between the Devil and the Deep Blue Sea: Merchant Seamen, Pirates and the Anglo-American Maritime World 1700–1750* (Cambridge, 1987).

ROBERTS, M., 'Sickles and scythes: women's work and men's work at harvest time', *History Workshop Journal*, 7 (1979), 3–28.

—— ' "Words they are women and deeds they are men": images of work and gender in early modern England', in L. Charles and L. Duffin (eds.), *Women and Work in Pre-industrial England* (1985), 122–80.

—— 'Women and work in sixteenth-century English towns', in P. J. Corfield and D. Keene (eds.), *Work in Towns 850–1850* (1990), 86–102.

ROBISHEAUX, T., 'Peasants and pastors: rural youth control and the Reformation in Hohenlohe 1540–1680', *Social History*, 6 (1981), 281–300.

ROCHE, D.,*The Culture of Clothing: Dress and Fashion in the Ancien Regime*, 1st pub. in France in 1989, trans. Jean Birrell (Cambridge, 1994).

ROCK, P., 'The sociology of crime, symbolic interactionism and some problematic qualities of radical criminology', in D. Downes and P. Rock (eds.), *Deviant Interpretations* (Oxford, 1979), 52–84.

ROPER, L., *The Holy Household: Women and Morals in Reformation Augsburg* (Oxford, 1989).

—— 'Blood and codpieces: masculinity in the early modern German town', in her *Oedipus and the Devil: Witchcraft, Sexuality and Religion in Early Modern Europe* (1994), 107–24.

ROSE-TROUP, F., *John White: The Patriarch of Dorchester* (1930).

ROSSER, G., *Medieval Westminster 1200–1540* (Oxford, 1989).

ROSSIAUD, J., *Medieval Prostitution*, trans. L. G. Cochrane (Oxford, 1988).

RUBIN, M., *Corpus Christi: The Eucharist in Late Medieval Culture* (Cambridge, 1991).

RULE, J., 'Employment and authority: masters and men in eighteenth-century manufacturing', in P. Griffiths, A. Fox, and S. Hindle (eds.), *The Experience of Authority in Early Modern England* (Basingstoke, 1996), 286–317.

RUSH, P., 'The government of a generation: the subject of juvenile delinquency', *Liverpool Law Review*, 14 (1992), 3–43.

SACKS, D. H., *The Widening Gate: Bristol and the Atlantic Economy, 1450–1700* (Berkeley, 1991)

SALERNO, A., 'The social background of seventeenth-century emigration to America', *Journal of British Studies*, 19 (1979), 31–52.

SCHNUCKER, R. V., 'Elizabethan birth control and puritan attitudes', *Journal of Interdisciplinary History*, 5 (1975), 655–67.

SCHOCHET, G., 'Patriarchalism, politics and mass attitudes in Stuart England', *Historical Journal*, 12 (1969), 413–41.

SCHOFIELD, R. S., 'Perinatal mortality in Hawkshead, Lancashire, 1581–1710', *Local Population Studies*, 4 (1970), 11–16.

—— and WRIGLEY, E. A., 'Infant and child mortality in England in the late Tudor and early Stuart period', in Charles Webster (ed.), *Health, Medicine and Mortality in the Sixteenth Century* (Cambridge, 1979), 61–95.

SCOTT, J. C., *Domination and the Arts of Resistance: Hidden Transcripts* (New Haven, 1990).

SCRIBNER, R. S., 'Reformation, carnival and the world turned upside down', in his *Popular Culture and Popular Movements* (1987), 71–102.

—— 'Is a history of popular culture possible?', *History of European Ideas*, 10 (1989), 175–91.

SEAVER, P. S., *Wallington's World: A Puritan Artisan in Stuart England* (Stanford, Calif., 1985).

—— 'A social contract? Master against servant in the Court of Requests', *History Today*, 39 (Sept. 1989), 50–6.

SHAHAR, S., *Childhood in the Middle Ages*, trans. Chaya Galai (1990).

SHARPE, J. A., *Crime in Early Modern England 1550–1750* (1984).

—— *Early Modern England: A Social History 1550–1750* (1987).

—— *Defamation and Sexual Slander in Early Modern England: The Church Courts at York* (Borthwick Papers, 58, York, 1980).

—— *Judicial Punishment in England* (1990).

—— ' "Such disagreement betwyx neighbours": litigation and human relations in early modern England', in John Bossy (ed.), *Disputes and Settlements: Law and Human Relations in the West* (Cambridge, 1983), 167–87.

—— ' "Last dying speeches": religion, ideology and public executions in seventeenth-century England', *Past and Present*, 107 (1985), 144–67.

SHARPE, P., 'Poor children as apprentices in Colyton 1598–1830', *Continuity and Change*, 6 (1991), 253–70.

SHOEMAKER, R. B., *Prosecution and Punishment: Petty Crime and the Law in London and Rural Middlesex c.1660–1725* (Cambridge, 1991).

SHORTER, E., *The Making of the Modern Family* (1976).

SLACK, P., *The Impact of Plague in Tudor and Stuart England* (paperback edn., Oxford, 1990).

—— *Poverty and Policy in Tudor and Stuart England* (1988).

—— 'Vagrants and vagrancy in England 1598–1664', in P. Clark and D. Souden (eds.), *Migration and Society in Early Modern England* (1987), 49–76 (1st pub. in *Economic History Review*, 2nd ser., 27 (1974)).

—— 'The public conscience of Henry Sherfield', in J. Morrill, P. Slack, and D. Woolf (eds.), *Public Duty and Private Conscience in Seventeenth-Century England: Essays Presented to G. E. Aylmer* (Oxford, 1994), 151–71.

SMITH, S. R., 'Religion and the conception of youth in seventeenth-century England', *History of Childhood Quarterly*, 2 (1975), 493–515.

—— 'The ideal and the reality: apprentice–master relations in seventeenth-century England', *History of Education Quarterly*, 21 (1981), 449–59.

—— 'The London apprentices as seventeenth-century adolescents', in P. Slack (ed.), *Rebellion, Popular Protest and the Social Order in Early Modern England* (Cambridge, 1984), 219–31 (1st pub. in *Past and Present*, 61 (1973)).

SNELL, K., *Annals of the Labouring Poor: Social Change and Agrarian England, 1660–1900* (Cambridge, 1985).

SOMMERVILLE, C. J., *The Discovery of Childhood in Puritan England* (Athens, G. 1992).

SOUDEN, D., 'Rogues, whores and vagabonds? Indentured servant emigration to North America, and the case of mid-seventeenth-century Bristol', *Social History*, 3 (1978), 23–41.

—— 'Migrants and the population structure of late seventeenth-century provincial cities and market towns', in P. Clark (ed.), *The Transformation of English Provincial Towns 1660–1800* (1984), 99–132.

SPAETH, D. A., 'Common prayer? Popular observance of the Anglican liturgy in Restoration Wiltshire', in S. J. Wright (ed.), *Parish, Church and People: Local Studies in Lay Religion 1350–1750* (1988), 125–51.

SPIERENBURG, P., *The Spectacle of Suffering: Executions and the Evolution of Repression from a Pre-industrial Metropolis to the European Experience* (Cambridge, 1984).

SPRINGHALL, J., 'The history of youth reaches middle age', *Social History Society Bulletin*, 19 (1994), 7–13.

SPUFFORD, M., *Contrasting Communities: English Villagers in the Sixteenth and Seventeenth Centuries* (Cambridge, 1974).

—— *Small Books and Pleasant Histories: Popular Fiction and its Readership in Seventeenth-Century England* (Cambridge, 1981).

STEVENSON, L. C., *Praise and Paradox: Merchants and Craftsmen in Elizabethan Popular Literature* (Cambridge, 1984).

STEVENSON, S. J., 'Social and economic contributions to the pattern of "suicide" in south-east England, 1530–1590', *Continuity and Change*, 2 (1987), 225–62.

STONE, L., *The Family, Sex and Marriage in England 1500–1800* (1977).

—— *Road to Divorce: England 1530–1987* (Oxford, 1990).

STRAUSS, G., *Luther's House of Learning: The Indoctrination of the Young in the German Reformation* (1978).

TAIT, J., 'The declaration of sports for Lancashire (1617)', *English Historical Review*, 32 (1917), 561–8.

THIRSK, J., 'The fantastical folly of fashion: the English stocking knitting industry 1500–1700', in N. B. Harte and F. C. Ponting (eds.), *Textile History and Economic History: Essays in Honour of Miss Julia de Mann* (Manchester, 1973), 50–73.

THISTLETON-DYER, T. F., *British Popular Customs Present and Past* (1876).
THOMAS, K., *Religion and the Decline of Magic: Studies in Popular Beliefs in Sixteenth- and Seventeenth-Century England* (1971).
—— *Man and the Natural World: Changing Attitudes in England 1500–1800* (1983).
—— 'Women and the civil war sects', *Past and Present*, 13 (1958), 42–62.
—— 'Age and authority in early modern England', *Proceedings of the British Academy*, 62 (1976), 1–46.
—— *Rule and Misrule in the Schools of Early Modern England*, University of Reading Stenton Lecture, 9 (Reading, 1976).
—— 'Numeracy in early modern England', *Transactions of the Royal Historical Society*, 5th ser., 37 (1987), 103–32.
—— 'Children in early modern England', in G. Avery and J. Briggs (eds.), *Children and Their Books: A Celebration of the Work of Iona and Peter Opie* (Oxford, 1989), 45–77.
—— 'Cases of conscience in seventeenth-century England', in J. Morrill, P. Slack, and D. Woolf (eds.), *Public Duty and Private Conscience in Seventeenth-Century England: Essays Presented to G. E. Aylmer* (Oxford, 1994), 29–56.
THOMPSON, E. P., 'The patricians and the plebs', in his *Customs in Common* (1991), 16–96.
—— 'Time, work-discipline and industrial capitalism', in his *Customs in Common* (1991), 352–403 (1st pub. in *Past and Present*, 38 (1967)).
—— 'Rough music', in his *Customs in Common* (1991), 467–538.
THOMPSON, R., *Women in Stuart England and America* (1974).
—— *Sex in Middlesex: Popular Mores in a Massachusetts County, 1649–1699* (Amherst, Mass., 1986).
—— 'Adolescent culture in colonial Massachusetts', *Journal of Family History*, 9 (1984), 127–44.
TITTLER, R., *Architecture and Power: The Town Hall and the English Urban Community c.1500–1640* (Oxford, 1991).
TREXLER, R., 'Ritual in Florence: adolescence and salvation in the Renaissance', in C. Trinkaus and H. O. Oberman (eds.), *The Pursuit of Holiness in Late Medieval and Renaissance Religion* (Leiden, 1974), 200–64.
TRUANT, C. M., *The Rites of Labor: Brotherhoods of Compagnonnage in Old and New Regime France* (Ithaca, NY, 1994).
TUDOR, P., 'Religious instruction for children and adolescents in the early English Reformation', *Journal of Ecclesiastical History*, 35 (1984), 391–413.
UNDERDOWN, D., *Revel, Riot and Rebellion: Popular Politics and Culture in England 1603–1660* (Oxford, 1985).
—— *Fire from Heaven: Life in an English Town in the Seventeenth Century* (1992).
—— 'The taming of the scold: the enforcement of patriarchal authority in early modern England', in A. Fletcher and J. Stevenson (eds.), *Order and Disorder in Early Modern England* (Cambridge, 1985), 116–36.

UNDERDOWN, D., 'Regional cultures? Local variations in popular culture during the early modern period', in Tim Harris (ed.), *Popular Culture in England, c.1500–1850* (Basingstoke, 1995), 28–47.

VON FRIEDEBURG, R., 'Reformation of manners and the social composition of offenders in an East Anglian clothing village: Earls Colne, Essex, 1531–1642', *Journal of British Studies*, 29 (1990), 347–79.

WALES, T., 'Poverty, poor relief, and the life-cycle: some evidence from seventeenth-century Norfolk', in R. M. Smith (ed.), *Land, Kinship and Life-Cycle* (Cambridge, 1984), 351–404.

WALL, R., 'The age at leaving home', *Journal of Family History*, 3 (1978), 181–202.

—— 'Leaving home and the process of household-formation in preindustrial England', *Continuity and Change*, 2 (1988), 77–109.

WALSHAM, A., ' "Out of the mouths of babes and sucklings": prophecy, puritanism, and childhood in Elizabethan Suffolk', in D. Wood (ed.), *The Church and Childhood* (Studies in Church History, 31, Oxford, 1994).

WALTER, J., 'A "rising of the people?" The Oxfordshire rising of 1596', *Past and Present*, 107 (1985), 90–143.

—— 'The social economy of dearth in early modern England', in J. Walter and R. Schofield (eds.), *Famine, Disease and the Social Order in Early Modern Society* (Cambridge, 1989), 75–128.

WATT, T., *Cheap Print and Popular Piety, 1550–1640* (Cambridge, 1991).

WHITING, R., *The Blind Devotion of the People: Popular Religion and the English Reformation* (Cambridge, 1989).

WIENER, M. J., *Reconstructing the Criminal: Culture, Law, and Policy in England, 1830–1914* (Cambridge, 1990).

WIESNER, M. E., *Working Women in Renaissance Germany* (New Brunswick, NJ, 1986).

—— *Women and Gender in Early Modern Europe* (Cambridge, 1993).

WOODWARD, D., 'The background to the statute of artificers: the genesis of labour policy 1558–1563', *Economic History Review*, 2nd ser., 33 (1980), 32–46.

WRIGHT, S. J., 'Confirmation, catechism and communion: the role of the young in the post-Reformation Church' in S. J. Wright (ed.), *Parish, Church and People: Local Studies in Lay Religion 1350–1750* (1988), 203–23.

—— ' "Churmaids, huswyfes and hucksters": the employment of women in Tudor and Stuart Salisbury', in L. Charles and L. Duffin (eds.), *Women and Work in Pre-industrial England* (1985), 100–21.

WRIGHTSON, K. E., *English Society 1580–1680* (1982).

—— 'Infanticide in earlier seventeenth-century England', *Local Population Studies*, 15 (1975), 10–22.

—— 'The nadir of English illegitimacy in the seventeenth century', in P. Laslett *et al.* (eds.), *Bastardy and its Comparative History* (1980), 176–91.

—— 'Two concepts of order: justices, constables and jurymen in seventeenth-century England', in John Brewer and John Styles (eds.), *An Ungovernable*

People: The English and Their Law in the Seventeenth and Eighteenth Centuries (1980), 21–46.

—— 'Alehouses, order and reformation in rural England 1590–1660', in E. Yeo and S. Yeo (eds.), *Popular Culture and Class Conflict 1590–1914* (Brighton, 1981), 1–27.

—— 'The social order of early modern England: three approaches', in L. Bonfield, R. Smith, and K. E. Wrightson (eds.), *The World We Have Gained: Histories of Population and Social Structure: Essays Presented to Peter Laslett* (Oxford, 1986), 177–202.

—— 'Estates, degrees and sorts: changing perceptions of society in Tudor and Stuart England', in P. Corfield (ed.), *Language, History and Class* (Oxford, 1991), 30–52.

—— ' "Sorts of people" in Tudor and Stuart England', in J. Barry and C. Brooks (eds.), *The Middling Sort of People: Culture, Society and Politics in England, 1550–1800* (Basingstoke, 1994), 28–51.

—— and LEVINE, D., *Poverty and Piety in an English Village: Terling 1525–1700* (1979).

—— 'The social context of illegitimacy in early modern England', in P. Laslett, K. M. Oosterveen, and R. M. Smith (eds.), *Bastardy and its Comparative History* (1980), 158–75.

WRIGLEY, E. A., 'Family limitation in pre-industrial England', in his *People, Cities and Wealth* (Oxford, 1987), 242–69.

—— and SCHOFIELD, R. S., *The Population History of England and Wales 1541–1871: A Reconstruction* (1981).

WURZBACH, N., *The Rise of the English Street Ballad 1550–1650*, trans. Gayna Walls (Cambridge, 1990).

YARBOROUGH, A., 'Apprentices as adolescents in sixteenth-century Bristol', *Journal of Social History*, 13 (1979), 67–81.

ZELL, M., 'Suicide in pre-industrial England', *Social History*, 11 (1986), 303–17.

5. Unpublished Work

ADAIR, R. L., 'Regional Variations in Illegitimacy and Courtship Behaviour in England 1538–1754' (unpublished University of Cambridge Ph.D. thesis, 1992),

BRODSKY ELLIOTT, V., 'Marriage and Mobility in Pre-industrial England . . .' (unpublished University of Cambridge Ph.D. thesis, 1978).

GRIFFITHS, P., 'Some Aspects of the Social History of Youth in Early Modern England, with Particular Reference to the Period *c.*1560–*c.*1640' (unpublished University of Cambridge Ph.D. thesis, 1992).

LORD, C. P., 'Image and Reality: The Chapbook Perspective on Women in Early Modern Britain' (unpublished University of St Andrews M.Phil. dissertation, 1988).

WRIGHTSON, K. E., 'The Puritan Reformation of Manners with Special Reference to the Counties of Lancashire and Essex 1640–1660' (unpublished University of Cambridge Ph.D. thesis, 1973).

INDEX